YUCATÁN
PENINSULA

LIZA PRADO & GARY CHANDLER

YUCATÁN
PENINSULA

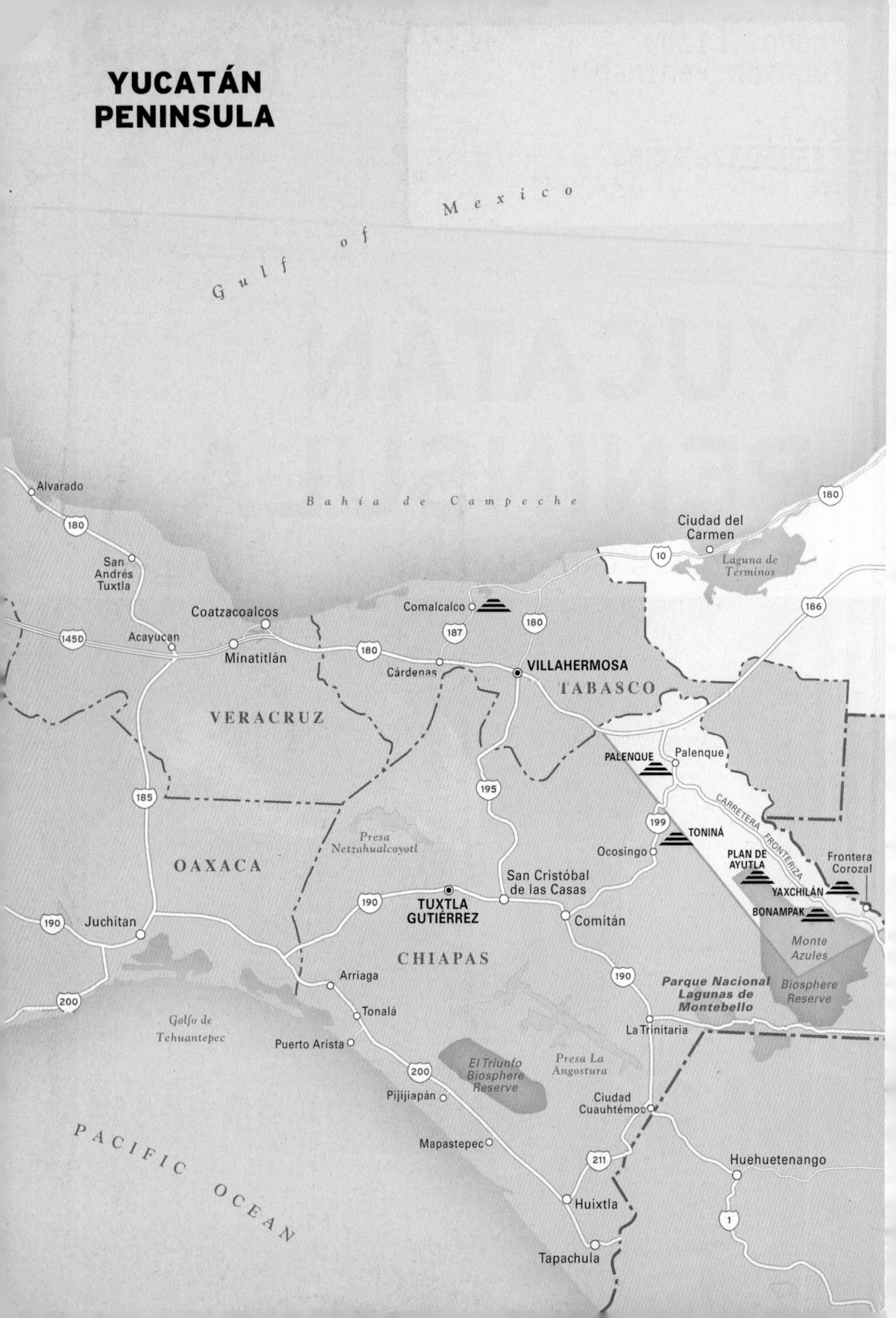

Gulf of Mexico

Bahía de Campeche

Alvarado

180

San Andrés Tuxtla

Coatzacoalcos

145D

Acayucan

Minatitlán

180

Cárdenas

Comalcalco

187

180

VILLAHERMOSA

TABASCO

Ciudad del Carmen

10

Laguna de Términos

180

186

VERACRUZ

185

195

PALENQUE

Palenque

Carretera Fronteriza

Presa Netzahualcoyotl

199

TONINÁ

Ocosingo

PLAN DE AYUTLA

Frontera Corozal

OAXACA

190

San Cristóbal de las Casas

TUXTLA GUTIÉRREZ

YAXCHILÁN

BONAMPAK

Monte Azules Biosphere Reserve

Juchitan

190

Comitán

190

Arriaga

CHIAPAS

200

Golfo de Tehuantepec

Tonalá

Parque Nacional Lagunas de Montebello

La Trinitaria

Puerto Arista

Presa La Angostura

200

Pijijiapán

El Triunfo Biosphere Reserve

Ciudad Cuauhtémoc

Mapastepec

211

Huehuetenango

PACIFIC OCEAN

Huixtla

1

Tapachula

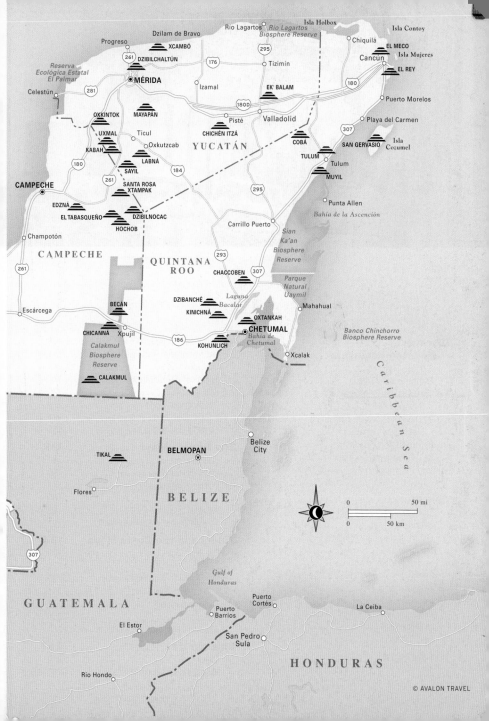

Contents

DISCOVER

Yucatán Peninsula

On the northern coast of the Yucatán Peninsula is a place called Uaymitún, where just a thin strip of land separates the ocean from a swampy coastal lagoon. But the swamp is not just a swamp—climbing a roadside tower, you discover it's also home to thousands of flamingos, their bright-pink feathers a stark contrast to the gray-green surroundings. Behind you are the emerald waters of the Gulf of Mexico, a favorite spot for windsurfers and kiteboarders. To the east is a small Maya ruin. To the south is the great colonial city of Mérida, and just down the road is the spot scientists believe a meteor smashed into the earth 65 million years ago, wiping out the dinosaurs and ushering in the age of humankind. Uaymitún is not a major tourist destination—except for the flamingos, it hardly rates a mention. But that's just it: The Yucatán has so much history, culture, and natural wonder, even a dusty roadside town is rich with stories and possibilities.

It's hard to exaggerate the number and variety of attractions here: stunning Maya ruins, vibrant colonial cities, wildlife-watching, a web of caves and underground rivers, and ideal conditions for kiteboarding and sportfishing. For divers,

Clockwise from top left: Mérida; handmade tortillas; Playa Norte on Isla Mujeres; Mérida's Mercado Municipal; Cobá's highest pyramid; Campeche's cathedral.

there are world-famous reefs at Isla Cozumel and eerie inland cenotes. And if you're looking for a beach vacation, well, you know you've come to the right place.

The Yucatán is also a place of many stories. Maya hieroglyphics tell complicated tales of gods, kings, and conquest. The exploits of its pirates and buccaneers are still the subject of fairy tales and feature films. The colonial era was rife with the boom and bust of products like henequen and chicle. The Maya have suffered unspeakable exploitation, but not passively—in the Caste War, they nearly drove European settlers off the peninsula for good. More recent is the remarkable story of Cancún, which in a matter of decades was transformed from a mosquito-infested sandbar into one of the world's top resort destinations.

The Yucatán Peninsula is all this, and even more—a place of endless mystery and beauty, fun and fascination. Enjoy!

Clockwise from top left: Hammocks are used instead of traditional beds in many Maya homes; *cabañas* on Isla Blanca; Restaurants specializing in ceviche and seafood cocktails are popular on the coasts; the waterfalls at Misol-Há.

If You Have...

- **ONE WEEK:** Visit Cancún, Isla Cozumel, or Isla Holbox; take a side trip to Valladolid and the ruins of Chichén Itzá.

- **TEN DAYS:** Add Mérida and the Puuc Route; go to Campeche City for a couple of days.

- **TWO WEEKS:** Add Tulum, the Riviera Maya, and Cobá ruins; join a one-day excursion in the Sian Ka'an Biosphere Reserve.

- **THREE WEEKS:** Add the Costa Maya, the Río Bec region, and Palenque.

Planning Your Trip

Where to Go

Cancún

Cancún has two parts: The **Zona Hotelera** (Hotel Zone) has Cancún's top resorts and nightclubs, plus miles of beautiful beaches. But if you don't mind hopping a bus to the beach, **downtown** has cheaper food and lodging, plus some unexpectedly cool bars and cafés. Most travelers visit **Isla Mujeres,** a sliver of an island offshore from Cancún, as a day trip, but nice hotels and a mellow ambience make it a tempting place to stay. **Isla Holbox** is even smaller, with sand roads and virtually no cars. The beaches aren't glorious, but the tranquility is sublime.

Isla Cozumel

Cozumel's pristine **coral reefs** and crystalline water attract divers the world over; fewer people realize the island also has a scenic **national park,** numerous beach clubs, a tournament golf course, even an important **Maya ruin.** Beat the cruise ship crowds by heading to the east side's isolated beaches and dramatic surf. Most people arrive by ferry—it's just a half-hour ride from Playa del Carmen—but there's also an airport with international arrivals.

The Riviera Maya

Stretching 130 kilometers (81 miles) from Cancún to Tulum, the Riviera Maya has megaresorts and boutique bed-and-breakfasts, busy cities and quiet villages, great reef diving and amazing cenotes (freshwater sinkholes). **Playa del Carmen** has the area's largest selection of hotels, food, nightlife, and services; try **Puerto Morelos** and **Akumal** for something a bit smaller, or isolated clusters of beachfront hotels like **Tankah Tres** and **Soliman Bay** for even more R&R.

Tulum and the Costa Maya

Tulum is justly famous for its stunning beaches, eco-chic bungalows, and namesake **Maya ruin,** with a dramatic view of the Caribbean. An hour away is **Cobá,** boasting the second-tallest Maya pyramid and a lovely forest setting teeming with birds. Directly south of Tulum is the pristine **Sian Ka'an Biosphere Reserve** and beyond that the isolated towns of the **Costa Maya.** There's a lovely freshwater lagoon, **Laguna Bacalar,** a short distance from **Chetumal,** the busy Quintana Roo state capital and gateway to Belize.

Chichén Itzá

Chichén Itzá is one of the most impressive and recognizable of all Maya ruins, especially its iconic main pyramid. There also is a nighttime sound and light show, and interesting villages and

Gulf of Mexico

Cancún

Chichén Itzá

MÉRIDA

Cancún

Valladolid

The Riviera Maya

0   50 mi
0   50 km

CAMPECHE

Isla Cozumel

Mérida, The Puuc Route, and Campeche

Tulum and The Costa Maya

CHETUMAL

MEXICO

Palenque

Caribbean Sea

Palenque

GUATEMALA

BELIZE

© AVALON TRAVEL

cenotes are nearby. The sister town of Pisté is unmemorable—better to base yourself in Valladolid, a lovely and convenient colonial city. **Ek' Balam** is a small but remarkable archaeological site, with an impressive stucco frieze. On the coast, Río Lagartos has tours into a neighboring biosphere reserve to see huge colonies of flamingos.

Mérida, the Puuc Route, and Campeche

Mérida, the Yucatán state capital, is a beautiful colonial city with excellent museums and nearly daily music and dance performances. Doable day trips from Mérida include the flamingo reserve at **Celestún,** the mellow beach town of **Progreso,** and the lovely colonial town of **Izamal.** South of Mérida, the **Puuc Route** includes must-see Maya ruins like **Uxmal** and myriad smaller sites, plus caves, cenotes, and colonial villages. Farther still, **Campeche City,** the capital of Campeche state, boasts a gorgeous colonial center and impressive walls and forts that once warded off pirate attacks. Southern Campeche state is home to numerous Maya sites, including **Calakmul,** a massive city now buried deep in a forest reserve that's home to parrots, monkeys, even jaguars.

Forget poolside dining—in Cozumel you can eat on the beach.

Palenque

Chiapas isn't technically part of the Yucatán Peninsula, but no tour of the Maya world is complete without seeing the intriguing temples and superb inscriptions at **Palenque.** From there, a series of lovely waterfalls makes a terrific day trip, as do the ruins of **Yaxchilán** and **Bonampak** in the Río Usumacinta valley. Palenque is also a jumping-off point for trips into the Lacandón rainforest, with its rich ecology and reclusive indigenous communities.

When to Go

Considering weather, prices, and crowds, the best times to visit the Yucatán Peninsula are from **late November to mid-December** and from **mid-January to early May.** You'll avoid the intense heat from June to August, the rain (and possible hurricanes) in September and October, and the crowds and high prices around the winter holidays.

The big caveats with those periods are spring break (March/April) and Semana Santa (the week before Easter), when American and Canadian students, and then Mexican tourists, turn out in force and prices spike temporarily.

Be aware that certain attractions are only available (or recommendable) during specific months, whether snorkeling with whale sharks (June-September) or visiting Chichén Itzá on the spring equinox. Even many year-round activities like sportfishing, kiteboarding, and bird-watching are better or worse according to the season.

Before You Go

Passports and Visas

American and Canadian travelers are required to have a valid passport to travel to and from Mexico. **Tourist visas** are issued upon entry; you technically are allowed up to 180 days, but agents often issue just 30 or 60 days. If you want to stay longer, request the time when you present your passport. To extend your visa, visit the immigration office in Cancún.

Vaccinations

No special vaccines are required for travel to the Yucatán Peninsula, but it's a good idea to be up to date on the **standard travel immunizations,** including hepatitis A, MMR (measles-mumps-rubella), tetanus-diphtheria, and typhoid.

Transportation

Cancún International Airport (CUN) is far and away the most common and convenient entry point to the region; airports at Mérida, Cozumel, Chetumal, Campeche, and Palenque are secondary options. There are plans (but nothing more) for a new airport outside Tulum; there also is an airport near Chichén Itzá, but it is used exclusively for charter flights. An excellent network of **buses, shuttles,** and **ferries** covers the entire region, though a rental car makes a world of difference in more remote areas.

What to Pack

Bring to the Yucatán Peninsula what you would to any beach destination: light cotton clothing, hat, sunscreen, sunglasses, flip-flops, etc. Beach buffs should bring two or even three **swimsuits,** plus **snorkel gear** if you've got it. **Water shoes** come in handy wherever the beach is rocky, while **sneakers** and **bug repellent** are musts for the Maya ruins. Finally, it's always smart to bring an extra pair of glasses or contacts, prescription medications, birth control, and a travel clock. If you do leave anything behind, no worries—there's a Walmart in all the major cities.

ziplining at Verde Lucero cenote

El Castillo

The Best of the Yucatán

See and do a little of everything in the Yucatán Peninsula in just two weeks. With beaches to enjoy, ruins to explore, museums to visit, cenotes to snorkel in, and cities to discover, this is a trip for travelers with plenty of energy and a hankering to see it all. Renting a car for the entire trip will give you added speed and flexibility, and ensure you have time to enjoy every stop. But if a rental car is out of your budget, most of the route can be done easily enough by bus. A good compromise is to rent a car for a few key days. Here goes:

Day 1

Arrive in Cancún but head south to **Playa del Carmen,** which is a better base for exploring the Riviera Maya. (**Puerto Morelos, Akumal, Tankah Tres, and Soliman Bay** also are good choices if you prefer something smaller.) If you plan to get in some serious diving, consider heading directly to **Isla Cozumel** to save

yourself the ferry ride the next day. That, or just fly straight there!

Day 2

Spend your first full day underwater in the Riviera Maya. Just about every town along the coast has a dive shop (usually several) offering **snorkeling and diving tours** on the ocean reef. The waters in front of **Puerto Morelos** and **Akumal** have less boat traffic than Playa del Carmen. Or take the plunge in one of the Riviera Maya's myriad **cenotes,** either at a park like **Dos Ojos** or on your own at a site like **Jardín del Edén.** Budget some beach time in the **afternoon.**

Day 3

Head inland. Get an early start and go straight to **Chichén Itzá,** getting there as close to opening time as possible. That way you'll have a jump on the big tour buses and can enjoy these magnificent ruins with fewer people to weave around. Budget at least three hours here. Check into a

A Family Affair

The Yucatán Peninsula is an excellent family destination, with plenty to see and do for kids and parents. From ecoparks on the Riviera Maya to cenotes and Maya ruins farther inland, you'll have no trouble keeping everyone happy, and good hotels and restaurants help take the stress out of traveling en masse. Here are a few recommended stops:

CANCÚN

Isla Mujeres: Super-calm water, a turtle farm, an ecopark, plus a ferry ride there and back—what's not to love?

Parque Las Palapas: Downtown Cancún's main plaza, where kids can run around and munch on chocolate-filled churros.

El Rey Archaeological Zone: Hundreds of beefy iguanas make this a fun stop for kids, even if they're lukewarm about piles of old rocks. (Hint: The iguanas love bananas!)

ISLA COZUMEL

Playa Chen Río: This protected ocean beach on Cozumel's east side is deserted midweek and busy with local families on weekends.

Parque Punta Sur: A scenic natural reserve with a nice beach and fantastic snorkeling, plus a maritime museum and a lighthouse you can climb.

Parque Chankanaab: This national park feels more like a beach club, with lounge chairs, snorkeling, ziplining, a sea lion show, even swimming with dolphins.

THE RIVIERA MAYA

Xcaret: This huge ecopark is an all-day excursion, with snorkeling, tubing, an aquarium, and a fun evening show.

Croco Cun Zoo: Charming little zoo near Puerto Morelos where you can see, pet, and even hold animals (including babies).

Dos Ojos Cenote: Great cenote snorkeling for all ages, either with a guide or on your own.

TULUM AND THE COSTA MAYA

Cobá: Renting bikes or bicycle taxis makes visiting these ruins especially fun for kids, while the thick forest provides cool shade and a chance to spot birds and insects.

Punta Laguna Spider Monkey Reserve: A great family outing, where you'll spot not only spider and howler monkeys, but also a slew of birds, tropical vegetation, and more.

Laguna Bacalar: Huge turquoise lagoon that's excellent for kayaking and swimming, and tranquil enough for little ones to enjoy. An 18th-century fort-turned-museum has pirate exhibits and lots of cannons to clamber on.

CHICHÉN ITZÁ

Chichén Itzá: Impressive ruins with several family-friendly hotels nearby. Cenote Sagrado Azul, just east of town, is a sure hit.

Valladolid: Charming colonial city, with three impressive cenotes nearby for swimming.

Río Lagartos: Fishing village with fun boat tours of the neighboring biosphere reserve, home to thousands of pink flamingos and nice beaches too.

MÉRIDA, THE PUUC ROUTE, AND CAMPECHE

Mérida: A city tour on an open-air double-decker bus is fun and easy, while older kids may appreciate the museums and outdoor dance performances.

Loltún Caves: Take a guided tour of the largest cave in the Yucatán, with huge stalagmites and stalactites, rock carvings dating to 1600 BC, and ancient handprints on the walls.

Izamal: A charming colonial town, painted in mustard yellow. Calesas, horse-pulled buggies, are a fun way to see the sights.

Campeche City: The city's colorful colonial center is enclosed by massive stone walls and forts that not only have interesting museums but also make for great exploring. The Lorencillo pirate-ship tour is a nice way to spend a couple of hours and see the coast.

PALENQUE

Aluxes Ecoparque Palenque: Families and school groups are the target audience at this ecopark and animal rehab center, with leafy pathways and a chance for close-up glimpses of recovering animals like jaguars and alligators.

Tulum is the only Maya ruin with its very own white-sand beach.

nearby hotel, have lunch, and spend the afternoon cooling off at **Cenote Sagrado Azul,** a popular site in Ik Kil ecopark. In the evening, head back to Chichén Itzá for its high-tech **sound and light show.**

Day 4

Get up early and head straight to **Mérida,** one of Mexico's great colonial cities. Go to the **anthropology museum** or the **modern art museum,** the market, or just visit the church, the murals in the government buildings, and the plaza. See what's happening that evening—there's a free cultural performance almost every night of the year.

Day 5

You can spend this day in a couple of different ways. There are a number of great day trips from Mérida, including a **flamingo tour** in the town of **Celestún,** or visiting the colonial town of Izamal and swimming in cenotes near **Cuzamá.** Then again, if you especially love the Maya ruins, you won't want to miss those along the **Puuc Route.** For this option, get an early start and visit **Uxmal** first—it is the biggest and the best of the sites here, and you don't want to shortchange your time there. Afterward, cross the road to the **Museo del Chocolate,** an engaging museum about the history of chocolate, which dates to the ancient Maya. Time permitting, visit one or two of the smaller Puuc ruins too. Check into a hotel in **Ticul** or **Santa Elena,** have dinner, and wind down with a relaxed evening in the town's central plaza.

Day 6

Plan to drive to the beautiful colonial town of **Campeche City** this morning. Check into a hotel and then pick a few of the sights to take in. The **museums** along the **city walls and at El Palacio Centro Cultural** or **Fuerte de San Miguel** are especially good. If it's a Saturday or Sunday, stroll down to the central park for a free musical performance and *elote* (corn on the cob) from a street cart. Most evenings, there's also a spectacular **sound and light show,** a multimedia celebration of Campeche's history.

Day 7

Start early for the long drive to **Palenque.** Check into your hotel and have dinner at **Don Mucho** in the jungle neighborhood of El Panchán. If you're up for it, stay late for live music and fire dancers.

Day 8

Spend the day visiting **Palenque archaeological zone.** Be sure to leave time for the terrific on-site **museum.**

Day 9

Stay another day in Palenque to see some of the nearby attractions. If you still haven't gotten enough of the Maya ruins, consider booking an all-day tour to **Yaxchilán** and **Bonampak.** Or visit the impressive waterfalls at **Misol-Há** and **Agua Azul** for a bit of outdoorsy fun.

Day 10

From Palenque, drive toward the southern Campeche town of **Xpujil.** Depending on your time and energy, visit one of the many small Maya ruins clustered along Highway 186 like **Balamkú** or **Becán.** Check into a hotel in Xpujil, or if your budget permits, at one along the highway.

Day 11

If you want to see even more ruins, a daylong trip into **Calakmul** is a terrific experience, albeit tiring. Otherwise, jump ahead in the itinerary—you can always use the extra day at Tulum, either for more beach time or for exploring more of the Sian Ka'an Biosphere Reserve.

Day 12

Drive to **Tulum,** where you can treat yourself to a beachside bungalow on one of Tulum's glorious beaches. Spend the afternoon relaxing.

Day 13

Spend another **beach day** on Tulum's quiet and dreamy southern beaches. If you get restless, get some snorkeling in at the great nearby **cenotes** of **Gran Cenote** or **Car Wash.** If you're tired of the car, walk to **Tulum ruins,** dramatically overlooking the turquoise Caribbean Sea. Be sure to take your bathing suit for a dip in the ocean from the site's small beach.

Day 14

Take a tour of the **Sian Ka'an Biosphere Reserve,** an ideal place for fishing, bird-watching, and snorkeling and a perfect way to end your vacation.

10 Days of Ecoadventure

Lazing on a beach or contemplating museum displays is all right, but some travelers crave a little more action. The Yucatán has plenty to offer active travelers, including kiteboarding, fly-fishing, kayaking, and mountain biking. This tour is a workout for the eyes too, taking you to some of the peninsula's most stunning (and little-visited) natural areas, from tangled mangrove forests to limestone caverns filled with the clearest, bluest water you've ever seen. The only thing this tour doesn't include is snorkeling or diving on the coast, which are covered in a list of their own.

Day 1

Ease into things by spending a day stand-up paddling (SUPing). It's challenging but fairly easy to master, and especially rewarding in the Riviera Maya's warm clear water. **Playa del Carmen, Isla Mujeres,** and **Cozumel** are all great places to start. Farther afield, **Xpu Há, Tulum,** and **Mahahual** are fine alternatives.

Day 2

Kayaking is another low-key, easy-to-learn activity that's perfect for exploring the region's rich mangrove forests. The **Sian Ka'an Biosphere Reserve, Laguna Bacalar,** and **Isla Holbox** all have fascinating kayak tours

a dramatic opening in the vast Loltún cave system

that include paddling through mangrove canals, spotting birds, and locating hidden beaches and lost Maya ruins.

Day 3

Today's the day for pushing yourself. Why not try kiteboarding? **Isla Blanca** and **Cozumel** are good for both, with perfect wind, forgiving surf for beginners, and some surprisingly challenging spots for the more advanced. If you want to head inland, **Isla Holbox** and **Progreso** also have first-rate kiting schools.

Day 4

You may want to spend a second day kiteboarding—few people master it in a day! Otherwise, dig out your sneakers and sign up for a mountain bike tour. Both **Tulum** and **Laguna Bacalar** have fun and moderately challenging rides, pedaling through the jungle to little-visited Maya ruins and remote beaches.

Day 5

You've gotta be getting tired by now. Spend the day fishing, either trolling in the ocean or fly-fishing in the region's vast coastal flats. **Cozumel** is ideal for the former, as is the latest craze: spearfishing. **Sian Ka'an** and **Xcalak** are world-class fly-fishing spots, brimming with tarpon, permit, bonefish, and snook.

Day 6

Get up bright and early to be at **Cobá archaeological zone** at opening. Of all the Maya ruins, this one is the best for **bird-watching.** It's not uncommon to spot toucans and parrots. Cobá also is an impressive ruin, with the second-highest pyramid in the Yucatán Peninsula, affording awesome views of the countryside. You can rent bikes near the entrance and explore the ruins on wheels. A short distance away is the **Punta Laguna monkey reserve,** a perfect place to visit after a late lunch.

Day 7

Drive to **Mérida.** If you get an early start, you'll have time to stop at the beautiful colonial town of **Izamal** or the **cenotes of Cuzamá,** where you'll take a horse-drawn cart through abandoned

Classics of Yucatecan Cuisine

Like many regions of Mexico, the Yucatán Peninsula has a cuisine all its own. The base is recognizably Mexican, but the dishes here are strongly influenced by traditional Maya ingredients and techniques, with dashes of Caribbean and Middle Eastern flavors. Some popular menu items include:

- **Cochinita Pibil:** pork that has been marinated in achiote, Seville orange juice, peppercorn, garlic, cumin, salt, and pepper, wrapped in banana leaves, and baked. It's typically served on weekends.

- **Dzoto-bichay:** tamales made of *chaya* (a leafy vegetable similar to spinach) and eggs. It comes smothered in tomato sauce.

- **Papadzules:** hard-boiled eggs chopped and rolled into a corn tortilla with a creamy pumpkin-seed sauce.

- **Poc-chuc:** slices of pork that have been marinated in Seville orange juice and coated with a tangy sauce. Pickled onions are added on the side.

- **Salbute:** handmade tortilla covered with shredded turkey, pickled onion, and slices of avocado.

- **Panucho:** handmade tortilla stuffed with re-fried beans and covered with shredded turkey, pickled onion, and slices of avocado. Like a *salbute* plus!

- **Sopa de Lima:** turkey-stock soup prepared with shredded turkey or chicken, fried tortilla strips, and juice from *lima*, a lime-like citrus fruit.

poc-chuc—a traditional Yucatecan dish

You can find Yucatecan dishes just about anywhere, from hole-in-the-wall taco joints to gourmet restaurants—discovering them is half the fun! But for a sure bet, check out **La Habichuela Sunset** (Zona Hotelera Cancún), **Quesadillas Tierra del Sol** (Downtown Cancún), **Jardín Maya** (Isla Mujeres), **La Candela** (Isla Cozumel), **La Gran Chaya** (Pisté), **La Palapita de los Tamales** (Valladolid), **La Chaya Maya** (Mérida), **Kinich** (Izamal), **El Príncipe Tutul-Xiu** (Maní), and **Marganzo** (Campeche City).

henequen fields, then descend ladders into underground caverns for a cool swim.

Day 8

Take a day trip to **Celestún** and take a **flamingo tour.** You can get there on your own or book a tour with one of Mérida's many tour operators. Head back to Mérida and check out a museum and one of the free nightly cultural performances.

Day 9

Spend the next day visiting some of the *grutas* (caves) along the Puuc Route south of Mérida. **Calcehtok** is the most adventuresome, with local guides offering 2-5-hour tours of this huge cave system. The longest tours go about four kilometers (2.5 miles) and reach a tiny chamber where human bones were left from ancient Maya ceremonies. Nearby, **Aktun Usil** offers a look in a sacred Maya cave, with hieroglyphics, cave paintings, rock carvings, even handprints, in silhouette, on the ceiling high above. Not far away, **Loltún caves** are much tamer, with paths and lighting, but fascinating nonetheless. Then make your way back to **Cancún, Cozumel, or the Riviera Maya** for your final night in the region.

Day 10

Spend your last day enjoying the Yucatán's other great natural wonder: the beach. The beaches in **Cancún, Cozumel, Isla Mujeres,** and **Playa del Carmen** all have plenty to keep you active—swimming, sailing, SUPing, kayaking, parasailing, volleyball, soccer, and more.

Pyramids and Palaces

For many people, the Maya ruins are the Yucatán Peninsula's greatest attraction, with their massive pyramids and palaces and amazing artistic and astronomical features. Few visitors have time to visit every site in a single trip; here is a description of each chapter's best Maya ruins to help you decide which ones to add to your itinerary—and which to save for next time! To dig a little deeper, so to speak, pair ruin hopping with a visit to one of the excellent **Maya museums** in **Cancún, Chetumal, Mérida,** and **Campeche City.**

Cancún and Isla Cozumel

- **El Rey, San Miguelito, and Yamil Lu'um:** These small ruins are found right in Cancún's Zona Hotelera. El Rey is the largest and best preserved of the group, and is home to hundreds of iguanas—almost as interesting to see as the structures themselves.

- **San Gervasio:** Isla Cozumel's main archaeological site has several modest temples connected by forest paths. Dedicated to the goddess of fertility, San Gervasio was an important pilgrimage site for ancient Maya women.

Tulum and the Costa Maya

- **Tulum:** Perched on a bluff overlooking the turquoise Caribbean Sea, Tulum's structures themselves are quite decayed, but a visit here is still worthwhile. Come early, as the site is often mobbed by day-trippers from nearby resorts.

- **Cobá:** With the second-highest pyramid on the peninsula, Cobá offers a great view of the countryside. Nestled in a forest near several

small lakes, it is also a good place to spot birds, including herons, parrots, and toucans.

- **Kohunlich:** Located in southern Quintana Roo, Kohunlich is best known for a series of imposing stucco masks. Nearby is a unique luxury resort with guided trips in the surrounding forest and river areas.

Chichén Itzá

- **Chichén Itzá:** Named one of the New Seven Wonders of the World, this site has the largest ball court of any Maya ruin and a pyramid recognizable the world over. Come early to beat the tour groups arriving from Cancún. Plan on spending several hours—it's huge—and checking out the worthwhile evening sound and light show.

- **Ek' Balam:** Near the city of Valladolid, Ek' Balam boasts one of the best-preserved stucco friezes in the Maya world and an all-embracing view from atop its main pyramid. Nearby cenotes provide a great place to cool off afterward.

Mérida, the Puuc Route, and Campeche

- **Uxmal:** This may be the chapter's most beautiful site, with intricate palaces and a massive pyramid with rounded corners—another must-see. The sound and light show here is also recommended.

- **The Puuc Route:** The Ruta Puuc is a series of four smaller ruins near Uxmal. Kabah and Labná are especially memorable, including beautiful archways and facades decorated with scores of identical rain-god masks. A

view of the Temple of the Count with Palenque's famous tower beyond

round-trip bus from Mérida hits all four plus Uxmal, but visiting by car will give you the freedom to appreciate them longer.

- Near the Puuc Route, other remarkable sites include the neatly organized **Mayapán** and the little-visited **Oxkintok,** with two impressive caves nearby; and **Dzibilchaltún,** with its first-rate museum and intriguing main temple.

- **Edzná:** A peaceful site, Edzná's Temple of Five Stories looks over a small acropolis and broad main plaza. It's located in the Chenes region, less than an hour's drive from Campeche City, but you still may be the only one there when you visit.

- **Calakmul:** Located in Campeche's Río Bec region, Calakmul was one of the most powerful Maya cities in its time and contains arguably the largest known Maya pyramid. What's more, the site is ensconced in a biosphere reserve, where you can spot monkeys and tropical birds.

- **Becán and Chicanná:** Also in the Río Bec region, Becán's many structures include two huge pyramids and an impressive multiroom palace, while Chicanná has gorgeously decorated temples and residential buildings.

- Other excellent sites in southern Campeche include **Balamkú, El Hormiguero,** and **Río Bec;** the latter two can be difficult to reach, however.

Palenque

- **Palenque:** This is the all-time favorite ruin of many travelers, thanks to its elegant design, intricate carvings, and superlative museum. Much of what archaeologists know about the Maya calendar, hieroglyphics, and astronomy emerged from studies conducted here.

- **Bonampak and Yaxchilán:** Sister cities located along the Guatemalan border, Bonampak and Yaxchilán are commonly reached on tours from Palenque. The former contains brilliantly colored murals, while the latter has beautifully carved stone panels and monoliths.

Best Diving and Snorkeling

The Yucatán Peninsula's underwater treasures are as compelling as its terrestrial ones. The region includes the world's second-longest coral reef, the longest known underground river system, and the Northern Hemisphere's largest coral atoll. Below are some of the top spots to get underwater:

Isla Cozumel's crystal clear water, vibrant coral reef, and myriad first-rate dive operators make the island a premier underwater destination. It's especially suited for expert divers, with challenging wall, deep, wreck, and drift dives—truly too many to name. Snorkelers should check out **Parque Punta Sur, Chankanaab,** and **Playa Azul,** which also have nice beach areas.

Puerto Morelos is a low-key town between Cancún and Playa del Carmen that's famous for the exceptionally rich and well-preserved coral reef just offshore. A local cooperative takes travelers on rewarding snorkeling tours, while local dive shops offer excellent reef dives.

The appealing beach town of **Akumal** has two great snorkeling options. **Laguna Yal-Ku** is an estuary zone, where fresh cenote water pours into the ocean, and is brimming with fish and sea plants. Unique sculptures adorn the water's edge, for added measure. **Akumal Bay,** meanwhile, has shallow protected water and is a known feeding ground for sea turtles.

From June to September, large numbers of whale sharks congregate between **Isla Holbox** and **Isla Mujeres,** gorging themselves on krill. Guided **whale shark trips** from either island allow you to snorkel beside these gentle giants.

Journey into the abyss! **The Riviera Maya** is dotted with hundreds of eerily beautiful cenotes (freshwater caverns and sinkholes) offering out-of-this-world snorkeling and diving for novices and experts alike. Tulum's dive shops specialize in cenote dives and courses, while snorkelers can grab their gear and spend the day cenote hopping. Try **Siete Bocas** and **Verde Lucero** on the Ruta de los Cenotes, just south of Puerto Morelos; **Jardín del Edén** and **Cenote Cristalino,** both on Highway 307 across from Xpu-Há; and the string of cenotes west of **Tulum** including **Car Wash** and **Gran Cenote. Dos Ojos,** near Tulum, also offers full-service guided tours for snorkelers and divers, in a gorgeous stalagmite-filled cavern.

Banco Chinchorro is the largest coral atoll on this side of the planet, and has spectacular diving and snorkeling. Getting there can be a bear—2-3 hours by boat each way—but the massive and pristine coral structure atoll is worth the time and expense. Dive shops in **Mahahual** or **Xcalak,** two small towns near the Belize border, offer Chinchorro trips. There's also fantastic snorkeling and diving right from the shore, including at night.

Cenote Hopping

The Yucatán Peninsula is dotted with hundreds of cenotes—pools of shimmering blue water fed by a vast underground freshwater river system. Some look like large ponds, others are deep sinkholes, and still others occupy gaping caverns or have dramatic rock formations. Many cenotes are open to the public (typically for a small entrance fee), and their cool clear water is perfect for swimming, snorkeling, and scuba diving. Facilities range from simple restrooms and snorkel rental to full-service "cenote parks" with guided tours. Some favorites in the region, by chapter, include:

The Riviera Maya

- **Ruta de los Cenotes:** Sure, some spots along the "Cenote Route" are tourist traps, but others are sublime, like Siete Bocas, a huge eerie cavern filled with shimmering water, and Verde Lucero, a gorgeous open-air pool filled with freshwater turtles and fish.

Into the Wild

The Yucatán Peninsula is best known for its Maya ruins and beautiful beaches, but it's also got some terrific places and opportunities to spot wildlife, including several biosphere reserves and extensive wetlands.

Sian Ka'an Biosphere Reserve: This sprawling coastal reserve south of Tulum is home to an astounding array of wildlife, including dolphins, howler monkeys, crocodiles, sea turtles, and hundreds of bird species. Harder to spot, but still there, are manatees, tapirs, and even jaguars.

Calakmul Biosphere Reserve: Home to a massive Maya ruin as well as to howler and spider monkeys that hang out in the treetops overlooking the ancient city's main plaza. If you're lucky, you might spot a puma or jaguar as well.

Ría Lagartos Biosphere Reserve and Ría Celestún Biosphere Reserve: These huge estuaries are the best place to observe American flamingos, which nest and feed there by the tens of thousands, plus ibis, herons, and myriad other species.

Isla Holbox: Come here to snorkel with whale sharks, gentle giants that congregate just offshore between June and September. Later, book a kayak or motorboat tour to visit the island's bird-rich lagoons.

Isla Cozumel: Cozumel's protected coral reef system teems with sponges, sea turtles, rays, eels, and countless tropical fish. Divers can get up close and personal, but even snorkelers get an eyeful in these pristine waters.

Punta Laguna Spider Monkey Reserve: This small reserve north of Cobá is home to several

Howler monkeys can be spotted in the Yucatán's interior.

families of rambunctious *monos arañas* (spider monkeys). A small lagoon has canoes to go looking for crocodiles.

Akumal: Yucatec Maya for "Place of the Turtle," Akumal is the center for turtle preservation along the Riviera Maya. A local organization welcomes visitors on nighttime excursions to find and protect sea turtle nests (May-July) and to release hatchlings back to the sea (August-October)

Xcalak Reef National Park: Xcalak sees far fewer visitors than elsewhere, and its reef is accordingly pristine, with rich colorful coral structures and large schools of fish, including silvery tarpon.

- **Jardín del Edén:** The best and biggest of a cluster of cenotes near Playa Xpu-Há, with a large cavern that forms a dramatic overhang.

- **Cenote Cristalino:** Next to Jardín del Edén, Cristalino also has an overhanging cliff but a smaller swimming area.

- **Cenote Azul:** A set of three cenotes near Playa Xpu-Há with impossibly clear waters and a small cliff for jumping into one of them.

- **Cenote Manatí:** Near Tankah Tres, this is actually a series of connected cenotes and lagoons that wind inland through a tangled scrub forest.

Tulum and the Costa Maya

- **Dos Ojos:** A cenote park with rentals, guides, and spectacular caverns.

- **Gran Cenote:** Lovely cavern with natural arches and stalactite formations; east of Tulum on the road to Cobá.

- **Car Wash:** Just past Gran Cenote, this innocuous-looking cenote has stunning rock formations below the surface.

- **Cenote Choo-Ha:** One of four dramatic cenotes near Cobá, with a high domed ceiling and iridescent blue water.

Chichén Itzá

- **Cenote Sagrado Azul:** Just three kilometers (1.9 miles) from Chichén Itzá, this huge deep cenote in Ik Kil ecopark can be crowded but is impressive all the same.

- **Cenote Yokdzonot:** This little-known gem near Chichén Itzá is all the more rewarding for being operated by a cooperative of enterprising local women.

- **Cenotes de Dzitnup:** Twin cenotes just outside Valladolid, both with huge domed ceilings and large swimmable pools beneath.

- **Cenote X'Canché:** A pretty 12-meter-deep (39-foot) cenote, a kilometer (0.6 mile) down a forest path from the Ek' Balam ruins.

- **Cenote Sak' Awa:** Like a sunken donut, this remote cenote has a flat rocky center encircled by teal-blue water and high overhanging cliffs.

Mérida, the Puuc Route, and Campeche

- **Cenotes de Cuzamá:** Getting to these three cenotes via horse-drawn carts is half the fun. Two have slippery ladders leading down to their cool azure waters.

- **Cenote Kankirixché:** North of Uxmal, this is considered one of the peninsula's prettiest cenotes. It's easy to see why, with its cool turquoise water, dangling tree roots, and a roof bristling with stalactites.

- **Grutas de X'tacumbilxuna'an:** This massive cavern was used for centuries by local Maya for collecting water, and is the subject of a famous drawing by 19th-century explorer-artist Frederick Catherwood.

Cancún

Highlights

★ **Playa Delfines:** Located at the far southern end of the Zona Hotelera, this is one of few spots without high-rise resorts gobbling up beach space and blocking the afternoon sun—and it has a refreshing mix of foreign and local visitors (page 36).

★ **Cancún Nightlife:** You don't have to be on spring break to enjoy Cancún's nightclubs—but it helps! If the all-night-every-nightclub scene isn't for you, head downtown for wine bars, jazz clubs, and cafés (page 37).

★ **Museo Subacuático de Arte (MUSA):** This remarkable "museum" has two sites featuring hundreds of statues of people of all ages and walks of life: one at Nizuc reef near Cancún, the other at Manchones reef near Isla Mujeres. Standing on the ocean floor in crystal clear water, the statues are made of material designed to promote coral growth, so they'll only get more interesting as time passes (pages 45 and 65).

★ **Isla Contoy:** Go island-hopping on this popular day trip from Isla Mujeres. A morning boat ride is followed by snorkeling on a rich coral reef, hiking and bird-watching, and digging into a fresh fish barbecue on the beach (page 65).

★ **Playa Norte:** Surfers need not apply—Isla Mujeres's best beach has virtually no waves, just soft white sand lapped by glassy turquoise water. It's great for families, couples, and single sun worshippers (page 67).

★ **Whale Shark Feeding Grounds:** Just because they weigh 10 tons and are longer than a Winnebago doesn't make whale sharks bad snorkeling partners. Get goggles-to-gills with the world's biggest fish (page 83).

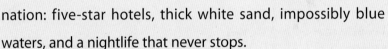

Cancún is a big, beautiful contradiction. For many people, it has all the makings of the ultimate vacation destination: five-star hotels, thick white sand, impossibly blue waters, and a nightlife that never stops.

Others chafe at Cancún for seeming more American than Mexican, a place where you need never speak a word of Spanish, never eat at a restaurant you couldn't find at a mall back home, and never convert your dollars into pesos.

Both perspectives are true, but one-sided. It's hard not to cringe at those loud tourists who don't bother to explore—or even care about—any part of Mexico beyond their beach chairs. Yet those who pooh-pooh Cancún are also selling the city short. Cancún is a working, breathing city that's vital to Mexico's economy and imbued with a fascinating history and plenty of "real" Mexican culture for those willing to seek it out. And contrary to impressions, Cancún has accommodations and services for visitors of all budgets and tastes.

Why not take advantage of both sides of Cancún? The resorts, beaches, and nightclubs will blow your mind—don't miss them! But be sure not to overlook Cancún's more subtle side, too, from live music in a bohemian downtown café to munching on *elote* (corn on the cob) sold from a cart in the city's pleasant central square.

And when you need to, just get away. A 15-minute ferry ride delivers you to the slow-paced island of Isla Mujeres, a sliver of sand surrounded by breathtaking blue waters. Farther north and even more laid-back is Isla Holbox; no cars, no banks, no post office—it's a world away from Cancún yet reachable in a morning.

HISTORY

Cancún is a new city in a new state. In the 1960s, the Mexican government set out to create the next Acapulco, and surveyors selected a swampy sandbar on the Caribbean coast as the country's most promising tourist town. Not everyone was convinced: The area was a true backwater—not even a state yet—with no infrastructure and few roads

---

Previous: Playa Norte on Isla Mujeres; Cancún's Playa Delfines. **Above:** El Meco Archaeological Zone.

Cancún

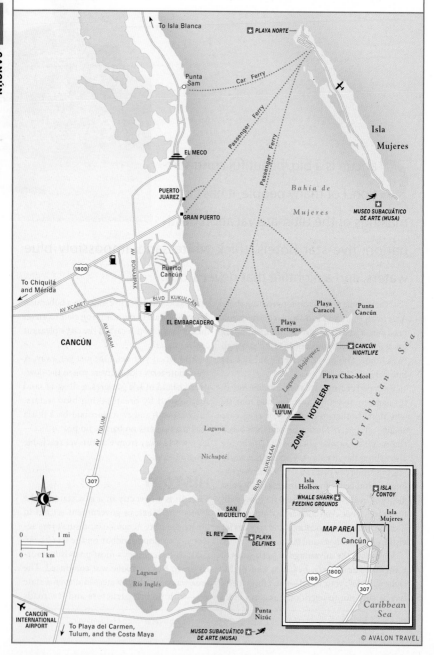

To Isla Blanca

PLAYA NORTE

Punta Sam

Car Ferry

EL MECO

PUERTO JUÁREZ

GRAN PUERTO

Passenger Ferry

Passenger Ferry

Bahía de Mujeres

Isla Mujeres

MUSEO SUBACUÁTICO DE ARTE (MUSA)

AV. BONAMPAK

Puerto Cancún

To Chiquilá and Mérida

180D

BLVD. KUKULCÁN

AV. XCARET

EL EMBARCADERO

CANCÚN

AV. KABAH

Playa Caracol

Punta Cancún

Playa Tortugas

CANCÚN NIGHTLIFE

Laguna Bojórquez

Playa Chac-Mool

YAMIL LU'UM

ZONA HOTELERA

Caribbean Sea

AV. TULUM

Laguna Nichupté

BLVD. KUKULCÁN

307

0   1 mi

0   1 km

SAN MIGUELITO

EL REY

PLAYA DELFINES

Laguna Río Inglés

Isla Holbox

WHALE SHARK FEEDING GROUNDS

ISLA CONTOY

MAP AREA

Cancún

Isla Mujeres

180   180D

307

Caribbean Sea

CANCÚN INTERNATIONAL AIRPORT

To Playa del Carmen, Tulum, and the Costa Maya

Punta Nizúc

MUSEO SUBACUÁTICO DE ARTE (MUSA)

© AVALON TRAVEL

in or out. But Mexico's planners forged on-ward, paving roads, building bridges, install-ing electrical lines. Thousands of mangroves were torn out, sadly, to expand the beaches and make room for hotels. Today's downtown Cancún started out as a small mainland fish-ing village that grew rapidly with the influx of workers; it serves much the same purpose today, though now has an economy and dy-namic unto itself, including banks, real estate, multinational companies, and more. Cancún officially "opened" in 1974, the same year the territory was elevated to statehood.

PLANNING YOUR TIME

A week will do just fine in Cancún, allowing time enough to get your tan on plus take a day trip or two, such as to Isla Mujeres or one of the nearby Maya ruins. Ten days gives you time to explore deeper and farther, turning a day trip to Isla Mujeres or the Maya ruins into an overnighter, or venturing north to the remote island of Isla Holbox. Isla Mujeres and Isla Holbox are small but wonderfully relax-ing; if either is your main destination, budget three or four days to experience them fully, but don't be surprised if you end up staying longer.

You don't *need* to rent a car to enjoy Cancún, Isla Mujeres, and Isla Holbox, es-pecially if you don't plan on moving around much; all can be navigated easily by bus, ferry, taxi, and foot. That said, having a car makes many excursions easier, quicker, and more fun, especially if you've got kids in tow. Rather than booking a crowded and expen-sive tour to, say, Chichén Itzá, you can drive there yourself, arriving before the big groups and then hitting a second ruin or an out-of-the way cenote on the way home. With the relatively low price of rental cars, and well-marked roads and highways, it's certainly worth considering.

ORIENTATION

Cancún's Zona Hotelera lies on a narrow white-sand island in the shape of a number 7. The 7's short upper arm leads directly into downtown Cancún, while the longer one (13 kilometers/8 miles) connects to the main-land near the airport. The elbow of the 7 is Punta Cancún—this is the fast-beating heart of the Zona Hotelera's nightlife, including all the major nightclubs, plus several resorts, hotels, restaurants, and shopping malls. The rest of the resorts and several more malls, restaurants, and water sports agencies are spread along the two arms, especially the southern one. The far southern tip of the 7 is called Punta Nizuc and has a few hotels, plus Cancún's largest archaeological site (El Rey). Busy Boulevard Kukulcán runs the en-tire length of the 7, and most addresses in the Zona Hotelera are simply a kilometer marker. Finally, the huge lagoon that's enclosed by the mainland and the Zona Hotelera is called Laguna Nichupté, and is a popular spot for fishing, waterskiing, and boating.

Downtown Cancún is on the mainland and is divided into numbered *super manza-nas* (square blocks, or SM for short). Avenida Tulum is downtown's main thoroughfare; west of Avenida Tulum is Parque Las Palapas (downtown's central plaza), and beyond that Avenida Yaxchilán. Most of downtown Cancún's hotels, restaurants, and music ven-ues are on or around Parque Las Palapas and Avenida Yaxchilán, primarily in SMs 22-25.

Isla Blanca is a thin peninsula just north of downtown Cancún. It's bordered by the white-sand beaches of the Caribbean on one side, and the huge saltwater Chacmochuch Lagoon on the other. It's virtually uninhab-ited, limited to a handful of private homes—both Maya huts and modern behemoths—plus a kiteboarding school and a rustic beach club. There's only one road on the peninsula; it be-gins as a paved road just north of the Isla Mujeres ferry terminals and quickly becomes a rutted sand road that leads almost to the very tip of the peninsula.

Sights

ARCHAEOLOGICAL ZONES

Cancún has three notable archaeological sites, two in the Zona Hotelera and a third north of town on Isla Blanca, near the Isla Mujeres ferry. None compare in size or wow factor to the Yucatán Peninsula's major sites, but they are still worth visiting, and the Zona Hotelera ones can be easily combined with a day at the beach.

El Rey Archaeological Zone

At the southern end of the Zona Hotelera, across from Playa Delfines, **Ruínas El Rey** (Blvd. Kukulcán Km. 17.5, 8am-4:30pm daily, US$3.50) consists of several platforms, two plazas, and a small temple and pyramid, all arranged along an ancient 500-meter (1,640-foot) roadway. The ruins get their name (Ruins of the King) from a skeleton found during excavation and believed to be that of, what else, a king. The ruins date from the late Postclassic period (AD 1200-1400); signage is available in English and Spanish. El Rey also is home to hundreds of iguanas, some quite beefy, which makes a visit here all the more interesting. Last visitors are admitted at 4:30pm.

Yamil Lu'um Archaeological Zone

Lodged between the Park Royal Cancún and the Westin Lagunamar, **Yamil Lu'um** (Blvd. Kukulcán Km. 12.5, 8am-5pm daily, free) consists of two small temples built between AD 1200 and 1550: **Templo del Alacrán** (Temple of the Scorpion) and **Templo de la Huella** (Temple of the Handprint); unfortunately, neither the scorpion nor the handprint that gave the temples their names is visible anymore. The temples were built on Cancún's highest point, suggesting they were used as watchtowers or navigational aids. The ruins can be reached through the Park Royal (nonguests may need to ask permission) and are visible from the beach at Playa Marlin.

El Meco Archaeological Zone

Archaeologists think **El Meco** (Av. López Portillo s/n, 8am-5pm daily, US$3.50) was a major gateway to and from Isla Mujeres—fitting considering it's located just north of the modern-day ferry terminal at Puerto Juárez. The ancient city started out as a fishing village in AD 300 but grew to be a thriving port town, building the tallest pyramid along this part of the coast before collapsing abruptly around AD 600. It was reoccupied four or five centuries later, probably as an outpost for the powerful Chichén Itzá kingdom before being abandoned in the 16th century. The site is smaller than El Rey, in the Zona Hotelera, but the structures are more substantial.

San Miguelito Archaeological Zone

Located on the grounds of the Museo Maya de Cancún, **San Miguelito** (Blvd. Kukulcán Km. 16.5, tel. 998/885-3842, www.inah.gob.mx, 9am-4:30pm daily, free with museum admission fee) was one of several Maya communities that occupied the present-day Zona Hotelera during the late Post-Classic period around AD 1200 until the arrival of European explorers in the late 1500s. (El Rey and Yamil Lu'um were others.) San Miguelito was apparently quite populous, though relatively few structures remain today—most were built of wood and palm and have long since disappeared. Most coastal Maya cities depended on fishing and maritime trade, and domination of the region likely shifted among them over the centuries. At that time, the long coastal island was covered in high sand dunes and dense mangrove forests, which served as a barrier against hurricanes and erosion. That natural protection has been mostly destroyed with the construction of Cancún's hotel "strip," the effects of which are only now becoming clear.

El Rey Archaeological Zone

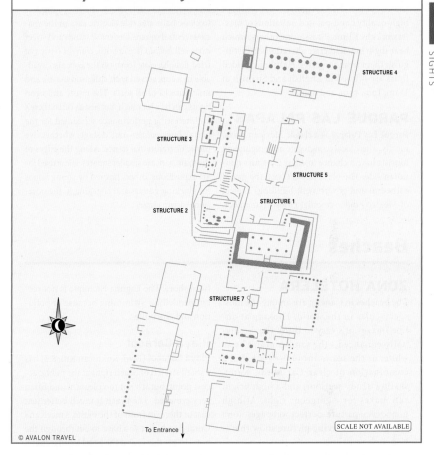

STRUCTURE 4

STRUCTURE 3

STRUCTURE 5

STRUCTURE 1

STRUCTURE 2

STRUCTURE 7

To Entrance

SCALE NOT AVAILABLE

© AVALON TRAVEL

MUSEUMS

Museo Maya de Cancún

Housed in a gorgeous, modern building in the Zona Hotelera, **Museo Maya de Cancún** (Blvd. Kukulcán Km. 16.5, tel. 998/885-3842, www.inah.gob.mx, 9am-5:30pm daily, US$4.50 including museum and archaeological site) has hundreds of Maya artifacts in bright, airy display rooms; vases, bowls, and masks figure prominently. Two permanent exhibition rooms are dedicated to finds from Quintana Roo and the greater Maya world, respectively, while a third room hosts temporary exhibits. Introductory signage is in Spanish and English, though many individual displays lack English translations. There also is a small archaeological site on the grounds—San Miguelito. The museum entrance fee includes admission to the ruins, though the site itself closes at 4:30pm daily.

Museo Pelopidas

Museo Pelopidas (La Isla Shopping Village, Blvd. Kukulcán Km. 12.5, cell tel. 998/146-5151, www.museopelopidas.com, 10am-10pm daily, free) is a large, sleek, somewhat gimmicky, yet mildly interesting art gallery on the 2nd floor of a Zona Hotelera mall. Check out the "New Originals": a roomful of high-quality hand-painted imitations of masterworks by Klimt, Picasso, and others, which bear slight but deliberate alterations to distinguish them from forgeries. Half-hour guided tours are offered in English and Spanish at 11am, 1pm, 4pm, and 6pm.

PARQUE LAS PALAPAS

Parque Las Palapas is a classic Mexican plaza, mostly, where locals congregate most nights and tourists have a chance to enjoy Cancún's quotidian side. The plaza doesn't have the grand cathedral and government buildings typical of Mexico's older colonial cities—remember, Cancún isn't even 50 years old—but it's still a place for adults to chat with friends, for teenagers and couples to circle about, and for youngsters to chase balls and ride electric cars in the spacious central square. Dozens of stands and street carts sell *helado* (ice cream), *churros* (strips of fried dough), *elote* (corn on the cob, also available in a cup, served with chile and mayo), and knickknacks of all sorts. The music and neon lights can be a bit much, but just as often there's an interesting performance scheduled for the plaza's huge *palapa*-roofed stage, whether live music or traditional dance. Along the edges of the main park are smaller squares, some used for art expositions, others favored by young bohos for plucking guitars and engaging in the occasional drum circle.

Beaches

ZONA HOTELERA

The beaches in Cancún are among the most spectacular in the world. Looking at online images, it's easy to think they're digitally enhanced—the sand couldn't be *so* white, or the sea *so* turquoise blue. But a combination of clear Caribbean water, shallow sandy seafloor, and a high bright sun makes for a gorgeous sight. At high noon, even picture-perfect webpages don't compare to the living picture show that is Cancún's coastline.

Be aware that the surf along the Zona Hotelera's long, east-facing arm, though beautiful, can be heavy, and drownings and near-drownings do occur. There are lifeguards near all public access points, and colored flags (Green is Safe, Yellow is Caution, Red is Closed) for reference. But nothing is more important than common sense: Don't swim if the conditions (or your own condition) aren't suitable. The beaches along the short, north-facing leg are much calmer. For really calm waters head to Isla Mujeres, where there are no waves and the water in places is only waist deep more than 75 meters (250 feet) from shore. The Laguna Nichupté is not recommended for swimming because of pollution and crocodiles.

Playa Caracol

Playa Caracol (Blvd. Kukulcán Km. 8.5) has a small stretch of beach right at the public access point, but it's not too pleasant and often very crowded. The beach is much better just east of there, in front of the Fiesta Americana Coral Beach, but you have to cut through the hotel to get there, and the hotel lounge chairs take up most of the beach.

Playa Gaviota Azul

The pathway to **Playa Gaviota Azul** (Blvd. Kukulcán Km. 10), a huge, beautiful beach, is between The City nightclub and Forum by the Sea mall, and it extends well north and south of there (merging with Playa Chac Mool just to the south) with plenty of room to set up a towel and umbrella. Parking can be tricky here—better to arrive by bus or taxi—but you've got plenty of eating and shopping options, if you need a break from the sun. If you're interested

Beach Access

Look for these signs in the Zona Hotelera for public access to the beach.

There's a notion that high-rise hotels have monopolized Cancún's best beaches, but this is only partly true. While most hotels *do* front prime real estate, all beach areas in Mexico are public (except for military zones). Hotels cannot, by law, prohibit you or anyone else from lying out on a towel and enjoying the sun and water. Many high-end hotels subvert this by making it difficult or uncomfortable for nonguests to use "their" beaches: Very few maintain exterior paths, and others spread guest-only beach chairs over the best parts. (In the hotels' defense, they also typically do a good job of keeping their areas clear of trash and seaweed, which can mar otherwise beautiful beaches.) If your hotel has a nice beach area, you're all set. If not, you can just walk through a hotel lobby to the beach—as a foreigner, you are very unlikely to be stopped. (Sadly, locals are likely to be nabbed if they do the same thing.) But even that is unnecessary: The city maintains several public access points marked with prominent blue and white signs along Boulevard Kukulcán. The area right around the access point is often crowded, but you can walk a couple hundred meters in either direction to have more breathing room. One public access point—Playa Delfines, at the southern end of the hotel zone—has no nearby hotels and is used by a refreshing mix of Mexican and foreign beachgoers.

in a beach club, **Mandala Beach** (Blvd. Kukulcán Km. 9.5, tel. 998/848-8385, www.mandalabeach.com, 10am-6pm daily, US$25 pp) is open to the public and has beach beds, a swimming pool, full bar and restaurant service, and a DJ. It can definitely be a scene, but that's pretty much the point.

Playa Marlín

Playa Marlín (Blvd. Kukulcán Km. 12.5) is a clean, attractive beach with an access point between Plaza Kukulcán mall and the police and fire station. There's plenty of parking on the road parallel to the beach, and the mall has restaurants just a few steps away.

Playa Ballenas

Playa Ballenas (Blvd. Kukulcán Km. 14.5) is a long, pretty beach, with an access path between the Hard Rock and Secrets The Vine resorts. There is no food or drink service on the beach, but look for a few small shops selling water and snacks on the frontage road rear the public access point.

Zona Hotelera

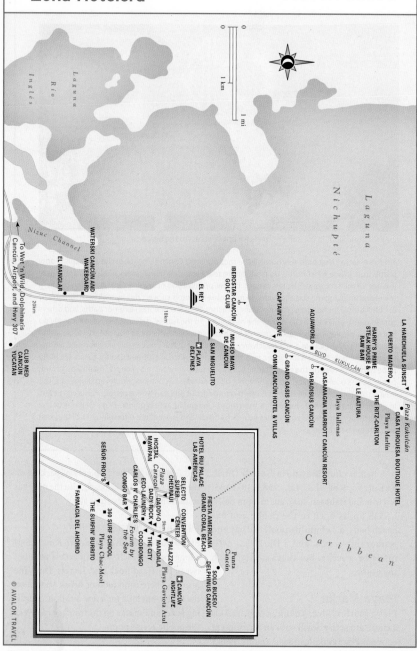

0
0

1 km

1 mi

Río Inglés

Laguna

Nichupté

Laguna

Nizuc Channel

To Wet 'n Wild, Dolphinaris Cancún, Airport, and Hwy 307

20km

18km

BLVD. KUKULCÁN

WATERSKI CANCÚN AND WAKEBOARD

EL MANGLAR

IBEROSTAR CANCÚN GOLF CLUB

EL REY

MUSEO MAYA DE CANCÚN

SAN MIGUELITO

PLAYA DELFINES

CLUB MED CANCÚN YUCATÁN

CAPTAIN'S COVE

AQUAWORLD

GRAND OASIS CANCÚN

OMNI CANCÚN HOTEL & VILLAS

PARADISUS CANCÚN

CASAMAGNA MARRIOTT CANCÚN RESORT

Playa Ballenas

LE NATURA

HARRY'S PRIME STEAK HOUSE & RAW BAR

THE RITZ-CARLTON

Playa Marlín

PUERTO MADERO

LA HABICHUELA SUNSET

Plaza Kukulcán

CASA TURQUESA BOUTIQUE HOTEL

HOSTAL MAYAPAN

Plaza Caracol

SELECTO SUPER CHEDRAUI

HOTEL RIU PALACE LAS AMÉRICAS

SEÑOR FROG'S

ECO-LAUNDRY

CARLOS N' CHARLIE'S

CONGO BAR

DADDY ROCK

360 SURF SCHOOL

Playa Chac-Mool

THE SURFIN' BURRITO

FARMACIA DEL AHORRO

DADY'O

CONVENTION CENTER

FIESTA AMERICANA GRAND CORAL BEACH

Forum by the Sea

MANDALA

PALAZZO

THE CITY

COCOBONGO

9km

CANCÚN NIGHTLIFE

Playa Gaviota Azul

SOLO BUCEO/ DELPHINUS CANCÚN

Punta Cancún

Caribbean

© AVALON TRAVEL

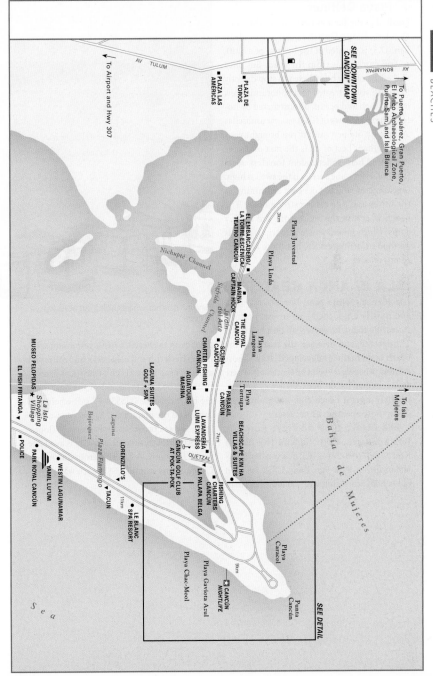

SEE "DOWNTOWN CANCÚN" MAP

To Puerto, Juárez, Gran Puerto,
El Meco Archaeological Zone,
Puerto Sam, and Isla Blanca

AV BONAMPAK

AV TULUM

To Airport and Hwy 307

PLAZA DE
TOROS

PLAZA LAS
AMÉRICAS

3km

Playa Juventud

Playa Linda

Nichupté Channel

EL EMBARCADERO/
LA TORRE ESCÉNICA/
TEATRO CANCÚN

MARINA
CAPTAIN HOOK

THE ROYAL
CANCÚN

Segurda Channel

Jardin
del Arte

SCUBA
CANCÚN

CHARTER FISHING
CANCÚN

AQUATOURS
MARINA

LAGUNA SUITES
GOLF + SPA

Playa
Langosta

Playa
Tortugas

PARASAIL
CANCÚN

BEACHSCAPE KIN HA
VILLAS & SUITES

7km

To Isla
Mujeres

Bahía de Mujeres

MUSEO PELOPIDAS

EL FISH FRITANGA

La Isla
Shopping
Village

YAMIL LU'UM

WESTIN LAGUNAMAR

PARK ROYAL CANCÚN

POLICE

Laguna
Bojórquez

LAVANDERÍA
LUMI EXPRESS

QUETZAL

CANCÚN GOLF CLUB
AT POK-TA-POK

LORENZILLO'S

LA PALAPA BELGA

FISHING
CHARTERS
CANCÚN

9km

Plaza Flamingo

11km

TACUN

LE BLANC
SPA RESORT

Playa Chac-Mool

Playa Gaviota Azul

CANCÚN
NIGHTLIFE

Playa
Caracol

Punta
Cancún

SEE DETAIL

Sea

★ Playa Delfines

Located at the far southern end of the Zona Hotelera, **Playa Delfines** (Blvd. Kukulcán Km. 17.5) is situated at the bottom of a bluff, so you can't see it from the road. But once parked, or off the bus (there is a stop directly in front), you're treated to a panoramic view of the beach and ocean, unobstructed by hotels. There are rows of fixed *palapa* umbrellas and plenty of open sand if you brought your own. Perhaps best of all is the mix of people you'll find here: independent travelers, local families, even some surfers if the swell is high. (Speaking of which, take care swimming as the waves and tide can be strong here.) The beach is across the road from the El Rey ruins, which makes a nice side trip. There is no food or drink service, but there are restrooms on-site.

ISLA BLANCA BEACHES

Isla Blanca's white-sand beaches are wild and mostly untouched—all to say, perfect! Accessing them, however, can be a bit tricky. Though the land between the road and the beach is virtually undeveloped, it is almost entirely privately owned and fenced off. There are occasional breaks between fences, but fortunately a great beach club makes hunting down those openings unnecessary.

Isla Blanca Club de Playa (formerly Pirata Morgan, Carr. Cancún-Isla Blanca Km. 9, tel. 998/240-2185, www.cabanasislablanca.com, 9am-5pm daily, US$2.50) is an old-school beach club with a handful of small

Cancún's beaches: where chilling out never looked so good

palapas on the beach, a rustic restaurant serving up fresh fish and cold beers, and miles and miles of beach. If you can't tear yourself away from the beach at the end of the day, there are basic *cabañas* (US$39-77 s/d) where you can spend the night. Each has screen walls to let in the sea breeze at night, cement floors, and private bathrooms; electricity is available 6pm-11pm only. A cab ride from downtown Cancún runs around US$15 each way.

Entertainment and Events

Cancún is justly famous for its raucous nightclubs, pulsing with lights and music and packed with revelers of all ages every night of the week. The club scene is especially manic during spring break, July, August, Christmas, and New Year's, but you can count on finding a party no matter when you visit. And those with quieter tastes will be happy to learn there's more to Cancún's nightlife than clubs, including a nice mix of small music venues, lounge bars, theaters, and cinemas.

★ NIGHTLIFE

Cancún's most popular nightclubs are within walking distance of each other in the **Zona Hotelera,** at Punta Cancún. The Zona Hotelera also has some great lounge bars. Downtown, meanwhile, has nightclubs specializing in Latin music, and the city's best live music, theater, and movies.

Cuncrawl (toll-free Mex. tel. 800/269-1317, toll-free U.S. tel. 800/975-4349, www.cuncrawl.com, US$80 pp) does fun guided bar/club crawls in the heart of Cancún, hitting three different clubs (they vary by night) with

VIP entrance and seating, open bar, and available transport to/from your resort (US$10 pp).

Nightclubs
ZONA HOTELERA

Nightclubs in the Zona Hotelera charge US$55-80 admission with open bar included. The clubs open every day, from around 10pm until 4am or later. Special events, like ladies night or bikini parties, vary by the day, club, and season; check the clubs' websites or Facebook pages for the latest info and deals, or ask the concierge at your hotel.

CocoBongo (Blvd. Kukulcán Km. 9.5, tel. 998/883-2373, www.cocobongo.com.mx) is a spectacular club featuring live rock and salsa bands, flying acrobats, and Rihanna, Michael Jackson, and KISS impersonators. Movie clips are also projected onto huge screens.

The City (Blvd. Kukulcán Km. 9, tel. 998/848-8385, www.thecitycancun.com) is a megaclub with three levels and a total capacity of 6,000 (and allegedly the world's biggest disco ball). Be sure to take a whirl on the

For clubs and nightlife, you've come to the right place.

Downtown Cancún

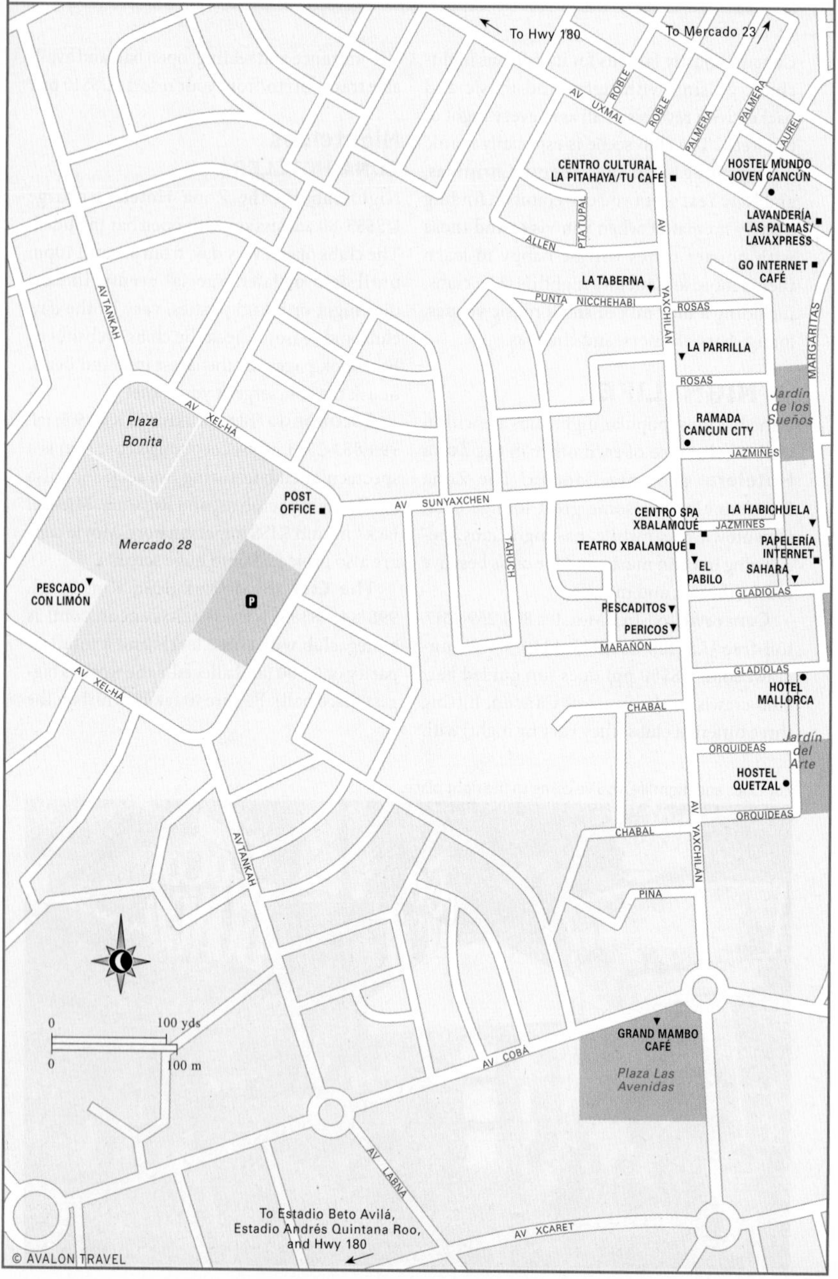

To Hwy 180

To Mercado 23

AV UXMAL
ROBLE
ROBLE
PALMERA
PALMERA
LAUREL

CENTRO CULTURAL
LA PITAHAYA/TU CAFÉ ■

HOSTEL MUNDO
JOVEN CANCÚN ■

PITAUPAL
AV
ALLEN

LAVANDERÍA
LAS PALMAS/
LAVAXPRESS ■

GO INTERNET ■
CAFÉ

LA TABERNA ▼

PUNTA NICCHEHABÍ

YAXCHILAN
ROSAS

LA PARRILLA ■

MARGARITAS

ROSAS

Jardín
de los
Sueños

RAMADA
CANCUN CITY ●

JAZMINES

AV TANKAH

Plaza
Bonita

AV XELHA

POST
OFFICE ■

AV SUNYAXCHEN

CENTRO SPA
XBALAMQUÉ ■

LA HABICHUELA
▼

Mercado 28

TAHUCH

JAZMINES

TEATRO XBALAMQUÉ ■

PAPELERÍA
INTERNET
SAHARA ■

EL
PABILO ■

PESCADO ▼
CON LIMÓN

P

GLADIOLAS

PESCADITOS ▼

PERICOS ▼

MARAÑON

GLADIOLAS

HOTEL ●
MALLORCA

AV XELHA

CHABAL

ORQUIDEAS

Jardín
del
Arte

HOSTEL
QUETZAL ●

ORQUIDEAS

AV TANKAH

CHABAL

YAXCHILAN

PIÑA

GRAND MAMBO ▼
CAFÉ

Plaza Las
Avenidas

0   100 yds

0   100 m

AV COBA

AV LABRIA

To Estadio Beto Avilá,
Estadio Andrés Quintana Roo,
and Hwy 180

AV XCARET

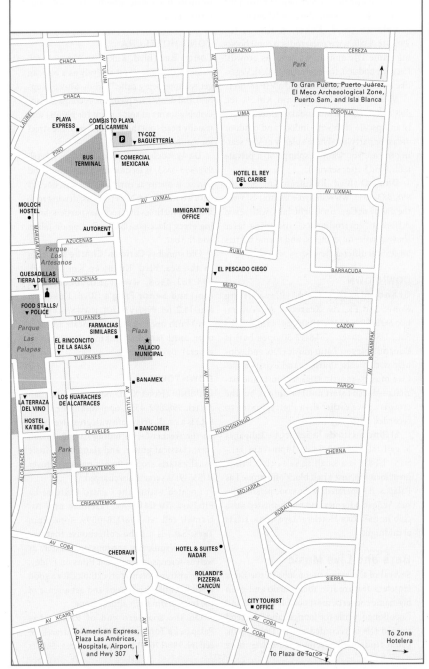

movable dance floor, which descends from the 3rd floor to the center of the club below.

Palazzo (Blvd. Kukulcán Km. 9, tel. 998/848-8380, www.palazzodisco.com) books big-name DJs and draws raucous crowds. Recently updated, the interior has a sleek Vegas-like look, huge chandeliers, and a VIP section.

Mandala (Blvd. Kukulcán Km. 9, tel. 998/848-8380, www.mandalanightclub.com) is an upscale club with indoor and outdoor areas for partying. There's plenty of VIP seating in case you want to splurge on a private table (and better service).

Dady-O (Blvd. Kukulcán Km. 9.5, tel. 998/883-3333, www.dadyo.com.mx) is, well, the daddy of Cancún's nightclubs, with seven different "environments," including laser shows, swimsuit contests, and theme parties on several different levels.

DOWNTOWN

Grand Mambo Café (Plaza Hong Kong, 2nd Fl., Av. Xcaret at Av. Tulum, tel. 998/884-4536, 10:30pm-4am Wed.-Sat., US$5 cover, US$8-12.50 open bar) is Cancún's biggest Latin music club, and popular with locals, tourists, and expats alike. Live music—mostly salsa, cumbia, and bachata—doesn't start until midnight, but the crowds arrive earlier than that, spinning to recorded Latin rhythms.

El Rinconcito de la Salsa (Av. Tulipanes 3, cell tel. 998/100-3429, 10pm-4am Fri.-Sun., US$5) is a smallish salsa club with a great location, just a half block off Parque Las Palapas. It's operated by the same person who ran Azúcar, a former and much-missed salsa club in the Zona Hotelera. Live music starts at midnight.

Bars and Live Music

Several of the major nightclubs in the Zona Hotelera feature live rock music and even big-name concerts, most notably Palazzo and CocoBongo, while the lounges and bars tend toward DJs or recorded music. Downtown, you'll find smaller venues featuring more intimate live music, whether jazz, solo guitarists, or trios.

ZONA HOTELERA

Congo Bar (Blvd. Kukulcán Km. 9.5, tel. 998/883-0563) is about as lively as a bar can get without being called a club. Music is upbeat and drinks are plentiful. A conga line inevitably forms at some point (or points) and usually heads out the door and onto the street for a quick spin.

Dady Rock (Blvd. Kukulcán Km. 9.5, tel. 998/883-3333) is technically a restaurant and bar, so it opens as early as 6pm and doesn't have a dance floor. Nevertheless, driving rock music, sometimes live, soon has partiers dancing every place possible, including on tables and the bar.

Old standbys **Carlos n' Charlie's** (Forum by the Sea, Blvd. Kukulcán Km. 8.5, tel. 998/883-4468, www.carlosandcharlies. com) and **Señor Frog's** (Blvd. Kukulcán Km. 14.2, tel. 998/193-1701, www.senorfrogs. com) both open at noon for meals and stay open until 3am for drinking, dancing, and general mayhem.

DOWNTOWN

El Pabilo (Hotel Xbalamqué, Av. Yaxchilán 31, tel. 998/892-4553, 6pm-midnight Mon.-Sat.) is a small, artsy café with great live music on the weekends, including Cuban, fusion jazz, classical guitar, and flamenco. Music usually starts around 9pm; a moderate cover (US$5-9) is sometimes charged.

Located within the Centro Cultural La Pitahaya, **Tu Café** (Av. Yaxchilán near Av. Uxmal, cell tel. 998/118-0099, 4pm-11pm Tues.-Sat.) is a boho coffeehouse that has open jazz/funk jam sessions on Tuesday as well as screens independent films on Friday. There also are rotating art exhibits. It's a good place to chill with friends and get a sense of the local art/music/cultural scene.

On the southern end of Parque Las Palapas, **La Terraza del Vino** (Alcatraces 29, cell tel. 998/126-0131, 6pm-3am Tues.-Sat.) is

portrait artist at the artisanal market Manos Mágicas

a pleasant open-air wine bar that books live guitar soloists most nights starting at 9pm.

La Taberna (Av. Yaxchilán at Punta Nicchehabi, tel. 998/887-5433, www.lataberna. com.mx, noon-4am daily) is a locals sports bar with lots of big-screen TVs and drink specials every night of the week. Free appetizers come with each drink, plus meals are free 1pm-6pm daily.

THE ARTS
Theater

Teatro Cancún (El Embarcadero, Blvd. Kukulcán Km. 4, tel. 998/849-5580, www.teatrodecancun.com.mx, ticket office on ground level 9am-9pm Mon.-Sat.) stages shows of all sorts, from music and dance to comedy and theater, both amateur and professional, mostly in Spanish. Ticket prices vary, but average US$5-30.

Teatro Xbalamqué (Hotel Xbalamqué, Av. Yaxchilán 31, www. teatroxbalamque. blogspot.com, tel. 998/204-1028) stages experimental and one-act theater performances

in a small space inside the hotel of the same name. Most shows are in Spanish; check website for showtimes.

Cinema

Cancún has two convenient movieplexes, one in the Zona Hotelera and one downtown, both offering the latest American and Mexican releases. Most Hollywood movies are subtitled, but be aware that those made for kids, and even teenagers, are likely to be dubbed. Look for "DOB" (for *doblado,* or "dubbed") or "SUB" for (*subtitulada,* or "subtitled") to be sure. Ticket prices average around US$6; early shows may be discounted, and there's two-for-one Tuesday at the Cinemex.

In the Zona Hotelera, there's a **Cinemex** at La Isla Shopping Village (Blvd. Kukulcán Km. 12.5, no phone, www.cinemex.com), while downtown has **Cinépolis** at Plaza Las Américas (Av. Tulum at Av. Sayil, tel. 998/884-0403, www.cinepolis.com). For a real treat, try **Cinépolis VIP,** which has reclining leather seats and wait service, with a menu that includes sushi, gourmet baguettes, cappuccinos, and cocktails (and popcorn and soda, too). Same location but tickets are sold at a separate window, costing around US$10.

FESTIVALS AND EVENTS

Held the first Saturday and Sunday of each month, **Manos Mágicas** (literally, magic hands) is an artisanal market held in the Jardín del Arte (across from Oasis Palm Hotel, Blvd. Kukulcán Km. 4.5, 3pm-10pm). Dozens of local artisans showcase their textiles, paintings, jewelry, and more alongside organic foods and treats. At 6pm, ballet *folklórico* (traditional Mexican folk dancing) is featured on a stage set up at the far end of the park.

Puerto Vallarta and Acapulco have long been Mexico's top destinations for gay travelers, but organizers of the **Cancún International Gay Festival** are working to put Cancún on the list. Inaugurated in 1995 and typically held in May, the festival includes beach parties, sunset cruises, city tours, and more.

Since 2001 the **Concurso Municipal de Artesanías,** a citywide handicraft competition, has been held annually in Cancún's Palacio Municipal. In addition to showcasing the city's best artisans, many participants also sell their work just in front of the building. Look for the large white tents—and the crowds—on Avenida Tulum in early August.

Shopping

Cancún has five major malls, a handful of open-air markets, and hundreds of independent shops, so you can buy just about anything. Most mall and independent shops accept credit cards, but plan on paying cash at the markets.

OPEN-AIR MARKETS

Mercado 28 (Av. Sunyaxchen at Av. Xel-Há, 9am-8pm daily) is a large open-air market featuring a wide variety of Mexican handicrafts: ceramics from Tonalá, silver from Taxco, hammocks from Mérida, *alebrijes* (wooden creatures) from Oaxaca, and handwoven shirts from Chiapas. You'll also find a fair share of T-shirts, key chains, coconut monkeys, and the like. A handful of restaurants in the center of the market offer traditional Mexican fare.

Adjacent to Mercado 28, **Plaza Bonita** (Av. Sunyaxchen at Av. Xel-Há, 9am-8pm daily) is a multilevel shopping center built to look like a colonial village—bright courtyards, fountains, greenery, and all. Folk art here is a bit more expensive than that in the market next door, but the quality is usually better.

On weekend evenings, stroll through **Parque Las Palapas** and **Parque Los Artesanos,** both great spots to pick up local handicrafts, Chiapanecan clothing, bohemian jewelry, and art.

MALLS

Recently renovated, **Plaza Caracol** (Blvd. Kukulcán Km. 8.5, www.caracolplaza.com, 8am-10pm daily) is the best place in the Zona Hotelera to get any beach essentials you left at home, with good brands and decent prices on bathing suits, flip-flops, sunglasses, sunscreen, etc. You can also grab a

Mercado 28 has souvenirs and keepsakes of all kinds.

Black Coral: A Disappearing Treasure

Despite its name, living black coral is not black at all, but a rich blue-green. It's only when the skeleton is stripped and polished that the namesake color emerges. Black coral belongs to a family of coral whose shells are semiflexible, and colonies grow into beautiful fanlike formations that bend and sway in the current. It's the world's slowest-growing coral, adding just 1-2 *hundredths of a millimeter* per year. (That's 200 times slower than human fingernails.) Black coral is among a handful of coral species recently discovered at extreme depths—300 meters (984 feet) down, and more—far deeper than previously thought possible for coral. And perhaps most remarkable of all was the finding, in 2009, that a colony of black coral near Hawaii is over 4,000 years old, making it the oldest known marine organism. Vast colonies of black coral once populated Cozumel's waters, and the island was for many years the center of black coral collection and trade. That's less true today, thanks partly to stricter regulation but also to the sad fact that the island's black coral is so diminished—the species is now considered endangered. Still, black coral retains a certain cachet, and the killing continues. Buying jewelry, souvenirs, and other items made with it only supports its continued destruction—please resist! Saving the black coral that lives in the region's waters is still very possible.

cup of Starbucks and good cheap grub at several small eateries.

Forum by the Sea (Blvd. Kukulcán Km. 9, www.forumbythesea.com.mx, 10am-11:30pm daily) is a horseshoe-shaped mall with three floors opening onto the airy main lobby. It's home to Hard Rock Cafe—you can't miss the huge guitar out front—the Rainforest Cafe (a jungle-themed family restaurant), a good steak house, and various mid- to high-end shops offering everything from T-shirts to expensive jewelry. There's a food court—and a spectacular view of the beach and ocean—on the 3rd floor.

A (mostly) open-air shopping center, **La Isla Shopping Village** (Blvd. Kukulcán Km. 12.5, tel. 998/883-5823, www.laislacancun.com.mx, 10am-10pm daily) is the most pleasant of the Zona Hotelera malls. It is set around an artificial river, with wide shady passageways, a nice variety of shops, and an excellent food court, including crepes, tacos, Italian, and more. The mall opens onto the lagoon, where there's a small marina and a nice boardwalk with half a dozen sit-down restaurants and a couple of water sports kiosks. A newer

enclosed section called El Palacio Boutique houses various luxury shops. La Isla is also home to the popular Interactive Aquarium and has a five-screen movie theater.

Plaza Kukulcán (Blvd. Kukulcán Km. 12.5, 10am-10pm daily) is a swanky Zona Hotelera mall, with a section called Luxury Avenue selling fine watches, jewelry, and couture clothing. The main mall area has some usual suspects like Sunglass Island and MixUp music store. Be sure to check out the **MUSA Visitor Center** (2nd floor, tel. 998/848-8312, www.musacancun.org, free) and its "dry" exhibit room; it describes the Subaquatic Museum of Art's underwater project through print and film plus has several sculptures on-site.

You don't have to go to the Zona Hotelera for your mall fix. **Plaza Las Américas** (Av. Tulum at Av. Sayil, tel. 998/887-3863, 9am-10pm daily) stretches almost a block and includes dozens of mid- to upscale shops, an arcade, and two movie theaters. **Plaza Las Avenidas** (Av. Cobá at Av. Tulum, tel. 998/887-7552, 9am-10pm daily) has similar offerings without the cinema.

Sports and Recreation

While relaxing by the pool or on the beach is more than enough sports and recreation for many of Cancún's visitors—and who can blame them?—there *are* a number of options for those looking for a bit more action. From golf and fishing to scuba diving and kiteboarding (and a whole bunch of things in between), Cancún has something for everyone.

BEACH ACTIVITIES

Parasailing (*paracaídas* in Spanish) can be booked as a traditional one-person ride (with takeoff from the shore) or a two-person ride, in which you can take off from the boat or the water. Prices and duration are fairly uniform: US$50-60 per person for a 10- to 12-minute ride. Look for independent operators on the beach, especially on Playa Tortugas (Blvd. Kukulcán Km. 6.5), Playa Chac-Mool (Blvd. Kukulcán Km. 10), Playa Ballenas (Blvd. Kukulcán Km. 14.5), and Playa Delfines (Blvd. Kukulcán Km. 17.5). Or sign up at **Parasail Cancún** (Playa Tortugas, Blvd. Kukulcán Km. 6.5, tel. 998/849-4995, www.parasailcancun. com, 9am-5:30pm) or **Aquaworld** (Blvd.

Kukulcán Km. 15.2, tel. 998/848-8326, toll-free U.S./Can. tel. 844/422-7235, www.aquaworld.com.mx, 7am-8pm daily).

WaveRunners are rented on the same beaches where parasailing is pitched. Prices average US$40-50 for 30 minutes; one or two people can ride at a time.

SNORKELING AND SCUBA DIVING

Cancún doesn't compare to Cozumel, Isla Mujeres, or really anywhere along the Riviera Maya for snorkeling and diving. Its coral and other sealife are less plentiful and far less healthy. That said, if you enjoy modern art, an underwater sculpture museum provides a special treat. Or consider arranging a snorkeling or diving trip in a cenote, the otherworldly freshwater caves that dot the coast south of Cancún. If you're really hankering for some bubbly, we recommend booking a trip with a shop in Isla Mujeres or Puerto Morelos, both easy to reach from Cancún. (Cozumel is harder to do as a day trip, requiring a ferry ride to and from Playa del Carmen.)

Small kiosks along the beach offer parasailing and other activities.

Snorkeling

For the best open-water and cenote snorkeling, book a trip with one of the dive shops listed below. All offer guided snorkeling trips in addition to diving, and are invariably better than the "jungle trips" hawked around Cancún, even for beginners.

★ MUSEO SUBACUÁTICO DE ARTE (MUSA)

A popular snorkeling site is Cancún's Nizuc reef, where an installation of the **Subaquatic Museum of Art** (www.musacancun.org) is located. Created by five artists, the site contains hundreds of life-size statues of everyday people—from nuns to tribal leaders. A breathtaking exhibit in and of itself, the works were created from a special cement that promotes coral and sealife formation. A second MUSA installation is located near Isla Mujeres, at Manchones reef.

Scuba Diving

A number of shops offer fun dives as well as certification courses at all levels. Hotels with their own dive shop may offer special rates to guests, but not necessarily.

Solo Buceo (Dreams Cancún Hotel, Blvd. Kukulcán Km. 9.5, tel. 998/883-3979, toll-free U.S./Can. tel. 800/310-6917, www.solobuceo. com, 9am-4:30pm daily) is a friendly shop with a strong reputation for service. Two-tank reef dives run US$80, while two-tank cenote trips cost US$175, including lunch; prices include all gear including wetsuit. Open-water certification classes (US$420, 3-4 days) can also be arranged.

Scuba Cancún (Blvd. Kukulcán Km. 5, tel. 998/849-7508, www.scubacancun.com. mx, 7am-8pm daily) was founded in 1980 and is still run by the same family. It offers the standard selection of dives, including one-tank (US$62), two-tank (US$77), and two-tank cavern and Cozumel dives (US$165 and US$180, respectively); all prices include equipment except wetsuit (US$10, recommended for cavern trips). Snorkel trips are offered in Cancún (US$39), Cozumel (US$125), and nearby cenotes (US$92). Trips can sometimes get crowded—ask about the size of your group before you book.

Aquaworld (Blvd. Kukulcán Km. 15.2, tel. 998/848-8326, toll-free U.S./Can. tel. 844/422-7235, www.aquaworld.com.mx, 7am-8pm daily) is Cancún's biggest, most commercialized water sports outfit, of which scuba diving is only a small part. Come here if you're looking for activities for the whole family, divers and nondivers alike, all in one spot. Otherwise, head to smaller shops for more personal attention.

KITEBOARDING

Ikarus (tel. 998/874-4245, www.kiteboard-mexico.com) is a full-service kiteboarding school on the lagoon side of Isla Blanca, just north of Cancún. Conditions for learning to kiteboard don't get much better than this: steady wind, kilometers of flat water with few boats or other obstacles, and water never more than waist deep. Private classes are US$75-95 per hour, while groups are US$58-70 per hour per person (maximum 3 to a group). Equipment is included for students or can be rented separately (US$95/day). Classes are held November-May, when the conditions are best. Simple lodging also is offered (US$8.50 pp hammock, US$10 pp tent, US$50 s/d). There's a restaurant on-site, too.

WATERSKIING, WAKEBOARDING, SURFING, AND SUP

Waterski Cancún and Wakeboard (Marina Manglar, Blvd. Kukulcán Km. 19.8, cell tel. 998/874-4816, www.waterskicancun. com, by appointment only) has three slalom courses and a number of ski sites at the southern end of Laguna Nichupté. Free-skiing and wakeboarding costs US$200 per hour, while the slalom courses are US$60 for 15 minutes. All equipment is included, except carbon skis.

360 Surf School (Blvd. Kukulcán Km. 9.5, cell tel. 998/241-6443, www.360surfschoolcancun.com, by appointment only) offers popular surfboarding classes on Playa Chac-Mool. Classes are geared toward beginners but can be tailored to any level. One-on-one classes run US$125 for 90 minutes; group lessons cost US$90 per person for 120 minutes (3 people maximum). Family packages and multiday packages also are offered. Surfing classes include surf equipment, Lycra tops, drinking water, and use of surfboard after the lesson. Stand-up paddleboard (or SUPing) classes also are offered for US$125 per person (1-3 students) or US$100 per person (4-8 students); each class is about two hours. Equipment rentals—body boards, short boards, long boards, fun boards, and paddleboards—also are available (US$15-75 per 24 hours).

SPORTFISHING

More than a dozen species of sport fish ply the waters off Cancún, including blue and white marlin, blackfin tuna, barracuda, dolphin dorado, wahoo, grouper, and more. **Fishing Charters Cancún** (Blvd. Kukulcán Km. 7.5, tel. 998/883-2517, U.S. tel. 954/283-8621, www.fishingcharterscancun.com, by appointment only) offers 4-8-hour trips on its fleet of custom fishing boats (US$280-3,200). Individual anglers also can sign up for "shared" trips (US$145-155, 4-6 hours). All trips include captain, mates, gear, bait, tackle, drinks, and, in some cases, lunch. Fly-fishing trips also can be arranged.

Charter Fishing Cancún (Blvd. Kukulcán Km. 6.5, cell tel. 998/2003240, www.charter-fishingcancun.com, by appointment only) offers excellent customer service on its small fleet of boats. Private charters range US$500-900 (4-8 hours); "shared" trips cost US$155 per person (6 hours). All trips include bait, tackle, ice, drinks (beer, soda, and water), fishing licenses, and passenger insurance. Round-trip transportation to/from your hotel is included for private charters only.

SWIMMING WITH DOLPHINS

Located within Wet n' Wild water park, **Dolphinaris Cancún** (Blvd. Kukulcán Km. 25, tel. 998/881-3030, toll-free Mex. tel. 800/365-7446, www.dolphinaris.com) offers dolphin interaction programs that include "fin shaking" and receiving a "kiss" (US$95, 1 hour), as well as swimming with and getting a foot push from them (US$139, 1 hour). For those toying with the idea of working with dolphins, visitors also can help out as Trainers for the Day (US$209, 8 hours).

Interactive Aquarium (La Isla Shopping Village, Blvd. Kukulcán Km. 12.5, tel. 998/206-3311, toll-free Mex. tel. 800/335-3461, www.aquariumcancun.com.mx, 10:30am-7pm daily, US$14) has a disappointingly small display of fish and other sea creatures, but its raison d'être are the interactive dolphin and shark exhibits. Dolphin program activities range from receiving a "kiss" and getting a "foot push" (US$109-159, 45-60 minutes) to a couples-only program (US$399, 75 minutes) that includes a review of the anatomy and physiology of dolphins. Shark "interactions" involve climbing into an acrylic booth and being lowered into the aquarium's huge shark tank to get a close-up look at bull, brown, and nurse sharks (US$34 pp, 30 minutes).

Delphinus Cancún (Blvd. Kukulcán Km. 7.5, toll-free Mex. tel. 800/335-3461, toll-free U.S./Can. tel. 888/526-2230, www.delphinus.com.mx) was being remodeled at the time of research. Check the website for updates.

ECOPARKS AND WATER PARKS
Ecoparks

Despite the deluge of advertising you'll see for Xcaret, Xel-Há, Xplor, and Parque Garrafón, none are actually in Cancún. Parque Garrafón is the closest, situated on the southern end of Isla Mujeres. The others are 60-90 minutes south of Cancún, nearer to Playa del Carmen and Tulum. You can buy tickets at the gates, though most people buy them online or at their hotels so bus transportation is included in the cost; discounted park tickets also are popular giveaways for taking part in a timeshare presentation.

Water Parks

Sometimes referred to as Parque Nizuc, **Wet n' Wild** (Blvd. Kukulcán Km. 25, tel. 998/193-2000, toll-free U.S. tel. 855/203-9863, www.wetnwildcancun.com, 9:30am-5pm daily, US$49 adult all-inclusive, US$43 child all-inclusive) is a small but classic water park with a handful of twisting slippery slides, high-speed water toboggans, and family-size inner tubing. It's a great way to cool off, especially if you're traveling with kids (or want to channel your own inner five-year-old). The all-inclusive plan includes all slides, meals, and drinks though, oddly enough, not the inner tubes. BYO towel too. The park is also home to **Dolphinaris Cancún** (Blvd. Kukulcán Km. 25, tel. 998/881-3030, toll-free Mex. tel. 800/365-7446, www.dolphinaris.com, US$95-209), a dolphin interaction program; the two parks often run specials together. Check either website for online deals.

GOLF

The **Iberostar Cancún Golf Club** (Blvd. Kukulcán Km. 17, tel. 998/881-8016, www.iberostargolfresorts.com/cancun, US$199/99 public/hotel guests, US$149/49 public/guests after 2pm) is considered one of the finer courses in the region. This 18-hole par 72 course hugs Laguna Nichupté and boasts a great view of the Maya ruins El Rey from the 16th hole. Alligators also are rumored to be in one of the water hazards, so consider leaving those water-bound balls behind.

The **Cancún Golf Club at Pok-ta-Pok** (Blvd. Kukulcán Km. 7.5, tel. 998/883-1230, www.cancungolfclub.com) is an 18-hole championship golf course designed by Robert Trent Jones Jr. It winds its way along the Caribbean and Laguna Nichupté and features its own Maya ruin near the 12th hole, discovered when the course was built. Greens fees are US$160 and drop to US$115 after 2pm. Rates include a shared golf cart and snacks and drinks on the course. Some Zona Hotelera hotels offer discounts—ask your concierge for details.

If you feel like a short round of golf and don't want to shell out the big bucks, there are two par-3 courses in the Zona Hotelera open to the public: **Paradisus Cancún** (Blvd. Kukulcán Km. 16.5, tel. 998/881-1100, www.melia.com, 7am-1pm last tee-off, US$45 greens fees, US$10 club rentals) and **Grand Oasis Cancún** (Blvd. Kukulcán Km. 16, tel. 998/885-0867, 8am-2:30pm last tee-off, US$27.50 greens fees including clubs).

You'll find two Jack Nicklaus courses at **Moon Palace Golf & Spa Resort** (Hwy. 307 Km. 340, tel. 998/881-6100, toll-free U.S. tel. 888/327-0655, www.moonpalacecancun.com, US$303 for 18 holes, US$187 for 9 holes), just 15 minutes south of the Zona Hotelera. It has three nine-hole courses spanning nearly 11,000 yards. Greens fees include a shared golf cart, snacks, drinks, and round-trip transportation to select hotels; from 2:30pm until closing at 6pm, greens fees are US$187 for as many holes as you can play. There's also a driving range, a green-side bunker, and putting and chipping greens. Club rentals are US$50.

SPECTATOR SPORTS

Bullfights

Cancún's **Plaza de Toros** (Av. Bonampak at Av. Sayil, tel. 998/884-8372, US$45, children under 12 free) hosts a bullfight every Wednesday at 3:30pm December-May. Bullfights here differ from traditional *corridas* (runnings) in that only four bulls are fought (versus five or six) and a mini-*charrería* (rodeo) is performed. Tickets can be purchased online (www.ticketmaster.com.mx) or at the box office.

Baseball

Baseball (*béisbol* in Spanish) is huge in Mexico, particularly in the north, where there are as many baseball diamonds as soccer fields. While still not having the pull in the Yucatán as it does elsewhere, it is a sport on the rise. The local team, **Tigres de Quintana Roo** (Quintana Roo Tigers, www.tigresqr.com), is one of the 16 teams that make up Mexico's professional baseball league, the

Liga Mexicana de Béisbol (www.lmb.com.mx). You can catch a game March-September at the **Estadio Beto Avilá** (Av. Xcaret s/n, behind Walmart, tel. 998/887-3113, US$1.50-10).

Soccer

Arriving in Cancún from Mexico City in 2007, **Atlante** (www.atlantefc.mx) is the city's first professional *fútbol* team. And arrive they did: Atlante won the Mexican League's championship and the Apertura 2007 Championship, both in their first year in residence. The following season Atlante won the 2008-09 CONCACAF Champions League, earning it a spot in the 2009 FIFA Club World Cup, where the team placed fourth. The team plays at the **Estadio Andrés Quintana Roo** (Av. Mayapán s/n, US$10-50), west of the baseball stadium, August-May.

SPAS AND GYMS

Many hotels and resorts have spas, but the following are some of the finest, and are open to the public. Reservations are strongly encouraged.

Le Blanc Spa (Le Blanc Spa Resort, Blvd. Kukulcán Km. 10, tel. 998/881-4740, toll-free U.S. tel. 888/327-0653, www.leblancsparesort.com/spa, 9am-8pm daily) is considered by many to be Cancún's best spa, and is a big reason Le Blanc Spa Resort as a whole gets such great reviews. The resort is adults-only, so the spa caters to couples, from joint massages and treatments to the Golden Spa Suite, a spa-within-a-spa.

Spas don't get much better, or bigger, than the new 40,000-square-foot **Gem Spa** (Fiesta Americana Grand Coral Beach, Blvd. Kukulcán Km. 9.5, tel. 998/881-3200, www.coralbeachcancunhotel.com, 10am-10pm daily) at the Fiesta Americana. There are dozens of available treatments, all said to be inspired by the precious stones of the Maya, Asian/South Pacific, and Baltic regions. Obsidian, amber, amethyst, even diamond dust are used to soothe and smooth your body and mind.

Downtown, the well-regarded **Centro Spa Xbalamqué** (Hotel Xbalamqué, Av. Yaxchilán 31, tel. 998/887-7853, 10am-8pm Mon.-Sat.) offers a full line of massages, facials, and body wraps, plus Reiki, crystal therapy, and *temascal* treatments. The spa's entrance is on Calle Jazmines, around the corner from the main hotel entrance. Prices are very reasonable, most ranging US$30-50.

TOURS

Jungle Tour

It sure *looks* like it would be fun to drive a WaveRunner or speedboat across the lagoon to a national marine park to snorkel. Unfortunately, the rules—Stay in line! Don't go too fast! Don't pass!—keep the boat part pretty tame. The snorkeling is also disappointing, with dozens of tourists swarming a small section of coral reef. We don't recommend this sort of trip, but dozens of agencies will gladly take your money (US$50-60 pp, 2 hours).

Aerial Tours and Views

AeroSaab (Playa Del Carmen Airport, 20 Av. Sur near Calle 1, tel. 998/865-4225, www.aerosaab.com) offers scenic full-day tours from Cancún—Chichén Itzá, Isla Holbox, Mérida, Uxmal, and as far as Palenque, with time to visit the area. Trips are in four- or five-seat Cessna airplanes and run US$95-800 per person, plus airport fees. Most trips require a minimum of 2-4 people.

If you prefer to stay (somewhat) grounded, board **La Torre Escénica** (Scenic Tower, El Embarcadero, Blvd. Kukulcán Km. 4.2, tel. 998/849-5582, 9am-9pm daily, US$15 during the day, US$18 at night), an 80-meter (262.5-foot) tower with a rotating passenger cabin, affording a beautiful 10-minute view of this part of the coastline. A brief history of the region also is played over the audio system. **Note:** Admission to this site is included in the Xcaret ticket; show your Xcaret wristband—it must still be on your wrist!—for free entry.

Food

Cancún has dozens of excellent restaurants—the finest are in the Zona Hotelera, mostly in the high-end resorts and along the west (lagoon) side of Boulevard Kukulcán. Be aware that eating out in the Zona Hotelera can be shockingly expensive, especially for dishes like lobster and imported steaks. There are a handful of Zona Hotelera gems, with great food at lower prices, and, of course, plenty of fast-food restaurants like McDonald's and Subway. For something more authentic but still affordable, downtown Cancún is the place to go. Parque Las Palapas and the surrounding streets have restaurants for all tastes and budgets, from fine dining to tasty street food, plus a number of great little cafés and sandwich shops.

ZONA HOTELERA
Mexican

Specializing in Yucatecan cuisine, **La Habichuela Sunset** (Blvd. Kukulcán Km. 12.6, tel. 998/840-6240, 1pm-midnight daily, US$15-40) is the sister restaurant of the popular **La Habichuela** (Parque Las Palapas, Calle Margaritas 25, tel. 998/884-3158, www.lahabichuela.com, noon-midnight daily) in downtown Cancún. The seafood is especially tasty—try the giant shrimp in tamarind sauce or *cocobichuela*, the house specialty, with lobster and shrimp in a sweet curry sauce. For dessert, ask for a Maya coffee flambé, Chiapanecan coffee made with cinnamon, brandy, and *Xtabentún* (a regional liqueur made with anise, rum, and fermented honey). Consider dining here on Monday, Wednesday, or Friday evening, when a colorful Maya dance show is presented at 8pm.

The Surfin' Burrito (Blvd. Kukulcán Km. 9.5, tel. 998/883-0083, 24 hours daily, US$5-10) is a hole-in-the-wall serving up a huge variety of burritos—pick your tortilla, protein (beef, chicken, or seafood), choice of salsas, and toppings. Rice and beans are a given.

Wash it down with a mammoth one-liter margarita (US$7) or fruit smoothie (US$4). Delivery is available.

Easy to miss, **Tacun** (Blvd. Kukulcán Km. 11.5, tel. 998/593-3638, 11am-10pm daily, US$5-10) is a roadside taco joint at heart, and one of the few places in the Zona Hotelera to get good, genuine Mexican food at reasonable prices. Try a taco sampler platter with shrimp, beef, chicken, and *al pastor* tacos, served piping hot with a variety of fresh salsas. The staff and ambience are friendly. Tacun is located across from the Flamingo Mall.

Seafood

A hidden gem in the Zona Hotelera, ★ **El Fish Fritanga** (aka Pescadillas, Blvd. Kukulcán Km. 12.7, tel. 998/840-6216, 11am-11pm daily, US$4-12) offers tasty homestyle seafood at great prices. If you're stumped, try the *pescadillas* or grilled nurse shark tacos, both house classics. The restaurant faces the lagoon and is below street level, making it easy to miss—look for a small parking lot under a bright Domino's Pizza sign.

Classy but unassuming, **Captain's Cove** (Blvd. Kukulcán Km. 16.5, tel. 998/885-0016, www.captainscoverestaurant.com, noon-11pm Tues.-Sat., 8am-11pm Sun., US$15-38) has a lovely lagoon-side location and excellent seafood, including fresh lobster, stuffed crab, and octopus and shrimp risotto. For a memorable dinner, call ahead to reserve a table on the patio at around sunset. It's located across from the Royal Mayan and Omni resorts.

The nautical-themed **Lorenzillo's** (Blvd. Kukulcán Km. 10.5, tel. 998/883-1254, www.lorenzillos.com.mx, 1pm-12:30am daily, US$18-45) is known as one of the best lobster houses in town. Live lobster is kept in an adapted rowboat tank at the entrance—select the one you want, weigh it on an old-time scale, and before you know it, dinner's on. (All of the lobster comes from the restaurant's lobster farm off Isla Blanca, just north of the Zona Hotelera). Seating is indoors under a *palapa* roof or outdoors on the narrow patio overlooking the lagoon.

Steak Houses

Puerto Madero (Marina Barracuda, Blvd. Kukulcán Km. 14.1, tel. 998/885-2829, www.puertomaderorestaurantes.com, 1pm-1am daily, US$15-65) is a longtime favorite serving carefully prepared meats in huge Argentinean-style portions. Choose a table in the warehouse-style dining room (an homage to the Puerto Madero shipyard in Argentina) or on the open-air patio with views of the lagoon. The menu includes salads, pastas, and excellent seafood, in addition to the many cuts of beef, some of which serve two. Prices are high, but not outrageously so, and you're sure to leave full.

Harry's Prime Steak House & Raw Bar (Blvd. Kukulcán Km. 14.2, tel. 998/840-6550, www.harrys.com.mx, 1pm-1am daily, US$25-100) specializes in best-of-the-best beef, expertly prepared (some cuts are dry-aged for up to four weeks) and cooked in blazing hot broilers. There's also a long menu of sashimi, oysters, ceviche, tartar, and other seafood dishes, plus salad and excellent wine and cocktails.

The prices are sky-high, but it's a memorable and worthwhile splurge for steak-lovers.

Other Specialties

Hidden in a small hotel near the Pok-ta-Pok golf course, **La Palapa Belga** (Hotel Imperial Laguna, Calle Quetzal 13, tel. 998/883-5454, www.lapalapabelga.com, 2:30pm-11pm Mon.-Sat., US$14-28) has been serving fine French-Belgian cuisine for almost two decades. It's worth searching out both for its views across the lagoon to the Zona Hotelera and its delicious food like beef tartar and escargot de Bourgogne. Reservations are recommended on weekends.

★ **Le Natura** (Blvd. Kukulcán Km. 14.2, tel. 998/883-0585, www.restaurantelenatura.mx, 7:30am-11pm daily, US$5-16) is a casual bistro serving up an amazing variety of whole foods and juices. The juice and smoothie menu alone is 33 items long (who knew carrots, beets, spinach, and celery could taste so good?); the breakfast menu has a good number of fruit and yogurt plates, egg dishes, and comfort food like waffles and pancakes; and lunch and dinner is just as varied with salads, bagel sandwiches, pastas, seafood, and Mexican classics like tacos and quesadillas. A vegetarian-only menu also is available.

Ceviche is a popular seafood dish on beaches in Mexico.

For a change of pace, **Elefanta** and **Thai Lounge** (La Isla Shopping Village, Blvd. Kukulcán Km. 12.5, tel. 998/176-8070, www. elefanta.com.mx and www.thai.com.mx, noon-midnight daily, US$15-42) are sister restaurants serving quality Indian and Thai food, respectively. The ambience at both is quite nice, despite being in a mall; the Thai Lounge, in particular, has private *cabañas* on stilts overlooking the lagoon and stays open late as a bar-lounge.

Groceries

Numerous small markets along Boulevard Kukulcán sell chips, water, sunscreen, and other beach basics. For a more complete—and upscale—grocery, head to **Selecto Súper Chedraui** (Blvd. Kukulcán Km. 9, tel. 998/830-0866, 7am-11pm daily). Opened in 2014, it's a three-story supermarket featuring organic foods, gourmet wines and cheeses, a sushi bar, a popular prepared food section, and great views over the lagoon.

DOWNTOWN
Mexican

★ **Quesadillas Tierra del Sol** (Margaritas near Tulipanes, 8am-midnight daily, US$2-4) is as great as ever. Hefty quesadillas (and *sopes, panuchos,* and *salbutes*) come with Oaxacan cheese and your choice of stuffing, from chorizo to *nopales* (cactus). Two will satisfy a decent appetite, four could push you over the edge. Fresh, fruity *aguas* help wash it down. Order at the register and they'll call your number.

On the southeast corner of Parque Las Palapas, **Los Huaraches de Alcatraces** (Alcatraces 31, tel. 998/884-3918, 8:30am-5pm Tues.-Sun., US$4-8) is a classic Mexican cafeteria serving traditional dishes like garlic-baked fish or chicken in homemade mole. All dishes come with a choice of two sides, such as veggies or beans. For something a little different, try one of the pre-Hispanic options, like quesadillas made with blue-corn tortillas.

Combine Disneyland and the Mexican Revolution and you might get **Pericos** (Av. Yaxchilán 61, tel. 998/884-3152, www.pericos. com.mx, noon-midnight daily, US$14-25), a classic Cancún family restaurant. *Bandito* waiters sport crisscrossed ammo belts, the bar has saddles instead of stools, and kids may get a rubber chicken on their plates as a joke. Low-key it is not, but Pericos has a solid reputation for serving good grilled meats and seafood in a fun, boisterous atmosphere. Live marimba and mariachi starts at 7:30pm most nights.

On the north end of Parque Las Palapas is a set of **food stalls** (8am-midnight daily, US$1.50-4) selling cheap Mexican and Yucatecan eats—tacos, quesadillas, tostadas, and *salbutes*. It's perfect if you're looking for some good street food or are on a tight budget.

Seafood

Pescaditos (Av. Yaxchilán 59, 11:30am-midnight Sun.-Thurs., 11:30am-1am Fri.-Sat., US$3-12) is the sort of restaurant you expect to see on the beach, complete with reggae music, a handful of tables, and a sign made from an old surfboard. And like the best beach shacks, Pescaditos will wow you with simple tasty meals, especially the seafood. The ceviche, beer-battered shrimp, and fish tacos and quesadillas are all outstanding, and very well priced. Wash it down with a frosty beer or homemade *limonada*.

A seafood eatery with an urban feel, **El Pescado Ciego** (Av. Nader btwn Rubia and Mero, tel. 998/898-1670, 1pm-11pm Mon.-Sat., noon-6pm Sun., US$6-15) serves up killer dishes like lobster quesadillas, octopus tostadas, swordfish carpaccio, and seafood bisque. It's popular with businesspeople during the week and couples on weekends.

Pescado Con Limón (Mercado 28, tel. 998/887-2436, 11:30am-7:30pm daily, US$6-12) may be a little short on ambience—plastic tables and chairs facing the Mercado 28 parking lot—but the seafood is as fresh and good as it comes, an open secret among locals and expats. For a sure thing, try a shrimp dish or one of the fried-fish platters. The tip is typically included (and somewhat hidden) in the bill.

Other Specialties

★ **Rolandi's Pizzeria Cancún** (Av. Cobá 12, tel. 998/884-4047, www.rolandirestaurants.com, noon-12:30am daily, US$11-17) is an institution, with sister pizzerias in Isla Mujeres, Playa del Carmen, and Cozumel. The food here—and at all of them—is consistently good; choose among thin-crust pizzas, calzones, and great homemade pastas. Pocket bread, warm and inflated, and a dish of olive oil come with every order. Sit on the veranda, which is draped in ivy that blocks out street noise.

Sahara (Calle Gladiolas 12, tel. 998/898-2222, 2pm-11pm Tues.-Sat., 2pm-6pm Sun., US$5-12) prepares authentic Lebanese food like hummus, falafel, and tabbouleh in a casual setting. A huge buffet, featuring the entire menu plus some extras, is served on Sunday only. Fun extras include hookah "hookups" (US$12.50) or having your coffee grounds read (US$12.50, including the coffee).

La Parrilla (Av. Yaxchilán 51, tel. 998/287-8119, www.laparrilla.com.mx, noon-2am daily, US$9-30) is one of the most popular of the restaurant-bars on this busy street, grilling a variety of delicious beef fillets, plus shrimp and lobster brochettes, chicken, fajitas, and tacos—the fiery spit in front is for *taquitos al pastor,* a Mexican classic. The breezy streetside eating area is comfortable and casual—good for families. There's also live mariachi music every night starting at 8pm.

Light Fare

El Pabilo (Hotel Xbalamqué, Av. Yaxchilán 31, cell tel. 998/129-9880, 5pm-1am daily, US$3-12) is an unassuming café serving up excellent coffee drinks, wine, and light meals. The space also serves as an art gallery, with rotating exhibits, and a multilingual bookstore. It is a great place to listen to live music, too—every night but Sunday, you can hear genres ranging from *bohemia cubana* to fusion jazz. Music starts at 9:30pm.

Get a tasty baguette sandwich at ★ **Ty-Coz Baguettería** (Av. Tulum at Av. Uxmal, tel. 998/884-6060, 8am-10pm Mon.-Sat., 8am-8pm Sun.), a cozy eatery tucked behind the Comercial Mexicana supermarket opposite the bus terminal. Popular with local professionals and students, the menu includes French- and German-inspired baguette sandwiches and *cuernos* (croissants). Most are US$3-5, but you can always order the *económica* baguette with ham, salami, and cheese for just US$1.25. If you don't want to head downtown for a sandwich, visit its **Zona Hotelera branch** (Blvd. Kukulcán Km. 9, 6am-9pm daily).

Groceries

Chedraui (Blvd. Kukulcán at Av. Tulum) and **Comercial Mexicana** (Av. Tulum at Av. Uxmal) are huge supermarkets with everything from produce and in-house bakeries to pharmacies and beach supplies. Both are open 7am-11pm daily and have ATMs just inside their doors.

Just a couple of blocks from the bus station, **Mercado 23** (Calles Ciricote and Cedro, three blocks north of Av. Uxmal via Calle Palmeras, 6am-6pm daily) has stands of fresh fruits and vegetables. The selection is somewhat limited, but the produce is the freshest around.

DINNER CRUISES

For couples, the **Lobster Dinner Cruise** (Aquatours Marina, Blvd. Kukulcán Km. 6.5, toll-free Mex. tel. 800/727-5391, toll-free U.S. tel. 866/393-5158, www.thelobsterdinner.com, US$99 dinner with open bar, no children under 14, departs at 5pm and 8pm nightly) offers a change of pace, serving three-course dinners aboard a Spanish-style galleon. The ship cruises the Laguna Nichupté for 2.5 hours, accompanied by live jazz.

If you've got kids, the **Galleon of Captain Hook** (Marina Captain Hook, Blvd. Kukulcán Km. 5, toll-free Mex. tel. 800/010-4665, www.capitanhook.com, US$65-102 adult with open bar, US$33-51 child, departs at 7pm nightly, 3.5 hours) offers dinner plus a costumed crew, tales of pirate conquest, and even a "disco party" on the deck while cruising the open sea. Hotel pickup is available for an extra fee.

Accommodations

Cancún has scores of hotels, varying from backpacker hostels to ultra-high-end resorts. They're also divided by their location: the Zona Hotelera and downtown. The Zona Hotelera has spectacular views, easy access to swimming pools and the beaches, and excellent restaurants, but prices are higher and you won't get much "authentic" interaction with local people. Downtown Cancún has a variety of food, shopping, and services (from Walmart to laundries) at generally lower prices, but staying downtown also means driving or taking a bus to the beach and not having access to hotel pools and amenities.

ZONA HOTELERA
Under US$100

Located on Laguna Nichupté, **El Manglar** (Blvd. Kukulcán Km. 19.8, tel. 998/885-1808, www.villasmanglar.com, US$90-100 s/d with a/c) has simple and spacious rooms, each with cable TV, air-conditioning, a king-size bed, and two couches that double as twin beds. There's a well-maintained pool on-site and beach access nearby at Playa Delfines. With the marina next door, it's especially popular with people who enjoy fishing, waterskiing, and wakeboarding.

The Zona Hotelera's one and only youth hostel, **Hostal Mayapan** (Mayfair Shopping Center, Blvd. Kukulcán Km. 8.5, tel. 998/883-3227, www.hostalmayapan.com, US$16-20 dorm with a/c, US$32 d with a/c) occupies, of all things, a defunct mall, complete with escalators and faux Maya artwork. The upside is you're within walking distance of the clubs and some nice beaches. The downside is, well, everything else: marginally clean linens and restrooms, ambivalent staff, paltry breakfast, no real common area, and air-conditioning that's on only intermittently. Private rooms aren't worth the extra cost.

US$100-200

Located alongside the Pok-ta-Pok golf course, **Laguna Suites Golf + Spa** (Paseo Pok-ta-Pok No. 3, tel. 998/891-5252, toll-free U.S./Can. tel. 866/384-0547, www.lagunasuites.com.mx, US$128 s/d with a/c, US$252 pp all-inclusive, children under 16 stay free) has just 47 suites, allowing for genuinely personalized service with none of the hubbub of a large beachfront resort. There's a small pool and a chic *palapa* lounge, plus free hourly shuttles to two nearby sister resorts—the Royal Sunset and Ocean Spa—where you can enjoy the pool, beach, restaurants, and other amenities like any other guest. A great option if you don't mind a little resort hopping.

An excellent value, **Beachscape Kin Ha Villas & Suites** (Blvd. Kukulcán Km. 8.5, tel. 998/891-5400, toll-free U.S. tel. 866/340-9082, www.beachscape.com.mx, US$119 s/d with a/c, US$212-476 suite with a/c) is a comfortable, low-key resort on a beautiful and spacious beach on the upper arm of the Zona Hotelera. The resort's one-, two-, and three-bedroom suites have fully equipped kitchens, living and dining areas, and ocean-view terraces; there also are a handful of standard hotel rooms. In addition to that huge beach, the property has a large (and rather plain) pool, restaurant-bar, and children's play area. Though lacking the style and ambience of Cancún's top resorts, Beachscape Kin Ha can hardly be beat for location and value. Coin-op laundry, an exercise room, and Wi-Fi (reception area only) is available.

US$200-400

With just 30 suites, **Casa Turquesa Boutique Hotel** (Blvd. Kukulcán Km. 13.5, tel. 998/193-2260, www.casaturquesa.com, US$240-280 s/d with a/c, US$406 suite with a/c) is a welcome change of pace from the massive resorts lining Boulevard Kukulcán. Units are spacious and spotless, if somewhat dated in style; ocean views and whirpool tubs more than make up for the old-school prints. Works of art also are featured throughout the property—paintings and sculptures from notable artists, mostly from Mexico. The hotel itself is perched above the beach, making for spectacular views from the pool. Service is warm and personalized.

CasaMagna Marriott Cancún Resort (Blvd. Kukulcán Km. 14.8, tel. 998/881-2000, toll-free U.S./Can. tel. 888/236-2427, www.marriott.com, US$249-299 s/d with a/c, US$349-449 suite with a/c) has over 400 rooms, all with private terraces and amenities like flat-screen TVs and wireless Internet. Guests can choose from eight eateries including an Argentinean steak house, a sushi restaurant, and a Thai restaurant. There's also a full-service spa, illuminated tennis courts, and a gym with separate men's and women's saunas. The hotel's main drawback is the pool—it's well maintained but small for the size and caliber of the resort; fortunately, it's just steps from the Caribbean.

Cancún has miles of inviting resorts.

Over US$400

★ **Fiesta Americana Grand Coral Beach** (Blvd. Kukulcán Km. 9.5, tel. 998/881-3200, www.coralbeachcancunhotel.com, US$390-415 junior suite with a/c, US$796 master suite with a/c) is an elegant hotel offering spacious and comfortable suites, all with spectacular ocean-view balconies. It features a series of infinity pools, lush and manicured gardens, and one of the calmest beaches of the Zona Hotelera. The hotel has five restaurants and cafés, a huge luxurious spa, a kids club, and activities ranging from Spanish lessons to golf.

The Ritz-Carlton (Blvd. Kukulcán Km. 13.9, tel. 998/881-0808, toll-free U.S/Can. tel. 800/542-8680, www.ritzcarlton.com, US$529-729 s/d with a/c, US$829-929 suite with a/c) is unparalleled in its elegance. Fine art, chandeliers, and marble floors greet you the moment the white-gloved porter opens the door. All rooms have stunning ocean views and boast features like goose down comforters, espresso machines, downpour showerheads,

and twice-daily housekeeping. Other high-end features of the resort include a full-service spa and gym, tennis courts, The Culinary Center (a gorgeous kitchen where guests can take cooking classes), and, of course, a well-maintained beach. The only hiccups are the unremarkable pools—nice enough but nothing special—an odd oversight given the luxuriousness of the rest of the hotel.

All-Inclusive Resorts

The Royal Cancún (Blvd. Kukulcán Km. 4.5, toll-free Mex. tel. 800/020-1421, toll-free U.S./Can. tel. 888/721-4431, US$155-176 pp all-inclusive) is a quiet resort that's especially well-suited for families. It's located on the short, north-facing part of the Zona Hotelera, so the beach has virtually no waves—a big difference from east-facing beaches, and a relief for parents with young children. There's also a popular kids club and lots of free sports gear like snorkeling equipment, sailboats, golf clubs, and bikes. The units themselves, while dated, are well maintained and spacious (all have two bedrooms and a full kitchen). Guests also enjoy access to two all-inclusive sister resorts, The Royal Sands in Cancún and The Royal Haciendas in Playa del Carmen.

Located at the southernmost tip of the Zona Hotelera, **Club Med Cancún Yucatán** (Blvd. Kukulcán Km. 20.6, tel. 998/881-8200, toll-free U.S. tel. 888/932-2582, www.clubmed. com, US$400 pp all-inclusive) is a secluded resort with a huge offering of activities—from wakeboarding and waterskiing to flying trapeze and salsa dancing. If you've got kids, the Mini Club keeps the little ones happy and busy all day long with activities like tennis and cooking lessons. There also are three good restaurants and a handful of bars—enough variety to keep most guests happy.

Hotel Riu Palace Las Américas (Blvd. Kukulcán Km. 8.5, tel. 998/881-4300, www. riu.com, US$284-304 s with a/c, US$392-420 d with a/c, US$364-402 s suite with a/c, US$500-555 d suite with a/c) is a Victorian-style hotel with 350-plus suites that, while not as elegant as the common areas, are quite nice nonetheless. Each has a separate sitting area, a minibar that's restocked daily, and standard amenities like satellite TV and in-room safe; most rooms also have ocean views. Beds are ultra firm—ask for a foam topper if that's an issue. Outside of the rooms, the beach is narrow but well maintained; there are also two infinity pools, endless water activities, six restaurants, and five bars.

A luxurious adults-only resort, ★ **Le Blanc Spa Resort** (Blvd. Kukulcán Km. 10, toll-free Mex. tel. 888/327-0654, toll-free U.S. tel. 888/327-0653, www.leblancsparesort.com, US$323-432 pp all-inclusive) offers all the amenities a vacationing couple could want: infinity pools, à la carte gourmet restaurants, a fully equipped gym and spa, Pilates and yoga classes, bars and lounges, and yards and yards of white-sand beach. The guest rooms are minimalist chic, all with views of the Caribbean or the lagoon. Each has a double whirlpool tub, marble bathroom with double showerheads, flat-screen TVs, a pillow menu, even in-room aromatherapy.

DOWNTOWN
Under US$50

A huge mural marks the entrance of ★ **Hostel Quetzal** (Jardín del Arte, Orquídeas 10, tel. 998/883-9821, www.quetzal.hostel.com, US$15-17 pp dorm with a/c, US$29 s with private bath and a/c, US$58 d with private bath and a/c), a dance studio turned hostel. An artsy place, it's got bright and airy rooms, all with air-conditioning, plus a verdant garden and a rooftop bar and lounge with views of downtown Cancún. A spiral staircase leads to the largest dorm (12 beds), which is spacious and colorful. Smaller dorms (5-6 beds) and private rooms are scattered around, all with terraces and plenty of natural light. All guests enjoy a full breakfast and family-style dinner as part of the rate. Nightly club outings also are included, and Wi-Fi is available.

Moloch Hostel (Margaritas 54, tel. 998/884-6918, www.moloch.com.mx, US$15 dorm with a/c, US$37/45 s/d with a/c) is a quiet and super-clean hostel with mini-split air conditioners in all the rooms, including the dorms, and an inviting kidney-shaped pool in back. Dorms are a bit cramped, but the beds are good; private rooms are larger and would even work for families. There's a fully equipped kitchen for all to use, as well as continental breakfast, a TV lounge, Wi-Fi, and free computers. All that, and it's just a block from the bus station and Parque Palapas.

Hostel Mundo Joven Cancún (Av. Uxmal 25, tel. 998/898-2104, www.mundojovenhostels.com, US$17 dorm with a/c, US$39 s/d with a/c and shared bath, US$46 with a/c and private bath) is a sleek affair with cool minimalist decor inside and out. Dorms are airy and bright, with outlets inside the lockers, so you can charge your devices without worrying they'll get swiped. Private rooms are equally stylish, and there's a rooftop lounge with a bar, whirlpool tub, hammocks, and nice views. Continental breakfast, kitchen access, and computers and Wi-Fi are all included.

A social place, **Hostel Ka'beh** (Calle Alcatraces at Calle Claveles, tel. 998/892-7902, www.cancunhostel.hostel.com, US$17-21 dorm with a/c, US$62 s/d with a/c) has welcoming lounge areas and daily activities like clubbing trips, movie night, and barbecue night. Breakfast—oatmeal, pancakes, eggs, waffles, PB&J—is self-service and available 24-7. There's also a full common kitchen, Wi-Fi, plus a huge lending library of travel guides. Dorms are mixed and comfortable enough; private rooms are too basic for the price.

US$50-100

★ **Hotel Mallorca** (Calle Gladiolas at Av. Alcatraces, tel. 998/884-4285, www.mallorcahotelandsuites.com, US$92 s/d with a/c, US$109 suite with a/c and kitchenette) has large comfortable rooms, friendly service, and a perfect location, just a half block from Parque Las Palapas. Rooms combine warm colors, wood furniture, and high ceilings with modern amenities like glass showers, flat-screen TVs, and Wi-Fi. A rooftop lounge has superb views of the park and city. All in all, it's a great downtown option.

Located just a short walk from Parque Palapas, **Hotel & Suites Nader** (Av. Nader near Av. Cobá, tel. 998/884-1584, www.suitesnadercancun.com, US$74 s/d with a/c, US$88 suite with a/c and kitchenette) is a comfortable and modern hotel. Rooms are somewhat sterile in decor but have updated amenities like flat-screen TVs, silent air-conditioning, and free Wi-Fi. The owners are often on-site, which makes for warm, personalized service. Another plus is the neighboring Café Nader, which is a tasty (and convenient) place for eats.

Ramada Cancun City (Av. Yaxchilán at Calle Jazmines, tel. 998/881-7870, toll-free Mex. tel. 800/640-7473, www.ramadacancun. com, US$75 s/d with a/c) is cool and sleek, yet affordable and centrally located. Rooms have stark white interiors accented by rust and brown furniture, with basin sinks and flat-screen TVs for a modern touch. Noise from nearby clubs can be a problem, and maintenance and service can be uneven. Still, it's a favorite among business travelers, and would suit travelers looking for a reliable, modern downtown hotel. There's a small pool and fitness room, and guests can take advantage of free transport and admission to **Mandala Beach** (Blvd. Kukulcán Km. 9.5, tel. 998/848-8385, www.mandalabeach.com, 10am-6pm daily), a hip beach club at Playa Gaviota Azul in the Zona Hotelera.

Cancún's hostels and small hotels can be great alternatives to all-inclusive resorts.

Over US$100

Bougainvillea and a gurgling fountain welcome you to **Hotel El Rey del Caribe** (Av. Uxmal at Nader, tel. 998/884-2028, www. reycaribe.com, US$111 s with a/c and kitchenette, US$125 d with a/c and kitchenette), an ecofriendly hotel two blocks east of the bus terminal. Rooms are clean and comfortable (those in the newer section are more spacious, with lovely wood floors), but it's the verdant tropical garden with hammocks, pool, and an outdoor dining area that really sets El Rey apart—you might even forget for a moment you're in the city. The hotel employs solar heating, rainwater recovery, and organic waste composting. Breakfast is included in the rate.

Information and Services

TOURIST INFORMATION

Downtown, the **City Tourist Office** (Av. Nader at Av. Cobá, tel. 998/887-3379, 9am-4pm Mon.-Fri.) is a bustling office with staffers who happily provide information on city and regional sights. A kiosk just outside of the office has brochures and maps. English is spoken.

Note: Be aware that booths with Tourist Information signs along Avenida Tulum and Boulevard Kukulcán are in fact operated by **time-share companies,** offering free tours and other goodies in exchange for attending a sales presentation.

There are also several publications that are worth picking up: *Cancún Tips* (www. cancuntips.com.mx) is a free tourist magazine with general information about Cancún and nearby sights; both *Restaurante Menu Mapa* and *Map@migo* (www.mapapocket-cancun.com) have maps, restaurant menus, reviews, and discount coupons; and *Agenda Cultural* has listings of Cancún's upcoming cultural events, exhibitions, and workshops. This last one can be hard to find—ask at the tourist office.

EMERGENCY SERVICES

There are several recommended private hospitals within a few blocks of each other in downtown Cancún. All have emergency rooms and English-speaking doctors and are open 24 hours daily: **Hospitén Cancún** (Av. Bonampak s/n, south of Av. Nichupté, tel. 998/881-3700, www.hospiten.com), **AmeriMed Hospital** (Av. Bonampak at Av. Nichupté, behind Las Américas mall, tel. 998/881-3400, www.amerimedcancun.com), and **Hospital Galenia** (Av. Tulum at Av. Nizuc, tel. 998/891-5200, www.hospitalgalenia.com).

For meds in the Zona Hotelera, try any of the malls or head to **Farmacia del Ahorro** (Blvd. Kukulcán Km. 9.5, tel. 998/892-7291, 24 hours). Downtown, **Farmacias Similares** (Av. Tulum near Calle Crisantemos, tel. 998/898-0190, 24 hours) is a reliable national chain.

The **police department, fire station,** and **ambulance** all can be reached by dialing toll-free 060 or 066 anytime. In the Zona Hotelera, all three are located in the same building next to Plaza Kukulcán (Blvd. Kukulcán Km. 12.5). Downtown, the main police station (Av. Xcaret at Av. Kabah, tel. 998/884-1913, 24 hours) faces the Carrefour supermarket, and there's a small office on Parque Las Palapas, near the food stalls, which is usually open 24 hours.

MONEY

You'll have no problem accessing or exchanging your money in Cancún. ATMs are ubiquitous, including at all the shopping malls, and give the best exchange rate. Many resorts will exchange dollars and euros, or simply accept them directly as payment. Ditto for many tour operators and even restaurants, especially in the Zona Hotelera. The exchange rate may be awful, however.

If you need an actual bank, head to **Plaza Caracol** (Blvd. Kukulcán Km. 8.5), where you'll find Bancomer, HSBC, and Banamex; or **Plaza Kukulcán** (Blvd. Kukulcán Km. 12.5), where there's a Banco Serfín. All have ATMs that accept foreign cards and are open roughly 9am-4pm Monday-Friday.

Downtown, the best-located banks are on Avenida Tulum between Avenida Cobá and Avenida Uxmal: **Bancomer** (Av. Tulum 20, 9am-5pm Mon.-Fri., 9am-2pm Sat.) and **Banamex** (Av. Tulum 19, 9am-4pm Mon.-Fri., 10am-2pm Sat.).

American Express (Av. Tulum at Calle Agua, tel. 998/881-4070, 9am-5pm Mon.-Fri., 9am-1pm Sat.) offers money exchange and other services to cardholding travelers.

MEDIA AND COMMUNICATIONS
Post Office
The **post office** (Av. Sunyaxchen at Av. Xel-Há, tel. 998/834-1418, 8am-4pm Mon.-Fri., 9am-12:30pm Sat.) is located in front of Mercado 28. There is no post office in the Zona Hotelera, though your hotel may mail postcards for you.

Internet and Telephone
Most hostels, hotels, and resorts now offer Wi-Fi, whether for free or at a small cost, and many have computers available for those without a laptop or mobile device of their own. Malls, restaurants, and even the Mexican government is following suit: Most Mexican cities, Cancún among them, have public Wi-Fi in their main plazas. If all else fails, you can get online at local cybercafes, scattered throughout downtown and in the main Zona Hotelera malls. Most have Skype-enabled computers, but also offer direct-dial national and international calls for US$0.20-0.50 per minute.

In the Zona Hotelera, Internet cafés are located at **Forum by the Sea** (Blvd. Kukulcán Km. 9, 8:30am-11pm Mon.-Sat., US$6/hour)

and at **Plaza Kukulcán** (Blvd. Kukulcán Km. 12.5, 10am-10pm daily, US$8.50/hour).

Downtown is far cheaper, including at **Go Internet Café** (Av. Uxmal near Margaritas, no phone, 24 hours daily), located near the bus station, with air-conditioning and fast Internet connections for around US$1.15 per hour.

Facing Parque Las Palapas, **Papelería Internet** (Margaritas near Gladiolas, 8am-1:30pm Mon.-Fri., 2pm-10:30pm Sat.-Sun.) charges US$0.95 per hour.

Newspapers
There are a handful of newspapers for local and regional news: In Spanish, *Novedades de Quintana Roo* (www.sipse.com/novedades) is the state's oldest newspaper, centrist in coverage, with a good classified section; *¡Por Esto!* (www.poresto.net) is a left-of-center paper with Quintana Roo and Yucatán versions; and *Diario de Yucatán* (www.yucatan.com.mx) is more conservative and covers the entire region. The Cancún version of the *Miami Herald Tribune* is a good English-language alternative.

IMMIGRATION
Cancún's **immigration office** (Av. Nader at Av. Uxmal, tel. 998/884-1749 or 998/881-3560, 9am-1pm Mon.-Fri.) is an efficient, welcoming office—worlds better than the one in Playa del Carmen.

LAUNDRY AND STORAGE
Downtown, **Lavandería Las Palapas** (Parque Las Palapas, Alcatraces near Gladiolas, 7am-10pm Mon.-Sat.) will do your laundry for US$5 per three kilos (6.6 pounds), or you can do it yourself for US$1.50 per wash or dry. Closer to the bus station, **Lavandería Las Palmas** (Av. Uxmal near Laurel, 7am-9pm daily) is slightly cheaper at US$3.25 per three kilos; next door, there's self-service laundry at **LavaXpress** (7am-9pm daily, US$1.40 per wash or dry).

In the Zona Hotelera, **Eco-Laundry**

(behind Dady-O, Blvd. Kukulcán Km. 9.5, tel. 998/883-4315, 8am-8pm Mon.-Sat., 10am-6pm Sun.) offers two-hour laundry service for US$8.50 for 4.5 kilos (9.9 pounds); self-service also is offered for US$6.15 per load. Another option is **Lavandería Lumi Express** (Blvd. Kukulcán Km. 8, tel. 998/883-3874, 8am-8pm Mon.-Sat., 9am-5pm Sun.), which will do your laundry for US$10 for four kilos (8.8 pounds).

On the 1st floor of the bus station, **Guarda Equipaje** (tel. 998/884-4352, ext. 2851, 6:30am-10pm daily) will store luggage for US$0.50-1.50 per hour, depending on the size, or a flat US$7.75 per day.

Storage lockers (US$6.50 per 24 hours) also can be rented in Terminal 3 at Cancún International Airport; they are big enough to hold carry-on bags only. Look for the lockers as you exit customs.

INSTRUCTION

The welcoming **Centro Cultural La Pitahaya** (Av. Yaxchilán near Av. Uxmal, cell tel. 998/118-0099, 4pm-11pm Tues.-Sat., prices vary) offers a wide range of classes in theater, music, art, even jewelry design. If you're going to be in town for a month or longer, consider checking out the offerings.

Getting There and Around

GETTING THERE
Air
The **Cancún International Airport** (CUN, Hwy. 307 Km. 22, tel. 998/848-7200, www.cancun-airport.com) is 20 kilometers (12.4 miles) south of Cancún. Most international flights arrive and depart from the airport's Terminal 3, which also has airline, taxi, bus, and car rental desks, as well as ATMs. In general, Terminal 2 is used for domestic flights with some overflow international flights; Terminal 1 is reserved for charter flights. A free shuttle ferries travelers between Terminals 2 and 3 only.

The following airlines serve Cancún International Airport:

- **Aeroméxico** (Av. Cobá at Av. Bonampak, tel. 998/849-2222, toll-free Mex. tel. 800/021-4000, toll-free U.S. tel. 800/237-6639, www.aeromexico.com)
- **AeroTucán** (toll-free Mex. tel. 800/640-4148, www.aerotucan.com.mx)
- **Air Canada** (toll-free Mex. tel. 800/719-2827, toll-free U.S./Can. tel. 888/247-2262, www.aircanada.com)
- **American Airlines** (toll-free Mex. tel. 800/904-6000, toll-free U.S./Can. tel. 800/433-7300, www.aa.com)
- **Continental** (toll-free Mex. tel. 800/900-5000, toll-free U.S./Can. tel. 800/864-8331, www.continental.com)
- **Copa Airlines** (toll-free Mex. tel. 800/265-2672, toll-free U.S. tel. 800/359-2672, www.copaair.com)
- **Cubana de Aviación** (Av. Tulum 232, tel. 998/887-7210, airport tel. 998/886-0355, toll-free Can. tel. 866/428-2262, www.cubana.cu)
- **Delta** (toll-free Mex. tel. 800/266-0046, toll-free U.S. tel. 800/241-4141, www.delta.com)
- **Frontier Airlines** (toll-free U.S. tel. 800/432-1359, www.frontierairlines.com)
- **InterJet** (Plaza Hollywood, Av. Cobá at Av. Xcaret, tel. 998/892-0278, toll-free Mex. tel. 800/011-2345, toll-free U.S. tel. 866/285-9525, www.interjet.com.mx)
- **LAN** (toll-free Mex. tel. 800/272-0330, toll-free U.S. tel. 866/435-9526, www.lan.com)

Cancún Bus Schedule

Cancún's **bus station** (tel. 800/702-8000) is located downtown at Avenidas Tulum and Uxmal. Departures listed below include both first- and second-class service; in many cases, second-class buses take significantly longer for only marginal savings.

DESTINATION	PRICE	DURATION	SCHEDULE
Cancún Int'l Airport	US$4.75	25 mins	every 30 mins 7am-10pm
Chetumal	US$18-35	5-6 hrs	every 30-90 mins 12:15am-11:45pm
Chichén Itzá	US$10.50-20	3.5-4.5 hrs	11 departures 2am-1pm or take any Pisté bus
Chiquilá	US$8.50	3 hrs	three departures 7:30am-12:50pm
Mahahual	US$29	4.5 hrs	6:45am
Mérida	US$25-45	4-4.5 hrs	every 30-60 mins 1am-11:59pm
Pisté	US$10.50	4-4.5 hrs	every 30-60 mins 12:30am-11:45pm
Playa del Carmen	US$2.50-7.50	1 hr	every 15-30 mins 12:15am-7:15pm
Puerto Morelos	US$1.75-3.25	40 mins	every 15-30 mins 12:15am-11:30pm
Tulum	US$7.25-13.50	2.5 hrs	every 60-90 mins 12:15am-11:59pm
Valladolid	US$8.25-14.50	2-3.5 hrs	every 15-60 mins 12:01am-11:45pm

- **Southwest Airlines** (toll-free U.S. tel. 800/435-9792, www.southwest.com)
- **Spirit Airlines** (toll-free Mex./U.S./Can. tel. 800/772-7117, www.spiritair.com)
- **United Airlines** (toll-free Mex. tel. 800/900-5000, toll-free U.S./Can. tel. 800/864-8331, www.united.com)
- **US Airways** (toll-free Mex. tel. 800/843-3000, toll-free U.S. tel. 800/428-4322, www.usairways.com)
- **Volaris** (toll-free Mex. tel. 800/122-8000, toll-free U.S. tel. 866/988-3527, www.volaris.com)

Bus

Buses leave Cancún's clean and modern bus terminal (Av. Tulum at Av. Uxmal) for destinations in the Yucatán Peninsula and throughout the interior of Mexico.

Combi

Combis, public shuttle vans, run between Cancún and Playa del Carmen. They queue up directly across Avenida Tulum from the bus terminal, near the Comercial Mexicana, and depart every 10-15 minutes 24 hours a day (US$2.75, 1 hour). For slightly more, **Playa Express** has larger, air-conditioned shuttles, departing on roughly the same schedule from the parking lot in front of the bus terminal (US$3, 50 minutes). Both services make stops along the way, including Puerto Morelos (US$2.50, 30 minutes).

GETTING AROUND
To and From the Airport

Cancún's airport is served by taxi, shuttle, and bus. The authorized airport taxi service, **Yellow Transfers** (toll-free Mex. tel. 800/021-8087, www.yellowtransfers.com), has two booths inside the airport and another at the exit, and has taxi and shuttle service, including luxury class and for the disabled, anywhere on the coast. Fares are fixed and prominently displayed at the airport and online (where rates are sometimes discounted). Rates to the Zona Hotelera or downtown are the same; private taxis and shuttles run US$48-100 (4-8 pax), while shared shuttles are US$12 per person. Yellow Transfers offers round-trip service at a discount, or you can hire an ordinary taxi; you'll end up paying roughly the same. Service down the coast includes Playa del Carmen (US$72-125 private, US$24 shared) and Tulum (US$124-190 private, US$40 shared).

ADO has a ticket counter right outside the airport; bear right as you leave the main doors. Comfortable, air-conditioned buses leave every half hour for downtown Cancún (7am-10pm daily, US$4.75, 25 minutes) and every 30 minutes for Playa del Carmen (9:15am-11:50pm daily, US$12, 1 hour); the latter stops in Puerto Morelos (US$7, 25 minutes) along the way. For other destinations, take any bus to Cancún or Playa del Carmen and transfer. ADO's airport buses do not enter Cancún's Zona Hotelera, however.

Bus

Frequent buses (US$0.75) run between downtown Cancún and the Zona Hotelera—you'll rarely have to wait more than five minutes for one to pass. The buses are red and have "R-1," "Hoteles," or "Zona Hotelera" painted on the front, and stop along Avenida Tulum, the bus station, and near most major hotels, beaches, and ferry ports.

Taxi

You'll have no trouble finding a taxi around town or in the Zona Hotelera—they are everywhere tourists are. Before getting into one, however, make sure to agree upon a price—meters are not used, and drivers sometimes overcharge. As of this writing, the rate around downtown is US$2.50, from downtown to the Isla Mujeres ferries US$4.75, and from downtown to the Zona Hotelera US$10-20, depending on the destination. Rates within the Zona Hotelera jump dramatically and depend on how far you're going. Ask your concierge for specific rates, but expect to pay US$8-20.

Car

Although you won't need a car to visit Cancún proper, renting one is a great way to visit the nearest archaeological sites (i.e., Tulum, Cobá, Ek' Balam, and Chichén Itzá) without being part of a huge tour group. A rental also makes exploring the Riviera Maya a little easier, though buses cover that route fairly well. Driving in the Cancún area is relatively pain-free—unexpected speed bumps and impatient bus drivers are the biggest concerns.

Most international car rental companies, and a few local ones, have offices at the airport (some are right at the terminal, others in a purpose-built rental center few miles away) as well as in select resorts and at offices downtown and in the Zona Hotelera. Various sizes and types of vehicles are available, from SUVs to Volkswagen bugs (optimistically dubbed VW sedans); prices with insurance and taxes start at around US$40 a day. The best rates are online with the international companies; you also can sometimes get discounted rates by spending half a day in a time-share presentation. Commonly used companies include:

- **America Car Rental** (Cancún Airport, tel. 998/253-6100; Flamingo Plaza, Blvd. Kukulcán Km. 11.5, tel. 998/883-0160, www.america-carrental.com)

- **AutoRent** (Av. Tulum at Calle Azucenas, tel. 998/887-0709)

- **Avicar** (Cancún Airport, toll-free Mex. tel. 800/212-0752, toll-free U.S./Can. tel. 866/577-1342, www.avicar.com.mx)

Driving Distances from Cancún

LOCATION	DISTANCE	LOCATION	DISTANCE
Airport	20 km (12.4 mi)	Puerto Aventuras	87 km (54 mi)
Akumal	105 km (65 mi)	Puerto Morelos	36 km (22.5 mi)
Bacalar	320 km (199 mi)	Punta Allen	182 km (109 mi)
Chetumal	382 km (237.5 mi)	Tulum	130 km (81 mi)
Chichén Itzá	178 km (110.5 mi)	Valladolid	158 km (98 mi)
Cobá	173 km (107.5 mi)	Xcalak	411 km (255.5 mi)
Mahahual	351 km (218 mi)	Xcaret	74 km (46 mi)
Mérida	320 km (199 mi)	Xel-Há	122 km (76 mi)
Paamul	82 km (51 mi)	Xpu-Há	101 km (63 mi)
Playa del Carmen	68 km (42.5 mi)		

- **Avis** (Cancún Airport, tel. 998/886-0221; La Isla Shopping Village, Blvd. Kukulcán Km. 12.5, tel. 998/883-1436, www.avis.com)

- **Hertz** (Cancún Airport, tel. 999/999-8040; La Isla Shopping Village, Blvd. Kukulcán Km. 12.5, tel. 999/118-040, www.hertz.com)

- **National** (Cancún Airport, tel. 998/881-8760; La Isla Shopping Village, Blvd. Kukulcán Km. 12.5, tel. 998/176-8117, www.nationalcar.com)

- **Thrifty** (Cancún Airport, tel. 998/886-0333; Westin Resort & Spa, Blvd. Kukulcán Km. 20, tel. 998/885-0086, www.thrifty.com)

Parking lots in the Zona Hotelera are in the shopping centers: La Isla Shopping Village, Forum by the Sea, Plaza Kukulcán, and Plaza Caracol. Rates are typically US$1.50 for the first hour and US$0.50 for each additional hour. Downtown, it's easiest—and relatively safe—to park on the street or in the public lots around Parque Las Palapas.

Travel Agencies

Most travelers handle their travel and hotel bookings online, but there are scores of travel agencies in Cancún for anyone who finds a need for their service—look especially on Avenidas Tulum and Uxmal. Worth noting is **American Express** (Av. Tulum at Calle Agua, tel. 998/881-4070, 9am-5pm Mon.-Fri., 9am-1pm Sat.), which has special services for cardholders.

Isla Mujeres

Just eight kilometers (5 miles) long and no more than a quarter mile wide, Isla Mujeres is a sliver of land fringed by white-sand beaches amid the wide turquoise sea. It actually was one of the first places in the Mexican Caribbean to have hotels and other tourist developments, but attention quickly shifted to Isla Cozumel and then Cancún proper. It may have been a blessing in disguise: As those areas exploded, rushing to build high-rise hotels and ports for cruise ships, Isla Mujeres developed more slowly, attracting backpackers and bohemians while remaining pretty much what it always was—a quiet, picturesque fishing community.

Of course, even slow change adds up, and today Isla Mujeres is a well-established tourist destination. Thousands of day-trippers come from Cancún to shop, eat, and relax on the island's calm beaches. While still popular with backpackers, Isla Mujeres now also attracts mid-range and upscale travelers with an ever-expanding selection of boutique hotels and bed-and-breakfasts.

Despite higher hotel prices and T-shirt shops, golf carts, and pushy tour operators, Isla Mujeres remains at its core a mellow tropical island with a friendly and laid-back population. Passersby greet one another, people stroll in the middle of the street, and many businesses close for long lunches. Add to that beautiful beaches and numerous options for snorkeling, biking, and other outdoor excursions, and it's no wonder so many visitors find themselves extending (and re-extending) their time here.

HISTORY

The precise origin of the name Isla Mujeres (Island of Women) is unknown, though not for lack of theories. Some say the name comes from the days of pirates trolling the Caribbean; they allegedly kept their female captives on Isla Mujeres while they ransacked boats sailing along the coast. Another more likely story is that the island served as a stopover (or secondary site) for Maya pilgrims on their way to Isla Cozumel to worship Ixchel, the female goddess of fertility. When Spanish explorers landed here, they reportedly found a large number of female-shaped clay idols and named the island after them.

ORIENTATION

The town of Isla Mujeres (known as the *centro,* or center) is at the far northwestern tip of the island; at just eight blocks long and five blocks deep, it is very walkable. This is where most of the hotels, restaurants, shops, and services are. There is no main street per se, although Avenida Hidalgo intersects with the town *zócalo* (central plaza) and has a bustling pedestrian-only section. Avenida Rueda Medina is the busy street that runs along the south side of the *centro* past the ferry piers and continues all the way to the island's other end, becoming Carretera Punta Sur at Parque Garrafón (and therefore also known as Carretera Garrafón). The road that runs along the north side of the island is Avenida Martínez Ross as it leaves the downtown area, becoming Carretera Perimetral partway down the island.

SIGHTS
Hacienda Mundaca

A sad dilapidated estate, **Hacienda Mundaca** (Av. Rueda Medina at Carr. Garrafón Km. 3.5, no phone, 9am-4pm daily, US$1.50) is not interesting enough to visit, but is just historical enough that tourism folks (including guidebook authors) can't just ignore it. It was built by a 19th-century retired slave trader, Antonio Mundaca, to woo a local woman; when she rejected his advances, Mundaca went crazy, holing up in the estate while it crumbled around him . . . and that's pretty much where things stand today (you'll find a small home, the

Isla Mujeres

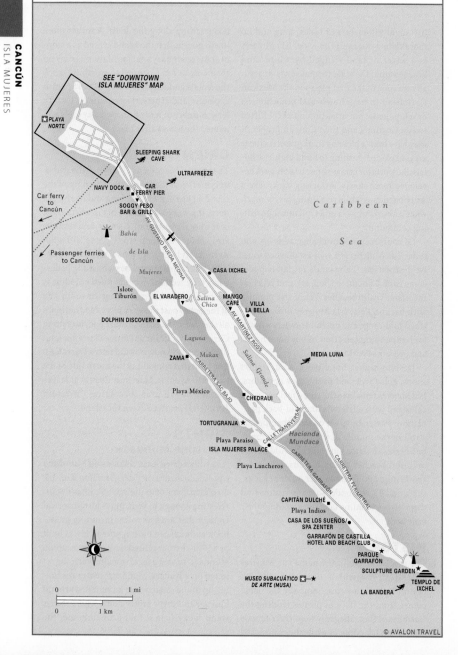

SEE "DOWNTOWN
ISLA MUJERES" MAP

★ PLAYA
NORTE

SLEEPING SHARK
CAVE

ULTRAFREEZE

Car ferry
to Cancún

NAVY DOCK ■   CAR
            FERRY PIER

SOGGY PESO
BAR & GRILL

Passenger ferries
to Cancún

Bahía

de Isla

Mujeres

Islote
Tiburón

EL VARADERO ■

Salina
Chico

MANGO
CAFÉ ■

VILLA
LA BELLA ■

DOLPHIN DISCOVERY ■

CASA IXCHEL ■

Laguna

Makax

ZAMA ■

Salina
Grande

MEDIA LUNA

Playa México

CHEDRAUI ■

AV GUSTAVO RUEDA MEDINA

AV MARTÍNEZ ROSS

CARRETERA SAC-BAJO

TORTUGRANJA ★

Playa Paraíso
ISLA MUJERES PALACE

Playa Lancheros

Hacienda
Mundaca

CALLE TRANSVERSAL

CARRETERA GARRAFÓN

CARRETERA PERIMETRAL

CAPITÁN DULCHÉ ■

Playa Indios

CASA DE LOS SUEÑOS/
SPA ZENTER

GARRAFÓN DE CASTILLA
HOTEL AND BEACH CLUB ■

PARQUE
GARRAFÓN ★

SCULPTURE GARDEN

TEMPLO DE
IXCHEL

LA BANDERA

MUSEO SUBACUÁTICO ✪ ★
DE ARTE (MUSA)

C a r i b b e a n

S e a

0   1 mi
0   1 km

© AVALON TRAVEL

platforms of a Maya ruin, two caged crocs, a lagoon, and lots and lots of mosquitoes).

Tortugranja

A modest sea turtle sanctuary on the island's southwestern shore, **Tortugranja** (Carr. Sac Bajo 5, tel. 998/888-0507, 9am-5pm daily, US$3) makes for an interesting stop on your golf-cart tour of the island. The one-room cement structure contains several enclosures with sea turtles of different ages and species. The tank of just-hatched *tortuguitas* is always a hit; please respect the rules (and huge signs) and refrain from touching or picking them up. Small aquariums along the walls also contain sea anemones, sea horses, lionfish, and the deadly rockfish, among others. Outside there are three tanks with more turtles as well as a large fenced-in area of the ocean that is home to a nurse shark. During the nesting season (May-October), one section of sand is fenced off, and eggs collected from nests are transplanted here for protection.

Between July and November, travelers may be able to accompany the center's workers to look for fresh sea turtle nests on the island's eastern shore and relocate eggs to protected areas, and, until October and November, help release hatchlings into the sea. Both activities take place in the evening several nights a week, typically starting around 9pm, but are not formal tours. Those interested should inquire at the center, and having basic Spanish (and possibly your own vehicle) will make participating much easier. There's no charge, but a tip is customary.

★ Museo Subacuático de Arte (MUSA)

Underwater sculpture is nothing new, but there's never been a project as ambitious— or as gorgeous, frankly—as the **Subaquatic Museum of Art** (www.musacancun.org). British sculptor Jason de Caires Taylor, along with four Mexican sculptors (Karen Salinas Martínez, Roberto Díaz Abraham, Rodrigo Quiñones Reyes, and Salvador Quiroz Ennis), created hundreds of life-size statues of everyday people—garbage men, pregnant women, wizened tribal leaders, and more—and sank them in two separate sites; one is near Cancún's Nizuc reef (approximately 12 feet deep), the other near Isla Mujeres's Manchones reef (approximately 24 feet deep). Striking for their lifelike quality, the figures were made from a special cement that will promote coral and other sealife, eventually forming an artificial reef system. Most dive shops offer dive and snorkeling trips to both sites.

Templo de Ixchel and Sculpture Garden

At the far southern tip of the island, a crumbling Maya temple stands on a cliff overlooking the sea. Its original function is unknown: The location suggests it was an observation post or even an astronomical observatory, but most experts believe it was related to Ixchel, the Maya goddess of the moon, fertility, weaving, and childbirth, possibly as a secondary pilgrimage site after Isla Cozumel. Whatever its history, the temple was abandoned long before Francisco Hernández de Córdoba first reported its existence in 1517.

The temple alone isn't too exciting, as time and weather have all but destroyed it. But a visit here also includes pondering a dozen or so multicolored modern sculptures lining the path to the ruins as well as enjoying an oceanside trail past the ruins that continues to the very tip of the island—the easternmost point of Mexico, in fact—before looping back along the craggy waterfront to the entrance. It's a decent side trip, with some fine photo ops along the way.

Admission to the Ixchel ruins is included in the ticket price to Parque Garrafón; all others must pay US$3 (9am-5pm daily).

★ Isla Contoy

Peeking out of a crystal clear sea and dotted with saltwater lagoons, mangrove trees, and coconut palms, Isla Contoy is home to over 150 species of birds, including herons, brown pelicans, frigates, and cormorants,

Downtown Isla Mujeres

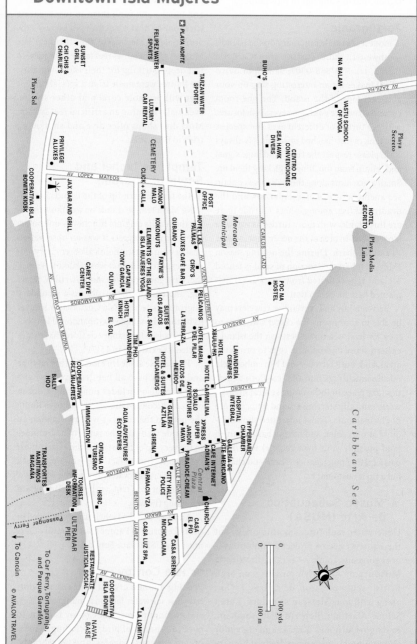

© AVALON TRAVEL

and is a preferred nesting ground for three different species of endangered sea turtles. The island was decreed a national park in 1998, and its only structures are a three-story viewing tower, a visitors center, and a small museum; a few trails allow for appreciating the otherwise pristine island environment. Just 24 kilometers (14 miles) north of Isla Mujeres, Isla Contoy is a popular and rewarding outing for nature buffs and average day-trippers alike.

Various tour operators on Isla Mujeres offer the same basic trip for a standard price (US$65-100, including the US$5 park entrance fee): Depart around 9am with a 30- to 45-minute stop for snorkeling along the way, then three hours to explore the island or just relax, including lunch on the beach (typically freshly grilled fish or chicken). Boats head back around 3pm, reaching Isla Mujeres at 4pm.

Recommended operators include **Captain Tony García** (Av. Matamoros near Av. Benito Juárez, tel. 998/260-4194, captaintonys@hotmail.com), a friendly English-speaking guide with over 20 years' experience whose house doubles as his office, and **Cooperativa Isla Bonita** (Av. Rueda Medina at Av. Allende, cell tel. 998/134-6103, 9am-5pm daily).

BEACHES
★ Playa Norte

Playa Norte (North Beach) is a long undulating strip of sand on the northern edge of Isla Mujeres. Its fine white sands descend ever so slowly into a gorgeous turquoise sea—you can wade almost a hundred yards out and still be only waist deep. The long, shallow shelf means Playa Norte has virtually no waves, adding to the beach's tranquility. It's a favorite spot for visitors of all ages: couples sunning themselves and sipping margaritas, backpackers on colorful beach towels, kids frolicking in the calm water, and older travelers relaxing under huge umbrellas.

You can rent beach chairs and umbrellas at a number of spots along Playa Norte, including **Buho's** (end of Av. Carlos Lazo, no phone, US$4.75 chair, US$4.75 umbrella); **Chi Chis & Charlie's** (southwestern end of Playa Norte, no phone, US$12.50 chair and umbrella); and **Tarzan Water Sports** (end of Av. Guerrero at Playa Norte, tel. 998/877-0679, US$11.50 chair and umbrella), where there also are lockers, restrooms, and free Wi-Fi.

Tarzan Water Sports (end of Av. Guerrero at Playa Norte, tel. 998/877-0679) also rents snorkel gear (US$10/day), single and double kayaks (US$15-20/hour), Hobie Cats

Brown pelicans are one of dozens of species of birds you'll see on Isla Contoy.

Island Murals

Mercado Municipal on Isla Mujeres

It's impossible to miss the massive ocean-themed murals dotting Isla Mujeres, their vibrant, colorful designs adorning sea walls, hotel exteriors, even City Hall. They extend up to a half block long or several stories high, and range from highly realistic, to psychedelic, to abstract modern, to urban street art. Painted mostly in 2013, the murals are the work of various artists belonging to **PangeaSeed** (www.pangeaseed.org), a nonprofit organization that uses education and "artivism" to promote marine conservation worldwide. Isla Mujeres is one of several communities selected for the group's "Sea Walls for Oceans" mural project; others are in Florida, New Zealand, Vietnam, Sri Lanka, and more. Of course, Mexico was once a muralist's mecca, the birthplace and inspiration of world-famous painters like Diego Rivera, José Orozco, and David Siqueiros. The murals in Isla Mujeres are not only gorgeous and impactful, but are a refreshing revival of the art form, connecting the greats of the early 20th century to contemporary street artists like Banksy and Shepard Fairey.

(US$45/hour), and stand-up paddleboards (US$12.50/hour) and can arrange snorkel tours (US$30 pp, 2 hours). **FeliPez Water Sports Center** (end of Av. Hidalgo at Playa Norte, tel. 998/593-3403) rents the same gear at similar prices.

Playa Sol

Around the corner, Playa Sol is also lovely, with deeper water and a wider beach than Playa Norte's. One end of the beach has long been packed with fishing boats, while the other end has recently been cordoned off for use by guests at a nearby resort. That said, there's still a large section in the middle where you can stretch out a towel. **Cooperativa Isla**

Bonita (cell tel. 998/134-6103) operates a small kiosk there with lounge chairs and umbrellas for rent.

Other Beaches

Zama (Carr. Sac Bajo s/n, tel. 998/877-0739, 10am-6pm daily) is a small beach club on the island's calm southwest shore that's gotten popular as a wedding spot, if that gives you an idea of how pretty it is. You can relax in a comfy beach bed on the large clean beach or in a hammock in the shady garden. The sand is a bit thin and there's sea grass in the shallows, but you can swim comfortably from the long pier or in one of the two appealing mosaic-tiled pools. The tidy open-air restaurant is reasonably priced and has everything from burritos to shrimp dishes, plus a kids menu (US$5-20). There's no admission or minimum consumption, but they charge US$7.75 for use of the lounge chairs, US$23 for the beach beds.

A new kid on the block, **Capitán Dulché** (Carr. Sac Bajo s/n, tel. 998/849-7594, www.capitandulche.com, 10am-6pm daily) is a beach club with a relaxed marina feel. It's divided into three sections—a well-tended beach with calm waters and *palapa* shade, a wide grassy area with antique anchors and thick tow chains, and a modern beachfront restaurant (US$8-17) with a solid menu of international dishes. Be sure to check out the bar that also happens to be housed in a repurposed sailboat. There's a small nautical museum (US$4) on-site, too—good if you're interested in model sailboats.

ENTERTAINMENT AND EVENTS

Isla Mujeres's nightlife ranges from laid-back lounges to nightclubs, and from beach bars to sports bars. Fortunately, the town is small enough that you can wander about until you find the scene that suits you best.

Bars

At the north end of Playa Norte, **Buho's** (end of Av. Carlos Lazo, no phone, 11am-10:30pm daily) is a classic beachfront watering hole, with swings instead of bar stools, shells and buoys as decoration, and hammocks and lounge chairs within easy reach.

Soggy Peso Bar & Grill (Av. Gustavo Rueda Medina, tel. 998/274-0050, www.soggypeso.net, 9am-8pm daily) is a favorite for daytime drinkin' Americans, open early and closed not long after sunset (the view of which, by the way, is terrific here). The vibe is casual and jocular, and every day there's a different special from the kitchen: Hot Wings Wednesdays, Cheeseburgers in Paradise Thursdays, BBQ Sundays, etc. It's located south of the center, on the waterfront.

Live Music

La Terraza (Av. Hidalgo at Av. Abasolo, tel. 998/236-3879, 5pm-midnight daily, no cover) has great live salsa, cumbia, and other Latin dance music most nights after 10pm. Drinks here are excellent—try the ginger margarita—and the food isn't bad, but it's the music and lively atmosphere that will draw you in, night after night.

Fayne's (Av. Hidalgo 12, tel. 998/877-0528, www.faynesbarandgrill.com, 5pm-midnight daily, no cover) features live nightly music, mostly Caribbean but with a smattering of rock and reggae acts as well. The high *palapa* roof and spacious bar area make it equally suited for dancing or just chilling out; you can even order dinner here, from pasta to seafood. Thursday-Sunday are the busiest nights, often with two bands starting as early as 6pm; otherwise, things get hopping around 10:30pm.

Down the street, the tiki-bar-themed **Kokonuts** (Av. Hidalgo near Av. López Mateos, tel. 998/125-1772, 7pm-3am daily, no cover) features cover bands, from salsa to Johnny Cash.

JAX Bar and Grill (Av. López Mateos at Av. Rueda Medina, tel. 998/877-1254, www.jaxsportfishing.com/bar.asp, 8am-11pm daily, no cover) has catered to Isla's yacht crews and visiting Joe Six-Packs since 2001, with utilitarian breakfasts and burgers during the day and live country blues and classic rock bands playing nightly 9pm-11pm during the high season (closed in September).

Farther down the island, the boutique hotel **Casa de los Sueños** (Carr. Garrafón s/n, tel. 998/888-0370, www.casasuenos.com) has live music—often acoustic guitar—during its fabulous poolside happy hour (4pm-6pm daily). Margaritas run US$2.50, beers US$1.50, plus the sunset views can't be beat. Music typically continues until 9pm.

SHOPPING

It's easy to be put off by the onslaught of kitschy souvenirs and cheap T-shirts that greet you as soon as you step off the ferry. But fear not: Isla Mujeres has a number of genuinely good specialty stores, especially for Mexican *artesanía,* if you keep your eyes open.

Located in a Caribbean clapboard house, **Galería Aztlán** (Av. Hidalgo at Av. Madero, tel. 998/887-0419, 9am-9pm Mon.-Sat.) sells gorgeous Mexican masks from every corner of the country. The owners, transplants from Mexico City, also make popular religious art that fills one section of the shop.

Mono Malo (Av. Hidalgo btwn Avs. Lopez Mateos and Matamoros, no phone, www.monomalo.com.mx, 2pm-10pm Fri.-Wed.) specializes in original high-end T-shirts, most inspired by Mexican skeleton art, Revolution heros, and *lucha libre* (wrestling) stars. If you don't find what you're looking for at the store, check out the website, which features the store's entire line.

Galería de Arte Mexicano (Parque Central, Av. Guerrero 3, tel. 998/877-1272, 10am-8pm daily) has fine Talavera pottery as well as an extensive selection of silver jewelry. The prices are somewhat higher here than elsewhere, but so is the quality.

La Sirena (Av. Morelos near Av. Hidalgo, tel. 998/877-0223, 10am-6pm Mon.-Sat.) is a tiny shop that's jam-packed with high-quality folk art from all over Mexico: textiles from Chiapas, masks from Guerrero, skeleton art from Mexico City, and *alebrijes* (wooden creatures) from Oaxaca.

SPORTS AND RECREATION
Scuba Diving

Beginner divers will appreciate the calm waters and vibrant sealife on Isla Mujeres's western side, while the east side presents more challenging options for advanced divers, with deeper water (up to 40 meters/131 feet), more varied terrain, and even a couple of shipwrecks. Favorite sites include La Bandera (a reef dive), Media Luna (a drift dive), Ultrafreeze (a shipwreck, in notoriously chilly water), and the famous Sleeping Shark Cave—a deep cave known to attract sharks, where they fall into a strangely lethargic and nonaggressive state. Explanations for this last phenomenon vary: Salinity of the water, low carbon dioxide, and underwater currents are some theories. Unfortunately, overfishing (and overdiving) has disrupted the slumber party, and there's only a 50-50 chance, at best, of seeing sharks on any given day. September seems to be the best month, but you just never know.

Isla Mujeres's dive shops charge fairly uniform rates: US$75-85 for two tanks; gear

shopping for *artesanía* on Isla Mujeres

and marine park admission is sometimes included; otherwise, they cost US$10-20 per day. The Sleeping Shark Cave and deep dives run a little higher, and most shops offer multi-dive specials. Open-water certification courses cost around US$395, including equipment and materials.

Aqua Adventures Eco Divers (Av. Juárez at Calle Morelos, tel. 998/236-4316, www. diveislamujeres.com, 9am-7pm Mon.-Sat., 10am-6pm Sun.) goes the extra mile to provide friendly, professional service.

Sea Hawk Divers (Av. Carlos Lazo at Av. López Mateos, tel. 998/877-0296, www.seahawkislamujeres.com, 9am-8pm daily) is a recommended dive shop owned and run by island locals Ariel and Bonnie Barandica. Sea Hawk has a half dozen comfortable rooms and studios attached to the dive shop, which it can include as part of a diving package.

Buzos de México (aka México Divers, Av. Madero at Av. Hidalgo, tel. 998/877-1117, www.buzosdemexico.com, 8am-8pm daily) is a popular dive shop with a youthful vibe.

Scualo Adventures (Av. Madero at Guerrero, tel. 998/274-1644, toll-free U.S./ Can. tel. 855/577-8256, www.squaloadventures.com, 8:30am-8pm daily) is another reliable option.

Carey Dive Center (Av. Matamoros near Av. Rueda Medina, tel. 998/877-0763, www. careydivecenter.com, 8am-8pm daily) is a recommended dive shop that enjoys lots of repeat customers.

Snorkeling

Isla Mujeres's western side has calm water and extensive coral reefs that make for excellent snorkeling, though relatively few spots are accessible from the shore. Snorkeling tours can be booked at **dive shops** or with one of the local cooperatives—**Cooperativa Isla Bonita** (Av. Rueda Medina at Av. Allende, cell tel. 998/134-6103, 9am-5pm daily) and **Cooperativa Isla Mujeres** (end of Av. Madero at pier, tel. 998/877-1363, 7am-7pm daily)—or from booths on Playa Norte and at the ferry pier. Most operators take snorkelers

to El Farito (The Lighthouse) and other spots near the northern end of the island, where the coral is decent but quite trafficked; tours run around US$25 per person. Dive shops are more likely to take you to less-visited spots.

You can also arrange to snorkel at **Museo Subacuático de Arte** (MUSA), the remarkable underwater sculpture park near Manchones reef, at the southern end of the island. Dive shops and other operators charge around US$35 per person for a trip combining MUSA and one other spot.

Yet another option is to take a trip to **Isla Contoy** (US$65-100 pp), which includes snorkeling on Ixlanche reef in addition to exploring the island. Boats depart Isla Mujeres around 9am and return at 4pm.

And you can snorkel on your own at **Garrafón de Castilla Hotel and Beach Club** (Carr. Punta Sur Km. 6, tel. 998/877-0107, 9am-5pm daily, US$4.75), at the southern tip of the island. The club itself is pretty desultory, but you can explore over 300 meters (894 feet) of coral reef, including the part used by its much-hyped neighbor, Parque Garrafón. Snorkel gear rents for US$6, and lockers and towels can be rented for around US$1.50 each.

Whale Shark Tours

Snorkeling with whale sharks, the world's largest fish, is an experience you won't soon forget. These gentle giants congregate along the northeastern tip of the Yucatán Peninsula mid-May-mid-September and typically measure 6-7.5 meters (20-25 feet) and weigh more than 10 tons. (They're known to grow upwards of 18 meters, or nearly 60 feet, though such behemoths are rare here.) From Isla Mujeres, whale shark tours leave around 8am for a 60- to 90-minute boat ride northwest past Isla Contoy toward Isla Holbox (where such tours first became popular). Once in the feeding grounds, you'll see the huge sharks trolling along the surface, feeding on krill. The boat is maneuvered nearby the shark, and a guide plus two guests slip overboard and swim alongside. The sharks are surprisingly fast, despite their languid appearance, and you have to kick hard to keep up and get a good look at their sleek spotted bodies and massive gaping mouths. The smaller your group, the more chances you'll have to get into the water, though most people welcome the short breathers between turns. Rules also require that boats not linger with any one shark more than 30 minutes; in all, each guest can expect to have 2-4 chances to jump in. Lunch and beverages are included. Boats typically return to Isla Mujeres by 3pm.

Two local cooperatives handle most whale shark tours, charging around US$110 per person: **Cooperativa Isla Bonita** (Av. Rueda Medina at Av. Allende, cell tel. 998/134-6103, 9am-5pm daily) and **Cooperativa Isla Mujeres** (end of Av. Madero at pier, tel. 998/877-1363, 7am-7pm daily). Most **dive shops** in Isla Mujeres also offer whale shark tours, charging around US$125 per person. Always confirm the departure times, how long the tour will last, and whether lunch and water are provided.

Swimming with Dolphins

Dolphin Discovery (end of Carr. Sac Bajo, toll-free Mex. tel. 800/727-5391, toll-free U.S. tel. 866/393-5158, www.dolphindiscovery.

com, US$109-199 adult, US$89-119 child) offers various dolphin interaction programs on the island's calm western shore, as well as ones with manatees and sea lions. Parque Garrafón, a nearby sister park with snorkeling, ziplines, and more, has packages combining Dolphin Discovery programs and admission to Garrafón, a good option if you'd like to make a day of it. Most visitors come from Cancún on Dolphin Discovery's private ferry (included in the price), though no transport is provided for guests staying on Isla Mujeres. Reservations are required.

Ecoparks

Built on a bluff at the southern end of Isla Mujeres, **Parque Garrafón** (Carr. Garrafón Km. 6, tel. 998/849-4748, toll-free U.S. tel. 866/393-5158, www.garrafon.com, 10am-5:30pm daily, US$89-199 adult, US$59-99 child) is a combo ecopark and water park. There's snorkeling, kayaking, ziplining, an interactive dolphin program (conducted at Dolphin Discovery, a nearby sister park), and, of course, just relaxing on the beach or by the pool. Ferry service to and from Cancún is included, as well as admission to Templo de Ixchel, a tiny Maya ruin nearby.

Parque Garrafón's scenic seaside walkway

Sportfishing

Cooperativa Isla Bonita (Av. Rueda Medina at Av. Allende, cell tel. 998/134-6103, 9am-5pm daily) and **Cooperativa Isla Mujeres** (end of Av. Madero at pier, tel. 998/877-1363, 7am-7pm daily) both offer *pesca deportiva* (sportfishing). Boats typically carry up to six people for the same price, and prices include nonalcoholic drinks, sandwiches, and bait. Two trips are usually available, depending on the season: Pesca Mediana (US$200, 4 hours) focuses on midsize fish, including snapper, grouper, and barracuda; and Pesca Mayor (US$350, 4 hours) goes after large catch such as marlin and sailfish. Reserve directly at the pier. **Sea Hawk Divers** (Av. Carlos Lazo at Av. López Mateos, tel. 998/877-0296, www.seahawkislamujeres.com, 9am-8pm daily) offers comparable services for half-day shore (US$350) and deep-sea fishing trips (US$450).

JAX Sportfishing (JAX Bar and Grill, Av. López Mateos at Av. Rueda Medina, tel. 998/877-1254, www.jaxsportfishing.com, US$950) has an experienced English-speaking captain and offers all-day charters for a maximum of four anglers, ensuring highly personalized service.

Spas

In downtown Isla, **Casa Luz Spa** (Av. Juárez btwn Calles Bravo and Allende, tel. 998/202-0081, 8am-8pm daily) has a loyal following among locals and repeat visitors thanks to the skill and personalized service of its founder, Josefina Rodriguez. Massages, facials, and body treatments include first-rate products, yet remain quite affordable. House calls can be made, too.

Spa Zenter (Casa de los Sueños, Carr. Sac Bajo s/n, tel. 998/888-0369, toll-free U.S. tel. 877/372-3993, www.casasuenos.com, 9am-8:30pm daily) is a full-service spa offering a wide range of massages, body treatments, and facials in a serene and luxurious setting.

Yoga

Vastu School of Yoga (Calle Zazil-Ha No. 118, tel. 561/200-6652, www.vastuyoga.com) offers yoga instruction in a breezy *palapa* studio at Na Balam Hotel. Classes are held every day at 7am, 9am, 11am, and 6pm. Kids yoga is also offered at 4pm on Tuesday and Thursday. All classes run US$12. Workshops and private sessions also are available.

Isla Mujeres Yoga (Av. Juárez btwn Avs. López Mateos and Matamoros, no phone, www.islamujeresyoga.com, US$12) offers yoga classes in a rooftop studio at Elements of the Island hotel. Offerings include vinyasa, ashtanga, and gentle flow. Guided meditation is also offered. Classes are typically held at 8:15am, 9am, and 10:15am every day, but check the website for the current schedule. Ask about monthly rates if you plan to stay awhile.

Yoga classes at **Poc Na Hostel** (Av. Matamoros near Av. Lazo, tel. 998/877-0090) are open to the public every morning at 9am. The price—US$3.85—can't be beat.

FOOD

Seafood is the specialty in Isla Mujeres, even more so than in Cancún. In fact, much of the lobster and fish served on the Riviera Maya is caught near Isla Mujeres, so it stands to reason that it's freshest here.

Mexican

Specializing in Yucatecan fare, ★ **Jardín Maya** (Av. Hidalgo near Av. Morelos, tel. 998/842-0758, 8am-8pm daily, US$4.50-10) is arguably one of the best restaurants on the island. The dishes are classic—*salbutes, panuchos, sopa de lima, cochinita pibil*—and prepared to perfection. Seating is either in a colorful dining room or just outside, overlooking the pedestrian walkway. Service is welcoming and responsive. This is definitely a place to go once, and then return again and again.

La Lomita (Av. Juárez near Av. Allende, tel. 998/826-6335, 9am-10pm Mon.-Sat., US$4-11), a brightly painted restaurant frequented by locals, offers tasty Mexican fare. *Comida corrida*—a two-course lunch special with drink—is offered daily and often includes chiles rellenos, tacos, and stews.

Ceviche, grilled whole fish, and other seafood meals also are featured at reasonable prices.

Mercado Municipal (Av. Guerrero at Av. Matamoros, 6am-4pm daily, US$2-4) has a handful of simple eateries that serve good cheap meals. On Sunday, *cochinta pibil* (slow-roasted pork marinated in achiote sauce and wrapped in banana leaves) is offered at a handful of stands. Get there by 9am to enjoy some before it sells out.

Seafood

Run and supplied by the fishermen's co-op, **Restaurante Justicia Social** (Av. Rueda Medina near Av. Allende, cell tel. 998/230-4803, 11am-7pm daily, US$6-12) serves up some of the freshest seafood on the island. Octopus, shrimp, oysters, conch, and all sorts of fish fillets are served on the patio overlooking the Caribbean or in the simple dining room. *Tikinxik* (TEEK-in-cheek), a whole grilled fish prepared using a spicy red sauce that's derived from pre-Hispanic Maya cuisine, is offered weekends only. Delivery is available.

Bally Hoo (Av. Rueda Medina near Av. Abasolo, cell tel. 998/108-4236, 6am-10pm daily, US$5-12) may be stuck behind a gas station and a slew of moored boats, but the Baja-style breaded fish tacos are to die for, and well worth any necessary searching. The fish and chips are great, too, and if you've got an appetite, the fish fillet or shrimp dishes are filling. Cold beers (US$1.50) and margaritas (US$3) are the perfect accompaniment.

On the tip of Playa Norte, **Sunset Grill** (Av. Rueda Medina, tel. 998/877-0785, www.sunsetgrill.com.mx, 10am-10pm daily, US$8-20) offers a great view with mellow beats on one of the best beaches on the island. Beachside chairs and umbrellas are also available for the day if you order from the menu. The food is solid, including grilled fish, ceviche, hamburgers, and even a kids menu.

Other Specialties

Upscale but homey, ★ **Olivia** (Av. Matamoros btwn Calle Juárez and Av. Rueda Medina, tel. 998/877-1765, www.olivia-isla-mujeres.com, 5pm-9:45pm Mon.-Sat., US$8-18) serves up the best Mediterranean cuisine on the island. Owned by an Israeli couple who pooled their families' recipes and opened shop, the menu is a phenomenal amalgam of specialties from Morocco, Greece, Bulgaria, and Turkey. Seating is either in the *palapa*-roofed dining room or in

Pick your pleasure at a local gelato shop.

the lush garden courtyard. Reservations are recommended, and it's cash only. Open on Monday January-March only.

Qubano (Av. Hidalgo btwn Avs. Matamoros and Mateos, cell tel. 998/214-2118, noon-10pm Mon.-Sat., US$10-15) is a colorful place offering up a tasty selection of Cuban sandwiches, burgers, and salads. Favorites include the Tostón (plantain slices stuffed with chicken, pork, or *picadillo*), the Cuban (grilled ham, pork, and cheese), and the goat-cheese-stuffed burger. Snag a table, enjoy a Cuban coffee while you wait, or take your eats to go.

In a clapboard house facing the lagoon, with fishing boats crowded up next to it, **El Varadero** (no phone, noon-10pm Tues.-Sun., US$10-19) doesn't really evoke the famous white-sand beach east of Havana that it's named for, but good food—and even better mojitos—have a way of trumping geography. Dig into classic Cuban fare while sitting at aluminum tables on an outdoor patio decorated with shipping buoys. Find it at the mouth of Laguna Makax, near Puerto Isla Mujeres.

Cafés

Located partway down the island, ★ **Mango Café** (Carr. Perimentral at Calle Payo Obispo, tel. 998/274-0118, 8am-3pm and 4pm-10pm daily, US$6.50-14) has a cheerful bohemian exterior that practically begs a closer look. You'll be glad you do: Dishes like coconut French toast and eggs Benedict with chaya and portabella mushrooms, plus drinks like ginger lemonade and bottomless organic coffee, make this small eatery an island favorite—and that's just breakfast!

Serving up organic products, **Elements of the Island Café** (Av. Juárez btwn López Mateos and Matamoros, tel. 998/274-0098, www.elementsoftheisland.com, 7:30am-1pm daily, US$5-10) serves up hearty and healthy meals. Breakfasts are especially popular, with homemade bread and marmalade, and cappuccinos to die for.

Aluxes Café Bar (Av. Matamoros btwn Avs. Hidalgo and Guerrero, no phone, 7am-10pm daily, US$3-14) is a small café offering up a huge variety of coffee drinks, amazing baked goods (try the banana bread), bagels, and breakfast dishes like granola with fruit and yogurt. Alcoholic drinks are also served up strong, and the menu extends to hearty lunch and dinner dishes like burritos, fajitas, and tuna steak.

Sweets

La Michoacana (Av. Bravo at Av. Hidalgo, 9am-11pm daily, US$1-2.50) offers homemade *aguas, paletas,* and *helados* (juices, popsicles, and ice cream). Choose from seasonal fruits including passion fruit, watermelon, pineapple, and mamey. Of course, chocolate- and vanilla-flavored treats are available, too.

Try **ParadICE-CREAM** (Av. Hidalgo at Av. Morelos, 10am-10pm daily, US$2.50-6.50) for terrific handmade gelato.

Groceries

For a big supermarket, head to **Chedraui** (www.chedraui.com.mx, 7am-8pm daily), about halfway down the island, across from the baseball diamond. To get there, simply follow Avenida Gustavo Rueda Medina; the supermarket will be on your right, just before a sharp bend known as "devil's curve."

Xpress Super (Av. Morelos 5, www.sanfranciscodeasis.com.mx, 7am-10pm Mon.-Sat., 7am-9pm Sun.) is the island's longtime local grocery store, facing the central plaza.

Mercado Municipal (Av. Guerrero at Av. Matamoros, 6am-4pm daily) has a good selection of fruits, vegetables, and meats, a *tortillería,* plus fresh-squeezed juices sold by the liter.

ACCOMMODATIONS

Isla Mujeres has a wide variety of lodging options, from youth hostels to upscale boutique hotels. Most budget and midrange places are in the *centro,* while higher-end resorts occupy secluded areas farther down the island (which may mean you'll need to rent a golf cart to get around).

Under US$50

Isla Mujeres's longtime backpacker haven, ★ **Poc Na Hostel** (Av. Matamoros near Av. Lazo, tel. 998/877-0090, www.pocna.com, US$6.25 pp camping, US$11-13 pp dorm, US$14.50 pp dorm with a/c, US$27 s/d with shared bath, US$30 d with private bath, US$25-38 with private bath and a/c) is a busy labyrinth of rooms, courtyards, and common areas, just steps from the island's best beach. Dorm rooms have 4-9 bunks each and are priced by the thickness of the mattress (thin, thinner, and thinnest); private rooms have cement floors and whitewashed walls. There's foosball, table tennis, and TV in the various common areas, plus a dining room with basic food service. The hostel hosts live music most nights starting at 9:30pm and organizes frequent events—from volleyball tournaments to Isla Contoy excursions. The drawbacks are no kitchen access and a serious risk of never leaving. Visa and MasterCard are accepted.

Hotel Maria del Pilar (Calle Abasolo 15, tel. 998/877-0071, www.mariadelpilar.hostel.com, US$48 s/d) is a small, well-located hotel with simple but tidy rooms, most with TV, air-conditioning, and minifridge, plus Wi-Fi and shared kitchen for all. It's a fine choice for budget travelers who want some of the conveniences of a hostel without the scene.

Hotel Carmelina (Av. Guerrero 4, tel. 998/877-0006, US$31 s/d with a/c) is a reliable budget choice. It has a slightly residential-motel feel (the family who runs it lives on the ground floor, and another room houses a manicure shop), but the rooms are clean, albeit small, with hot water, TV, and air-conditioning. Larger double and triple rooms are available (US$50-57).

US$50-100

A charming place, ★ **Casa El Pío** (Av. Hidalgo near Av. Bravo, tel. 998/229-2799, www.casaelpio.com, US$80-95 s/d with a/c) is a five-room boutique-ish hotel with cool minimalist decor accented with artsy touches and splashes of color. Rooms are spacious and comfortably equipped with good beds, separate seating areas, balconies (two with ocean view), and Wi-Fi; each also has a mini-fridge, coffeemaker, and a cutting board for light food preparation. There's also a small mosaic-tile plunge pool for cooling off after a day at the beach. Adults only; reservations are highly recommended.

Hotel Kinich (Av. Juárez near Av. Matamoros, tel. 998/888-0909, www.islamujereskinich.com, US$95 s/d, US$115 suite) is a great find in downtown Isla: Rooms are simple but elegant with warm wood furnishings, muted colors, and Mexican wall art from Guadalajara. All rooms have quiet air-conditioning, cable TV, and Wi-Fi, and more than half of them also have king-size beds. Two gorgeous suites occupy the top floor—modern one-bedroom apartments with state-of-the-art kitchens, outdoor whirlpool tubs, and views of town. The only downer is that the hotel occupies a four-story building with no elevator, but, hey, at least you'll get your workouts in.

Elements of the Island (Av. Juárez btwn Avs. López Mateos and Matamoros, tel. 998/274-0098 or cell tel. 998/117-8651, www.elementsoftheisland.com, US$85 s/d with a/c) has three lovely studio apartments, each with fine wood furnishings, flowing white curtains, and bursts of color. All rooms have king-size beds and basic kitchenettes, plus Wi-Fi and TVs with DVD players. Guests pass through a leafy courtyard with a gurgling fountain to access the rooms, which are behind the hotel's recommended restaurant. Common spaces include a hot tub and hammock area as well as a rooftop yoga studio. Kind and attentive owners provide excellent service.

Simple and well located, **Suites Los Arcos** (Av. Hidalgo near Av. Abasolo, tel. 998/877-1343, US$70-90 s/d with a/c) has large, colorful rooms with gleaming bathrooms and heavy wood furnishings. All have a small fridge, microwave, and coffeemaker, plus TV, air conditioner, and Wi-Fi. Four of the 12 rooms have balconies—two overlook the pedestrian walkway and are great for people-watching (but can be noisy), while the others face the opposite direction and are huge and sunny.

Hotel Xbulu-Ha (Av. Guerrero btwn Avs. Abasolo and Madero, tel. 998/877-1783, www. islamujeres.biz, US$46 s with a/c, US$52 d with a/c, US$73-83 suite with kitchenette and a/c) offers bright and airy rooms with modern amenities like cable TV, mini-split air conditioners, and safety deposit boxes. The beds are double sized—something to consider if you plan on sharing. Suites are larger versions of the standard rooms, with fully equipped kitchenettes and king-size beds. Wi-Fi and beach towels and chairs are included in the rate. The hotel is located just one block from the Caribbean.

Hotel & Suites Bucaneros (Av. Hidalgo near Av. Madero, tel. 998/877-1228, toll-free Mex. tel. 800/227-4765, www.bucaneros. com, US$45-62 s/d with a/c, US$80-90 d/t with a/c and kitchenette) has 16 nicely appointed rooms, all with modern bathrooms, air-conditioning, and Wi-Fi, plus continental breakfast. The budget rooms are quite small, though not uncomfortable, while larger ones have small equipped kitchens (hot plate or gas stove, minifridge, and toaster) and in some cases a sofa bed, balcony, and separate dining area. The location couldn't be more central, but it can be noisy at night.

US$100-200

A colonial-style home turned boutique inn, ★ **Casa Sirena** (Av. Hidalgo near Av. Bravo, no phone, www.sirena.com.mx, US$145-165 s/d with a/c) has just six rooms, all sumptuously appointed with teak furnishings, Tiffany lamps, stone-tiled bathrooms, and extras like iPod docks and laptop-size safes; some rooms also boast beautiful Talavera tile floors. A full Mexican breakfast—*huevos divorciados, enfrijoladas,* chicken enchiladas—is served daily (except Sunday) on the small, leafy patio. Every evening (Monday-Saturday), guests also enjoy a happy hour with the gregarious owner, who serves up potent cocktails on the rooftop terrace. Other features include

two plunge pools (one with Venetian glass tiles), a sundeck with almost 360-degree views of the Caribbean, and Wi-Fi. Online reservations are required; adults only.

The adults-only **Villa La Bella** (Carr. Perimetral s/n, tel. 998/888-0342, www.villalabella.com, US$150 s/d with a/c, US$165 suite, US$185 honeymoon suite with a/c) is run by an amiable American couple who give warm, personalized service to all their guests. There are just six units: three bright pool-front rooms with whimsical decor, two 2nd-floor *palapa*-roofed units with hanging beds (but no air-conditioning), and a colorful honeymoon suite with fantastic ocean views from its two terraces. There also is a well-maintained pool on-site. A gourmet breakfast is included (except Monday) and served in the eclectic open-air lounge, where you can also score great cocktails and ice-cold beer.

Hotel Las Palmas (Av. Guerrero near Av. López Mateos, cell tel. 998/236-5803, www. laspalmasonisla.com, US$100-110 s/d with a/c, US$120-150 penthouse) is a homey hotel run by a friendly mother-daughter team from Canada. Rooms are small but tastefully decorated, with creature comforts like good water pressure, pillow-top beds, even full-length mirrors. There's lots of common space for relaxing and socializing, including a rooftop lounge with hammocks, shared kitchen, and a plunge pool. Most guests enjoy the camaraderie, but those seeking seclusion may find it overly hostel-like. (It doesn't help that most rooms open right onto the common areas.) Complimentary use of snorkel gear, coolers, and yoga mats also is available (first-come, first-served). There's a five-night minimum in high season.

The boutique **Casa Ixchel** (Av. Martínez Ross at Carr. Perimetral, tel. 998/888-0107, www.casaixchelisla.com, US$73-157 s/d with a/c, US$240 1-bdrm apartment with a/c, US$407 3-bdrm apartment with a/c) has just 10 rooms, all with names like Grace, Karma, and Serenity. Standard rooms are tiny, suites have a bit more breathing room, and you can actually unpack your bags in the apartments.

But even in the small quarters, each room has a deep bathtub, luxurious beds, and classy decor; the apartments have fully equipped kitchens, too. There are great ocean views from the pool and patio area, though it's too rough and rocky for swimming here. A top-floor restaurant serves mostly Italian, American, and seafood dishes. Children over 12 only, except during Easter, Christmas, and summer, when all ages are welcome.

Over US$200

Hotel Secreto (Sección Rocas 11, tel. 998/877-1039, www.hotelsecreto.com, US$259-289 s/d with a/c) is a classy glass and stucco hotel that's good for couples who want a quiet getaway without having to go down island. The beach here isn't swimmable (Playa Norte is a short walk away), but there are gorgeous views from the rooms and the hotel's long, narrow infinity pool. Rooms have native stone floors, plasma TVs, iPod docks, pillow-top mattresses, and huge private balconies. Upkeep can be lacking, but not egregiously. Continental breakfast is included, and there's a small gym.

★ **Casa de los Sueños** (Carr. Garrafón s/n, tel. 998/888-0370, toll-free U.S. tel. 877/372-3993, www.casasuenos.com, US$249-399 s/d with a/c, US$599 presidential suite) is a gorgeous boutique hotel with 10 immaculate rooms. Located on a bluff at the southern end of the island, the hotel has gorgeous views, including from the large infinity pool. There's no beach, unfortunately, but a large pier does well for swimming, sunbathing, and spa treatments, while the hotel's excellent restaurant-bar is on the water's edge. Bikes, kayaks, and snorkel gear are available for exploring.

All-Inclusive

Privilege Aluxes (Av Lopez Mateos at Gustavo Rueda Medina, tel. 998/848-8470, www.privilegehotels.com, US$285 s/d with a/c, US$318 pp all-inclusive) is a newish resort with both all-inclusive and B&B options. The beach club is lovely and a highlight for most travelers, despite having to walk across the street to get there. The hotel's pool is sleek and clean (though oddly chilly), and rooms, though somewhat sterile in decor, are large and comfortable. All in all, it's a good option if you're looking for a resort experience in downtown Isla.

Isla Mujeres Palace (Carr. Sac Bajo s/n, tel. 998/999-2020, toll-free U.S. tel. 888/563-7805, www.palaceresorts.com, US$498-598 s/d with a/c) is an upscale, couples-only all-inclusive resort with just 62 rooms and an exclusive getaway vibe. Suites have king-size beds and muted modern decor. There's only one restaurant, but it's a good one, with international cuisine and even a dress code. The beach and pool areas are lovely, though noise from neighboring beach clubs can be annoying at times.

Apartments and Private Homes

If you feel like lingering for a while in Isla Mujeres—and who doesn't?—consider booking an apartment or private home. There are a surprising number available, both in town and down island, running the gamut in size and price, and available by the week or month. Check out the options at agencies like Lost Oasis (www.lostoasis.net) and Isla Beckons (www.islabeckons.com), which specialize in Isla Mujeres, or at Vacation Rentals by Owner (www.vrbo.com).

INFORMATION AND SERVICES
Tourist Information

The **Oficina de Turismo** (Av. Rueda Medina 130, tel. 998/877-0307, www.islamujeres.gob. mx, 9am-4pm Mon.-Fri.) sometimes has maps and useful information. There's also a **tourist information desk** (9am-4pm daily) at the passenger ferry pier.

The English-language website **www. islamujeres.info** has concise and accessible descriptions of various aspects of Isla Mujeres, including activities, tours, taxis, ferry schedules, and history, plus a Q&A section frequented by longtime expats.

Soul de Isla Mujeres (www.souldeisla.com) also has information and recommendations about Isla Mujeres, from restaurants to wedding planners. Also try www.isla-mujeres.net for information about visiting Isla.

MapChick Isla Mujeres (www.cancunmap.com, US$15) is a fantastic professional-quality color map of Isla Mujeres. It is extremely detailed, including annotated listings of almost every restaurant, hotel, and point of interest on the island. It is available at a handful of Isla's restaurants and hotels, and also can be ordered online.

Emergency Services

General practitioner **Dr. Antonio E. Salas** (Av. Abasolo btwn Avs. Hidalgo and Benito Juárez, tel. 998/877-0021, 24-hour tel. 998/877-0477, drsalas@prodigy.net.mx, 9am-3pm and 4pm-9pm daily) is highly recommended by islanders. He speaks fluent English and basic German.

If you need immediate assistance, **Hospital Integral Isla Mujeres** (Av. Guerrero 7, tel. 998/877-0117, 24 hours) is equipped to handle walk-in consultations, simple surgeries, and basic emergencies. In case of a serious injury or illness, patients are taken to a Cancún hospital.

For diving-related injuries, Isla Mujeres's primary **hyperbaric chamber** (tel. 998/877-0819, 9am-4pm daily), or *cámera hiberbárica* in Spanish, is on the pedestrian-only extension of Avenida Morelos, just north of the *zócalo*.

Farmacia YZA (Av. Benito Juárez at Calle Morelos, tel. 998/999-0234, 24 hours) has sunscreen, bug repellent, and toiletries in addition to medications.

The **police station** (tel. 998/999-0051, 24 hours) is on the central plaza.

Money

HSBC has a bank and ATMs across from the UltraMar pier (Av. Rueda Medina btwn Avs. Madero and Morelos, tel. 998/877-0005, 9am-5pm Mon.-Fri., 9am-3pm Sat.) and an ATM only at Xpress Super grocery store on the central plaza.

Media and Communications

Like many cities in Mexico now, Isla Mujeres has **free public Wi-Fi** in the central plaza, available to anyone with a computer or mobile device. Most hotels offer Wi-Fi to guests, too.

There are a handful of Internet cafés around town, including **Café Internet Adrian's** (8am-11pm daily, US$1.75/hour Internet, US$0.35/minute international calls), facing the central plaza, and **Click + Call** (Av. Benito Juárez near Av. López Mateos, 9am-8pm daily, US$1.75/hour Internet, US$0.25/minute to U.S./Can., US$0.50/minute all other international calls).

The **post office** (Av. Guerrero at Av. López Mateos, tel. 998/877-0085) is open 9am-5pm Monday-Friday, and 9am-12:30pm Saturday.

Immigration

The **immigration office** (Av. Rueda Medina near Av. Morelos, tel. 998/877-0189, 9am-4pm daily) issues tourist cards to those arriving by boat from another country; for all other matters, including visa extensions, visitors should go to Cancún.

Laundry and Storage

Lavandería Cienpies (Av. Vicente Guerrero at Av. Madero, no phone, 7am-9pm Mon.-Sat.) will wash, dry, and fold for US$4.75 per four kilos (8.8 pounds).

Tim Pho Lavandería (Av. Juárez at Abasolo, no phone, 8am-8pm Mon.-Sat., 8am-2pm Sun.) offers same-day service with a two-hour wait. Loads cost US$5.50 per four kilos (8.8 pounds).

Storage lockers (US$5.50 per 24 hours) are available at the Ultramar ferry pier; they are big enough to hold carry-on bags only. If it's really early or late in the day and there's no staffer around, ask for help from the parking lot attendant, just east of the pier.

GETTING THERE

A number of ferries ply the turquoise waters of the Bahía de Mujeres (Bay of Women) between Isla Mujeres and various mainland ports in and around Cancún. There is no

Ferries to Isla Mujeres

Various passenger ferries (and also a car ferry) leave for Isla Mujeres from Cancún every day. Those leaving from the Zona Hotelera are more expensive and take longer but may be more convenient. In case you've got a car, there's also a vehicle ferry. **Note:** During the high season, additional departures are occasionally offered.

ZONA HOTELERA

El Embarcadero
UltraMar (Blvd. Kukulcán Km. 4, tel. 998/881-5890, www.granpuerto.com.mx, US$14/19 one-way/round-trip, 30 minutes). **Departure:** 9:15am, 10:30am, 11:45am, 1pm, 2:15pm, and 4:30pm. **Return:** 9:45am, 11am, 12:15pm, 1:30pm, 4pm, and 5:15pm.

Playa Tortugas
UltraMar (Blvd. Kukulcán Km. 7, tel. 998/881-5890, www.granpuerto.com.mx, US$14/19 one-way/round-trip, 30 minutes). **Departure:** hourly 9am-2pm, 4pm, and 5pm. **Return:** hourly 9:30am-1:30pm, 3:30pm, 4:30pm, and 5:30pm.

Playa Caracol
UltraMar (Blvd. Kukulcán Km. 9.5, tel. 998/881-5890, www.granpuerto.com.mx, US$14/19 one-way/round-trip, 30 minutes). **Departure:** 9am, 10:15am, 11:30am, 12:45pm, 2pm, and 4:45pm. **Return:** 9:45am, 11am, 12:15pm, 1:30pm, 4pm, 5:15pm.

DOWNTOWN

To get to either of the passenger ferries in downtown Cancún, take the red R-1 bus (US$0.75) on Boulevard Kukulcán or Avenida Tulum; continue past the downtown bus terminal and north out of the city. **Gran Puerto** is easily located by its tall observation tower. (Be aware that you may be approached by people dressed in UltraMar uniforms who are in fact selling time-shares here.) **Puerto Juárez** is two blocks past Gran Puerto. It's the original Isla Mujeres ferry pier, but the boats and waiting area are older. The vehicle ferry at **Punta Sam** is located on Avenida López Portillo, about five kilometers (3 miles) north of Gran Puerto. On Isla Mujeres, the car ferry pier is a few hundred meters south of the passenger piers, past the naval dock.

Gran Puerto
UltraMar (Av. López Portillo s/n, tel. 998/881-5890, www.granpuerto.com.mx, US$6 each way, 15 minutes) boats feature comfy seats in an air-conditioned cabin and an open-air deck, with televisions playing a short promotional program on Isla Mujeres. There's often live music on the open deck. **Departure:** every 30 minutes 5am-8:30pm, then hourly 9:30pm-11:30pm. **Return:** every 30 minutes 5:30am-9pm, then hourly 10pm-midnight.

Puerto Juárez
Transportes Marítimos Magaña (Av. López Portillo s/n, tel. 998/877-0618, US$6 each way, 15 minutes). **Departure:** every 30 minutes 6:30am-8:30pm, then midnight. **Return:** every 30 minutes 6am-8pm, then 11pm.

Punta Sam (vehicle ferry)
The lumbering vehicle ferry to Isla Mujeres is run by **Marítima Isla Mujeres** (Av. López Portillo s/n, tel. 998/878-4171, www.maritimaislamujeres.com, 45-60 minutes). Rates are according to vehicle: US$22.50 for cars, US$33 for SUVs and vans, US$7.75 for motorcycles or mopeds, and US$7.15 for bicycles. Rates include the driver only—each additional passenger costs US$3.15. Arrive about an hour early to get in line; tickets go on sale 30 minutes prior to departure. **Departure:** 7:15am, 11am, 2:45pm, 5:30pm, and 8:15pm Mon.-Sat. and 9:15am, 1:30pm, 5:30pm, and 8:15pm Sun. **Return:** 6am, 9:30am, 12:45pm, 4:15pm, and 7:15pm Mon.-Sat. and 8am, noon, 4:15pm, and 7:15pm Sun.

direct ferry service from Isla Cozumel, however, and despite having an airstrip, no regular air service either.

Passenger Ferries

Passenger-only ferries leave for Isla Mujeres from Cancún in the Zona Hotelera and from Puerto Juárez, about three kilometers (1.9 miles) north of downtown Cancún. If you are just visiting for the day, reconfirm the return times and remember that service to the Zona Hotelera ends earlier than service to Puerto Juárez.

Car Ferries

A vehicle ferry operates from Punta Sam, about eight kilometers (5 miles) north of Cancún past Puerto Juárez.

GETTING AROUND

Isla Mujeres is a small and mostly flat island. In town you can easily walk everywhere. Buses and taxis are available for exploring farther afield, but definitely consider renting a golf cart, moped, or bike for more flexibility and independence.

Bus

There are two bus lines on Isla Mujeres (US$0.30), running the same route but in opposite directions, from downtown to Playa Lancheros and back. They stop in local neighborhoods, but do not reach the far southern tip. Theoretically the buses run every 30 minutes, but be prepared to wait longer than that. There are some official stops, but you can just flag one down wherever you see it.

Taxi

Isla Mujeres has many more taxis than seem necessary—in town, it feels more likely that you'd be hit by a taxi than have trouble finding one. Out of town, you shouldn't have to wait too long for a taxi to pass, either, and Parque Garrafón, Dolphin Discovery, and Playa Lancheros all have fixed taxi stands. From downtown, rates are US$1-2 around town (including the beaches) and US$2-5

elsewhere on the island. Official rates are posted wherever taxis line up, including Parque Garrafón, Punta Sur, and downtown. Taxis are per trip, not per person, and drivers may pick up other passengers headed the same direction. You can also hire a taxi to give you a private driving tour of the island for US$13 per hour. **Note:** Taxi fares double after dark until 6am.

Golf Cart, Moped, and Bicycle Rental

Most rental operations on the island share the same fixed rates: golf carts US$14 per hour, US$43 per day (store hours), and US$50 for 24 hours; mopeds US$8.50 per hour, US$25 per day, US$29 for 24 hours; and bicycles (including lock but often not helmet) US$2.50 per hour, US$10 per day, US$11.50 for 24 hours.

Note: Isla Mujeres has a regular occurrence of serious accidents involving tourists driving mopeds. Riding double is a major culprit: Mopeds are much harder to control with two people riding instead of one. Poor roads and wet and windy conditions also are dangerous, not to mention unpredictable. Better to rent a bike or golf cart, or at least separate mopeds.

Agencies right at the ferry pier sometimes charge slightly more than those a few blocks away. Solid choices include **Ciro's** (Av. Guerrero near Av. Matamoros, cell tel. 998/183-9971, 9am-5pm daily), **El Sol** (Av. Juárez btwn Avs. Abasolo and Matamoros, tel. 998/877-0791, 9am-5pm daily), **Luxury Car Rental** (Av. Hidalgo near Playa Norte, tel. 998/877-0392, 8am-6pm daily), and **Pelícanos** (Av. Matamoros near Av. Guerrero, no phone, 8am-5pm daily).

Isla Mujeres Golf Cart Rentals (cell tel. 998/242-6558, www.islamujeresgolfcartrentals.com) is a convenient new service that makes renting a golf cart easy. Rates are slightly higher than you'd pay normally, but you can reserve and pay online, the cart can be delivered to your hotel, and someone even comes by every day or two to fill the gas tank. Four- and six-seat carts are available; discounts for longer rentals.

Isla Holbox

At the northeastern tip of Quintana Roo, where the Caribbean Sea mingles with the Gulf of Mexico, and completely within the Yum Balam reserve, Isla Holbox (hole-BOASH) is one of the last reasonably obscure islands along the Yucatán Peninsula. The town of Holbox is a fishing village with sand roads, golf carts instead of cars, no hospital, and no post office. (There *are* three ATMs on the island, though they're often empty.) Instead, you'll find brightly painted homes, *palapa*-roofed hotels, and a handful of Italian and Spanish expats who have opened bed-and-breakfasts and small restaurants. The water here is emerald—not the clear turquoise of Cancún and Tulum—and while the sand is thinner, the beach is loaded with seashells and is no less scenic. Holbox is becoming well known as a place to snorkel with behemoth but harmless whale sharks—present June-September—and also has great opportunities for bird-watching, kayaking, and sportfishing. Above all, Holbox offers a sense of peace and tranquility that is increasingly hard to find on Mexico's Caribbean coast, and the feeling of a place as yet untouched by big business.

HISTORY

Indigenous Maya inhabited Holbox for centuries but abandoned the island more than 300 years before the first Europeans arrived. The name of the island and town is a matter of some dispute. Some say *holbox* is derived from a Maya term meaning "black water" and is a reference to the island's natural springs, whose dark depths make the water appear black. A more popular, albeit fantastical, story is that the pirate Francisco de Molas buried a treasure on the island and cut off the head of his African bodyguard so that his ghost would watch over the spot for eternity. De Molas was promptly killed by a snakebite, but the disembodied head of his bodyguard has appeared occasionally to islanders, trying to divulge the treasure's location but succeeding only in scaring everyone away. By this latter account, the island originally would have been called *poolbox* (black head), and was altered later by European settlers.

Snorkel with whale sharks, the biggest fish in the world, from Isla Holbox.

Isla Holbox

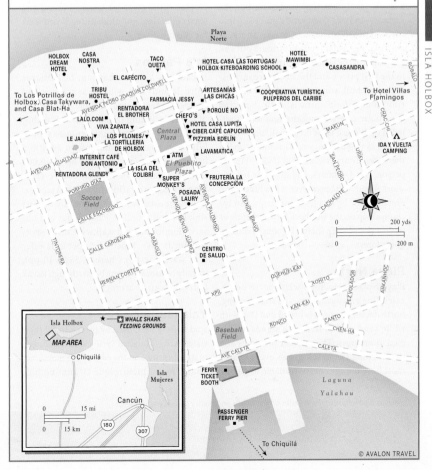

© AVALON TRAVEL

Storms are serious business on this low, flat island, which is regularly buffeted by tropical conflagrations. In fact, the town was originally located farther west but was destroyed by a hurricane and rebuilt in its current location about 150 years ago. *Nortes* are fall and winter storms that sweep down the Gulf coast bringing rain and turbid seas. *Maja' che* is the Maya name for sudden winds that can knock over trees; they are most common in April and May. In major storms, the whole island is evacuated.

SIGHTS
★ Whale Shark Feeding Grounds

From June to September, large numbers of whale sharks—the world's largest fish, typically measuring 6-7.5 meters (20-25 feet) and weighing more than 10 tons—congregate in shallow waters about 16 kilometers (10 miles) east of Holbox village. Despite their size, the sharks are completely harmless, eating plankton, krill, and other tiny organisms, much like baleen whales. Snorkeling with whale sharks is a unique and (to some) nerve-wracking experience. The captain pulls the boat alongside a shark—at Holbox they tend to feed on the surface—and two guests and a guide slip into the water with life jackets, masks, snorkels, and fins. The water tends to be murky (it's all the sealife in the water that attracts the sharks in the first place), and the sharks are surprisingly fast. Still, you get a good view of these enormous, gentle animals, with their tiny eyes, bizarre shovel mouths, and dark spotted skin. It's best to be on a small tour—since you go in two by two, you'll get more time in the water. Tours cost around US$95-115 per person, last 4-6 hours, and typically include snorkel gear, a life preserver, a box lunch, and nonalcoholic beverages. Some trips also include a stop on the way back for snorkeling or to visit the island's inland lagoons and mangrove forest.

Playa Norte

Playa Norte is Holbox's scenic main beach, extending eastward along the island's long, north-facing shore; it is broad and flat, with white sand, and dotted with stands of tangled dune grass. The number of homes and hotels along the beach grows every year—most have lounge chairs available to guests, but there's less and less open space for everyone else to lay out a towel. That said, Playa Norte is still great for beachcombing and shell collecting, and sunbathing if you walk far enough down.

Isla Pájaros

Located in Yalahau Lagoon, Isla Pájaros (Bird Island) is a wildlife sanctuary and the permanent home to some 150 species of birds, including frigate birds, white ibis, double-crested cormorants, roseate spoonbills, and boat-billed herons. In addition, between May and September up to 40,000 flamingos nest on Holbox before their long winter migration to South America. Environmental restrictions mean you can't simply wander on Isla Pájaros, but two observation towers and walkways make spotting birds easy. Most tour operators offer bird-watching trips here (US$25-40 pp), usually by *lancha* (motorboat), though kayak tours also can be arranged.

Yalahau Spring

Said to have been used by pirates to fill their water barrels, Yalahau Spring is an *ojo de agua* (natural spring) on the edge of the mainland. Today, it is a picturesque swimming hole

Head to Isla Holbox for long walks on the beach and plenty of peace and quiet.

Bug Patrol

Isla Holbox's famous whale sharks may weigh 10 tons and have mouths that measure five feet across, but it's the island's itty-bitty residents that pack the meanest bite. Mosquitoes, sand flies, and *tábanos* (horseflies) can be fierce, particularly in the summer and after heavy rains. Bring bug repellent and use it liberally, day and night. Another tip: Always dry off and reapply repellent immediately after swimming—horseflies love skin that's moist, especially with seawater.

complete with a large *palapa*, picnic area, and pier. A trip here typically is combined with a stop to Isla Pájaros.

Isla de la Pasión

Just 15 minutes from town by boat, Isla de la Pasión is a tiny deserted island just 50 meters (164 feet) wide. It's known for its white-sand beach and beautiful emerald waters—perfect for a relaxing day at the beach. There are trees and a large *palapa* for shade. Be sure to bring plenty of water and snacks—there are no services on the island.

Street Art: Murals

Walking around Holbox, it's impossible to miss the gorgeous and dramatic murals around the island. They're the product of two projects: *Soñando por Holbox* (Dreaming for Holbox) and the *Festival Internacional de Arte Público* (International Festival of Public Art). The prior was a Kickstarter project that funded two of the murals; the latter funded the rest. Both projects involved artists from Mexico and beyond who met with islanders and explored the island for inspiration. Ask at your hotel for a map of the murals.

ENTERTAINMENT AND EVENTS
Cinema

Opened in 2011, the island's first (and only) **movie theater** (El Pueblito Plaza, Av. Benito Juárez near Porfirio Díaz, no phone, US$2.15) is located in El Pueblito Plaza, a small commercial center just off the main square. It may diminish the deserted-island feel somewhat, but locals certainly appreciate not having to trek to Cancún for the latest *Hunger Games* flick. Films are screened at 8pm on Friday, Saturday, and Sunday only.

Festivals and Events
FESTIVAL DE SAN TELMO

Most of Holbox's residents live by fishing, and the island has over 400 fishing boats and numerous fishing cooperatives. It's no surprise, then, that San Telmo, the patron saint of fishermen, is celebrated here with fervor. The party lasts for two weeks in mid-April, with food stands, live performances, and special events, including a popular sportfishing tournament. The festival ends on April 19 when fishermen and their families participate in a huge boat procession followed by general revelry in the decked-out main square.

FESTIVAL DE LA VIRGEN DE FATIMA

In mid-May, Holbox celebrates the Virgin of Fatima, the community's official patron saint. Held just a month after the San Telmo blowout, this festival is more austere, with religious processions and more folksy music and other performances. That said, it's still a party.

ENVIRONMENTAL WEEK

What started as an effort to educate children about the environment has turned into an annual island-wide event known as "Environmental Week." The first week of July is dedicated to environmental education and action, still focused on schoolkids, but involving parents and even visitors. Tourists can join the students in one of the week's biggest events: picking up trash from the beach.

SHOPPING

Holbox isn't exactly a shopper's paradise, but there is a **string of boutiques** along Avenida Igualdad (just east of the central plaza) selling everything from handcrafted jewelry to whale shark magnets. Among them, **Artesanías Las Chicas** (tel. 984/875-2430, 9am-3pm and 6pm-10pm Tues.-Sun.) stands out for its high-end folk art, mostly from central and southern Mexico. It's a bit pricey, but the items are unique.

If you're into shells, **Lalo.com** (Av. Abasolo near Av. Pedro Joaquín Coldwell, tel. 984/875-2118) is jam-packed with beautifully polished *conchas* from around the world. The owner, *maestro* Lalo, lives below the shop—just ring his bell, and he'll open up the shop.

Inaugurated in 2011, **El Pueblito Plaza** (Av. Benito Juárez near Porfirio Díaz) is as close as you'll get to a mall in these parts. Located just off the central plaza, it has a handful of boutiques, eateries, and the island's one and only movie theater, a one-screen affair showing reasonably recent Hollywood films (US$2.15).

SPORTS AND RECREATION

There is a lot to do on Holbox, and various excursions can be arranged through your hotel, local tour operators, or done on your own. Most of Holbox's tour operators offer the full gamut of excursions, at comparable prices. Recommended outfits include **Cooperativa Turística Pulperos del Caribe** (Av. Igualdad near Calle Carito, tel. 984/875-2347) and **Turística Moguel** (tel. 984/875-2028, www.holboxislandtours.com).

Snorkeling

Besides swimming with whale sharks, the best place to snorkel on Isla Holbox is **Cabo Catoche,** a coral reef in about 2-4 meters (6.5-13 feet) of water at the far eastern end of the island. The water isn't as clear as in the Riviera Maya, but the reef here is more pristine and the animal life more abundant, including stingrays, moray eels, nurse sharks, sea stars, conch, and myriad fish. Because it is so far from town, tours cost around US$75 per person (minimum 4 people). Alternatively, a stop at Cabo Catoche can be combined with another outing, such as an island tour or a whale shark excursion.

Holbox has great conditions for kiteboarding.

Wind Sports

Holbox's steady winds and shallow, nearly waveless coastal waters make it ideal for wind sports, particularly kiteboarding and windsurfing. The strongest winds are September-March, while July and August tend to have lighter, novice-friendly breezes. Gabriel Olmos Aguirre (aka Gabo) is a popular and accomplished instructor offering courses at all levels through his outfit, **Holbox Kiteboarding School** (Hotel Casa Las Tortugas, Av. Igualdad s/n, cell tel. 984/144-2227, www.holboxkiteboarding.com), and in association with shops elsewhere in the Riviera Maya. Instruction prices, including gear, range US$75 per hour (private lessons) to US$65 per hour (group lessons, 3 students maximum). Rentals also are available. Wakeboarding classes are offered on those days the wind dies down (US$65-80/hour).

Kayaking

Kayaking is a great way to see the interior lagoons of the island, and especially for spotting birds. A fun and challenging option is to hire a golf-cart taxi to drive you and your boat—balanced on the back—to the main inlet where you can put in. From there it's possible to wend through the lagoons to the other side of the island, then paddle along the shore to the main ferry dock, passing Isla Pájaros along the way. Several shops and hotels rent kayaks (US$10-15/hour), while **Andrés Limón** (tel. 984/875-2220, kayak_holbox@hotmail.com) is a popular private guide.

Bird-Watching

Holbox has more than 30 species of birds, including herons, white and brown pelicans, double-crested cormorants, roseate spoonbills, and greater flamingos (the brightest pink of the five flamingo species). Most hotels can arrange a standard bird-watching excursion (US$30-45 pp, 4 hours, minimum 4 people), which generally includes taking a motorboat or kayaks through the mangroves to Isla Pájaros and the flamingo nesting grounds at Punta Mosquita. More specialized bird-watchers may want to contact **Juan Rico Santana** (aka Juan Karateca, tel. 984/875-2347 or cell tel. 984/100-9132)—a certified birder who leads many of the hotel trips, but also often arranges separate, more focused trips that are tailored to your interests.

Fishing

Holbox is an excellent spot for **sportfishing,** yet it's still relatively unknown. A deep-sea fishing excursion costs US$450-500, depending on how long you go out. It typically includes gear, bait, drinks, and lunch. A coastal fishing tour with a local fisherman, going after smaller and more plentiful catch, lasts 4-5 hours and costs around US$150-200. Local tour operators, and most hotels, can help you organize either trip.

Holbox also has great **fly-fishing,** with 100-plus-pound giant tarpons cruising the coastal waters, and smaller juveniles plying the interior lagoons, along with snook and jack. **Holbox Tarpon Club** (tel. 984/875-2144) offers personalized tours, running US$450 per boat (8 hours, lunch included, maximum 2 anglers per boat).

Horseback Riding

Los Potrillos de Holbox (across from airport, Av. Pedro Joaquin Coldwell s/n, tel. 984/129-9995) offers horseback riding tours into the interior of the island, along the beach, or both. Most tours last approximately 2.5 hours and cost US$30 per person.

Baseball

Holbox has an amateur baseball team, known as **Tiburones de Holbox** (Holbox Sharks). Their season lasts all spring, and games against visiting teams are held most Sundays at noon at the baseball "stadium" on Avenida Benito Juárez, a few blocks from the pier. It's a popular outing for island families, who typically bring tostadas and huge bowls of homemade ceviche to go with the cold beer and soda on sale in the stands. Admission is US$1-2; bring a hat as there is little shade.

Pirates of the Caribbean

For most of the colonial era, pirates were a major and constant threat to ships and port towns throughout the Yucatán Peninsula. They launched attacks throughout the region, creating virtual pirate colonies. Some of the region's more notorious and colorful nemeses include:

- **Francisco de Molas:** Said to have lived on present-day Isla Holbox for nearly four decades, attacking ships that approached looking for drinking water. The story goes that Molas had an African slave help him bury his treasure, then killed him so that his ghost would watch over the spot. Islanders say a wailing disembodied head haunts the island, and that the name Holbox is an alteration of the Maya term "pool box," or Black Head.

- **Henry Morgan and Jean Lafitte:** Pirates who used Isla Cozumel as a refuge and a base to launch attacks on the Yucatecan mainland and various Caribbean islands. Lafitte is said to have often used the island's safe northern harbors to hide from pursuers.

- **Pierre de Sanfroy:** A French corsair who occupied Cozumel's small village for several weeks in 1579, making the church his home, including sleeping on the altar, and harassing the local townspeople.

- **Lorencillo:** Born Laurent de Graff, the French buccaneer is best known for attacking Campeche City in 1685 with a pirate army of 700 men and holding the city ransom for two months. According to legend, he was captured in Valladolid after being lured there by a woman he captured on a ship. Held in the Ex-Convento San Bernardino, he was rescued by his crew before authorities could jail or execute him.

- **Peg Leg:** Cornelius Jol was one of the first privateers known to use a wooden prosthetic—and to go by the now-iconic pirate name. Technically an admiral in the Dutch navy, Peg Leg terrorized Spanish and Portuguese ships and ports, including a 10-ship assault on Campeche City in 1663.

Other notable pirates who sailed Yucatán's waters and figure in the region's lore include Sir Francis Drake, John Hawkins, Michel de Grammond, and Jacobo Jackson.

Yoga

Hotel Casa Las Tortugas (Av. Igualdad s/n, cell tel. 984/115-4244, www.islandholbox.eu, US$14) offers hatha yoga sessions every day at 9am in its gorgeous beachfront yoga studio; all classes are led by certified instructors.

About a 15-minute walk from the central plaza, **Casa Blat-Ha** (Calle Caguama at Calle Charral, cell tel. 984/137-6721, www.casablatha.com, US$9.25) offers rooftop yoga at 9am and 7pm every day but Wednesday. Afterward, stay for a cucumber smoothie or vegan meal at the on-site café.

FOOD

There are only a handful of restaurants on Isla Holbox, so anyone staying more than a day or two could easily sample them all. It wouldn't even take much effort, as virtually all face the central plaza or are less than a block off it. A quick stroll around the plaza lets you whet your appetite while sizing up the options.

Mexican and Seafood

Viva Zapata (Av. Igualdad btwn Av. Benito Juárez and Abasolo, 5pm-11:30pm daily, US$6.50-20) is a sand-floored *palapa* restaurant near the central plaza. It's all about seafood here, with dishes made from locally caught fish, shrimp, octopus, and other seafood. There's a kids menu, too, with tasty treats for the little ones like fish burgers and quesadillas. Come early to beat the crowd, or order a beer and kick back at the swing bar while you wait for a table to open up.

★ **Taco Queta** (Av. Palomino near Av. Pedro Joaquín Coldwell, 6pm-midnight daily,

US$3-8) is a classic Mexican restaurant, down to the plastic chairs and tables, the tarp, and the spit of *al pastor* meat prominently placed toward the front of the joint. As the name suggests, the specialty is street tacos—small tortillas stacked and heaped with the yummy goodness of meats and toppings. The burritos are huge and delicious, too—jam-packed with meat, chicken, or beans, and doused in *crema*. Come hungry—the portions are hearty. It's located just half a block from the beach.

A colorful clapboard house, **La Isla del Colibrí** (central plaza, Av. Benito Juárez at Av. Porfirio Díaz, tel. 984/875-2162, 8am-1pm and 6pm-11pm daily, US$4-9) is a decent breakfast place offering fresh fruit juices and big *licuados,* egg dishes, and Mexican classics. It's open for lunch and dinner, too, but there are better places for those meals.

Italian

The beachfront **Casa Nostra** (Hotel La Palapa, Av. Morelos at the beach, tel. 984/875-2121, 7:30am-10pm daily, US$8-25) may have a long list of pizzas, but it's much more than a simple pizza joint. This is first-class Italian cuisine, featuring handmade sausage, perfect pasta, and expertly prepared seafood, including whole lobster and octopus salad. (And, yes, the pizza's good, too.) Breakfasts are less successful, but dinner is a worthwhile splurge. You'll find a strong wine list and excellent service here.

Decked out with kitschy Mexican wrestling memorabilia, **Los Pelones** (central plaza, Av. Benito Juárez btwn Avs. Porfirio Díaz and Igualdad, no phone, 6:30pm-11pm daily, US$10-25) is a small 2nd-floor restaurant overlooking the central plaza. It specializes in classic Italian dishes, including great handmade pasta and seafood. Grab a table on the balcony for the best view and sea breeze.

Pizzería Edelín (central plaza, Av. Palomino at Av. Porfirio Díaz, tel. 984/875-2024, 11am-11pm daily, US$5-17) manages to stay busy even in the low season, serving decent thin-crust pizza—try the lobster or olive-and-caper ones for a treat—plus a smattering

of fish, pasta, and Mexican dishes. The ovens can really heat up the place, so nab a table on the porch for the breeze.

Light Fare and Sweets

★ **La Tortillería de Holbox** (central plaza, tel. 984/875-2443, 7:30am-4pm daily, US$3-7) is a breakfast favorite in a central location, with great fresh-brewed coffee to go along with omelets, yogurt and fresh fruit, and more—all with friendly service. For lunch, the Spanish tortilla feeds two and is to die for.

El Cafécito (Av. Pedro Joaquín Coldwell near Av. Palomino, 8am-3pm daily, US$4-8) is a cozy café just steps from the central plaza. Diners enjoy croissant and focaccia sandwiches, hummus platters, lasagna, and—the pièce de résistance—giant crepes with fillings like Nutella, caramel and nuts, and fruit.

An artisanal French bakery, **Le Jardin** (no-name street near Av. Pedro Joaquín Coldwell, 8am-noon daily, US$2-5) specializes in simple breakfasts made with homemade breads like croissants, brioche, and baguettes. Diners order at the register and take a seat under the *palapa*-roofed dining room. Come early to be sure to get a meal—once the bread runs out (and it does), the place closes for the day.

Porqué No (Av. Igualdad near Av. Bravo, no phone, noon-10:30pm daily, US$1.50-3) specializes in artisanal gelato. Flavors change periodically but include varieties like Oreo, pomegranate, coconut, and pistachio.

Groceries

Supplies ebb and flow in Isla Holbox, so you might have to go to more than one store to find everything you're looking for.

The souped-up **Super Monkey's** (Av. Benito Juárez near Calle Escobedo, 6am-midnight daily) has a decent selection of canned and packaged food, bug repellent, sunscreen, and toiletries.

For late-night munchies, check out **Chefo's** (central plaza, 24 hours daily).

The best selection of fruits and vegetables on the island is at **Frutería La Concepción** (Calle Escobedo near Av. Palomino, cell tel.

984/129-1240, 6am-10pm daily). You'll also find eggs, honey, and spices. Delivery is available.

ACCOMMODATIONS

For most travelers, Holbox's most appealing accommodations are its beachfront bunga-lows; they vary in style, amenities, and price, but all offer simple rest and relaxation in a peaceful seaside setting. Alternatively, ho-tels in town offer comfortable rooms at more accessible rates, and you're still just a short distance from the beach. Be aware that rates typically rise during whale shark season (mid-May-mid-September).

Under US$50

Holbox's best budget choice is ★ **Tribu Hostel** (Av. Pedro Joaquín Coldwell s/n, tel. 984/875-2507, www.tribuhostel.com, US$10.50-12 pp dorm, US$36-40.50 s/d). Set in two-story *palapa*-roofed buildings with polished wood floors, each room is named after one of the world's tribes—Maori, Huli, Woodabe, etc.—and is decorated accordingly. Dorms have 3-5 bunks apiece, fans, en suite bathrooms, and private balconies. Sheets and big lockers (BYO lock) are included in the rate. Private rooms are similarly outfitted but smaller. Common areas are first-rate, too: a fully equipped kitchen, an outdoor dining room, a rooftop lounge with lots of hammocks and stellar views, a bar with swings for seats, and even a screening room with a small li-brary of movies. Wi-Fi, laundry, yoga, kayaks, and Spanish classes also are available.

Though the mosquitos can be a problem (bring bug repellent), **Ida y Vuelta Camping** (Calle Plutarco Elias Calles btwn Róbalo and Chacchi, tel. 984/875-2358, www.holboxhos-tel.com, US$12 pp hammock, US$12 pp camp-ing, US$14 pp dorm, US$47 s/d bungalow with shared bath, US$51 s/d *cabaña,* US$66 house) has a good range of options—from hammock and tent sites to fully equipped houses. The most popular choices are the garden bun-galows, which have sand floors, screened windows, and shared bathrooms, and the *cabañas*—wood plank cabins on stilts, each with two basic rooms with private bathrooms. All guests have access to a fully equipped kitchen, colorfully tiled bathrooms with 24/7 hot water, and free Wi-Fi.

Located on a quiet residential street, **Posada Laury** (Calle Cardenas near Av. Palomino, tel. 984/875-2133, US$46 s/d with a/c) offers stark rooms with unexpected creature comforts: air-conditioning, cable TV, and minifridges, plus hot water and decent beds, too. It's a great deal, especially considering it's just two blocks from the central plaza. If you want to check in and there's no staff on-site, go around the corner to the nearest house on Avenida Palomino, where the owner lives (look for the "Posada Laury" sign above the doorbell).

US$50-100

Located about half a mile west of the central plaza, **Casa Blat-Ha** (Calle Caguama at Calle Charral, cell tel. 984/137-6721, www.casab-latha.com, US$50 s/d) is a small B&B with a welcoming boho-off-the-grid feel. It has 12 simple and clean rooms that are divided be-tween two buildings: the main one, where the rooms have ocean views and private balconies, and a building across the sand road, which has smaller, dark rooms. The main building also has a cozy lounging area, a rooftop medita-tion and yoga center, an organic garden, and a vegetarian café where a complimentary con-tinental breakfast is served. The beach is just a block away.

Opening onto the central plaza, **Hotel Casa Lupita** (Av. Palomino near Av. Igualdad, tel. 984/875-2017, www.casalupita-holbox.com, US$65 s/d with a/c, US$83-107 suite with a/c) has simple, comfortable rooms with colorful linens and Mexican tilework. Units are divided between two buildings with a courtyard between them serving as a com-mon area (and the best place to use the Wi-Fi). Suites have large terraces with chairs and hammocks—a peaceful place to chill out after a day at the beach, not so peaceful when chat-ter from late-night partyers wafts through the terrace doors.

US$100-200

★ **Hotel Mawimbi** (Av. Igualdad s/n, tel. 984/875-2003, www.mawimbi.net, US$115-145 s/d with a/c, US$175 s/d with a/c and kitchenette, US$197 suite with a/c) offers modern rooms and comfortable bungalows with a touch of boho flair. Guatemalan bedspreads, colorful tiles, and shell accents all lend an artistic touch, while quiet air-conditioning and free Wi-Fi keep you cool and connected. The shady garden has plenty of lounge chairs and hammocks, and is just steps from one of the best-kept stretches of beach. The low-key Italian owners maintain a friendly, welcoming atmosphere and offer recommended island excursions. There also is a good restaurant on-site, El Barquito, where a complimentary continental breakfast is served.

About a 10-minute walk from town, **Casa Takywara** (Av. Pedro Joaquín Coldwell s/n, tel. 984/875-2255, www.casatakywara. com, US$132-165 s/d with a/c and kitchenette) offers six spacious and lovely units in a circular three-story building. All have fully equipped kitchenettes (down to blenders and lime presses) and share wood floor porches. The oceanfront, just steps away, has plenty of lounge chairs, hammocks, and other places to relax. Continental breakfast is delivered to rooms daily. Service is friendly and efficient.

Holbox Dream Hotel (Av. Pedro Joaquín Coldwell s/n, tel. 984/875-2433, www.holbox-dream.com, US$116-144 s/d with a/c, US$160 deluxe s/d with a/c, US$181 deluxe s/d with a/c and whirpool tub) is a refreshing alternative to the deserted-isle getaways that make up most of Holbox's hotels. Standard rooms are comfortable and modern, with air-conditioning, good mattresses, stone basin sinks, and balconies with partial ocean views; deluxe rooms are bigger, with minifridges, security boxes, and better balcony views, plus some even have whirpool tubs. There's free Wi-Fi in all the rooms. The hotel also has a well-maintained stretch of beach, two small inviting pools, and a newly opened restaurant, which is perfect for leisurely meals.

Over US$200

★ **CasaSandra** (Calle Igualdad s/n, tel. 984/875-2171, www.casasandra.com, US$263 s/d with a/c, US$343-386 suite) is one of Holbox's most exclusive boutique hotels, though it still maintains the welcoming feel of a home. The main building looks like a Swiss ski lodge (it houses ocean-view rooms, the library, and a restaurant), but it

Hotel Mawimbi is a beachfront oasis.

also has a handful of smaller *palapa*-roofed buildings, more in style with their island neighbors. Rooms vary from shabby chic to tropical safari in decor and have features like claw-foot tubs and original art. Outside, guests can relax on the well-tended beach or by the large pool. A full breakfast is included in the rate.

Recently remodeled, **Hotel Villas Flamingos** (Paseo Kuka s/n, tel. 984/875-2167, www.villasflamingos.com, US$200-230 s/d with a/c, US$315-385 suite with a/c) is one of the nicest places to stay on the beach. Units are modern with boho flair: conch shell showerheads, coconut lamps, bamboo accents, and gorgeous mosaic tile bathrooms. All rooms have air-conditioning, private balconies, and ocean views (some partial, some dramatically expansive), and some even have private plunge pools and whirpool tubs. There is a well-tended pool just feet from the ocean, as well as a high-end restaurant/bar. Full breakfast is included in the rate.

INFORMATION AND SERVICES

While Holbox is making it onto more travelers' radars, there still is no bank (though there is one bank-affiliated ATM) and no post office. Also, note that hours of operation on the island are decidedly flexible—"open all day" usually means "closed for a couple of hours in the middle of the day for lunch."

Tourist Information

There is no tourist information office in Holbox, but **www.holboxisland.com** usually has useful information and listings.

Emergency Services

Holbox's **Centro de Salud** (Av. Benito Juárez btwn Oceano Atlántico and Adolfo López Mateos, tel. 998/875-2158, 8am-2pm and 4pm-8pm Mon.-Sat., until 6pm Sun.) offers basic health services and occasionally runs out of medicine. For more advanced medical attention, head to Cancún or Mérida; in emergencies, you may be able to charter a small plane.

Farmacia Jessy (Av. Igualdad near Av. Bravo, no phone, 9am-3pm and 5pm-10pm Mon.-Sat., 9am-2pm Sun.) usually has a moderate selection of medications and basic toiletries.

Money

There is **no bank** on Isla Holbox, but there is one **Bancomer ATM** on the 2nd floor of the Alcaldía (City Hall, central plaza, Av. Porfirio Díaz s/n). There also are two **unaffiliated ATMs** in El Pueblito Plaza (Av. Benito Juárez near Porfirio Díaz) that charge an arm and a leg in fees. **Note:** The ATMs on the island often run out of money, so plan accordingly.

Though more hotels, restaurants, and tour operators are accepting credit cards, don't count on using plastic; be sure to **bring enough cash** for the length of your stay (plus an extra day or two, in case you decide to extend your visit).

Media and Communications

Internet Café Don Antonio (corner of Avs. Porfirio Díaz and Morelos, 9am-2pm and 4pm-9:30pm Mon.-Sat., US$1.50/hour) is one of a handful of Internet places on the island. Another good option is **Ciber Café Capuchino** (Av. Palomino near Porfirio Díaz, 9am-midnight daily, US$1.25/hour), which overlooks the central plaza from the 2nd floor of a small building. No cappuccino is sold, in case you're wondering.

Laundry

Just half a block from the central plaza, **Lavamatica** (Av. Palomino near Porfirio Díaz, tel. 998/883-0530, 8:30am-5:30pm Mon.-Fri., 8:30am-4:30pm Sat.) does a good job of washing, drying, and folding clothes; it charges US$6.15 per five kilos (11 pounds).

GETTING THERE
Car, Ferry, Bus, and Taxi

To get to Holbox, you first need to get to the small coastal village of Chiquilá. There are buses from Cancún, Playa del Carmen, and Mérida. If you're driving, take old Highway

180 (not the *autopista*) to El Ideal, about 100 kilometers (62 miles) west of Cancún. Turn north onto Highway 5 and follow that about 140 kilometers (87 miles) to Chiquilá, passing though the town of Kantunilkín. (There are shortcuts from both Mérida and Cancún, but they follow smaller, less-maintained roads.) You'll have to leave your car in Chiquilá. Several families run small overnight parking operations, charging around US$4-8 per day, depending on the proximity to the dock; ask about weekly rates.

Ferries are operated by two (very competitive) companies: **9 Hermanos** (cell tel. 984/120-8655) and **Holbox Express** (tel. 984/875-2029). The boats themselves are not remarkably different—9 Hermanos has a newer fleet, but Holbox Express's boats have cushioned seats. Between the two, boats leave Chiquilá for Isla Holbox (US$7.75/13.85 one-way/round-trip, 25 minutes) at 6am, 8am, then hourly 10am-8pm, and 9:30pm. Returning boats leave Holbox at 5am, 7am, then hourly 9am-8pm. Going to Holbox, it's a good idea to get to the dock a half hour early, as boats occasionally leave ahead of schedule. Private boatmen also make the trip in either direction for approximately US$35-45 for up to six people; ask at the dock. **Note:** Private

boats are prohibited from ferrying passengers to/from Holbox after dark.

From Chiquilá, **second-class buses** to Cancún (US$8.50, 3.5 hours) leave the dock parking area at 5:45am, 7:45am, and 1:45pm. To Mérida, there's just one bus at 5:30am (US$15, 7 hours). All buses wait for the ferry arriving from Holbox. **Note:** For Playa del Carmen and other destinations on the Riviera Maya, take a bus to Cancún and transfer to one headed south.

Taxis also often are available at the dock to take travelers door-to-door to Cancún (US$75), Cancún International Airport (US$90), Playa del Carmen (US$100), and Valladolid (US$45); be sure to agree upon a price before you step into the car.

If you get stuck in Chiquilá, the **Hotel Puerta del Sol** (tel. 984/267-1004, US$28 s/d with fan, US$35 s/d with a/c) is your only option, located a short distance back down the main road from the dock. Rooms here are very simple but have TVs and private baths. If you can swing it, opt for a room with air-conditioning—they are newer and considerably nicer than the fan rooms. There also is a string of basic restaurants, most with a focus on seafood, facing the dock.

Golf carts are an easy way to get around Holbox.

Air

If you've got the money and the stomach for itty-bitty planes, **AeroSaab** (tel. 998/873-0501, www.aerosaab.com) offers a full-day tour to Isla Holbox departing from Cancún, Playa del Carmen, or Cozumel. Using Cessna airplanes, the trip begins with a scenic flight up the coast to Holbox, followed by a tour of Isla Pájaros and Yalahau Spring, lunch, and a chance to explore the village and beach (US$311-392 pp, minimum 4 people). Overnight trips and/or whale shark excursions also can be arranged.

GETTING AROUND

Holbox is very easy to get around on foot. Even the farthest hotels are no more than a half hour's walk from town, and it's very safe day or night. The only time you may really need a lift is when you're lugging your bags between the pier and your hotel.

Taxi

Golf carts serve as the island's taxis (some are even painted in yellow-and-black checkers). A ride from the pier into town is US$1.50-3 or US$3-5 to the hotels farther down the beach. They are almost always parked on the plaza, or your hotel can call one.

Golf Cart

Though you really don't need a golf cart to get around Holbox, you may enjoy the convenience of one. Rates, though not cheap, are relatively uniform: US$12 per hour, US$40 for 4 hours, US$62 for 12 hours, and US$77 for 24 hours.

Recommended outfits include **Rentadora Glendy** (Av. Porfirio Díaz at Av. Morelos, tel. 984/875-2093, 7am-11pm daily) and **Rentadora El Brother** (Av. Benito Juárez at Av. Igualdad, tel. 998/875-2018, 8am-10pm daily).

Bicycle

Other than walking, the easiest—and most affordable—way of getting around town is by bike. **Cooperativa Turística Pulperos del Caribe** (Av. Igualdad near Calle Carito, tel. 984/875-2347) rents bikes with locks for US$1.50 per hour or US$9.50 per 24 hours.

Isla Cozumel

Look for ★ to find recommended sights, activities, dining, and lodging.

Highlights

★ **Santa Rosa Wall:** Sit back and enjoy the ride at one of Cozumel's marquee dive sites. A strong current whisks you past a long wall that's home to massive sea fans, translucent sponges, and colorful tropical fish (page 104).

★ **Palancar:** With five sections spread over nearly five kilometers (3 miles), this massive dive site has something for everyone. Snorkelers can check out Palancar Shallows, while divers can explore the winding ravines and natural arches of Palancar Horseshoe (page 104).

★ **San Gervasio:** Smack-dab in the middle of the island, Cozumel's best and biggest Maya ruin is thought to be dedicated to Ixchel, the goddess of fertility; in ancient times, it attracted women from all over the Yucatán seeking her favor (page 105).

★ **Playa Chen Río:** Heavy surf makes most of Cozumel's east side unswimmable, except here, where a rocky arm forms a calm natural pool. Come midweek to have it all to yourself, or on a Sunday to *convivir* (literally, "share life") with local families (page 110).

★ **Parque Punta Sur:** Snorkel the colorful ocean reef, or stay above water on the long curving beaches of this scenic nature reserve. There's also a small maritime museum, a Maya ruin, and a

lighthouse you can climb for a bird's-eye view of the gorgeous surroundings (page 122).

All around Isla Cozumel, the Caribbean Sea glitters a hundred shades of blue. Beneath the waves, pristine coral reefs make for spectacular diving and snorkeling, the island's number one draw.

San Miguel de Cozumel—usually just called Cozumel, since it's the only city on the island—is where the ferries from Playa del Carmen land. It's also where cruise ships, as many as 30 per week in the high season, arrive; it's then that the waterfront promenade becomes a human river, flowing slowly down a channel of jewelry stores, souvenir shops, and open-air restaurants.

Just a few blocks from the promenade, another Cozumel emerges—a small, friendly community where old folks sit at their windows and dogs sleep in the streets. In spring, masses of orange *framboyán* (poinciana) flowers bloom on shade trees in the plaza, and festivals and religious celebrations are widely attended.

Cozumel's interior—including an important Maya ruin—and its eastern shore are yet another world, lacking even power lines and telephone cables. Heavy surf makes much of the eastern shore too dangerous for swimming, but you easily can spend a day beachcombing or relaxing on the unmanicured beaches and lunching at small restaurants overlooking the sea.

As Mexico's third-largest island, it shouldn't be surprising to discover that it's so multifaceted. But it's hard not to marvel at how stark the differences are. Come for the diving and snorkeling, but leave time to experience a side of Cozumel you may not have expected.

HISTORY

Cozumel has been inhabited since 300 BC and was one of three major Maya pilgrimage sites in the region (the others were Chichén Itzá and Izamal in Yucatán state). The name is derived from the island's Maya name, *Cuzamil* (Land of Swallows). The height of its pre-Hispanic occupation was AD 1250-1500, when Putún people (also known as the Chontol or Itzás, the same group who built Chichén

---

Previous: Isla de la Pasión; stingray. **Above:** painted maracas.

Isla Cozumel

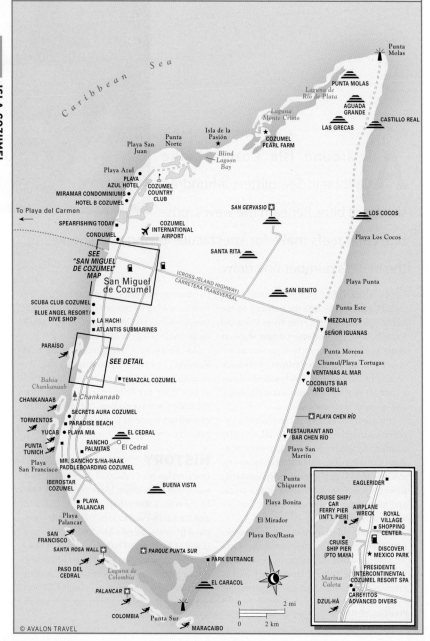

Caribbean Sea

Punta Molas

PUNTA MOLAS

Laguna de Río de Plata

AGUADA GRANDE

CASTILLO REAL

LAS GRECAS

Laguna Monte Cristo

Playa San Juan

Punta Norte

Isla de la Pasión

COZUMEL PEARL FARM

Blind Lagoon Bay

Playa Azul

PLAYA AZUL HOTEL

MIRAMAR CONDOMINIUMS

HOTEL B COZUMEL

COZUMEL COUNTRY CLUB

SAN GERVASIO

LOS COCOS

To Playa del Carmen

SPEARFISHING TODAY

CONDUMEL

COZUMEL INTERNATIONAL AIRPORT

Playa Los Cocos

SEE "SAN MIGUEL DE COZUMEL" MAP

San Miguel de Cozumel

SANTA RITA

(CROSS-ISLAND HIGHWAY) CARRETERA TRANSVERSAL

SAN BENITO

Playa Punta

Punta Este

SCUBA CLUB COZUMEL

BLUE ANGEL RESORT/ DIVE SHOP

LA HACH!

ATLANTIS SUBMARINES

MEZCALITO'S

SEÑOR IGUANAS

PARAÍSO

Punta Morena

Chumul/Playa Tortugas

SEE DETAIL

VENTANAS AL MAR

COCONUTS BAR AND GRILL

Bahía Chankanaab

Chankanaab

CHANKANAAB

PLAYA CHEN RÍO

TORMENTOS

SECRETS AURA COZUMEL

PARADISE BEACH

YUCAB

PLAYA MIA

EL CEDRAL

PUNTA TUNICH

RANCHO PALMITAS

El Cedral

RESTAURANT AND BAR CHEN RÍO

Playa San Martín

Playa San Francisco

MR. SANCHO'S/HA-HAAK PADDLEBOARDING COZUMEL

IBEROSTAR COZUMEL

BUENA VISTA

Punta Chiqueros

PLAYA PALANCAR

Playa Bonita

Playa Palancar

SAN FRANCISCO

El Mirador

Playa Box/Rasta

SANTA ROSA WALL

PARQUE PUNTA SUR

PASO DEL CEDRAL

Laguna de Colombia

PARK ENTRANCE

PALANCAR

EL CARACOL

COLOMBIA

Punta Sur

MARACAIBO

0   2 mi

0   2 km

EAGLERIDER

CRUISE SHIP/ CAR FERRY PIER (INT'L PIER)

AIRPLANE WRECK

ROYAL VILLAGE SHOPPING CENTER

CRUISE SHIP PIER (PTO MAYA)

DISCOVER MEXICO PARK

PRESIDENTE INTERCONTINENTAL COZUMEL RESORT SPA

Marina Caleta

CABEYITOS ADVANCED DIVERS

DZUL-HÁ

© AVALON TRAVEL

Itzá's most famous structures) dominated the region as seafaring merchants. Capitan Don Juan de Grijalva arrived on the island in 1518 and dubbed it Isla de Santa Cruz, marking the beginning of the brutal dislocation of the native people by Spanish explorers and conquistadors. It eventually was overrun by British and Dutch pirates who used it as a base of operations. By the mid-1800s, however, the island was virtually uninhabited. The henequen, chicle, and coconut-oil booms attracted a new wave of people to the Quintana Roo territory (it didn't become a state until 1974), and Cozumel slowly rebounded, this time with a mostly Mexican mestizo population.

Cozumel benefitted mightily from the worldwide popularity of Jacques Cousteau's early underwater films (which were not filmed there, contrary to legend, but inspired others that were) and later, of course, the establishment of Cancún in the 1970s.

PLANNING YOUR TIME

Don't let the cruise ship hubbub on Avenida Rafael Melgar turn you off from the town altogether. Besides the fact that most of the hotels, dive shops, banks, and other services are here, the town itself has much to offer, including a pleasant central plaza and a great museum. Budget a day or two to rent a car and explore the rest of the island, including the beach clubs, Maya ruins, family-friendly ecoparks, and the wild beaches and deserted coastline of Cozumel's eastern side.

ORIENTATION

The town of San Miguel de Cozumel (aka "Downtown Cozumel") is located on the west side of the island. The main passenger ferry lands here, across from the central plaza.

Avenida Benito Juárez is one of the main streets in Downtown Cozumel, beginning at the central plaza, crossing town, and becoming the Carretera Transversal (Cross-Island Highway). The highway passes the turnoff to the San Gervasio ruins before intersecting with the coastal road. The coastal road follows Cozumel's eastern shore, which is dotted with a few beach clubs and restaurants. Rounding the southern tip, the road heads north along the west shore before becoming Avenida Rafael Melgar and returning to the central plaza. Continuing north, the road passes turnoffs to the airport and a country club before turning to dirt and eventually dead-ending.

Sights

PARQUE BENITO JUÁREZ

Downtown Cozumel's central plaza has long maintained a surprisingly peaceful atmosphere, despite the mass of humanity that disembarks at the nearby ferry pier and cruise ship ports. It's been a place where locals and tourists come to stroll about, enjoy live music and dancing on weekends, and snack at small-time food vendors. The city municipal building, which occupies most of the plaza's east side and was beautifully restored in 2005, houses an airy commercial center on the ground floor and civic offices above. But a major renovation may (or may not) change all that. A M$95 million project has sparked fierce debate, mostly over the price tag, but also over changes such as lowering the plaza and removing the central kiosk. Proponents say the changes will make the plaza more accessible, especially for tourists and the handicapped, and will allow upgrades to underground water and sewage systems. Critics worry the project will spoil the plaza's traditional character while lining the pockets of well-connected developers.

San Miguel de Cozumel

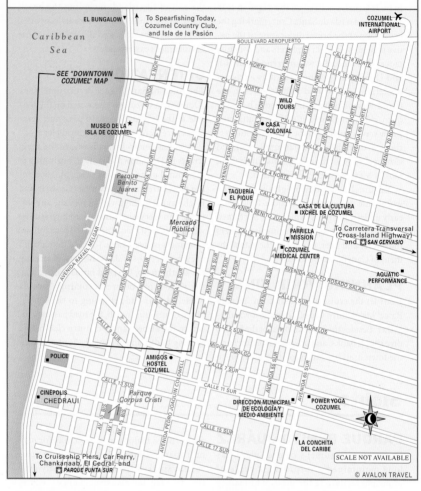

EL BUNGALOW ▼

To Spearfishing Today,
Cozumel Country Club,
and Isla de la Pasión

COZUMEL ✈
INTERNATIONAL
AIRPORT

*Caribbean
Sea*

BOULEVARD AEROPUERTO

SEE "DOWNTOWN
COZUMEL" MAP

WILD
TOURS

MUSEO DE LA ★
ISLA DE COZUMEL

● CASA
COLONIAL

*Parque
Benito
Juárez*

▼ TAQUERÍA
EL PIQUE

CASA DE LA CULTURA
■ IXCHEL DE COZUMEL

*Mercado
Público*

AVENIDA BENITO JUÁREZ

PARRILLA
■ MISSION

To Carretera Transversal
(Cross-Island Highway)
and ✚ SAN GERVASIO

■ COZUMEL
MEDICAL CENTER

AQUATIC ■
PERFORMANCE

AVENIDA ADOLFO ROSADO SALAS

JOSÉ MARÍA MORELOS

MIGUEL HIDALGO

■ POLICE

AMIGOS ●
HOSTEL
COZUMEL

CINÉPOLIS ■
CHEDRAUI

*Parque
Corpus Cristi*

DIRECCIÓN MUNICIPAL ■
DE ECOLOGÍA Y
MEDIO AMBIENTE

■ POWER YOGA
COZUMEL

To Cruiseship Piers, Car Ferry,
Chankanaab, El Cedral, and
✚ PARQUE PUNTA SUR

▼ LA CONCHITA
DEL CARIBE

SCALE NOT AVAILABLE

© AVALON TRAVEL

MUSEO DE LA ISLA DE COZUMEL

The town's small but excellent museum, **Museo de la Isla de Cozumel** (Av. Rafael Melgar at Calle 6, tel. 987/872-1434, 9am-4pm daily, US$4) is on the waterfront in what was once a turn-of-the-20th-century hotel. Well-composed exhibits in English and Spanish describe the island's wildlife, coral reefs, and the fascinating, sometimes tortured, history of human presence here, from the Maya pilgrims who came to worship Ixchel, the fertility goddess, to present-day survivors of devastating hurricanes. The museum also has a small bookstore and a library. For a good photo op head to the terrace, which has a great view of the main drag, ferry pier, and—on a clear day—Playa del Carmen. It's also home to a popular restaurant (7am-11pm daily, US$7-18) serving mostly Mexican fare.

COZUMEL PEARL FARM BEACH

Located on a remote private island on Cozumel's northern shore, the **Cozumel Pearl Farm Beach** (cell tel. 984/114-9604, www.cozumelpearlfarm.com, US$110 adult, US$85 child age 6-12, free age 5 and under) is a fun place to spend a day and learn about these unique nature-made jewels. The six-hour trip includes touring the farm's facilities to learn how and why pearls form, and how they are farmed and harvested, then snorkeling around the underwater installations. Lunch on the beach is included (think burgers, chips, and drinks), plus time for relaxing in hammocks and "power snorkeling"—snorkeling while being tugged by a boat. Service is friendly and professional, and transportation from the Aqua Safari Pier (Av. Rafael Melgar near Calle 5) is included.

DISCOVER MEXICO PARK

Discover Mexico Park (Carr. Costera Sur Km. 5.5, no phone, www.discovermexico.org, 8am-4pm Mon.-Sat., US$26-70 adult, US$14-40 child) boasts hundreds of enthusiastic reviews from visitors, but we're hard-pressed to understand the appeal. Exhibits include a video on Mexican history, scale-models of various iconic Mexican structures (the cathedral in Mexico City, the pyramid at Chichén Itzá, etc.), a gallery of Mexican folk art, tequila tasting, and, of course, plenty of opportunities for eating, drinking, and shopping. The center's tour guides are peppy and well informed, and Mexican art never fails to impress, but the overall experience is too gimmicky to be truly satisfying.

CORAL REEFS

Cozumel's coral reef—and the world-class diving and snorkeling it provides—is the main reason people come to the island. The reef was designated a national marine reserve more than two decades ago, and the waters have thrived under the park's rigorous protection and cleanup programs. Dozens of dive and snorkeling sites encircle the island, and the 1,000-meter-deep (3,281-foot) channel between Cozumel and the mainland provides spectacular drift and wall dives. Here is a list of some of the most popular dives, though by no means all the worthwhile ones.

Airplane Wreck

A 40-passenger Convair airliner lies on Cozumel's seabed, about 65 meters (213 feet) from the shore near El Cid hotel. Sunk in 1977

Cozumel is justly famous for its pristine coral reef.

Downtown Cozumel

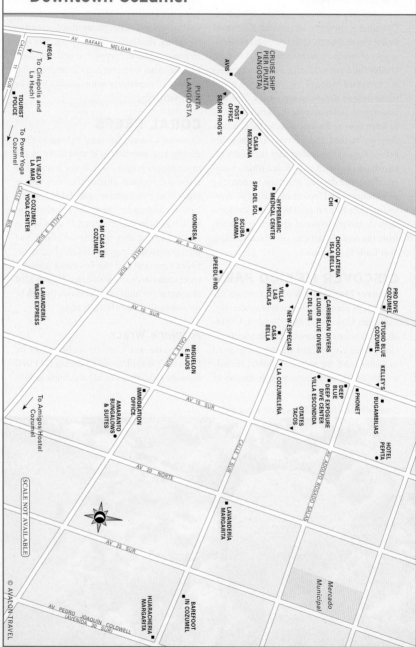

AV RAFAEL MELGAR

CALLE 11

CALLE 1 SUR

MEGA

To Cinépolis and La Hach!

TOURIST POLICE

To Power Yoga Cozumel

CRUISE SHIP PIER (PUNTA LANGOSTA)

AVIS

PUNTA LANGOSTA

POST OFFICE

SEÑOR FROG'S

CASA MEXICANA

EL VIEJO Y LA MAR

CALLE 9 BIS

CALLE 9 SUR

COZUMEL YOGA CENTER

MI CASA EN COZUMEL

SPA DEL SOL

HYPERBARIC MEDICAL CENTER

CHI

SCUBA GAMMA

KONDESA

CHOCOLATERIA ISLA BELLA

PRO DIVE COZUMEL

AV 5 SUR

CALLE 7 SUR

SPEEDL@ND

CARIBBEAN DIVERS

LIQUID BLUE DIVERS

DEL SUR

VILLA LAS ANCLAS

STUDIO BLUE COZUMEL

LAVANDERIA WASH EXPRESS

AV 10 SUR

NEW ESPECIAS

CASA BELLA

KELLEY'S

CALLE 5 SUR

MIGUELON E HIJOS

LA COZUMELEÑA

DEEP BLUE

DEEP EXPOSURE DIVE CENTER

VILLA ESCONDIDA

PHONET

BUGAMBILIAS

To Amigos Hostel Cozumel

AMARANTO BUNGALOWS & SUITES

IMMIGRATION OFFICE

AV 15 SUR

OTATES TACOS

AV ADOLFO ROSADO SALAS

HOTEL PEPITA

AV 20 NORTE

CALLE 3 SUR

(SCALE NOT AVAILABLE)

LAVANDERIA MARGARITA

Mercado Municipal

AV 25 SUR

HUARACHERIA MARGARITA

BAREFOOT IN COZUMEL

AV PEDRO JOAQUIN COLDWELL (AVENIDA 30 SUR)

© AVALON TRAVEL

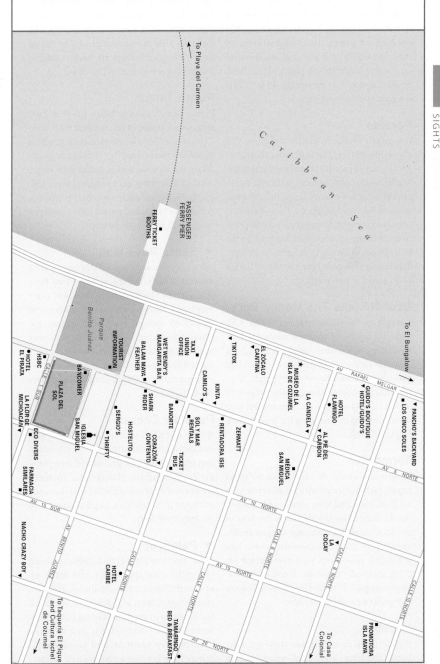

To Playa del Carmen

C a r i b b e a n S e a

PASSENGER FERRY PIER
FERRY TICKET BOOTHS

To El Bungalow

Parque Benito Juárez

TOURIST INFORMATION

TAXI UNION OFFICE

WET WENDY'S MARGARITA BAR
BALAM MAYA FEATHER

TIKI TOK

EL ZOCALO CANTINA

MUSEO DE LA ISLA DE COZUMEL

LA CANDELA

AV RAFAEL MELGAR

HOTEL FLAMINGO

GUIDO'S BOUTIQUE HOTEL/GUIDO'S

PANCHO'S BACKYARD
LOS CINCO SOLES

HOTEL EL PIRATA
HSBC

BANCOMER

PLAZA DEL SOL

CAMILO'S

KINTA

SOL Y MAR RENTALS

ZERMATT

RENTADORA ISIS

AL PIE DEL CARBON

MEDICA SAN MIGUEL

AV 5 NORTE

SHARK RIDER
BANORTE

CORAZON CONTENTO

SERGIO'S
HOSTELITO
THRIFTY
IGLESIA SAN MIGUEL

TICKET BUS

LA FLOR DE MICHOACÁN
ECO DIVERS
FARMACIA SIMILARES

AV 10 NORTE

CALLE 6 NORTE

LA COCAY

CALLE 8 NORTE

AV 15 SUR

NACHO CRAZY BOY

AV 15 NORTE

CALLE 2 NORTE

HOTEL CARIBE

CALLE 4 NORTE

CALLE 10 NORTE

PROMOTORA ISLA MAYA

BENITO JUÁREZ

To Taquería El Pique and Cultura Ixchel de Cozumel

AV 20 NORTE

TAMARINDO BED & BREAKFAST

To Casa Colonial

for the Mexican movie production of *Survive II,* the plane has been broken into pieces and strewn about the site by years of storms. The site itself is relatively flat, though with parrot fish, damselfish, and a host of sea fans and small coral heads, there's plenty to see. With depth ranges of 3-15 meters (10-49 feet), this is a good site for snorkelers.

Paraíso

Just south of the international pier, and about 200 meters (656 feet) from shore, lies Paraíso, an impressive three-lane coral ridge. Medium-size coral—mostly brain and star—attract sergeant majors, angelfish, grunts, squirrel fish, and snappers. This site also is popular for night dives because of its proximity to hotels, which means less time on the boat. Depth ranges 5-13 meters (16-43 feet). Snorkeling is decent near the shore, but be very careful of boat traffic.

Dzul-Há (aka The Money Bar)

Located off the old coastal road (Km. 6.5), Dzul-Há is one of the best spots for DIY snorkeling, with small coral heads and sea fans that support a colorful array of fish like blue tangs, parrot fish, and queen angels. Steps lead into the ocean, where depths range 3-10 meters (10-33 feet). You can rent snorkel gear on-site for US$15, including the marine park fee (US$3).

Tormentos

At this site divers can see about 60 coral heads, each decorated with an assortment of sea fans, brain and whip corals, and sponges. Invertebrates like to hide out in the host of crevices—look for flamingo tongue shells, arrow crabs, and black crinoids. Lobster like the scene, too—keep your eyes peeled for them, especially at the north end of the site. Depth ranges 5-15 meters (16-49 feet). The site is popular with photographers.

Yucab

A perfect drift dive, Yucab has archways, overhangs, and large coral heads—some as tall as

three meters (10 feet)—that are alive with an incredible array of creatures: Lobsters, octopus, scorpionfish, banded coral shrimp, and butterfly fish can almost always be found here. Videographers typically have a field day. Depth ranges 5-15 meters (16-49 feet).

Punta Tunich

Punta Tunich usually has a 1.5-knot current, which makes it an excellent drift dive. The site itself has a white-sand bottom with a gentle downward slope that ends in a drop-off. Along the way, the reef is dotted with finger coral and elephant ear sponges. Divers regularly encounter eagle rays, barracuda, sea horses, bar jacks, and parrot fish. The depth ranges 5-18 meters (16-59 feet).

★ Santa Rosa Wall

With a sensational drop-off that begins at 22 meters (72 feet), the spectacular Santa Rosa Wall is known for its tunnels, caves, and stony overhangs. Teeming with sealife, it's home to translucent sponges, mammoth sea fans, file clams, horse-eyed jacks, fairy basslets, gray angelfish, and black groupers. Strong currents make this a good drift dive, especially for experienced divers. Depth ranges 5-27 meters (16-89 feet).

Paso del Cedral

A strip reef lined with small corals like disk and cactus, this site attracts large schools of fish like blue-striped grunts and snapper—perfect for dramatic photographs. Southern stingrays often are seen gliding over the sandy areas just inside the reef. Depths range 10-20 meters (33-66 feet).

★ Palancar

This spectacular five-kilometer-long (3.1-mile) dive spot is actually made up of five different sites—Shallows, Garden, Horseshoe, Caves, and Bricks. It is known for its series of enormous coral buttresses. Some drop off dramatically into winding ravines, deep canyons, and passageways; others have become archways and tunnels with formations 15 meters (49 feet) tall. The most popular site here is Palancar Horseshoe, which is made up of a horseshoe-shaped series of coral heads at the top of a drop-off. All the sites, however, are teeming with reef life. Palancar ranges in depth 5-40 meters (16-131 feet).

Colombia

An enormous coral buttress, Colombia boasts tall coral pillars separated by passageways, channels, and ravines. Divers enjoy drifting past huge sponges, anemones, and swaying sea fans. Larger creatures—sea turtles, groupers, nurse sharks, and southern stingrays—are commonly seen here. The site is recommended for experienced divers. Depths range 5-40 meters (16-131 feet).

Maracaibo

At the island's southern tip, Maracaibo is a deep buttress reef interspersed with tunnels, caves, and vertical walls. It is known for its immense coral formations as well as for the possibility of spotting large animals—sharks (black tip and nurse) as well as turtles and eagle rays. A deep-drift dive, this site is recommended for advanced divers only. Depths range 30-40 meters (98-131 feet).

ARCHAEOLOGICAL ZONES

Isla Cozumel played a deeply significant role in the Maya world as an important port of trade and, more importantly, as one of three major destinations of religious pilgrimages (the others were Izamal and Chichén Itzá, both in Yucatán state). The island's primary site—known as San Gervasio today—was dedicated to Ixchel, the Maya goddess of fertility as well as of the moon, childbirth, medicine, and weaving. Archaeologists believe that every Maya woman was expected, at least once in her lifetime, to journey to Cozumel to make offerings to Ixchel for fertility—her own, and that of her family's fields. Cozumel's draw was powerful, as inscriptions there refer to places and events hundreds of miles away.

Over 30 archaeological sites have been discovered on the island, though only four are easily accessible, and only the largest—San Gervasio—can properly be called a tourist attraction. San Gervasio is certainly not as glorious as ruins found on the mainland, but it's worth a visit all the same.

★ San Gervasio

The area around **San Gervasio** (Cross-Island Hwy. Km. 7.5, www.cozumelparks.com, 8am-4pm daily, US$9.50) was populated as early as AD 200 and remained so after the general Maya collapse (AD 800-900) and well into the Spanish conquest. In fact, archaeologists excavating the ruins found a crypt containing 50 skeletons along with numerous Spanish beads; the bodies are thought to be those of 16th-century Maya who died from diseases brought by the conquistadors.

Today's visitors will find a modest ruin, whose small square buildings with short doors are typical of those found elsewhere on the island. This style, known as *oratorio,* almost certainly developed in response to climatic imperatives: Anything built here needed to withstand the hurricanes that have pummeled Cozumel for millennia.

San Gervasio has three building groups that are accessible to the public—Las Manitas, Plaza Central, and Murciélagos; all are connected by trails that follow the same ancient causeways used by the city's original inhabitants. A fourth building group—El Ramonal—is not yet open to the public.

Entering the site, you'll come first to the building group named after the structure **Las Manitas** (Little Hands), for the red handprints still visible on one of its walls. This structure is thought to have been the home of one of San Gervasio's kings, Ah Huneb Itza, and the inner temple was likely a personal sanctuary. Just east of the Las Manitas building is **Chi Chan Nah;** consisting of two rooms, it is the smallest structure in San Gervasio. The exact purpose of this building is unknown, though it is theorized that it was used for rituals.

San Gervasio

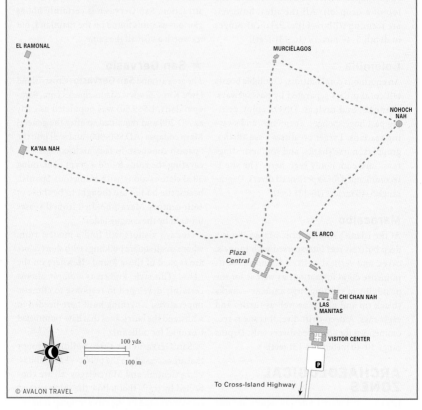

EL RAMONAL

MURCIÉLAGOS

NOHOCH
NAH

KA'NA NAH

EL ARCO

Plaza
Central

CHI CHAN NAH

LAS
MANITAS

VISITOR CENTER

P

0   100 yds
0   100 m

To Cross-Island Highway

© AVALON TRAVEL

Bearing left, the trail leads to the **Plaza Central,** a large courtyard surrounded by nine low structures in various states of decay; it is believed that the structures were made taller with wood extensions. The Plaza Central served as the seat of power in San Gervasio's latest era, from AD 1200 onward. At the northwest side of the Plaza Central is the somewhat precarious-looking **El Arco** (The Arch), which served as an entrance to this section of the city.

At 0.5 kilometer (0.3 mile) from the Plaza Central is the **Murciélagos** (Bats) building group, containing the site's largest and most important structure: **Ka'na Nah** (Tall House).

Also dating to San Gervasio's later era, this was the temple of the goddess Ixchel, and in its heyday would have been covered in stucco and painted red, blue, green, and black.

Finally, on the northeastern edge of San Gervasio rests **Nohoch Nah** (Big House), a boxy but serene temple. With an interior altar, the temple might have been used by religious pilgrims to make an offering upon entering or leaving San Gervasio. It was originally covered in stucco and painted a multitude of colors.

Guides can be hired at the visitors center for a fixed rate: US$20 for a one-hour tour in Spanish, English, French, or German. Prices are per group, which can include up to four people. Tips are customary and are not included in the price.

El Cedral

El Cedral is the "other town" on Cozumel, a sleepy village south of San Miguel that's home to a small historic church and modest Maya structure of the same name. It's got a pleasant central plaza, and tour operators, including horseback riding guides, often bring visitors here to visit the church and temple, and to peruse the souvenir stands normally set up here. Once a year, El Cedral hosts one of Cozumel's largest festivals, a 10-day blowout celebration of the Catholic holy cross.

Although overshadowed by San Miguel today, El Cedral is actually the older settlement. It was here that a group of 18 families of indigenous Christian converts fled in 1847 to escape persecution by fellow Maya during the War of the Castes. They came bearing a small wooden cross known as *Santa Cruz de Sabán* (Holy Cross of Sabán) and founded their church and village alongside a Maya temple that they discovered just inland from their landing site. The group was led by Casimiro Cárdenas, whose descendants still serve as caretakers, or *mayordomos,* of the temple and church; there's a statue of Don Casimiro in the central plaza.

El Cedral is famous for its **Fiesta de la Santa Cruz** (Festival of the Holy Cross), which begins in late April and culminates on May 3. The celebration includes food, music, dance, performances, rodeos, and fireworks aplenty, and even some traditions of distant Maya origin. The party is open to everyone, including tourists, and makes for a fun and fascinating outing if your visit happens to coincide with it.

A well-marked turnoff just south of Playa San Francisco leads 5 kilometers (3.1 miles) to the village. El Cedral's **Maya ruin** (8am-5pm daily, free) is small and underwhelming, though it still bears a few traces of the original paint and stucco. The church is directly adjacent and contains the original wooden cross borne by El Cedral's founders.

El Caracol

Located inside **Parque Punta Sur** (Carr. Costera Sur Km. 27, tel. 987/872-0914, www.cozumelparks.com, 9am-4pm daily, US$14 adult, US$8 child under 12), El Caracol is a small, conch-shaped structure that dates to AD 1200. It's believed to have been a lighthouse where Maya used smoke and flames to

ancient archway at San Gervasio archaeological zone

lead boats to safety. Small openings at the top of the structure also acted as whistles to alert Maya to approaching tropical storms and hurricanes. Admission to the reserve includes access to this small site.

Castillo Real

Castillo Real is a partially excavated site with a temple, two chambers, and a lookout tower.

It is believed to have been a Maya watchtower to protect against approaching enemies. It's located on the remote northeastern corner of the island, along the sand road leading to Punta Molas. The road is quite treacherous, such that even ATVs and motorcycles can have trouble making it. Ask at the tourist office for the latest before making any plans to head up there.

Beaches and Beach Clubs

Cozumel isn't famous for its beaches, but it is not without a few beautiful stretches of sand. The best swimming beaches are on the protected southwestern coast, with soft white sand and calm azure waters. The best stretches are occupied by large beach clubs, which have conveniences like lounge chairs, umbrellas, restrooms, restaurants, and water sports; a few even have swimming pools. Most beach clubs charge either a cover or a minimum consumption, but neither is exorbitant. The clubs cater to cruise shippers and range from peaceful and low-key to boisterous and loud. Independent travelers are perfectly welcome too, of course.

Beaches on Cozumel's east side are wild and picturesque, with virtually no development beyond a few small restaurants. The surf can be fierce here, though a few sheltered areas have good swimming and are popular with locals. The municipal government has been steadily improving the road on the east side, including adding signs, stairways, and parking, but it remains a far different experience than the west-side beach clubs.

NORTHWESTERN COZUMEL
Isla de la Pasión

One of Cozumel's loveliest beaches is **Isla de la Pasión** (no phone, www.isla-pasion. com, US$70 pp), a privately owned island and beach club just off Cozumel's north shore.

Although aimed squarely at cruise ship passengers, anyone can sign up for a package tour, which includes a buffet, open bar, and free beach activities. The beach is gorgeous—one of Corona's commercials was filmed here—and the island is covered, oddly, with wispy pine trees. (Scientists believe their seeds were washed or blown from the Atlantic coast of the United States.) The price is a bit steep, but the main bummer is you only get four hours at the beach. Additional packages are offered, including off-roading, kayaking, and speedboating (US$65-70 pp).

It's possible, though not easy, to visit Isla de la Pasión on your own; the beach itself is public, after all, and you can stay as long as you like. From the northern end of Avenida Rafael Melgar, a dirt road continues 5 kilometers (3.1 miles) past a water treatment plant to the port at Bahia Ciega. (The road isn't bad, but drive carefully, as your vehicle's insurance is probably void here.) At the port, ask around for a fisherman to take you across (around US$10, 20 minutes). Be sure to arrange a time for him to return, and cross your fingers he's got a good memory; otherwise, you'll be left begging a ride with a tour group. Bring food, water, and an umbrella—you won't be allowed to use the beach club facilities, but there's plenty of beach to lay out a towel. If you do book a tour, you can save US$20 per person by getting to the port yourself.

SOUTHWESTERN COZUMEL

The majority of beach clubs are clustered on Playa San Francisco, a three-kilometer (1.9-mile) stretch of white-sand beach that begins just south of Secrets Aura Cozumel resort. Another beach, Playa Palancar, is farther south, near the tip of the island, and has a beach club of the same name.

Paradise Beach

Paradise Beach (Carr. Costera Sur Km. 14.5, tel. 987/120-0027, www.paradise-beach-cozumel.com, 9am-sunset daily, US$10 minimum consumption) has a gorgeous pool and a spacious picture-perfect beach, dotted with palm trees. Oddly, they charge US$3 for beach chairs and US$12 for use of the water sports gear, like kayaks, trampoline floats, paddleboards, and snorkel gear. Nevertheless, it's a lovely and not-too-raucous place to spend a day at the beach.

Playa Mia

Playa Mia Grand Beach & Water Park (Carr. Costera Sur Km. 14.25, tel. 987/872-9030, www.playa-mia.com, 9am-6pm daily, US$30/25 adult/child, US$45/35 adult/child with buffet, US$60/50 adult/child with buffet and drinks) is big, busy, and energetic without being crass or obnoxious, like other clubs. The beach is decent, though often very crowded, and there's an excellent beachside pool. There's also a small water park with two additional pools with features like water cannons and sprays as well as a pair of 61-meter-long (200-foot) waterslides. The restaurant-buffet area is cool and pleasant, thanks to a high-peaked, circus-like tent. And there's certainly no shortage of activities: volleyball, table tennis, a kids' play structure, massage, snorkeling, parasailing, catamaran rides, water trampoline, even a huge inflatable "iceberg" and more.

Mr. Sancho's

Though you can pay as you go at **Mr. Sancho's** (Carr. Costera Sur Km. 15, tel. 987/871-9174, www.mrsanchos.com, 8am-5pm Mon.-Sat., US$55 adult, US$40 teen, US$35 child), it's known best for its all-inclusive packages. It has a decent Mexican restaurant, fairly mellow ambience, and plenty of extras, from snorkeling to massage. There's also a floating aquatic park with trampolines, water tubes, climbing walls, and more (US$12 pp extra). The beach is a bit narrow, meaning the lounge chairs are squeezed pretty tight, but it's a lovely spot all the same, and a great option for a no-brainer beach day.

Playa Palancar

With a calm atmosphere to match the calm turquoise waters, **Playa Palancar** (Km. 19.5, cell tel. 987/118-5154, www.buceopalancar.com, 8am-5pm daily, no cover or minimum consumption) is just the place to relax in a hammock under a palm tree or dig into a long book while digging your toes into the thick white sand. Playa Palancar has gotten busier over the years, now with music and even parasailing, but it's still the mellowest of Cozumel's main beach clubs. And there happens to be great diving and snorkeling at nearby Palancar and Columbia reefs; an on-site dive shop offers fun dives (US$65/90 one/two tanks) and guided snorkeling trips (US$35-45, 60-90 minutes), with daily departures at 9am, noon, and 2pm. Snorkel gear can be rented separately (US$10), but there's not much to see close to shore. A *palapa*-roofed restaurant serves classic Mexican seafood and a wide range of drinks (US$6-17). The club is 750 meters (0.5 mile) off the main road.

SOUTHEASTERN COZUMEL

On the east side of the island, you'll find a wild and windswept coastline dotted with beaches facing the open ocean. The surf here can be quite rough, and only a few beaches are safe for swimming.

Parque Punta Sur

As the name suggests, **Parque Punta Sur** (Carr. Costera Sur Km. 27, tel. 987/872-0914, www.cozumelparks.com, 9am-4pm daily, US$14 adult, US$8 child under 12) covers Cozumel's southern point, but the entrance is on the east side, and the ambience and appeal is certainly akin to that of the eastern beaches. It is an important natural reserve that happens to have a fine beach and outstanding snorkeling. Because it faces south, the surf tends to be light. There's a small eatery, plus restrooms, a changing area, and a kiosk renting snorkel gear.

Playa Box (Playa Rasta)

Playa Box (pronounced boash, Yucatec Maya for head) is better known as Playa Rasta for the two reggae-themed bars—**Freedom in Paradise** (no phone, www.bobmarleybar. com, 9am-sunset daily) and **Rasta's Bar** (no phone, 9am-sunset daily)—that occupy it. It's just past Punta Sur, where the road turns north along Cozumel's eastern shore. It's a rocky stretch of coastline with only a few sandy inlets and the two restaurant/bars blasting reggae at each other. It's not really the best place to spend the day—unless you like rambling on rocks and have a serious craving for jerk chicken.

El Mirador

Spanish for The Lookout, this is the best place to appreciate Isla Cozumel's dramatic ironshore formations, including a natural arch and exposed huge bulges of the black jagged stone. Ironshore is formed when waves, wind, and especially microscopic organisms erode the ancient limestone cap that underlies much of the island. Be very careful walking on the ironshore; flip-flops are not recommended considering how sharp and slippery it can be.

Playa Bonita and Punta Chiqueros

Playa Bonita is another picturesque curve of sand with plenty of room to lay out a towel and soak in the sun. Heavy surf usually makes swimming here inadvisable, but it's definitely dramatic. The northern end of the beach is Punta Chiqueros, where a small **beach restaurant** (no phone, 10am-5pm daily) serves hamburgers, fresh fish, and other standards at decent prices.

Playa San Martín

A wooden stairway leads from the road down to the beach at this long, scenic, windswept beach. There are a handful of permanent *palapa* umbrellas near the stairway that are popular with couples and families, but otherwise you're likely to have the beach virtually to yourself.

★ Playa Chen Río

The best place to swim on the east side of the island is **Playa Chen Río** (1 kilometer/0.6 mile south of Coconuts Bar), where a rocky spit blocks the waves, forming a huge natural pool, and lifeguards are on duty on weekends. Quiet during the week, it's lively and bustling most Sundays, when local families turn out in force. **Restaurant and Bar Chen Río** (no phone, 11am-6pm daily, US$12-18) is located here, but it's a bit pricey for the quality so it's not uncommon to see families with coolers and baskets and even small grills.

Chumul (Playa Tortugas)

About six kilometers (3.7 miles) south of the Carretera Transversal intersection is Chumul, also known as Playa Tortugas, a broad beautiful beach on the north side of the Ventanas al Mar hotel. The scenic windswept beach is good for surfing—and has nesting turtles May-November—but it is often too rough for swimming or snorkeling. Still, it makes a good place to watch the wild and crashing waves anytime.

A few steps away is **Coconuts Bar and Grill** (no phone, www.coconutscozumel.com, 10am-sunset daily, US$7-18). Set on a dramatic palm-studded bluff—the only piece of elevated land on the island, in fact—the tables are arranged for diners to enjoy the fabulous views of the beach below and the Caribbean beyond. Classic beach fare is served—ceviche, tacos, nachos—and plenty of cold beer. There's rum punch and live music 2pm-3pm daily.

Punta Morena

This scenic and little-used stretch of beach has a small restaurant with restrooms. Like elsewhere on the eastern shore, swimming here can be hazardous because of heavy surf and rocky outcrops, but it's still a nice place to relax or search for shells on the beach.

Mezcalitos and Señor Iguanas

These two low-key restaurants—**Mezcalito's** (no phone, www.mezcalitos.com, 9am-sunset daily) and **Señor Iguanas** (no phone, 8am-6pm Mon.-Sat., 9am-6pm Sun.)—are located side by side, right where the Carretera Transversal hits the coast. Longtime Cozumel institutions, they have similar menus (ceviche, fried fish, hamburgers, US$7-15), drinks (beer, margaritas, and tequila shots, US$2.50-5), and services (beachside chairs, hammocks, and *palapas*, free if you buy something from the restaurant). Boogie boards also are available for rent at Señor Iguanas (US$5 for 2 hours)—a lot of fun if you can handle the rough surf.

NORTHEASTERN COZUMEL

Cozumel's northeastern shoulder is its long-lost coast, the wildest and least-visited part of the island. The 25-kilometer (15.5-mile) stretch from the Carretera Transversal north to Punta Molas includes coastal dunes, scrub forest, and deserted beaches, plus the ancient Maya site of **Castillo Real** at around the 22-kilometer (14-mile) mark. This untended coast also is the final resting spot of a shockingly large amount of trash and jetsam, an ugly reminder of civilization in the one place on the island it ought to be easy to forget.

The road itself is a challenge—four-wheel drive is essential to avoid becoming mired in deep sand—and hurricanes and other storms can render it impassable. The area also is at the center of a bitter, on-again off-again land dispute and is occasionally closed without warning.

If you do go, be aware that there are no facilities whatsoever, or any other people most of the time. If you plan to camp, take plenty of water and food, a flashlight, extra batteries, bug repellent, and a mosquito net. Remember, too, that most car insurance policies (including all policies sold by rental agencies on the island, regardless of the vehicle) specifically exclude this and other dirt roads from coverage.

Playa Chen Río is protected by a long rocky spit, making it the east side's best place for swimming.

Sea Turtles of the Yucatán

sea turtle hatchlings waiting to be released into the sea

All eight of the world's sea turtle species are endangered, thanks to a combination of antiquated fishing practices, habitat destruction, and a taste for turtle products. Four turtle species—hawks-bill, Kemp's ridley, green, and loggerhead—nest on the shores of the Yucatán Peninsula, and until fairly recently, were a common supplement to the regional diet. Turtles make easy prey, especially females clambering on shore to lay eggs. They are killed for their meat, fat, and eggs, which are eaten or saved for medicinal purposes, as well as for their shells, which are used to make jewelry, combs, and other crafts.

Various environmental organizations collaborate with the Mexican government to protect sea turtles and their habitats; they maintain strict surveillance of known nesting beaches to stop poaching and have developed breeding programs, too. This, in combination with laws that prohibit the capture and trade of sea turtles or their products, has tremendously increased awareness about their protection.

On Isla Cozumel, travelers can volunteer to monitor nests and to release hatchlings into the sea. Nesting season runs May-September, and during that period volunteers join biologists on nighttime walks of Cozumel's beaches, locating and marking new nests, and moving vulnerable eggs to protected hatcheries. From July to November, volunteers release hatchings, typically at sundown, by encouraging the tiny turtles to move toward the water (without touching them) and scaring off birds in search of an easy meal.

Dirección Municipal de Ecología y Medio Ambiente (Calle 11 at Av. 65, tel. 987/872-5795) monitors Cozumel's sea turtles and manages volunteer opportunities. It maintains a **visitors center** (9:30am-2pm and 3:30pm-5:30pm daily May-Nov. only) in a small trailer, usually parked on the roadside near Playa San Martín on the eastern side of the island. Inside are a handful of aquariums, Plexiglas-enclosed nests, and more; stop by for information on upcoming beach walks and hatchling releases, or just to learn more about these endangered creatures. Donations are appreciated. Spanish is useful but not required.

Similar volunteer opportunities also are available in Akumal at the **Centro Ecológico Akumal** (CEA, tel. 984/875-9095, www.ceakumal.org) as well as on Isla Mujeres at **Tortugranja** (Carr. Sac Bajo 5, tel. 998/888-0507).

Entertainment and Events

NIGHTLIFE

Most of the partying on Cozumel happens during daylight hours, when cruise ships disgorge thousands of tourists eager to stretch their legs and see some new faces. Beach clubs can get raucous, and many bars in town are open before lunch. Still, there are enough locals, expats, and overnight visitors to support a cadre of lounges and nightclubs. Most places don't charge a cover; if they do, it's on select nights, like when there's a live band.

Nightclubs

Tiki Tok (Av. Rafael Melgar btwn Calles 2 and 4, tel. 987/869-8189, 9am-2am Mon.-Wed., 10am-4am Thurs.-Sun., no cover) sports a hodgepodge of beach-isle decor, from Polynesian lamps to Jamaican carved masks and figures. The plastic tables and chairs are a killjoy, but the upstairs beach patio, complete with sandy floor and nice sea views, is a nice touch. A live salsa band gets the crowd moving Friday and Saturday nights, starting at around 9:30pm; free salsa classes are at 8pm.

El Zócalo Cantina (Av. Rafael Melgar btwn Calles 2 and 4, tel. 987/871-0668, 7pm-4am Wed.-Sun.) is an eclectic 2nd-floor cantina with long high tables, music and dancing most nights, and frequent special events, from major sports games projected on a huge screen to surprise happy hours where everyone drinks for free.

El Bungalow (Av. Rafael Melgar at Blvd. Aeropuerto, cell tel. 987/120-2927, 11am-midnight Sun.-Fri., 11am-4am Sat.) is a large open-air *palapa* with wood floors and killer views, especially at sunset. It's a great place for happy hour (5pm-7pm daily) and is known for its live rock bands on Saturday nights.

Bars and Lounges

Wet Wendy's Margarita Bar (Av. 5 Norte btwn Av. Benito Juárez and Calle 2, tel. 987/872-4970, www.wetwendys.com, 9:30am-12:30am Mon.-Sat.) is your classic expat island bar, with usual features like Monday Night Football, giant bacon burgers, and a jocular atmosphere. There's occasionally live music, too. But more than anything, Wet Wendy's is famous for its huge hand-crafted margaritas: potent creations that look more like sundaes than cocktails and range from mango and strawberry to ginger and key lime pie.

Pitched as a "Husband Day Care Center," **Kelley's** (Av. 10 btwn Calles 1 and Rosado Salas, tel. 987/878-4738, noon-11pm Mon. and Wed.-Fri., 11am-11pm Sat., 10:30am-11pm Sun.) is an outdoor sports bar with 12 screens airing major sporting events, including pay-per-view. As expected, it also pours Guinness. Be sure to pay with pesos, as the exchange rate is set at 10:1, regardless of the market. Decent, but pricey, American and Irish food is available, too.

Perennially packed, **La Hach!** (Carr. Costera Sur Km. 2.9, tel. 987/120-1806, www.lahachcozumel.com, 9am-midnight Mon.-Thurs., 9am-4am Fri.-Sat., noon-midnight Sun.) is just steps from the cruise ship ports, making it a convenient and popular stop for cruise ship passengers. But its gorgeous sunsets and live reggae and classic rock (beginning at 11pm most nights) help draw in independent travelers. The food is just okay—stick to the drinks, which are 2-for-1 all day.

For a spring break atmosphere all day (and all year) long, head to the Punta Langosta shopping center, where **Señor Frog's** (Av. Rafael Melgar at Calle 9, tel. 987/869-1648, www.senorfrogs.com, 10am-1am Mon.-Fri., 10am-4am Sat.) makes driving beats, drink specials, and dancing on tables the norm.

THE ARTS

Cultural and Music Performances

Every Sunday evening, the city hosts an **open-air concert** in the central plaza. Locals and expats come out to enjoy the show—put on a clean T-shirt and your nicest flip-flops, and you'll fit right in. Concerts typically last two hours, beginning at 7pm in the summer, 8pm in the winter. Simple food stands selling homemade flan, churros, and other local goodies set up around the park these nights, too.

Casa de la Cultura Ixchel de Cozumel (Av. 50 btwn Av. Benito Juárez and Calle 2 Norte, tel. 987/872-1471, 9am-5pm Mon.-Fri.) hosts free concerts, movies, and art exhibits year-round. If you'll be on the island for an extended (or permanent) stay, a variety of classes—dance, art, music, drama, creative writing—also are offered, with a wide selection for children.

Cinema

You can catch relatively recent releases at **Cinépolis** (Av. Rafael Melgar btwn Calles 15 and 17, tel. 987/869-0799, www.cinepolis.com.mx, US$5.25 adult, US$4.25 child, US$3.25 before 3pm), which is located in the Chedraui shopping center.

FESTIVALS AND EVENTS
Carnaval

Cozumel is one of the few places in Mexico where Carnaval is celebrated with vigor. Held in February, the one-night celebration centers on a parade of floats and dance troupes, all decked out in colorful dress, masks, and glitter. Entire families come to participate and watch. Spectators dance and cheer in the streets as the floats go by, and many join the moving dance party that follows the floats with the largest speakers. Eventually the parade ends up in the center of town, where more music, dancing, and partying continue late into the night.

Festival de El Cedral

Residents of the village of El Cedral celebrate their namesake festival beginning in late April and culminating on May 3, the Day of the Holy Cross. Traditionally, the festival entails daily prayer sessions and ends with a dance called the *Baile de las Cabezas de Cochino* (Dance of the Pigs' Heads). The festival, started by a survivor of the Caste War to honor the power of the cross, has morphed over the years into a somewhat more secular affair, with rodeos, dancing, music, and general revelry.

Rodeo de Lanchas Mexicanas

Every May, Cozumel hosts a popular sport-fishing tournament known affectionately as the Mexican Boat Rodeo. Anglers from all over Mexico participate—including nearly 200 boats—and international anglers are welcome as long as they register their boats in Mexico. The tournament is timed to coincide with the arrival of big game to Cozumel's waters; tuna, dorado, marlin, and sailfish are often among the fish caught.

Fiesta de San Miguel Arcángel

You'd be forgiven for not knowing that the main town on Cozumel is officially called San Miguel. Hardly anyone, local or tourist, calls it that, preferring just Cozumel instead. One story, among many, is that the city got its name when construction workers unearthed a centuries-old statue of the winged saint on September 29, the very day Saint Michael the Archangel is traditionally celebrated. San Miguel was designated the town's patron saint, and every year September 29 is marked with a citywide celebration, including special masses and religious processions, a rodeo, food stands, music, and general revelry, mostly in and around the central square and San Miguel church.

Festival de Aves

Held in early November, the **Festival de Aves** (Festival of Birds, tel. 987/872-4689, US$20-35) is a three-day event that brings birders to the island to sneak a peek or learn more about the almost 350 species of birds found in Cozumel. Bird-watching outings are the highlight of the event, but bird-related conferences, workshops, and exhibits also are quite interesting.

Gran Fondo Cozumel

The Italian-born international bicycle racing craze that is *Il Gran Fondo* made its Cozumel debut in 2014, with over 400 riders participating in the inaugural event. Like all Gran Fondo races, Cozumel's features a mass start, individual chip timing, and an atmosphere that's both jocular and competitive. The main 100-mile Gran Fondo takes riders twice clockwise around the island; a "Medio Fondo" option is 50 miles and just one lap. A "King of the Wind" medal is given to the racer with the fastest intermediate time along the 19-kilometer section from Punta Sur to Mezcalitos, infamous for punishing "Maya winds." Gran Fondo New York (www.gfnycozumel.com) has good information about the race.

Ironman Cozumel

Ironman Cozumel (www.ironmancozumel.com) is the only qualifying event in the Ironman series to be held in Mexico, featuring a course that's as beautiful as it is grueling. The swim (3.8 kilometers/2.4 miles) is certainly the most distinctly *cozumeleño* part, starting and ending at Chankanaab, with gorgeous underwater vistas, and scuba divers and sea creatures observing from below. The bike ride (180 kilometers/112 miles) entails three laps around the island, with lovely sea views but crosswinds strong enough to topple unwitting racers. The run is oddly uninspired, three laps between downtown and the airport, although the sunsets there are spectacular (and you've got until midnight to finish). Ironman Cozumel is usually held in late November and attracts around 2,800 triathletes from around the world.

Cozumel Scuba Fest

Every December, hundreds of divers from around the world converge on Cozumel for the annual **Cozumel Scuba Fest** (www.cozumelfest.com), a six-day celebration of the island's unique underwater wonderland. The marquee event is the "Jean Michel Cousteau Route," a four-day, nine-dive circuit that retraces signature dives made by Jean Michel's famous father. The festival also includes dive competitions, lectures, film screenings, equipment demos and sales, gala events, and plenty of impromptu carousing in venues throughout the island. Many hotels and dive shops offer special packages for what is arguably the premier diving festival in the Americas.

Shopping

Shopping in Cozumel is aimed straight at cruise ship passengers—and it's no wonder, since they tend to spend a lot of money quickly. Avenida Rafael Melgar is where most of the action is, with a succession of marble-floored shops blasting air-conditioning to entice sweaty passersby in for a refreshing look around. For better prices and more variety, head inland a block or two.

AVENIDA MELGAR

Populated with a mix of high-end jewelry shops and souvenir chain stores, Avenida Melgar has the highest prices in town for items that, on the whole, can be found back home. None of the shops are open to bargaining—at least when there is a cruise ship in port—so if you're looking for a deal, head inland a couple of blocks. In fact, unless you find something you absolutely can't live without, you're uniformly better off shopping elsewhere on the island.

The one exception to this general rule is **Los Cinco Soles** (Av. Rafael Melgar at Calle 8, tel. 987/872-9004, www.loscincosoles.com, 9am-8pm Mon.-Sat., 11am-5pm Sun.). A labyrinth of rooms at the northern end of Avenida Melgar, it's filled with high-end Mexican folk art from every state in the country: pre-Columbian replicas, *barro negro* pottery, colorful *rebosos* (shawls), hand-carved furniture, silver jewelry, handmade wood toys, alabaster sculptures, wool rugs, and more. The prices are higher than others in town, but it's reflected in the quality. It's definitely worth a stop, if only to admire the artisanship.

CENTRAL PLAZA AND BEYOND

Acquatic Performance (Calle 1 btwn Avs. 85 and 90, tel. 987/869-8116, www.cozumelscubarepair.com, 8:30am-5pm Mon.-Fri., 8:30am-1pm Sat.) is a highly recommended shop selling and renting snorkel and dive equipment. It also repairs dive equipment, often with 24-hour turnaround times, and provides loaners if needed. If you plan to return to Cozumel to dive, long-term storage of equipment is available for US$100 per year and includes a complete regulator servicing, too.

Though pricey, **Pro Dive Cozumel** (Calle Rosado Salas at Av. 5, tel. 987/872-2420, 9am-9pm Mon.-Sat., 1pm-9pm Sun.) is centrally located and has a great selection of snorkel and dive equipment—perfect if you've forgotten your mask or lost a fin.

Sergio's (Av. Benito Juárez btwn Avs. 5 and 10, tel. 987/872-7632, www.sergiosilver.com.mx, 10am-8pm daily) is a longtime mom-and-pop shop that specializes in high-end jewelry made from silver from Taxco, Mexico's silver mining capital. Most of the items are made by local artisans, which means you'll find unique and beautiful pieces of jewelry. Unlike other shops, there's no pressure to buy and prices are non-negotiable. If you don't find what you're looking for here, head to its second location one block east on Avenida Juárez between Avenidas 10 and 15 (same phone and hours).

If you're in the market for a pair of traditional leather sandals, check out **Huaracheria Margarita** (Av. 30 at Calle 3, no phone, 10am-8pm Mon.-Sat., 10am-2pm Sun.). Among the colorful jellies and flip-flops, you'll find rows and rows of handmade huaraches, many brought from the mainland. The leather inventory is well priced, especially considering the craftsmanship that goes into making each sandal.

Bugambilias (Av. 10 Sur btwn Calles Rosado Salas and 1, tel. 987/872-6282, 9am-6pm Mon.-Sat.) sells traditional handmade linens and clothing, most incorporating

Artists can be found demonstrating their skills and plying their wares in Cozumel's central plaza.

embroidery and lace. The quality is excellent, and prices range from moderate to high.

True to its name, which is Spanish for beautiful house, **Casa Bella** (Calle 3 btwn Avs. 5 and 10, no phone, 9am-6pm Mon.-Sat.) sells beautiful household items created by artisans from around the country. Items include pewter trays, *talavera* pottery, and whimsically painted mirrors.

For more local art, check out the small shop **Miguelon e Hijos** (Calle 5 Sur btwn Avs. 10 and 15, tel. 987/872-5549, 9am-6pm Mon.-Sat.), which specializes in conch shells with intricately carved portraits and ancient Maya tableaus. It's not exactly everyone's taste, but the craftsmanship is remarkable.

Balam Mayan Feather (Av. 5 at Calle 2, tel. 987/869-0548, 10am-10pm daily) trades in a unique and dying art, selling oil paintings created on the feathers of regional birds. Most feathers depict scenes of traditional villages or ancient Maya people, but there is a decent variety beyond that, including tropical flowers and underwater creatures. If you're lucky, an artist will be working on a new feather painting while you're browsing—feel free to watch. Prices range US$30-150.

SHOPPING CENTERS

Punta Langosta (Av. Rafael Melgar btwn Calles 7 and 11, 9am-8pm daily) is downtown Cozumel's swankiest shopping center. The ultramodern open-air building is home to high-end clothing boutiques, air-conditioned jewelry stores, and fancy ice cream shops. It's a good place to window shop, especially if you want to buy a memento but aren't sure exactly what you'd like.

Located in a yellow building on the east side of the main plaza, **Plaza del Sol** (Av. 5 Norte btwn Av. Benito Juárez and Calle 1, 9am-8pm Mon.-Sat., 11am-5pm Sun.) houses a labyrinth of small souvenir shops selling everything from bad T-shirts to quality silver jewelry. You'll have to poke around a bit to find items worth buying, but a little perseverance will go a long way, especially if you're on a tight budget.

Located across from the Puerto Maya and TMM International piers, **Royal Village Shopping Center** (Carr. Sur Km. 4.5, tel. 987/857-0457, 9am-6pm Mon.-Sat.) is squarely aimed at cruise ship travelers. Shops are higher end and international—think Swarovski, Zingara, Harley-Davidson, even Sunglass Island. A new Hard Rock Cafe was in the works when we passed through, too.

Sports and Recreation

SCUBA DIVING

Cozumel is one the world's best (and best known) places to scuba dive and snorkel, so it's no surprise that the island is home to dozens of dive shops—more than 100 at last count. Virtually all offer diving, snorkeling, and all levels of certification courses; there are a handful of dive "resorts," too, which offer packages that include lodging, diving, gear, and sometimes food.

Rates can vary considerably from shop to shop, and season to season, so be sure to clarify all the details up front. For most of the year, a two-tank fun dive costs US$72-93, plus US$15-32 per day if you need gear. Low-season rates can be significantly lower, and often include gear rental. PADI open-water certification courses (3-4 days) generally cost US$350-535, including all equipment and materials. Most shops also offer advanced courses, Nitrox and night diving, and multi-dive packages. All divers also must pay US$3 per day for marine park admission and to support Cozumel's hyperbaric chambers and marine ambulance; ask if the fees are included in a shop's rates or charged separately.

Dive Shops

Cozumel's diver safety record is good, and there are many competent outfits in addition to those listed here. Consider this list a starting point, to be augmented by the recommendations of trusted fellow divers, travelers, locals, and expats. Most important, go with a shop you feel comfortable with, not just the cheapest, the cheeriest, or the most convenient. Dive shops are generally open 8am-8pm daily, closing during those business hours only if no one's around to run the shop during a dive trip.

- **Blue Angel Dive Shop** (Carr. Costera Sur Km. 2.2, tel. 987/872-1631, www.blueangel-resort.com)

- **Careyitos Advanced Divers** (Marina Caleta, tel. 987/872-1578, www.careyitosadvanceddivers.com)

- **Caribbean Divers** (Calle 3 btwn Avs. Rafael Melgar and 5, tel. 987/872-1145, cdivers@prodigy.net.mx)

- **Deep Blue** (Calle Rosado Salas at Av. 10 Sur, tel. 987/872-5653, www.deepbluecozumel.com)

- **Deep Exposure Dive Center** (Av. 10 Sur btwn Calles 3 Sur and Rosado Salas, tel. 987/872-3621, toll-free U.S. tel. 866/670-2736, www.deepexposuredivecenter.com)

- **Eco Divers** (Av. 10 at Calle 1 Sur, tel. 987/872-5628, www.ecodiverscozumel.com)

- **Liquid Blue Divers** (no storefront, tel. 987/111-0311, www.liquidbluedivers.com)

- **Scuba Gamma** (Calle 5 near Av. 5 Sur, tel. 987/878-4257, www.scubagamma.net)

- **Scuba Tony** (no storefront, tel. 987/113-3706, U.S. tel. 310/272-9943, www.scubatony.com)

- **Studio Blue Cozumel** (Calle Rosado Salas btwn Avs. 5 and 10 Sur, tel. 987/872-4414, toll-free U.S. tel. 866/341-1090, www.studioblue.com.mx)

Dive Insurance

Although diving and snorkeling accidents are relatively rare on Cozumel, especially among beginning divers, you might consider purchasing secondary accident and/or trip insurance through the **Divers Alert Network** (DAN, toll-free U.S. tel. 800/446-2671, 24-hour emergency Mex. tel. 919/684-9111, accepts collect calls, www.diversalertnetwork.org), a highly regarded, international, nonprofit medical organization dedicated to the health and safety of snorkelers and recreational divers. Dive accident plans cost just US$30-75 per year, including medical and decompression coverage and limited trip and lost equipment coverage. More complete trip insurance—not a bad idea in hurricane country—and life and disability coverage are also available. To be eligible for insurance, you must be a member of DAN (US$35 per year).

SNORKELING

Snorkelers have plenty of options in Cozumel, from cheap-and-easy snorkeling tours to renting gear and exploring on your own, right from shore.

Most dive shops offer snorkeling as well as diving, usually visiting 2-3 sites for a half hour each (US$50-70 pp). Snorkelers often go out with a group of divers and either snorkel in the same general location or go to a nearby site while the divers are underwater. This can mean some extra downtime as divers get in and out of the water, but the advantage is that you typically go to better and less crowded sites.

For a quick and easy snorkeling tour, stop by one of the booths that flank the ferry pier. These trips are somewhat less expensive (though with larger groups) and can be booked right as you disembark from the ferry. Most offer two tours daily at around 11am and 2pm; some use a glass-bottom boat for extra pizzazz. The standard trip (US$45, including equipment) lasts 2-3 hours, visiting two or three sites, spending 30-45 minutes

How to Choose a Dive Shop

Dive sites, here we come!

There are more than 100 dive shops on Isla Cozumel, and scores more at Isla Mujeres, Playa del Carmen, Cancún, Tulum, and elsewhere. Choosing just one—and then placing all your underwater faith into its hands—can be daunting.

Safety should be your number one concern in choosing a shop. Fortunately, the standards in Cozumel and the Riviera Maya are almost universally first-rate, and accidents are rare. Still, don't dive with a shop that doesn't ask to see your certification card or logbook. Also ask how long the shop has been in business, how much experience the dive guides have, how long the captain and crew have been with the shop, and how many divers per guide will be on the tour. "Cattle boats" are a sign of shops trying to maximize profits; even if they're not unsafe, they often make for a less enjoyable experience.

Equipment is another crucial issue. You should ask to inspect the shop's equipment, and the dive shop should be quick to comply. Although few casual divers are trained to evaluate gear, a good dive shop will appreciate your concern and be happy to put you at ease.

The most important equipment is not what's on the rack but what you actually use. On the day of your dive, get to the shop early so you can **double-check your gear.** Old equipment is not necessarily bad, but you should ask for a different BCD, wetsuit, or regulator if the condition of the one assigned to you makes you uneasy. Learn how to check the O-ring (the small rubber ring that forms the seal between the tank and the regulator), and do so before every dive. You also should attach your regulator and open the valve, to listen for any hissing between the regulator and the tank, or in the primary and backup mouthpieces. If you hear any, ask the dive master to check it and, if need be, change the regulator. Arriving early lets you do all this before getting on the boat—ideally before leaving the shop—so you can swap gear if necessary.

Feeling free to ask questions or raise concerns (of any sort at any time) is a crucial factor in safe diving. That's where a dive shop's **personality** comes in. Every dive shop has its own culture or style, and different divers will feel more comfortable in different shops. Spend some time talking to people at a couple of different dive shops before signing up. Try to meet the person who will be leading your particular dive—you may have to come in the afternoon when that day's trip returns. Chances are one of the shops or dive masters will click with you.

Finally, there are some specific questions you should ask about a shop's practices. Has their air been tested and certified? Do they carry radios and oxygen? Does the captain always stay with the boat? How many people will be going on your dive? How advanced are they? How many dive masters or instructors will there be? And how experienced are they? Above all, be vocal and proactive about your safety, and remember, *there are no stupid questions.*

snorkeling at each one. Among many operators vying for your business are **Dive Cozumel 1** (tel. 987/869-2591) and **Cozumel Tours** (tel. 987/869-3746).

There are several terrific snorkeling spots near town and just offshore where you don't need a boat or a guide at all. Cozumel's boat drivers are careful about steering clear of snorkelers, but even so, do not swim too far from shore, look up and around frequently, and stay out of obvious boat lanes. If you plan to do a lot of snorkeling, especially outside of established snorkeling areas, consider bringing or buying an inflatable personal buoy. Designed for snorkelers, they are brightly colored and have a string you attach to your ankle or to a small anchor weight, alerting boat drivers of your presence. Also be aware of the current, which typically runs south to north and can be quite strong.

KITEBOARDING

Kiteboarding has quickly and thoroughly morphed from a novelty act to one of the most popular beach sports worldwide. Cozumel is no exception, with a dedicated cadre of kiteboarders and a growing number of options for travelers who want to learn or practice the sport.

De Lille Sports (no storefront, tel. 987/103-6711, www.delillesports.com) is operated by Cozumel native Raul de Lille, a former Olympic-level windsurfer and now one of Mexico's top kiters and instructors. Raul doesn't come cheap, but he's an outstanding instructor, not least for his calm demeanor and excellent English. Private lessons are US$125 per hour or US$500 per day. An intensive three-day introductory kiteboarding course includes 15 hours of instruction and costs US$900 per student (maximum 2 students per instructor); it also can be broken into modules depending on your time and previous experience. Kiteboarding rentals are US$150 per day for a full kit. For experienced kiters, de Lille offers clinics on kite control, tricks, and other specialties, plus adventuresome tours like downwinding the entire island.

Another locally run option is **Cozumel Kiteboarding** (no storefront, tel. 987/876-1558, www.cozumelkiteboarding.com). The shop offers kiting excursions around the island (4 hours, US$250 for 1-2 people), including to the little-visited northern lagoons: Río de Plata, Monte Cristo, and Blind Bary. Kiteboarding instruction for beginners and more experienced students also is offered.

Cozumel is one of the Riviera Maya's best places for kiteboarding.

STAND-UP PADDLING

Stand-up paddling (or SUPing) is the sport du jour in Cozumel and around the world, and for good reason: It's fun and easy to learn yet challenging to master; it's also a unique way to experience Cozumel's rich coastline and extraordinarily clear waters. The glassy waters on Cozumel's western shore are perfect for the sport, which involves standing upright on an oversized surfboard-like board and using a long paddle to cruise around. Fitness buffs appreciate the full-core workout SUPing provides, while the elevated perspective allows you to see surprisingly well into the surrounding water—significantly better than in a kayak, in fact. It's not uncommon to see fish, rays, even sea turtles and dolphins swimming below and around you. Numerous resorts have SUP boards available for guests, and a handful of agencies offer instruction, rentals, and tours.

De Lille Sports (no storefront, tel. 987/103-6711, www.delillesports.com) is operated by windsurfing and kiteboarding legend (and Cozumel native) Raul de Lille, but he's big on SUPing too, even designing his own line of boards. The sports complement each other well: If there's not enough wind for kiting, it's probably perfect for SUPing, and vice versa. The agency offers private and group lessons, plus tours in remote areas of the island. SUP instruction runs US$75 per student (2-3 hours, maximum 8 students), while high-quality SUP rentals are US$25 per hour or US$85 per day.

Based out of Mr. Sancho's beach club, **Ha-Haak Paddleboarding Cozumel** (Carr. Costera Sur Km. 15, cell tel. 987/800-3022, www.supcozumel.com, 8am-4pm daily) offers friendly one-on-one instruction (US$35/hour) as well as paddleboard rentals (US$35/hour or US$60/day). It also has a variety of tours that depart from different parts of the island, depending on the weather (US$60, 1.5 hours). All guides are bilingual.

SURFING

Owned and operated by professional surfer Nacho Gutierrez, **Cozumel Surfing** (no storefront, tel. 987/111-9290, www.cozumel-surfing.com, price varies) provides beginner surf lessons to adults and children of all ages. Instruction is given on the east side of the island in either a private or group setting. Classes typically begin with a 30- to 60-minute lesson on land to learn and practice the basics of surfing. Then it's straight to the water for two separate 75-minute sessions alongside Nacho and his team. Snacks and drinks are provided, and rentals are available, too.

KAYAKING

Cozumel's calm, clear waters make it a nice place to kayak. Most **all-inclusive resorts** and some **beach clubs** have a handful of kayaks available for guests to use (free to US$10/hour). If you plan to swim or snorkel along the way—a great way to enjoy little-visited spots on the reef—be sure the kayak has a small anchor to prevent it from floating away.

SPORTFISHING AND SPEARFISHING

Cozumel boasts good deep-sea fishing year-round. It's one of few places anglers can go for the grand slam of billfishing: hooking into a blue marlin, a white marlin, a sailfish, and a swordfish all in a single day. It's also got plentiful tuna, barracuda, dorado, wahoo, grouper, and shark. For an extra challenge, jump out of the boat and give spearfishing a try.

Albatros Charters (tel. 987/872-7904, toll-free U.S. tel. 888/333-4643, www.albatroscharters.com, US$445-500 for 4 hours, US$525-600 for 6 hours, US$600-675 for 8 hours) has a variety of boats, each able to carry at least six anglers. Trips include hotel pickup and drop-off, beer and soda, snacks, bait, and gear. Other recommended outfits include **Aquarius Fishing** (tel. 954/317-3743, toll-free U.S. tel. 800/371-2924, www.cozumelflatsfishing.com) and **Wahoo Tours** (tel. 987/869-8560, toll-free U.S./Can. tel. 866/645-8977, www.wahootours.com).

Spearfishing Today (Puerto de Abrigo, Carr. Costera Norte Km. 1.5, tel. 987/876-0862, www.spearfishingtoday.com, US$250-700 for 2-7 people) gets rave reviews for its excellent service and wide variety of spearfishing excursions, from mellow first-timer and family tours to private "deep blue" outings for intermediate and advanced hunters. Half-day trips include gear, instruction, refreshments, and complimentary fish cleaning at the end of the tour. Although Cozumel is known for its currents, most trips head to the calmer protected waters at the island's north end (and outside the marine park, of course).

ECOPARKS AND WATER PARKS
★ Parque Punta Sur

Parque Punta Sur (Carr. Costera Sur Km. 27, tel. 987/872-0914, www.cozumelparks. com, 9am-4pm daily, US$14 adult, US$8 child under 12) is a massive natural reserve on the southern tip of Cozumel. The park spans thousands of acres of coastal dunes, beaches, mangroves, and wetlands, and extends well out into the ocean, including large areas of coral reef. It's home to a vast array of land and sea creatures, including 30 types of seabirds and some huge crocodiles that live in the park's large inland lagoons. There's a small Maya ruin known as El Caracol, which dates to AD 1200 and is believed to have been used for navigation, plus the park's famous lighthouse (which you can climb for great views) and a small but rewarding maritime museum. At the park's long, lovely beach—about a kilometer past the lighthouse—there are beach chairs, restrooms, a small eatery, and a shop to rent snorkel gear (US$10) and kayaks. The snorkeling here is outstanding, including sea fan "forests" that wave gently in the current.

Most visitors visit on package tours, but it's perfectly easy to visit independently; there's even a separate area away from the volleyball nets and buffet lines for people arriving on their own. You'll need a car—there used to be shuttle service into the park, but no longer—and you should arrive no later than 1pm in order to take full advantage of all the park has to offer.

Chankanaab

Some 9 kilometers (5.6 miles) south of town, **Chankanaab** (Carr. Costera Sur Km. 9, tel. 987/872-0914, www.cozumelparks.com, 8am-4pm daily, US$21 adult, US$14 child under 12) is a national park that operates mainly as a beach club and water park; that is to say,

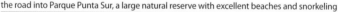

the road into Parque Punta Sur, a large natural reserve with excellent beaches and snorkeling

Parque Punta Sur

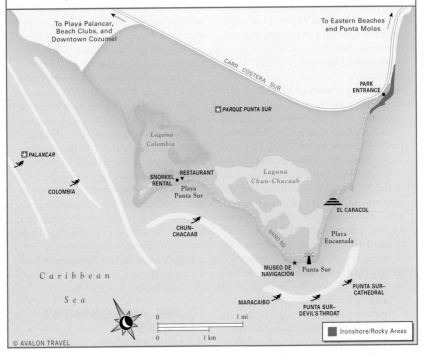

To Playa Palancar, Beach Clubs, and Downtown Cozumel

To Eastern Beaches and Punta Molas

CARR COSTERA SUR

PARK ENTRANCE

PARQUE PUNTA SUR

Laguna Colombia

PALANCAR

Laguna Chun-Chacaab

SNORKEL RENTAL
RESTAURANT
Playa Punta Sur

COLOMBIA

EL CARACOL

CHUN-CHACAAB

SAND RD

Playa Encantada

Caribbean Sea

MUSEO DE NAVIGACIÓN
Punta Sur

PUNTA SUR-CATHEDRAL

MARACAIBO

PUNTA SUR-DEVIL'S THROAT

0   1 mi
0   1 km

Ironshore/Rocky Areas

© AVALON TRAVEL

more Xcaret than Punta Sur. A visit here includes sunbathing by the pool, snorkeling in the ocean, relaxing in a hammock, and watching the sea lion shows (included in the ticket price); there is also a zipline course, a crocodile sanctuary, replicas of various Maya ruins, and a small tequila "museum" (i.e., a bar with a hacienda feel, old photos, and a small agave patch). **Dolphin Discovery** (toll-free U.S. tel. 866/393-5158, www.dolphindiscovery.com) has a facility within the park, with various interactive programs with dolphins and sea lions, for an additional fee. Reserve in advance or right upon arrival, as they fill up fast. Chankanaab also has a fully equipped dive shop on-site, plus two thatch-roofed restaurants, a handful of gift shops, lockers, and restrooms. Chankanaab may be a bit commercialized for independent travelers—consider Punta Sur instead—but it's a great option for families looking for an easy all-day option.

GOLF

Jack Nicklaus designed the par-72 championship course at **Cozumel Country Club** (Carr. Costera Norte Km. 6.5, tel. 987/872-9570, www.cozumelcountryclub.com.mx, 6:30am-6pm daily), located at the far end of the northern hotel zone. Greens fees are US$99 before 8am (and all day Sunday), US$134 until 1:30pm, and US$89 afterwards. Carts are required and included in the rate. In addition to the slightly rolling, moderately challenging course, the club has a driving range, putting and chipping areas, overnight bag storage, a retail shop, and lessons from PGA golf pros. Book online for a discount.

SPAS

Spa del Sol (Calle 5 btwn Avs. 5 and Rafael Melgar, tel. 987/872-6474, www.spadelsolcozumel.com, 9am-7pm Mon.-Sat.) provides a variety of traditional and holistic treatments in its quaint downtown location. Almost a dozen types of massages are offered, including Swedish, Thai, and Aquasana (a treatment performed in open water—who knew?). Acupuncture, Reiki, and ear candling, among other alternative treatments, also are performed regularly. One-hour treatments run US$50-80. Walk-ins are very welcome, and shorter and longer sessions are available, too.

Barefoot in Cozumel (Calle 3 btwn Avs. 25 and 30, tel. 987/878-4662, www.barefootincozumel.com, 9am-7pm daily by appointment only, US$60/85 per 60/90 minutes) is the one-woman business of U.S. certified massage therapist Sally Hurwitch. She offers a popular Ashiatsu massage, which is administered using her feet to help clients who suffer from chronic back pain. Swedish massages as well as Reiki treatments are also offered.

Temazcal Cozumel (Xcan-Ha Reserve, tel. 987/869-8201, www.temazcalcozumel.com, US$80) provides a traditional Maya steam lodge experience. It's a favorite practice of health- and spiritual-minded folks of all stripes, and especially popular in the region. Temazcal Cozumel has an especially lovely spot to experience this unique treatment, a leafy retreat well inland from Cozumel's busy western shore. A session here begins by addressing the cardinal directions before entering the low, circular brick hut, where a guide leads guests through additional exercises and visualizations, related to ancient Maya beliefs as well as one's own experiences, all intended to further the cleansing and mind-opening process. Afterward, you can take a dip in a nearby freshwater cenote and relax in hammocks with a fresh-made juice.

FITNESS

The most modern gym on the island, **EGO** (Calle 11 at Av. 5, tel. 987/872-4897, 5am-11pm Mon.-Fri., 6am-6pm Sat.) is a full-service facility complete with free weights, weight machines, cardio machines (plus personal trainers to help), and a slew of classes including Pilates, yoga, spinning, and kickboxing. Monthly membership is US$65, while visitors pay US$9 for the day. All that, plus the air-conditioning can't be beat!

Cozumel Yoga Center (Av. 5 btwn Calles 9 and 9 Bis, tel. 987/869-1065, www.yogacozumel.com, US$5-8) offers a wide variety of yoga classes—26 styles at last count. Yoga and meditation workshops as well as teacher trainings are also a regular part of the programming. Classes are held either in the studio, in an oceanfront *palapa*, or on the beach.

Power Yoga Cozumel (Calle 7 at Av. 65 Bis, tel. 987/564-3200, www.poweryogacozumel.com) offers all levels of vinyasa and hatha classes—group or private—in a large airy space. Instruction is in either Spanish or English and is held early morning and late afternoon Monday-Saturday. Sessions cost US$10, but packages are available, too.

TOURS AND COOKING CLASSES

Horseback Riding

Located on the inland side of the highway across from Nachi-Cocom beach club, **Rancho Palmitas** (Carr. Costera Sur Km. 16, cell tel. 987/118-3032, palmitas_ernesto@hotmail.com, 8am-4pm daily) offers two horseback tours. A 2.5-3-hour tour (US$40 pp) includes stops at a cavern with a cenote, the archaeological site of El Cedral, and a few unexcavated Maya ruins. A shorter 1.5-hour tour (US$35 pp) leads to the cavern only. Call to set up a tour or just drop in—the last excursion leaves at 3pm.

ATV Excursions

Though catering to cruise ship passengers, **Wild Tours** (Av. 45 at Calle 14, tel. 987/872-5876, toll-free U.S./Can. tel. 888/497-4283, www.wild-tours.com) offers ATV excursions to everyone. Tours include off-roading through the jungle, visiting a cenote and inland cave, exploring isolated Maya ruins, relaxing and snorkeling at Playa Uva's beach club, even a 45-minute ride in a high speed jet boat (US$65-85 adult, US$90-110 child with adult, 4 hours). Tours leave from a staging area in front of MEGA supermarket (Av. Rafael Melgar at Calle 11).

Submarine Tour

Atlantis Submarines (Carr. Costera Km. 4, tel. 987/872-5671, toll-free Mex. tel. 800/715-0804, www.atlantissubmarines.com, US$105 adult, US$65 child) offers 40-minute underwater excursions near Chankanaab national park. The subs have oversized portholes with low seats in a long row down the center. Staff members describe what you're seeing outside. The sub dives as deep as 120 feet; you're sure to see plenty of fish and coral formations, and, if you're really lucky, a shark or sea turtle. It's pretty pricey considering how short the actual tour is, but it's a memorable way for youngsters and nondivers to admire Cozumel's marine riches.

Cooking Classes

Josefina's Cocina Con Alma (no phone, www.cozumelchef.com, US$80 adult, US$70 teen 13-17, US$30 child 6-12, by appointment only) is a small cooking school offering private bilingual instruction in Yucatecan and classic Mexican dishes. Classes begin with a field trip to the market to select fresh ingredients, then it's straight to the kitchen to learn to create a preselected meal. Dishes offered range from *cochinita pibil* (pork marinated in orange juice, achiote, and other spices and baked in banana leaves) and *sopa de lima* (a citrus-based soup with shredded turkey and fried tortilla strips) to *chiles en nogada* (poblano peppers stuffed with meat or cheese and topped with a walnut-based cream sauce and pomegranate seeds) and tamales (seasoned meat, cheese, or vegetables stuffed in a cornmeal dough and wrapped in corn husks). Afterward, students enjoy their creations at a sit-down meal. Chef Josefina gets rave reviews for her expertise and warm manner.

Promotora Isla Maya (Av. 15 near Calle 10, tel. 987/872-4493, lilianam1313@yahoo.com.mx, cost varies) is a small school offering a variety of cooking classes, mostly for locals and expats. If you'll be in town for a while, check out the chocolate-making courses and cooking classes for kids. Art, photography, and jewelry-making workshops are also offered.

Food

Cozumel's food scene is steadily improving, with an ever-increasing variety and quality of restaurants. Like most islands, it has terrific seafood, always served fresh, from gourmet restaurants with executive chefs to simple eateries operated by local fisherman's cooperatives. (You may be surprised to learn, though, that much of the catch actually comes from around Isla Mujeres because the waters around Cozumel are protected.) The island's popularity with Americans, especially hungry divers, means you'll never want for steak, pizza, or big breakfasts, but there's a growing number of fine international options, including Italian, Argentinean, and, of course, Mexican.

MEXICAN AND YUCATECAN

Kinta (Av. 5 btwn Calle 2 and 4 Norte, tel. 987/869-0544, www.kintacozumel.com, 5pm-11pm daily, US$8-21) is a chic bistro serving gourmet Mexican dishes and knockout cocktails. Seating is indoors in a modern, welcoming space or outdoors in a leafy tropical garden. The menu includes such specialties as chile relleno, a poblano chile stuffed with ratatouille and Chihuahua cheese, and *peskado pastor,* catch of the day marinated in achiote with caramelized pineapple salsa and served with cilantro rice. Be sure to try the tamarindo martini—unforgettable! Enjoy live jazz and bossa nova on Saturday nights. Reservations are recommended.

★ **Kondesa** (Av. 5 btwn Calles 5 and 7, tel. 987/869-1086, www.kondesacozumel.com, 5pm-11pm daily, US$8-18) may well be Cozumel's classiest restaurant, with its sister restaurant, Kinta, its closest competition. Seating is in a lush garden with tables under a high *palapa*, on a central wooden platform, or right under the stars. The menu has some classic Mexican and Mediterranean dishes, but is mostly contemporary fusion. The guacamole trio and lionfish tortas are popular appetizers and go well with the restaurant's creative cocktails, including mojitos and sangria. The catch of the day is always flavorful and inventive, while homemade churros and coffee make a perfect dessert.

Parrilla Mission (Calle 1 btwn Avs. 50 and 55, tel. 987/869-2463, www.parrillamission.com, 4pm-11pm daily, US$3-8) specializes in tacos, served on delicious handmade corn tortillas and heaped with fresh grilled steak, chicken, or everyone's favorite, *al pastor* (spicy grilled pork). A self-serve "sides bar" includes not just salsa, cilantro, and lime, but Spanish rice, beans, and grilled onions as well. The rest of the menu is pretty outstanding too, including mole, chiles rellenos, and fajitas, all very reasonably priced. This place is a favorite among locals and a highlight for tourists willing to venture beyond the main downtown area.

The breezy *palapa*-roofed **La Candela** (Av. 5 at Calle 6 Norte, tel. 987/878-4471, 8am-11:30pm Mon.-Sat., US$4-14) offers an extensive lineup of Mexican and traditional Yucatecan dishes in a cafeteria-style setting. Check out what's steaming behind the glass window cases, find a seat, then place your order with your waiter. Lunch specials typically include soup or pasta, a main dish, and a drink (US$5-6).

★ **Otates Tacos** (Av. 15 btwn Calles Rosado Salas and 3, tel. 987/120-1076, noon-4am daily, US$2-6) is a bustling taco joint serving authentic Mexican grub at nearly street-cart prices. Tacos are just the beginning, served piping hot on tiny corn tortillas; the quesadillas, *tortas* (Mexican-style sandwiches), and *pozole* (pork and hominy soup) are all terrific, and the guacamole is rave-worthy. Service is fast and friendly, with menus in Spanish and English.

Taquería El Pique (Av. Pedro Joaquín Coldwell btwn Av. Benito Juárez and Calle 2, tel. 987/872-4628, 7pm-midnight daily, US$2-5) is a classic taco joint serving pint-size

a plate of huevos rancheros, a classic Mexican breakfast—perfect before a morning dive

tacos, chunky guacamole, gooey *queso fundido* (melted cheese), and more. It's a locals' favorite, though a small stream of expats and tourists make their way here, too.

Opened since 1962, **La Cozumeleña** (Av. 10 Sur at Calle 3, tel. 987/872-0189, 7am-5pm daily, US$3-7) is a longtime favorite with local families and professionals, serving classic dishes in a quiet air-conditioned dining area. For breakfast, try *chilaquiles* (fried tortilla strips, scrambled eggs, and chicken doused in green or red salsa) or eggs with *chaya*. Lunch specials include a main dish, like fish tacos or baked chicken, and a drink. There's a bakery next door, too, for fresh breads and pastries.

Corazón Contento (Av. 10 Sur at Calle 2, no phone, 7am-2pm Mon.-Sat., US$3-6) has a peaceful and welcoming ambience befitting its name (Contented Heart), while the stenciled walls and colorful tile floors are reminiscent of Mérida. Service is friendly, with great bottomless coffee and simple breakfast and lunch specials. Watch out: The bread basket is charged per item, and the chocolate-filled croissants are almost impossible to resist!

SEAFOOD

★ **El Viejo y La Mar** (Av. 5 Sur btwn Calles 9 and 9 Bis, no phone, noon-8pm daily, US$5-15) is a low-key eatery run by a local fisherman's cooperative, so the fish is especially fresh and well-priced. Whole fried fish is US$9 per kilo (2.2 pounds); a half kilo makes for a hefty meal. There are a dozen different ceviche and cocktail options, and just as many fillets. Eat in the large open-air dining area, or order to go if it's near closing time.

Camilo's (Av. 5 btwn Calles 2 and 4, tel. 987/872-6161, 11am-9pm daily, US$8-16) is a small place offering an abundance of fresh seafood: ceviche, shrimp cocktail, lobster tail, fried fish, grilled fish—you name it, they've probably got it. It's popular with locals, and travelers are beginning to trickle in now, too.

A family-run restaurant, **La Conchita del Caribe** (Av. 65 btwn Calles 13 and 15, tel. 987/869-1218, laconchitadelcaribe.mx, 11:30am-7:30pm daily, US$10-18) is another

locals' favorite, in a spacious location. When ordering whole fish—the house specialty, served grilled or fried—you'll be asked to pick the fish out of a cooler by the counter and will be charged according to size. And whether you order fish, shrimp, or other seafood, it was almost certainly swimming earlier in the day. This is a great off-the-tourist-path option; takeout is also available.

OTHER SPECIALTIES

La Cocay (Calle 8 btwn Avs. 10 and 15, tel. 987/872-5533, www.lacocay.com, noon-4:30pm and 5:30pm-11pm Mon.-Sat., 6pm-11pm Sun., US$15-22) offers Mediterranean cuisine with flair. The menu changes seasonally, but expect to see dishes like fish of the day with Cajun spice and mango sauce and blue-cheese-filled phyllo dough rolls with black cherry sauce. Seating is in a candlelit dining room or on the breezy garden patio—perfect for a special night out.

Al Pie del Carbon (Calle 6 at Av. 5, cell tel. 987/101-2599, 11am-11pm Mon.-Fri., 3pm-11pm Sat., US$9-18) is a popular Argentinean steak house serving up excellent cuts of beef, plus tasty salads and sides, and a decent wine list. Steaks are grilled over an open flame and can be enjoyed in the restaurant's air-conditioned dining room or open-air patio. The empanadas, another Argentinean classic, make great appetizers.

Founded in 1978 and passed from father to daughter, ★ **Guido's** (Av. Rafael Melgar btwn Calles 6 and 8, tel. 987/872-0946, www.guidoscozumel.com, 11am-11pm Mon.-Sat., 3pm-9:30pm Sun., US$13-20) is a bit pricey but worth every peso, serving unique Italian dishes like brick-oven baked lasagna, homemade pastas, memorable seafood dishes (like prosciutto-wrapped sea scallops served with risotto and orange beurre blanc sauce), and excellent sangria and desserts. The leafy courtyard setting makes a meal here all the more worthwhile.

Cruise ship crew members beeline to **Chi** (above Pizza Hut, Calle 3 at Av. Rafael Melgar, tel. 987/869-8156, www.chicozumel.com,

9:30am-11pm Mon.-Sat., noon-11pm Sun., US$8-15) for its gorgeous ocean views and extensive pan-Asian menu, including Chinese, Thai, Japanese, and Filipino dishes. The sushi is mediocre (ham nigiri?), but the rest is quite tasty, and a nice change of culinary pace. There's also a second location across from the Puerto Maya pier (Carr. Sur Km. 4.5), but the food there is hit or miss.

Though not so new anymore, **New Especias** (Calle 3 btwn Avs. 5 and 10, tel. 987/869-7947, 6pm-11:30pm Thurs.-Tues., US$8-18) continues to serve up excellent Italian dishes along with friendly service. The restaurant occupies the 2nd floor of the building, including a narrow patio with street views and a breezy dining area in the rear. That makes room for a lively wine bar downstairs, with guests migrating from one to the other, and even to the bistro tables set up on the sidewalk in front.

Del Sur (Av. 5 at Calle 3, tel. 987/871-5744, 5pm-11pm Mon.-Sat., US$4-21) serves crispy Argentinian empanadas and hearty steak (plus seafood, chicken, and salads) in a homey and attractive dining room. Order a couple of empanadas as a starter, or several for a full meal; either way, they go great with a cold beer. If you're ordering from the grill, ask for a recommendation from the restaurant's excellent wine list. There's also live tango on Friday nights starting at 8:30pm.

SWEETS

At **Zermatt** (Av. 5 Norte at Calle 4, tel. 987/872-1384, 7am-8:30pm Mon.-Sat., US$1-2.50) you may have to jostle with locals for a crack at the island's best fresh breads, pastries, and other traditional Mexican baked goods. Consider getting a little something extra for the stray pooch that is often hanging around out front.

★ **Nacho Crazy Boy** (Av. 20 Sur btwn Av. Benito Juárez and Calle 1, 8am-11pm Mon.-Sat., 10am-2pm Sun., US$2-3) serves outstanding juices and smoothies right from the patio of the owner's modest house. Fruits fresh from the market are squeezed and blended on the spot by Nacho Crazy Boy himself, an earnest and interesting guy who makes time for conversation with customers.

Rave reviews keep the small **Chocolateria Isla Bella** (Calle 3 btwn Av. 5 and Rafael Melgar, tel. 987/103-9409, noon-8pm Mon.-Thurs., noon-6pm Fri.-Sat., US$1-5) hopping. Its friendly owners churn out exquisite handmade chocolates in a variety of flavors, including Nutella, vanilla, lime and coconut,

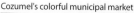
Cozumel's colorful municipal market

a luscious dark chocolate called The Black Panther, and more. New creations and holiday specials are announced on the restaurant's Facebook page, as well as special events, like truffle-making classes: a fun and informative (and tasty!) way to spend a couple of hours.

La Flor de Michoacán (Calle 1 near Av. 10, 9am-11pm daily, US$1-2) serves cool treats, including *aguas* (fruit drinks), *helados* (ice cream), and *paletas* (popsicles).

GROCERIES

Whatever groceries you need, you'll find them and more at **MEGA** (Av. Rafael Melgar at Calle 11, tel. 987/872-3658, 7:30am-10:30pm daily), the island's largest supermarket.

For a traditional market experience, Cozumel's **Mercado Municipal** (Av. 25 btwn Calles 1 and Rosado Salas, 7am-3pm daily) has stalls brimming with colorful produce, freshly butchered chickens, eggs, cheese, spices, and more, all at reasonable prices.

Accommodations

DOWNTOWN COZUMEL
Under US$50

Just one block from the central plaza, **Hostelito** (Av. 10 btwn Av. Benito Juárez and Calle 2 Norte, tel. 987/869-8157, www.hostelcozumel.com, US$15 dorm, US$18-20 dorm with a/c, US$40 s/d with a/c, US$50-60 suite with a/c and kitchenette) is a stylish hostel with a large coed dorm packed with 13 bunks, lockers, and fans. Groups of four or more should ask about the air-conditioned dorm with private bathroom—at US$18-20 per head, it's a steal. Private doubles have air-conditioning, minifridges, and TVs. There also are a couple of spacious suites with kitchenettes and lots of natural light. A fully equipped rooftop kitchen also is available for all to use, as is a great lounge and solarium with Wi-Fi and hammocks for just kicking back. A tiny plunge pool was in the works when we passed through.

Though a long way from the center of town, **Amigos Hostel Cozumel** (Calle 7 btwn Avs. 25 and 30, tel. 987/872-3868, www.cozumelhostel.com, US$12 dorm, US$45 s/d/t) is a great option for budget travelers looking for a peaceful place to stay. The hostel sits on a sprawling verdant property complete with a well-tended pool, a fully equipped communal kitchen, an open-air game room (with a pool table, no less), and lots of hammocks and lounge chairs. There

are two mixed dorms with four bunks apiece and en suite bathrooms. There's also one private room with a kitchenette that sleeps three comfortably. All units have air-conditioning, but it's only turned on May-October (10pm-8am).

Hotel Pepita (Av. 15 Sur btwn Calles 1 and Rosado Salas, tel. 987/872-0098, US$35 s/d with a/c) is a good value for traveler 'tweens: post-hostel but pre-B&B. The friendly owners keep the rooms very clean, though some of the beds are saggy and the decor could use some serious updating. All have air-conditioning, ceiling fans, cable TV, minifridges, and two double beds. There's also fresh coffee every morning in the long inner courtyard.

Hotel Caribe (Calle 2 Norte btwn Avs 15 and 20, tel. 987/872-0325, US$42-50 s/d with a/c) has a small, appealing pool in a leafy central garden—a rare and welcome feature in the ranks of budget hotels. Rooms are plain but clean, with one, two, or three beds, okay bathrooms, and old-school air conditioners. Service can be ambivalent, but you can't argue with the value.

Optimally located a half block from the central plaza, **Hotel El Pirata** (Av. 5 near Calle 1, tel. 987/872-0051, US$46-55 s/d with a/c) is a solid budget option. Recently updated, rooms are modern in decor and have thick beds, flat-screen TVs, and mini-split air conditioners. More expensive rooms have views of the park. Wi-Fi is available in the lobby, too. The only bummer about the place is that guests must climb a steep set of stairs to access rooms—a challenge for some.

US$50-100

★ **Mi Casa en Cozumel** (Av. 5 btwn Calles 7 and 9, tel. 987/111-9512, www.micasaencozumel.com, US$45-60 s/d, US$65 s/d with a/c, US$70 suite with a/c and kitchenette, US$160 penthouse) is a terrific boutique hotel and an architectural gem—the curves of the spiral staircase and interior walls are counterbalanced by triangular patios and angled nooks occupied by whirlpool tubs. All nine units have contemporary Mexican decor, private balconies or patios, minifridges, and cable TV; one has a kitchenette. Several units have airconditioning, while the others were designed for natural ventilation and are quite comfortable with fans only. The split-level penthouse is stunning, with full kitchen, outdoor hot tub, front and rear patios, and great views. The hotel's lofty structure is equally impressive, but could be difficult for guests who have trouble climbing stairs. A complimentary (and tasty!) breakfast is served in a cozy ground-floor dining area. Weekly rates are available.

★ **Tamarindo Bed and Breakfast** (Calle 4 btwn Avs. 20 and 25 Norte, tel. 987/872-6190, www.tamarindobedandbreakfast.com, US$59 s/d, US$63 s/d bungalow, US$69 s/d with a/c, US$75 suite with a/c and kitchenette) is a pleasant B&B owned by a friendly French expatriate who lives on-site. The hotel has seven units bordering a large, leafy garden. Each room is different from the other, from two boxy but comfortable hotel rooms to a whimsical *palapa* bungalow with boho flair. All have cable TV and Wi-Fi. Full breakfast is included during the high season for those units without cooking facilities; there's also a small communal kitchen. Rinse tanks and storage facilities are provided for guests with dive gear, too. The same owner also rents four units known as **Tamarindo Apartments & Bungalow** (US$89-99 s/d with a/c); located south of the center near the waterfront, they've got one or two bedrooms, air-conditioning, kitchen, cable TV, Wi-Fi, and a small pool. Reservations are highly recommended.

Amaranto Bungalows & Suites (Calle 5 btwn Avs. 15 and 20 Sur, cell tel. 987/106-6220, www.amarantobedandbreakfast.com, US$65 s/d bungalow with a/c, US$65 s/d suite, US$75 s/d suite with a/c) offers seclusion and privacy, while still within easy walking distance from downtown. The shining stars are the suites, in a three-story tower, each with a sitting area and 360-degree views; the lower unit has air-conditioning, high ceilings, and a modern feel, while the upper one has a *palapa* roof that offers a bird's-eye view. There also are three thatch-roofed bungalows with modern bathrooms and beachy decor; rooftop solariums were in the works for two of them. Each room has either a king-size or two queen-size beds, minifridge, microwave, cable TV, and security box. There's a plunge pool onsite—perfect for cooling off after a day in the sun—and Wi-Fi runs throughout the entire place. Amaranto doesn't have a full-time attendant, so it's best to reserve in advance.

Hotel Flamingo (Calle 6 btwn Avs. Rafael Melgar and 5 Norte, tel. 987/872-1264, toll-free U.S. tel. 800/806-1601, www.hotelflamingo.com, US$79-89 s/d with a/c, US$220 penthouse) offers classy, well-priced rooms with modern furnishings, mosaic tile bathrooms, and colorful Guatemalan decor, all in a quiet north-of-center location. Rooms have mini-split air conditioners, electronic safes, and cable TV. Three common areas provide lots of extra outdoor space for guests—a rooftop solarium with lounge chairs and whirpool tub, a shady midlevel area with hammocks, and a garden courtyard with tables and chairs. Wi-Fi is available in the lobby and bar areas. Families and groups should consider the penthouse, a two-bedroom apartment with full-size kitchen, private whirlpool tub, even a rooftop grill.

Located in the heart of San Miguel, **Villa**

Escondida (Av. 10 Sur btwn Calles 3 Sur and Rosado Salas, tel. 987/120-1225, US$100 s/d with a/c) is an adults-only B&B with just four guest rooms. Each is modern—if a bit sparse—in style, with comfortable beds and spacious bathrooms. All look onto a well-tended garden complete with an inviting swimming pool, lounge chairs, hammocks, and Wi-Fi. A full breakfast—from pancakes to *chilaquiles*—is served on the hotel terrace. Complimentary bicycles and snorkeling gear also are available to guests.

Over US$100

★ **Villa Las Anclas** (Av. 5 Sur btwn Calles 3 and 5, tel. 987/872-5476, www.hotelvillalasanclas.com, US$105 1-bdrm apartment) is a great option for those who want a little home away from home. Seven pleasantly decorated apartments open onto a leafy, private garden, each with a fully equipped kitchenette, a living room, and a loft master bedroom accessed by spiral stairs. Using the sofas as beds, the apartments can accommodate up to four people while still not feeling overcrowded. All units also have air-conditioning and Wi-Fi. There's also a new mosaic tile pool on-site plus an outdoor area for grilling and just hanging out. There's a great friendly vibe here, too.

Guido's Boutique Hotel (Av Rafael Melgar btwn Calles 6 and 8 Norte, tel. 987/872-0946, www.guidosboutiquehotel.com, US$110-130 1-bdrm apartment) is less a hotel and more do-it-yourself apartments, but the location, amenities, and price make Guido's an outstanding option. Masters have king beds, while juniors have queens; all are spacious, with full-size kitchens, stylish decor, and satellite TV and Wi-Fi. Each has a small balcony overlooking the street and ocean—traffic can get noisy but the views are priceless. The hotel is located just north of the center, above Guido's Restaurant, one of the island's best. There's no formal reception, so reserve ahead.

Casa Mexicana (Av. Rafael Melgar btwn Calles 5 and 7, tel. 987/872-9080, toll-free Mex. tel. 800/277-2639, toll-free U.S. tel. 877/228-6747, www.casamexicanacozumel.com, US$88-126 s/d with a/c) is a modern beauty with a soaring interior courtyard and gorgeous views of the Caribbean from the oceanside rooms, including cruise ships gliding in and out of port. Rooms are spacious and bright, though less inspired than the building itself, with good beds and quiet air conditioners but dated decor. There's a small infinity pool overlooking the water on one end of the lobby, too (though, admittedly, it's a little strange to take a dip so close to the front desk). Rates include a well-stocked buffet breakfast.

A long walk from town but worth every step, **Casa Colonial** (Av. 35 btwn Calles 8 and 10, U.S. tel. 954/284-4318, www.cozumelrentalvillas.com, US$1,075/week with a/c) has four fully equipped Mexican-style villas. All are two stories with two bedrooms, 2.5 bathrooms, a living room, a dining room, a modern kitchen, cable TV, Wi-Fi, even a washer and dryer. And unlike many longer-term rentals, you still get daily maid service and complimentary concierge service. All villas face a lush courtyard with a large pool and hot tub. Dive rinse tanks are available, too.

NORTHWESTERN COZUMEL
Under US$150

The intimate **Miramar Condominiums** (Zona Hotelera Norte Km. 3.4, toll-free U.S. tel. 866/564-4427, www.cozumelvillas.com/miramar, US$140-180 1-bdrm condo, US$200 2-bdrm condo) is a well-maintained complex with units varying in style, though all are updated and very comfortable. There's a fabulous infinity pool overlooking the Caribbean and entry points to the ocean that make snorkeling easy. The staff does a good job of making guests feel welcome—from fresh flowers upon arrival to concierge services like booking rental cars. There's no on-site beach, which is a drawback, but if you enjoy exploring the island, this is a great place to stay. It's especially suitable for families and those traveling in small groups.

Maya stelae decorate the facade of **Condumel** (Zona Hotelera Norte Km. 1.5, tel. 987/872-0892, www.condumel.com, US$142 up to 4 people with a/c), an old-school but very agreeable oceanfront condo complex, located a 15-minute walk from downtown. Ten spacious one-bedroom apartments have king-size beds, Wi-Fi, fully equipped kitchens, and daily maid service. Oversized sliding-glass doors offer awesome views of the Caribbean and incoming airplanes. The coast here is ironshore, so there's just a small patch of sand; steps and a ladder make swimming and snorkeling easy.

Over US$150

Playa Azul Hotel (Zona Hotelera Norte Km. 4, tel. 987/869-5160, www.playa-azul.com, US$180 s/d with a/c, US$225-270 suite with a/c) caters mostly to golfers—guests pay no greens fees at Cozumel Country Club—but has packages for divers and honeymooners as well. Medium-size rooms and spacious suites all have fairly modern furnishings, large bathrooms, and excellent ocean views from balconies and terraces; master suites have private outdoor whirlpool tubs, too. Full breakfast is included in the rates. The pool is clean and attractive, but the beach (already small) can get crowded with day-trippers visiting the hotel's beach club.

Oozing cool, ★ **Hotel B Cozumel** (Zona Hotelera Norte Km. 2.5, tel. 987/872-0300, www.hotelbcozumel.com, US$210-265 s/d with a/c, US$304 suite with a/c) is a boutique hotel that combines midcentury aesthetic with traditional Mexican decor. Rooms have clean lines, lots of natural light, and feature gorgeous Mexican folk art. All have a balcony or patio and the amenities you'd expect—silent air-conditioning, cable TV, and Wi-Fi. Most have ocean views, too. Outdoors, there's a breezy restaurant, a great half-moon pool, a whirpool tub, plus lots of sandy areas with hammocks and beach chairs. The main thing missing is a beach; the waterfront is mostly ironshore, so the hotel has done its best to create plenty of entry points to the water. Customer service, also, can be hit or miss.

SOUTHWESTERN COZUMEL
Under US$150

A laid-back dive resort, **Blue Angel Resort** (Carr. Sur Km. 2.2, tel. 987/872-0819, www.blueangelresort.com, US$119 s/d with a/c) provides all the amenities a diver could want: a reputable dive shop, reliable boats, an on-site

words of wisdom at the bottom of the pool at Hotel B Cozumel

dock, and drying racks and lockers for gear. The rooms themselves are modern but basic; all have great ocean views and private balconies. There's also an open-air restaurant, a well-tended pool, and plenty of shady places to sit back and relax. The only thing really missing is a beach. If you can live with that, this a perfect place to stay awhile.

Scuba Club Cozumel (Carr. Sur Km. 1.5, tel. 987/872-0853, toll-free U.S. tel. 800/847-5708, www.scubaclubcozumel.com, US$130 pp all-inclusive) is an old-school dive hotel with great packages, an on-site dock, and drying racks for your gear. Rooms are basic—clean and bare bones (good beds and a balcony yes, cable TV and Wi-Fi no). There's a small pool and a sandy area on the water, too. Meals are typically included in the rate and are served in a bustling dining room with plastic tables and chairs. Not exactly a tropical getaway, but perfect if you'll be underwater most of the time anyway.

Over US$150

★ **Presidente InterContinental Cozumel Resort Spa** (Carr. Sur Km. 6.5, tel. 987/872-9500, toll-free Mex. tel. 800/000-6633, toll-free U.S. tel. 800/327-0200, www.intercontinentalcozumel.com, US$292-490 s/d with a/c, US$580-2,456 suite with a/c) may well be the best resort in Cozumel, with sleek sophisticated rooms that have high-end amenities as well as niceties like twice-daily maid service and turndown service. While the views are of either garden or ocean, all roads lead to a mellow and welcoming pool scene and a great beach—despite the ironshore—thick white sand and calm, turquoise waters with plenty of access points for snorkelers and shore divers. A well-regarded dive shop, two lighted tennis courts, three restaurants, and a full-service spa round out this elegant hotel. If anything can be improved, it's the Wi-Fi connection, which can be spotty during high traffic hours.

A far cry from its advertised 5-star rating, **Iberostar Cozumel** (Carr. Sur Km. 17.8, tel. 987/872-9900, toll-free U.S. tel. 888/923-2722, www.iberostar.com, US$142-225 pp all-inclusive) is a basic all-inclusive with well-kept, lush grounds. It's a good option if you're traveling on a budget but want a resort experience. The rooms, for instance, are located in two-story bungalows but are smallish and pretty dated. The beach is wide but has lots of rocky areas—great for snorkeling, not so great for wading (bring water shoes). The food is fine for a long weekend—there's an extensive buffet and snack bar plus two reservations-only restaurants (dinner only). Service is consistently good too, and there are plenty of activities like water aerobics and yoga. There's also an on-site dive and snorkel shop. All in all, this is a good value if you find an online deal. If it's rack rates only, head elsewhere.

The adults-only **Secrets Aura Cozumel** (Carr. Sur Km. 12.9, toll-free U.S. tel. 866/467-3278, www.secretsresorts.com, US$155-276 pp all-inclusive) is a small all-inclusive resort sitting on a lush oceanfront property. It has features like four à la carte dining options (only one buffet here), top-shelf drinks, a 14,000-square foot spa, tennis courts, and an on-site dive shop. Rooms are modern and spacious with private balconies and whirpool tubs; if you can swing it budget-wise, opt for a "swim-up" room, which provides direct access to one of the resort's winding pools (as in open the patio door and step right in).

SOUTHEASTERN COZUMEL

The only hotel on the east side of the island, **Ventanas al Mar** (south end of Playa Tortugas, cell tel. 987/105-2684, www.ventanasalmar.com.mx, US$128 s/d with kitchenette, US$200 s/d suite with kitchenette) has 12 large rooms and two suites, all with high ceilings and private patios or decks, many with marvelous ocean views. The interiors lack the detailing and upkeep you'd expect at this price but suit the hotel's isolated feel. All have kitchenettes with microwaves, but none have air-conditioning, as the hotel runs almost entirely on wind and solar power. Fortunately, the constant sea breeze keeps rooms cool.

There's also a new beachfront pool, which is a huge plus since the ocean is often too rough to swim in. If you want a bit of action, there's a popular restaurant and beach club next door, but you'll probably want a car, as the east side has no ATM, grocery stores, or other services. Or you can embrace the isolation: Many guests spend a week or more without going to town at all. Rates include full breakfast.

Information and Services

TOURIST INFORMATION

The **city tourist office** (Plaza del Sol, Av. 5 Norte btwn Av. Benito Juárez and Calle 1, tel. 987/872-0966, 8am-3pm Mon.-Fri.) is located on the central plaza. It also has **information booths** in the central plaza (8am-2pm and 4pm-9pm Mon.-Sat., 9am-2pm Sun.), the international pier (8am-3pm daily), and at the Puerta Maya pier (8am-3pm daily). English is spoken at all locations.

The *Free Blue Guide to Cozumel* has good maps and listings for a range of services, from restaurants to dive shops. Look for the booklet as you get off the ferry.

There are numerous websites with news, tips, maps, special deals, discussion groups, and other information about Cozumel, including www.thisiscozumel.com, www.cozumelinsider.com, www.cozumelmycozumel.com, www.cozumeltoday.com, and even www.cruiseportinsider.com.

EMERGENCY SERVICES

Cozumel Medical Center (CMC, Calle 1A Sur at Av. 50, tel. 987/872-9400, toll-free U.S. tel. 888/409-0504, www.costamed.com.mx, 24 hours daily) accepts many foreign insurance plans, though the prices tend to be high.

A good alternative is the **Médica San Miguel** (Calle 6 Norte btwn Avs. 5 and 10, tel. 987/872-0103, www.medicasanmiguel.com, 24 hours daily), offering general medical services.

Cozumel's **Hyperbaric Medical Center** (Calle 5 btwn Avs. Rafael Melgar and 5 Sur, tel. 987/872-1430, 24 hours daily) specializes in diver-related medical treatment, though nondiving ailments also are treated.

For meds, try **Farmacia Similares** (Calle 1 Sur at Av. 15 Norte, tel. 987/869-2440, 9am-10pm Mon.-Sat., 9am-2pm Sun.). Mexico now requires a prescription for many antibiotics; this pharmacy has an on-site *consultorio* (doctor's office), open roughly the same hours.

The **tourist police** (Calle 11 Sur near Av. Rafael Melgar, 8am-11pm daily) are stationed in a kiosk near Punta Langosta, though officers often can be found patrolling the central plaza.

The **police station** (Palacio Municipal, Calle 13 btwn Avs. 5 and Rafael Melgar, tel. 987/872-0092, 24 hours) can be reached toll-free at 066.

MONEY

Accessing your money is not difficult in Cozumel, especially near the central plaza. **HSBC** (Av. 5 Sur at Calle 1, 9am-5pm Mon.-Fri.), **Bancomer** (Av. 5 Sur btwn Av. Juárez and Calle 1, 8:30am-4pm Mon.-Fri.), and **Banorte** (Av. 5 Norte btwn Av. Juárez and Calle 2, 9am-5pm Mon.-Fri.) all have ATMs and exchange foreign cash.

MEDIA AND COMMUNICATIONS

Cozumel's **post office** (Av. Rafael Melgar at Calle 7, no phone, 9am-4pm Mon.-Fri., 9am-1pm Sat.) is next to Punta Langosta shopping center.

There are myriad Internet cafés where you can get online, make international phone calls, burn photos to CDs, and more. **Phonet** (Calle Rosado Salas at Av. 10, no phone, 8am-11pm daily) is a quiet, reliable place charging US$0.75 per hour for Internet use and US$0.35 per minute for calls to the United States, Canada, and Europe. Another good option is **Speed1@ nd** (Calle 5 near Av. 5, tel. 987/878-4390, 7am-midnight Mon.-Sat., 10am-midnight Sun.), which charges US$1 per hour for Internet, US$.020 per minute for calls to the United States and Canada, and US$0.20-.040 for calls to Europe.

IMMIGRATION AND CONSULATES

The **immigration office** (Av. 15 Sur at Calle 5, tel. 987/872-0071) is open 9am-1pm Monday-Friday. There are immigration agents at the airport, too (7am-9pm daily).

LAUNDRY AND STORAGE

Lavandería Margarita (Av. 20 btwn Calle 3 and Av. Rosado Salas, cell tel. 987/112-5740, 7am-9pm Mon.-Sat., 8am-4pm Sun.) charges US$7.75 per load to wash and dry up to eight kilos (17.5 pounds). There also are self-service machines (US$2.50/washer, US$1.50/dryer); detergent, fabric softener, and dryer sheets are sold separately.

Lavandería Wash Express (Av. 10 btwn Calles 7 and 9, no phone, 7:30am-9pm Mon.-Sat., 8am-3pm Sun.) charges US$1.25 per kilo (2.2 pounds); drop off early for same-day service.

Storage lockers (9am-5pm Mon.-Sat., US$4-6) can be rented at the passenger ferry pier. Most are big enough to hold carry-on bags and backpacks only; larger bags are placed on top of the lockers and "watched" by an attendant (leave at your own risk!). Look for the lockers near the ticket booths.

Getting There and Around

GETTING THERE
Air
Cozumel International Airport (CZM, tel. 987/872-2081, www.asur.com.mx) is approximately three kilometers (1.9 miles) from downtown. The airport has an ATM in the departures area, AmEx currency exchange at arrivals, and a few magazine stands and duty-free shops. The **airport taxi cooperative** (tel. 987/872-1323) provides private and shared transport to the center and to resorts along the western coast. Prices vary by destination. Private taxis are US$11-24 per person, while shared transport costs US$5-11 per person and utilizes 10-person shuttles or Suburbans; departures are every 5-20 minutes. A taxi stand near the exit sells tickets and has prices prominently displayed.

The following airlines service Cozumel International Airport:

- **Aeroméxico** (toll-free Mex. tel. 800/021-4000, toll-free U.S. tel. 800/237-6639, www.aeromexico.com)
- **Air Canada** (toll-free Mex. tel. 800/719-2827, toll-free U.S./Can. tel. 888/247-2262, www.aircanada.com)
- **American Airlines** (toll-free Mex. tel. 800/904-6000, toll-free U.S./Can. tel. 800/433-7300, www.aa.com)
- **Continental** (toll-free Mex. tel. 800/900-5000, toll-free U.S./Can. tel. 800/864-8331, www.continental.com)
- **Delta** (toll-free Mex. tel. 800/266-0046, toll-free U.S. tel. 800/241-4141, www.delta.com)
- **Frontier Airlines** (toll-free U.S. tel. 800/432-1359, www.frontierairlines.com)
- **United Airlines** (toll-free Mex. tel.

800/900-5000, toll-free U.S./Can. tel. 800/864-8331, www.united.com)

- **US Airways** (toll-free Mex. tel. 800/843-3000, toll-free U.S. tel. 800/428-4322, www.usairways.com)

- **Volaris** (toll-free Mex. tel. 800/122-8000, toll-free U.S. tel. 866/988-3527, www.volaris.com)

Bus

Ticket Bus (Calle 2 at Av 10 Sur, tel. 987/869-2553, www.ticketbus.com.mx, 8am-9pm Mon.-Sat., 8am-8pm Sun.) sells tickets for ADO buses leaving from Playa del Carmen at no extra charge, a handy service for when you're ready to move on.

Ferry

Passenger ferries to Playa del Carmen (US$13 each way, 30 minutes) leave from the passenger ferry pier across from the central plaza. **UltraMar** (www.granpuerto.com.mx) and **Mexico Water Jets** (www.mexicowaterjets.com) alternate departures and charge the same amount, though UltraMar's boats are newer. Their ticket booths are opposite each other partway down the pier, with the time of the next departure displayed prominently. The ticket seller may try to sell you a round-trip ticket, but there's no savings in doing so; better to buy a *sencilla* (one-way ticket) and wait to see which company's ferry is departing when you're ready to leave. Between the two companies, there are ferries every 1-2 hours on the hour 6am-9pm daily.

GETTING AROUND

In town, you can walk just about anywhere or else grab a public van, or *combi,* circulating on various routes between the city center and outskirts (US$0.50, every 10-25 minutes 6am-8pm, less frequently on Sunday). However, the powerful taxi union has succeeded in quashing any and all efforts to start public bus service out of town and around the island. It is a shame, really, since it would be so easy and convenient to have a fleet of buses making loops around the island, or even just up and

down the western shore. Until that changes (don't hold your breath), you'll need a car, moped, or bike to explore the rest of the island on your own.

Bicycle

A bike can be handy for getting to beach clubs and snorkel sites outside of town. Traffic on Avenida Rafael Melgar can be heavy south of town, but once clear of that, the roadway is relatively unhurried.

A highly recommended biking outfit is **Rent A Bike Cozumel** (no storefront, tel. 987/113-1082, www.rentabikecozumel.com, US$12-45/day), which has a wide variety of bicycles—from beach cruisers and mountain bikes to hybrids and cyclocrosses. All rentals include a helmet and lock. Extras like lights and saddlebags also can be rented. Bikes are brought to your hotel or location of choice; rates go down the longer you rent. Reserve in advance, especially during the high season.

If you want a last-minute rental, consider renting a bicycle from **Rentadora Isis** (Av. 5 Norte btwn Calles 2 and 4, tel. 987/872-3367, www.rentadoraisis.com.mx, 8am-6:30pm daily, US$10/day) or **Shark Rider** (Av. 5 Norte btwn Av. Benito Juárez and Calle 2, tel. 987/120-0231, 8am-7pm daily, US$15/day).

Taxi

Taxis are everywhere—you can easily flag one down on Avenida Rafael Melgar, near the main passenger pier, and around the plaza. If you want to be picked up at a specific place and time, call the **taxi union office** (Calle 2 btwn Avs. 5 and 10, tel. 987/872-0041, 24 hours daily). Cabs typically charge US$4 around town and US$6.50 from the center to the airport, for up to four people. For hotels and beach clubs on the western shore south of town, you'll pay US$6-26, depending on the distance. Fares to the east side are a bit more, US$13.50-32, while San Gervasio and Punta Sur cost US$50-60. A trip around the island, including stops, runs around US$100-120 for four hours. Most taxi stands have the current fares prominently displayed; always agree on a price before getting into a taxi.

Car and Moped Rental

Renting a car is a nice way to get out of downtown and see the rest of the island. It is virtually impossible to get lost, and you can visit all the main spots in a day or two.

If you do decide to rent some wheels, go to the agency yourself—do not allow one of the friendly guys at the pier to lead you there. They are *comisionistas,* freelancers who earn hefty commissions for bringing tourists to particular shops, which then pass the cost on to you. Shop owners go along begrudgingly; if they decline the "service," the same freelancers will actively steer future tourists away from the shop, saying it's closed, burned down, fresh out of cars—you get the idea.

Excluding commissions, rental cars in Cozumel start at around US$40-50 for a compact car, including insurance and taxes. Mopeds rent for around US$25 per day. Be aware that scooters account for the majority of accidents here, as speed bumps, potholes, and windy conditions can upend even experienced drivers; having a second person on the back is even more dangerous. Also remember that unpaved roads are not covered by most rental car insurance plans.

Rentadora Isis (Av. 5 Norte btwn Calles 2 and 4, tel. 987/872-3367, www.rentadorai-sis.com.mx, 8am-6:30pm daily) consistently has the island's best rates, and friendly service to boot; their Internet specials often are good, too. Another good local option is **Sol y Mar Rentals** (Calle 2 near Av. 5 Norte, tel. 987/869-0545, 8am-7pm daily).

International companies have newer fleets, and often have good rates if you book online. Try **Avis** (Punta Langosta Pier, Av. Rafael Melgar btwn Calles 7 and 11, tel. 987/872-5383, airport tel. 987/872-0219, www.avis.com), **Hertz** (airport tel. 987/869-8184, www.hertz.com), or **Thrifty** (Av. Juárez at Av. 10 Norte, tel. 987/869-8090, airport tel. 987/869-2957, www.thrifty.com).

Motorcycle Rental

To explore the island in style, head to **Eaglerider** (Palmar Plaza, Carr. Costera Sur Km. 3.8, tel. 987/857-0106, toll-free U.S. tel. 888/900-9901, www.eaglerider.com, US$159-199/day), which rents several types of Harley-Davidson motorcycles, from Sportsters to Road Kings and Electra Glides.

Mopeds are convenient for getting around town.

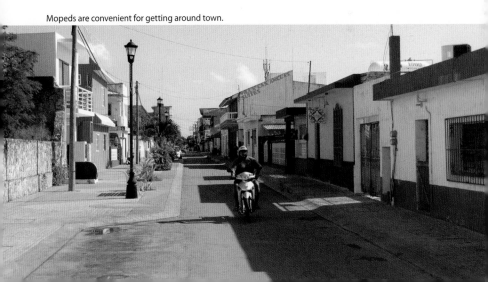

Highways and Road Conditions

The distance around the island—on paved roads, and including the northwestern arm that dead-ends after Cozumel Country Club—is approximately 93 kilometers (58 miles). Driving without stopping, it takes a little under two hours to circumnavigate the island. If doing this, consider going counter-clockwise so there's nothing between your vehicle and the ocean, especially on the east side. Biking around the island is possible but challenging, given the strong crosswinds.

Cozumel has three **PEMEX gas stations** (7am-midnight daily). Two are in town on Avenida Benito Juárez (at Avs. Pedro Joaquin Coldwell and 75), and the third is four kilometers (2.5 miles) south of town on the Carretera Costera Sur, across from Puerta Maya, the main cruise ship pier.

Note: Most streets are one-way in town; if you're driving, be aware that *avenidas* (avenues) run north-south and have the right-of-way over *calles* (streets), which run east-west. Once you leave town, there is a single road that circles the entire island.

The Riviera Maya

Look for ★ to find recommended sights, activities, dining, and lodging.

Highlights

★ **Puerto Morelos's Coral Reef:** Go snorkeling where the reef is still healthy, the water uncrowded, and the price unbeatable (page 143).

★ **Playa del Carmen's Quinta Avenida:** Ever growing yet still walkable, Playa's 5th Avenue has block after block of tempting restaurants, hipster boutiques, and lively bars (page 155).

★ **Playa del Carmen's Beaches and Beach Clubs:** Playa's beaches are among the Riviera Maya's most beautiful, and its beach clubs make them some of the most enjoyable, too. **Playa Tukán** takes the cake with ankle-deep white sand, mild surf, and two beach clubs—one mellow, one hoppin' (page 158).

★ **Xcaret:** The Riviera Maya's elaborate eco-parks are a hit with parents looking for a safe, active, friendly place to take the kids. Xcaret is the most ambitious of them all, with tubing and snorkeling, an aquarium, and an end-of-the-day extravaganza (page 159).

★ **Laguna Yal-Ku:** A long elbow of water fed by freshwater cenotes and flowing into the sea, this lagoon is a snorkeler favorite for its colorful fish and jumble of underwater rocks (page 182).

★ **Playa Xcacel:** Just off the highway down an easy-to-miss sand road, this glorious stretch

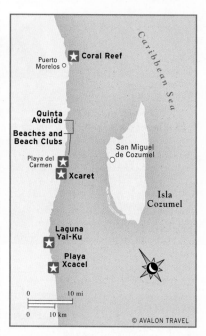

of white-sand beach has nary a beach bed or banana boat in sight. The secret? It's a sea-turtle nesting area protected from development—at least for now (page 190).

Cancún may be the name everyone recognizes, but for many people—especially repeat visitors—the best of Mexico's Caribbean coast is the Riviera Maya.

Stretching more than 130 kilometers (81 miles) south from Cancún to Tulum, the Riviera Maya is home to fast-growing cities like Playa del Carmen, low-key towns like Puerto Morelos, and tiny beachfront settlements like Tankah Tres. It boasts megaresorts and tiny bed-and-breakfasts, and is flanked by the world's longest underground river on one side and the world's second-longest coral reef on the other. And, of course, the Riviera Maya has the same spectacular beaches Cancún is famous for.

There's plenty to see and do, much of it do-it-yourself: Go snorkeling in freshwater cenotes and lagoons, help release newly hatched sea turtles into the sea, explore little-visited Maya ruins, or spend the day at a family-friendly ecopark. For party hounds, Cancún still has a lock on over-the-top nightspots, though Playa del Carmen has several of its own, and there are plenty of lounge bars, beach clubs, and resort nightclubs where visitors can kick back or cut loose.

PLANNING YOUR TIME

You'll probably want to pick a home base (or two) for your time here and make day trips from there. Playa del Carmen is the area's only real city, with all the expected urban amenities, including nightlife. (It's also the gateway to Isla Cozumel.) Puerto Morelos and Akumal are smaller but still have a decent selection of hotels and restaurants. If isolation is more important than convenience, the Riviera Maya has some secret getaways, like Xpu-Há and Tankah Tres. If you've got a week or more, consider spending half your time in the northern section—around Playa del Carmen, for example—and then move farther south, to enjoy Akumal, Tankah Tres, and even Tulum.

A rental car isn't absolutely necessary but will certainly make exploring the Riviera Maya a lot easier. Cheap public shuttles zip up and down the coast, but they only stop along the highway, which in most places is about a kilometer (0.6 mile) from the ocean. That leaves you to make the hot, dusty walk

---

Previous: orchids; Puerto Morelos's main pier. **Above:** a perfect spot.

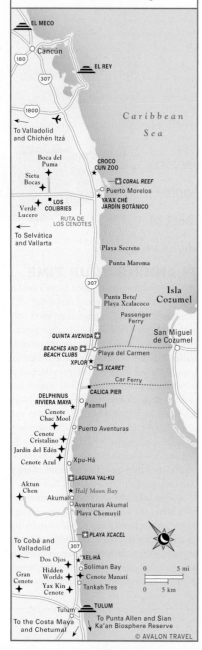

The Riviera Maya

EL MECO

Cancún

180

EL REY

307

180D

Caribbean Sea

To Valladolid
and Chichén Itzá

Boca del
Puma

CROCO
CUN ZOO

CORAL REEF

Sieta
Bocas

Puerto Morelos

YA'AX CHÉ
JARDÍN BOTÁNICO

Verde
Lucero

LOS
COLIBRIES

RUTA DE
LOS CENOTES

To Selvática
and Vallarta

Playa Secreto

Punta Maroma

307

Isla
Cozumel

Punta Bete/
Playa Xcalacoco

Passenger
Ferry

QUINTA AVENIDA

San Miguel
de Cozumel

BEACHES AND
BEACH CLUBS

Playa del Carmen

XPLOR

XCARET

Car Ferry

CALICA PIER

DELPHINUS
RIVIERA MAYA

Paamul

Cenote
Chac Mool

Cenote
Cristalino

Puerto Aventuras

Jardín del Edén

Cenote Azul

Xpu-Há

LAGUNA YAL-KU

Aktun
Chen

Half Moon Bay

Akumal

Aventuras Akumal

Playa Chemuyil

To Cobá and
Valladolid

307

PLAYA XCACEL

Dos Ojos

XEL-HÁ

Gran
Cenote

Hidden
Worlds

Soliman Bay

Cenote Manatí

Yax Kin
Cenote

Tankah Tres

0   5 mi

0   5 km

Tulum

TULUM

To the Costa Maya
and Chetumal

To Punta Allen and Sian
Ka'an Biosphere Reserve

© AVALON TRAVEL

up and down the access roads, especially in more rural areas where taxis are uncommon.

Puerto Morelos

Puerto Morelos has largely escaped the mega-development that has swept up and down the Riviera Maya, despite being squeezed between the booming cities of Cancún and Playa del Carmen. It remains, for the most part, a quiet seaside town. Yes, the town fills up with tourists in the high season—and more and more condos and resorts are cropping up—but it is still a place where a substantial part of the local population lives by fishing, where life revolves around the central plaza, and where kids and dogs romp in the streets.

The beach in Puerto Morelos has improved significantly in the last few years, and more and more travelers are spending lazy afternoons in the sun and sand. But Puerto Morelos is best known for the reef system just offshore. Local residents fought tirelessly (and successfully) to have a large section in front of town designated a national reserve, and as a result, the snorkeling and diving are superb. A town cooperative and several local dive shops offer tours of various sorts, most highly recommended and quite affordable. Puerto Morelos also is gaining popularity as a destination for yoga and meditation groups—no surprise given its serene atmosphere—and a growing number of hotels and resorts cater to that market.

Be aware that the low season here is *very* low, and many businesses close in May, September, and/or October.

SIGHTS AND BEACHES
Playa Principal

Over the years, Puerto Morelos has improved its beachfront area considerably, with leafy arbors and palm-shaded benches. The beach itself, however, lacks the creamy white sand found elsewhere in the Riviera Maya, and the same regulations

Puerto Morelos

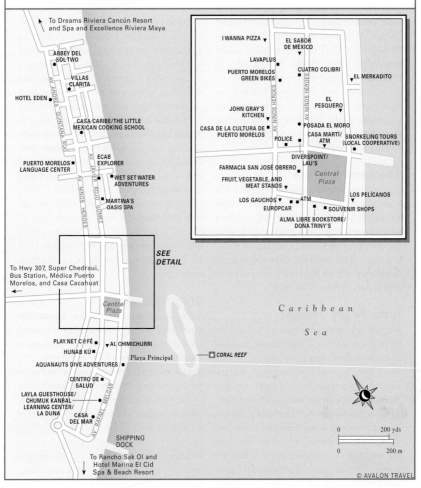

that protect the town's famous coral reef also prevent the removal of sea grass in the shallow areas. Fishing boats also moor on the beach, though there's still plenty of room to lay out a towel, especially toward the northern and southern ends. A good beach option is **Club de Playa Los Pelícanos** (central plaza, 9am-3pm Mon.-Sat.), which has lounge chairs, umbrellas, and kayaks. It's located off one corner of the main plaza, in front of the restaurant of the same name.

★ Coral Reef

Puerto Morelos's top attraction is snorkeling on the reef. Directly in front of the village, around 500 meters (0.3 mile) offshore, the reef here takes on gargantuan dimensions—up to 30 meters (99 feet) wide. Winding passages and large caverns alive with fish and sea flora make for great exploring. And since it's a marine reserve, and fishing and motor traffic are limited, the reef is more pristine here than almost any place along the Riviera. A **local cooperative** (central plaza, Av. Rafaél Melgar s/n, cell tel. 998/121-1524, 9am-3pm Mon.-Sat., US$25 pp for 2 hours) offers guided tours of the reef, with boats leaving every 30 minutes—or sooner, if there are four snorkelers—from the municipal pier. The tour includes visits to two snorkeling sites, gear, and a certified guide. The **dive shops** in town also offer snorkeling tours to the town reef and beyond, for slightly higher prices.

The Central Plaza

Puerto Morelos's peaceful central plaza is a highlight of the town, with shaded benches, a basketball court, and a new play structure for kids, making it a great place to while away the early evening hours, especially for families. Many of Puerto Morelos's best restaurants face the plaza or are just a block away, so you're sure to pass by more than once.

Ruta de los Cenotes

Marked by an enormous mustard-yellow arch on Highway 307, the "Cenote Route" is one of the newest developments along the Riviera Maya, and a sign, for better or worse, that the megaresorts are finally starting to appreciate cenotes. The route is simply a paved road, which begins just south of Puerto Morelos and extends nearly 20 kilometers (12.4 miles) into the scrub forest, passing several cenotes along the way. The most popular stops, at least for tour groups, are cenotes like **Boca del Puma** and **Selvática,** which also have ATV tours, ziplines, paintball—you get the picture. But the route also has some true gems: gorgeous and remote cenotes, undeveloped and all but overlooked by the package tours, and well worth the drive to reach them.

Independent travelers will particularly enjoy **Siete Bocas** (Carr. Pto. Morelos-Vallarta Km. 15.5, tel. 998/208-9199, 8am-4pm daily, US$19), so named for its seven openings (or "mouths"). Three openings have steep wood stairways leading straight into the cool, clear water; another is a jumping-screaming-cannon-ball-entry spot for the more adventurous (apparently, the cenote is 492 feet deep); the other three allow sunlight into the underground chamber, lighting up the water dramatically, especially around midday. Inside, you can swim or float through the cave, with its spectacular stalagmites and stalactites, often with no one else around (BYO snorkel gear and underwater flashlight).

Just down the road from Siete Bocas is **Verde Lucero** (Carr. Pto. Morelos-Vallarta Km. 18, cell tel. 998/224-3731, 8am-5pm daily, US$12), an open-air cenote surrounded by huge tropical trees. Completely different from its neighbor but no less dramatic, Verde Lucero is like an enormous swimming hole with clear turquoise water and seemingly no bottom. There's a zipline as well as a thick safety line stretching across the cenote. Look for the freshwater turtles that make their home here.

Croco Cun Zoo

A nice little tropical petting zoo, **Croco Cun Zoo** (Hwy. 307, tel. 998/850-3719, www.crococunzoo.com, 9am-5pm daily, US$30 adult, US$20 child 6-12, free 5 and under) is located five kilometers (3.1 miles) north of the Puerto Morelos turnoff. Seventy-five-minute guided tours, offered in English or Spanish, bring visitors up close and personal to all sorts of local creatures. You can feed spider monkeys and white-tailed deer, walk through a crocodile enclosure, be "kissed" by macaws, and hold boas and baby crocs. Well managed and reasonably affordable, Croco Cun is a hit for youngsters and adults alike.

Ya'ax Ché Jardín Botánico

Just south of the Puerto Morelos turnoff, a peaceful botanical garden, **Ya'ax Ché Jardín Botánico** (Hwy. 307 Km. 320, tel. 998/206-9233, www.ecosur.mx, 8am-4pm daily Nov.-Apr., 9am-5pm daily May-Oct., US$11.50 adult, US$5 child), has four kilometers (2.4 miles) of trails winding through diverse habitat, from tropical forest to

Cenotes: Then and Now

divers exploring the otherworldly depths of the Riviera Maya's cenotes

One of the Yucatán Peninsula's most intriguing features is its cenotes, freshwater sinkholes, sometimes hundreds of meters deep and filled with crystalline freshwater that is fed by underground rivers. Cenotes owe their formation to the massive meteorite that hit the Yucatán Peninsula 65 million years ago. The impact shattered the peninsula's thick limestone cap like a stone hitting a car windshield, and in the millions of years that followed, rainwater seeped into the cracks, carving huge underground caverns and hundreds of kilometers of channels out of the highly soluble limestone. Cenotes are former caverns whose roofs collapsed—cave-ins are extremely rare today, however—and together the channels form the world's longest underground river system.

Cenotes were sacred to Maya, who relied on them for water and viewed them as apertures to the underworld. (The name is derived from the Yucatec Maya word *dz'onot,* meaning "well.") Sacrificial victims were sometimes thrown into their eerie depths, along with finely worked stone and clay items, and archaeologists have learned a great deal about early Maya rituals by dredging cenotes near archaeological sites, most notably Chichén Itzá. Indeed, the name Chichén Itzá means Well of the Itzá, undoubtedly a reference to the ancient city's dramatic cenote.

Today the peninsula's cenotes attract worshippers of a different sort: snorkelers and scuba divers. The unbelievably clear water—100-meter (328-foot) visibility in places—is complemented by what other inland and underground diving environments (like lakes and flooded mines) lack: stunning stalactites and stalagmites. During early ice ages, water drained from the cenotes, giving time for the slow-growing features to form. When the climate warmed, the cenotes filled with water once again, their depths now forested with dramatic stone spires, pillars, and columns.

Divers with open-water certification can dive in the cenotes. Though "full-cave" diving requires advanced training, most cenote tours are actually "cavern" dives, meaning you are always within 40 meters (130 feet) of an air pocket. It's a good idea to take some open-water dives before your first cenote tour—buoyancy control is especially important in cenotes, and you'll be contending with different weights and finning technique.

mangrove swamp. In addition to hundreds of marked plants, there's a scenic lookout tower, a 130-foot suspension bridge, the remains of a small Maya ruin, and re-creations of a modern Maya home and *chicle* camp. Monkeys can be sometimes spotted in the afternoon. Wear long sleeves, pants, and plenty of bug repellent.

ENTERTAINMENT AND EVENTS
Festival de Música de Puerto Morelos

Held between late January and early March, the **Festival de Música de Puerto Morelos** (www.festivalmusicapuertomorelos.com, free) is a three-day event that brings local and international musicians together to celebrate their art. Music genres vary from blues and jazz to reggae and merengue. Held in the central plaza, all proceeds benefit Puerto Morelos's Casa de Cultura.

SHOPPING

A so-called **Mayan Jungle Market** (Calle 2, Zona Urbana, tel. 998/208-9148, 9:30am-2pm Sun., Dec.-Easter only) is held at Casa Cacahuate bed-and-breakfast in the residential part of Puerto Morelos, on the other side of the highway. This cheerful, family-friendly event is facilitated by the nonprofit founded by the bed-and-breakfast's owners. The market includes a variety of handicrafts produced by local women, as well as tasty food and drink. A traditional Maya dance is held at 11:30am.

Cuatro Colibrí (Av. Javier Rojo Gómez s/n, cell tel. 998/198-1235, 9am-3pm and 5pm-10pm Mon.-Sat.) specializes in high-end *artesanía* and jewelry from around the country. You'll find everything from *corazónes de latón* (tin hearts) to Huichol-inspired T-shirts. Prices are somewhat higher here, but the quality is tough to beat.

The artisan's market of **Hunab Kú** (Av. Javier Rojo Gómez s/n, 9am-8pm daily) may be your best bet for finding local handicrafts in Puerto Morelos. Here you'll find a bunch of stands with colorful blankets, ceramics, hammocks, masks, jipi hats, and shell art. A **string of souvenir shops** (8am-8pm daily) on the central plaza sell similar items, in case you don't find what you're looking for at the market.

One of the best bookstores on the peninsula, **Alma Libre Bookstore** (central plaza, tel. 998/251-1206, www.almalibrebooks.com, 10am-6pm daily, closed May-mid-Nov.) has a whopping 20,000 titles, new and used, ranging

shopping in Puerto Morelos

from "beach trash to Plato," in the words of the friendly Canadian owners. There's Maya culture, Mexican cooking, ecology, mysteries, guidebooks, maps, and more, and not just in English but Spanish, French, German, Dutch, Italian, and others. The store's website is an outstanding resource for everything Puerto Morelos, too.

SPORTS AND RECREATION
Snorkeling

Puerto Morelos is justly famous for its snorkeling, with a protected stretch of coral reef running very near shore. A **local cooperative** (central plaza, Av. Rafaél Melgar s/n, no phone, 9am-3pm Mon.-Sat.) offers excellent and affordable guided tours, visiting two spots on the reef for 45 minutes apiece, and using boats with sunshades. Prices are fixed: US$25 per person, including certified guide, equipment, park fees, and a bottle of water. Boats leave every 30 minutes from the municipal pier; if there are fewer than three people, you'll have to wait up to 30 minutes (but no more) for additional passengers to come. Sign up at the cooperative's kiosk at the northeast corner of the plaza; late morning is the best time to go, as the sun is high but the afternoon winds haven't started. The **dive shops** in town also offer snorkeling tours to the town reef and beyond, for slightly higher prices.

Caution: *Do not swim to the reef* from anywhere along the beach. Although it's close enough for strong swimmers to reach, boats use the channel between the reef and the shore, and tourists have been struck and killed in the past.

Scuba Diving

Puerto Morelos has over two dozen dive sites within a 15-minute boat ride, virtually all in protected marine reserve waters. Add to that the nearby cenotes, plus night and wreck diving, and divers have plenty to keep them happy and interested. The dive shops in town tend to have small groups and offer a full range of fun dives and certification courses.

Prices range US$55-80 for one tank, US$75-100 for two tanks, and US$415-460 for open-water certification. Be sure to ask about any extra fees, like equipment, taxes, and marine park fee. Shop hours are irregular, and reservations are strongly recommended.

Wet Set Water Adventures (Hotel Ojo de Agua, Av. Javier Rojo Gómez s/n, tel. 998/206-9204, www.wetset.com) is one of the longest-running dive shops around, offering top-to-bottom service and extensive area expertise.

Aquanauts Dive Adventures (Hotel Hacienda Morelos, Av. Rafaél Melgar 5, cell tel. 984/126-7966, www.aquanautsdiveadventures.com) is another long-operating dive shop offering personalized service.

Diverspoint (Av. Javier Rojo Gómez s/n, tel. 998/206-9051, www.diverspoint.com) is a small shop run by a friendly Dutch couple.

Sportfishing

The dive shops in Puerto Morelos also offer fishing trips, whether trolling for barracuda or marlin, or dropping a line for "dinner fish" like grouper or snapper. **Wet Set Water Adventures** (Hotel Ojo de Agua, Av. Javier Rojo Gómez s/n, tel. 998/871-0198, www.wetset.com) has been taking visitors fishing for many years; a **local cooperative** (central plaza, Av. Rafaél Melgar s/n, no phone, 9am-3pm Mon.-Sat.) does the same. Both charge around US$60-70 per hour.

Another popular—though pricier—option is the fishing fleet at **Marina El Cid** (Hotel Marina El Cid Spa & Beach Resort, Blvd. El Cid Unidad 15, tel. 998/871-0185, www.elcidmarinas.com). Trips run US$500-1,000 for 4-8 hours, but the boats tend to be newer and faster. The cost includes captain, crew, fishing license, tackle, ice, and insurance; food and beverages are optional. Taxidermy, filleting, and cooking are offered, too.

Tours

ECAB Explorer (cell tel. 998/123-5062, www.ecabexplorer.com) is a small but reliable tour operator run by a longtime Puerto Morelos resident (and former purveyor of fine shrimp tacos). Tours include not only the main destinations—Chichén Itzá, Cobá, Ek' Balam, Sian Ka'an, etc.—but also whale shark snorkeling tours and interesting add-ons like bird-watching and visits with a local family. Groups are small and rates reasonable considering the tours' length and depth: around US$95-150 adult, with discounts for children and groups. Check the website for scheduled outings or to arrange a private tour.

Chumuk Kanbal Learning Center (Layla Guesthouse, Av. Rafaél Melgar s/n, cell tel. 998/104-9831, www.laylaguesthouse.com, US$62) offers a popular cenote tour to a little-visited site about 90 minutes from Puerto Morelos. The trip includes a guided nature walk, a visit to a dry cave, a swim in a gorgeous cenote, and a traditional lunch at a local Maya home. Tours run 8am-5pm and must be booked in advance.

Over 50 visual artists live in the Zona Urbana of Puerto Morelos, located on the west side of the highway. Get an inside look at some of these artists' studios through the **Art Tour of Puerto Morelos** (tel. 998/245-9308, nadjabvd@gmail.com, US$35 for up to 3 people), a three-hour tour of 4-5 workshops led by a bilingual guide. Tours include meeting the artists and learning about their processes. Discounts are available if you provide your own transportation.

Spas

The **Ixchel Jungle Spa** (Casa Cacahuate, Calle 2, Zona Urbana, tel. 998/208-9148, www.mayaecho.com, 10am-3:30pm Tues.-Sat., Sun. by appointment only) is one of several community projects undertaken by Maya Echo, a nonprofit founded by the owners of Casa Cacahuate B&B. Local women provide professional massage and traditional Maya treatments for far less than at ordinary spas. Treat yourself to one of various available treatments, from a four-handed full-body massage (US$80, 1 hour) to a chocolate body wrap and massage (US$60, 1 hour). Group massage or *temascal* (traditional Maya sweat

lodge) also can be arranged with advance notice. A cab ride from Puerto Morelos's central plaza runs about US$5.

Martina's Oasis Spa (Calle Rojo Gómez 7, tel. 998/213-4595, www.martinasoasis.com, by appointment only) draws on the considerable skills of its owner, Martina, a licensed massage therapist with an uncanny ability to zero in on the precise source of discomfort and know just how to alleviate it. Prices are reasonable: US$40-85 for facials, manipedis, etc., and US$65-165 for one- and two-hour massages, including Swedish, Thai, deep tissue, and hot stone. Treatments are also offered off-site.

Set on a jungle plot along the Ruta de los Cenotes, **Los Colibries** (Ruta de los Cenotes Km. 15, cell tel. 998/105-2016, www.loscolibries.mx, 9am-5pm daily) offers Maya massages, *temascal* sessions, and outdoor bath treatments. Prices range US$35-80 for 1-2.5 hours. It's an especially nice way to end a day of cenote hopping.

Cooking Classes

The Little Mexican Cooking School (Casa Caribe, Calle Rojo Gómez 768, tel. 998/251-8060, www.thelittlemexicancookingschool.com, 10am-3:30pm Tues.-Fri., US$110 pp, including complimentary recipe book and apron) offers a fun and unique introduction to Mexican cuisine. Smallish classes (12 maximum) begin with a light breakfast and a discussion of Mexican food and ingredients, followed by demonstrations and hands-on practice of 7-8 recipes, from pumpkin seed salsa to chicken mole. Class ends with a luncheon from the dishes you helped create. Cooking and lodging packages are available.

FOOD

Who knows how it happened, but modest little Puerto Morelos is home to an amazing array of restaurants and eateries, from cheerful holes-in-the-wall to international cuisine that draws diners all the way from Cancún and Playa del Carmen.

Mexican and Seafood

A colorful open-air restaurant, **El Sabor de México** (Av. Javier Rojo Gómez, cell tel. 998/115-2244, 8am-11pm daily, US$4-7) is owned and run by a friendly family from Oaxaca and serves up delicacies from around the country. Favorites include mole dishes (a thick spicy sauce, often incorporating chocolate), chiles rellenos (stuffed peppers), tamales (meat or veggies wrapped in a cornmeal dough), and breakfast combos.

A *palapa*-roofed eatery with sand floors and plastic tables, ★ **El Pesquero** (Av. Rafaél Melgar, tel. 998/206-9129, 12:30pm-7:30pm daily, US$6-14) specializes in fresh seafood—everything from *chipachole* soup (a seafood medley of shrimp, fish, octopus, and squid) and ceviche to whole fish and lobster tail. Portions are generous and often include sides like coleslaw, rice, beans, and cucumber salad. The service is friendly and efficient, too.

El Merkadito (Av. Rafaél Melgar, tel. 998/871-0774, www.elmerkadito.mx, noon-9pm daily, US$5-20) is one of the only beachfront restaurants in town, which is a huge plus. The food is solid—ceviches, tacos, tostadas, carpaccio, pastas—and beautifully presented. The rub is that it might take an hour (or more) to get your appetizers. If you can handle the slow service, this is a great option on a beautiful afternoon.

Asian

A spin-off of the much-loved (and now closed) "David Lau's" restaurant, **Lau's** (Av. Javier Rojo Gómez, tel. 998/254-0601, 3pm-10pm Tues.-Sat. US$8-13) serves terrific Asian-inspired dishes like sesame beef with broccoli, chicken lo mein, and coconut shrimp dishes. Meals are made to order and are served in a small dining room that feels a bit like a fast-food joint; delivery is available, too.

La Duna (Av. Rafaél Melgar s/n, cell tel. 998/104-8454, 8am-4:30pm Wed.-Sun., US$6-9) is a cozy open-air eatery offering traditional breakfasts (think omelets, fruit plates, and fresh-squeezed juices) as well as Asian-themed lunch dishes like Indian curries, spring rolls, Thai noodles, and sushi. The menu changes weekly using local and fresh ingredients.

Other Specialties

Though ★ **Al Chimichurri** (Av. Javier Rojo Gómez s/n, tel. 998/252-4666, www.alchimichurri.com, 5pm-1am Tues.-Sun., US$9-20) serves up a variety of tasty Uruguayan specialties, the shining stars are the grilled meats,

Fish tacos are a Riviera Maya staple: simple, classic, delicious.

chicken, and homemade sausage (don't be afraid to ask for extra chimichurri sauce, for dipping). Food is served at candlelit tables in an open-air dining room and along the sidewalk, which is great for people watching and simply enjoying the evening breeze. If you have room, finish off your meal with the flambéed apple crepe topped with vanilla ice cream.

John Gray's Kitchen (Av. Niños Héroes s/n, tel. 998/871-0665, 2pm-10pm Mon.-Sat., US$14-25) is, without question, the fanciest restaurant in Puerto Morelos. The menu changes every day, though a few perennial favorites are almost always available, like mac n' cheese with jumbo shrimp and white truffle oil as well as pan-roasted duck breast with chipotle, honey, and tequila. Fine cuts of meat, inventive sauces, and fresh pastas and vegetables are a given. Occupying a boxy building two blocks from the plaza, the dining room is elegant and understated.

Considered one of the best pizza joints in town, ★ **I Wanna Pizza** (Av. Niños Héroes s/n, tel. 984/281-3036, 4pm-11pm Tues.-Sun, US$8-10) lives up to the hype. Pizzas are made in a hot brick oven, with a soft-on-the-inside-crisp-on-the-outside crust and a range of toppings varying from pepperoni to red onion reduction with prosciutto, mushrooms, and feta cheese. Tables are set up on an outdoor patio with soft lighting, plastic tables, and inch-thick tree rounds for plates. Bring bug repellent—the restaurant backs into the mangrove, which can be buggy, especially in the rainy season.

There's great homemade pasta at **Los Gauchos** (Calle Tulum s/n, cell tel. 998/167-6703, 1pm-11pm Wed.-Mon., US$5-15), but don't leave without trying the empanadas: a classic Argentinean snack made of puffy, crispy fried dough stuffed with cheese, olives, or other goodies. At just US$1.50-2.50 apiece, a plate of five or six and a couple of sodas make a great cheap meal for two. Live tango is presented most Friday or Saturday nights starting around 8pm (with plenty of room to join, if you're inclined to dance).

Groceries

Casa Martín (central plaza, 6:30am-10pm daily) has a fairly large selection of canned foods, pastas, snacks, and drinks; there's also a small produce section near the back.

Every Wednesday, **fruit, vegetable, and meat stands** (Calle Tulum near Av. Javier Rojo Gómez, 7am-2pm) set up a half block from the central plaza. Prices are by the kilo.

For a bigger shopping run, head to **Super Chedraui** (Hwy. 307, 7am-11pm daily), located in front of the highway underpass. It's a traditional supermarket with a big produce section, in-house bakery, and even beach supplies.

ACCOMMODATIONS
Under US$50

Casa Cacahuate (Calle 2, Zona Urbana, tel. 998/208-9148, www.mayaecho.com, US$40 s, US$55 d, breakfast included) is a bed-and-breakfast located in Puerto Morelos's residential area on the inland side of the highway, offering a rare opportunity to experience the nontouristed side of the Riviera Maya. Homey even by bed-and-breakfast standards, the house has two tidy guest rooms upstairs and the personable owners below, with a large lush garden space. The owners maintain close ties with the community and host a popular crafts market and Jungle Spa on-site. The beach and central plaza are a bit of a hike—and that's the main drawback to staying here—but taxis are plentiful and inexpensive.

US$50-100

A 10-minute walk from the central plaza, **Hotel Edén** (Av. Andrés Quintana Roo near Calle Lázaro Cardenas, tel. 998/871-0450, www.puertomoroloseden.com, US$69 1-bdrm apartment with a/c and kitchenette) is rather more austere than its name suggests, but is a fine budget option all the same. Decent-sized one-bedroom apartments have cable TV, Wi-Fi, clean hot-water bathrooms, and small but well-equipped kitchenettes. Air-conditioning is in the bedrooms only. Weekly (US$400) and monthly (US$850) rates are also available.

Posada El Moro (Av. Javier Rojo Gómez near central plaza, tel. 998/871-0159, www.posadaelmoro.com, US$72 s/d, US$78-95 s/d with a/c and TV, US$106 suite with a/c, TV, and kitchenette) is a homey hotel with spacious units, most with polished cement floors and lots of natural light. There's Wi-Fi throughout most of the hotel, plus a pleasant little pool surrounded by hammocks and lounge chairs toward the back. Continental breakfast is included in the rate, and weekly rates are available.

★ **Rancho Sak Ol** (1 kilometer/0.6 mile south of the central plaza, tel. 998/871-0181, www.ranchosakol.com, US$93 s/d with a/c, US$99 s/d, US$145 suite, 2-night minimum) is a relaxing *palapa* hideaway located a 15-minute walk south of town. Rooms have hanging beds and private patios with hammocks. A buffet breakfast is included in the rate, and guests can use the well-stocked community kitchen. The beach here is just okay—very clean, with good snorkeling offshore, but boxed in by the cargo ferry on one side and a condo complex on the other. Still, there's enough breathing room so as not to spoil Rancho Sak Ol's quiet, isolated feel. The resort is for adults and teens only, except during the school holidays, when children over the age of three are welcome. The use of snorkel equipment and bicycles also is included in the rate.

US$100-200

★ **Layla Guesthouse** (Av. Rafaél Melgar s/n, cell tel. 998/104-9831, www.laylaguesthouse.com, US$100 studio with a/c) has two modern studios with aesthetic flair and the comforts a traveler looks for. Each opens onto a well-tended tropical garden and integrates the outdoors through skylights, a tiny interior patio with hammocks, and even an indoor/outdoor shower. Each studio has a well-equipped kitchenette, plush king-size bed, foldout sofa, flat-screen TV, and details like coffee-table books, fine art, soak shower heads, and tropical wood details. A two-bedroom apartment also is in the works. The welcoming owners, Robin and Steve, are a wealth of information on area activities and sights.

Just down the street, **Casa del Mar** (Av. Rafaél Melgar s/n, cell tel. 998/130-0968, www.lacasadelmar.com.mx, US$120 studio with a/c, US$250 penthouse, 2-night minimum) offers eight studios with a modern, airy feel—think white walls, clean lines, and splashes of color here and there. Each unit has a kitchenette and includes use of beach chairs, beach umbrellas, and bicycles. There's also a gorgeous two-bedroom penthouse with full kitchen and ocean views. A small, well-tended pool with teak lounge chairs makes for a great place to unwind. Weekly and monthly rates are also available.

Occupying a converted hacienda-style house, **Casa Caribe** (Av. Javier Rojo Gómez near Calle Lázaro Cardenas, tel. 998/251-8060, U.S. tel. 512/410-8146, www.casacaribepuertomorelos.com, US$135 s/d with or without a/c) has four bright 2nd-floor rooms with whitewashed walls, colorful paintings, and large glass doors opening onto private ocean-view terraces. They don't have air-conditioning, but between the ceiling fan and ocean breezes, you really don't miss it. (A fifth room on the ground floor has air-conditioning but no views.) Casa Caribe is home to The Little Mexican Cooking School, so naturally the rates include a full delicious breakfast, served in the hotel's interior patio-garden. Hotel/cooking class packages can be arranged; beach gear is available free of charge.

A perfect place if you're planning a longer stay, **Abbey del Sol Two** (Av. Niños Héroes s/n, tel. 998/871-0127, U.S. tel. 651/690-3937, www.abbeydelsol.com, US$99 s/d with a/c, US$157-230 1- and 2-bdrm apartments with a/c) offers nicely appointed units with king-size beds, balconies or private patios, and fully equipped kitchens (all except one). There's a small pool in the leafy garden and a rooftop patio with *palapa*-shaded hammocks. Complimentary use of bicycles also is included. If it's booked, check the website for availability in its other properties around town.

Villas Clarita (Av. Niños Héroes near Calle Benito Juárez, tel. 998/240-1762, www.villasclaritamexico.com, US$120-175 with a/c) has eight comfortable one- and two-bedroom apartments that open onto two courtyards: One courtyard has a large pool with lots of lounge chairs and tables, the other has an open-air yoga studio and shady garden. Most of the apartments have a hacienda-like feel and feature heavy wood Mexican furnishings. (The better ones open onto the garden courtyard, though families may like having an apartment right next to the pool.) All have full kitchen, air-conditioning, cable TV, Wi-Fi, purified water, and even daily maid service.

Over US$200

Dreams Riviera Cancún Resort and Spa (Hwy. 307 Km. 324, tel. 998/872-9200, toll-free U.S. tel. 866/237-3267, www.dreamsresorts.com, US$290-339 s with a/c, US$482-583 d with a/c, US$851-979 suite) is a bustling all-inclusive resort north of downtown Puerto Morelos. Aesthetically, it has a South Pacific feel with airy rooms that feature tropical woods and bamboo accents. The amenities are high-end and luxurious. Outside there are lots of pools and a long, wide beach with plenty of places to relax (no need to get up at 6am to save a spot!). Nine restaurants and a wide variety of activities round out the resort nicely, providing enough options to keep most people happy during their stay.

Located south of town, **Hotel Marina El Cid Spa & Beach Resort** (Blvd. El Cid Unidad 15, tel. 998/872-8999, toll-free U.S. tel. 888/733-7308, www.elcid.com, US$336 s with a/c, US$400 d with a/c, US$481-495 suite, US$542 1-bdrm apartment) is Puerto Morelos's first all-inclusive resort—a milestone that didn't please everyone in this tightly knit town. The resort gets high marks from families though, with a kids club, waterslide, and manageable size, though the beach is smallish. There is a full-service spa on-site—including beachfront massage tables—as well as a great gym with floor-to-ceiling windows facing the Caribbean. Rooms have modern, tasteful decor and lots of natural light; ask for one in building 21, 22, or 23—these were inaugurated in 2014 and have even more updated and luxurious amenities (not to mention views over a new infinity pool).

The adults-only **Excellence Riviera Maya** (Hwy. 307 Km. 324, toll-free U.S. tel. 866/540-2585, www.excellence-resorts.com, US$380-430 s with a/c, US$516-618 d with a/c) is a rambling resort located north of town. The size can be overwhelming, but it gets points for the number of options it provides: eight restaurants, six pools, an expansive beach area, a sports center, a spa, and an entertainment complex. The rooms themselves are modern and comfortable, with king-size beds, whirlpool tubs, and private patios or balconies. This is a great choice if you're traveling with a group—given the number of options here, there's something for almost everyone.

INFORMATION AND SERVICES

Although this town sees a good number of tourists, the services remain somewhat sparse.

Emergency Services

Médica Puerto Morelos (Calle Ignacio López Rayón, Zona Urbana, tel. 998/251-1478 or 998/201-2456, 24 hours) is the small but well-equipped medical office of Dr. Víctor Ballestros, a Mexico City-trained surgeon and general practitioner. Look for signs leading to his office along the access road, near the highway. English is spoken.

Centro de Salud (no phone, 8am-2pm and 4pm-6pm daily) is south of the plaza, on an unmarked connector street between Avenidas Javier Rojo Gómez and Rafaél Melgar.

Farmacia San José Obrero (central plaza, Av. Javier Rojo Gómez, tel. 998/871-0053, 8am-2pm and 4pm-10pm daily) is a mom-and-pop pharmacy selling basic meds and toiletries.

The **police station** (central plaza, Av. Javier Rojo Gómez) can be reached toll-free at 066.

Money

There is no bank in Puerto Morelos, but there are three **ATMs**—an HSBC one in front of Casa Martín, a Santander ATM in front of the police station, and a Banco Norte ATM inside the OXXO mini-mart on the west corner of the central plaza.

Media and Communications

Play.net C@fé (Av. Javier Rojo Gómez s/n, no phone, 9am-9pm daily, US$3/hour) is located just off the central plaza. And like many Mexican towns, there's **free Wi-Fi** (24 hours) in the central plaza.

Laundry

The bustling **LavaPlus** (Av. Niños Héroes s/n, cell tel. 998/198-4850, 8am-8pm daily) charges US$1.15 per kilo (2.2 pounds). For service in five hours, the rate jumps to US$1.40 per kilo. Coin-operated machines are also available.

Language and Instruction

Puerto Morelos Language Center (Av. Niños Héroes 46, tel. 998/871-0162, www.puertomorelosspanishcenter.com) has a variety of Spanish language course for all levels of students. Courses are taught by native Spanish speakers trained to teach Spanish as a second language. Classes are limited to five students and range 1-12 weeks; fees range US$100-240 per week depending on the course. Private instruction also is available for US$25 per hour. Weekly activities like Latin dance classes, social hours, and area excursions are offered. Homestays also can be arranged with local families.

December-May, **Chumuk Kanbal Learning Center** (Layla Guesthouse, Av. Rafaél Melgar s/n, cell tel. 998/104-9831, www.laylaguesthouse.com, US$5) offers weekly lectures covering diverse regional topics such as Maya history, the Caste War, marine biology, and local ecology. Speakers are experts in their respective fields. Lectures are held in a casual outdoor setting on Monday at 7pm with offerings in English and Spanish. Buddhist meditation classes—both practice and theory—also are offered on Tuesday at 7pm.

If you'll be in town for a longer period of time, **Casa de Cultura de Puerto Morelos** (Av. Niños Héroes s/n, cell tel. 998/150-2857, www.casaculturapuertomorelos.mx.tl) has multiweek courses and workshops that are open to all. Courses include theater, yoga for kids, capoeira, and *danza folkorica* (traditional Mexican dance).

GETTING THERE AND AROUND

Puerto Morelos is almost exactly halfway between Cancún (36 kilometers/22 miles, 40 minutes driving) and Playa del Carmen (35 kilometers/21 miles, 35 minutes). The Cancún airport is closer, just 18 kilometers (11 miles, 20 minutes) north of Puerto Morelos. A rental car isn't really necessary around town, but makes exploring the Riviera Maya beyond Puerto Morelos significantly easier.

Europcar (Calle Tulum near Av. Javier Rojo Gómez s/n, tel. 998/206-9372, www.europcar.com.mx, 8am-6pm daily) has a small office just off the main plaza, making it the most convenient option for renting a car. Otherwise, Cancún airport has a large number of agencies, and you can often find excellent deals online.

Bus

ADO buses pass the Puerto Morelos turnoff on Highway 307 but do not enter town. The northbound stop is right at the turnoff, while the southbound bus stop is across the highway and a block south. Headed north to Cancún (US$1.75-3.25, 45 minutes) or south to Playa del Carmen (US$1.50-6.25, 35 minutes), second-class buses and *combis* (shared vans) pass every 10-15 minutes 5:30am-10pm daily, and less frequently throughout the night. A handful continue to Tulum, but it may be quicker to go to Playa and transfer. Buses to the Cancún airport (US$7, 25 minutes) pass roughly every 30-60 minutes 7:55am-8:45pm daily. Buy your ticket a day in advance, as buses often fill in Playa del Carmen.

Taxi

Taxis line up day and night at the taxi stand on the northwest corner of the central plaza. Prices are fixed and prominently displayed on a signboard at the taxi stand. A ride to the highway or the ADO bus stops costs around US$2.

Bicycle

Puerto Morelos Green Bikes (Av. Niños Héroes s/n, tel. 998/734-8132, ride@greenbikesrentals.com, US$10 per 24 hours) rents comfortable bikes that include a basket, a lock, a rear rack, blinking lights, and a bell. Email or check them out on Facebook.

Another good option is the dive shop **Diverspoint** (Av. Javier Rojo Gómez s/n, tel. 998/206-9051, www.diverspoint.com), which rents bicycles for US$2 per hour, US$10 per 24 hours, and US$40 per week.

PUNTA BETE AND PLAYA XCALACOCO

It used to be that the only way to find Punta Bete and its main beach, Playa Xcalacoco, was to look for the big Cristal water plant. That's still the best landmark, but a flurry of new construction, and renovation of existing locations, has prompted hoteliers to finally add signs along the highway as well. The beach here is decent—the sand is clean but coarse, and the shoreline rocky in places—but the snorkeling is good, and the isolation has always been a big plus. It's still a quiet place, but all the new development—including a huge condo complex—may mark a new chapter for this long-overlooked stretch of beach.

Food

Coco's Cabañas (Hwy. 307 Km. 296, cell tel. 998/185-7798, www.cocoscabanas.com, 8:30am-8pm daily, US$6-18) has a small outdoor bar and restaurant that specializes in wood-oven pizzas, though there are lots of seafood dishes as well. It's a bit pricey for the location, but then again you don't often see prosciutto, arugula, and Brie pizza around here.

Accommodations

★ **Hotel Petit Lafitte** (Hwy. 307 Km. 296, tel. 984/877-4000, www.petitlafitte. com, US$189-208 s with a/c, US$214-256 d with a/c, US$231-277 s bungalow with a/c, US$265-311 d bungalow with a/c) offers the comfort of a full-scale hotel on this isolated stretch of beach, including a large pool, plenty of lounge space, and a well-maintained beach area with *palapas* and hammocks. Accommodations are either in the main building, where all the rooms have at least partial ocean views, or in spacious beachfront bungalows. All accommodations have one or two beds, cable TV, air-conditioning, minibar, and Wi-Fi.

Owned by a Mexican-Swiss couple, **Coco's Cabañas** (Hwy. 307 Km. 296, cell tel. 998/185-7798, www.cocoscabanas.com, US$90-110 s/d with a/c, US$130 suite with kitchenette) has a handful of charming *palapa*-roofed bungalows on a small garden plot. The *cabañas* are comfortable and attractive, with large paintings and artful stonework, plus patios with hammocks. The suites have kitchenettes, too. There's a heart-shaped pool next to the open-air restaurant and bar, and the beach is just 30 meters (100 feet) away.

Getting There and Around

From the highway, follow the access road two kilometers (1.2 miles) until it forks at the Viceroy Riviera Maya resort. Bear left to reach the listed hotels and beach.

There is no taxi stand in this tiny community; when guests need one, hotels call cabs from Playa del Carmen or Puerto Morelos. A ride to the airport costs around US$50, to Playa del Carmen US$10.

Playa del Carmen

Playa del Carmen (or Playa for short) has long been a favorite among travelers looking for an alternative to Cancún, a place where boutique hotels and lounge bars outnumber glitzy high-rises and all-night clubs. There also are more opportunities for tourists and locals to interact in Playa, and it's easier to find "authentic" Mexican outlets, especially compared to Cancún's Zona Hotelera. And while Cancún is an American playground, Playa attracts many more Europeans, especially Italians.

But Playa is no longer the small seaside town many remember. Its population has exploded in recent years, with tourist and residential development stretching farther and farther up the coast every year. The main tourist strip, Quinta Avenida (5th Avenue) is still mostly pedestrian, but walking from end to end is no longer the casual jaunt it once was; a bike path along 10 Avenida is a smart and welcome addition. And while lounge bars and beach clubs are still the mainstay of Playa's nightlife, the opening of nightclubs like Coco Bongo Playa, an offshoot of the famous Cancún club, has fanned fears of

an impending "Cancúnification" of Playa del Carmen.

Playa still has plenty of small hotels, hipster bars, and boho charm, and remains a genuine alternative to Cancún. It's got stellar beaches, and the atmosphere remains decidedly mellow, even with all the changes. Playa's location also makes it a convenient base from which to explore the rest of the Riviera Maya and Yucatán Peninsula, whether snorkeling in cenotes, diving on Isla Cozumel, or visiting inland Maya ruins.

SIGHTS AND BEACHES
★ Quinta Avenida

Playa's main pedestrian and commercial drag is Quinta Avenida, or 5th Avenue, which stretches more than 20 blocks from the ferry dock northward. Pronounced KEEN-ta av-en-EE-da, you may see it written as 5 Avenida or 5a Avenida, which is akin to "5th" in English. The southern section, especially near the ferry dock, is packed with typical tourist traps: souvenir shops, chain restaurants, etc. North of Calle 12, and even farther past Avenida

Playa's Quinta Avenida has it all, from fine dining and boho shops to open-air bars and tourist traps.

Playa del Carmen

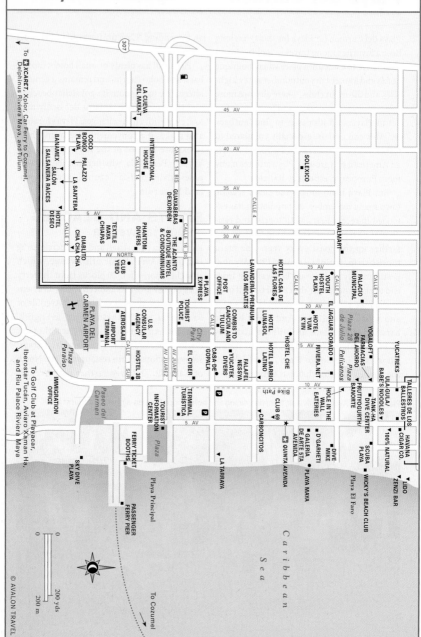

To XCARET, Xplor, Car Ferry to Cozumel,
Dolphinus Riviera Maya, and Tulum.

307

45 AV

40 AV

35 AV

CALLE 4

30 AV

30 AV

25 AV

WALMART

SOLEXICO

LA CUEVA DEL MAYA-T

CALLE 14 BIS

CALLE 14

5 AV

CALLE 16 BIS

CALLE 12

INTERNATIONAL HOUSE

COCO BONGO PLAYA

PALAZZO

LA SANTERA

BANAMEX SALON
SALSANERA RAICES

GUAYABERAS
DEXORDEN

THE ACANTO
BOUTIQUE HOTEL
& CONDOMINIUMS

PHANTOM DIVERS

TEXTILE MAYA CHIAPAS

HOTEL DESEO

DIABLITO CHA CHA CHA

CLUB YEBO

1 AV NORTE

HOTEL CASA DE LAS FLORES

CALLE 8

CALLE 6

CALLE 10

PALACIO MUNICIPAL

YOGALOFT
FARMACIAS
DEL AHORRO

Plaza 28
de Julio

Plaza
Pelicanos

YUCATREKS
ULA-GULA
BABE'S NOODLES

TANK-HA
DIVE CENTER

FRUTIYOGURTH/
BANORTE

TALLERES DE LOS
BALLESTEROS

HAVANA
CIGAR CO.

100% NATURAL

LIDO

ZENZI BAR

SCUBA
PLAYA

WICKY'S BEACH CLUB

Playa El Faro

LAVANDERIA PREMIUM
LOS MECATES

PLAYA EXPRESS

POST OFFICE

TOURIST POLICE

CALLE 2

City Park

PLAYA DEL CARMEN AIRPORT

Plaza Paraiso

U.S. CONSULAR AGENCY

AEROSAAB
AIRPORT TERMINAL

AV JUAREZ

CALLE 1 SUR

HOSTEL 3B

EL CYBER

CASA DE GOPALA

COMBIS TO CANCÚN AND TULUM

HOTEL LUNASOL

YUM K'IIN

HOTEL RIVIERA.NET

EL JAGUAR DORADO

YOUTH HOSTEL PLAYA

20 AV

15 AV

HOTEL CHE

YUCATEK DIVERS

FALAFEL NESSYA

HOTEL BARRIO LATINO

HOSTEL LATINO

Bike Path

10 AV

HOLE IN THE WALL
EATERIES

DIVE MIKE

D'GARNETI

GALERIA DE ARTE 5TA AVENIDA

PLAYA MAYA

DIVE MIKE

To Golf Club at Playacar,
Iberostar Tucán, Aviaro Xaman Ha,
and Riu Palace Riviera Maya

Paseo del Carmen

IMMIGRATION OFFICE

TOURIST INFORMATION CENTER

TERMINAL TURISTICA

Plaza

FERRY TICKET BOOTHS

PASSENGER FERRY PIER

SKY DIVE PLAYA

Playa Principal

EL CYBER

5 AV

CLUB 69

CARBONCITOS

QUINTA AVENIDA

CARBONCITOS

LA TARRAYA

Caribbean Sea

To Cozumel

0   200 yds
0   200 m

© AVALON TRAVEL

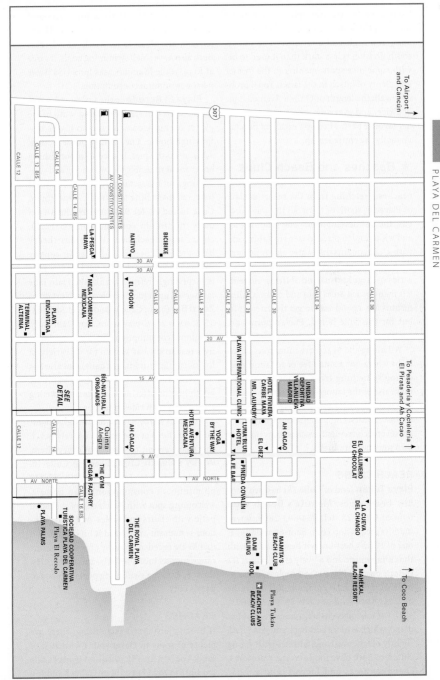

To Airport
and Cancún

307

CALLE 12
CALLE 12 BIS
CALLE 14
AV CONSTITUYENTES
AV CONSTITUYENTES
LA PESCA MAYA
NATIVO
BICIBIKE
CALLE 14 BIS
30 AV
30 AV
MEGA COMERCIAL MEXICANA
EL FOGÓN
CALLE 20
CALLE 22
CALLE 24
CALLE 26
CALLE 28
CALLE 30
CALLE 34
CALLE 38
PLAYA ENCANTADA
TERMINAL ALTERNA
20 AV
15 AV
BIO-NATURAL ORGANICS
SEE DETAIL
Quinta Alegra
AH CACAO
PLAYA INTERNATIONAL CLINIC
HOTEL RIVIERA CARIBE MAYA
MR. LAUNDRY
UNIDAD DEPORTIVA VILLANUEVA MADRID
To Pesadería y Coctelería
El Pirata and Ah Cacao
HOTEL AVENTURA MEXICANA
YOGA BY THE WAY
LUNA BLUE HOTEL
PINEDA COVALIN
LA FE BAR
EL DIEZ
AH CACAO
EL GALLINERO DU CHOCOLAT
5 AV
CALLE 12
CALLE 14
THE GYM
CIGAR FACTORY
1 AV NORTE
1 AV NORTE
LA CUEVA DEL CHANGO
SOCIEDAD COOPERATIVA TURISTICA PLAYA DEL CARMEN
Playa El Recodo
PLAYA PALMS
CALLE 16 BIS
THE ROYAL PLAYA DEL CARMEN
DANI SAILING
MAMITA'S BEACH CLUB
KOOL
Playa Tukán
BEACHES AND BEACH CLUBS
MAHEKAL BEACH RESORT
To Coco Beach

Constituyentes, the atmosphere is somewhat more sophisticated, with more bistros, cool bars, and high-end boutiques. The north-south division is less stark than it used to be, with some nice spots opening in the former and plenty of kitsch in the latter. You'll probably walk the length of Quinta Avenida once or twice, and everyone seems to find his or her favorite part. There are excellent beaches virtually the entire length.

★ Beaches and Beach Clubs

Playa del Carmen is blessed with gorgeous beaches stretching from the resort enclave of Playacar, south of town, all the way north past the last development. The sand is thick and white, and in places dozens of yards wide, with clear aquamarine water and mild surf. It's a change from several years ago, when a series of large storms and shifting currents left many beach areas thin and rocky. Online forums are a good way to get the latest info, but for the time being, Playa's *playas* are spectacular.

All along the beach are numerous beach clubs where, for a small fee or for simply ordering something from the menu, you can make use of the lounge chairs, umbrellas, restrooms, even swimming pools and changing rooms. If beach clubs aren't your thing, there are several convenient beaches to lay out your own towel and umbrella.

BEACH CLUBS

Playa Tukán (end of Calle 28) has two popular beach clubs. **Mamita's Beach Club** (end of Calle 28, tel. 984/803-2868, www.mamitasbeachclub.com, 8am-6pm daily) is one of Playa's best-known beach clubs, with thumping music and a lively atmosphere. It's the one place in Playa where topless sunbathing is permitted and common. Just down the beach is **Kool** (end of Calle 28, tel. 984/803-1961, www.koolbeachclub.com.mx, 8am-6pm daily), which is more laid-back and good for a slightly older crowd and families with young children. Both have food service, restrooms, changing areas and lockers, and similar

prices: around US$3 apiece for chairs and umbrellas, US$15-25 for beach beds and large *palapas*, and US$5-15 for snacks and drinks. Both also have small swimming pools; it's free at Kool, while Mamita's asks for a US$13 per person minimum consumption.

Playa El Recodo is the little-used name for the stretch of sand stretching south of the pier at Avenue Constituyentes to Playa's historic lighthouse. The northernmost section, adjacent to the pier, is used to moor fishing boats and is unusable for swimming and sunbathing, but the rest is gorgeous and benefits from relatively little foot traffic. **Lido** (btwn Calle 10 and 12, tel. 984/803-1090, 8am-8pm daily, minimum consumption US$12.50, chairs free, beach beds US$8) has cheery lime-green umbrellas and faces an equally smile-inducing beach. The food service here is surprisingly refined, unlike the Plain Jane fair served up at most beach clubs. Next door, **Zenzi Bar** (btwn Calle 10 and 12, tel. 983/803-5738, www.zenzi-playa.com, 8am-2am daily, minimum consumption US$18 pp) is primarily a restaurant-bar known for its variety of live music (5pm-midnight daily), but also has umbrellas and beach beds for rent. Nearby are beach booths offering massages, snorkeling trips, catamaran rides, and more.

Playa El Faro, named for the large lighthouse (or *faro*) at one end, is a lovely beach that's convenient to just about everywhere. **Wicky's Beach Club** (Beach at Calle 10, tel. 984/873-3541, 7am-11pm daily, US$13 pp minimum consumption) is an upscale, welcoming spot with beach chairs, a shaded patio with chairs and tables, and a large indoor restaurant area. Food is hit or miss, but drinks are excellent. Nearby operators can arrange snorkel tours, Jet Skis, and more. Alas, the very enticing swimming pool is for condo guests only.

BEACHES

If beach clubs aren't your thing, there are plenty of spots to claim your own patch of sand. The best are **Playa Tukán** (end of Calle 28) and **Playa El Faro** (btwn Calles 8 and 16);

while both have beach clubs, they also boast long lovely stretches of open sand and are popular with independent travelers and locals. Note that Playa Tukán is popular with Europeans, and topless sunbathing is not uncommon. Another option, if you don't mind the walk (or taxi or bike ride), is **Coco Beach;** located between Calles 38 and 46, it's ideal for lying out on your towel, listening to the waves, and chilling out. And just north of there is **Chunzubul Reef,** one of Playa's best spots for snorkeling.

★ Xcaret

Just five kilometers (3.1 miles) south of Playa, **Xcaret** (Hwy. 307 Km. 282, tel. 984/206-0038, toll-free Mex. tel. 800/292-2738, www.xcaret.com.mx, 8:30am-9:30pm daily, US$99/49.50 adult/child, US$129/64.50 adult/child including buffet and snorkeling equipment) is a mega-ecopark offering water activities like snorkeling in underground rivers and swimming with dolphins and sharks; up-close animal viewing areas including jaguar and puma islands, a butterfly pavilion, and an aquarium; a phenomenal folk art museum that's brimming with *artesanía* from around Mexico; and spectacular shows, like a Maya ball game, regional dances, and music performances.

Xcaret is thoroughly touristy and pre-packaged, yes, but also surprisingly well done and a worthwhile day trip, especially for families. There are numerous packages and prices, including combo visits with sister parks **Xplor** and **Xel-Há;** be sure you know what you're getting (and not getting) when you book. Discounts are available for booking online.

Xplor

One of the youngest of Xcaret company's family of ecoparks, **Xplor** (Hwy. 307 Km. 282, tel. 984/803-4403, toll-free Mex. tel. 800/009-7567, www.xplor.travel, 9am-5pm daily, US$139/69.50 adult/child) is adjacent to the mother ship and focused on adventure activities. The park has a zipline circuit with 14 segments, including tandem lines and a splashdown in the mouth of a cavern. Other activities include swimming and rafting through caverns bristling with stalactites, and driving amphibious ATVs through the forest and underground passages. Admission includes lockers, showers, buffet lunch, and fresh-made juices and smoothies. Xplor also offers evening-only admission (5:30pm-10:30pm daily, US$99/49.50 adult/child), with colored lights and torches lighting up the park and its activities, adding an additional rush.

Traditional Maya costumes and dancing are part of the end-of-the-day extravaganza at Xcaret.

Aviario Xaman Ha

A short distance inside the Playacar entrance off 10 Avenida, the small bird sanctuary **Aviario Xaman Ha** (Paseo Xaman Ha s/n, tel. 984/873-0593, 9am-5pm daily, US$25 adult, child under 12 free) is home, or a stopover, for more than 60 species of tropical birds, including toucans, flamingos, cormorants, and parrots. Some birds are in enclosures, but many are not, and a stone path meanders through the leafy grounds. It's a pleasant place to spend an hour, though the admission price is ridiculously inflated. If you do go, be sure to bring bug repellent.

ENTERTAINMENT

Playa del Carmen's nightlife has long been dominated by bars and lounges, as if deliberately leaving the raucous clubs and discotheques to Cancún. While that's still mostly the case, Playa is definitely getting rowdier, with several major nightclubs and the increasingly boisterous cluster of club-like bars at the corner of 1 Avenida and Calle 12.

Lounges and Bars

With retro tables and armchairs, low beats, and even lower lights, **Diablito Cha Cha Cha** (1 Av. at Calle 12, tel. 984/803-3416, 7pm-3am daily) is certainly one of the most stylish of the bars in this up-and-coming area. Order anything under the sun from the bar, and munch on unlikely Mexican-Japanese fusion snacks and meals.

A **cluster of small bars** (5pm-2am daily) on 5 Avenida between Calles 26 and 30 make it an easy area to wander over to after dinner. Among several worth checking out are **La Fe Bar,** the *mezcalería* **Rufino, Santa Remedio,** the Brazilian-style **La Choperia,** and **La Casa del Hábano,** a cigar shop by day and cocktails and hookah joint at night.

At sunset, the 2nd-floor patio at **Hotel Deseo** (5 Av. at Calle 12, tel. 984/879-3620, www.hoteldeseo.com, 5pm-2am daily) transforms into a sleek lounge, with DJs spinning urban beats and a reliable crowd of local and foreign hipsters. A candlelit stone stairway leads from the street to the open-air terrace, where a long swimming pool is surrounded by queen-size cushions and billowing curtains. There's food service until midnight, and the poolside bar stirs up creative cocktails.

Nightclubs

Coco Bongo Playa (Av. 10 at Calle 12, tel. 984/803-5939, toll-free U.S. tel. 800/841-4636, www.cocobongo.com.mx, 10:30pm-3:30am Mon.-Sat., US$60-65 including open bar) is a satellite of the famous nightclub in Cancún. Like the original, Coco Bongo Playa features a slew of celebrity impersonations, from Elvis to Rihanna, plus acrobats, light shows, and multiple DJs to keep everyone dancing. The space here is fairly small, but the crowds can be huge and boisterous—tons of fun, assuming you're not claustrophobic. Check Facebook for current promos, and with your hotel concierge about VIP tickets and party-hopper tours; shows begin at 11:30pm.

There are two more clubs nearby, which either benefit from or are overshadowed by the crowds amassing outside Coco Bongo. Directly next door to Coco Bongo is another Cancún offshoot, **Palazzo** (Av. 10 at Calle 12, tel. 984/803-0730, www.palazzodisco.com, 10:30pm-3:30am Tues.-Sun., US$45-55), a sister club to The City and Palazzo Cancún in the Zona Hotelera. It offers a somewhat more traditional techno nightclub scene, while aiming to inject old-school glamour through its decor and image. Across the street, **La Santanera** (Av. 10 at Calle 12, tel. 984/803-2856, www.lasantanera.com, 11pm-7am daily, US$4) has an edgier ambience and a host of "resident DJs." Check out the rooftop lounge bar for a change of scenery (music and otherwise). It's especially popular in the wee hours of the night, after partiers have hit other places.

One of Playa's only gay clubs, **Club 69** (off 5 Av. between Calles 4 and 6, tel. 984/876-9466, 9pm-6am Tues.-Sun.) doesn't get interesting until after 1am, and sometimes later. There are regular drag shows and exotic dancers, and, of course, music and dancing. Drinks are so-so and the place could use a good scrub, but it's not bad considering Playa's slim pickings for gay travelers. The entrance is easy to miss—look for the 7-Eleven mini-mart on the west side of Quinta Avenida, then follow the rainbow sign down an alley. If the club is super slow, check out **La Cueva del Maya-T** (Calle 1 Bis btwn 40 and 45 Avs., tel. 984/803-0186, 9pm-6am Tues.-Sun., US$4), a new gay bar with a strikingly similar theme—drag shows and exotic dancers—that caters to locals.

Salón Salsanera Raíces (Calle 12 btwn 5 and 10 Avs., cell tel. 984/128-2854, 9:30pm-5am Tues.-Sun, US$11) is a hot new salsa club with live bands featured every night. Come strut your stuff on the open-air dance floor or learn a few new moves during the free salsa lessons at 9:30pm and 10:30pm. Drink specials are often offered on Tuesday and Thursday nights (mojitos, mostly).

SHOPPING

Playa del Carmen offers some of the best shopping on the Riviera Maya, and Quinta Avenida is (mostly) where it's at. Here you'll find numerous souvenir shops, from small to gargantuan, open all day every day. For something more unique, try the following stores.

Artesanía

D'Garheti (5 Av. btwn 6 and 8 Avs., tel. 984/803-1370, www.dgarheti.com, 10am-11pm daily) is a two-story boutique selling gorgeous Mexican handicrafts from around the country. Items include Oaxacan pottery, amber and silver jewelry from central Mexico, hand-embroidered shawls from Chiapas, sculptures from Jalisco, leather bags from the northern states—a true representation of works of everyday art produced throughout Mexico.

Textile Maya Chiapas (5 Av. near Calle 14, no phone, 9am-2am daily) is a huge open-air shop bursting with colorful handicrafts from Chiapas. Piles of handwoven blankets and runners, baskets of handmade wool toys, shelves upon shelves of embroidered clothing, countless traditional garments hanging from the rafters—the abundance and the quality are breathtaking. Prices are fair (and fixed).

Pineda Covalín (5 Av. btwn Calle 26 and 28, no phone, www.pinedacovalin.com, 10am-11pm daily) has gorgeous high-end accessories, including purses, scarves, and wallets, made from silk and other luxurious fabrics printed with traditional Mexican and indigenous images. This is the largest Pineda Covalín store in the Riviera Maya, with

Textiles make a memorable souvenir—and are easy to get home!

smaller displays in the Cancún and Cozumel airports.

Just two blocks from Quinta Avenida, and well worth veering off the beaten path, **El Jaguar Dorado** (Calle 8 btwn 10 and 15 Avs., cell tel. 984/147-2705, www.eljaguardorado. com, 10am-1pm and 5pm-10pm Mon.-Sat.) sells whimsical and unique art and textiles. Many of the objects are made on-site; others have been created by cooperatives of artists from the Yucatán and Chiapas. You'll find embroidered masks, handmade dolls, lithographs, T-shirts, bags, and more.

Specialty Items

Opening onto a leafy courtyard, **Galería de Arte 5ta Avenida** (5 Av. near Calle 6, tel. 984/879-3389, www.galerialaquinta.com, 10am-10pm daily) is a collection of about a dozen galleries featuring modern art paintings, sculptures, and wood carvings inspired by Mexican culture and traditions. Items are by no means cheap, but can be quite special.

Guayaberas Dexorden (Calle 16 Bis btwn 1 and 5 Avs., cell tel. 984/131-7204, www. dexorden.com, noon-9pm daily) specializes in high-end *guayaberas,* classic button-down shirts worn by men in Latin America and the Caribbean. The shop has a wide variety of styles and sizes, and is known for its knowledgeable staff.

Though pricey, **Talleres de los Ballestros** (5 Av. btwn. Calles 10 and 12, cell tel. 984/149-2530, www.ballesteros.net, 9am-11pm daily) is a well-respected silver shop selling gorgeous items from Taxco, Mexico's silver capital. Jewelry and home decor figure prominently. For more options, check out the like-named **sister shop,** located in the Paseo del Carmen mall (tel. 984/803-3939, 10am-10pm daily). Light haggling is welcome at both stores.

With workers rolling cigars at the front of the store, it's tough to walk by **Cigar Factory** (5 Av. at Calle 16, no phone, 9am-11pm daily) without taking a second look. Inside you'll find a good variety of Cuban and Mexican *puros* sold individually (US$7-17) or by the box (US$60-450). If you don't find what you're looking for, head down Quinta Avenida to **Havana Cigar Co.** (5 Av. btwn Calles 10 and 12, tel. 984/803-1047, 9am-11pm daily) for a different selection of stogies.

Shopping Centers

At the southern end of Quinta Avenida, **Paseo del Carmen** (5 Av. at Calle 1, no phone, 10am-10pm daily) is a shady outdoor shopping center with high-end clothing boutiques, jewelry stores, art galleries, and restaurants. Its series of modern fountains make it an especially pleasant place to window-shop or enjoy a nice lunch after a morning at the beach.

Toward the other end of the pedestrian walkway, the newly constructed **Quinta Alegria** (5 Av. at Av. Constituyentes, tel. 984/803-2358, www.quintaalegria.com.mx, 10am-11pm daily) is an airy and verdant three-story shopping center with big-name shops like Nike, Levi's, Victoria's Secret, Forever 21, Bebe, and, of course, Starbucks. Not exactly a slice of Mexico but a pretty place to shop nonetheless.

SPORTS AND RECREATION
Scuba Diving

Playa del Carmen has decent offshore diving—virtually all drift dives, thanks to prevailing currents—and relatively easy access to Cozumel and inland cenotes. It's a logical base if you want a taste of all three, plus the convenience of being in a major town. However, if diving is the main reason you came, consider basing yourself on Cozumel itself, or closer to the cenotes, such as at Akumal or Tulum. This will save you the time, money, and effort of going back and forth.

Diving prices in Playa del Carmen are reasonable, and fairly uniform from shop to shop. Two-tank reef dives cost US$65-80, Cozumel trips run US$80-135, cenote trips are around US$110-160, and open-water certification courses run US$390-430. Gear is included in the courses but may be charged separately for fun dives (US$15-20/day). Most shops do not include the price of taking the ferry to Cozumel (US$25 round-trip), and additional fees, like marine park and cenote admissions, may also apply.

Tank-Ha Dive Center (Calle 10 btwn 5 and 10 Avs., tel. 984/873-0302, www.tankha. com, 8am-10pm daily) is one of the longest-operating shops in Playa and a PADI Gold Palm resort and instructor training facility.

Dive Mike (Calle 8 btwn 5 Av. and the beach, tel. 984/803-1228, www.divemike. com, 7am-9pm daily) is a very friendly, professional, and reasonably priced shop. Check out its excellent website for additional info and pictures.

Phantom Divers (1 Av. Norte at Calle 14, tel. 984/879-3988, www.phantomdivers.com, 8am-8pm Mon.-Sat., 8am-7pm Sun.) is one of a handful of locally owned dive shops offering lower-than-average prices.

Yucatek Divers (15 Av. btwn Calles 2 and 4, tel. 984/803-2836, www.yucatek-divers.com, 7:30am-5pm daily) is a longtime shop with instruction available in several languages. Notably, all fun dives are led by instructors.

Scuba Playa (Calle 10 btwn 1 and 5 Avs., tel. 984/803-3123, www.scubaplaya.com, 8am-8pm daily) specializes in small groups and offers a six-dive package that includes two tanks apiece in Cozumel, the cenotes, and the reef.

Snorkeling

In Playa itself it's best to go snorkeling with a boat tour, since the snorkeling off the beach isn't too rewarding. There are also numerous cenotes near Playa that make for unique snorkeling, including several you can visit on your own.

Most of Playa's dive shops offer guided snorkeling tours to excellent sites. Ocean trips cost US$40-50, while cenote trips are US$60-70, all gear included. Be sure to clarify how many reefs or cenotes you'll be visiting and for how long. A wetsuit is strongly recommended, even if it means paying extra to rent one. Cenotes can be quite cold, while sunburn is a serious concern in the open ocean; wetsuits

protect against both, as well as against accidental scrapes and cuts.

Dani Sailing (Calle 28 near the beach, cell tel. 984/136-3363, www.danisailing.com, 9am-5pm daily) offers fun catamaran trips (US$65) with an hour spent sailing and another hour snorkeling. Or rent snorkel gear (US$11.50/hour) and a kayak or stand-up paddleboard (US$23/hour) and find a spot of your own. Instruction is available. Look for the small shop where Calle 28 hits the beach.

Sociedad Cooperativa Turística Playa del Carmen (Playa El Recodo, end of Calle 14, no phone, 7am-6pm daily) is a local fisherman's cooperative offering snorkeling tours from a kiosk on the beach (US$35/50 pp for one/two sites).

Wind Sports

Kiteboarding, sailboarding, and sailing have grown in popularity along the Caribbean, a trickle-down effect from the world-famous wind belt on the Gulf coast. You can catch at least some breeze almost any time of the year, but the strongest, most consistent winds blow November-March.

Dani Sailing (Calle 28 near the beach, cell tel. 984/136-3363, www.danisailing.com, 9am-5pm daily) offers catamaran rentals and tours, with or without snorkeling, as well as kiteboarding rentals and instruction. Prices vary.

Arguably a wind sport, **Sociedad Cooperativa Turística Playa del Carmen** (Playa El Recodo, end of Calle 14, no phone, 7am-6pm daily) offers parasailing—either single or double seated. Rides last 12-15 minutes (US$60 pp).

Ikarus (tel. 984/871-0748, www.kiteboardmexico.com) is the region's first full-service kiteboarding school. Once based in Playa, it now only offers classes off Isla Blanca, in the massive flat-water Chacmochuch Lagoon north of Cancún; the location is ideal for kiting but is nearly two hours by car from Playa del Carmen (and around three hours by public transportation, if you time it right). Ikarus offers simple, clean lodging on Isla Blanca (US$8 hammock, US$8 pp tent, US$55 s/d); there's also an on-site restaurant. Private classes are US$83 per hour or US$450 for six hours, while groups are US$65 per hour per person (maximum 3 to a group) or US$350 for six hours. Equipment is included for students or can be rented separately (US$65-95/day). Classes are mainly held November-June, when the conditions are best.

Stand-Up Paddling and Kayaking

Stand Up Paddle Playa del Carmen (cell tel. 984/168-0387, www.suppdc.com) is a one-man operation offering hour-long lessons for US$65 (US$50 pp for 2 people) at the beach nearest you, with an hour's free rental afterward to practice your skills. There's no fixed storefront, so reservations are recommended; otherwise, look for SUP gear near the pier at Avenida Constituyentes or near Fusion beach bar (end of Calle 6). Rental gear is available (US$30/hour, US$80/halfday).

Do-it-all beach sports outfit **Dani Sailing** (Calle 28 near the beach, cell tel. 984/136-3363, www.danisailing.com, 9am-5pm daily) rents kayaks (US$18/hour single, US$23/hour double) and stand-up paddleboards (US$23/hour). Hour-long instructional courses (US$25) are available for anyone new to "SUPing."

Sociedad Cooperativa Turística Playa del Carmen (Playa El Recodo, end of Calle 14, no phone, 7am-6pm daily) also rents stand-up paddleboards for US$25 per hour.

Swimming with Dolphins

With swimming pens set up in the ocean, **Delphinus Riviera Maya** (Hwy. 307 Km. 282, tel. 998/206-3304, toll-free Mex. tel. 800/212-9071, toll-free U.S./Can. tel. 888/526-2230, www.delphinus.com.mx, US$89-399) is about as good as it gets for performing dolphins. There are various packages, from 30-minute group interactions to hour-long one-on-one encounters. Check the website for complete descriptions, photos, and a 15 percent discount for booking online. Prices are a

There's a stand-up paddleboard waiting for you in the Riviera Maya.

bit higher at Delphinus Riviera Maya, mainly because round-trip transportation is included.

Sportfishing

Playa de Carmen has excellent sportfishing and bottom fishing, with plentiful wahoo, dorado, mackerel, snapper, barracuda, and—especially April-June—sailfish and marlin. Trips depend mostly on the size and power of the boat that's used, but a 4-5-hour trip for 1-4 people usually costs US$240-300, including tackle and drinks. Many dive shops offer tours, as does **Sociedad Cooperativa Turística Playa del Carmen** (Playa El Recodo, end of Calle 14, no phone, 7am-6pm daily).

Golf

The **Golf Club at Playacar** (Paseo Xaman-Há s/n, toll-free Mex. tel. 800/314-9712, www.palace-resorts.com, 6am-sundown daily) is a challenging 7,144-yard championship course designed by Robert Van Hagge and located in Playacar, the upscale hotel and residential development south of Playa del

Carmen proper. Greens fees are US$180 per adult, US$120 after 2pm, and US$80 for kids under 16 (accompanied by adult), including cart and all-inclusive food and drinks from the beverage carts that travel the course and at the on-site restaurant; free hotel pickup is included for full-price rounds. Reserve at least a day in advance November-January.

Skydiving

Gleaming white beaches and brilliant turquoise seas make the Riviera Maya a spectacular place for skydiving. If you're up for it, **Sky Dive Playa** (Plaza Marina, just south of the ferry dock, tel. 984/873-0192, www.skydive.com.mx, 9am-4pm Mon.-Sat.) has been throwing travelers out of planes at 10,000 feet since 1996. You freefall for 4,500 feet—about 45 seconds—then the chute opens for a 7-8-minute ride down to a soft landing on the beach. Tandem dives (you and an instructor, US$269) are scheduled every hour; walkups are accepted, but reservations are highly recommended. For an additional US$159, a cameraman also can be booked to **freefall** alongside you to record your jump either in an eight-minute video or 50-60 digital photographs.

Tours

YucaTreks (10 Av. btwn Calles 10 and 12, tel. 984/803-1265, www.yucatreks.com, 9:30am-2pm Mon.-Fri., 10am-1pm Sat.) offers highly recommended tours to a variety of sites in the region: archaeological zones like Cobá and Chichén Itzá, snorkeling (cenote or reef), whale shark tours, and sailboat excursions. Trips are limited to small groups and are led by knowledgeable and enthusiastic (and punctual) people. Private tours also can be arranged.

    Alltournative (Hwy. 307 Km. 287, tel. 984/803-9999, toll-free Mex. tel. 800/466-2848, toll-free U.S. tel. 877/437-4990, toll-free Canada and other countries tel. 877/432-1569, www.alltournative.com, 9am-7pm daily, US$85-139 adult, US$65-109 child under 12) offers a variety of full-day

conservation-minded tours, including a combination of activities like canoeing, ziplines, ATVing, and snorkeling, plus visits to the Tulum or Cobá archaeological zone—even to a small Maya village. To book in person, stop at any of the informational kiosks on Quinta Avenida.

    AeroSaab (Playa del Carmen Airport, 20 Av. Sur near Calle 1, tel. 998/865-4225, www.aerosaab.com) offers stunning panoramic flights of Playa del Carmen and the Riviera Maya (US$195-1,064, 4-6 passengers, 15 minutes-2 hours), as well as scenic full-day tours to places like Ek' Balam, Isla Holbox, and Mérida/Uxmal (US$140-546 pp). Trips are in 4-6-seat Cessna airplanes and typically require a minimum of 2-4 people.

Spas and Gyms

The Gym (Av. 1 near Calle 16 Bis, tel. 984/873-2098, www.thegymplaya.com, 6am-midnight Mon.-Fri., 7am-7pm Sat., 8am-5pm Sun.) is a modern facility offering state-of-the-art equipment and a host of classes, including yoga, Pilates, spinning, and jiu jitsu. There are personal trainers on-site, too. Day passes are US$16; multiday and monthly passes also are available.

    Yoga By The Way (Calle 26 btwn 5 and 10 Avs., tel. 984/873-3583, www.yogabytheway.com, hours vary Mon.-Sat., US$11.50/class) is a popular 2nd-floor studio just steps from Quinta Avenida. Instruction focuses on vinyasa yoga, with classes for all levels of students. If you prefer a bigger studio, check out **Yogaloft** (Plaza Pelícanos, Calle 10 btwn 10 and 15 Avs., www.yogaloftplaya.com, hours vary Mon.-Sun., US$11.50/class), which has two airy and modern studios and a wider variety of classes. Private instruction is available at both studios, too.

    You can get a **massage on the beach** at various locations—look for the white tents and massage tables—for about US$20 per hour.

    The recently renovated **Unidad Deportiva Villanueva Madrid** (10 Av. near Calle 30, no phone, 6am-10pm daily) is Playa del Carmen's public sporting facility, with a gym, tennis and basketball courts, track, and soccer field. All have night lighting and are open to the public free of charge, but you need to bring your own gear.

FOOD

Playa del Carmen has restaurants and eateries for all tastes and budgets. Those on Quinta Avenida are pricier, of course, many for good reason, others less so. Cheaper eats tend to be off the main drag.

Mexican

★ **La Cueva del Chango** (Calle 38 near 5 Av., cell tel. 984/147-0271, www.lacuevadelchango.com, 8am-11pm Mon.-Sat., 8am-2pm Sun., US$6-13) means The Cave of the Monkey, but there's nothing dim or primitive about it: The covered dining area has light-hearted decor (and a back patio ensconced in leafy vegetation), while the menu features crepes, empanadas, and innovative items like eggs with *chaya*, cactus, and Oaxacan cheese. It's often packed with Playa's upper crust, though the prices make it accessible to all.

Carboncitos (Calle 4 btwn Avs. 5 and 10, tel. 984/873-1382, 7:30am-11pm daily, US$5-22) is a traveler favorite in Playa, serving terrific Mexican food (and some things you may be missing from home, like fresh salads) in a friendly and welcoming setting. Prices and portions are reasonable by Playa standards, and the restaurant gets the little things right, like tasty guacamole and homemade salsas.

A popular taco place, **El Fogón** (Av. Constituyentes btwn 25 and 30 Avs., tel. 984/803-0885, noon-2am daily, US$3-12) serves up mean plates of grilled food—everything from tacos and fajitas to brochettes and T-bone steaks. There are some options for vegetarians—cheese-based dishes like quesadillas and fondue, mostly. Drinks are cheap and strong, and lines can be long but move fast. Get here early to beat the crowds or head to its second location at Avenida 30 at Calle 6 Bis (same hours).

Frutiyogurth (Plaza Pelícanos, Av. 10 near Calle 10, tel. 984/803-2516, www.frutiyogurth. com.mx, 8:30am-10:30pm daily, US$4-9) is a bustling little eatery, serving classic Mexican *tortas* (sandwiches) piled high with fillings like chipotle chicken and *milanesa* (chicken-fried steak), plus a monster selection of fresh juices and smoothies.

Seafood

★ **Pesadería y Coctelería El Pirata** (Calle 40 btwn Avs. 5 and 10, no phone, 10am-6pm daily, US$12-54 per kg) serves up freshly caught fish, shrimp, octopus, and lobster—all sold by the kilo (2.2 pounds)—and prepared to your liking. Sides are à la carte and include rice, beans, and tortillas. Seating is in the casual dining room or on the sidewalk under big umbrellas. It's a bustling place, especially on weekends; live music is often featured streetside.

A classic beachfront restaurant, **La Tarraya** (Calle 2 at the beach, no phone, noon-9pm daily, US$2.50-11.50) serves up tasty fish and seafood dishes that are easy on the wallet: think ceviche, shrimp cocktail, and fish tacos for under 10 bucks. Someone not into seafood? There also are hamburgers and chicken nuggets for the disinclined.

Unassuming and off-the-beaten track, **La Pesca Maya** (30 Av. near Av. Constituyentes, tel. 984/873-1037, www.langosteriamaya.com, 11am-11pm daily, US$5-14) specializes in super-fresh seafood, including hefty fish and shrimp plates, tasty ceviche, and great fish tacos. It's a bit of a hike from the center and has a view of a supermarket parking lot, but it is a tasty way to get off Quinta Avenida.

Ula Gula Bar & Restaurant (5 Av. at Calle 10, 2nd Fl., tel. 984/803-0597, 11am-1am daily, US$15-27) serves outstanding gourmet meals in an appealing dining area overlooking Quinta Avenida. The seafood is the real standout here, whether appetizers like tuna with wasabi and soy sauce, or the fish of the day prepared with a parsley Gorgonzola sauce. For dessert, try the chocolate fondant—a small chocolate cake filled with rich chocolate syrup and accompanied by ice cream.

Vegetarian

BÍO-Natural Organics (Av. 10 btwn Av. Constituyentes and Calle 16, cell tel. 984/267-2208, www.bio-natural.com.mx, 9am-9:30pm daily, US$4-9) specializes in vegan and vegetarian dishes, all organic, with lots of gluten-free options. The menu includes items like quinoa bowls, hummus and baba ganoush plates, vegetarian paella, and lots of fresh fruits, veggies, and nuts. Look for it behind the Quinta Alegria mall.

Popular with locals, **Nativo** (Calle 30 near Av. Constituyentes, tel. 984/873-0758, 7am-1am daily, US$4-10) serves up gigantic plates of Mexican classics and fruit-based meals. The fruit plate is something to write home about—a heaping bowl of cut fruit (at least six different types) with granola, yogurt, and honey. The freshly squeezed juices and smoothies also are no joke. Served in one-liter-size cups, you'll find combos like Alma Grande (*chaya*, pineapple, guava, and orange juice) and Indio Mora (spinach, kiwi, strawberry, and OJ). The restaurant sits in a two-story *palapa*-roofed building, with an airy 2nd floor decked out in dramatic murals.

★ **Falafel Nessya** (Calle 4 btwn 10 and 15 Avs., cell tel. 984/187-6491, noon-10pm Sun.-Thurs., noon-6pm Fri., US$4-8) is a hole-in-the-wall serving up some of the best falafel outside of Israel. The menu has just two main items: Pita and Plate (how's that for efficient?). The "Pita" is a light and fluffy pita pocket stuffed with hot falafel, hummus, and the classic fixins. The "Plate" comes with falafel, hummus, fresh salad, and homemade potato chips. Order at the register and grab a seat at one of the three tables, or join other diners curbside.

100% Natural (5 Av. btwn Calles 10 and 12, tel. 984/873-2242, 7am-11pm daily, US$6-15) serves mostly vegetarian dishes and a large selection of fresh fruit juices. Service can be hit or miss, but the food is well prepared. Tables are scattered through a leafy garden area and covered patio—great for taking a break from the sun.

Other Specialties

Although occasionally missing the mark, old-timer **Babe's Noodles and Bar** (Calle 10 btwn 5 and 10 Avs., tel. 984/879-3569, www.babesnoodlesandbar.com, 1pm-midnight Tues.-Sun., US$8-18) still serves up delicious Thai-fusion meals in a retro-hip bistro setting. Dishes come in half and full orders. Don't miss a chance at ordering the *limonmenta*, an awesome lime-mint slushie. It's not a huge

La Tarraya

place, so you may have to wait for a table during high season.

On a fun, busy block at the north end of Playa, **El Diez** (5 Av. at Calle 30, tel. 984/803-5418, www.eldiez.com.mx, 1pm-midnight daily, US$12-25) is an Argentinean steak house, borrowing the nickname of Argentina's larger-than-life footballer, Diego Maradona. The specialties here are grilled meats, but the long menu also includes items like burgers, pizzas, and empanadas. Service can be a bit slow, but the large outdoor dining area is perfect for enjoying the goings-on.

If you're looking for cheap eats, check out the string of **hole-in-the-wall eateries** (Av. 10 btwn Calles 8 and 10, US$1.50-4) across the street from Plaza Pelícanos. Here you'll have your choice of tacos, *tortas* (Mexican-style sandwiches), crepes, pizza by the slice, and smoothie stands, all at decent prices. Most are open 9am-10pm daily.

Sweets

A puff of pink on Quinta Avenida, ★ **El Gallinero du Chocolat** (5 Av. at Calle 38, cell tel. 984/130-1458, www.elgallineroduchocolat.com, 9am-11pm daily, US$2-7) is a dreamy place for anyone with a sweet tooth. Specializing in all that is sugar, you'll find artisanal chocolates, homemade ice cream, freshly made baked goods, plus a mouthwatering number of crepes and waffles. Take your time. Peruse the menu. Enjoy the sugar high.

Chocolate lovers will melt over **Ah Cacao** (5 Av. at Av. Constituyentes, tel. 984/803-5748, www.ahcacao.com, 7:15am-11:30pm daily, US$3-6), a chocolate café where every item on the menu—from coffees to cakes—is homemade from the finest of beans. **Two sister shops** are located nearby, with the same operating hours (Calle 30 near 5 Av., and 5 Av. btwn Calles 38 and 40).

Groceries

MEGA Comercial Mexicana (30 Av. at Av. Constituyentes, tel. 984/876-2236, www.comercialmexicana.com, 7am-11pm daily) is a huge supermarket that sells everything from clothes, shoes, and snorkel gear to groceries, prepared food, and booze. If you don't find what you're looking for, head three blocks north to **Walmart** (Calle 8 btwn Avs. 20 and 25, toll-free Mex. tel. 800/710-6352, www.walmart.com.mx, 7am-midnight daily), which is located right behind city hall—how's that for a metaphor?

ACCOMMODATIONS

Playa del Carmen has a huge selection and variety of accommodations, from youth hostels to swanky resorts to condos and long-term rentals. Though there are a couple of all-inclusives in town, most are located in Playacar, just south of Playa.

Under US$50

A hostel with hipster style, ★ **Hostel 3B** (10 Av. at Calle 1, tel. 984/803-2901, www.hostel3B.com, US$20-23 dorm with a/c, US$70 s/d with a/c and private bath) offers clean and comfortable dorms—mixed and female only—on the southern end of town. Each has custom-designed bunk beds with matching lockers, individual bed lamps, air-conditioning, and muted decor. Private rooms open onto the spacious rooftop lounge, which has a pool, grill, and popular bar—a party zone really, complete with guest DJs Tuesday-Sunday (don't expect to go to bed early). There's a small but well-equipped galley kitchen and lots of indoor common areas for chilling out, eating, and using Wi-Fi. Why the name "3B"? In homage to the Mexican saying about good bargains: *"Bueno, Bonito, Barato."* Good, Pretty, and Cheap. An accurate description for this place too, we'd say.

Youth Hostel Playa (Calle 8 near 25 Av., tel. 984/803-3277, www.hostelplaya.com, US$14 dorm, US$34/49 d/t with shared bath) has long been one of Playa del Carmen's most popular hostels, despite being somewhat removed from downtown and the beach. The dorm rooms are narrow but clean and have thick, comfortable mattresses, individual fans, mosquito nets, and free lockers. The private rooms are spotless, although light sleepers may be bothered by street noise. There's a clean, well-equipped kitchen and free PCs and Wi-Fi. Best of all is the hostel's enormous common area, which is perfect for eating, playing cards, reading, watching TV, or just kicking back. There's also a nice aboveground pool. Breakfast is included.

Hostel Che (Calle 6 btwn 15 and 20 Avs. 984/147-1741, www.hostelche.com.mx, US$18-20 dorm with a/c, US$50 s/d with a/c and private bath) is a cool hostel, with a party atmosphere and reasonably comfortable accommodations. The higher-priced dorms are worth the investment, and there's a nice terrace with a full bar and music and activity into the wee hours. It's a good option if you're looking to meet people and have fun, less so if you're an early sleeper. There's also kitchen access, free breakfast, and Wi-Fi.

Hotel Yum K'iin (20 Av. btwn Calles 6 and 8, tel. 984/873-0173, www.hotelyumkiin.com, US$46 s/d with a/c) is a clean, well-located budget alternative that won't break the bank. Rooms are well maintained and perfectly comfortable, all with flat-screen TVs and mini-split air-conditioning. All open onto a long, leafy courtyard. The recently renovated lobby also makes a good place to use the Wi-Fi.

US$50-100

Hotel Barrio Latino (Calle 4 btwn 10 and 15 Avs., tel. 984/873-2384, www.hotelbarriolatino.com, US$69 with a/c) offers charming rooms with mosaic-tile bathrooms, stone-inlaid floors, and private balconies. A complimentary continental breakfast is served in a leafy courtyard with a *palapa*-roofed lounge— a good place to write postcards or play cards. Wi-Fi and most international phone calls are also included in the rate. Be sure to confirm online reservations—the system experiences occasional glitches (which may mean no reservation).

An old-school hotel, **Casa de Gopala** (aka Paraíso Azul, Calle 2 btwn 10 and 15 Avs., tel. 984/873-0054, www.casadegopala.com, US$65 s/d, US$75 s/d with a/c, US$85 s/d with

a/c and kitchenette) has 19 spacious rooms, with rustic Mexican furnishings and colorful fabrics, that open onto shared leafy terraces. All have air-conditioning, minifridges, and TV—they're comfortable but unremarkable. Head upstairs for the breathtaking feature—a rooftop solarium with a small, well-kept pool and an enviable view of Playa del Carmen, the Caribbean, and, on a clear day, Cozumel.

Hotel Riviera Caribe Maya (10 Av. at Calle 30, tel. 984/873-1193, www.hotelrivieramaya.com, US$60-131 s/d with a/c) offers bright rooms with modern amenities like silent air conditioners, cable TV, in-room phones, and minifridges. Many have patios or balconies that look out onto a pleasant courtyard and the hotel's inviting pool. The more expensive rooms are located in a newer building and are larger, with wood-floor balconies and deluxe features like king-size beds and whirlpool tubs. Wi-Fi is available in the lobby only.

US$100-150

Hotel Casa de las Flores (20 Av. btwn Calles 4 and 6, tel. 984/873-2898, www.hotelcasadelasflores.com, US$95-120 s/d with a/c) offers a cheerful hacienda-esque exterior that gives way to a leafy courtyard and garden, with a small stone-paved pool and rooms arranged on two levels in back. All units have comfortable beds and warm artful decor; the "plus" rooms have king-size beds, larger flat-screen TVs, iPod docks, and more space and light, and are well worth the higher rate. Wi-Fi is available in the common areas. Concierge service and bicycle rental are available onsite too.

Tucked into a leafy courtyard, ★ **Club Yebo** (Av. 1 at Calle 14, tel. 984/803-3966, toll-free Mex. tel. 800/681-9510, toll-free U.S./Can. tel. 888/676-4431, www.clubyebo.com, US$65 s/d with a/c, US$95-115 studio with a/c, US$130 1-bdrm apartment with a/c, US$160 2-bdrm with a/c) is a small hotel offering tasteful studios and apartments with modern furnishings and fully equipped kitchens (plus a couple of basic hotel rooms). All have quiet air-conditioning, cable TV, Wi-Fi, and daily maid service. Common areas include a small pool and two *palapa* lounges with hammocks. Each room also comes with a "beach kit," which includes beach chairs, towels, and a cooler—perfect for a DIY beach day.

Hotel LunaSol (Calle 4 btwn 15 and 20 Avs., tel. 984/873-3933, www.lunasolhotel. com, US$100-110 s/d with a/c) offers 16 comfortable rooms, all with private balconies or terraces, on spacious leafy grounds. The rooms are a bit sparse but have nice tile bathrooms, minifridges, and flat-screen TVs; 2nd-floor rooms have higher ceilings and better light. Though well located for eating out, the hotel has a fully equipped outdoor kitchen if you'd rather stay in, plus a sparkling swimming pool and whirlpool tub.

A (mostly) adults-only hotel (teens 14 and over welcome), ★ **Luna Blue Hotel** (Calle 26 btwn 5 and 10 Avs., tel. 984/873-0990, www. lunabluehotel.com, US$89-115 s/d with a/c, US$125 suite) is a leafy oasis, and an excellent value, just off busy Quinta Avenida. Rooms are tidy and cool, with pithy travel-related quotes stenciled on the wall, and range from standard hotel rooms to suites with balconies and kitchens. A pleasant garden has colorful Adirondack chairs and a sunken pool, all beneath a canopy of tropical trees. The friendly American owners also provide Wi-Fi, beach club passes, purified water, and morning coffee and baked goods.

US$150-250

Playa Palms (Av. 1 Bis near Calle 14, tel. 984/803-3966, toll-free Mex. tel. 800/681-9510, toll-free U.S./Can. tel. 888/676-4431, www.playapalms.com, US$176-272 s/d with kitchenette and a/c, US$232 1-bdrm suite with kitchenette and a/c) is a classy beachfront hotel, with airy and colorful rooms, kitchenettes, and fine ocean views. A thin pool winds through the hotel's leafy interior courtyard; it's picturesque though not really practical for actually swimming in. Likewise, the beach area is comfortable, but fishing boats moored there can make it hard to enjoy the water.

Still, the location and amenities made this a popular option. Rooms have Wi-Fi and iPod docks. Complimentary continental breakfast is included.

Playa Maya (on the beach btwn Calles 6 and 8, tel. 984/803-2022, toll-free U.S./Can. tel. 888/866-2988, www.playa-maya.com, US$165-225 s/d with a/c, US$195 suite with a/c and kitchenette) is one of the few small hotels in Playa with direct beach access. All 20 rooms are modern and comfortable, including some with kitchen, balcony, and ocean views. There are a tiny pool, whirlpool tub, and sundeck, located somewhat awkwardly at the entrance. The beach is lovely and relaxing, though, with lounge chairs, shaded tables, and food and drink service. Note that even the entrance faces the beach, so you may need a porter to help carry bags across the sand. There's a 4-5-night minimum, depending on the season (though shorter stays are possible, depending on the occupancy). Breakfast is included in the rate.

Hotel Aventura Mexicana (Calle 24 btwn 5 and 10 Avs., tel. 984/873-1876, www. aventuramexicana.com, US$193-212 s/d with a/c, US$212 deluxe s/d with a/c, US$225-257 suite with a/c) has two sections: The newer adults-only area has deluxe rooms with muted colors, elegant furnishings, and a nicely manicured garden and pool. The older section is somewhat plain and has a long, thin pool squeezed in the center of the courtyard; it's also slightly cheaper and open to families. Guests give both areas top marks, though, making it a versatile option.

Over US$250

Totally renovated in 2014, **Mahékal Beach Resort** (Calle 38 near 5 Av., tel. 984/873-0611, toll-free Mex. tel. 800/836-8942, toll-free U.S. tel. 877/235-4452, www.mahekalplaya.com, US$305-380 s/d with a/c, US$560 casita with a/c, including breakfast and dinner) is a huge yet tranquil resort on the northern end of town. All units are in thatch-roofed one- and two-story bungalows, each with a modern beachy feel. Each features a private terrace with hammocks and purposefully do not have TV, phone, or Wi-Fi in the rooms. The resort's beach is gorgeous—a good thing since that's where you're sure to end up most days.

On a shady street just a block from the beach, **The Acanto Boutique Hotel & Condominiums** (Calle 16 Bis btwn 1 and 3 Avs., toll-free U.S. tel. 888/331-2177, www. acantohotels.com, US$315 1-bdrm condo, US$310-405 2-bdrm condo, US$355-475 3-bdrm condo) is a lovely and peaceful place to call home. The 21 apartments have modern kitchens, spacious living-dining rooms, and balconies. Each is decked out in dark woods, marble floors, luxurious fabrics, and fine art. A small swimming pool sits in the lush central courtyard, where complimentary continental breakfast is served each morning. There's also a rooftop lounge, complete with several grills and a whirlpool tub—a fine place for a sunset dinner.

All-Inclusive Resorts

Though most of Playa del Carmen's all-inclusives are in Playacar, an upscale development south of town, a couple have recently popped up in town (with more surely on the way).

Located smack-dab in the middle of Playa del Carmen, ★ **The Royal Playa del Carmen** (Av. Constituyentes at Av. 1, toll-free U.S./Can. tel. 800/760-0944, www.realresorts. com, US$414-789 s, US$467-705 d all-inclusive) is an adults-only Mediterranean-style resort with gleaming white walls, lots of ironwork, and manicured gardens. A winding pool (one of many) runs through the center of it, leading to one of Playa's beautiful beaches. All of the units are suites, which means ocean views, private terraces, and luxurious amenities, with extras like a minibar stocked with top-shelf liquors, soft bathrobes, even umbrellas. There are a dozen buffet and à la carte restaurants as well as a spa, tennis courts, and lounges. Almost best of all, Playa is right outside your door.

Iberostar Tucán (Playacar, Av. Xaman-Ha s/n, tel. 984/877-2000, www.iberostar.com, US$294 s all-inclusive, US$482 d all-inclusive,

US$348 s junior suite all-inclusive, US$590 d junior suite all-inclusive) has a spacious lobby-entryway and wide attractive beach with palm trees, beach chairs, and mild surf. Separating the lobby and the beach is a broad patch of healthy coastal forest, where you can spot monkeys, parrots, and other native creatures in the treetops. After so many sterile and manicured resorts, the Tucán makes for a welcome change of scenery. The main pool is huge and near the beach. Rooms occupy large buildings along the property's edges and are clean and comfortable, though plain. Junior suites have sea views.

Riu Palace Riviera Maya (Playacar, Av. Xaman-Ha s/n, tel. 984/877-2280, www.riu. com, US$424-588 s all-inclusive, US$585-811 d all-inclusive) is one of six all-inclusive Riu resorts clustered together in Playacar and the most upscale, though each resort in the group has its own appeal. The Palace Riviera Maya has an old-world look, with a soaring marble-floored lobby, ornate ironwork, and Renaissance-style paintings and artwork. Suites feature additional sitting areas, understated colors and decor, top-shelf liquors, and modern bathrooms, including hydromassage tubs. The beach and pool areas are spacious and appealing, and there are well-supplied gym and spa areas. Nightlife here can be a bit sedentary, but the advantage of the Palace category is that you have access to the other more lively Riu resorts, like the Tequila or Yucatán.

Rental Properties

Playacar has scores of houses for rent, of all sizes and styles. Prices vary considerably, but expect to pay a premium for ocean views and during peak seasons. A number of property-management companies rent houses, including **Playacar Vacation Rentals** (Calle 10 s/n, tel. 984/873-0418, toll-free U.S. tel. 866/862-7164, www.playacarvacationrentals.com) and **Playa Beach Properties & Rentals** (Plaza Antigua, Calle 10 s/n, tel. 984/873-2952, U.S. tel. 205/332-3458, www.playabeachrentals. com). Both offices are south of Avenida Juárez near the Playacar entrance.

INFORMATION AND SERVICES

Tourist Information

There is no tourist information office in Playa, but there's a **tourist information kiosk** on the plaza (5 Av. at Av. Juárez, 8am-8pm), which is stocked with brochures and maps and often is manned by a reasonably knowledgeable staffer.

Sac-Be (www.sac-be.com) and *In the Roo* (www.intheroo.com) are online magazines that usually offer a handful of useful articles, listings, and events calendars.

Emergency Services

Hospiten Riviera Maya (Hwy. 307 s/n, tel. 984/803-1002, www.hospiten.com, 24 hours daily) is a private hospital offering modern, high-quality medical service at reasonable rates. Many of the doctors have U.S. training and speak English, and are accustomed to treating foreign visitors and expats. It is located along the east side of the highway, near the entrance to Playacar.

Playa International Clinic (10 Av. at Calle 28, tel. 984/803-1215, emergency tel. 984/873-1365, www.sssnetwork.com, 9am-8pm daily) offers specialized medical care for recreational and commercial scuba divers. It has a hyperbaric chamber and lab on-site.

For emergency **ambulance service,** call 065 from any phone.

Prescriptions are required for many antibiotics now, unlike years past. **Farmacias del Ahorro** (10 Av. at Calle 10, toll-free Mex. tel. 800/711-2222, 9am-10pm daily) has a full pharmacy on the 1st floor and a **free walk-in clinic** on the 2nd floor, where a doctor can write prescriptions after a short interview or exam; the clinic is closed 3pm-5pm and weekends.

The **tourist police** (tel. 984/877-3340, or 060 from any pay phone) have an office on Avenida Juárez and 15 Avenida.

Money

Banamex (Calle 12 at 10 Av., 9am-4pm Mon.-Fri.) and **Banorte** (Plaza Pelícanos, 10 Av. btwn Calles 8 and 10, 9am-6pm Mon.-Fri., 10am-2pm Sat.) are full-service banks with ATMs and foreign exchange. There also are several freestanding **ATMs** around town; use ones that are affiliated with recognizable banks to avoid exorbitant service charges.

Media and Communications

The **post office** (Calle 2 at Av. 20, 9am-4pm Mon.-Fri., 9am-1pm Sat.) is easy to miss—look for the pink-striped building near the *combi* terminal.

Internet cafés have gone from ubiquitous to nearly obsolete, thanks to the proliferation of mobile devices and the availability of free Wi-Fi at most hotels. Among the remaining locations include **El Cyber** (10 Av. btwn Av. Juárez and Calle 2, 9am-10pm Mon.-Sat., US$1/hour) and **Riviera.net** (Calle 8 btwn 10 and 15 Avs., no phone, 8am-1am daily, US$1.15/hour).

Immigration and Consulates

Playa del Carmen's **immigration office** (Plaza Antigua mall, 2nd Fl., Calle 10 s/n, tel. 998/881-3560, 9am-1pm Mon.-Fri.) is located on the road to Playacar. Avoid using it, however, as the one in Cancún is more efficient. A tourist visa extension, or *prórroga,* can take a week or more in Playa and involves considerable documentation; in Cancún, the same process is simplified and takes as little as two hours.

The **U.S. Consular Agency** (Calle 1 btwn 15 and 20 Avs., tel. 984/873-0303, conagencyplayadelc@state.gov) is open 9am-1pm Monday-Friday.

Laundry and Storage

At the north end of town, **Mr. Laundry** (10 Av. btwn Calles 28 and 30, 7am-10pm Mon.-Sat., 8am-5pm Sun.) charges US$1.25-2 per kilo with a two-kilo (4.4-pound) minimum. **Lavandería Premium Los Mecates** (Calle 4 near 20 Av., 8am-9pm Mon.-Sat.) charges US$0.80-1.25 per kilo and has a three-kilo (6.6-pound) minimum. At both places, the lower rate is for 1-2-day service, the higher is for express.

Luggage storage is available at both bus stations. **Guarda Plus** (6am-10pm daily) charges US$0.50-1.25 per hour depending on the size of the bag, or US$7.75 per day.

Language and Instruction

Playa del Carmen is becoming a popular place to study Spanish, with several schools, plenty of options for cultural and historical excursions, and, of course, great beaches and nightlife.

Solexico (Calle 6 btwn 35 and 40 Avs., tel. 984/873-0755, toll-free U.S./Can. tel. 800/263-5580, www.solexico.com) is a highly recommended school with a welcoming campus and reputation for professionalism. Classes are offered one-on-one or in groups no larger than eight, and for 15, 20, 25, 35, or 40 hours per week (US$197-645/week). All levels of courses are offered, including instruction geared toward professionals who have regular contact with Spanish speakers. Students can stay with local families (US$215-245/week), at the school's 10-room student residence (US$225-280/week), or arrange for hotel and condo rentals. Ask about volunteer opportunities.

International House (Calle 14 btwn 5 Av. and 10 Av., tel. 984/803-3388, www.ihrivieramaya.com) occupies a pretty and peaceful colonial home, with a large classroom, garden, and café on-site. Group classes (US$220/week) meet 20 hours per week with a maximum of eight students, though typically just 3-4, and can be paired with instruction in things like diving, Mexican cooking, and Latin dancing. Private and two-person classes are also available, as well as custom courses for medical professionals, teachers, and other groups. Family stays can be arranged for US$231-273 per week, with breakfast or half board, while a variety of student rooms, single and shared, with or without meals, run US$182-343 per week.

GETTING THERE
Air

Playa del Carmen has a small airport a few blocks from the ferry pier, but it's used for private and charter flights only. Commercial service is available at Cancún's international airport.

Bus

Playa del Carmen has two bus stations: **Terminal Turística** (aka Terminal Riviera, 5 Av. and Av. Juárez) is in the center of town and has frequent second-class service to destinations along the coast, including Cancún, Tulum, and everything in between; and **Terminal Alterna** (Calle 20 btwn Calles 12 and 12 Bis) has first-class and deluxe service to interior destinations such as Mérida, Campeche, and beyond. There is some overlap, and you can buy tickets for any destination at either station, so always double-check from which station your bus departs.

Combi

Combis (shuttle vans) are an easy way to get up and down the Riviera Maya. In Playa, northbound *combis* line up on Calle 2 near 20 Avenida, with service 24 hours a day (every 10 minutes until 11pm, then every 30 minutes, US$2.75). For slightly more, **Playa Express** has larger, air-conditioned shuttles, departing from a lot on Calle 2 between 20 and 25 Avenidas 5:15am-11:15pm daily (US$3). The final destination of both services is Cancún's main bus terminal (50 minutes), but you can be dropped off anywhere along the highway, including Puerto Morelos (US$2.50, 30 minutes). *Combis* do not enter Cancún's Zona Hotelera, but you can catch a bus there from outside the terminal.

South from Playa del Carmen, ordinary *combis* leave from the same corner around the clock, going as far as the Carrillo Puerto bus station (US$6.15, 2 hours), passing the turnoffs for Puerto Aventuras (US$2, 10 minutes), Xpu-Há (US$2.50, 20 minutes), Akumal (US$2.75, 25 minutes), Tankah Tres (US$3, 45 minutes), Tulum Ruins (US$3, 50 minutes), and Tulum (US$3, 1 hour). To return, flag down a *combi* anywhere along the highway.

Playa del Carmen Bus Schedules

Terminal Turística (5 Av. and Av. Juárez, tel. 984/873-0109, ext. 2501, toll-free Mex. tel. 800/702-8000) is located near the ferry dock and has frequent service along the Caribbean coast and throughout the Yucatán Peninsula. Long-distance buses to other parts of the country use the **Terminal Alterna** (Calle 20 btwn Calles 12 and 12 Bis, tel. 984/803-0944, toll-free Mex. tel. 800/702-8000).

Most Tulum-bound buses stop at the turnoffs for destinations along the way, including **Paamul** (US$1.50-3.75, 15 minutes), **Puerto Aventuras** (US$1.75-3.75, 20 minutes), **Xpu-Há** (US$2.25-4.25, 25 minutes), **Akumal** (US$2.75-4.75, 30 minutes), **Xel-Há** (US$2.85-5.50, 45 minutes), and **Dos Ojos** (US$3.25-5.25, 40 minutes).

Most Chetumal-bound buses stop at **Carrillo Puerto** (US$6.75-13.50, 2-2.5 hours) and **Bacalar** (US$14-18.50, 4.5 hours).

Most Cancún-bound buses stop at **Puerto Morelos** (US$1.75-6.15, 35 minutes), but *not* the airport or Cancún's Zona Hotelera.

Destination	Price	Duration	Schedule
Cancún	US$2.50-8.75	1 hr	every 15-30 mins 12:15am-7:30pm
Cancún Int'l Airport	US$12	1 hr	every 30-60 mins 4:30am-10:10pm
Chetumal	US$16.50-29.50	4.5 hrs	every 60-90 mins 1am-11:58pm
Chichén Itzá	US$10.15-26.75	4-4.5 hrs	2 departures 7:30am and 8am
Chiquilá	US$11.50	3.5 hrs	1 departure 9:10am
Cobá	US$6.25-9.25	2 hrs	every 30-90 mins 6:10am-6:55pm
Mérida	US$31.50-34.75	4.5-5.5 hrs	every 60-90 mins 1:30am-11:59pm
Tulum	US$3-5.50	1 hr	every 15-30 mins 12:25am-11:40pm
Valladolid	US$9.25-14.50	2.5 hrs	every 15-90 mins 1:30am-10:30pm
Xcaret (main entrance)	US$1-4.50	20 mins	every 30-60 mins 12:25am-11:30pm

Car

If you are driving to Playa del Carmen, look for the two main access roads to the beach—Avenida Constituyentes on the north end of town and Avenida Benito Juárez on the south. Playacar has its own entrance from the highway but can also be reached by turning south on Calle 10 off Avenida Juárez.

Ferry

Passenger ferries to Cozumel (US$12.50/7.50 adult/child each way, 30 minutes) leave from the pier at the end of Calle 1 Sur. **UltraMar** (www.ultramarferry.com) and **Mexico Water Jets** (www.mexicowaterjets.com.mx) alternate departures and charge the same amount, though UltraMar's boats are newer. Their ticket booths are side by side at the foot of the pier, with the time of the next departure displayed prominently. The ticket seller will try to sell you a round-trip ticket, but there's no disadvantage to buying a *sencilla* (one-way ticket) and waiting to see which ferry has the next departure when you're ready to return. Between the two companies, there are ferries every 1-2 hours on the hour 7am-10pm daily.

Car ferries operated by **Transcaribe** (tel. 987/872-7688, www.transcaribe.net) depart from the Calica dock south of Playa at 4am, 8am, 1:30pm, and 6pm Monday-Saturday; and 6am and 6pm on Sunday. Returning from Cozumel, the ferry leaves from the international pier at 6am, 11am, 4pm, and 8:30pm Monday-Saturday; and 8am and 8pm on Sunday. The trip takes about an hour and 15 minutes and costs US$60 for a passenger car including driver, and US$5.50 per additional passenger. Reservations are available online, by phone, or at the pier, and are strongly recommended.

GETTING AROUND

Playa del Carmen is a walking town, although the steady northward expansion is challenging that description. The commercial part of Quinta Avenida now stretches over 40 blocks and keeps getting longer. Bicycles are a great way to get around town, especially since Calle 10 has a dedicated bike path. Cabs also are a good option, especially if you have luggage.

Bicycle

BiciBike (Av. 30 at Calle 20, tel. 984/803-4618, lety.goma@gmail.com, 9am-9pm Mon.-Sat.) is a bike shop that also rents bicycles by the day (US$5.75) and week (US$40). Another good option is **Playa Encantada** (Calle 12 Bis at Av. 20, tel. 984/803-5602, 7am-11pm daily), which rents bikes for US$10 per day, including helmet and safety vest.

Taxi

Taxis around town cost US$2.50-5.50, or a bit more if you use a taxi stand or have your hotel summon one. All taxi drivers carry a *tarifário*—an official fare schedule—which you can ask to see if you think you're getting

taken for a ride (so to speak). Prices do change every year or two, so ask at your hotel what the current rate is, and always be sure to agree on the fare with the driver before setting off.

Car Rental

Playa has myriad car rental agencies, and prices can vary considerably. Major agencies like Hertz, National, Avis, and Executive are the most reliable and often have great deals if you reserve online.

Parking in Playa in the high season can be a challenge, especially south of Avenida Constituyentes. Many hotels have secure parking; there are also parking lots around town, including on Calle 2 at 10 Avenida (8am-10pm daily) and at Calle 14 Bis and 10 Avenida (8am-10pm daily), charging around US$1.25 per hour or US$15 per day.

PAAMUL

What started out as an unassuming trailer park on a beautiful stretch of beach has now become a seaside community all its own. Located about 20 kilometers (12.4 miles) south of Playa del Carmen, Paamul has everything from RVs with elaborate wood and *palapa* structures over them to hotel rooms, a restaurant, and even a dive shop.

Beach

Paamul stretches over a wide curving beach. It's clean and classically pretty with white sand and turquoise water—perfect for swimming and exploring. Watch your step on the south end of the beach, as its waters harbor prickly sea urchin—consider wearing water shoes.

Snorkeling and Scuba Diving

Scuba-Mex (Hwy. 307 Km. 85, tel. 984/807-7866, toll-free U.S. tel. 888/871-6255, www.scubamex.com, 8am-5pm daily) is a full-service shop offering fun dives, dive packages, and dive courses at good prices. If you're just interested in snorkeling off the beach, the shop also rents snorkel gear.

Food

Open-air, modern, and with a great view of the Caribbean, the **Reefs of Paamul Restaurant and Bar** (Hwy. 307 Km. 85, tel. 984/875-1050, 8am-8pm daily, US$6-18) serves up classic Mexican dishes along with a variety of international meals. There's something for everyone, which makes it an easy choice. (Good thing, since it's the only place to eat.)

For groceries, the very mini **Mini Super Paamul** (7am-8pm Mon.-Sat., 7am-2pm Sun.) sells basic foodstuffs. It's located at the highway turnoff to Paamul.

Accommodations

Sitting alone on a gorgeous bay is ★ **Paamul Hotel & Cabañas** (Hwy. 307 Km. 85, tel. 984/875-1050, U.S. tel. 612/597-0888, www.paamul.com, US$11.50 pp camping, US$47 s/d RVs, US$125-140 s/d *cabañas*, US$145-170 s/d suite with a/c, TV, Wi-Fi, and kitchenette). From elegant hotel rooms to simple campsites, it appeals to travelers of all budgets. The hotel rooms are simple and elegant with features like minifridges and microwaves, quiet air-conditioning, Wi-Fi, and gorgeous ocean views from private terraces. The *cabañas* are rustic freestanding wood cabins on short stilts. The tent and trailer spaces are just steps from the Caribbean, have electricity and running water, and share clean hot-water bathrooms. Considering the on-site restaurant and dive shop, this place is a truly rare find.

Information and Services

There are no health, banking, postal, or laundry services in Paamul. The closest town for a full range of services is Playa del Carmen, 20 kilometers (12.4 miles) north.

Paamul's beach

Puerto Aventuras

Puerto Aventuras is an odd conglomeration of condos, summer homes, and hotels, organized around a large marina, including a swim-with-dolphins area. It's more than a resort but not really a town. Whatever you call it, Puerto Aventuras's huge signs and gated entrance are impossible to miss, located a few minutes north of Akumal on Highway 307.

SIGHTS
Museo Sub-Acuático CEDAM

Short for Conservation, Ecology, Diving, Archaeology, and Museums, CEDAM runs the worthwhile **Museo Sub-Acuático CEDAM** (Bldg. F, no phone, 9am-1pm and 2:30pm-5:30pm Mon.-Sat., donation requested), displaying a wide variety of items: Maya offerings that were dredged from the peninsula's cenotes, artifacts recovered from nearby colonial shipwrecks, early diving equipment, and photos of open-water and cenote explorations, some from the halcyon days of diving when *jeans* were the preferred getup.

SPORTS AND RECREATION
Snorkeling and Scuba Diving

Some 25 dive sites lie within a 10-minute boat ride from town, each boasting rich coral, abundant sealife, and interesting features, like pillars and swim-throughs, found up and down the coast.

Aquanauts (Bldg. A, tel. 984/873-5041, toll-free U.S. tel. 877/623-2491, www.aquanauts-online.com, 8am-5pm daily) is a full-service shop that enjoys lots of repeat guests. The shop offers the full range of dives and courses, including reef dives (US$60/one tank, US$110/two tanks), cenote dives (US$130/two tanks) and all levels of certification courses. The shop also offers snorkel tours, including one with a stop at the Tulum ruins (US$55-100). Reservations are recommended, especially during the high season.

Another great option is **Planet Scuba** (Calle Bahía Xcacel s/n, cell tel. 984/182-0227, www.planetscubamexico.com, 8am-6pm daily), which offers specialized cavern (US$140-250/two tanks), cave (US$180/one tank, US$210/two tanks), and tech (US$180/one tank, US$210/two tanks) dives. A full range of reef dives and certification courses (including completing confined water sessions in local cenotes) is also offered.

Swimming with Dolphins

Dolphin Discovery (Marina, tel. 984/873-5078, toll-free U.S. tel. 866/393-5158, www.dolphindiscovery.com, 9am-5pm daily) offers several dolphin encounter activities; prices vary according to the duration and degree of interaction (US$89-149 adult, US$89 child). The center also has a manatee program that can be taken in combination with dolphin activities. Programs start at 9:30am, 11:30am, 1:30pm, and 3:30pm daily; free round-trip shuttle service is available from area hotels.

Sportfishing

Captain Rick's Sportfishing Center (past Omni Puerto Aventuras Beach Resort, tel. 984/873-5195, toll-free U.S. tel. 888/449-3562, www.fishyucatan.com, office 8am-7pm daily) offers customized fishing trips, both trolling and deep-sea fishing, utilizing a fleet of a dozen boats, including a 48-foot yacht with room for up to 12 people. You can also arrange time for visiting a deserted beach or Maya ruin, snorkeling on the reef, or just cruising by upscale homes and hotels. Rates are for half day (US$450-685), three-quarter day (US$580-825), and full day (US$690-1,050).

Sailing

Fat Cat (Bldg. E, cell tel. 984/116-3040, toll-free Mex. tel. 800/724-5464, www.fatcatsail.com, 8:30am-5pm Mon.-Sat.) offers a spacious, custom-designed catamaran used for

CEDAM and the Riviera Maya

Maya artifacts have been found in cenotes, probably thrown in as offerings to the gods.

In 1948, a small group of Mexican divers—active frogmen during World War II—created a non-profit organization called Club de Exploración y Deporte Acuáticos de México (Exploration and Aquatic Sports Club of Mexico, or CEDAM). Their mission was to promote ocean conservation and educate others about its treasures and resources.

In 1958, the group set about salvaging the *Mantanceros,* a Spanish galleon that foundered offshore in 1741. It set up camp in present-day Akumal, then just an uninhabited beach owned by a man named Argimiro Arguelles. Arguelles leased CEDAM an old work boat for their project, the SS *Cozumel,* and worked as its captain.

It was this relationship that sealed Akumal's—and arguably, the Riviera Maya's—destiny. Sitting around the campfire one night, Arguelles sold Pablo Bush Romero, one of CEDAM's founders, the bay of Akumal and thousands of acres of coconut palms north and south of it. For the next 12 years, CEDAM continued its work in the rustic and beautiful place—replacing their tents with sturdy *palapa* huts, and using the creaky SS *Cozumel* to carry divers to work sites along the coast.

It wasn't long before the idea of promoting tourism on Mexico's forgotten Caribbean coast arose. In 1968, the group—which had changed the words behind its initials to Conservation, Ecology, Diving, Archaeology, and Museums—donated 5,000 acres of land to the government, including the Cove of Xel-Há, to create a national park. The aim was to open the isolated area to tourists and, in so doing, create jobs for local residents. CEDAM also provided housing, food, electricity, running water, a school for the children, and a first-aid station with a trained nurse.

Still based in Akumal, CEDAM has grown into an important scientific and conservation organization. The group plays an active role in the archaeological exploration of cenotes, among other things, and hosts regular symposiums and seminars. A small but worthwhile museum in Puerto Aventuras—**Museo Sub-Acuático CEDAM** (Bldg. F, no phone, 9am-1pm and 2:30pm-5:30pm Mon.-Sat., donation requested)—displays some of the items the group has recovered in the region's waters over the years, mostly from shipwrecks and cenotes.

half-day excursions (US$110 adult, US$78 child 3-11) that include sailing north toward Bahía Ihna or south toward Xpu-Há—both with good snorkeling in shallow and protected waters. Trips include a picnic boxed lunch.

Golf

Puerto Aventuras Club de Golf (across from Bldg. B, tel. 984/873-5109, www.puertoaventuras.com/golf.html, 7:30am-dusk daily, US$88) offers a nine-hole, par-36 golf course right in town. The course, designed in 1991 by Tom Lehman, is flat but has two par 5s over a total 2,961 yards (3,255 championship).

FOOD

Latitude 20 (Calle Bahía Xcacel s/n, tel. 984/802-9372, www.restaurantlatitude20.com, 12:30pm-9:30pm daily, US$6-15) is a popular place serving up simple Caribbean and Mexican dishes, including lots of seafood. There's live jazz on Wednesday and Saturday nights 7pm-9:30pm and happy hour every day 3pm-6pm. Cash or PayPal only.

Café Olé in Puerto Aventuras (Bldg. A, tel. 984/873-5125, 8am-10pm daily, US$8-20) has an extensive international menu with something for just about everyone. It's best known, though, for its filet mignon and homemade desserts like coconut cream pie and dulce de leche cheesecake. A friendly, welcoming place, there's karaoke on Tuesday and Thursday nights and live music (by professionals) on weekends.

For gourmet takeout food, head to **El Quijote Gourmet** (Bldg. F, tel. 984/802-9309, 11am-2:30pm and 4:30pm-8pm Mon.-Fri., 11:30am-7pm Sat., 11:30am-5pm Sun.), which has a daily case full of freshly prepared dishes ranging from meat and fish entrées to salads. Paella is on the menu on Saturday and Sunday, too. Quality cheeses, wines, and other high-end foods are also in stock.

If you're cooking for yourself or just want some fresh fruit, check out the outdoor **fruit and vegetable market** (8:30am-3pm), which is held every Wednesday and Saturday next to the town's kiosk.

Located across from the Omni hotel, **OXXO** (9am-9pm Mon.-Sat., 9am-1pm Sun.) is a convenience store with basic foodstuffs. For serious shopping—and better prices—head to the mega-store **Chedraui** (tel. 984/802-8773, 7am-8pm daily), located directly across Highway 307 from the Puerto Aventuras entrance.

ACCOMMODATIONS

The road into town bumps right into **Omni Puerto Aventuras Beach Resort** (tel. 984/875-1950, toll-free U.S. tel. 888/444-6664, www.omnihotels.com, US$214-249 s/d with a/c), a small upscale resort with the marina on one side and a fine, palm-shaded beach on the other. There are just 30 rooms, all reasonably spacious and attractive, with colorful regional decor and private patio and hot tub; ocean-view rooms are particularly nice. The resort's small size and low-key atmosphere make it easy to meet other guests, and nighttime typically finds everyone around the main hot tub/beach bar overlooking the ocean.

Casa del Agua (Punta Matzoma 21, tel. 984/873-5184, www.casadelagua.com, US$525-1,500 s/d with a/c) is a beacon of class and charm amid the cookie-cutter commercialism of Puerto Aventuras. What looks like a private home is actually a boutique hotel with a handful of spacious suites. Each has elegant decor, a king-size bed, and luxurious bathrooms and amenities. There is a small sunny pool and private beach as well as complimentary kayaks and snorkeling gear. Daily maid service and a private chef are included in the rate. The per night rate is based on private use of the entire villa (maximum 8 guests). There's a seven-night minimum during Thanksgiving and the Christmas/New Year holidays, three-night minimum the rest of the year.

INFORMATION AND SERVICES
Tourist Information

Despite the numbers of travelers who come to Puerto Aventuras, there is no tourist information office. Nevertheless, the town website—**www.puertoaventuras.com**—is a good resource.

Emergency Services

There is one pharmacy in town: **Emergency 911 Pharmacy** (Bldg. A, tel. 984/873-5305, 8am-10pm daily, or by telephone 24 hours).

Money

Puerto Aventuras doesn't have a bank, but there's a **Banamex ATM** next to Captain Rick's Sportsfishing Center and a **Santander ATM** near the entrance of Museo CEDAM. Both are accessible 24 hours.

Media and Communications

The **post office** (9am-11:30am Mon.-Thurs.) is in a large kiosk a short distance from the golf club entrance.

The small office supply shop **Papelería y Ciber** (Bldg. F, tel. 984/802-9309, 11am-2:30pm and 4:30pm-8pm Mon.-Fri., 11:30am-7pm Sat., 11:30am-5pm Sun.) has Internet service for US$3 per hour.

GETTING THERE AND AROUND

Arriving by public transportation, you can take a *combi* from Cancún, Playa del Carmen, or Tulum. Let the driver know where you're going, and he'll drop you off on the side of the highway. From there, it's 500 meters (0.3 mile) into town. Arriving by car, you'll pass through a large control gate, but no one who looks like a tourist is stopped.

In Puerto Aventuras, you can walk just about everywhere, as virtually all shops and services are centered around the marina.

Xpu-Há

This long, picturesque beach has clusters of development on either end and practically nothing in between. It seems only a matter of time before the owners of this enviable stretch of sand give their blessing to a megaresort, but for now it's a gorgeous and peaceful spot where you could easily while away the whole day, or several.

SPORTS AND RECREATION

Beach Clubs

La Playa Xpu-Há (Hwy. 307 Km. 265, tel. 984/106-0024, www.laplayaxpuha.com, 10am-6pm daily) is a bustling club that offers a slew of classic beach activities, including fishing, snorkeling, and kayaking, all at standard prices. On weekends and holidays, there's a US$3 per person "toll" at the entrance, charged by the landowner for upkeep of the access road. You get it back, though, as a credit on restaurant bills over US$10. There's live music on Sunday.

Just down the beach, **KSM Beach Club** (Hwy. 307 Km. 265, tel. 984/140-2339, 8am-5pm daily, US$4) has a hipper vibe with more areas to chill out, away from the scene. There's also a hut to rent snorkeling gear, kayaks, paddleboards, and kiteboarding equipment. A *palapa*-roofed restaurant is a good option for eats and drinks. There's also plenty of parking, though, like La Playa Xpu-Há, there's a US$3 "toll" at the entrance. To get here, look for a narrow dirt road with a small sign, just south of the Catalonia Royal Tulum resort.

Scuba Diving

Bahía Divers (Hwy. 307 Km. 265, cell tel. 984/116-4963, www.bahiadivers.com) operates out of a small hut a short distance down the beach from La Playa Xpu-Há beach club. It offers the full gamut of ocean and cenote dives, plus certification courses, all with the advantage of small groups (6 divers maximum) and personalized service. They also provide transport to and from your hotel, which is very handy. Ocean dives cost US$90 for two tanks, while cenote diving runs US$120 for two tanks, all including gear.

Snorkeling

In addition to the ocean reef, there's great snorkeling in the numerous cenotes along the inland side of Highway 307, including a cluster just north of Xpu-Há. They vary in size, but most are like large ponds, some with high or overhanging limestone walls, and all filled with cool crystalline water—heaven on a hot day. The cenote floor is often a jumble of stone slabs and in places quite deep—some even have gaping underwater caves that descend out of sight. The cenotes near Xpu-Há are not, however, the huge stalactite-laden caverns you may have seen in photos; for those, head south to Dos Ojos cenote parks, near Tulum.

Half-moon-shaped **Cenote Cristalino** (Hwy. 307, 2 kilometers/1.2 miles north of Xpu-Há, 8am-6pm daily, US$5.50, no rental gear available), much of which is shallow and covered in algae, has a unique section that extends under a deep, overhanging rock ceiling.

Jardín del Edén (formerly Ponderosa Cenote, Hwy. 307, 1.75 kilometers/1 mile north of Xpu-Há, 8am-5pm Sun.-Fri., US$6.25 adult, US$4 child, US$4.25 mask and snorkel, US$4.25 life vest) is much larger than most cenotes—almost like a small lake—with a craggy floor that makes for fun snorkeling. At one end, the floor falls away into a deep underwater cave, where you can see divers emerging—or disappearing—into the abyss, their halogen lights piercing the shadows. A six-meter (19.7-foot) cliff is fun to jump off; just be alert for divers who may be coming up. Between cave-diving classes, snorkeling groups, and independent travelers, Jardín del Edén can get busy but is generally big enough to make a stop here worthwhile.

Cenote Azul (Hwy. 307, 1.5 kilometers/0.9 mile north of Xpu-Há, 8:30am-5pm daily, US$5.50 adult, US$3 child under 8) is made up of three refreshing pools with teal waters: two small ones toward the front that are teeming with tiny fish and surrounded by thin leafy trees, and one large pool with a section of overhanging rock (great for jumping off of) and walkways along the edges for exploring or easing into or out of the cenote. Snorkel gear rentals also are available (US$2.50 mask and snorkel, US$2.50 life vest).

Kiteboarding and Stand-Up Paddling

A small hut on the beach, **KSM Kiteboarding & Paddle Surfing Center** (Hwy. 307 Km. 265, tel. 984/140-2339, 9am-5pm daily) offers kitesurfing instruction to all levels of students (US$80-500, 1-9 hours). Classes include transportation to and from your hotel, KSM Beach Club entrance fee, and all equipment. Stand-up paddling instruction (US$50 per hour) is also available, though most folks opt to take a combo paddleboarding-snorkel tour (US$50 pp, 1.5 hours), which includes paddleboarding to a nearby reef and snorkeling before heading back to land.

FOOD AND ACCOMMODATIONS

Hotel Esencia (Hwy. 307 Km. 265, tel. 984/873-4835, toll-free U.S./Can. tel. 844/373-6242, toll-free Mex. tel. 800/561-9162, www.hotelesencia.com, US$897 s/d with a/c, US$1,012-1,438 suite, US$3,493 2-bdrm cottage with pool) is a luxurious private estate turned resort. It boasts 29 gorgeous units, including classy garden-view rooms (some with private plunge pools), larger ocean-view suites, and stunning split-level cottages with private swimming pools and amenities like surround-sound audio systems and electronic window shades. The beach is just steps away and stretches, virtually untouched, for over a mile. Meal plans are available at the hotel's gourmet restaurant, and there's a full-service spa on-site. Service, as expected, is impeccable.

KSM Beach Club (Hwy. 307 Km. 265, tel. 984/140-2339, 8am-5pm daily, US$5-12) has a cool restaurant bar with a high *palapa* roof, sand floor, tree trunks for chairs, and a bar with swing-style seats. The food is solid—mostly tacos, empanadas, seafood, salads, and nibblers like nachos and fries. The bar, as expected, is fully loaded, though at US$2.75, the *chelas* (a combo of beer, lime juice, and hot spices) are tough to pass up.

INFORMATION AND SERVICES

There are no services in Xpu-Há, save what's available to guests at the hotels. For Internet cafés, laundry, ATM, and other services, head to Akumal or Puerto Aventuras.

GETTING THERE AND AROUND

Each of the listings for Xpu-Há has its own access road, marked with large or small signs, and located at or near Kilometer 265 on the main coastal highway (Hwy. 307). Catalonia Royal Tulum resort is the largest and most obvious landmark; the other access roads are within a few hundred yards. La Playa and KSM Beach Clubs, at the southern end of the beach, are the best access points if you're only staying the day, and are located 25 kilometers (15.5 miles) south of Playa.

Akumal

Unreachable by land until the 1960s, Akumal (Yucatec Maya for Place of the Turtle) is a quiet destination community that has developed on two bays, known as Akumal Bay and Half Moon Bay. It's a very agreeable mid-range place with sand roads and dozens of condominiums and rental homes. The beach in town is quite nice, if you don't mind the boats occasionally parked on the sand; the beach at Half Moon Bay is long and curving with soft white sand, though it's narrow in places. Just offshore, a spectacular portion of barrier reef makes for great diving and snorkeling, and protects Akumal's bays from heavy surf.

A short distance south of Akumal proper is **Aventuras Akumal,** another small bayside development. It doesn't have the town-like feel or activity that Akumal does, but a good condo-hotel and a truly gorgeous beach make this a tempting alternative. Aventuras Akumal has a separate access road from the highway, and walking there along the beach takes about 45 minutes.

SIGHTS AND BEACHES
Beaches
Akumal Bay—the one right in front of town—has a long, slow-curving shoreline, with soft sand shaded by palm trees. The water is beautiful and there's great snorkeling,

including a good chance at spotting sea turtles. It's a bit rocky underfoot, and you should be aware of boat traffic when swimming or snorkeling. **Half Moon Bay** also is equally nice for swimming and snorkeling, with a white-sand beach to match. Water shoes are handy in both areas.

★ Laguna Yal-Ku

At the mouth of an elbow-shaped lagoon at the north end of Akumal, an endless upwelling of underground river water collides with the tireless flow of seawater—the result is a great place to snorkel, teeming with fish and plants adapted to this unique hybrid environment. Once a secret snorkeler's getaway, **Laguna Yal-Ku** (9am-5pm daily, US$14 adult, US$5 child 4-12, free 3 and under, US$5 apiece for mask, fins, and life vest, US$3 locker) now has a spot in every guidebook and tour group itinerary—come before 10am or anytime on Sunday for the least traffic. (That, and a shot at snagging a private picnic area [US$30], complete with *palapa* shade, a table, and chairs). Use a T-shirt or wetsuit instead of sunscreen, as even the biodegradable kind can collect on plants and coral. The lagoon is dotted with 34 intriguing bronze sculptures by Mexican artist Alejandro Echeverría.

Centro Ecológico Akumal

Next to Akumal Dive Shop, the **Akumal Ecological Center** (CEA, tel. 984/875-9095, www.ceakumal.org, 9am-1pm and 2pm-6pm Mon.-Fri.) is a nonprofit founded in 1993 to monitor the health of Akumal's ecosystems, particularly related to coral and sea turtles. May-July, you can join CEA volunteers on nighttime turtle walks, helping move newly laid eggs to protected hatcheries. August-October, visitors can help release hatchlings into the sea. Both activities are free, but a US$25 donation is appreciated. The center also has free displays and frequent evening lectures on ocean ecology in the high season.

CEA operates long-term volunteer projects on reef monitoring, sea-turtle monitoring, and environmental education projects. Volunteers stay in the center's dorms, with kitchen and Internet access; minimum age is 21, and some fees are required. See the website for details.

Aktun Chen

Yucatec Maya for Cave with an Underground River, **Aktun Chen** (Hwy. 307 Km. 107, tel. 984/806-4962, www.aktun-chen.com, 9am-5pm Mon.-Sat., last tour 1 hour before closing,

US$33-110 adult, US$16.50-55 child) is certainly that, plus a cenote for swimming and snorkeling, and a canopy/zipline route. You can do all three activities, or just the ones that interest you. The cave tour is a walk of about 0.6 kilometer (0.3 mile) amid a breathtaking array of stalactites and stalagmites; at the end is a 12-meter-deep (39-foot) cenote filled with crystalline water. Lighting and a pathway make it accessible to all. You can't swim in that cenote, but there's another nearby, with stairs and platforms for getting in and out. Lastly, the canopy tour is made up of 10 ziplines and two wobbly suspension bridges, covering a full kilometer (0.6 mile). Between activities, check out the park's small "zoo," with spider monkeys, toucans, and more. Admission adds up fast, especially for families, but the experience is memorable.

Tours are offered in English and Spanish and last about 90 minutes. Round-trip transportation is available, or you can go independently—look for the turnoff just across from Aventuras Akumal, and continue three kilometers (1.9 miles) to the entrance. Mosquito repellent and a bottle of water are recommended. You'll encounter the least crowding before 11am and on weekends.

Laguna Yal-Ku is a snorkelers' favorite.

Akumal

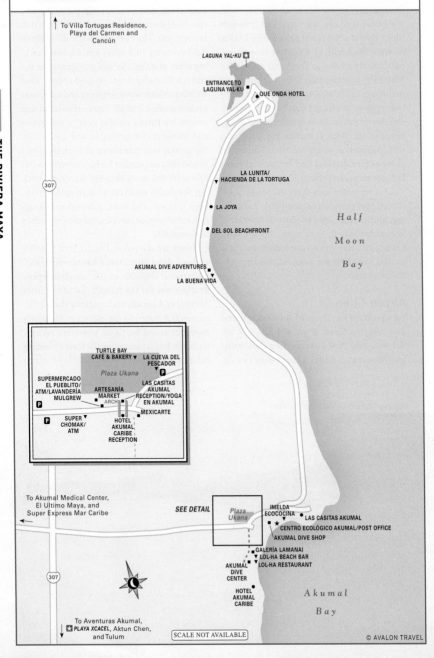

To Villa Tortugas Residence,
Playa del Carmen and
Cancún

307

LAGUNA YAL-KU

ENTRANCE TO
LAGUNA YAL-KU
QUE ONDA HOTEL

LA LUNITA/
HACIENDA DE LA TORTUGA

LA JOYA

DEL SOL BEACHFRONT

Half

Moon

Bay

AKUMAL DIVE ADVENTURES

LA BUENA VIDA

TURTLE BAY
CAFÉ & BAKERY
LA CUEVA DEL
PESCADOR

Plaza Ukana

SUPERMERCADO
EL PUEBLITO/
ATM/LAVANDERÍA
MULGREW

ARTESANÍA
MARKET
ARCH

LAS CASITAS
AKUMAL
RECEPTION/YOGA
EN AKUMAL

SUPER
CHOMAK/
ATM

MEXICARTE

HOTEL
AKUMAL
CARIBE
RECEPTION

To Akumal Medical Center,
El Ultimo Maya, and
Super Express Mar Caribe

SEE DETAIL

Plaza
Ukana

IMELDA
ECOCOCINA

LAS CASITAS AKUMAL

CENTRO ECOLÓGICO AKUMAL/POST OFFICE

AKUMAL DIVE SHOP

GALERÍA LAMANAI

LOL-HA BEACH BAR

LOL-HA RESTAURANT

AKUMAL
DIVE
CENTER

HOTEL
AKUMAL
CARIBE

Akumal

Bay

307

To Aventuras Akumal,
PLAYA XCACEL, Aktun Chen,
and Tulum

SCALE NOT AVAILABLE

© AVALON TRAVEL

SHOPPING

MexicArte (tel. 984/875-9115, 8am-9pm daily) is the small, bright-pink shop just inside the arches on your right. The owner hand-selects the best folk art from around the region and country. Prices are high, but so is the quality and artisanship.

Galería Lamanai (tel. 984/875-9055, www.galerialamani.com, 8am-9pm daily) offers similar wares, both in quality and price. The shop is located on the beach near Snack Bar Lol Ha.

There is an open-air *artesanía* market (8am-6pm daily) behind Playa Ukana, facing the town basketball court. The items are standard Mexican handicrafts, like colorful ceramics from Puebla and textiles from Chiapas.

SPORTS AND RECREATION
Scuba Diving

Some of the Riviera Maya's first scuba divers waded into the waves right here at Akumal Bay, and the area has been special to the sport ever since. Akumal's diving is easy and fun, with a mellow current and moderate depths; few profiles go below 20 meters (66 feet). The reef here is predominantly boulder coral, which isn't as picturesque as other types, but it still teems with tropical fish and plant life.

Founded more than 30 years ago, **Akumal Dive Shop** (Akumal Bay, tel. 984/875-9032, toll-free Mex. tel. 800/462-1212, www.akumaldiveshop.com, 8am-5pm daily) was the first dive shop in the Riviera Maya. Still located on the beach, the shop offers fun dives and various certification courses in both open-water and cave/cavern diving. Divers can take one- or two-tank reef dives (US$50/80), cavern dives (US$140-200), or buy dive packages. Fun dives don't include equipment rental (US$18/day, US$70/week, US$12/day wetsuit). Open-water certification courses take 3-4 days and cost US$485, equipment and materials included. Just down the beach, **Akumal Dive Center** (tel. 984/875-9025, U.S. tel. 719/359-9672, www.akumaldivecenter.com, 8am-5pm) offers the same dives and courses for slightly less.

On Half Moon Bay, **Akumal Dive Adventures** (next to La Buena Vida restaurant, tel. 984/875-9157, toll-free U.S. tel. 888/425-8625, www.akumaldiveadventures.com, 8am-5pm daily) offers somewhat lower prices than the other shops, as well as dive and accommodation packages starting at three nights of lodging and four reef dives for US$325/425 per person double/single occupancy. Rooms are at the affiliated Vista del Mar hotel.

Aventuras Akumal has excellent diving and snorkeling, with a calm bay and less traffic than Akumal proper. **Aquatech Dive Center** (Villas DeRosa Resort, tel. 984/875-9020, U.S. tel. 801/619-9050, www.cenotes.com) has many years of experience and offers a complete range of dives and courses, with special emphasis on cenote and cave diving. Reef dives run US$50/75 for one/two tanks, while cenote dives are US$95/140. Open-water certification as well as cavern, cave, and technical diving instruction are also available.

Snorkeling

Laguna Yal-Ku (9am-5pm daily, US$14 adult, US$5 child 4-12, free 3 and under, US$5 apiece for mask, fins, and life vest, US$3 locker) is a favorite among many snorkelers for its large area, calm water, and unique mix of fresh- and saltwater ecosystems.

The dive shops also offer **guided snorkel tours,** which typically last 60-90 minutes and cost around US$30-40 per person, including gear.

You can **rent snorkel gear** at any of Akumal's dive shops for around US$12 per day or US$60 per week and head out on your own in either Akumal Bay or Half Moon Bay; both have nice coral, plentiful fish, and a good chance of seeing sea turtles. Be alert for boats, especially in Akumal Bay.

Sailing

Akumal Dive Shop (Akumal Bay, tel. 984/875-9032, toll-free Mex. tel. 800/462-1212, www.akumaldiveshop.com, 8am-5pm daily) offers a popular Robinson Crusoe cruise: a five-hour excursion on a catamaran sailboat, with stops for fishing and snorkeling (US$95 pp including lunch and equipment). Or try the two-hour Sunset Cruise, which doesn't include snorkeling, but offers beautiful evening views of the bay (US$45 pp).

Sportfishing

Akumal's dive shops also offer fishing tours year-round. The price, duration, and group size vary considerably based on the season, what kind of fishing you want to do, and the type of boat that's available. That said, expect to pay US$100-200 for a basic 2-3-hour tour with 2-6 anglers; you can usually extend the tour for an additional fee. Fishing is excellent year-round, but April-August are when sailfish and marlin are most prevalent.

Spas and Gyms

Yoga en Akumal (town arch, 2nd Fl., cell tel. 984/745-3488 or 984/876-2652, www.akumalyoga.com) offers a variety of hatha classes for all experience levels in a breezy studio inside the arch at the entrance to town. Sessions are led by certified instructors; they cost US$15 per class, US$45 for four classes, or US$85 for an unlimited two-week pass; check online for the monthly schedule.

FOOD
In Town

Lol-Ha Restaurant (Hotel Akumal Caribe, tel. 984/875-9014, www.hotelakumalcaribe.com, 6:30pm-10pm daily, closed Oct.-mid-Nov., US$10-25) is Akumal's finest restaurant, with a beautiful wood and stucco dining room topped with a high *palapa* roof that opens onto a pleasant veranda. Expect excellent seafood and Mexican and American specialties, including prime USDA steaks and ahi tuna. During high season, enjoy flamenco performances on Wednesday, and jazz and blues singers Thursday and Saturday nights starting at 7:30pm; additional events are posted at the restaurant, and a small per-person cover charge is sometimes added to the bill. Reservations are highly recommended.

Next door, **Lol-Ha Beach Bar** (no phone, 11am-9pm daily, US$8-14) serves the best hamburgers on the beach, and tasty tacos, too (the *tacos de cochinita* are particularly good). Three flat-screen TVs at the bar always have a sporting event on, whether Monday Night Football, March Madness, or the Kentucky Derby; hundreds of people turn out for the annual Super Bowl and Academy Awards parties (proceeds of which go to local community groups). Kids will love the adjacent game room with air hockey and foosball.

For a fresh, healthy meal, try **Imelda Ecococina** (no phone, 8am-9pm Mon.-Sat., US$4-7), next to Centro Ecológico Akumal. Breakfast options include eggs, omelets, pancakes, and French toast. For lunch, the *comida corrida* (lunch special) comes with a choice of main plate and a side dish or two. On Monday and Thursday, the restaurant hosts a popular Maya buffet (7pm, US$20, reservations recommended) followed by *cumbia* tunes and dancing.

In Plaza Ukana, ★ **Turtle Bay Café & Bakery** (tel. 984/875-9138, www.turtlebaycafe.com, 7am-9pm daily, US$5-19) offers creative comfort food like crab cakes, seafood-stuffed chiles rellenos, and "Black and Bleu" salad. For breakfast, try the famous sticky buns and eggs Benedict. Enjoy your meal surrounded by palm trees, either in the outdoor *palapa*-roofed dining room or on the porch of the main building. Free Wi-Fi is available.

For fresh seafood, check out **La Cueva del Pescador** (Plaza Ukana, tel. 984/875-9205, noon-9pm daily, US$6-22). Sink your teeth into fish kabobs, shrimp prepared nine different ways (e.g., grilled, à la tequila, with curry salsa, and so on), and lobster—most caught the day you order it. If you've been fishing, bring in your catch and have it cooked by the chef. The bar is especially popular on weekends.

For groceries, the best prices are across from the Akumal turnoff on Highway 307 in **Super Express Mar Caribe** (Av. Gonzalo Guerrero, 7am-11pm daily); look for the store about 100 meters (328 feet) west of the highway. Otherwise, just outside the arch, **Super Chomak** and **Supermercado El Pueblito** (both 7am-9pm daily) charge an arm and a leg for canned and dried food, soups and pastas, fresh and packaged meat, booze, and basics like sunscreen and bug repellent. All the markets also sell fresh fruit and veggies, but you may find a better selection at the **farmers market** held Wednesday and Saturday in Plaza Ukana.

Half Moon Bay

A fantastic flying serpent skeleton greets diners at **La Buena Vida** (Beachfront, tel. 984/875-9061, http://labuenavidarestaurant.com, 7am-11pm daily, US$6-24), where clients enjoy the varied menu—from hamburgers to shrimp ceviche—under *palapa*-shaded tables on the beach. If you've already had a meal, stop in for a drink at the swing-lined bar; happy hour runs 5pm-7pm.

La Lunita Restaurant (Hacienda de la Tortuga, tel. 984/875-9070, www.lalunita-akumal.com, 1:30pm-11pm daily, US$15-38) is an intimate bistro serving gourmet Mexican and international dishes, both small plates or full entrées. Seafood is king here, though there are plenty of options for vegetarians and serious meat eaters. With only a handful of tables, some overlooking the Caribbean, La Lunita is a perfect place for a romantic dinner—just be sure to make reservations.

Aventuras Akumal

★ **Beached Bikini Bar and Grill** (Beachfront, no phone, 10am-last person leaves, US$9-16) is a classic chilled-out beach joint with swing seats at the bar, plastic tables on the beach, and palm tree shade. It's a friendly, jocular place where everyone is treated like a regular. Stick to the basics—nachos, burgers, and ceviche—and you won't be disappointed. Order a mango jalapeño margarita to wash it all down.

ACCOMMODATIONS

Akumal draws a number of long-term visitors and has a large number of fully equipped condos and villas, in addition to ordinary hotels. There's no hostel, but backpackers might be able to snag a dorm room at CEA.

In Town

Centro Ecológico Akumal (CEA, next to Akumal Dive Shop, tel. 984/875-9095, www.ceakumal.org, US$27 pp dorm) has several large, comfortable dorms—most even have air-conditioning—and a well-outfitted communal kitchen. CEA's volunteers have priority for the rooms, and they are usually full, but if not, they're available to walk-ins (BYO linens).

Just across the highway, **El Ultimo Maya** (Av. Gonzalo Guerrero s/n, tel. 984/875-9042, US$31 s/d with a/c) offers sparse but clean rooms with cable TV, air-conditioning, and Wi-Fi. There's nothing particularly special about the place other than it's a great deal, especially since it's just a short walk (300 meters/0.2 mile) to the main beach.

Hotel Akumal Caribe (reception in the arches at the entrance to town, tel. 984/206-3500, toll-free U.S. tel. 800/351-1622, toll-free Can. tel. 800/343-1440, www.hotelakumalcaribe.com, US$149 s/d bungalow, US$179 s/d with a/c, US$184 s/d with a/c and kitchenette) is the oldest hotel in town. Though some of the units show their age (think bamboo furnishings and flower prints), many have been updated and have such features as sleek espresso furnishings, stainless steel minifridges, mini-split air conditioners, and Wi-Fi. Hotel rooms have balconies with ocean views, too. The property fronts an enviable stretch of palm-tree-laden beach, plus there's a great pool with a small waterfall. Continental breakfast is included in the rate.

On the eastern end of town, **Las Casitas Akumal** (tel. 984/875-9071, toll-free U.S./Can. tel. 800/525-8625, www.lascasitasakumal.com, US$351-398 2-bdrm condo with a/c) has 18 airy condominiums, each with two bedrooms, two baths, living room, fully equipped kitchen, and private patio. Some have two floors and space for six people, and most feature bright, colorful Mexican artwork. All have ocean views and direct access to a semiprivate section of the beach. There's a seven-night minimum in the high season.

Half Moon Bay

Del Sol Beachfront (tel. 984/875-9060, toll-free U.S. tel. 888/425-8625, www.akumalinfo.com, US$110-130 s/d with a/c, US$170-270 studio to 3-bdrm condo with a/c) has 16 spacious condos plus 15 smallish hotel rooms, all overlooking a lovely stretch of beach. Condos have long balconies or porches, fully equipped kitchens, separate living and dining rooms, and master bedrooms with king-size beds. Colorful Mexican decor complements modern amenities like flat-screen TVs, mini air conditioners, in-room safes, Wi-Fi, and (in some) whirlpool tubs. Hotel rooms are comfortable but may feel a bit cramped for longer stays. All units have daily maid service and share a well-tended beach with lounge chairs and *palapa* shades. All that, plus a beachfront pool too.

Hacienda de la Tortuga (tel. 984/875-9068, www.haciendatortuga.com, US$171 1-bdrm condo, US$228 2-bdrm condo) has just 16 rooms and cultivates a quiet, relaxed atmosphere geared toward couples. Roomy one-bedroom and two-bedroom condos all have huge ocean-view windows, plus a living room, kitchen, king-size bed(s), and air-conditioning in the bedrooms. Each is uniquely decorated, many with fine Mexican artwork and homey touches like a well-stocked bookcase. There's a small pool just steps from the beach, and a well-regarded Mexican restaurant, La Lunita, on-site.

★ **La Joya** (toll-free U.S. tel. 800/448-7137, www.akumalvacations.com, US$127-171 1-bdrm condo, US$220 2-bdrm condo, 5-night minimum) is a great little condominium complex with seven one- and two-bedroom units on three floors. The condos are individually owned, so they vary in decor and amenities, but all share a high level of comfort and charm, not to mention a lovely beach (with excellent snorkeling), a small pool,

and stellar views from the rooftop terrace. Parking, daily maid service, 24-hour security, an on-site management office, and a nearby convenience store are all added bonuses.

Just a block from Laguna Yal-Ku, **Que Onda Hotel** (tel. 984/875-9101, maribel.ondarte@gmail.com, US$85-100 s/d, US$125-150 suite) has seven rooms, each lovingly decorated with beautiful fabrics and unique works of art. Two suites are similar in style, can accommodate up to six guests, and include terrific upper-floor views of the Caribbean and Yal-Ku. All face a verdant garden with a pool. None have air-conditioning, unfortunately, which means 1st-floor rooms can get a little stuffy (those on the 2nd floor have terraces that let in nice sea breezes). The on-site restaurant can get a bit busy, but fortunately it stops receiving guests at 10pm. Use of snorkel gear is included in the rate.

Aventuras Akumal

★ **Villa Las Brisas** (tel. 984/875-9263, www.aventuras-akumal.com, US$100 s/d, US$75 studio, US$150 1-bdrm condo, US$200 2-bdrm condo) has just three units, two of which can be combined to make a two-bedroom condo. All are spacious, spotless, and meticulously furnished, down to a stocked spice rack in the kitchen. The condos have large terraces with hammocks and stunning views; the smaller units have balconies that overlook a tidy garden. With comfortable beds, modern Mexican-style furnishings, and space to stretch out, it's easy to feel at home here. Snorkel gear and kayaks are included in the rate. There's a simple mini-mart at the entrance (8am-4pm Mon.-Sat.), but you'll have to go to Akumal for additional shopping and services. There is free Wi-Fi but no air-conditioning.

Outside of Town

Located on the inland side of Highway 307, **Villa Tortugas Residence** (Hwy. 307 Km. 256, cell tel. 984/157-5318, www.villatortugas.com, US$75 s/d with a/c) is a great little place offering six studios set in a leafy jungle setting. Each unit is a colorful casita with a kitchenette, one or two firm beds, a private patio, air-conditioning, and Wi-Fi; they are spic-and-span, with daily maid service. The grounds include a mosaic-tiled pool and an outdoor lounge area, both surrounded by a well-tended garden. Located 3 kilometers (1.8 miles) north of Akumal, it's a peaceful place to base yourself, especially if you have a car and don't mind being a few miles from the beach.

Rental Properties

The majority of rooms for rent in Akumal are in privately owned homes and condos, especially along Half Moon Bay. Most are managed and rented by one of various property management companies; browse the listings of several agencies to get the best selection. Some reliable agencies include **Caribbean Fantasy** (www.caribbfan.com, toll-free U.S. tel. 800/523-6618), **Akumal Villas** (www.akumalvillas.com, toll-free U.S. tel. 866/535-1324), **Akumal Rentals** (www.akumal-rentals.com, U.S. tel. 815/642-4580), and **Loco Gringo** (www.locogringo.com, toll-free U.S. tel. 800/478-0081).

INFORMATION AND SERVICES
Tourist Information

Akumal doesn't have an official tourist office, but it's a small town, and you can probably find what you're looking for by asking the first person you see. If that fails, the folks at **Centro Ecológico Akumal** (CEA, Akumal Bay, tel. 984/875-9095, www.ceakumal.org, 9am-1pm and 2pm-6pm Mon.-Fri.) are friendly and well informed, and most speak English.

Emergency Services

Across the highway, **Akumal Medical Center** (Av. Gonzalo Guerrero s/n, tel. 984/875-9090, cell tel. 984/806-4616, 24 hours daily) is the medical office of long-time Akumal provider Dr. Néstor Mendoza Gutiérrez. He also has a small office facing

Plaza Ukana. Pharmacy, ambulance, and house calls are available.

The **police** can be reached by calling 060 from any public phone.

Money

There is no bank in town, but there are **ATMs** inside Akumal's small supermarkets, near the town arch: **Super Chomak** and **Supermercado El Pueblito** (both 7am-9pm daily). They are sometimes out of cash, however, so plan accordingly.

Media and Communications

Many hotels offer Wi-Fi to guests, as does **Turtle Bay Café & Bakery** (tel. 984/875-9138, www.turtlebaycafe.com, 7am-9pm daily) in Plaza Ukana.

Laundry

Lavandería Mulgrew (7am-noon and 5pm-7pm Mon.-Sat.) charges US$1.75 per kilo (2.2 pounds) and provides same-day service if you drop off your load before 8:30am (2-kilo/4.4-pound minimum). Look for it next to Supermercado El Pueblito, near the town arch.

GETTING THERE AND AROUND

The turnoff to Akumal is between kilometers 254 and 255 on the main highway. For Aventuras Akumal, the access road is just south of the main Akumal entrance; look for the sign to Hotel Villas DeRosa, as the community itself isn't well signed.

Bus and *Combi*

Combis and second-class buses stop at the Akumal turnoff, but it's a kilometer (0.6 mile) walk into town. Likewise, you can manage the center area by foot, but walking to and from Half Moon Bay can be long, hot, and dusty. Consider hiring a cab, which are often parked just outside the town arches.

Combis and second-class buses also stop at the Aventuras Akumal entrance; it's only about 500 meters (0.3 mile) into the community from there.

Car

If you drive into town, there is a small **town parking lot** (7am-4pm daily, US$1.25/hour) in front of Plaza Ukana. Some shops and restaurants can validate your parking—be sure to bring your receipt. There also are a handful of **public parking lots** just outside the town arches charging US$4 per day.

Taxi

Taxis gather near the Super Chomak grocery store at the entrance of Akumal, just outside of the arches. A ride from town to Laguna Yal-Ku costs US$5.

Bicycle

Bicycles can be rented from the hotel **Del Sol Beachfront** (Half Moon Bay, tel. 984/875-9060, toll-free U.S. tel. 888/425-8625, www.akumalinfo.com) for US$11 per day or US$66 per week.

★ PLAYA XCACEL

For all the breakneck construction along the Riviera Maya, much of the coastline remains virtually untouched, including some gorgeous stretches of white-sand beach. **Playa Xcacel** (Hwy. 307 Km. 247.5, 9am-6pm daily, US$2) is one of those, a gently curving band of thick white sand, with only a small parking lot, restrooms, and changing area, and popular with local residents. Xcacel's pristine state is thanks in part to the fact that sea turtles nest here, and development is restricted by federal law. Along the inland edge of the beach are scores of wood blades with dates on them, marking where and when sea turtles laid eggs; needless to say, do not move the markers or disturb the nests! A small freshwater cenote is located down a slippery path, about 350 meters (0.2 mile) south of the main entrance. The turnoff to Playa Xcacel is easy to miss, but it's located 11 kilometers (7 miles) north of Tulum, just south of Chemuyil community.

The Riviera Maya still has long stretches of untouched beach, including gorgeous Playa Xcacel.

Tankah Tres and Soliman Bay

Tucked innocuously between Akumal and Tulum, Tankah Tres and Soliman Bay see only a fraction of the tourist traffic that their better-known neighbors do. But that's just the way visitors to this little stretch of coastline prefer it, enjoying excellent snorkeling, diving, and pretty beaches, with a sense of isolation that's hard to find in these parts. The area has three small bays. The scattered hotels, villas, and private homes along their shores were once connected by a U-shaped access road, but development cut the *U* in half; the southern entrance is still marked Tankah Tres, while the northern entrance has a sign for Soliman Bay.

SIGHTS AND BEACHES
Playa Tankah
The handful of hotels here have nice beachfronts along three sandy bays. If you aren't staying at one of the hotels, **Casa Cenote** (Tankah Tres, 1.5 kilometers/0.9 mile from the southern turnoff, tel. 521/984-6996, www.casacenote.com) allows nonguests to enjoy the hotel beach and lounge chairs if they order something at the restaurant.

Cenote Manatí
Across from Casa Cenote (and sometimes called by the same name), **Cenote Manatí** (Tankah Tres, 1.5 kilometers/0.9 mile from the southern turnoff, no phone, sunrise-sunset, US$4 snorkelers, US$7 divers) is a series of interconnected cenotes and lagoons extending from the road well inland. (An underground channel drains into the ocean.) The crystal clear water, winding channels, and tangle of rocks, trees, and freshwater plants along the edges and bottom all make for terrific snorkeling. Look for schools of tiny fish near the surface and some bigger ones farther down. Snorkel gear rental is available for US$6.

Yax Kin Cenote
Located just north of the Soliman Bay access road, **Yax Kin Cenote** (Hwy. 307 Km. 242, tel. 984/135-0636, 9:30am-5pm, US$5.50 adult, US$3 child under 9) is a pool of shimmering teal water with a limestone shelf that makes entering the cool water easy (and less stressful for parents of small children). Snorkeling equipment can be rented (US$2.50) to get a better view of the small fish darting about. Camping (US$11.50 pp, BYO gear) is permitted in two-story towers located about 50 meters (164 feet) from the cenote.

SPORTS AND RECREATION
Scuba Diving and Snorkeling
There are excellent dive and snorkel sites in and near Tankah Tres and Soliman Bay. Located inside the Tankah Inn, **Tankah Divers** (Tankah Tres, tel. 984/128-2000, www.tankahdivers.com, hours vary) is a full-service shop offering guided trips (US$45/80 one tank reef/cenote, US$75/125 two tank reef/cenote) and all levels of PADI dive instruction. The shop also offers snorkeling excursions (US$40/60 reef/cenote) and rents snorkel gear for US$10 per day.

FOOD
The restaurant at **Casa Cenote** (Tankah Tres, 1.5 kilometers/0.9 mile from the southern turnoff, tel. 521/984-6996, www.casacenote.com, 8am-9pm daily, US$8-18) has a breezy *palapa*-roofed dining area just steps from the ocean. You can order beach food such as quesadillas or a guacamole plate, or something heftier—the seafood is always tasty and fresh. Every Sunday at noon, the hotel hosts an awesome Texas-style barbecue (US$13) that is popular with expats up and down the Riviera Maya.

The restaurant at **Blue Sky Hotel** (Tankah Tres, 1.7 kilometers/1 mile from the southern turnoff, tel. 998/800-1371, www.blueskyhotel.com.mx, 7:30am-9pm Mon.-Thurs., 7:30am-10pm Fri.-Sun., US$10-24) specializes in Italian food, prepared to order, with simple but beautiful presentation. The pizza is famously good, handmade with fresh ingredients and baked in a custom brick oven. But appetizers like ceviche and mains like grilled calamari with vegetables are also worth sampling—you'll just have to come back more than once! With only a handful of tables, it's ideal for an intimate dinner.

Set in a large palm tree grove along the curving Soliman Bay, ★ **Chamico's** (Soliman Bay, end of road, no phone, 10am-4pm daily, US$8-17) is a family-run restaurant serving up unbelievably fresh seafood and fish dishes. "Restaurant" is a bit of a stretch, though; it's more like a handful of plastic tables and chairs set under swaying palm trees, and a Maya-style hut with a couple of open-fire grills and rickety wood tables serves as the kitchen. Meals range from whole grilled fish and lobster tail to fish ceviche and seafood stews.

ACCOMMODATIONS

Tankah Inn (Tankah Tres, 1.1 kilometers/0.6 mile from the southern turnoff, U.S. tel. 918/582-3743, www.tankah.com, US$131 s/d with a/c) has five spacious rooms with murals of Maya temples. Each room has a private terrace and ocean views; all feature minifridges, drinking water, and remote-controlled air-conditioning. A breezy common room has sweeping views of the Caribbean—comfy chairs and tables, lots of board games, and an honor bar make this a popular place to hang out. The beach, with its lounge chairs and hammocks, is a tempting alternative. À la carte breakfast is included, as is use of kayaks, snorkel gear, and Wi-Fi.

The first hotel on this bay, **Casa Cenote** (Tankah Tres, 1.5 kilometers/0.9 mile from the southern turnoff, tel. 521/984-6996, www.casacenote.com, US$125 s/d with shared bath, US$175 s/d with a/c) has spacious beachfront rooms with air-conditioning, one or two large beds, Wi-Fi, and fine ocean views. Decor is tasteful but low-key, with a large stucco relief of a Maya god in each room. There also are "eco accommodations"—very basic bungalows with shared bathroom and outdoor kitchen—that are too pricey considering how rustic they are. There's a well-tended beachfront pool in

the view from Chamico's in Soliman Bay

the center of it all, and Cenote Manatí is just across the street. Use of kayaks and snorkeling gear is included in the rate. À la carte breakfast is included, too.

Blue Sky Hotel (Tankah Tres, 1.7 kilometers/1 mile from the southern turnoff, tel. 998/800-1371, www.blueskyhotel.com.mx, US$175-250 s/d with a/c) is a boutique hotel offering nine breezy units with views of the Caribbean or jungle. Units are simple but elegant with large, private terraces and amenities like luxurious linens, high-pressure showers, and a state-of-the-art sound system. Turndown service, complete with aromatherapy, is provided each night. There's a refreshing pool facing the beach. Kayaks and snorkel gear are available to guests, too.

A gorgeous boutique hotel, ★ **Jashita Hotel** (Soliman Bay, 1.2 kilometers/0.7 mile from the northern turnoff, cell tel. 984/139-5131, www.jashitahotel.com, US$210 s/d with a/c, US$440-1,450 suite) sits on the curving Soliman Bay. It's an intimate place with elegant rooms that have marble floors, fine hardwoods, basin sinks, rainfall showerheads—some even have private plunge pools. The common areas are just as sophisticated without losing a sense of hominess; if anything, the fine art and high-end furnishings make you feel like you're staying at a very wealthy friend's home. There's also a great pool, a gourmet restaurant, and a breathtaking beach. Use of kayaks, stand-up paddleboards, and snorkel gear is included in the rate, as is breakfast. There's a minimum three-night stay; five-night minimum December 20-January 10.

If you have camping gear, make a beeline to ★ **Chamico's** (Soliman Bay, end of road, no phone, US$8 pp camping). A basic restaurant is located in a gorgeous palm tree grove, and tents can be set up at the far end of the beach. Rustic bathrooms are the only bummer, but it seems a small price to pay considering the location—swaying palms, gentle ocean waves, and, on a clear night, an endless array of stars. All to say, a slice of heaven.

INFORMATION AND SERVICES

There are no formal services here, because it's not really a formal town. Head to Tulum for ATMs, medical services, Internet, groceries, and more.

GETTING THERE AND AROUND

The turnoff to the southern portion of Tankah Tres is between kilometers 237 and 238 on the main highway, and marked with a large road sign. Driving south from Cancún, you'll have to overshoot the entrance a short distance until a break in the median (at Dreams Tulum Resort and Spa) allows you to make a U-turn and return to the turnoff; this access road makes a beeline for the shore, then turns abruptly to the left, hugging the beach and passing the listed hotels and sights. The access road to the northern section is a bit farther and is marked with a large sign for Oscar & Lalo's Restaurant, which is actually on the west side of the highway. If you don't have a car, you can ask a *combi* to drop you at either turnoff, but it will not enter Tankah Tres or Soliman Bay itself.

Tulum and the Costa Maya

Tulum has long been favored by travelers who cringe at the splashy resorts and package tourism found in Cancún (and increasingly the Riviera Maya).

In that sense, Tulum is a fitting bridge between Quintana Roo's booming northern section and its far-less-traveled south. Tulum has so far managed to avoid the impulse to fill the coast with ever-bigger resorts; prices have certainly gone up, but there are still no megadevelopments here, or even power lines for that matter. Its beaches and *cabañas* remain as idyllic as ever.

If Tulum is the anti-Cancún, you might call southern Quintana Roo, or the "Costa Maya," the non-Cancún. Though fairly close in distance, it's worlds apart by any other measure. Immediately south of Tulum is the massive Sian Ka'an Biosphere Reserve, one of the Yucatán's largest and richest preserves, whose bays, lagoons, mangrove stands, and inland forests support a vast array of plants and animals, from dolphins to jaguars; there's even a large Maya ruin and several smaller temples. Beyond Sian Ka'an is the Costa Maya, the sparsely populated stretch of coast reaching down to the Belize border; the largest towns are Mahahual and Xcalak, with numerous small bed-and-breakfasts and seaside hotels in both (and a highly incongruous cruise ship port in Mahahual). Most of the beaches aren't postcard perfect like Tulum's, but the isolation—not to mention the far-less-expensive lodging—are hard to match. Inland and farther south is the multicolored Laguna Bacalar and several significant but all-but-forgotten Maya ruins. Chetumal, the state capital, isn't much of a destination itself but has some unexpectedly appealing areas nearby, and is the gateway to Belize.

Less than an hour from Tulum—and a great alternative to the overcrowded ruins there—is the ancient city of Cobá (42 kilometers/26 miles from Tulum), home of the second-tallest known Maya pyramid. Unlike many other ruins, Cobá is ensconced in a thick tropical forest that teems with birdlife, including parrots and toucans.

PLANNING YOUR TIME

Tulum is the first stop, of course, and for many people their main destination. From Tulum

---

Previous: Tulum's scenic Maya ruins; Mahahual beach. **Above:** mural in Tulum.

Look for ★ to find recommended sights, activities, dining, and lodging.

Highlights

★ **Tulum's Southern Beaches:** Mile after mile of powdery white sand, tranquil turquoise water, cozy bungalows peeking out from behind softly bending palm trees . . . these are the beaches you've been dreaming of (page 203).

★ **Cenotes near Tulum:** Sure the ocean reefs are gorgeous, but don't miss a chance to explore these eerie and unforgettable limestone caverns, bristling with stalagmites and stalactites, and filled with the crystalline water of the world's longest underground river system (page 204).

★ **Cobá Archaeological Zone:** Just an hour from Tulum are the terrific jungle-cloaked ruins of Cobá, where you can climb the Yucatán's second-highest pyramid and rent bikes to get from temple to temple (page 222).

★ **Cenotes near Cobá:** A visit to Cobá just got better, with the opening of three impressive cenotes a short distance from the ruins. Each is unique, but all are massive caverns, with stalactites above and easy-to-use stairs descending to the cool shimmering water below (page 227).

★ **Bahía de la Ascensión:** A huge protected expanse of calm ocean flats and tangled mangrove forests make this a world-class destination for bird-watchers and anglers (page 231).

★ **Banco Chinchorro:** A punishing two-hour boat ride across the open sea is rewarded

with spectacular diving on one of the world's largest coral atolls (page 239).

★ **Fuerte San Felipe Bacalar:** Housed in a stout star-shaped fort, this small-town museum has fascinating and innovative displays on piracy and the Caste War (page 251).

Tulum and the Costa Maya

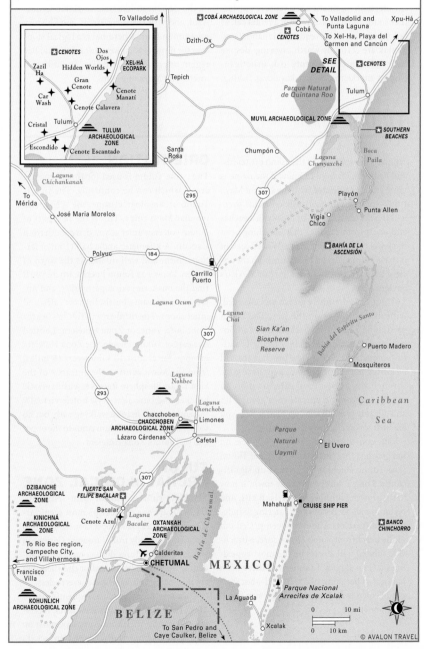

To Valladolid

★ CENOTES

Dos Ojos

Zazil Ha

Hidden Worlds

★ XEL-HÁ ECOPARK

Gran Cenote

Cenote Manatí

Car Wash

Cenote Calavera

Cristal

Tulum

≈ TULUM ARCHAEOLOGICAL ZONE

Escondido

Cenote Escantado

★ COBÁ ARCHAEOLOGICAL ZONE

Cobá

CENOTES

To Valladolid and Punta Laguna

To Xel-Ha, Playa del Carmen and Cancún

Xpu-Há

Dzith-Ox

Tepich

SEE DETAIL

★ CENOTES

Parque Natural de Quintana Roo

Tulum

MUYIL ARCHAEOLOGICAL ZONE

★ SOUTHERN BEACHES

Santa Rosa

Chumpón

Laguna Chunyaxché

Boca Paila

Laguna Chichankanah

295

307

Playón

Punta Allen

To Mérida

José Maria Morelos

Vigía Chico

★ BAHÍA DE LA ASCENSIÓN

Polyuc

184

Carrillo Puerto

Laguna Ocum

Laguna Chai

Sian Ka'an Biosphere Reserve

Bahía del Espíritu Santo

Puerto Madero

Mosquiteros

Caribbean Sea

293

Laguna Nohbec

Laguna Chonchoba

Chacchoben

CHACCHOBEN ARCHAEOLOGICAL ZONE

Limones

Lázaro Cárdenas

Cafetal

Parque Natural Uaymil

El Uvero

307

DZIBANCHÉ ARCHAEOLOGICAL ZONE

FUERTE SAN FELÍPE BACALAR

KINICHNÁ ARCHAEOLOGICAL ZONE

Bacalar

Cenote Azul

Laguna Bacalar

OXTANKAH ARCHAEOLOGICAL ZONE

Mahahual

CRUISE SHIP PIER

★ BANCO CHINCHORRO

To Río Bec region, Campeche City, and Villahermosa

Calderitas

CHETUMAL

Bahía de Chetumal

MEXICO

Francisco Villa

KOHUNLICH ARCHAEOLOGICAL ZONE

La Aguada

Parque Nacional Arrecifes de Xcalak

0   10 mi

0   10 km

BELIZE

To San Pedro and Caye Caulker, Belize

Xcalak

© AVALON TRAVEL

you can take day trips or short overnighters to the Sian Ka'an reserve and Cobá archaeological site, both fascinating. To venture any farther south you'll probably want a rental car, as bus service grows infrequent. Mahahual and Xcalak are certainly worth savoring; despite their isolation, there's plenty to do in both, including snorkeling, diving, kayaking, fishing, and, of course, just relaxing. Laguna Bacalar is worth a day or possibly two, to take a boat trip on the Caribbean-like water, swim in Cenote Azul, and visit the surprisingly good history museum in town. Chetumal is a logical stopover for those headed west toward the Río Bec region or crossing into Belize, and it has an interesting Maya museum.

Tulum

Tulum is the subject of a thousand postcards, and justly so. It's hard to know if the name is more closely associated with the ancient Maya ruins—perched dramatically on a cliff overlooking the Caribbean—or the idyllic beaches and oceanfront *cabañas* that have long been the jewel of the Riviera Maya. What's certain is that Tulum manages to capture both the ancient mystery and modern allure of Mexico's Riviera Maya.

Tulum has definitely grown and changed, with more changes on the way. The beach used to be a haven for backpackers and bohemians, with simple *cabañas* facing beautiful untouched beaches. The beaches are still beautiful, but the prices have long since gone through the *palapa* roof, catering more to urban escapists and upscale yoga groups. It's still a lovely place to stay, no matter who you are, just not as cheap as it used to be.

One consequence of the spike in prices on the beach is that the inland village of Tulum (aka Tulum Pueblo) has perked up significantly. Long a dumpy roadside town, it now has a growing number of hotels, B&Bs, and recommendable restaurants catering to independent travelers who have been priced out of the beachfront hotels. To be sure, a beachside *cabaña* will always be the most appealing place to stay in Tulum—and there are a handful of bargains still to be had—but staying in town is no longer the huge step down that it once was.

ORIENTATION

The name Tulum is used for three separate areas, which can be confusing. The first is Tulum archaeological zone, the scenic and popular Maya ruins. This is the first part of Tulum you encounter as you drive south from Cancún. A kilometer and a half (1 mile) farther south (and well inland) is the town of Tulum, known as Tulum Pueblo, where you'll find the bus terminal, supermarket, and numerous restaurants, hotels, Internet cafés, and other shops. The third area is Tulum's beachfront hotel zone, or Zona Hotelera. Located due east of Tulum Pueblo, the Zona Hotelera extends for almost 10 kilometers (6 miles) from the Maya ruins to the entrance of the Sian Ka'an Biosphere Reserve, with fantastic beaches and bungalow-style hotels virtually the entire way. There's a walking path, but no road, connecting the Tulum ruins to the upper end of Tulum's Zona Hotelera.

TULUM ARCHAEOLOGICAL ZONE

The Maya ruins of **Tulum** (8am-5pm daily, US$4.50) are one of Mexico's most scenic archaeological sites, built atop a 12-meter (40-foot) cliff rising abruptly from turquoise Caribbean waters. The structures don't compare in grandeur to those of Cobá, Uxmal, or elsewhere, but are interesting and significant nevertheless.

Tulum is the single most frequently visited Maya ruin in the Yucatán Peninsula, receiving thousands of visitors every day, most on package tours from nearby resorts. (In fact, it's

Tulum Archaeological Zone

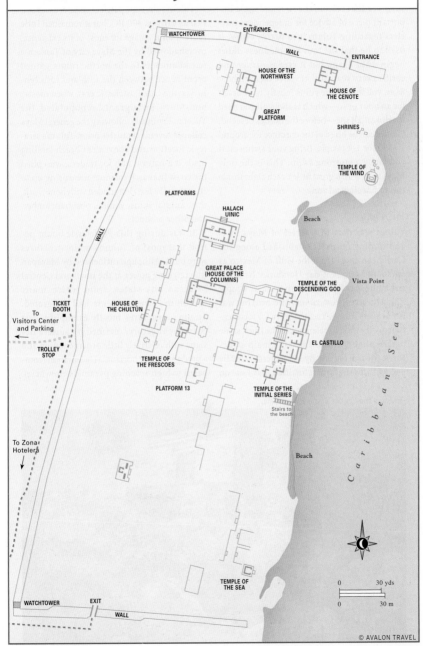

WATCHTOWER
ENTRANCE
WALL
ENTRANCE

HOUSE OF THE NORTHWEST

HOUSE OF THE CENOTE

GREAT PLATFORM

SHRINES

TEMPLE OF THE WIND

PLATFORMS

HALACH UINIC

Beach

GREAT PALACE (HOUSE OF THE COLUMNS)

TEMPLE OF THE DESCENDING GOD

Vista Point

HOUSE OF THE CHULTÚN

TICKET BOOTH

To Visitors Center and Parking

TROLLEY STOP

TEMPLE OF THE FRESCOES

EL CASTILLO

PLATFORM 13

TEMPLE OF THE INITIAL SERIES

Stairs to the beach

To Zona Hotelera

Caribbean Sea

Beach

WATCHTOWER

EXIT

WALL

TEMPLE OF THE SEA

0   30 yds
0   30 m

© AVALON TRAVEL

second only to Teotihuacán, near Mexico City, as the country's most visited archaeological site.) For that reason, the first and most important piece of advice for independent travelers regarding Tulum is to *arrive early.* It used to be that the tour bus madness didn't begin until 11am, but it creeps earlier and earlier every year. Still, if you're there right at 8am, you'll have the ruins mostly to yourself for an hour or so—which is about all you need for this small site—before the hordes descend. Guides can be hired at the entrance for around US$50 for 1-4 people. Bring your swimsuit if you fancy a morning swim: This is the only Maya ruin with a great little beach right inside the archaeological zone.

History

Tulum was part of a series of Maya forts and trading outposts established along the Caribbean coast from the Gulf of Mexico as far south as present-day Honduras. Its original name was Zamá-Xamanzamá or simply Zamá (derived from *zamal,* or dawn) but was later called Tulum, Yucatec Maya for fortification or city wall, in reference to the thick stone barrier that encloses the city's main structures. Measuring 380 by 165 meters (1,250 by 540 feet), it's the largest fortified Maya site on the Quintana Roo coast (though small compared to most inland ruins).

Tulum's enviable patch of seashore was settled as early as 300 BC, but it remained little more than a village for most of its existence, overshadowed by the Maya city of Tankah a few kilometers to the north. Tulum gained prominence between the 12th and 16th centuries (the Late Postclassic era), when mostly non-Maya immigrants repopulated the Yucatan Peninsula following the general Maya collapse several centuries prior. Tulum's strategic location and convenient beach landing made it a natural hub for traders, who plied the coast in massive canoes measuring up to 16 meters (52 feet) long, laden with honey, salt, wax, animal skins, vanilla, obsidian, amber, and other products.

It was during this Postclassic boom period that most of Tulum's main structures were built. Although influenced by Mayapán (the reigning power at the time) and Central Mexican city-states, from which many of Tulum's new residents had emigrated, Tulum's structures mostly exemplify "east coast architecture," defined by austere designs with relatively little ornamentation and a predominantly horizontal orientation (compared to high-reaching pyramids elsewhere).

House of the Cenote at the Tulum ruins

Rediscovering the Maya

The Maya ruins of the Yucatán Peninsula were all but unknown in the United States and Europe until well into the 19th century. Although Spanish explorers and colonizers had occupied the peninsula for more than two centuries, conflicts with local Maya and Catholic antipathy for all things pagan probably account for the Spaniards' lack of research or even apparent interest. To be fair, the immensity of the task was surely daunting—by the time the Spanish reached the Yucatán in the early 1500s, the majority of sites had been abandoned for at least 300 years, and in some cases double or triple that. Many were piles of rubble, and those still standing were mostly covered in vegetation. Just getting to the sites was a task in itself.

And so it was an American and an Englishman—diplomat **John Lloyd Stephens** and artist-architect **Frederick Catherwood**—who brought the Maya world to worldwide attention. Between 1839 and 1841, they conducted two major explorations of the Maya region, including present-day Yucatán, Chiapas, and Central America, visiting a total of 44 ruins. Stephens kept a detailed account of their travels, making many observations on the nature of Maya civilization that proved remarkably prescient. He correctly surmised that Maya writing contained detailed dynastic and historical accounts, and rejected the prevailing notion that Mesoamerican civilizations were descended from Egyptian or other Old World societies, declaring the mysterious ruins "a spectacle of a people skilled in architecture, sculpture, and possessing the culture and refinement attendant upon those, not derived from the Old World, but originating and growing here without models or masters like the plants and fruits of the soil, indigenous." Meanwhile, Catherwood made incredibly precise drawings of numerous structures, monuments, hieroglyphs, and scenes of peasant life. (Though they've been widely reprinted, you can see a rare collection of original Catherwood prints in Mérida, at the highly recommended museum-gallery Casa Catherwood.)

Stephens and Catherwood published their work in two volumes, both of which were instant sensations in the United States and Europe, awakening immense interest in ancient Maya civilization. Their books now are condensed into a single, very readable volume, *Incidents of Travel in Yucatán* (Hard Press, 2007), available in English and in many bookstores in the Yucatán. It is a fascinating read, not only for the historical value but also as a backdrop for your own travels throughout the region.

Ironically, construction in these later eras tended to be rather shoddy, thanks in part to improvements in stucco coverings that meant the quality of underlying masonry was not as precise. Today, with the stucco eroded away, Tulum's temples appear more decayed than structures at other sites, even those built hundreds of years prior.

The Spanish got their first view of Tulum, and of mainland indigenous society, on May 7, 1518, when Juan de Grijalva's expedition along the Quintana Roo coast sailed past the then brightly colored fortress. The chaplain of the fleet famously described the city as "a village so large that Seville would not have appeared larger or better." Tulum remained an important city and port until the mid-1500s, when European-borne diseases decimated its population. The once-grand city was effectively abandoned and, for the next three centuries, slowly consumed by coastal vegetation. In 1840, Spanish explorers referred to an ancient walled city known as Tulum, the first recorded use of its current name; two years later the famous American/English team of John Lloyd Stephens and Frederick Catherwood visited Tulum, giving the world its first detailed description and illustrations of the dramatic seaside site. During the Caste War, Tulum was occupied by members of the Talking Cross cult, including the followers of a Maya priestess known as the Queen of Tulum.

House of the Cenote

The path from the ticket booth follows Tulum's wall around the northwest corner to two low corbel arch entryways. Using the second entrance (closest to the ocean), you'll first see the Casa del Cenote. The two-room structure, with a third chamber added later, is less impressive than the gaping maw of its namesake cenote. The water is not drinkable, thanks to saltwater intrusion, but that may not have been the case a half millennium ago; it's unlikely Tulum could have grown to its size and prominence without a major water source, not only for its own residents but passing traders as well. Cenotes were also considered apertures to Xibalba, or the underworld, and an elaborate tomb discovered in the floor of the House of the Cenote suggests it may have had a ceremonial function as well.

Temple of the Wind

Following the path, the next major structure is the Temple of the Wind, perched regally atop a rocky outcrop overlooking a picturesque sandy cove. If it looks familiar, that's because it appears on innumerable postcards, magazine photos, and tourist brochures. (The view is even better from a vista point behind El Castillo, and of course from the ocean.) The name derives from the unique circular base upon which the structure is built: In Central Mexican cosmology, the circle is associated with the god of the wind, and its presence here (and at other ruins, like San Gervasio on Isla Cozumel) is evidence of the strong influence that Central Mexican migrants/invaders had on Postclassic Maya societies.

Temple of the Descending God

One of Tulum's more curious structures is the Temple of the Descending God, named for the upside-down winged figure above its doorway. Exactly who or what the figure represents is disputed among archaeologists—theories include Venus, the setting sun, the god of rain, even the god of bees (as honey was one of the coastal Maya's most widely traded products). Whatever the answer, it was clearly a deeply revered (or feared) deity, as the same image appears on several of Tulum's buildings, including the upper temple of Tulum's main pyramid. The Temple of the Descending God also is notable for its cartoonish off-kilter position, most likely the result of poor construction.

El Castillo

Tulum's largest and most imposing structure is The Castle, a 12-meter-high (40-foot) pyramid constructed on a rocky bluff of roughly the same height. Like many Maya structures, El Castillo was built in multiple phases. The first iteration was a low broad platform, still visible today, topped by a long palace fronted by a phalanx of stout columns. The second phase consisted of simply filling in the center portion of the original palace to create a base for a new and loftier temple on top. In the process, the builders created a vaulted passageway and inner chamber, in which a series of intriguing frescoes were housed; unfortunately, you're not allowed to climb onto the platform to see them. The upper temple (also off-limits) displays Central Mexican influence, including snakelike columns similar to those found at Chichén Itzá and grimacing Toltec masks on the corners. Above the center door is an image of the Descending God. Archaeologists believe a stone block at the top of the stairs may have been used for sacrifices.

Temple of the Frescoes

Though quite small, the Temple of the Frescoes is considered one of Tulum's most archaeologically significant structures. The name owes to the fading but remarkably detailed paintings on the structure's inner walls. In shades of blue, gray, and black, they depict various deities, including Chaac (the god of rain) and Ixchel (the goddess of the moon and fertility), and a profusion of symbolic imagery, including corn and flowers. On the temple's two facades are carved figures with elaborate headdresses and yet another image of the Descending God. The large grim-faced masks on the temple's corners are believed to represent Izamná, the Maya creator god.

Halach Uinic and the Great Palace

In front of El Castillo are the remains of two palatial structures: the House of the Halach Uinic and the Great Palace (also known as the House of the Columns). Halach Uinic is a Yucatec Maya term for king or ruler, and this structure seems to have been an elaborate shrine dedicated to Tulum's enigmatic Descending God. The building is severely deteriorated, but what remains suggests its facade was highly ornamented, perhaps even painted blue and red. Next door is the Great Palace, which likely served as residential quarters for Tulum's royal court.

Practicalities

Tulum's massive parking lot and strip-mall-like visitors complex ought to clue you in to the number of tourists that pass through here every day. (Did we mention to get here early?) You'll find a small museum and bookshop amid innumerable souvenir shops and fast-food restaurants. (If this is your first visit to a Maya ruin, don't be turned off by all the hubbub. Tulum is unique for its excessive and obnoxious commercialization; most sites have just a ticket booth and restrooms.)

The actual entrance and ticket booth are about one kilometer (0.6 mile) from the visitors center; it's a flat mild walk, but there are also **trolleys** that ferry guests back and forth for US$2.25 per person round-trip (kids under 10 ride free).

Getting There

The Tulum archaeological zone is a kilometer (0.6 mile) north of Tulum Pueblo on Highway 307. There are two entrances; the one farther south is newer and better, leading directly to the main parking lot (parking US$5.75). Arriving by bus or *combi*, be sure to ask the driver to let you off at *las ruínas* (the ruins) as opposed to the town. To return, flag down a bus or *combi* on the highway.

The road from Tulum Pueblo hits the coast near the upper end of the Zona Hotelera, which stretches from the archaeological zone down to the entrance of the Sian Ka'an reserve, almost exactly 10 kilometers (6 miles). The area north of the Tulum/Zona Hotelera junction has two easy-to-reach beach areas that are ideal for people staying in town.

Playa El Paraíso (Carr. Tulum-Punta Allen, 2 kilometers/1.2 miles north of junction, cell tel. 984/113-7089, www.elparaisohoteltulum.com, 8am-11pm daily) is a popular beach club on a scenic beach of the same name. Once little more than a bar and some hammocks, the beach club has grown popular with tour groups and has morphed into a bustling expanse of lounge chairs, beach beds, and umbrellas (US$5-20/day), with waiters weaving between them and the full restaurant and beach bar. It's busy but still scenic and relaxing.

Directly north of Playa El Paraíso is **Playa Mar Caribe** (Carr. Tulum-Punta Allen, 2.3 kilometers/1.4 miles north of junction), named after the rustic bungalows that have long fronted this portion of beach. Broad and unspoiled, this is a great place to come to lay out your towel on the soft white sand, which you share with a picturesque array of moored fishing boats. There are no services here, so be sure to bring snacks and plenty of water. Don't feel like carting lunch to the beach? Head to **Adelita Tulum** (tel. 984/116-7645, 10am-midnight, US$10-19), a laid-back restaurant on the beach just a few steps to the south.

★ Southern Beaches

Tulum's very best beaches—thick white sand, turquoise-blue water, gently bending palm trees—are toward the southern end of the Zona Hotelera. Not surprisingly, Tulum's finest hotels are in the same area, and there are no official public access points. That said, hotels rarely raise an eyebrow at the occasional nonguest cutting through to reach the beach. You can also grab breakfast or lunch at one of the hotel restaurants and cut down to the beach afterward; in some cases, you can even use the lounge chairs.

Aimed at an older crowd, **Ana y José Beach Club** (Carr. Tulum-Punta Allen, 2.4 kilometers/1.5 miles south of junction, no phone, www.anayjosebeachclub.com, 10am-6pm daily, free) is located about a kilometer (0.6 mile) north of the resort of the same name and is open to guests and nonguests alike. An airy, sand-floored dining area serves mostly seafood, including ceviche, shrimp cocktail, and grilled fish, at decent prices (US$6-14) and has a full bar (US$2-6). Chaise lounges and four-poster beach beds (US$5-20/day) are arranged a bit too close together, but they are comfy and relaxing nonetheless.

Ziggy Beach (Carr. Tulum-Punta Allen, 3.5 kilometers/2.1 miles south of junction, cell tel. 984/745-8023, www.beach-tulum. com, 9am-5pm daily, free) is a mellow beach club with rows of thick queen-size beach beds and lounge chairs plus hammocks strung from palm trees. They're free to use as long as you buy something from the restaurant bar. (Drinks often come with a complimentary round of chips and salsa, too). The beach, as expected, is as gorgeous here as pretty much anywhere along this coast.

A popular spot for weddings, **Ak'iin Beach Club** (Carr. Tulum-Punta Allen, 4 kilometers/2.4 miles south of junction, cell tel. 984/113-7293, www.akiintulum.com, 8:30am-5pm daily, free) is truly a beautiful spot. A wood plank walkway snakes through the leafy property before arriving at the white-sand beach. Along the way, guests pass the restaurant, a spacious high-roofed *palapa* structure, with a solid menu of Mexican and international dishes. There's also a two-for-one happy hour 5pm-7pm most days. Like neighboring beach clubs, use of the comfy beach couches, beds, and chairs are complimentary with the purchase of pretty much anything on the menu.

★ Cenotes

Dos Ojos (Hwy. 307 Km. 244, tel. 984/105-1048, www.divedosojos.com, 8am-5pm daily), or Two Eyes, is a reference to twin caverns that are the largest openings—but far from the only ones—into the labyrinthine river system that runs beneath the ground here. You can snorkel on your own (US$11.50), but you'll see a lot more on a guided snorkeling tour (US$46 pp, no reservations required); be sure to ask to visit the Bat Cave. After the tour, you're free to keep snorkeling on your own; in

one of Tulum's gorgeous southern beaches

fact, there are hammocks and benches, so you can bring food and drinks and make a day of it. Diving trips (US$120/two tanks, US$80/one tank, US$20/day for gear; maximum 4 divers/guide) should be arranged in advance. It's two kilometers (1.2 miles) from the entrance to the cenotes, so a rental car is handy. Discounts are available if you have your own gear. Cash only.

Once a bustling tourist attraction with a well-respected dive shop, **Hidden Worlds** (Hwy. 307 Km. 243, no phone, 9am–sunset daily) is now like most cenote businesses: a couple of people running the show from a simple *palapa*. Nevertheless, it remains a great introduction to underground snorkeling, with a gorgeous on-site cenote system. A 1.5-hour snorkeling tour runs US$35. (DIY snorkeling is not permitted—in fact, staffers drive visitors to the cenote entrance, deep in the jungle.)

One of the only cenotes in the Zona Hotelera that's open to the public, **Cenote Encantado** (aka Cenote Yax Chen, Carr. Tulum-Punta Allen Km. 10, 8am–sunset) is a winding channel of cool clear water with freshwater plants along the edges. Measuring about 300 meters (984 feet) in length, it's part of an intricate network of about 100 cenotes on the jungle side of Tulum. Three small hotels—Cabañas Xbalamque, Cenote Encantado, and Cenote El Encantado Cabañas—provide easy access (US$3.85 pp) as well as rent kayaks (US$4-7) and snorkel gear (US$4) to better explore it. Look for schools of tiny fish (and some say baby crocs) in the water as well as herons in the low-lying trees.

Other favorite cenotes include **Zazil Ha, Car Wash, Gran Cenote,** and **Calavera Cenote** (all west of Tulum on the road to Cobá); **Cristal** and **Escondido** (Hwy. 307 just south of Tulum); **Casa Cenote** (at Tankah Tres); and **Cenote Cristalino, Jardín del Edén,** and **Cenote Azul** (Hwy. 307 just north of Xpu-Há). All can be visited on a tour or by yourself, and most have snorkel gear for rent (US$6-8). Most are on private or *ejido* (collective) land and charge admission fees, usually US$4-7 for snorkelers and US$9-10 for divers. If you take a tour, ask if admission fees are included in the rate. Most cenotes are open 8am–5pm daily.

TOURS OF SIAN KA'AN BIOSPHERE RESERVE

Community Tours Sian Ka'an (Calle Osiris Sur near Calle Sol Ote, tel. 984/871-2202, www.siankaantours.org, 7am–7pm daily) is an excellent community-run agency offering

Despite being deep underground, most of the Riviera Maya's popular cenotes are quite accessible, with stairways and interior lighting.

a variety of tours (US$75-109, 3-7 hours) to the Sian Ka'an Biosphere, a 1.3-million-acre reserve of coastal and mangrove forests and wetlands, with pristine coral reefs and a huge variety of flora and fauna. Among the most popular outings are the "Muyil" route, which begins with a visit to the Muyil archaeological zone, then a boat tour of Muyil and Chunyaxche lagoons, including a chance to jump in and float down a long mangrove-edged canal; "Mayaking" in Sian Ka'an, a bird- and animal-spotting tour by kayak through the lagoons and mangroves; and a "Chicle" tour, where you learn about the practice of tapping chicle (gum) trees, from Maya times to today, followed by a swim in the lagoon.

Visit Sian Ka'an (Sian Ka'an Biosphere Reserve, Carr. Tulum-Punta Allen Km. 15.8, cell tel. 984/141-4245, www.visitsiankaan. com) offers many of the "standard" Sian Ka'an tours—boating, snorkeling, bird-watching, ruin exploration—but will run a tour with just two guests (there's a maximum of 6). Though pricier, it also offers customized tours of the reserve, tailored to your interests. All excursions include a typical Maya lunch plus snacks and drinks. Guides are enthusiastic and knowledgeable; all are bilingual.

ENTERTAINMENT AND SHOPPING
Entertainment
ZONA HOTELERA

The lounge bar at **La Zebra** (Carr. Tulum-Punta Allen, 4.8 kilometers/3 miles south of junction, cell tel. 984/800-1943, www.lazebratulum.com, 8am-10pm Mon.-Sat., 8am-midnight Sun.) serves up shots and mixed drinks, including its signature Zebra margarita, made with pineapple and ginger and served on the rocks. On Sunday, it hosts a salsa party 8pm-midnight, with a free dance class at 6pm. Dinner reservations are recommended if you want to feast on pulled-pork tacos between sets.

Papaya Playa Project (Carr. Tulum-Punta Allen, 1.5 kilometers/1 mile south of junction, cell tel. 984/116-3774, www. papayaplayaproject.com, hours vary) has a regular lineup of live musical acts, plus full-moon parties, bongo drum sessions, and an overall counterculture vibe. Saturday is the main night, but look for schedules online or around town for upcoming events. Papaya Playa is actually a rustic-chic resort, hence all the *cabañas,* but is better known (and better liked, really) as a place to party. Most shows begin around 10pm; cover is US$5-10.

The upscale boutique resort **Mezzanine** (Carr. Tulum-Punta Allen, 1.3 kilometers/0.8 mile north of junction, cell tel. 984/131-1596, www.mezzaninetulum.com) is known as the go-to bar on Friday nights, with cool cocktails and a hip vibe on a relaxed beachfront patio.

Gitano (Carr. Tulum-Punta Allen, 3 kilometers/1.8 mile south of junction, cell tel. 984/188-2184, www.gitanotulum.mx, 6pm-12:30am) is a hipster jungle restaurant/bar, known for its mixologists, DJs, and dance floor. It's definitely a scene—down to the beautiful people inside and the velvet ropes keeping out the riffraff. That said, if you like mezcal, can clean up nicely, and want to run with the "it" crowd, this is a great option.

IN TOWN

El Curandero (Av. Tulum at Calle Beta, tel. 984/871-2414, www.curanderotulum.com, 7pm-2am daily) is the best of several local bars cut from the same cloth: small, mood lit, with great music and a relaxed, welcoming vibe. There's live music weekdays, electronica on Saturday, and movies on Thursday. Look for the crowd spilling out—and partying—right outside its doors.

Just off the main drag, **El Batey** (Calle Centauro Sur btwn Av. Tulum and Calle Andromeda Ote., no phone, 7am-2am Mon.-Sat., 7am-1am Sun.) is a hopping bar that features live jazz, blues, and Mexican *bohemia* groups most nights starting at 9pm. There's a leafy courtyard in the back where bands set up, an artsy little bar in front, and a VW bug converted into a mojito bar on the street in front (with drinks made with real sugar cane!).

Waye'Rest-Bar (Av. Tulum btwn Calles Beta and Osiris, tel. 984/806-4206, 7am-3am daily) is a bigger *palapa*-roofed place playing mostly reggae and *norteños* (Mexican music from the northern states). It doesn't have the hipster atmosphere of other bars in town, but its drinks are cheap and strong, making it a popular stop.

Shopping

Tulum's main drag is peppered with *artesanía* and knickknack shops. You'll find everything from T-shirts and magnets to high-end Maya replicas and custom-made jewelry. Consider window-shopping a bit—it won't take long to peruse most of the shops. A couple of standouts include:

MexicArte (Av. Tulum btwn Calles Alfa and Jupiter, tel. 984/871-2136, 10am-10pm daily) has a large selection of quality folk art, from green copper suns to carved wooden angels and masks. Cool T-shirts, jewelry, cards, and more also are sold. There's a sister shop of the same name in the Zona Hotelera (Punta Piedra, Carr. Tulum-Punta Allen, 1 kilometer/0.6 mile south of junction, same hours).

Casa Hernández (Av. Tulum at Calle Centauro, no phone, 9am-5pm daily except Thurs.) specializes in handcrafted pottery and ceramics, mostly from Puebla. Items range from mugs and picture frames to finely painted plates and dinner sets.

SPORTS AND RECREATION
Scuba Diving

The reef here is superb, but Tulum's diving claim to fame is the huge and easily accessible network of freshwater cenotes, caverns, and caves, offering truly one-of-a-kind dive environments. Divers with open-water certification can dive in cenotes (little or no overhead) and caverns (no more than 30 feet deep or 130 feet from an air pocket) without additional training. Full-cave diving requires advanced certification, which is also available at many of Tulum's shops. If you haven't dived in a while, definitely warm up with some open-water dives before doing a cenote or cavern trip. Buoyancy control is especially important in such environments because of the roof above and the sediment below, and is complicated by the fact that it's freshwater instead of saltwater, and entails gear you may not be accustomed to, namely thick wetsuits and a flashlight.

Prices for cenotes and caverns are fairly uniform from shop to shop: around

painted *calaveras*, a kind of *artesanía*

US$85-120 for one tank or US$120-165 for two. Be sure to ask whether gear and admission to the cenotes are included. Shops also offer multidive packages, cave and cavern certification courses, and hotel packages if you'll be staying awhile. As always, choose a shop and guide you feel comfortable with, not necessarily the least-expensive one.

If you plan on doing as much cave and cavern diving as possible, **Xibalba Dive Center** (Calle Andrómeda btwn Calles Libra and Geminis, tel. 984/871-2953, www.xibalbadivecenter.com, 9am-7pm daily) not only has an excellent record for safety and professionalism, but now has an on-site hotel with comfortable rooms, a small swimming pool, and space to dry, store, and repair gear. Good lodging and diving packages are available. Xibalba also fills its own tanks and offers free Nitrox to experienced clients. The shop's name, aptly enough, comes from the Yucatec Maya word for the underworld.

Koox Dive Center (Av. Tulum btwn Calles Beta and Osiris, tel. 984/141-5502, www.kooxdiving.com, 9am-sunset daily) is another reliable option for diving and snorkeling, on the reef and in cenotes.

Mot Mot Diving (Av. Tulum at Calle Beta, tel. 984/802-5442, www.motmotdiving.com, 8am-9pm daily) is recommended by several hotel owners.

Cenote Dive Center (Calle Centauro at Calle Andrómeda, cell tel. 984/876-3285, www.cenotedive.com, 8am-4pm Sun.-Fri.) offers a large variety of tours and courses, in Tulum and beyond.

In the Zona Hotelera, **Mexi-Divers** (Punta Piedra, Carr. Tulum-Punta Allen, 1.5 kilometers/0.9 mile south of junction, tel. 984/807-8805, www.mexidivers.com, 8:30am-5pm daily) is located opposite Zamas Hotel in the Punta Piedra area and has regularly scheduled snorkeling and diving trips, in the ocean and nearby cenotes.

Snorkeling

Like divers, snorkelers have an embarrassment of riches in Tulum, with great reef snorkeling and easy access to the eerie beauty of the area's many cenotes. **Dive shops in Tulum** offer snorkel trips of both sorts; prices vary considerably, so be sure to ask which and how many reefs or cenotes you'll visit, for how long, and what's included (gear, entrance fees, transport, snacks, etc.). Reef trips cost US$30-45 visiting 1-3 different spots, while cenote trips run US$50-65; snorkel gear can also be rented.

Kiteboarding

Extreme Control (no storefront, tel. 984/745-4555, www.extremecontrol.net) is Tulum's longest-operating kiteboarding outfit, offering courses and rentals for all experience levels and in various languages. Classes are held on Tulum's southernmost beach at Rosa del Viento Hotel (Carr. Tulum-Punta Allen Km. 10) as well as at Caleta Tankah, just a short drive north of town. Private classes are US$75 per hour, or US$225-390 for 3-6-hour introductory packages, including equipment; group classes are somewhat less.

Mexican Caribbean Kitesurf & Paddlesurf (Ahau Tulum, Carr. Tulum-Punta Allen Km. 4.4, tel. 984/168-1023, www.mexicancaribbeankitesurf.com, 9am-5:30pm daily) is a friendly shop with IKO-certified instructors and top-of-the-line equipment. Private and group instruction is offered in 3-9-hour courses (US$165-405 group, US$240-600 private). Wave-kitesurfing—a hybrid of kiting and surfing—classes are also offered (US$55-80/hour).

A well-respected kiting shop, **Ocean Pro Kite** (Av. Tulum btwn Calles Centauro and Orion Sur, cell tel. 984/119-0328, www.oceanprokite.com, 9am-5pm daily) offers classes on 100 meters (300 feet) of empty (or near-empty) beach in front of the Villa Las Estrellas hotel (Carr. Tulum-Punta Allen Km. 8). Instruction is offered to beginners as well as experts. Ninety-minute private classes run US$100, group classes US$80. Packages and rentals are also available.

Morph Kiteboarding (Hotel Playa Azul, Carr. Tulum-Punta Allen Km. 7, cell tel. 984/114-9524, www.morphkiteboarding.

com, 9am-sunset daily) also offers classes to all levels of kiteboarders. Rates are for private classes, though group lessons can be arranged as well: US$235, US$390, and US$468 for three-, five-, and six-hour courses, respectively.

Stand-Up Paddling

Stand-up paddling, or "SUPing," has exploded in popularity, a challenging but relatively easy sport to learn, and especially well-suited to the calm clear waters found in much of the Riviera Maya. You can see a surprising amount of sealife doing SUP instead of kayaking, thanks simply to the improved vantage point.

Ocean Pro Kite (Av. Tulum btwn Calles Centauro and Orion Sur, cell tel. 984/119-0328, www.oceanprokite.com, 9am-5pm daily) offers SUP lessons for all levels, starting with safety and theory on the beach, graduating to kneeling paddling, then standing and catching waves. Private classes are US$40 per hour, while groups of two or three start at US$25 per person per hour. Classes typically are held in the Zona Hotelera at Villa Las Estrellas (Carr. Tulum-Punta Allen Km. 8). Gear and refreshments are included, and rentals are also available.

Mexican Caribbean Kitesurf & Paddlesurf (Ahau Tulum, Carr. Tulum-Punta Allen Km. 4.4, tel. 984/168-1023, www.mexicancaribbeankitesurf.com, 9am-5:30pm daily) offers paddleboarding and paddlesurfing classes (US$50/hour). Once the lesson is over, students are free to use the paddleboards for as long as they'd like. Several SUPing-snorkeling tours are also offered (US$80-90, 4 hours). Rentals are available, too, with free delivery.

Extreme Control (no storefront, tel. 984/745-4555, www.extremecontrol.net) offers SUPing lessons (US$70 private, US$50 pp 2 pax, US$40 pp 3+ pax; 2 hours) plus tours in area cenotes and on the oceanfront, including transport to and from Tulum, Akumal, and Tankah. Hourly and weekly paddleboard rentals are also available.

Ecoparks

Built around a huge natural inlet, **Xel-Há** (Hwy. 307, 9 kilometers/5.6 miles north of Tulum, toll-free Mex. tel. 800/009-3542, toll-free U.S./Can. tel. 855/326-2696, www.xel-ha.com, 9am-6pm daily, US$80 adult all-inclusive, US$40 child under 12, child under 5 free) is all about water—being in and around it. Activities include snorkeling, snuba, tubing,

For some, stand-up paddling is a family affair.

TULUM AND THE COSTA MAYA

TULUM

aquatic ziplines, and interactive programs with dolphins, manatees, and stingrays. Although it doesn't compare to snorkeling on the reef, there's a fair number of fish darting about, and it makes for a fun, easy intro for children and beginners. A buffet lunch and open bar are included. Check the website for online deals and combo packages with sister parks Xcaret and Xplor.

Bicycling

In town, **iBike Tulum** (Av. Cobá Sur at Calle Venus, tel. 984/802-5518, www.ibiketulum. com, 9am-5:30pm Mon.-Sat.) offers mountain bike tours through jungle trails to cenotes and dry caves. Prices vary depending on the tour; they typically last 4-5 hours and are limited to eight cyclists.

Spas

Set on the jungle side of the road, the luxurious **Yaan Wellness Energy Spa** (Carr. Tulum-Punta Allen Km. 10, tel. 984/179-1530, www.yaanwellness.com, 9:30am-9pm daily) offers a wide range of spa services. Massages, body treatments, facials, soaking baths— even energy healing and traditional *temascal* (pre-Hispanic sweat lodge) ceremonies. All treatments begin with a "Healing Water Circuit," which includes leisurely stops in the sauna, steam room, and hot and cold massage pools. Most services run around US$175-200 per hour—pricey for sure, but totally worthwhile.

Overlooking the beach at Azulik Hotel, **Maya Spa Wellness Center** (Carr. Tulum-Punta Allen Km. 5, toll-free Mex. tel. 800/681-9537, www.maya-spa.com, 8am-8pm daily) offers a variety of massages, facials, and body wraps in a gorgeous setting. Massages run US$80 to US$185 (45-90 minutes), while other treatments include body wraps (US$185, 90 minutes) and facials (US$90, 60 minutes).

Located at the Ana y José hotel, **Om...Spa** (Carr. Tulum-Punta Allen Km. 7, tel. 984/871-2477, www.anayjose.com, 9am-5pm daily) is a full-service spa set in a chic beachfront setting. Choose from a menu of massages ranging from Swedish and Thai to Reiki and Maya

(US$80-130, 60-90 minutes) and body treatments like exfoliations, facials, and body wraps (US$70-100, 60-80 minutes). Packages for individuals and couples are also available.

Yoga

Surrounded by lush vegetation, **Yoga Shala Tulum** (Carr. Tulum-Punta Allen Km. 7.4, cell tel. 984/141-8116, www.yogashalatulum. com, 8:30am-6pm Mon.-Fri., 10am-6pm Sat.-Sun.) offers a wide range of yoga instruction in its gorgeous open-air studio. Classes cost US$15 each or US$50 per week for unlimited classes. There also is an affordable hotel on-site. Look for it on the inland side of the Zona Hotelera road.

Yaan Wellness Energy Spa (Carr. Tulum-Punta Allen Km. 10, tel. 984/179-1530, www.yaanwellness.com, 9:30am-9pm daily) offers drop-in yoga classes—vinyasa and hatha, mostly—in its 2nd story open-air studio. Classes are at 10am and 5pm every day and run US$20 per person.

Maya Spa Wellness Center (Azulik Hotel, Carr. Tulum-Punta Allen Km. 5, toll-free Mex. tel. 800/681-9537, www.maya-spa. com, 8am-8pm daily) also offers hatha and vinyasa yoga sessions at 7am and 9am daily. Classes cost US$15 per person; private instruction is also available.

FOOD
Zona Hotelera

Adelita Tulum (Carr. Tulum-Punta Allen, 2.2 kilometers/1.3 miles north of junction, tel. 984/116-7645, 10am-midnight, US$10-19) is a hip-without-the-attitude beachfront restaurant/bar with a strong menu of gourmet seafood dishes and beach munchies. Tables and hammocks are set up under slatted wood structures, *palapas,* or on the beach. There's also a great bar with swings for seats and dreamy cocktails.

Located well down the coastal road, ★ **Hechizo** (Carr. Tulum-Punta Allen Km. 10.2, tel. 984/879-5020, 6:30pm-11pm Mon.-Sat., US$19-30) is considered by many to be Tulum's finest restaurant. Specializing in gourmet Mexican fare, it features innovative creations like lobster and green tomato *pozole* and seared ahi tuna on jicama-green apple salad. Prix fixe five-course dinners (US$50-60) also are offered nightly. Seating is at long handmade tables in a softly lit dining room or outside, under the stars with a view of the surf. The chefs and owners, who also happen to be married, are Ritz-Carlton transplants.

Thai is the specialty at **Mezzanine** (Carr. Tulum-Punta Allen, 1.3 kilometers/0.8 mile north of junction, cell tel. 984/131-1596, www.mezzaninetulum.com, 8am-10pm daily, US$10-23), one of Tulum's chicest hotels on the beach. Curries—red, green, sweet potato, pineapple—and house specialties like crispy-style whole fish and lemongrass soup are among the dishes served in a fashionable dining area or on a shaded outdoor patio, both with fine sea views. A full bar and cool music make this a place to linger.

La Zebra (Carr. Tulum-Punta Allen, 4.8 kilometers/3 miles south of junction, cell tel. 984/800-1943, www.lazebratulum.com, 8am-10pm Mon.-Sat., 8am-midnight Sun., US$10-23) serves up classic Mexican dishes like tortilla soup, chicken in mole sauce, and chiles rellenos (stuffed peppers). For lighter fare, check out the ceviche bar, with everything from fish and shrimp to octopus and tuna (there's even a vegan option!). Tables are set up on a lovely beachfront patio and in a *palapa*-roofed dining area; at night, the long entry path is lit by lanterns. On Sunday there's a popular barbecue and salsa party starting at 8pm (free dance classes at 6pm).

Posada Margherita (Carr. Tulum-Punta Allen, 2.4 kilometers/1.5 miles south of junction, tel. 984/801-8493, www.posadamargherita.com, 7am-9:30pm daily, US$10-30) specializes in homemade pastas and breads. Service is personalized to the point of having no menus—instead, the waiter pulls up a chair to discuss the dishes being prepared that night (ask for prices before ordering—many customers are shocked when the bill arrives). It's busy most nights, so expect a wait—fortunately, the cocktails and the view are killer.

In Town

One of the best breakfast places in town, ★ **Azafrán** (Av. Satélite near Calle Polar, cell tel. 984/129-6130, www.azafrantulum.com, 8am-3pm daily, US$5-11) serves up superb morning meals made with gourmet products: homemade bagels with prosciutto and Brie, crepes stuffed with an assortment of fresh fruits, *chaya* omelets, and pâté platters with freshly baked bread. Organic coffee is a must, as is the fresh-squeezed orange juice. The only bummer about this place is that it gets crowded fast—come early to beat the morning rush.

★ **El Asadero** (Av. Satélite near Calle Sagitario, tel. 984/157-8998, 4:30pm-11:30pm Mon.-Sat., US$6-19) is the go-to steak house for locals and expats looking for a spectacular meal without breaking the bank. Meat, chicken, and yes, even veggies, are grilled in the open kitchen, the flavorful smells wafting throughout the dining room and out to the streetside tables. Try the hearty taco plate with your choice of fillings, cooked to order. All meals come with crispy tortilla chips and a trio of homemade salsas.

Taquería El Carboncito (Av. Tulum btwn Calles Acuario and Jupiter; 6pm-2am Wed.-Mon., US$1-5) serves up hot tacos at plastic tables in the driveway of an auto shop that's closed for the night. That is, it's a great place for a cheap tasty meal, and popular with local families.

For seafood, don't miss **La Barracuda** (Av. Tulum near Calle Luna Norte, tel. 984/160-0325, noon-8pm Tues.-Sun., US$6-13), a popular Mexican eatery with plastic tables and chairs located on the main drag. Ceviche and fish soup are the specialty, but the shrimp cocktail and made-to-order fish dishes are mouthwatering. All to say, the seafood here is super fresh, super tasty, and served in generous portions.

Cetli (Calle Polar Norte at Calle Orion Norte, cell tel. 984/108-0681, 5pm-10pm Thurs.-Tues., US$10-20) serves up modern Mexican creations by Chef Claudia Pérez, a Mexico City transplant and a graduate of one of Mexico's top culinary schools. The menu is full of the unique and unexpected, from chicken and *chaya* roll in peanut mole to *agua de pepino con yerba buena* (mint cucumber water). Chef Pérez herself is a delight and often comes out to chat with diners. Reservations are required and can be made via Facebook.

Le Bistro (Calle Centauro near Av. Tulum, cell tel. 984/134-4507, 8:30am-11:30pm daily, US$4-15) is a bustling café offering a full range of French delicacies—from freshly baked croissants to duck confit. Tables are set up outdoors, either on the front porch or under umbrellas in the back courtyard; neither is particularly charming, but the food is so good, it's easy to overlook.

Don't let the nautical theme fool you: **La Nave** (Av. Tulum between Calles Beta and Osiris, tel. 984/871-2592, 7am-11pm Mon.-Sat., US$7-14) is more about thin crispy pizza than fish fry. Whether you go all out with a Brie and prosciutto pizza or stick with a classic margherita, you'll leave satisfied. Pasta dishes and hefty appetizers are excellent alternatives.

El Pequeño Buenos Aires (Av. Tulum btwn Calles Orion and Beta, tel. 984/871-2708, 11am-11pm daily, US$7-30) serves excellent cuts of beef, including a *parrillada Argentina,* which comes piled with various cuts, plus chicken and sausage. The menu also includes crepes, a few vegetarian dishes, and lunch specials.

For home-style Mexican cooking, head to **Don Cafeto's** (Av. Tulum btwn Calles Centauro and Orion, tel. 984/871-2207, 7am-11pm daily, US$5-18), serving Mexican staples like mole and enchiladas, plus ceviche plates that are meals unto themselves. On a hot day, try a tall cold *chayagra,* an uplifting blend of pineapple juice, lime juice, cucumber, and *chaya* (similar to spinach).

Sweets and Groceries

A classic Mexican bakery, **Pan del Carmen** (Av. Tulum near Calle Osiris, 6am-11pm daily, US$0.50-1.50) is a bustling shop offering everything from fresh rolls to chocolate-filled *cuernos* (croissants). Be sure to grab a metal tray and tongs to make your selections.

La Reyna de Michoacan (Calle Alfa Sur at Calle Sol Ote, no phone, 7:30am-11:30pm, US$1.50-3) specializes in *paletas* (frozen ice pop), *helado* (ice cream), *aguas* (juices), and *licuados* (smoothies), all made with fresh fruits. There's a huge variety of flavors—from coconut and strawberry to guava and pineapple with chile. It's a perfect stop while strolling about town.

The Zona Hotelera's largest market is a **convenience store** (Punta Piedra, 9am-9pm daily), which is filled with snack food, canned goods, water, liquor, and sunscreen.

For a supermarket with the basics and then some, head to the **Chedraui** (Av. Cobá s/n, 7am-10pm daily), located between Tulum town and the Zona Hotelera; beyond fresh, dry, and canned food, you'll find a bakery, a beachwear and shoe section, even home appliances.

Tulum Pueblo has a great local fruit and vegetable shop, **Huerta del Eden** (Av. Tulum at Calle Alfa Norte, no phone, 7am-9pm daily). On Sunday, check out the **Tianguis Orgánico y Natural** (central plaza, 10am-3pm), a farmers market featuring organic produce, artisanal products, and homeopathic medicines.

ACCOMMODATIONS

Chances are you've come to Tulum to stay in one of the famous beachside bungalow-type hotels. There are many to choose from, each slightly different but most sharing a laid-back atmosphere and terrific beaches. However, some travelers are surprised by just how rustic some accommodations are, even those charging hundreds of dollars per night. The root of the matter is that there are no power lines or freshwater wells serving the beach. Virtually all accommodations have salty water in the showers and sinks. Most have fans, but not all, and electricity may be limited to nighttime hours only. Air-conditioning is available in only a handful of places. At the same time, some hotels use generators to power their restaurants and reception, so it's worth asking for a room away from the generator; nothing is a bigger killjoy than a diesel motor pounding outside your window when the point of coming here was to enjoy the peace and quiet.

If staying on the beach is out of your budget (join the club!), staying in town is a perfectly good alternative. The options have improved significantly, with a crop of new bed-and-breakfasts and boutique hotels to go along with a burgeoning number of hostels and budget digs. The beach is just a short drive or bike ride away, and prices for food, Internet, and laundry are much lower.

Zona Hotelera
UNDER US$50

Fronting a winding cenote, ★ **Cenote Encantado** (Carr. Tulum-Punta Allen Km. 10, cell tel. 984/142-5930, www.cenoteencantado.com, US$15.50 pp tent) is, in some ways, a throwback to Tulum's beginnings: a haven for backpackers with boho spirit. The hotel is more like a camping village with 17 tents set up around the leafy property. Each has an airbed with sheets, a bedside table, a lamp and fan (there's electricity), Wi-Fi, even a rug. There's also a clean communal kitchen and a cozy wood-floor lounge for meditating, yoga classes (US$8-15), and just hanging out; both structures are breezy but enclosed with strong mosquito netting. Open-air showers and dry toilets round out the camping-plus experience. Use of bikes is complimentary—and a necessity, really, if you want to go to the beach. Admission to the cenote also is included, as are inflatable rafts and floaties (snorkel gear extra).

Next door, **Cabañas Xbalamque** (Carr. Tulum-Punta Allen Km. 10, cell tel. 984/140-3156, xbalamquetulum@gmail.com, US$45-65 s/d with shared bathroom) has eight simple *palapa*-roofed cabins on a palm-tree-laden property. Each has a decent bed with mosquito netting, big screened windows, and electricity (5:30pm-2am only). There's also an open-air kitchen with a gas-operated fridge to keep your perishables kicking, as well as a

comfortable lounge with Wi-Fi. Admission to Cenote Yax Chen (in the backyard) is included in the rate as is use of kayaks and snorkel gear.

Santa Fe (Carr. Tulum-Punta Allen, 2.5 kilometers/1.5 miles north of junction, tel. 984/136-5248, US$8 pp tent) is a beachfront restaurant (8am-6pm daily) that welcomes campers on its property. The facilities are very basic—wear your flip-flops in the shower—and there's no electricity after 10pm. (All the better to enjoy the night sky!)

US$50-100

A private home turned yoga hotel, **Yoga Shala Tulum** (Carr. Tulum-Punta Allen Km. 7.5, cell tel. 984/141-8116, www.yogashalatulum.com, US$49/79 s/d with shared bath, US$99/109 s/d) offers simple but comfortable rooms on a jungly plot on the inland side of the Zona Hotelera. Rooms have whitewashed walls, polished cement floors, and good beds and linens, with a bit of boho flair, too. Outside is an impressive open-air yoga studio with a high *palapa* roof and gorgeous wood floors. There's also a restaurant on-site and Wi-Fi in the common areas.

Ahau Tulum (Carr. Tulum-Punta Allen Km. 4.4, cell tel. 984/802-5632, www.ahautulum.com, US$79 s/d) is not exclusively a budget place—it's got rooms that go for over US$400—but its guesthouse units (with shared bathrooms) and stick-built "Bali Huts" are among the cheapest digs on the beach. Gaps in the walls and bathrooms that never get truly clean are the price you pay to be on the sand for this cheap—a bargain for boho beach hounds.

US$100-200

Although sharing a bathroom for over US$150 a night doesn't seem quite right, **Coco Tulum** (Carr. Tulum-Punta Allen Km. 8, cell tel. 984/157-4830, www.cocotulum.com, US$155-180 s/d with shared bath, US$225-330 s/d) does the basics with style. Tidy *palapa*-roofed bungalows have cement floors, comfy beds, hanging bookshelves, fans, and sleek black exteriors with private patios. The

Tulum Town and Zona Hotelera

SCALE NOT AVAILABLE

To Cenote Cristal, Escondido, Muyil Archaeological Zone, Mahahual, and Chetumal

307

AVENIDA TULUM

HOTEL DON DIEGO DE LA SELVA

JARDÍN DE FRIDA

LA BARRACUDA

SECRET GARDEN

KELLY BIKE RENTAL

HOSPITAL DE TULUM

POSADA LUNA DEL SUR

TAQUERÍA EL CARBONCITO

CENTRO DE SALUD TULUM

FARMACIA SIMILARES

BUS STATION

LAVANDERÍA

HUERTA DEL EDEN

MEXICARTE

LA REYNA DE MICHOACAN

Central Plaza

CHAN-CHEN

ZAZILHA

KUKULCAN

ACUARIO NORTE

AVENIDA TULUM NORTE

LUNA NORTE

LUNA PTE.

CENTAURO PTE.

SATURNO NORTE

LUNA PRIV.

SATURNO SUR

MERCURIO OTE

LUNA SUR

ACUARIO SUR

JÚPITER SUR

MERCURIO SUR

AEROLITO

LEO SUR

ARIES SUR

NEPTUNO SUR

PLUTÓN SUR

ALFA SUR

PRIV. ALFA SUR

OMEGA

BETA SUR

OSIRIS SUR

ZONA

To Sian Ka'an, Sol Caribe, Visit Sian Ka'an, and Punta Allen

To Sian Ka'an, Sol Caribe, Visit Sian Ka'an, and Punta Allen

Cenote Encantado

HECHIZO

CENOTE ENCANTADO

CABAÑAS XBALAMQUE

YAAN WELLNESS ENERGY SPA

DOS CEIBAS

SUEÑOS TULUM

TULUM'S SOUTHERN BEACHES

LA ZEBRA

YOKTE BIKES

YOGA SHALA TULUM

ZIGGY BEACH

AHAU TULUM/MEXICAN CARIBBEAN KITESURF & PADDLESURF

AK'IIN BEACH CLUB

TITA TULUM

HOTEL NUEVA VIDA DE RAMIRO

OM.. SPA

GITANO

CABAÑAS LA LUNA

MORPH KITEBOARDING

POSADA MARGHERITA

POSADA LAMAR

COCO TULUM

Caribbean Sea

© AVALON TRAVEL

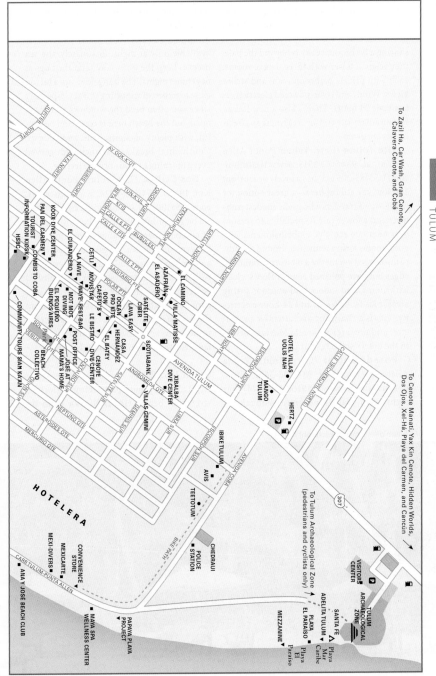

To Zazil Ha, Car Wash, Gran Cenote,
Calavera Cenote, and Cobá

To Cenote Manatí, Yax Kin Cenote, Hidden Worlds,
Dos Ojos, Xel-Há, Playa del Carmen, and Cancún

To Tulum Archaeological Zone
(pedestrians and cyclists only)

307

VISITORS
CENTER

TULUM
ARCHAEOLOGICAL
ZONE

Playa
Mar
Caribe

Playa
El
Paraíso

SANTA FE
ADELITA TULUM
PLAYA
EL PARAÍSO

MEZZANINE

PAPAYA PLAYA
PROJECT

MAYA SPA
WELLNESS CENTER

ANA Y JOSÉ BEACH CLUB

CARR TULUM-PUNTA ALLEN

MEXI-DIVERS

MEXICARTE
CONVENIENCE
STORE

CHEDRAUI

POLICE
STATION

TEETOTUM

AVIS

IBIKE TULUM

BIKE PATH

HOTELERA

COMMUNITY TOURS SIAM KA'AN

MERCURIO OTE
ASTEROIDES OTE
NEPTUNO OTE

VENUS
Parque Otte

SOL OTE
MAMA'S HOME

BEACH
COLECTIVO
JOSÉ ALT-OTE

BUENOS AIRES
EL PEQUEÑO

MOT MOT
DIVING

POST OFFICE

CENOTE
DIVE CENTER

EL BATEY

LE BISTRO

CASA
HERNÁNDEZ

ANDROMEDA OTE

VILLAS GEMINI

SCOTIABANK
DIVE CENTER

XIBALBA
DIVE CENTER

MANGO
TULUM

HERTZ

HOTEL VILLAS
UOLIS NAH

AVENIDA TULUM

VILLA MATISSE

EL CAMINO

AZAFRÁN
EL ASADERO

SATÉLITE
CIBER

LAVA EASY

PRO KITE
CAFETO'S
OCEAN

DON
MOVISTAR
NAVE-REST-BAR
LA NAVE

CETLI
EL CURANDERO

KOOX DIVE CENTER
PAN DEL CARMEN

TOURIST
INFORMATION KIOSK

COMBIS TO COBÁ

HSBC

ALTA NORTE

JÚPITER NORTE

SAGITARIO PTE
POLAR PTE

CALLE 2 PTE

CALLE 4 PTE
CALLE 6 PTE

BR KI'IS
TUN K'UL

AV OOK-K'OT

BUBUL-EK
CALLE 8 PTE

SATÉLITE NORTE

GÉMINIS NORTE

CENTAURO NORTE
TUN-KUL NORTE
ORIÓN NORTE

LIBRA
VIBAL
LEPTO

ESCORPIÓN NORTE

ESCORPIÓN SUR

AVENIDA COBÁ

CALLE LUCIÉRNAGA

CALLE SATÉLITE SUR
SATURNO SUR

shared bathrooms are actually quite nice, with modern basin sinks, rainshower heads, hot water, and thrice-daily cleaning. And if sharing a bathroom really is beyond the pale, they've got a tower with three deluxe rooms, each with private bathroom, fan, and stellar views. Wind- and solar-powered electricity is available 24 hours. There's also a new Italian restaurant on-site and an area where spa treatments are given.

Tita Tulum (Carr. Tulum-Punta Allen Km. 8, tel. 984/877-8513, www.titatulum. com, US$185-205 s/d) has a lovely beachfront and low-key atmosphere—a great option for families and travelers who prefer modest comforts and a lower rate (especially off-season) over boutique eco-chic embellishments. Ten guest rooms form a semicircle around a sandy, palm-fringed lot; they're a bit worn around the edges but have polished cement floors, clean bathrooms, and indoor and outdoor sitting areas, plus fans, Wi-Fi, and 24-hour electricity. Tita is a charming and attentive proprietor, and prepares authentic Mexican dishes in the hotel's small restaurant.

Posada Lamar (Carr. Tulum-Punta Allen Km. 6, cell tel. 984/106-3682, www. posadalamar.com, US$160-220 s/d) has eight comfortable and artful bungalows, with salvaged-wood detailing and rich colors and fabrics. There are no fans or air-conditioning, and electricity (solar powered) is available only at night; fortunately, the sea breezes keep the units cool (and the bugs at bay) most nights. The bungalows are a bit too close together, diminishing privacy, especially since you often need the windows and doors open, but the beach here is clean and beautiful, with plenty of chairs, beds, and *palapas.* Continental breakfast is included, served every morning on your private terrace.

Dos Ceibas (Carr. Tulum-Punta Allen Km. 10, tel. 984/877-6024, www.dosceibas. com, US$100-190 s/d) has eight comfortable, if a bit garish, bungalows on a beautiful stretch of beach. Bungalows range from a top-floor honeymoon unit to a "bargain" bungalow with a detached bathroom (and near enough the road to hear passing cars). Most have polished cement floors, brightly painted walls, and firm beds with mosquito nets hanging from the *palapa* roof; all but the two breezy oceanfront rooms and budget rear unit have ceiling fans (electricity available at night only).

OVER US$200

Nestled in a jungly plot facing a glorious stretch of beach, **Hotel Nueva Vida de**

Tulum offers idyllic beachfront hotels.

Ramiro (Carr. Tulum-Punta Allen Km. 8.5, tel. 984/877-8512, www.tulumnv.com, US$115-413 s/d) has a large number (and variety) of accommodations, from spacious suites with pillow-top mattresses and gorgeous ocean views to simple thatch-roof bungalows, including some with kitchenette, and even an adults-only area. (The oldest rooms can be dark, however, and aren't a great value, despite being cheaper.) There's 24-hour clean power, but no air-conditioning, just fans and sea breezes. Complimentary continental breakfast (including a bottomless cup of joe) is served at the hotel's restaurant, Casa Banana Steakhouse, located across the street.

Artful, spirit-minded decor is nothing new in Tulum, but ★ Sueños Tulum (Carr. Tulum-Punta Allen Km. 8.5, cell tel. 984/115-4338, www.suenostulum.com, US$220-285 s/d, US$485 s/d with hot tub) takes the theme further than most. Each of the hotel's 12 suites is decorated according to an essential force—Earth, Rain, Moon, etc.—and there's Maya imagery inside and out. All have ceiling fans, most rooms have ocean views, and two are reserved for families. A small clean pool is an added bonus, even with beaches as gorgeous as these. Located at the far southern end of the hotel zone, Sueños is quiet and isolated, even by Tulum's standards. Continental breakfast is included.

Accommodations at the lovely and well-liked Cabañas La Luna (Carr. Tulum-Punta Allen Km. 6.5, U.S. tel. 818/631-9824, Mex. cell tel. 984/146-7737 [urgent matters only], www.cabanaslaluna.com, US$125-250 s/d, US$290-530 2- and 4-bdrm villas) range from cozy beachfront bungalows to spacious split-level villas, but share essential details like comfortable mattresses, high ceilings, fans and 24-hour electricity, and bright artful decor. The beach is stunning, of course, and the property is big enough for a sense of isolation, yet within walking distance of shops and restaurants in Punta Piedra. Service is excellent.

In Town
UNDER US$50

Known for its elaborate daily breakfasts, José at Mama's Home (Calle Orion Sur btwn Calles Venus and Sol Ote., tel. 984/871-2272, US$10 pp dorm, US$12 pp dorm with a/c, US$50 s/d with a/c) is a popular spot for budget travelers. Two mixed dorms and eight private rooms—all with thick mattresses—open onto a colorful courtyard with Maya-inspired murals, hammocks, and long tables. There's a small communal kitchen plus a living room with a couple of computers for Internet access (there's also Wi-Fi). Weekly themed events like "Margarita Night," "Flamenco & Sangria," and "Hollywood Movie Night" make it easy to meet other travelers.

Mango Tulum (Calle Polar Pte. near Av. Cobá, tel. 984/169-9097, www.mangotulum.com, US$20 pp dorm with a/c, US$70-75 s/d with a/c) is a pleasantly sparse hotel with whitewashed walls, polished cement floors, and a spacious garden with mature trees and a refreshing pool. Dorms are limited to two bunk beds with en suite bathroom; sheets, towels, and lockers are included. The private rooms are bright and airy; some have king-size beds. Continental breakfast is provided, but there's no communal kitchen, unfortunately. Look for the hotel behind the OXXO convenience store on Avenida Cobá.

Villa Matisse (Av. Satélite at Calle Sagitario, tel. 984/871-2636, villamatisse@hotmail.com, US$50 s/d) has six simple, comfortable rooms, a pleasant garden and reading area (with book exchange), and a community kitchen. The rooms are spotless, and the grounds and common areas are equally well maintained; the multilingual owner sets out coffee and small snacks in the morning and often supplies rooms with fresh flowers. There's no air-conditioning, but rooms have fans and good cross ventilation. Use of the hotel's bikes is included in the rate.

US$50-100

Tucked into a quiet residential street, ★ **Secret Garden** (Calle Sagitario near Calle Acuario, tel. 984/157-8001, www.secretgardentulum.com, US$55-65 s/d with a/c, US$75 s/d with a/c and kitchenette, US$65-75 *palapa* bungalow with fan and kitchenette) offers stylish, comfortable rooms at affordable rates (guests over age 16 only). Units vary in size and layout (some with kitchenettes, some with lofts), but all have fashionable colors, artful stencils, and high-end linens. Rooms open onto a long, leafy central garden with hammocks and low couches, perfect for relaxing day or night. Service is outstanding; purified water, fruit, and baked goods are offered daily.

Located on the southern end of town, **Jardín de Frida** (Av. Tulum near Calle Kukulcán, tel. 984/871-2816, www.fridastulum.com, US$16 pp dorm, US$62 s/d, US$81 s/d with kitchenette, US$92 s/d with kitchenette and a/c) is an artsy hotel with a jungly garden replete with mango and palm trees, a lounge that feels like a global traveler's living room (think tapestries, eclectic furnishings, artworks, and an intriguing library), a spacious common kitchen, and lots of outdoor spaces for hanging out. All the units have spectacular murals—from jungle scenes to modern art. Dorms have twin beds (no bunks here) and en suite bathrooms. Private rooms are different in style and size but are comfortable and homey. Continental breakfast and Wi-Fi are included in the rate.

Hotel Don Diego de la Selva (Av. Tulum s/n, cell tel. 984/114-9744, www.dondiegodelaselva.com, US$85-110 s/d with a/c) offers spacious rooms and bungalows with classy understated decor, comfortable beds, and large glass doors looking onto a shady rear garden. There's a large pool, and the hotel restaurant serves good French-Mexican cuisine; half-board options are available. The only catch is the location, about a kilometer (0.6 mile) south of the plaza. The hotel rents bikes, but most guests find a rental car indispensable. It's very popular with French travelers; wireless Internet and continental breakfast are included.

Set in a leafy garden on the road to Cobá, **Hotel Villas Uolis Nah** (Carr. Tulum-Cobá Km. 0.2, tel. 984/876-4965, www.uolisnah. com, US$63 s/d with kitchen, US$80 s/d with kitchen and a/c) has six simple studios with little touches like mosquito-net canopies, mosaic-tile bathrooms, and *palapa*-shaded terraces with hammocks. All units have fully equipped kitchens (even ovens), and one of Tulum's main supermarkets is just down the street. There's also a well-kept pool near the front of the property—perfect for cooling off. Continental breakfast, bike rentals, and wireless Internet are included in the rate.

US$100-200

Rooms at **Posada Luna del Sur** (Calle Luna Sur near Av. Tulum, tel. 984/871-2984, www. posadalunadelsur.com, US$120 s/d with a/c) are compact but tidy and pleasant, with whitewashed walls, comfortable beds (king or two twins), and small terraces overlooking a leafy garden. Each has a kitchenette for light food prep—there aren't microwaves or hot plates—though you may not use it much considering the full à la carte breakfast and the many restaurant recommendations of the food-savvy owner who lives on-site. The rooftop lounge is a great evening hangout, with plenty of tables, chairs, and Wi-Fi. Service is friendly and accommodating. The hotel is for ages 16 and over only.

A short distance from town on the road to the beach, **Teetotum** (Av. Cobá Sur s/n, cell tel. 984/143-8956, www.hotelteetotum.com, US$130 s/d with a/c) has four sleek minimalist rooms—ceramic basin sinks, low bed stands—and artful decor throughout, including playful oversized murals in the dining room. All rooms have air-conditioning, Wi-Fi, and iPod docks, but no TV or telephone. Guests enjoy free continental breakfast and bike rentals, and a lovely plunge pool and rooftop sun beds, too. Various massages and other spa treatments are available on request. The restaurant serves a little of everything, from vegetable dumplings to bacon cheeseburgers, with an equally varied (and enticing) drink menu.

★ **Villas Geminis** (Calle Andrómeda at Calle Gemini, tel. 984/871-3556, www.villas-geminis.com, US$145 s/d with a/c, US$170 penthouse studio with a/c, US$155 1-bdrm condo with a/c, US$205 2-bdrm condo with a/c) has spacious penthouse studios and one- and two-bedroom condos with modern kitchens and private terraces (there's also one hotel room); all are simple but elegant in decor. There's 24-hour security and daily maid service, and the owners and staff are attentive and capable. The interior courtyard has a nice swimming pool surrounded by a leafy garden. There's a large supermarket nearby, plus restaurants, bars, and dive shops. The property has cable TV and Wi-Fi, and bikes for rent. All in all, this is an amazing deal, especially considering most units sleep four people.

INFORMATION AND SERVICES
Tourist Information
A **tourist information kiosk** (no phone, 9am-5pm daily) is located on the central plaza, across from the HSBC bank. The chief attendant is quite knowledgeable, her teenage disciples less so. You often can glean useful information from the stacks of brochures there. The website **www.todotulum.com** also offers good information on current goings-on and offerings in Tulum.

Emergency Services
Hospital de Tulum (Av. Tulum btwn Calles Luna and Acuario Norte, tel. 984/871-2271, www.hospitaldetulum.com, 24 hours daily) is a small private hospital offering emergency and preventative services with a bilingual staff. For minor medical issues, Tulum's local clinic, **Centro de Salud Tulum** (Calle Andrómeda btwn Calles Jupiter and Alfa, tel. 984/871-2050, 24 hours) is a decent option. For serious health problems, head to Playa del Carmen or Cancún.

Farmacia Similares (Av. Tulum at Calle Jupiter Sur, tel. 984/871-2736) is open 8am-10pm Monday-Saturday and 8am-9pm Sunday; it also has a doctor on staff for simple consultations 9am-9pm Monday-Saturday and 9am-3pm Sunday.

The **police** (toll-free tel. 066, 24 hours) share a large station with the fire department, about two kilometers (1.2 miles) from Tulum Pueblo on the road to the Zona Hotelera.

Money
HSBC (Av. Tulum at Calle Alfa next to city hall, 9am-5pm Mon.-Fri.) has reliable ATM machines and will change foreign cash and AmEx travelers checks. If there's a line, **ScotiaBank** (Av. Tulum at Calle Satélite, 8:30am-4pm Mon.-Fri.) is a good option, too.

Media and Communications
Tulum's **post office** (Calle Orion Sur at Calle Andrómeda Sur) is open 8am-4:30pm Monday-Friday and 8am-noon Saturday.

In the Zona Hotelera, most hotels offer free Wi-Fi in the reception or restaurant area for guests. In town, **Satélite Ciber** (Av. Satélite near Av. Tulum, 8:30am-10:30pm daily, US$1/hour) has flat-screen computers and killer air-conditioning. Another good option is **Movistar** (Av. Tulum at Calle Orion, 9am-10pm daily, US$1/hour), which has Skype-enabled computers plus direct-dial international calls (US$0.25-0.40/minute).

Laundry and Storage
Lava Easy (Av. Tulum btwn Av. Satélite and Calle Centauro, 8am-8pm Mon.-Sat.) charges US$1.15 per kilo (2.2 pounds), with a three-kilo (6.6-pound) minimum.

Near the bus station, a **no name** *lavandería* (Av. Tulum near Calle Jupiter Norte, 7am-7pm Mon.-Sat.) charges US$1.50 per kilo for two-hour service with a three-kilo (6.6 pound) minimum.

The **bus terminal** (Av. Tulum btwn Calles Alfa and Jupiter, tel. 984/871-2122, 24 hours) has luggage storage for US$1.50 per hour or US$7.75 per 8-24 hours.

Language and Instruction
El Camino (Av. Satélite Norte at Calle 4 Pte., tel. 984/135-8118, www.elcaminotulum.com,

Tulum Bus Schedule

Departures from the **bus terminal** (Av. Tulum btwn Calles Alfa and Jupiter, tel. 984/871-2122) include:

Destination	Price	Duration	Schedule
Cancún	US$7.15-9.25	2-2.5 hrs	every 15-60 mins midnight-11:15pm
Carrillo Puerto	US$4.75-7.15	1.5 hrs	every 15-90 mins 12:30am-11:30pm
Chetumal	US$13.50-24	3.5-4 hrs	every 30-90 mins 12:30am-11pm
Chichén Itzá	US$7.50-14.75	3-3.5 hrs	8:30am and 9am
Cobá	US$3.25-5.25	45-60 mins	every 30-60 mins 7:15am-11am and 3:30pm-8pm
Mahahual	US$18.50	2.5 hrs	1 departure 9am
Mérida	US$23	4 hrs	5 departures 2:30am-8:30pm
Playa del Carmen	US$3-5.50	1 hr	every 30-60 mins 12:15am-11:15pm
Valladolid	US$6.50-8.50	1.5-2hrs	every 30-90 mins 2:30am-8:30pm

8am-8pm daily) is a language school offering all levels of Spanish language instruction. Classes are offered one-on-one (US$15/hour) or in small groups (US$215-375 for 15-45 hours). Homestays with local families as well as accommodations at local hotels or condos can be arranged by the school.

GETTING THERE
Bus

Tulum's **bus terminal** (Av. Tulum btwn Calles Alfa and Jupiter, tel. 984/871-2122) is at the south end of town, a block from the main plaza.

Combi

Combis are white collective vans that zip between Tulum and Playa del Carmen all day, every day (US$3.25, 1 hour, every 10 minutes 5am-10pm). They leave more frequently than buses and are handier for intermediate stops, like Dos Ojos, Akumal, and Xpu-Há. Flag them down anywhere on Avenida Tulum or Highway 307.

Combis also go to Cobá (US$4.75, 1 hour), stopping at cenotes along the way. They leave hourly 8am-5pm from a stop on Avenida Tulum at Calle Osiris Norte. You can also catch them at the intersection of Highway 307 and the Cobá/Zona Hotelera road.

Tukan Kin (tel. 984/871-3538, www.from-cancunairport.com) operates an **airport shuttle** from Tulum to Cancún airport (US$45 adult, US$22.50 child), with six designated pickup stops around Tulum town and door-to-door service from the Zona Hotelera. Service from the airport to Tulum also is available for the same one-way rate. The trip takes just under two hours; advance reservations are required.

Car

Highway 307 passes right through the middle of Tulum Pueblo, where it is referred to as

Avenida Tulum. Coming south from Cancún or Playa del Carmen, you'll first pass the entrance to Tulum archaeological site, on your left. A kilometer and a half later (1 mile) you'll reach a large intersection, where you can turn left (east) toward the beach and Zona Hotelera, or right (west) toward Cobá. Continuing straight ahead takes you into Tulum Pueblo, then onward to the Costa Maya.

GETTING AROUND
Bicycle
A bike can be very handy, especially for getting to or from the beach, or anywhere along the now-paved road through the Zona Hotelera.

In the Zona Hotelera, check out **Yokte Bikes** (Carr. Tulum-Punta Allen Km. 7.5, cell tel. 984/145-4061, 9am-6pm daily), which rents beach cruisers for US$9.25 per 24 hours, including helmet, lock, and safety vest. Drop-off and pickup at your hotel is included.

In town, **iBike Tulum** (Av. Cobá Sur at Calle Venus, tel. 984/802-5518, www.ibiketulum.com, 9am-5:30pm Mon.-Sat.) rents a variety of bikes, including beach cruisers and mountain bikes (US$10-19 per 24 hours), most in top condition. All come with helmet, lock, lights, and roadside assistance. Child seats and bikes are also available. The shop also offers enjoyable tours, including to cenotes and dry caves.

Another option in town is **Kelly Bike Rental** (Av. Tulum at Calle Acuario, cell tel. 984/114-4657, 8:30am-8pm daily), which has decent bikes for US$5 per 12 hours; helmet, lock, and safety vest are included.

Beach Shuttle
There is a local *colectivo* (US$1.15) labeled "Cabañas" that goes from Tulum town to the arch at the southern end of the Zona Hotelera and back again, every 20-30 minutes 6am-8pm. Another *colectivo* (US$0.75), labeled "Ruínas," goes from town to the northern end of the Zona Hotelera at 8am, 8:30am, 5:30pm, and 6pm. Both routes start at the corner of Calle Sol Ote and Orion Sur. You also can catch both *colectivos* along Avenida Tulum and on the road to and along the beach. Schedules often change, so be sure to confirm the current departures (and return times!).

Car
A car can be very useful in Tulum, especially in the Zona Hotelera, even if you don't plan on using it every day. Renting a car from the airport in Cancún is the easiest and most affordable option for most travelers, especially if you book online and in advance. In Tulum, agencies include **Avis** (Av. Cobá Sur at Calle Sol Ote, cell tel. 984/120-3972, toll-free Mex. tel. 800/288-8888, www.avis.com, 8am-8pm daily) and **Hertz** (Hwy. 307 at Carr. Tulum-Cobá, toll-free Mex. tel. 800/709-5000, www.hertz.com, 7am-10pm daily), located next to Super San Francisco supermarket.

Taxi
Taxis are plentiful, and fares run about US$3 in town and US$8-12 to get to the Zona Hotelera (depending on where exactly you're going). In the Zona Hotelera, there is a taxi stand in Punta Piedra; rates are roughly the same within the Zona Hotelera or back into Tulum Pueblo. From either area, a ride to Tulum ruins costs about US$5.

Cobá

The Maya ruins of Cobá make an excellent complement—or even alternative—to the memorable but vastly overcrowded ruins at Tulum. Cobá doesn't have Tulum's stunning Caribbean view and beach, but its structures are much larger and more ornate—in fact, Cobá's main pyramid is the second tallest in the Yucatán Peninsula, and it's one of few you are still allowed to climb. The ruins are also surrounded by lakes and thick forest, making it a great place to see birds, butterflies, and tropical flora.

★ COBÁ ARCHAEOLOGICAL ZONE

Cobá (8am-5pm daily, US$4.50) is especially notable for the complex system of *sacbeob,* or raised stone causeways, that connected it to other cities, near and far. (The term *sacbeob*—whose singular form is *sacbé*—means white roads.) Dozens of such roads crisscross the Yucatán Peninsula, but Cobá has more than any other city, underscoring its status as a commercial, political, and military hub. One road extends in an almost perfectly straight line from the base of Cobá's principal pyramid to the town of Yaxuna, more than 100 kilometers (62 miles) away—no small feat considering a typical *sacbé* was 1-2 meters (3.3-6.6 feet) high and about 4.5 meters (15 feet) wide, and covered in white mortar. In Cobá, some roads were even bigger—10 meters (32.8 feet) across. In fact, archaeologists have uncovered a massive stone cylinder believed to have been used to flatten the broad roadbeds.

History

Cobá was settled as early as 100 BC around a collection of small lagoons; it's a logical and privileged location, as the Yucatán Peninsula is virtually devoid of rivers, lakes, or any other aboveground water. Cobá developed into an important trading hub, and in its early existence had a particularly close connection with the Petén region of present-day Guatemala. That relationship would later fade as Cobá grew more intertwined with coastal cities like Tulum, but Petén influence is obvious in Cobá's high steep structures, which are reminiscent of those in Tikal. At its peak, around AD 600-800, Cobá was the largest urban center in the northern lowlands, with some 40,000 residents and over 6,000 structures spread over 50 square kilometers (31 square miles). The city controlled most of the northeastern portion of the Yucatán Peninsula during the same period before being toppled by the Itzás of Chichén Itzá following a protracted war in the mid-800s. Following a widespread Maya collapse—of which the fall of Cobá was not the cause, though perhaps an early warning sign—the great city was all but abandoned, save as a pilgrimage and ceremonial site for the ascendant Itzás. It was briefly reinhabited in the 12th century, when a few new structures were added, but had been abandoned again, and covered in a blanket of vegetation, by the time of the Spanish conquest.

Cobá Group

Passing through the entry gate, the first group of ruins you encounter is the Cobá Group, a collection of over 50 structures and the oldest part of the ancient city. Many of Cobá's *sacbeob* initiate here. Its primary structure, **La Iglesia** (The Church), rises 22.5 meters (74 feet) from a low platform, making it Cobá's second-highest pyramid. The structure consists of nine platforms stacked atop one another and notable for their round corners. Built in numerous phases beginning in the Early Classic era, La Iglesia is far more reminiscent of Tikal and other Petén-area structures than it is of the long palaces and elaborate facades typical of Puuc and Chenes sites. Visitors are no longer allowed to climb

Cobá Archaeological Zone

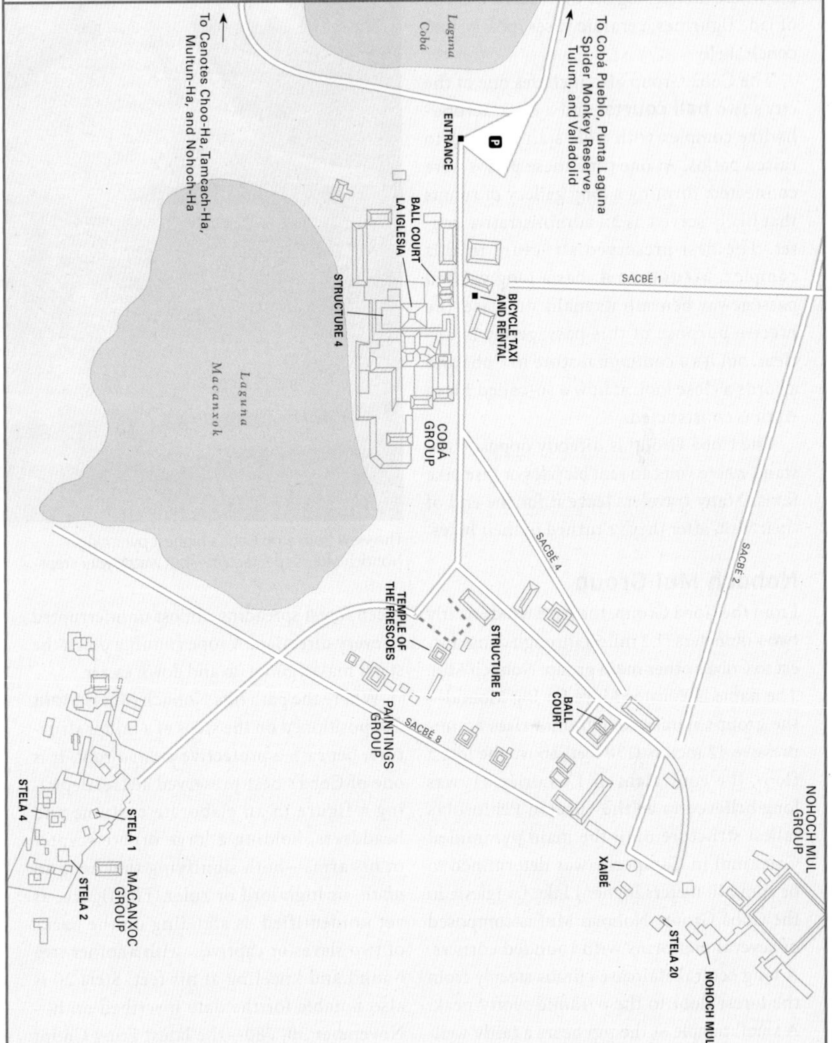

To Cenotes Choo-Ha, Tamcach-Ha, Multun-Ha, and Nohoch-Ha

Laguna Cobá

To Cobá Pueblo, Punta Laguna Spider Monkey Reserve, Tulum, and Valladolid

ENTRANCE

P

Laguna Macanxok

BALL COURT
LA IGLESIA

STRUCTURE 4

BICYCLE TAXI AND RENTAL

COBÁ GROUP

SACBÉ 1

SACBÉ 2

SACBÉ 4

STRUCTURE 5

TEMPLE OF THE FRESCOES

PAINTINGS GROUP

SACBÉ 8

BALL COURT

NOHOCH MUL GROUP

XAIBÉ

STELA 20

NOHOCH MUL

STELA 4

STELA 1

MACANXOC GROUP

STELA 2

SCALE NOT AVAILABLE

© AVALON TRAVEL

the Iglesia pyramid due to the poor state of its stairs, but it is crowned with a small temple where archaeologists discovered a cache of jade figurines, ceramic vases, pearls, and conch shells.

The Cobá Group also includes one of the city's two **ball courts,** and a large acropolis-like complex with wide stairs leading to raised patios. At one time these patios were connected, forming a long gallery of rooms that likely served as an administrative center. The best-preserved structure in this complex, **Structure 4,** has a long vaulted passageway beneath its main staircase; the precise purpose of this passageway is unclear, but it's a common feature in Cobá and affords a close look at how a so-called Maya Arch is constructed.

The Cobá Group is directly opposite the stand where you can rent bicycles or hire bike taxis. Many travelers leave it for the end of their visit, after they've turned in their bikes.

Nohoch Mul Group

From the Cobá Group, the path winds nearly two kilometers (1.2 miles) through dense forest to Cobá's other main group, Nohoch Mul. The name is Yucatec Maya for Big Mound—the group's namesake pyramid rises an impressive 42 meters (138 feet) above the forest floor, the equivalent of 12 stories. (It was long believed to be the Yucatán Peninsula's tallest structure until the main pyramid at Calakmul in Campeche was determined to be some 10 meters higher.) Like La Iglesia in the Cobá Group, Nohoch Mul is composed of several platforms with rounded corners. A long central staircase climbs steeply from the forest floor to the pyramid's lofty peak. A small temple at the top bears a fairly well-preserved carving of the Descending God, an upside-down figure that figures prominently at Tulum but whose identity and significance is still unclear. (Theories vary widely, from Venus to the god of bees.)

Nohoch Mul is one of few Maya pyramids that visitors are still allowed to climb, and the view from the top is impressive—a flat

The view from atop Cobá's highest pyramid, Nohoch Mul, is spectacular—but watch your step!

green forest spreading almost uninterrupted in every direction. A rope running down the stairs makes going up and down easier.

Where the path hits Nohoch Mul is **Stela 20,** positioned on the steps of a minor structure, beneath a protective *palapa* roof. It is one of Cobá's best-preserved stelae, depicting a figure in an elaborate costume and headdress, holding a large ornate scepter in his arms—both signifying that he is an *ahau,* or high lord or ruler. The figure, as yet unidentified, is standing on the backs of two slaves or captives, with another two bound and kneeling at his feet. Stela 20 is also notable for the date inscribed on it—November 30, 780—the latest Long Count date yet found in Cobá.

Xaibé and the Ball Court

Between the Cobá and Nohoch Mul Groups are several smaller but still significant structures. Closest to Nohoch Mul is a curiously conical structure that archaeologists have dubbed **Xaibé,** a Yucatec Maya word for crossroads. The name owes to the fact that it's near the intersection of four major *sacbeob*, and for the same reason, archaeologists believe it may have served as a watchtower. That said, its unique design and imposing size suggest a grander purpose. Round structures are fairly rare in Maya architecture, and most are thought to be astronomical observatories; there's no evidence Xaibé served that function, however, particularly since it lacks any sort of upper platform or temple. Be aware that the walking path does not pass Xaibé—you have to take the longer bike path to reach it.

A short distance from Xaibé is the second of Cobá's **ball courts.** Both courts have imagery of death and sacrifice, though they are more pronounced here: a skull inscribed on a stone in the center of the court, a decapitated jaguar on a disc at the end, and symbols of Venus (which represented death and war) inscribed on the two scoring rings. This ball court also had a huge plaque implanted on one of its slopes, with over 70 glyphs and dated AD 465; the plaque in place today is a replica, but the original is under a *palapa* covering at one end of the court, allowing visitors to examine it more closely.

Paintings Group

The Paintings Group is a collection of five platforms encircling a large plaza. The temples here were among the last to be constructed in Cobá and pertain to the latest period of occupation, roughly AD 1100-1450. The group's name comes from paintings that once lined the walls, though very little color is visible now, unfortunately. Traces of blue and red can be seen in the upper room of the **Temple of the Frescoes,** the group's largest structure, but you aren't allowed to climb up to get a closer look.

Although centrally located, the Paintings Group is easy to miss on your way between the more outlying pyramids and groups. Look for a sign for **Structure 5,** where you can leave your bike (if you have one) and walk into the group's main area.

Macanxoc Group

From the Paintings Group, the path continues southeasterly for about a kilometer (0.6 mile) to the Macanxoc Group. Numerous stelae have been found here, indicating it was a place of great ceremonial significance. The most famous of these monuments is **Stela 1,** aka the Macanxoc Stela. It depicts a scene from the Maya creation myth—"the hearth stone appears"—along with a Long Count date referring to a cycle ending the equivalent of 41.9 billion, billion, billion years in the future. It is the most distant Long Count date known to have been conceived and recorded by the ancient Maya. Stela 1 also has reference to December 21, 2012, when the Maya Long Count completed its first Great Cycle, equivalent to 5,125 years. Despite widespread reports to the contrary, there is no known evidence, at Cobá or anywhere, that the Maya believed (much less predicted) that the world would end on that date.

Flora and Fauna

The name Cobá (Water Stirred by the Wind in Maya) is surely a reference to the group of shallow lagoons here (Cobá, Macanxoc, Xkanha, and Sacakal). The archaeological site and the surrounding wetlands and forest are rich with birdlife—herons, egrets, motmot, parrots, and the occasional toucan are not uncommon. Arrive early to see the most birds—at the very least you'll get an earful of their varied songs and cries. Later, as the temperature climbs, you'll start to see myriad colorful butterflies, including the large, deep-blue morphidae and the bright yellow-orange barred sulphur.

If you look on the ground, you'll almost certainly see long lines of leaf-cutter ants. One column carries freshly cut leaves to the burrow, and the other marches in the opposite direction, empty-jawed, returning for more. The vegetation decays in their nests, and the fungus that grows on the compost is an important staple of the ants' diet—a few scientists even claim that this makes leaf-cutter ants the world's second species of agriculturists. Only

Deciphering the Glyphs

Maya glyphs

For years, scholars could not agree whether the fantastic inscriptions found on Maya stelae, codices, and temple walls were anything more than complex records of numbers and dates.

Mayanist and scholar Michael D. Coe's *Breaking the Maya Code* (Thames and Hudson, 2012) is a fascinating account of the decipherment of Maya hieroglyphics. Coe describes how, in 1952, reclusive Russian scholar Yuri Valentinovich Knorosov made a crucial breakthrough by showing that Maya writing did in fact convey spoken words. Using a rough alphabet recorded by Fray Diego de Landa (the 16th-century bishop who, ironically, is best known for having destroyed numerous Maya texts), Knorosov showed that ancient texts contain common Yucatec Maya words such as *cutz* (turkey) and *tzul* (dog).

But Knorosov's findings were met with staunch resistance by some of the field's most influential scholars, which delayed progress for decades. By the mid-1980s, however, decipherment picked up speed; one of many standouts from that era is David Stuart, the son of Maya experts, who went to Cobá with his parents at age eight and passed the time copying glyphs and learning Yucatec Maya words from local playmates. As a high school student he served as chief epigrapher on a groundbreaking exploration in Belize, and at age 18 he received a US$128,000 MacArthur Fellowship (aka "Genius Award") to, as he told Michael Coe, "play around with the glyphs" full-time.

Researchers now know that Maya writing is like most other hieroglyphic systems. What appears at first to be a single glyph can have up to four parts, and the same word can be expressed in pictorial, phonetic, or hybrid form. Depending on context, one symbol can have either a pictorial or phonetic role; likewise, a particular sound can be represented in more than one way. One of David Stuart's great insights was that for all its complexity, much of Maya glyphic writing is "just repetitive."

But how do scholars know what the symbols are meant to sound like in the first place? Some come from the Landa alphabet, others are suggested by the pictures that accompany many texts, still others from patterns derived by linguistic analyses of contemporary Maya languages. In some cases, it is simply a hunch that turns out to be right. If this seems like somewhat shaky scientific ground, it is—but not without a means of being proved.

Hundreds of glyphs have been deciphered, and most of the known Maya texts can be reliably translated. Some archaeologists lament, not unreasonably, that high-profile glyphic studies divert attention from research into the lives of everyday ancient Maya, who after all far outnumbered the nobility but are not at all represented in the inscriptions. That said, the effort has lent invaluable insight into Maya civilization, especially dynastic successions and religious beliefs.

particular types of leaves will do, and the columns can be up to a kilometer (0.6 mile) long.

Practicalities

Cobá's main groups are quite spread apart, and visiting all of them adds up to several kilometers. Fortunately, you can rent a bicycle (US$3) or hire a *triciclo* (US$9.50 for 80 minutes, US$15 for 2 hours) at a large stand a short distance past the entryway, opposite the Cobá Group. Whether you walk or ride, don't forget a water bottle, comfortable shoes, bug repellent, sunscreen, and a hat. Watch for signs and stay on the designated trails. Guide service is available—prices are not fixed but average US$52 per group (1.5 hours, up to 6 people). Parking at Cobá is US$3.

Cobá is not nearly as crowded as Tulum (and is much larger), but it's still a good idea to arrive as early as possible to beat the ever-growing crowds.

COBÁ PUEBLO

It's fair to say that the town of Cobá, a rather desultory little roadside community, has never regained the population or stature that it had as a Maya capital more than 1,000 years ago. Most travelers visit Cobá as a day trip from Tulum or Valladolid, or on a package tour from resorts on the coast. There are two decent hotels in town, used mostly by those who want to appreciate Cobá's rich birdlife, which means being at the gate right when the site opens at 8am; if you're lucky, the gatekeeper may even let you in early.

Sights

Cobá Pueblo itself doesn't have much in the way of sights—besides the ruins, of course—but a number of small eco-attractions have cropped up, all a short distance from town.

RESERVA DE MONOS ARAÑAS PUNTA LAGUNA

The **Punta Laguna Spider Monkey Reserve** (cell tel. 985/107-9182, puntalagunamexico@gmail.com, 7:30am-5:30pm daily, US$5) is a nationally protected forest that's home to various families of boisterous spider monkeys, as well as smaller groups of howler monkeys—it's estimated that there are up to 800 individual monkeys living in the reserve. There are also numerous bird species as well as coati, white-tailed deer, and even pumas. A short path winds through the reserve, passing a small unexcavated Maya ruin and a large lagoon where you can rent canoes (US$8.50). There's also a zipline and a place to rappel into a cenote, but it's typically reserved for large groups. Your best chance of spotting monkeys is by going in late afternoon, and by hiring one of the guides near the entrance (US$10 pp, minimum 2 people). The reserve (whose official name is Otoch Ma'ax Yetel Kooh, Yucatec Maya for House of the Spider Monkey and Puma) is operated by a local cooperative, whose members live in the nearby village and serve as guides; most speak at least some English. Be sure to wear good walking shoes and bring plenty of bug repellent. The reserve is located 18 kilometers (11 miles) north of Cobá, on the road toward Nuevo X'can.

★ CENOTES

If you've got a car, a cluster of three well-maintained and well-run cenotes (no phone, 8am-5pm daily) are a great addition to a day spent at Cobá. **Choo-Ha, Tamcach-Ha,** and **Multun-Ha** are southwest of Cobá and are operated jointly (US$5/7/10 for 1/2/3 cenotes); a fourth cenote called **Nohoch-Ha** is a bit farther and requires a separate entrance fee (US$4). Each is slightly different—one has a high roof and platform for jumping, another is wide and low—but all are impressive enclosed chambers bristling with stalactites, filled with cool crystalline water that's heaven on a hot day. Cement or wooden stairways lead down to pools; showers and changing areas are available at Choo-Ha. To get there, continue past the Cobá ruins on the road to Tepich and follow the signs.

Food

With a large raised patio overlooking the lagoon, **La Pirámide** (Calle Principal at Laguna

Cobá, no phone, 7:30am-9pm daily, US$6-15) is a nice place for lunch après-ruins or beer and snacks in the evening. The restaurant receives a number of tour groups, and it often has a buffet set up (US$12.50); otherwise, the menu has grilled fish, chicken, and meat dishes as well as typical Mexican fare.

A few doors down, **Nicte Ha** (facing Laguna Cobá, tel. 984/206-7025, 8am-7pm daily, US$3-8) is a small place serving tacos, enchiladas, and various pork dishes.

Across the street from the church, **Abarrotes Neftali** (Calle Principal s/n, 7am-11pm daily) is a mini-mart that sells canned goods, bread, and some fresh produce.

Accommodations

The low-key **Hotel Sac Be** (Calle Principal, tel. 984/206-7140, US$34 s/d, US$42 s/d with a/c) has friendly service and spotless rooms with one or two beds, televisions, Wi-Fi, and a small desk. All have private bathrooms and open onto a long outdoor corridor. Guests get 10 percent off at the hotel restaurant (which is the small one right above the mini-mart reception area; the much larger attached restaurant has a different owner). If it's booked, consider heading to Tulum or Valladolid, each

about 45 minutes away by car or bus—the other options in town are pretty grim.

Information and Services

Cobá has neither an official tourist office nor a health clinic. There also are no banks or ATMs—the nearest banking and medical services are in Tulum and Valladolid.

Facing the lagoon, **Farmacia El Porvenir** (Calle Principal s/n, no phone, 9am-1pm and 2pm-9pm Mon.-Sat.) is a small shop selling basic medicines and toiletries.

The **police station** (toll-free tel. 066) is halfway down the main drag, before you hit the lagoon.

Getting There and Around

You can easily walk to any of the listed businesses in town; the archaeological site is a five-minute walk down the main road, alongside the lagoon.

BUS

A tiny bus station operates out of El Bocadito restaurant (Calle Principal). For the coast, the lone first-class bus departs Cobá at 3:10pm, with stops in Tulum (US$5.15, 1 hour), Playa del Carmen (US$9.25, 2.5 hours), and Cancún (US$14.50, 3.5 hours). Second-class buses to

Hotel Sac Be

the same destinations cost a bit less but take longer; departures are at 9:30am, 10:30am, 1:30pm, 3:30pm, 4pm, and 6pm.

CAR

Getting to Cobá is easiest by car. No matter what direction you're coming from, the roads are smooth and scenic, cutting through pretty farmland and small towns. Keep your speed down, however, as there are innumerable *topes* (speed bumps) and occasional people and animals along the shoulder. Buses ply the same routes, but somewhat infrequently.

Three different roads lead to Cobá; none are named or marked, so they are known by the towns on either end. There are no formal services along any of the roads, save a gas station in the town of Chemax.

The Cobá-Tulum road (45 kilometers/28 miles) is the busiest, cutting southeast to Tulum and the coastal highway (Hwy. 307). The other two roads connect to Highway 180, the main highway between Cancún and Chichén Itzá. The Cobá-Nuevo X'Can road (47 kilometers/29 miles) angles northeast, connecting with Highway 180 about 80 kilometers (50 miles) outside Cancún and passing places like the Punta Laguna monkey reserve along the way. The Cobá-Chemax road (30 kilometers/19 miles) angles northwest to the town of Chemax; from there it's another 20 kilometers (12.4 miles) to Valladolid and Highway 180, connecting to the highway about 40 kilometers (25 miles) from Chichén Itzá.

All three roads, plus the short access road to Cobá, intersect at a large roundabout just north of Cobá village. Pay close attention to which road you want to avoid a long detour.

Sian Ka'an Biosphere Reserve

Sian Ka'an is Yucatec Maya for "where the sky is born," and it's not hard to see how the original inhabitants arrived at such a poetic name. The unkempt beaches, blue-green sea, bird-filled wetlands and islets, and humble accommodations are manna for bird-watchers, artists, snorkelers, and kayakers. But most visitors come here for the fishing. Sian Ka'an is one of the best fly-fishing spots in the world, with all three Grand Slam catches: bonefish, tarpon, and permit.

The reserve was created in 1986, designated a UNESCO World Heritage Site in 1987, and expanded in 1994. It now encompasses around 1.3 million acres of coastal and mangrove forests and wetlands, and some 113 kilometers (70 miles) of pristine coral reefs just offshore. A huge variety of flora and fauna thrive in the reserve, including four species of mangrove, many medicinal plants, and about 300 species of birds, including toucans, parrots, frigate birds, herons, and egrets. Monkeys, foxes, crocodiles, and boa constrictors also populate the reserve and are spotted by locals and visitors with some regularity. Manatees and jaguars are the reserve's largest animals but also the most reclusive: You need sharp eyes and a great deal of luck to spot either one. More than 20 Maya ruins have been found in the reserve, though most are unexcavated.

Spending a few days in Sian Ka'an is the best way to really appreciate its beauty and pace. Hotels and tour operators there can arrange fishing, bird-watching, and other tours, all with experienced local guides. But if time is short, a number of tour operators in Tulum offer day trips into the reserve as well.

SIGHTS
Muyil Archaeological Zone

The most accessible Maya site within the Sian Ka'an reserve is **Muyil** (Hwy. 307, 25 kilometers/15.5 miles south of Tulum, 8am-5pm daily, US$4), on the western edge of the park. Also known as Chunyaxché, it is one of the oldest archaeological sites in the

Muyil Archaeological Zone

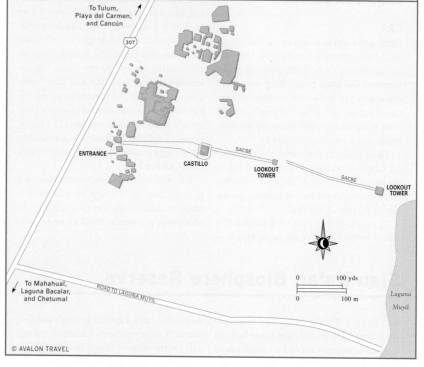

To Tulum, Playa del Carmen, and Cancún

307

ENTRANCE

CASTILLO

SACBÉ

LOOKOUT TOWER

SACBÉ

LOOKOUT TOWER

To Mahahual, Laguna Bacalar, and Chetumal

ROAD TO LAGUNA MUYIL

0   100 yds
0   100 m

Laguna Muyil

© AVALON TRAVEL

Maya world, dating back to 300 BC and occupied continuously through the conquest. It's believed to have been primarily a seaport, perched on a limestone shelf near the edge of Laguna Muyil; it is connected to the Caribbean via a canal system that was constructed by ancient Maya traders and still exists today.

Only a small portion of the city has been excavated, so it makes for a relatively quick visit. There are six main structures ranging from two-meter-high (6.6-foot) platforms to the impressive **Castillo.** At 17 meters (56 feet), it is one of the tallest structures on the peninsula's Caribbean coast. The Castillo is topped with a unique solid round masonry turret from which the waters of the Caribbean Sea can be seen. Unfortunately, climbing to the top is prohibited.

A *sacbé* (raised stone road) runs about a half kilometer (0.3 mile) from the center of the site to the edge of the **Laguna Muyil.** Part of this *sacbé* is on private property, however, so if you want to access the lagoon from the ruins—you also can get to it by car—there is an additional charge of US$4 per person. Along the way, there is a lookout tower with views over Sian Ka'an to the Caribbean.

Once you arrive at the water's edge, it's possible to take a **boat tour** (US$46 pp) that crosses both Muyil and Chunyaxché Lagoons, which are connected by a canal that was carved by the ancient Maya in order to reach the ocean. It's a pleasant way to enjoy the water, and you'll also get a view of several otherwise inaccessible ruins along the lagoons' edges and through the mangroves, with the final stop being **Xlapak ruins,** a small site thought to have been a trading post. If arriving by car, look for signs to Muyil Lagoon on Highway 307, just south of the similarly named archaeological site. More thorough tours of this part of Sian Ka'an can be booked in Tulum.

★ Bahía de la Ascensión

Ascension Bay covers about 20 square kilometers (12.4 square miles), and its shallow flats and tangled mangrove islands teem with bonefish, tarpon, and huge permit—some of the biggest ever caught, in fact. It is a fly fisher's dream come true, and it has been attracting anglers from around the world since the mid-1980s. Don't fly-fish? No worries: The spin fishing is also fantastic, while the offshore reef yields plenty of grouper, barracuda, dorado, tuna, sailfish, and marlin.

SPORTS AND RECREATION
Sportfishing

Sportfishing is world-class in and around Sian Ka'an—it's hard to go wrong in the flats and mangrove islands, or with the Caribbean lapping at its shores. All the hotels listed in this section arrange fishing tours, and most specialize in it, using their own boats and guides.

If you prefer to go with an independent operator, recommended outfits include **Pesca Maya** (7 kilometers/4.3 miles north of Punta Allen, tel. 998/848-2496, toll-free U.S. tel. 888/894-5642, www.pescamaya.com, 8am-7pm daily); the **Palometa Club** (Punta Allen, north of the central plaza, toll-free U.S. tel. 888/824-5420, www.palometaclub.com, 8am-6pm daily); and **Club Grand Slam** (near the entrance to Punta Allen, cell tel. 984/139-2930, www.grandslamfishinglodge.com).

Weeklong fly-fishing trips range US$3,400-4,000 per person, in shared room and shared boat, depending largely on the style and comforts afforded by the lodge. Most packages include airport transfer, daily guided fishing, meals, and admission to the reserve, but it's always a good idea to confirm this before booking. For private room or private boat, expect to pay an additional US$100-200 per day; shorter trips are available, but may incur extra transportation costs to and from the airport. Fishing day trips can be arranged through most hotels; rates start at around US$360 for a private full-day tour, including lunch and admission and license fees. Variations like renting gear, adding people, and half-day options can also be arranged.

dolphin spotting in the Sian Ka'an Biosphere Reserve

Sport- and Game Fishing

Cozumel and the Riviera Maya are well known for trolling and deep-sea fishing, while Ascension Bay and the Costa Maya have terrific fly-fishing. Although you can hook into just about any fish at any time of the year, below is information on the peak and extended seasons for a number of top target species. Those fish not listed—tuna, barracuda, yellowtail, snapper, grouper, and bonefish—are prevalent year-round.

SPORTFISHING

Fish	Peak Season	Extended Season	Description
Sailfish	Mar.-June	Jan.-Sept.	Top target species, with a dramatic dorsal fin and a high-flying fighting style.
Blue Marlin	Apr.-Aug.	Mar.-Sept.	Largest Atlantic billfish, up to 500 pounds locally, but much larger elsewhere.
White Marlin	May-July	Mar.-Aug.	Smaller than the blue marlin, but still challenging.
Wahoo	Nov.-Jan.	June-Feb.	Lightning fast, with torpedo-like shape and distinctive blue stripes.
Dorado	May-July	Feb.-Aug.	Hard fighter with shimmery green, gold, and blue coloration; aka dolphin or mahimahi.

FLAT-WATER FISHING

Fish	Peak Season	Extended Season	Description
Tarpon	Mar.-Aug.	Feb.-Oct.	Big hungry tarpon migrate along the coast in summer months.
Snook	July-Aug.	June-Dec.	Popular trophy fish, grows locally up to 30 pounds.
Permit	Mar.-Sept.	year-round	March and April see schools of permit, with some 20-pound individuals.

Bird-Watching

Sian Ka'an is also an excellent place for bird-watching. Trips to Bird Island and other spots afford a look at various species of water birds, including male frigates showing off their big red balloon-like chests in the winter. Tours often combine bird-watching with snorkeling and walking around one or more bay islands. Hotels in Punta Allen and along the coastal road can arrange tours, as can outfits in Tulum. Prices are typically per boat, so don't be shy to approach other travelers in town about forming a group.

In Punta Allen, **Punta Allen Coop** (no phone, 6:30am-2pm daily) is a local cooperative that offers bird-watching tours (US$120-145, 2-3 hours, up to 6 pax); look for their two-story wooden shack along the main road near the entrance to town. Other operators to consider include **Community Tours Sian Ka'an** (Calle Osiris Sur near Calle Sol Ote, tel. 984/871-2202, www.siankaantours.

org, 7am-7pm daily); and, if your budget permits, **Visit Sian Ka'an** (Sian Ka'an Biosphere Reserve, Carr. Tulum-Punta Allen Km. 15.8, cell tel. 984/141-4245, www.visitsiankaan. com), which offers customized private tours.

Kayaking

The tangled mangrove forests, interconnected lagoons, and scenic bays make Sian Ka'an ideal for kayaking. **Community Tours Sian Ka'an** (Calle Osiris Sur near Calle Sol Ote, tel. 984/871-2202, www.siankaantours.org, 7am-7pm daily) offers several kayak excursions, with tours starting at US$75 per person.

FOOD

Punta Allen isn't a foodie's village, but it does have a handful of eateries, all specializing in fresh seafood. A few mini-marts and a tortilleria round things out a bit, especially if you're planning on staying more than a couple of days.

With a gorgeous view of the Caribbean, **Muelle Viejo** (just south of the central plaza, no phone, 11am-10pm Mon.-Sat., US$6-14) serves up fresh seafood dishes and cold beers—perfect for a long lazy lunch.

Casa de Ascensión (tel. 984/801-0034, 8am-10pm daily, US$4-17) offers a wide variety of Mexican dishes, pizza and pasta, and (of course) seafood. Seating is outdoors, under a large *palapa*. It's located two blocks from the beach, near the entrance to town.

There are three **mini-marts** in town: on the north end (near the road to the lagoonside dock), south end (two blocks west of Cuzan Guesthouse), and near the central plaza (one block west). Each sells basic foodstuffs and snacks, though you may have to visit all three to find what you're looking for. If you plan to cook a lot, stock up on supplies in Tulum.

ACCOMMODATIONS

Punta Allen is the only town on the peninsula and has the most options for lodging, food, tours, and other services. Along the long unpaved road leading there is a smattering of lodges and private homes, amid miles and miles of deserted coastline. **Note:** The town of Punta Allen often switches off the electricity grid at midnight—and hotels outside of town are entirely off the grid—so air-conditioning and TV are not functional unless the establishment has a generator. (Fans work as long as the hotel has solar or wind power.) If you're staying in a room with kitchen facilities, keep the fridge shut as much as possible to conserve the cold.

Toward Punta Allen

Eight kilometers (5 miles) north of Punta Allen, ★ **Sol Caribe** (cell tel. 984/139-3839, www.solcaribe-mexico.com, US$185 s/d, US$175-250 *cabaña,* US$100/40 extra per adult/child all-inclusive) offers modern rooms and *cabañas* set on a breezy, palm-tree-laden beach. All feature tropical wood furnishings, terraces with hammocks, 24-hour electricity (fan only), and gorgeous views of the ocean—a true hidden getaway of the Riviera Maya. There's a full-service restaurant on-site, too.

For more luxury than you'd rightly expect in a remote natural reserve, **Grand Slam Fishing Lodge** (cell tel. 984/139-2930, www. grandslamfishinglodge.com, US$370 s/d with a/c) has gigantic guest rooms in two-story villas, each with one or two king-size beds, fully stocked minibars, marble bathrooms, and satellite service on large flat-screen TVs, plus 24-hour electricity for air-conditioning and Wi-Fi. The grounds include a tidy beach and aboveground pool, both with drink service, and a spacious restaurant-lounge. Guides and boats are first-rate.

Punta Allen

Facing the central plaza, ★ **Posada Sirena** (cell tel. 984/139-1241, www.casasirena. com, US$38-75 s/d) offers simple Robinson Crusoe-style rooms. Most are quite spacious, sleeping 6-8 people, and all have private bathrooms, fully equipped kitchens, and plenty of screened windows to let in the ocean breeze. Area excursions, including fly-fishing, snorkeling, and bird-watching, can be arranged on-site.

The accommodations at **Serenidad Shardon** (road to the lighthouse, cell tel. 984/107-4155, www.shardon.com, US$150 s/d, US$200 s/d with kitchen, US$375 2-bdrm apartment for up to 4 guests, US$500 beach house for up to 8 guests) vary from oceanfront *cabañas* to a large beach house; all have basic furnishings but are clean and well equipped. You also can camp using your own gear, or rent deluxe tents with real beds, electric lighting, and fans; access to hot showers and a full kitchen is included, too.

A dedicated fishing lodge, **The Palometa Club** (north of the central plaza, toll-free U.S. tel. 888/824-5420, www.palometaclub.com) has just six rooms in a two-story structure facing the beach. Each has two double beds, air-conditioning, and a private bathroom. Meals are served family-style, with cocktails and snacks (including freshly made ceviche) available at the club's outdoor bar, après fishing. The Palometa is designed for serious anglers, with a fly-tying study, one-to-one guiding, and an emphasis on landing permits (*palometa* in Spanish, hence the name). The all-inclusive seven-night/six-day rate is US$3,650 per person (non-anglers US$2,000/

person). Rates are for shared room and boat. Private add-ons and shorter packages are also available.

INFORMATION AND SERVICES

Don't expect much in the way of services in Sian Ka'an—if there is something you can't do without, definitely bring it with you. There are **no banking services,** and few of the hotels or tour operators accept credit cards. There is one **Internet café** (9am-9pm Mon.-Fri., 9am-2pm Sat., US$1/hour), located inside a mini-mart near the southwest corner of the central plaza; many hotels have Wi-Fi. Cell phones typically don't work in Sian Ka'an, but there are **public telephones** in town. Punta Allen also has a modest **medical clinic**—look for it on the main road as you enter town. There is **no laundry,** but most hotels will provide the service.

Volunteer Work

Global Vision International (www.gvi. co.uk) operates a popular volunteer-for-pay program in Sian Ka'an in partnership with Amigos de Sian Ka'an, a local nonprofit. GVI "expedition" fees are reasonable considering how much diving is involved (including

A handful of beachfront hotels dot the road between Tulum and Punta Allen.

open-water scuba certification, if needed): US$2,767-8,932 for 4-24 weeks, including room, board, and equipment, but not airfare. Advance registration is required.

GETTING THERE

Many of the hotels include airport pickup/drop-off, which is convenient and helps you avoid paying for a week's car rental when you plan on fishing all day. That said, a car is useful if you'd like to do some exploring on your own.

Bus

Public transport to and from Punta Allen is unpredictable at best—build some flexibility into your plans in case of missed (or missing) connections.

A privately run **Tulum-Punta Allen shuttle** (cell tel. 984/115-5580, US$22, 4 hours) leaves Tulum at 2pm most days. You can catch it at the taxi station on Avenida Tulum between Calles Centauro and Orion, or anywhere along the Zona Hotelera road; advance reservations are required. To return, the same shuttle leaves Punta Allen for Tulum at 5am.

You also can get to Punta Allen from Carrillo Puerto, a slightly cheaper but much longer and more taxing trip. State-run *combis* leave from the market in Carrillo Puerto (a block from the main traffic circle) for a bone-jarring four-hour trip down a private road to the small settlement of Playón (US$10, 10am and 3pm daily), where water taxis wait to ferry passengers across the lagoon to Punta Allen (US$2.50 pp, 15 minutes). The *combi* back to Carrillo Puerto leaves Playón at 6am.

Car

To get to Punta Allen by car, head south along the coast through (and past) Tulum's Zona Hotelera. About eight kilometers (5 miles) from the Tulum/Zona Hotelera junction is *el arco* (the arch), marking the reserve boundary where you register and pay a US$2.85 per person per day park fee. From there it's 56 kilometers (35 miles) by dirt road to Punta Allen. The road is much improved from years past, and an ordinary car can make it in 2-3 hours. It can be much more difficult after a heavy rain, however. Be sure to fill the tank in Tulum—there is no gas station along the way or in Punta Allen, though some locals sell gas from their homes.

The Costa Maya

The coastline south of Tulum loops and weaves like the tangled branches of the mangrove trees that blanket much of it. It is a mosaic of savannas, marshes, lagoons, scattered islands, and three huge bays: Bahía de la Ascensión, Bahía del Espiritu Santo, and Bahía de Chetumal. Where it's not covered by mangroves, the shore has sandy beaches and dunes, and just below the turquoise sea is one of the least-impacted sections of the great Mesoamerican Coral Reef. Dozens of Maya archaeological sites have been discovered here, but few excavated, and much remains unknown about pre-Hispanic life here. During the conquest, the snarled coastal forest proved an effective sanctuary for indigenous rebels and refugees fleeing Spanish control, not to mention a haven for pirates, British logwood cutters, and Belizean anglers.

In the 1990s, Quintana Roo officials launched an effort to develop the state's southern coast, which was still extremely isolated despite the breakneck development taking place in and around Cancún. (It has always been a famous fly-fishing area, however.) The first order of business was to construct a huge cruise ship port, which they did in the tiny fishing village of Mahahual. They also needed a catchy name, and came up with the "Costa Maya." The moniker generally applies to the coastal areas south of Tulum, particularly the Sian Ka'an Biosphere Reserve; the towns of

Mahahual and Xcalak; Laguna Bacalar; and Chetumal, the state capital and by far the largest city in the area.

It's hard not to be a little cynical about cruise liners coming to such a remote area, whose entire population could fit comfortably on a single ship. The town of Mahahual, nearest the port, is utterly transformed when cruise ships arrive, their passengers moseying about Mahahual, beer bottles in hand, the beaches packed with sun worshippers serenaded by the sound of Jet Skis. Then again, it's doubtful the area would have paved roads, power lines, or telephone service if not for the income and demand generated by cruise ships. Driving down the old rutted coastal road to Xcalak (an even smaller town south of Mahahual) used to take a half day or more; today, a two-lane paved road has cut the trip to under an hour. The state government has vowed to control development by limiting hotel size and density, monitoring construction methods, and protecting the mangroves and coral reef. Small, ecofriendly bed-and-breakfasts have thrived, not surprisingly, and more and more independent travelers are drawn to the Costa Maya for its quiet isolation and pristine natural beauty.

CARRILLO PUERTO

Highway 307 from Tulum to Chetumal passes through Carrillo Puerto, the gateway to the Costa Maya. It's a small city that holds little of interest to most travelers except an opportunity to fill up on gas. Historically, however, it played a central role in the formation of Quintana Roo and the entire peninsula.

History

Founded in 1850, the town of Chan Santa Cruz (present-day Carrillo Puerto) was the center of a pivotal movement during the Caste War. As the Maya lost ground in the war, two indigenous leaders enlisted a ventriloquist to introduce the *Cruz Parlante* (Talking Cross) in Chan Santa Cruz. The cross "spoke" to the battle-weary population,

urging them to continue fighting, even issuing tactical orders and predicting victory in the long, bitter conflict. Thousands joined the sect of the cross, calling themselves Cruzob (a Spanish-Maya conflation meaning People of the Holy Cross). Some accounts portray the talking cross as little more than political theater for a simpleminded audience, while others say most Cruzob understood it as a ruse to instill motivation. Some people, of course, believe in the cross's divinity. Whatever the case, it reinvigorated the Maya soldiers, and Chan Santa Cruz remained the last redoubt of organized indigenous resistance, finally submitting to federal troops in 1901. Once residing in Carrillo Puerto's Santuario de la Cruz Parlante, the Talking Cross is today housed in a small sanctuary in the town of Tixacal.

The town's name was changed in 1934 in honor of a former governor of Quintana Roo, much revered by indigenous and working-class people for his progressive reforms, for which he was ultimately assassinated.

Sights

The **Santuario de la Cruz Parlante** (Calle 69 at Calle 60, no phone, irregular hours, free) is a sacred place where the Talking Cross and two smaller ones were originally housed (they now reside in the nearby town of Tixacal). Today, there are several crosses in their place, all dressed in *huipiles*, which is customary in the Yucatán. Shoes and hats must be removed before entering. Be sure to ask permission before snapping any photographs.

Carrillo Puerto's main church, the **Iglesia de Balam Nah** (facing the central plaza, no phone), was reportedly built by white slaves—mostly Spaniards and light-skinned Mexicans—who were captured during the Caste War. It was constructed in 1858 to house the Talking Cross and its two companion crosses because the original sanctuary had become too small to accommodate its worshippers. Unfortunately, at the end of the Caste War, federal troops used the church as an army storeroom,

The Caste War

On July 18, 1847, a military commander in Valladolid learned of an armed plot to overthrow the government that was being planned by two indigenous men—Miguel Antonio Ay and Cecilio Chí. Ay was arrested and executed. Chí managed to escape punishment and on July 30, 1847, led a small band of armed men into the town of Tepich. Several officials and Euro-Mexican families were killed. The military responded with overwhelming force, burning villages, poisoning wells, and killing scores of people, including many women, children, and elderly. The massacre—and the longstanding oppression of indigenous people at its root—sparked spontaneous uprisings across the peninsula, which quickly developed into a massive, coordinated indigenous rebellion known as the Caste War.

Indigenous troops tore through colonial cities, killing and capturing scores of non-Maya. In some cases, the Maya turned the tables on their former masters, forcing them into slave labor, including building the church in present-day Carrillo Puerto's central plaza. Valladolid was evacuated in 1848 and left abandoned for nearly a year, and by 1849, the peninsula's indigenous people were close to expelling the colonial elite. However, as they were preparing their final assaults on Mérida and Campeche City, the rainy season came early, presenting the Maya soldiers with a bitter choice between victory and (were they to miss the planting season) likely famine. The men turned their backs on a hard-fought and near-certain victory to return to their fields to plant corn.

Mexican troops immediately took advantage of the lull, and the Maya never regained the upper hand. For the next 13 years, captured indigenous soldiers (and increasingly *any* indigenous person) were sold to slave brokers and shipped to Cuba. Many Maya eventually fled into the forests and jungles of southern Quintana Roo. The fighting was rekindled when a wooden cross in the town of Chan Santa Cruz (today, Carrillo Puerto) was said to be channeling the voice of God, urging the Maya to keep fighting. The war ended, however, when troops took control of Chan Santa Cruz in 1901. An official surrender was signed in 1936.

desecrating it in the eyes of many Maya; this led to the transfer of the Talking Cross to the town of Tixacal.

Museo Maya Santa Cruz (central plaza, no phone, 9am-8:30pm Mon.-Fri., 10am-2pm and 5pm-9pm Sat.-Sun., free) is a small museum located in an exterior wing of the main church. Inside you'll find a mishmash of folk art, modern paintings, and modern Maya woodwork. It's not worth making a special stop but is a nice diversion if you're spending the night in Carrillo Puerto.

Despite outward appearances, Maya nationalism is still very much alive, and its adherents are not blind of the sometimes invasive effects of mass tourism. Don't miss the beautifully painted **Central Plaza Mural,** next to the Casa de Cultura, that reads: *La zona Maya no es un museo etnográfico, es un pueblo en marcha* (The Maya region is not an ethnographic museum, it is a people on the move).

Food

El Faisán y el Venado (Av. Benito Juárez at Calle 67, tel. 983/834-0043, 6am-10pm daily, US$5-8) is Carrillo Puerto's best-known restaurant, as much for its location and longevity than for any particular noteworthiness of its food. The menu is filled with reliable Yucatecan standards, including 8-10 variations of fish, chicken, and beef, plus soup and other sides.

Located just off the central plaza, **Café Luna Violeta** (Calle 63 at Calle 68, tel. 983/700-3847, 7am-noon and 7pm-midnight Mon.-Sat., US$3-8) is a cozy little place serving light fare like sandwiches and pastries plus a variety of coffee drinks and teas.

Information and Services

The **tourist office** (Av. Benito Juárez at Av. Santiago Pacheco Cruz, tel. 983/267-1452) is open 8am-2pm and 6pm-9pm Monday-Friday.

The **Hospital General** (Calle 51 btwn

Carrillo Puerto Bus Schedule

Departures from the **bus terminal** (Calle 65 near central plaza, tel. 983/834-0815) include:

Destination	Price	Duration	Schedule
Bacalar	US$5	1.5-2 hrs	17 departures 2am-11pm
Cancún	US$11.50	3.5-4 hrs	23 departures 1am-11:30pm
Chetumal	US$6.75	2-2.5 hrs	17 departures 2am-11pm
Limones	US$3.50	45-60 min	17 departures 2am-11pm
Mérida	US$15.25	6 hrs	13 departures midnight-9pm
Tulum	US$4.50	1-1.5 hrs	23 departures 1am-11:30pm
Valladolid	US$7	2.5 hrs	3 departures 9:30am-10:30pm

Av. Benito Juárez and Calle 68, tel. 983/834-0092) is open 24 hours daily. Try **Farmacia Similares** (Av. Benito Juárez at Av. Lázaro Cárdenas, tel. 983/834-1407, 8am-10:30pm Mon.-Sat., 9am-10:30pm Sun.) for meds.

The **police department** (central plaza, tel. 983/834-0369, 24 hours) is located in the Palacio Municipal (city hall).

Next to the PEMEX station, **HSBC** (Av. Benito Juárez at Calle 69, 9am-5pm Mon.-Fri., 9am-3pm Sat.) has one 24-hour ATM. There also are two ATMs—HSBC and Santander—inside the bus terminal (Calle 65 near the central plaza).

The **post office** (Calle 69 btwn Calles 64 and 66) is open 9am-4pm Monday-Friday. Facing the central plaza, **Balam Nah Internet** (8am-midnight daily) charges US$0.75 per hour.

Accommodations

Owned by one of the founding families of the city, **Hotel Esquivel** (Calle 63 btwn Calles 66 and 68, tel. 983/834-0344, US$44 s/d with a/c, US$52 suite with a/c and kitchenette) offers 37 rooms in four buildings, each with private bathroom, cable TV, and Wi-Fi. The main building has by far the best rooms—gleaming tile floors, simple furnishings, decent beds, and even some with balconies overlooking a pleasant park. The suites are in a large building across the street—recently remodeled, they are spacious and sparse with kitchenettes for basic cooking (microwave only). They open onto a large garden with swing sets and even a wading pool—perfect if you're traveling with small children (or are desperate to cool off).

Getting There

Carrillo Puerto's **bus terminal** (Calle 65 near the central plaza, tel. 983/834-0815) has second-class service to Mahahual, Chetumal, Cancún, Mérida, and elsewhere.

If traveling by car, **fill your gas tank** in Carrillo Puerto, especially if you're headed to Mahahual or Xcalak. There are other roadside gas stations ahead (and in Chetumal), but they get less and less reliable—having either no gas or no electricity to pump it—as the stretches of empty highway grow longer and longer.

Mahahual

SHOPPING CENTER
MAIN STREET
LAS CASITAS
CRUISE SHIP PIER
AV PASEO DEL PUERTO CHICLE
AV MAYA CACAO
AV DEL MANGLAR
PRIVATE ROAD (RESTRICTED USE)
RIO HONDO
OXTANKAH
CALDERITAS
CHETUMAL
KOHUNLICH
LAVANDA
MINISUPER BERE
BACALAR
THE NATIVE CHOICE
CHACCHOBEN
CHINCHORRO
MOBIUS INTERNET
CARRETERA CAFETAL MAHAHUAL
← To gas station, Xcalak, Mayan Beach Garden Inn, and Hwy 307
BLUE KAY
AV MALECON MAHAHUAL
HUACHINANGO
BUS TERMINAL
PARGO
Caribbean Sea
RUBIA
LAVANDERIA 4 HERMANOS
PHARMACY MÉRIDA
HOSTAL JARDÍN
SARDINA
CHERNA
CAFÉ COLONIAL
KI'I TACO
MARTILLO
POLICE
COSTA MAYA YOGA
POSADA PACHAMAMA
UNDERTOE MEXICO/DOLCE VITA
HOTEL CABALLO BLANCO/DOCTOR DIVE
CENTRO DE SALUD
CORONADO
DIVINO DELICIA ITALIANA
NACIONAL BEACH CLUB AND BUNGALOWS
BARRACUDA
MERO
ROBALO
MOJARRA
LIZA
CAZON
NOHOCH KAY
ATÚN
CENTRO DE ACOPIO DE LANGOSTA
ALMEJA

0   500 yds
0   500 m

To Maya Luna, Balamku Inn on the Beach, Travel In', Kohunbeach, and Almaplena Eco Resort and Beach Club ↓
LAS CABAÑAS DEL DOCTOR
TRITONES
DREAMTIME DIVE RESORT

© AVALON TRAVEL

MAHAHUAL

Mahahual is a place of two faces: cruise ship days, when the town's one road is packed with day-trippers looking to buy T-shirts and throw back a few beers; and non-cruise-ship days, when Mahahual is sleepy and laid-back, and the narrow white-sand beaches are free to walk for miles. Whether you stay here a night or a week, you're likely to see both, which is a good thing. You can be in a major party zone one day, and the next be the only snorkeler in town—all without changing hotels. If you seek long quiet days every day, though, definitely stay outside of town.

Whether or not there is a cruise ship in town, Mahahual is pretty easy to manage. Most of its hotels and services are located on, or just off, Avenida Mahahual (aka El Malecón), the three-kilometer (1.9-mile) pedestrian walkway that runs through town until it meets up with the coastal road heading south, the Carretera Antigua (literally, Old Highway). Just northwest of town, the tiny residential community of Las Casitas has additional services like an Internet café and a laundry.

Sights

★ BANCO CHINCHORRO

Chinchorro Bank is by some measurements the largest coral atoll in the Northern Hemisphere and a paradise for divers and snorkelers alike. About 44 kilometers (27 miles) east of Mahahual and 65.4 kilometers (40 miles) northeast of Xcalak, Chinchorro is a marine reserve and is known for its spectacular coral formations, massive sponges, and abundant sealife. Scores of ships have foundered on the shallow reefs through the years, but (contrary to innumerable misreports) the wrecks cannot be dived. Not only are they protected as historical sites, but most are on the eastern side of the atoll, where the surf and currents are too strong for recreational diving. The famous **40 Cannons wreck,** in about three meters (10 feet) of water on the atoll's northwest side, is good for snorkeling but not diving, and thanks to looters there are far fewer than 40 cannons there. There are small government and fishermen's huts on Cayo Centro, one of the three cays; as of 2010, tourists are permitted to stay overnight, which means spectacular multiday diving and snorkeling opportunities. To get to Chinchorro, it's a 1.5- to 2-hour boat ride, which can be pretty punishing depending on conditions. Groups typically set out around 7am and return to port around 5pm. Dive shops usually require at least five divers or six snorkelers (or a combination of the two) and may not go for days at a time if the weather is bad (summer months are best).

Sports and Recreation
SCUBA DIVING
Mahahual has terrific diving on the coral reef just offshore, with dozens of sites a short boat ride away. It's also one of two jumping-off points for trips to Chinchorro Bank, the largest coral atoll in the Northern Hemisphere. The other departure point is Xcalak, south of Mahahual.

Tritones (Av. Mahahual Km. 2.4, cell tel. 983/123-7639, www.tritonesdemahahual.com, 8am-6pm daily) is a friendly shop offering a wide array of dives to local sites (US$100 one tank, US$190 two tanks). It also offers fantastic overnight trips to Banco Chinchorro (US$500 pp, 1 night) that include six dives, meals (including a lobster dinner), drinks, and basic lodging in a stilt house on the water's edge. Snorkelers are welcome, too (US$200 pp). Longer trips to Chinchorro also can be arranged.

Doctor Dive (Malécon at Calle Coronado, cell tel. 983/125-2140, www.doctordive.com, 8am-6pm daily) is a small shop offering personalized service for independent travelers; fun dives are US$55 for one tank, US$85 for two; gear is an extra US$15 per day. Specialty trips, including lionfish hunting and diving unexplored locations, also can be arranged.

Don't be deterred by the slew of cruise shippers who crowd into **Dreamtime Dive Resort** (Av. Mahahual Km. 2.5, cell tel. 983/124-0235, U.S. tel. 904/730-4337, www.dreamtimediving.com, 9am-7pm daily)—the shop is an indie operation at heart and sends its students and "regular" guests on separate boats in groups of six divers or fewer. Fun dives cost US$55 for one tank, US$85 for two, and US$110 for three; rental equipment is an additional US$20 per day. The shop also offers Chinchorro Bank trips, all-day exploration trips, night dives, and a full menu of diving instruction and courses.

SNORKELING
You can rent snorkel gear for around US$8-10 a day from the dive shops or from the kiosks that pop up on cruise ship days. Swim or kayak out to the reef for a do-it-yourself experience, or join a guided tour, where you'll likely see more sealife, plus have extra safety and convenience. Mahahual's dive shops all offer guided snorkel trips for US$30-40 per person, including gear and about 90 minutes in the water.

STAND-UP PADDLING
UnderToe Mexico (Calle Coronado near Malécon, cell tel. 983/117-8995, www.undertoemexico.com, hours vary) offers introductory paddleboarding lessons (US$40 for 90 minutes) from certified bilingual instructors. If you already know the basics, rentals are available (US$35/hour) as are a number of SUPing excursions to nearby rivers and lagoons (prices vary).

YOGA
Located in a breezy studio overlooking the Caribbean, **Costa Maya Yoga** (Calle Martillo near Malécon, cell tel. 983/105-8040, www.costa-maya-yoga.com, hours vary) offers vinyasa, hatha, and restorative yoga classes from a handful of talented instructors. Classes run US$20 per person; check the website for the current schedule.

TOURS
The Native Choice (Las Casitas, Av. Paseo del Puerto at Calle Chinchorro, tel. 998/869-3346, www.thenativechoice.com) offers a range of area tours, all led by guides who are

Lionfish

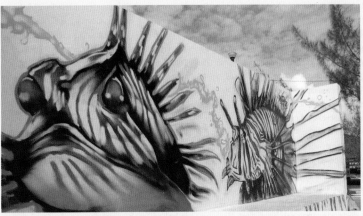
lionfish mural in Puerto Morelos

The lionfish is a spectacular striped fish with a "mane" of fins and poisonous spines that is changing the underwater landscape of the entire Caribbean. Historically found only in the warm regions of the Pacific and Indian Oceans, lionfish were first sighted in Atlantic waters in 1992 in Biscayne Bay, Florida; it's believed they were released into the wild after a private aquarium was swept into the ocean by Hurricane Andrew. Since then, lionfish have been documented in the Florida Keys, the Bahamas, Cuba, and elsewhere; the first lionfish sighting in the region was in Cozumel in January 2009. Voracious hunters with no natural predators, lionfish can grow to 20 inches long and devour everything from small reef fish to commercial fish like snapper and juvenile grouper. They thrive at depths of just a few feet to over 500 feet, and their coloring makes them especially well-suited for coral environments. Government agencies have taken proactive efforts to help curb the growth of this invasive fish, garnering widespread community support. There now are fishing tournaments targeting lionfish, and spear-fishing training for local sport divers; experts are even trying, with some success, to "train" wild sharks and mature grouper to prey on lionfish by introducing them into known hunting grounds. Restaurants are doing their part by creating innovative and tasty dishes from lionfish meat.

extremely knowledgeable about Maya history, culture, and belief systems. Tours include visiting the archaeological sites of Chacchoben, Kohunlich, or Dzibanché (US$55-100 adult, US$45-85 child), a "Mayan Experience Tour," which includes touring Chacchoben ruins and a visit to a home in Chacchoben village (US$75 adult, US$65 child), plus a kayaking and hiking trip on and around Laguna Bacalar (US$55 adult, US$40 child). The tours are geared toward the cruise ship crowd, but hotel owners warmly recommend the outfit to independent travelers as well.

Food
IN TOWN

An open-air eatery and beach club, ★ **Nohoch Kay** (Big Fish in English, Malecón btwn Calles Liza and Cazón, no phone, 8am-7pm Mon.-Tues., 8am-10pm Wed.-Sun., US$5-14) serves up some of the best fish tacos in town. Thick pieces of fish—fried or grilled—are served with small tortillas, onion, cilantro, and plenty of lime. On cruise ship days, it gets overrun with clients, but otherwise it's a laid-back place to get a beachfront meal.

Ki'i Taco (Calle Huachinango at Calle Cherna, no phone, 11am-10pm Mon.-Sat., US$2-6) offers equally good fish tacos without the cruise ship scene. For a treat, order the garlic shrimp tacos.

A breezy restaurant with hanging shell lamps and a *palapa* roof, ★ **Divino Delicia Italiana** (Calle Huachinango at Calle Coronado, no phone, 5pm-11pm Tues.-Sun., US$7-14) serves up freshly made pastas, seafood salads, and wooden tablets loaded with gourmet cheeses and meats. Thin-crust pizzas also are baked in the wood-burning stove, visible from the dining room. An extensive wine list combined with friendly service round out a meal nicely.

Café Colonial (Calle Sierra near Malécon, no phone, 7am-5pm daily, US$3-6) is a good place to grab breakfast. Package deals include a hearty plate of eggs with bread, coffee, and juice for US$6. À la carte items like fruit plates and breakfast sandwiches also are offered. Tables are in a small wood house or on the pedestrian walkway in front.

Dolce Vita (Malécon at Calle Coronado, no phone, 8am-10pm daily, US$3-7) is a small shop specializing in homemade gelato, pastries, crepes, and milkshakes. And if you're looking for a mean cappuccino, look no further.

If you're cooking for yourself, consider buying fresh lobster from the local lobster fisherman's co-op, **Centro de Acopio de Langosta** (Calle Huachinango near Calle Almeja, no phone, 7am-7pm daily). At this roadside shack, you can take your pick of lobsters; they generally sell for US$30 per kilo (2.2 pounds). Fresh conch also is sold here for about US$16 per kilo.

OUTSIDE OF TOWN

A longtime favorite, **Travel In'** (Carr. Antigua Km. 5.8, cell tel. 983/110-9496, www.travel-in.com.mx, 5:30pm-9pm Tues.-Sat., US$5-20) is a great little restaurant a few kilometers down the coastal road. Homemade pita bread is baked fresh every day—order it as an appetizer with an assortment of homemade dips. Daily seafood specials vary according to the day's catch. Open on Monday Christmas-Easter.

For basic groceries, try **Minisuper Bere** (Las Casitas, Av. Paseo del Puerto near Calle Kohunlich, 8am-11pm daily).

Even the waves take it easy in Mahahual.

Accommodations

Many of Mahahual's lodgings, especially the ones with beachfront, are outside of the village itself, along the Carretera Antigua that hugs the coast south of town. The rest are in town, either on the Malecón or a stone's throw away.

IN TOWN

Under US$50: ★ **Hostal Jardín** (Calle Sardina near Calle Sierra, tel. 983/834-5722, hostal.jardin.mahahual@gmail.com, US$10 pp dorm, US$27 s/d, US$35 s/d with a/c) is an appealing hostel with a small interior garden and a friendly staff. The eight-bed dorm has overhead fans, thick mattresses, and spotless single-sex bathrooms. Four private rooms are located on the other side of the garden, with whitewashed walls, polished cement floors, and artsy touches. The only bummer—there's no communal kitchen.

Near the entrance to town, **Blue Kay** (Malecón btwn Carretera Cafetal and Calle Pargo, tel. 983/834-5868, www.bluekaymahahual.com, US$7.50 pp camping, US$11.50 pp dorm, US$32-39 s/d cabin with shared bathroom) has 27 tiny wood-plank cabins, lined up in three tidy rows in front of a long, gorgeous beach. Except for the waterbeds (yes, waterbeds), the cabins are basic—wood floor, a bed, a light—with a private porch for relaxing in the evenings; campers can set up in a garden just steps from the beach (BYO gear). Shared bathrooms are located in a *palapa*-roofed building—they're huge and clean enough. All guests enjoy use of the hotel's beach club and its amenities, though on cruise ship days, it can get pretty busy.

Set on a grassy lot facing the ocean, **Las Cabañas del Doctor** (Av. Mahahual Km. 2, tel. 983/832-2102, www.lascabanasdeldoctor.com, US$7 pp camping, US$37-50 s/d *cabaña*, US$50 s/d, US$69 s/d with a/c) has a good range of accommodations: camping on the beach with access to cold-water bathrooms (BYO gear); simple *palapa*-roofed *cabañas* with tile floors and fans; and hotel rooms with recently remodeled bathrooms, modern

decor, and private porches. All units—and camping spots—have Wi-Fi, too.

US$50-100: Posada Pachamama (Calle Huachinango btwn Calles Martillo and Coronado, tel. 983/834-5762, www.posadapachamama.net, US$68-76 s/d with a/c) is a small hotel a block from the beach. Rooms are small but appealingly decorated with modern furnishings and stone-inlaid floors; they are starting to show a bit of wear and tear, but nothing that impedes a comfortable stay. All have air-conditioning, wireless Internet, and satellite TV. The higher-priced rooms have small balconies, some with partial beach views. Guests also enjoy complimentary use of the beach club at Barba Roja, just in front.

With direct access to the beach and a rooftop bar with a spectacular view, **Hotel Caballo Blanco** (Malecón btwn Calles Martillo and Coronado, tel. 983/834-5830, www.hotelelcaballoblanco.com, US$77-115 s/d suite with a/c) is a great place to land. Rooms are modern and comfortable with air-conditioning, flat-screen TVs, mini-fridges, and Wi-Fi. All have private balconies, the more expensive ones overlooking the Caribbean. The only quirk about the place? Dramatic murals of old-world villages.

Over US$100: ★ **Nacional Beach Club and Bungalows** (Malécon near Calle Coronado, tel. 983/834-5719, www.nacionalbeachclub.com, US$62-112 s/d bungalows, US$112-127 s/d with a/c) is a tasteful beachfront hotel with spectacular ocean views and excellent service. Units vary from thatched-roof bungalows with private terraces to spacious hotel rooms with high ceilings and Mexican tile bathrooms. There's a small pool right on the Malécon and a good restaurant on-site. Guests are welcome to use the hotel beach club and its amenities, too.

OUTSIDE OF TOWN

US$50-100: Kohunbeach (Carr. Antigua Km. 7, cell tel. 983/700-2820, www.kohunbeach.com, US$54-77 s/d) offers three simple and spacious *cabañas* on the beach. Each has a queen bed, a foldout futon sofa, picture windows, and a mosaic-tile bathroom. All are solar powered. Kayaks and plenty of hammocks are available to guests, too.

Owned and operated by friendly Canadian expats, ★ **Balamku Inn on the Beach** (Carr. Antigua Km. 5.7, tel. 983/732-1004, www.balamku.com, US$85 s, US$95 d) offers artfully decorated rooms in a handful of *palapa*-roofed buildings. All run on solar power, wind turbines, and a nonpolluting wastewater system. Full breakfast is included, as is use of the hotel's kayaks, board games, and library. Wi-Fi is available in all the rooms, too.

Maya Luna (Carr. Antigua Km. 5.6, tel. 983/836-0905, www.hotelmayaluna.com, US$89 s/d) has four modern bungalows with 24-hour solar/wind power, rainwater showers, and *palapa*-shaded porches. Each has a private rooftop terrace with views of the Caribbean in front and the jungle in back; all have Maya- or ocean-themed murals, too. A hearty and healthy breakfast is included in the rate. Pets are welcome (and will join a cadre of friendly cats and a dog who live on-site).

Over US$100: About 20 minutes south of town, **Almaplena Eco Resort and Beach Club** (Carr. Antigua Km. 12.5, cell tel. 983/137-5070, www.almaplenabeachresort. com, US$135-145 s/d) is a small boutique resort with just eight rooms facing a gorgeous isolated stretch of beach. All have king-size beds, ceiling fans (no air-conditioning), cool stone floors, and tasteful decor. Suites are on the top floor and have private terraces, while standards share a wooden patio with direct access to the beach. All have Wi-Fi, too. Continental breakfast is included, and the on-site restaurant serves fine Mediterranean and Mexican meals.

About 21 kilometers (13 miles) north of Mahahual, **Mayan Beach Garden Inn** (cell tel. 983/130-8658, www.mayanbeachgarden. com, US$96-125 s/d, US$125 s/d with kitchenette, US$25 extra for a/c at night) is a quiet hotel (children over age 12 only) with several rooms and one *cabaña,* all with whitewashed walls and Mexican-style decor, most with ocean views. A hearty breakfast is included in the rate, as are Wi-Fi and the use of kayaks. All-inclusive meal packages are also available. In the high season, there's a three-night minimum.

Information and Services

Cruise ships have brought considerable modernization to this once-isolated fishing village, but services are still somewhat limited.

EMERGENCY SERVICES

The **Centro de Salud** (Calle Coronado btwn Calles Huachinango and Sardina, no phone, 8am-2:30pm daily, after 5pm emergencies only) offers basic health services. For serious health matters, head to Chetumal.

For meds, try **Pharmacy Mérida** (Calle Sardina btwn Calles Rubia and Sierra, cell tel. 983/132-1845, 7am-11pm Mon.-Fri., 9am-11pm Sat.-Sun.), the best-stocked pharmacy in town.

The **police department** (Calle Huachinango near Calle Martillo, toll-free Mex. tel. 066) is open 24 hours.

MONEY

There is no bank in town, but there are a handful of **ATMs,** all along El Malecón. At the time of research, however, none were affiliated with local banks, so withdrawal charges were hefty. Another option is to go to the gas station outside of town, where there's an **HSBC ATM** (though it often runs out of cash); alternatively, consider bringing enough money to get you through your stay.

MEDIA AND COMMUNICATIONS

The only Internet café is in Las Casitas, where **Mobius Internet** (Calle Chinchorro near Av. Paseo del Puerto, 9am-10pm Mon.-Fri., 9am-2pm and 5pm-10pm Sat.) charges US$1.50 per hour and offers international telephone service, too (US$0.35-0.45/minute calls to the United States and Europe). Most hotels and some restaurants offer wireless Internet as well.

LAUNDRY

Lavandería 4 Hermanos (Calle Huachinango near Calle Rubia, 7am-8pm daily) offers same-day laundry service for US$1.50 per kilo (2.2 pounds).

In Las Casitas, try **Lavanda** (Av. Paseo del Puerto at Calle Chetumal, 9am-6pm daily), which charges US$1.25 per kilo (2.2 pounds).

Getting There and Around

Just south of the grubby roadside town of Limones, a good paved road with signs to Mahahual breaks off Highway 307 and cuts through 58 kilometers (36 miles) of coastal forest and wetlands tangled with mangroves. It's a scenic stretch, whether in a car or on a bus, along which you can occasionally see egrets, herons, and other water birds.

Mahahual proper is very walkable—in fact, the main road that runs through town, El Malecón, is a three-kilometer (1.9-mile) pedestrian walkway. If you're staying outside of town, a car certainly comes in handy, but plenty of people manage without; dive shops and tour operators typically offer hotel pickup, and there are cabs and a local bus.

BUS

Mahahual's bus terminal is a modest affair near the entrance to town—basically, a parking lot in front of Koox Quinto Sole Hotel. Buses to Cancún (US$28.50, 4.5 hours) leave at 5pm daily, stopping at Carrillo Puerto (US$10.25, 2 hours), Tulum (US$18.50, 3 hours), Playa del Carmen (US$24, 3.5 hours), and Puerto Morelos (US$23, 4 hours) along the way. To Chetumal (US$6.25, 2.5 hours) and Laguna Bacalar (US$5.75, 1.5 hours), buses depart at 7:40am and 5:40pm daily. All buses stop in Limones (US$3.50, 1 hour).

Note: Buses entering Mahahual stop in Las Casitas before arriving at the bus terminal; be sure you get off at the latter if you're headed to the beach or any of the hotels.

CAR AND TAXI

There is a PEMEX gas station (24 hours) on the main road to Mahahual, just east of the turnoff to Xcalak. It occasionally runs out of gas, so definitely fill your tank in Carrillo Puerto or Chetumal on your way here.

Note: There's often a military checkpoint set up just west of the turnoff to Xcalak, where officials conduct searches for illicit drugs and other contraband. As long as you or your passengers don't have anything illegal in the car, the longest you should be delayed is a couple of minutes.

Cabs abound in this town, especially on cruise ship days. Rates are set by zone; in general, rates run around US$1 per kilometer (0.6 mile). If in doubt, ask to see the *tarifario* (official rate chart).

AIRPORT

Mahahual has a small airport just outside of town. Well, it's more like a well-maintained airstrip with a nice shelter. At the time of research, it was only used by private or chartered planes.

XCALAK

The tiny fishing village of Xcalak lies just a short distance from the channel that marks the Mexico-Belize border, and a blessed long way from anything else. The town started out as a military outpost and didn't get its first real hotel until 1988. Villagers had to wait another decade to get a paved road; before that, the only way in or out of town was by boat or via 55 kilometers (34 miles) of rutted beach tracks. Electrical lines were installed in 2004 but only in the village proper, so many outlying areas (including most of the better hotels) still rely on solar and wind power, as well as generators. The town has no bank, no public phones, and no gas station. That is to say: perfect!

The area doesn't have much beach but makes up for it with world-class fly-fishing, great snorkeling and diving, and a healthy coral reef and lagoon. A growing contingent of expats, mostly American and Canadian, have built homes here, some for personal use, others for rent, others as small hotels. Large-scale tourism may be inevitable but still seems a long way off, and Xcalak remains a small and wonderfully laid-back place, perfect for those looking for some honest-to-goodness isolation.

Sights

PARQUE NACIONAL ARRECIFES DE XCALAK

Xcalak Reef National Park was established at the end of 2003, affording protection to the coastal ecosystem as well as Xcalak's nascent tourist economy. The park spans nearly 18,000 hectares (44,479 acres), from the Belize border to well north of town, and includes the reef—and everything else down to 100 meters (328 feet)—as well as the shoreline and numerous inland lagoons.

The main coral reef lies just 90-180 meters (100-200 yards) from shore, and the water is less than 1.5 meters (5 feet) deep almost the whole way out. Many snorkelers prefer the coral heads even closer to shore, which have plenty to see and less swell than the main reef. The shallow waters keep boat traffic to a minimum, and anglers are good about steering clear of snorkelers (you should still stay alert at all times, however).

Divers and snorkelers also can explore the reef at 20 or so official sites and many more unofficial ones. Most are a short distance from town, and shops typically return to port between tanks. **La Poza** is one of the more distinctive dives, drifting through a trench where hundreds, sometimes thousands, of tarpon congregate, varying in size from one-meter (3-foot) "juveniles" to two-meter (7-foot) behemoths.

A fee of US$4 per day technically applies to all divers and snorkelers (and kayakers and anglers) in the Parque Nacional Arrecifes de Xcalak; dive shops typically add it to their rates, while most hotels have a stack of wristband permits to sell to guests who want to snorkel right from shore.

Sports and Recreation

SCUBA DIVING AND SNORKELING

XTC Dive Center (north end of town, across bridge, no phone, www.xtcdivecenter.com, 8am-6pm daily) is a highly recommended full-service dive shop offering dives to dozens of sites within Xcalak Reef National Marine Park (US$70 for one tank, US$110 for two tanks). It also specializes in trips to Chinchorro Bank (US$239 for two tanks or US$179 per person for snorkelers, including lunch, drinks, and a hike on Cayo Centro, the main cay; overnight trips are also offered). A variety of dive classes also are available; a nice three-meter-deep (9-foot) pool on-site is used for the open-water certification course. Snorkeling tours run US$40-75 per person depending on how long and far you go; five-hour trips include jaunts into Chetumal Bay and Bird Island, which can be fascinating, especially in January and February when the birds are most plentiful.

STAND-UP PADDLING

XTC Dive Center (north end of town, across bridge, no phone, www.xtcdivecenter.com, 8am-6pm daily) offers SUPing instruction for US$35-50 (30-60 minutes), including the equipment. Just want to take a board out on your own? Paddleboard rentals also are offered for US$35-55 (half-full day).

SPORTFISHING

Xcalak boasts world-class sportfishing, with huge saltwater and brackish flats where hooking into the grand slam of fly-fishing—tarpon, bonefish, and permit—is by no means impossible. Add a snook, and you've got a super slam. Oceanside, tarpon and barracuda abound, in addition to grouper, snapper, and others.

Costa de Cocos (3 kilometers/1.9 miles north of town, no phone, www.costadecocos. com) is the area's oldest fishing resort, with highly experienced guides and numerous magazine write-ups. Three- to seven-night packages include transfer to and from the airport, lodging, meals, open bar, fishing license, marine park wristband, and, of course, non-stop fly-fishing (US$2,030-4,305 s, US$1,620-3,295 d). The resort also offers half- and full-day fishing trips (US$175-350), in case you want to fish while in Xcalak without making it a full-on fishing vacation.

Hotel Tierra Maya (2.1 kilometers/1.3 miles north of town, tel. 983/839-8012, www.tierramaya.net) also offers fly-fishing packages for 6-7 nights (US$3,040-3,684 s, US$1,950-2,400 d), though they don't include all the perks—like airport transportation, open bar, and fishing license fees—that the Costa de Cocos packages do.

XTC Dive Center (north end of town, across bridge, no phone, www.xtcdive-center.com, 8am-6pm daily) offers half-day and full-day fly-fishing excursions (US$249-349) that include drinks, snacks, and a guide. BYO gear.

Food

Locally run **Restaurant Toby** (center of town, across from volleyball court, cell tel. 983/107-5426, 11am-9pm Mon.-Sat., US$7-14) is a popular seafood restaurant serving up, among other tasty dishes, heaping plates of ceviche, coconut shrimp, and fish soup. It's a friendly, low-key place perfect for a beer

and a good meal after a day of diving or relaxing on the beach. Wi-Fi is available, too.

The Maya Grill (Hotel Tierra Maya, 2.1 kilometers/1.3 miles north of town, tel. 983/839-8012, www.tierramaya.net, 6:30am-9pm daily, US$6-14) is a hotel beachfront restaurant with spectacular floor-to-ceiling windows with views of the Caribbean. The menu is solidly Mexican—tacos, quesadillas, enchiladas—with a fair share of seafood, too. Ingredients are fresh and portions are hearty.

The restaurant at Costa de Cocos, **The Reel Inn** (3 kilometers/1.9 miles north of town, no phone, www.costadecocos.com, 7am-8:30pm daily, US$6-28) serves up breakfast classics, burgers, steak, pizza, and all manner of tall tales—though with fishing as good as it is, many just happen to be true. The service is seriously lacking, but the schedule, reservations policy (none required), and full bar make it a reliable option.

If you are cooking for yourself, a **grocery truck** passes through town and down the coastal road several times per week—ask at your hotel for the current schedule. It comes stocked with eggs, yogurt, grains, basic produce, fresh meats, and canned food. You also

The Costa Maya is home to some of the world's best fishing.

can buy a broom or two. In town, there are a handful of small **mini-marts** selling basic canned and dried foods. Most are open 9am-9pm daily.

Accommodations

Xcalak's most appealing accommodations are on the beach road heading north out of town. Few places accept credit cards on-site, but many have payment systems on their websites.

UNDER US$50

Next to Restaurant Toby, **Hotel Caracol Caribe** (center of town, across from volleyball court, tel. 983/839-8381, US$27-31 s/d) is a simple, if aging, hotel offering the basics: a decent bed, a clean bathroom, a bare bulb, and a fan. There are two extras though: 24-hour electricity (huge in this part of the world) and a full breakfast (huge anywhere). Service is friendly, too.

US$50-100

Part of the XTC Dive Center, **Flying Cloud Hotel** (north end of town, across bridge, no phone, www.xtcdivecenter.com, US$45-55 s/d, US$65 s/d with kitchenette) is a three-room hotel with whitewashed walls, polished cement floors, and spectacular ocean views. Mattresses are thick and bathrooms are spotless. While each room is different—a collection of dive magazines, a private solarium, a king-size bed—each is comfortable. Guests enjoy use of the dive shop's pool and sea kayaks, too. When we passed through, plans were in the works to build a larger hotel just next door.

★ **Hotel Tierra Maya** (2.1 kilometers/1.3 miles north of town, tel. 983/839-8012, www.tierramaya.net, US$90-100 s/d, US$150 apartment) is a pleasant hotel with ample rooms decorated with simple furnishings and colorful Mexican rugs. All have private terraces or balconies with views of the Caribbean. Continental breakfast is included in the rate and served in the hotel's excellent beachfront restaurant. Fly-fishing and dive packages are also available.

US$100-150

It's hard not to feel at home at ★ **Sin Duda** (8 kilometers/5 miles north of town, Can. tel. 306/500-3240, www.sindudavillas.com, US$84 s/d, US$110 studio, US$120 apartment), a gem of a hotel with beautifully decorated rooms and apartments featuring Mexican folk art and breathtaking views. Evening often brings cocktail hour, when guests can join the friendly Canadian hosts for margaritas in the cozy lounge that doubles as a common kitchen and library. Kayaks and bicycles are available for guests, as are a rooftop solarium and hammocks on the beach. A healthy continental breakfast is included in the rate.

Four cheerful units with fully equipped kitchenettes make **Casa Carolina** (2.5 kilometers/1.6 miles north of town, U.S. tel. 678/446-9817, www.casacarolina.net, US$120 s/d) a great choice for indie travelers. Add ocean views from private balconies and a wide beach with palm trees, and it's a classic beach vacation. Full breakfast is included in the rate and is served in a pleasant *palapa*-roofed dining area. Kayaks, snorkel gear, and bicycles are available to guests free of charge, too. Snorkeling and fishing trips also can be arranged, with pickup at the hotel's private dock.

OVER US$150

Playa Sonrisa (6.9 kilometers/4.3 miles north of town, no phone, www.playasonrisa.com, US$150-175 s/d, US$175-250 suite) is a clothing-optional resort on a palm-tree-laden stretch of beach. Units are clean and comfortable, though they lack the charm that you'd expect for the rate. What you mostly pay for is the freedom to enjoy the Caribbean in the buff. A continental breakfast is included in the rate, as is Wi-Fi. Geared at naturist couples, the hotel welcomes naturist families during the low season only.

Information and Services

Xcalak has **no bank, ATM, or**

currency-exchange office, and only a few places take credit cards—plan accordingly!

There's a basic **health clinic** (no phone, 8am-noon and 2pm-6pm Mon.-Fri.) two blocks from the soccer field, near the entrance of town.

The **police station** (toll-free Mex. tel. 066) is located behind the lighthouse.

Most hotels have Wi-Fi; in a pinch many hotel owners will let you use their computers to send a quick email. For more time on the net, **San Jordy** (center of town, hours vary, US$2/hour) is a reliable Internet café. To make an international or domestic call, head to **Telecomm/Telégrafos** (2 blocks north of the lighthouse, 9am-3pm Mon.-Fri.).

Getting There and Around

Bus service is somewhat erratic in Xcalak. Theoretically, buses bound for Chetumal (US$7.75, 4-5 hours) with stops in Mahahual (US$3, 1 hour) and Limones (US$5.50, 2.5 hours) leave twice daily, typically around 5am and 2pm, but it's not unusual for one or both departures to be delayed or canceled. Upon arrival, your hotel may send a car to pick you up; otherwise, a taxi from town is about US$10. A cab from Mahahual runs around US$40.

Most travelers come in a rental car, which certainly simplifies life here. The closest gas station is on the main road to Mahahual, near the turnoff for Xcalak. However, it occasionally runs out of gas, so you should fill up on Highway 307 as well—Carrillo Puerto is a good spot. In a pinch, a few Xcalak families sell gas from barrels in their front yards; ask your hotel owner for help locating them.

If your budget permits, there also is a well-maintained airstrip approximately 2 kilometers (1.2 miles) west of town. Despite rumors that commercial flights will begin using it regularly, at the time of research, it was only used sporadically by private or chartered planes.

CHACCHOBEN ARCHAEOLOGICAL ZONE

Chacchoben (8am-5pm daily, US$4) got its name from archaeologists who, after uncovering no inscription indicating what the city's original residents called it, named it after the Maya village to which the land pertained. The meaning of that name is also lost, even to local villagers, though the accepted translation is Place of Red Corn. The area may have been settled as early as 1000 BC, and most of the building activity probably took place AD 200-700, the Classic period.

Chacchoben's Temple 24 has unusual, rounded corners.

Chacchoben Archaeological Zone

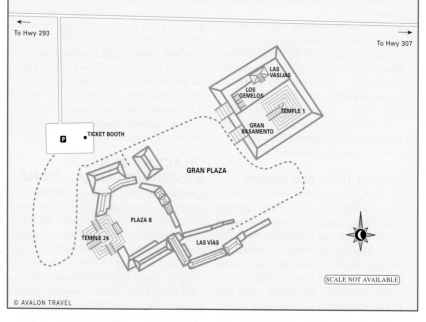

← To Hwy 293

→ To Hwy 307

LAS VASIJAS
LOS GEMELOS
TEMPLE 1
GRAN BASAMENTO

P ▪ TICKET BOOTH

GRAN PLAZA

PLAZA B

TEMPLE 24

LAS VÍAS

SCALE NOT AVAILABLE

© AVALON TRAVEL

Visiting the Ruins

Entering the site, a short path leads first to **Temple 24,** a squat pyramid that is the primary structure of a small enclosed area called **Plaza B.** Across that plaza—and the larger Gran Plaza beyond it—is a massive raised platform, the **Gran Basamento,** with the site's largest pyramid, **Temple 1,** atop it; this pyramid is believed to have served astronomical and religious purposes. Also on the platform, two smaller structures, dubbed **Las Vasijas** and **Los Gemelos,** were likely used for ceremonial functions. The site has some well-preserved stucco and paint, and for that reason none of the pyramids can be climbed.

Though it can get crowded when there's a cruise ship at Mahahual, Chacchoben has an appealingly remote feel, nestled in the forest with towering mahogany and banyan trees, and paths dotted with bromeliads.

Practicalities

Chacchoben is located about 70 kilometers (43 miles) north of Mahahual and 4 kilometers (2.5 miles) west of Limones. By **car,** take Highway 307 and turn west at the sign to Chacchoben ruins and like-named town, about 3 kilometers (1.9 miles) down a well-paved road. Alternatively, take a **bus** to Limones and then a **cab** (US$5) to the ruins.

Laguna Bacalar

Almost 50 kilometers (31 miles) long, Laguna Bacalar is the second-largest lake in Mexico and certainly among the most beautiful. Well, it's not technically a lake: A series of waterways do eventually lead to the ocean, making Bacalar a lagoon, but it is fed by natural springs, making the water on the western shore, where the hotels and town are, 100 percent *agua dulce* (fresh water).

The Maya name for the lagoon translates as Lake of Seven Colors. It is an apt description, as you will see on any sunny day. The lagoon's sandy bottom and crystalline water turn shallow areas a brilliant turquoise, which fades to deep blue in the center. If you didn't know better, you'd think it was the Caribbean.

The hub of the Laguna Bacalar region is the town of Bacalar. Located on the west side of the lake, it won't win any prizes for charm, but it does have a terrific museum, one of the best hotels around, a handful of decent restaurants, and, of course, gorgeous views of the lagoon.

SIGHTS AND EVENTS
★ Fuerte San Felipe Bacalar

The mid-18th-century **Fuerte San Felipe Bacalar** (central plaza, no phone, Av. 3 at Calle 20, 9am-7pm Tues.-Sun., US$2.50 adult, US$1.25 child) was built by the Spanish for protection against English pirates and Maya that regularly raided the area. In fact, attacks proved so frequent—and successful—that the fort was captured in 1858 by Maya during the Caste War. It was not returned to Mexican officials until 1901. Today, the star-shaped stone edifice has been restored to its former glory: drawbridge, cannons, moat, and all. The fort also houses the excellent **Museo del Fuerte de San Felipe Bacalar,** a modern museum with exhibits on the history of the area, including details on the pirates who regularly attacked these shores.

Cenote Azul

As good or better than Laguna Bacalar for swimming, **Cenote Azul** (Hwy. 307 Km. 15) is two kilometers (1.2 miles) south of town. It's the widest cenote in Mexico, some 300 meters (984

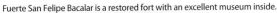
Fuerte San Felipe Bacalar is a restored fort with an excellent museum inside.

TULUM AND THE COSTA MAYA
LAGUNA BACALAR

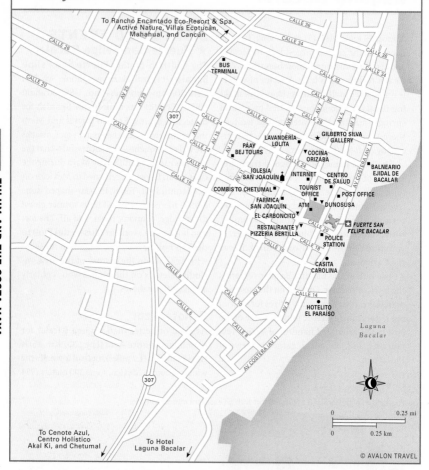

Laguna Bacalar

To Rancho Encantado Eco-Resort & Spa, Active Nature, Villas Ecotucán, Mahahual, and Cancún

CALLE 36
CALLE 34
CALLE 36
CALLE 34
CALLE 28
CALLE 26
CALLE 20
CALLE 20
CALLE 32
CALLE 30
CALLE 24
CALLE 22
CALLE 20
CALLE 18
CALLE 16
CALLE 14
CALLE 10
CALLE 8
CALLE 8

307

BUS TERMINAL

AV. 23
AV. 21
AV. 15
AV. 13
AVE. 9
AV. 7
AV. 5
AV. 3
AV. COSTERA (AV. 1)

LAVANDERÍA LOLITA
GILBERTO SILVA GALLERY
PAAY BEJ TOURS
COCINA ORIZABA
IGLESIA SAN JOAQUÍN
INTERNET
CENTRO DE SALUD
BALNEARIO EJIDAL DE BACALAR
COMBIS TO CHETUMAL
TOURIST OFFICE
POST OFFICE
FARMICA SAN JOAQUÍN
ATM
DUNOSUSA
EL CARBONCITO
RESTAURANTE Y PIZZERIA BERTILLA
FUERTE SAN FELIPE BACALAR
POLICE STATION
CASITA CAROLINA
HOTELITO EL PARAÍSO

Laguna Bacalar

AV. COSTERA (AV. 1)

To Cenote Azul, Centro Holístico Akal Ki, and Chetumal

To Hotel Laguna Bacalar

307

0   0.25 mi
0   0.25 km

© AVALON TRAVEL

feet) across at its widest, and 150 meters (492 feet) deep, with crystalline blue water. A rope stretches clear across, so even less-conditioned swimmers can make it to the far side. A large, breezy **restaurant** (tel. 983/834-2038, 7:30am-8pm daily, US$6-16) has the only entrance to the cenote, and charges a small admission fee (US$0.75) only if you don't order something.

Gilberto Silva Gallery

Gilberto Silva, an accomplished sculptor of Maya art, has a small **gallery and workshop**

(Calle 26 btwn Calles 5 and 7, tel. 983/834-2657, hours vary) where some of his works are displayed and sold. Most are intricately carved limestone pieces, which are then cast in clay. Notably, his works have been displayed at the Museum of Natural History in New York City.

Festival Mágico Bacalar

Held in early June, the Festival Mágico Bacalar (www.festivalmagicobacalar.com) is a five-day event showcasing Bacalar's water sports and culture. The festival features a two-day, 74-kilometer (44.5-mile) **Paddle Marathon** for adult sea kayakers and paddleboarders; for youths, there's a 2-kilometer (1.2-mile) **regatta.** Other popular events include a two-day **kayaking film festival** (who knew there were so many movies about kayaking?) as well as several live music and dance performances and art exhibits. There's also an expo of the latest paddle-sport gear, with top vendors and professionals on-site—a go-to stop if you're an aficionado or just curious about developments in the industry.

Fiesta de San Joaquín

Every July, the town of Bacalar celebrates San Joaquín, its patron saint. For nine consecutive days, different neighborhoods host festive celebrations, each trying to outdo the other for the year's best party. Visitors are welcome and should definitely join the fun—expect plenty of food, music, dancing, and performances of all sorts. Cockfights also are popular, and a three-day **hydroplane race** usually follows the festivities in early August.

SPORTS AND RECREATION
Ecotours

A friendly German couple founded **Active Nature** (Hotel Villas Ecotucán, Hwy. 307 Km. 27.3, cell tel. 983/120-5742, www.active-naturebacalar.com) after fate and car trouble cut short their planned tour of the Americas and left them in lovely Laguna Bacalar. Tour options include kayaking through mangrove channels, outrigger canoe tours, sunrise birding walks, and more. Day trips cost US$12.50-60 per person, including gear and often lunch and water; children under 10 are free, under 14 half off. Tours begin at Villas Ecotucán, whose guests get a 10 percent discount. Overnight tours can also be arranged.

Páay bej Tours (Posada Casa Madrid, Av. 22 btwn Calles 11 and 13, tel. 983/154-7580, www.bacalar-tours-paaybej.com) offers mellow hiking and kayaking trips in the lagoon (US$38.50 pp) and guided tours of Maya ruins like Kohunlich, Dzibanché, and Chacchoben

(US$42-69 pp, including transport and entrance fees), led by a friendly multilingual guide. You can also rent bikes here (US$0.75/hour, US$7.75/day).

Swimming

Though you'll have to walk through a bit of mud to get to the entrance, the **Balneario Ejidal de Bacalar** (Av. Costera near Calle 26, no phone, 7am-7pm, US$0.25) is a public swimming area complete with *palapas* for rent (US$3/day), bathrooms, and a restaurant (9am-7pm, US$3-10). Located just 250 meters (0.2 mile) from the central plaza, it's a convenient and inexpensive place to enjoy the water.

Other good swimming spots on Laguna Bacalar include **Rancho Encantado** (2 kilometers/1.2 miles north of town, tel. 998/884-2071, www.encantado.com) and **Hotel Laguna Bacalar** (Blvd. Costero 479, tel. 983/834-2205, www.hotellagunabacalar.com); plan on ordering something from the hotel restaurant to be able to use the waterfront.

FOOD

For good cheap eats, **Cocina Orizaba** (Av. 7 btwn Calles 24 and 26, tel. 983/834-2069, 8am-6pm daily, US$4.50-12) serves a variety of classic Mexican dishes. The daily *comida corrida* (lunch special) includes an entrée, main dish, and drink.

On the main plaza, the Italian-owned and operated **Restaurante y Pizzeria Bertilla** (Av. 5 at Calle 20, cell tel. 983/123-4567, 4pm-11pm Tues.-Sun., US$6-15) specializes in authentic homemade pasta and pizza. Service can be a bit grumpy, but think of it as part of the experience. Some traditional Mexican dishes are available, too.

El Carboncito (central plaza, Av. 5 near Calle 20, tel. 983/117-7167, 5pm-11pm daily, US$2.50-8) is a popular *puesto* (food stand) that serves up grilled favorites like hot dogs, hamburgers, and tacos. If you want your meal to go, let the cook know it's *"para llevar."*

Dunosusa (Calle 22 btwn Avs. 3 and 5, 7:30am-9pm Mon.-Sat., 8:30am-8pm Sun.) is a well-stocked supermarket on the central plaza.

ACCOMMODATIONS
In Town

One of the area's most charming and convenient accommodations, ★ **Casita Carolina** (Av. Costera btwn Calles 16 and 18, tel. 983/834-2334, www.casitacarolina.com, US$37.50-54 s/d, some with shared kitchen) offers lagoon-front units that open onto a large grassy garden. Units are either standalone or occupy a converted home, but all have a private bathroom, a fan, and a homey feel. The friendly American owner lives on-site and is a wealth of information on area sights.

Hotelito el Paraíso (Av. Costera at Calle 14, tel. 983/834-2787, www.hotelitoelparaiso.com.mx, US$61/73 d/t with a/c) has 14 stark hotel rooms, with minifridges, cable TV, and Wi-Fi. All open onto a large grassy area that runs to the lakeshore; there's a *palapa* shade, plenty of chairs, and even a grill.

Outside of Town

Villas Ecotucán (Hwy. 307 Km. 27.3, cell tel. 983/120-5743, www.villasecotucan.info, US$73 s/d) has ten solar-powered, *palapa*-roofed *cabañas*, each spacious and artfully decorated, with a veranda to enjoy the view of the lake and surrounding tropical forest. The verdant grounds included a bird-watching tower, shady hammocks throughout, a dock, and complimentary kayaks. The hotel specializes in guided nature excursions, by bike, kayak, outrigger boat, and on foot.

Built on a bluff just south of town, **Hotel Laguna Bacalar** (Blvd. Costero 479, tel. 983/834-2205, www.hotellagunabacalar.com, US$80-92 d/t with fan, US$100-119 d/t with a/c) has spacious rooms with tolerable nautical-themed decor; pay a bit more for a room with a balcony and dramatic views of the lagoon. Stairs zigzag down to the water, where a pier, a ladder, and a diving board make swimming in the lagoon easy. There's a moderately sized pool and simple restaurant; breakfast can be included for an extra US$5.50 per person.

Rancho Encantado Eco-Resort & Spa (Hwy. 307 Km. 24, tel. 998/884-2071, www.encantado.com, US$140-250, breakfast included) has spacious *palapa*-roofed casitas and modern suites, both featuring Mexican tile floors, good beds, and views of either the lush garden or the lagoon; all but one have air-conditioning. The prettiest spot here, however, is a pier that leads to a shady dock strung with hammocks—it's perfect for swimming and relaxing. Guests

Find utter peace and tranquility at little-visited Laguna Bacalar.

Bacalar Bus Schedule

Departures from the **bus terminal** (Hwy. 307 near Calle 30, no phone) are almost all *de paso* (mid-route service), which means there's often a limited availability of seats. Destinations include:

Destination	Price	Duration	Schedule
Cancún	US$17.75-26.75	5-6 hours	every 30-60 minutes 12:45am-11:50pm
Carrillo Puerto	US$5.25-9.25	1.5-2 hours	take Cancún bus
Chetumal	US$2.50-2.75	50 minutes	every 30-60 minutes 12:30am-11:30pm
Mahahual	US$5.75	1.5-2 hours	6:30am and 5pm
Playa del Carmen	US$14.25-21.75	4-4.5 hours	take Cancún bus
Tulum	US$11.50-15	3 hours	take Cancún bus

can receive massages and body treatments in a small kiosk built over the lake; a hot tub is nearby. The only downer here is the persistent hum of traffic from nearby Highway 307.

Set on the dramatic waters of Laguna Bacalar, ★ **Centro Holístico Akal Ki** (Hwy 307, Km. 12.5, tel. 983/106-1751, www.akalki.com, US$207-330 s/d) is a whole body experience—from the yoga classes and holistic body treatments to the organic foods and breathtaking views. Eleven *cabañas* and suites are simple and elegant, with white-washed walls, tropical wood floors, thick mattresses, and luxurious linens (and no outlets in any of them, to help guests fully disconnect). Best of all, most units are built over the water—fall asleep to the gentle lapping of the lagoon (or jump in, from your private sundeck, first thing in the morning). Complimentary use of kayaks and bicycles is included. Service is gracious and accommodating.

INFORMATION AND SERVICES
Tourist Information

Bacalar's municipal **tourist office** (Calle 22 between Avs. 3 and 5, 8am-5pm Mon.-Fri., 9am-noon Sat., tel. 983/834-2886) is located on the central square. Also, **www.bacalarmosaico.com** is a bilingual website with useful information on the area's sights, activities, and businesses.

Emergency Services

The **Centro de Salud** (Av. 3 btwn Calles 22 and 24, tel. 983/834-2756, 24 hours) offers basic medical care; for serious matters, head to Chetumal. For meds, try **Farmacia San Joaquín** (Av. 7 btwn Calles 20 and 22, no phone, 8am-3pm and 6pm-9pm daily). The **police station** (Calle 20 near Av. 3, toll-free Mex. tel. 066, 24 hours) is located across from the Fuerte San Felipe Bacalar.

Money

There is no bank in town, but there is a **Banorte ATM** on the west side of the central plaza. If you need other money services or the ATM has run out of cash, the closest bank is in Chetumal.

Media and Communications

The **post office** (Av. 3 near Calle 24, 8am-4:30pm Mon.-Fri., 8am-noon Sat.) is just east of the Fuerte San Felipe Bacalar. For email try the **no name Internet** (Av. 5 near Calle 24, 9am-10pm daily, US$1/hour), operated out of a private home.

Laundry

Lavandería Lolita (Av. 7 btwn Calles 24 and 26, tel. 983/834-2069, 9am-8pm daily) offers same-day service for US$1.25 per kilo (2.2 pounds). Pickup and delivery are available.

GETTING THERE AND AROUND

You can easily walk to all the sites of interest in Bacalar, with the exception of Cenote Azul. A taxi there from town costs around US$3; cabs typically wait for passengers around the central plaza and on Avenida 7 in front of Iglesia San Joaquín.

Bus

Bacalar's modest **bus terminal** (Hwy. 307 near Calle 30) is on the highway, about a 20-minute walk from the central plaza. The buses are almost exclusively *de paso* (mid-route) service, which means there's often limited availability (i.e., as soon as you know your schedule, buy your ticket).

Combi

Combis and *taxi colectivos* (US$2-3, every 30 minutes) run between Bacalar and Chetumal daily. You can catch either in front of Iglesia San Joaquín (Calle 22 near Av. 7), one block up from the central plaza.

Chetumal

Chetumal is the capital of Quintana Roo and the gateway to Central America. It's not the prettiest of towns, and most travelers just pass through on their way to or from Belize or southern Campeche. However, Chetumal's modern Maya museum is one of the best you'll find in the region (albeit with few original pieces) and is well worth a visit. And if you're dying to see the Guatemalan ruins of Tikal, a shuttle from Chetumal can get you there in eight hours (cutting through Belize) and back again just as fast; a 90-minute boat ride also will take you to San Pedro, Belize, for a quick overnighter. The area around Chetumal is worth exploring, too, whether the bayside town of Calderitas or the intriguing and little-visited Maya ruins of Kohunlich, Dzibanché, Kinichná, and Oxtankah. North of town is Laguna Bacalar, a beautiful multicolored lake with great swimming and kayaking.

SIGHTS

Museo de la Cultura Maya

One of the best museums in the region, the **Maya Culture Museum** (Av. de los Héroes at Calle Cristóbal Colón, tel. 983/832-6838, 9am-7pm Tues.-Thurs., 9am-8pm Fri.-Sun., US$5 adult, US$2 child) extends over three levels—the upper represents the world of gods, the middle the world of humans, and the lower Xibalba, the underworld. Each floor has impressive, well-designed exhibits describing Maya spiritual beliefs, agricultural practices, astronomy, and more, all in English and Spanish. In fact, the only thing lacking is original artifacts. (The replicas, however, are quite good.) The exhibition area past the ticket booth usually has good temporary art shows, plus a cinema that hosts free screenings of independent films.

Monumento al Mestizo

Across from the Museo de la Cultura Maya is the **Monumento al Mestizo** (Av. de los Héroes s/n), a striking sculpture symbolizing the creation of a new race—the mestizo—through the union of the shipwrecked Spanish sailor Gonzalo Guerrero and Zazil Há, a Maya woman. Hernán Cortés offered to take Guerrero back to Spain, but Guerrero chose to stay in the Americas, wedding Zazil Há in a Maya marriage ritual. Note that the Maya symbol for the number zero as well as the cycle of life, the snail shell, provides the framework for the entire work of art.

Museo de la Ciudad

The **city museum** (Calle Héroes de Chapultepec btwn Avs. Juárez and de los Héroes, tel. 983/832-1350, 9am-7pm Tues.-Sun., US$1) is small and well organized, and describes the political, economic, and cultural history of Chetumal, spanning the period from its founding in 1898 to the present day. Signage is in Spanish only.

El Malecón

Running six kilometers (3.7 miles) on the Boulevard Bahía, this breezy promenade makes for a fine bayfront stroll. Along it you'll find cafés, monuments, a lighthouse, government buildings, and, hopefully, a cooling breeze. Of particular note are two impressive **murals** found within the **Palacio Legislativo** (end of Av. Reforma, 9am-10pm Mon.-Fri.), a shell-shaped building that houses the State Congress. Created by local artist Elio Carmichael, one mural outlines the state's history—from the creation of man to the devastating effects of Hurricane Janet in 1955—while the other depicts the law of the cosmos. Both are located in the reception area and are open to the public.

Maqueta Payo Obispo

The **Maqueta Payo Obispo** (Calle 22 de Enero near Av. Reforma, 9am-7pm Tues.-Sun., free) is a scale model of Chetumal as it looked in the 1930s, with brightly colored clapboard houses, grassy lots, and plenty of palm trees. It's a reproduction of a model made by long-time resident Luis Reinhardt McLiberty. Look for it in a glass-enclosed building across the street from the Palacio Legislativo, though glare on sunny days can make it hard to see the exhibit. A small history museum of the city also is on-site; signage is in Spanish only.

Trolley Tours

For a breezy overview of Chetumal's attractions, consider taking **Bule Buzz** (cell tel. 983/120-5223, US$7.75 adult, US$4 child), a guided trolley tour of the city. Sites visited include the murals in the Palacio Legislativo, the sculptures along Boulevard Bahía, the Maqueta Payo Obispo, and the Museo de la Cultura Maya. The trolley leaves from the Monumento al Mestizo at noon and 3pm Tuesday-Saturday and 11am Sunday; admission to the Museo de la Cultura Maya also is included.

The Museo de la Cultura Maya in Chetumal has fascinating displays on Maya sculpture, writing, mathematics, astronomy, and more.

Chetumal

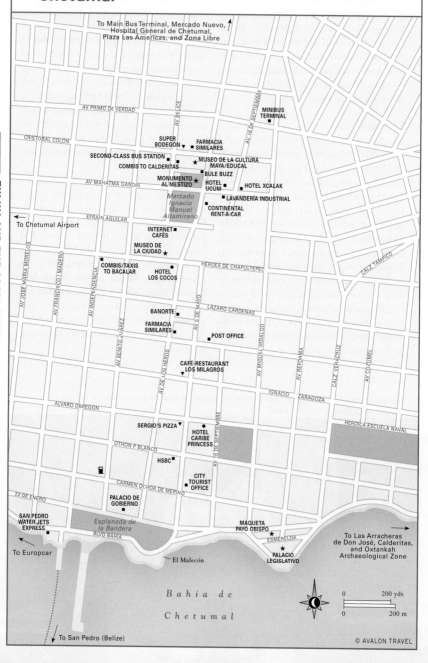

To Main Bus Terminal, Mercado Nuevo,
Hospital General de Chetumal,
Plaza Las Américas, and Zona Libre

AV PRIMO DE VERDAD

CRISTOBAL COLON

AV BELICE

AV 16 DE SEPTIEMBRE

MINIBUS
TERMINAL

SUPER
BODEGON

FARMACIA
SIMILARES

SECOND-CLASS BUS STATION

COMBIS TO CALDERITAS

MUSEO DE LA CULTURA
MAYA/EDUCAL

BULE BUZZ

MONUMENTO
AL MESTIZO

HOTEL
UCUM

HOTEL XCALAK

AV MAHATMA GANDHI

Mercado
Ignacio
Manuel
Altamirano

LAVANDERÍA INDUSTRIAL

EFRAIN AGUILAR

CONTINENTAL
RENT-A-CAR

To Chetumal Airport

INTERNET
CAFÉS

MUSEO DE
LA CIUDAD

AV JOSE MARIA MORELOS

AV FRANCISCO I MADERO

AV INDEPENDENCIA

COMBIS/TAXIS
TO BACALAR

HOTEL
LOS COCOS

HEROES DE CHAPULTEPEC

CALZ TAMPICO

BANORTE

FARMACIA
SIMILARES

AV 5 DE MAYO

LÁZARO CARDENAS

AV BENITO JUAREZ

POST OFFICE

AV DE LOS HEROS

CAFÉ-RESTAURANT
LOS MILAGROS

AV MIGUEL HIDALGO

AV REFORMA

CALZ VERACRUZ

AV COZUMEL

IGNACIO ZARAGOZA

ALVARO OBREGON

HEROICA ESCUELA NAVAL

SERGIO'S PIZZA

OTHON P BLANCO

HOTEL
CARIBE
PRINCESS

HSBC

AV 16 DE SEPTIEMBRE

CITY
TOURIST
OFFICE

CARMEN OCHOA DE MERINO

22 DE ENERO

PALACIO DE
GOBIERNO

SAN PEDRO
WATER JETS
EXPRESS

Esplanada de
la Bandera

BLVD BAHIA

MAQUETA
PAYO OBISPO

To Las Arracheras
de Don José, Calderitas,
and Oxtankah
Archaeological Zone

ESMERELDA

To Europcar

El Malecón

PALACIO
LEGISLATIVO

To San Pedro (Belize)

Bahía de
Chetumal

0   200 yds
0   200 m

© AVALON TRAVEL

ENTERTAINMENT AND SHOPPING

Sunday on El Malecón

Every Sunday at 6pm, locals gather at the **Esplanada de la Bandera** (southern end of Av. de los Héroes) to enjoy city-sponsored events, typically performances by the municipal band or local musicians and singers. The events are free and family friendly, with vendors selling drinks and munchies.

Cinema

If you're hankering to watch the latest Hollywood film, head to **Cinépolis** (Plaza Las Américas, Av. Insurgentes s/n, tel. 983/837-6044, www.cinepolis.com, US$5-8), an 11-screen theater where most films are in English with Spanish subtitles.

Shopping

Educal (Av. de los Héroes at Calle Cristóbal Colón, cell tel. 983/129-2832, www.educal.com.mx, 9am-7pm Tues.-Sat., 9am-2pm Sun.) is a good bookstore located inside the Museo de la Cultura Maya.

Mercado Ignacio Manuel Altamirano (Efraín Aguilar btwn Avs. Belice and de los Héroes, 8am-4pm daily) is a two-story building mostly selling everyday items, from clothing to kitchenware. For travelers, it's a good place to buy a pair of flip-flops, a travel clock, or kitschy souvenirs.

Plaza Las Américas (Av. Insurgentes s/n, 9am-10pm daily) is a classic shopping mall with clothing and shoe boutiques, a Chedraui supermarket, a megaplex movie theater, and all the typical amenities, like ATMs, food court, and public bathrooms.

The **Zona Libre** (Corozal Duty Free Zone, 9am-7pm daily) is an area just across the Belize border that's jam-packed with stores selling products from around the world, including shoes, clothing, alcohol, and household items. Bring your passport along, but guard it carefully.

FOOD

A buzzing little place, ★ **Café-Restaurant Los Milagros** (Calle Ignacio Zaragoza near Av. 5 de Mayo, tel. 983/832-4433, 7:30am-9pm Mon.-Sat., 7:30am-1pm Sun., US$3-7) serves up strong coffee drinks and especially good breakfasts. The best seating is outdoors—snag a table where you can, as it can get crowded fast.

Located on the Malecón, ★ **Las Arracheras de Don José** (Blvd. Bahía at Calle Josefa Ortiz de Dominguez, tel. 983/837-6103, 11am-10pm daily, US$4-10) serves some of the best tacos in town. Try the *tacos de arrachera* (broiled skirt steak marinated in lemon and spices), which are only improved when followed with a cold beer.

Sergio's Pizza (Av. 5 de Mayo at Av. Alvaro Obregón, tel. 983/108-1438, 7am-11:30pm daily, US$5-17) serves much more than pizza in its dimly lit dining room. The extensive menu covers the gamut of Italian and Mexican dishes—from meat lasagna to *molletes rancheros*. Meals are hearty, making it popular with families.

Super Bodegón (Calle Cristóbal Colón btwn Avs. Belice and de los Héroes, 5am-9pm Mon.-Sat., 5am-3pm Sun.) has an impressive selection of fresh fruits and veggies. Canned goods, dry foods, and basic toiletries are also sold.

ACCOMMODATIONS

Chetumal's status as the state capital and its location on the Belize border make it a busy town, and reservations are recommended.

Under US$50

★ **Hotel Xcalak** (Av. 16 de Septiembre at Av. Mahatma Gandhi, cell tel. 983/129-1708, www.hotelxcalak.com.mx, US$33 s/d with a/c) is one of the best deals in town: modern rooms with tasteful decor, strong but quiet air-conditioning, SKY TV, and wireless Internet. The hotel restaurant also provides room service (though you've got to order in person). The hotel is located one block from the Museo de la Cultura Maya.

Next door, the moss-colored **Hotel Ucúm** (Av. Mahatma Gandhi btwn Avs. 5 de Mayo and 16 de Septiembre, tel. 983/832-0711, US$19 s/d with fan, US$23 s/d with fan and cable TV, US$32 s/d with a/c and cable TV) has aging but clean rooms. Beds are hit or miss, unfortunately, and some rooms can be downright stuffy (ask for one on the top floor for the best breeze). There's a decent pool on-site with a separate wading area for kids. There's also a secure parking lot.

Over US$50

Hotel Caribe Princess (Av. Alvaro Obregón btwn Avs. 5 de Mayo and 16 de Septiembre, tel. 983/832-0900, toll-free Mex. tel. 866/337-7342, US$39 s with a/c, US$54 d with a/c) has comfortable nondescript rooms with decent beds, cable TV, and powerful air-conditioning. There's Wi-Fi in the lobby and a self-serve breakfast (i.e., toast, cereal, fruits) every day. Ask for a room facing the interior of the building; the karaoke bar in front blasts music—and keeps the windows rattling—until late.

Hotel Los Cocos (Av. de los Héroes at Calle Héroes de Chapultepec, tel. 983/835-0430, toll-free Mex. tel. 800/719-5840, www.hotelloscocos.com.mx, US$50-65 s/d with a/c) has three categories of rooms, all pleasant with updated furnishings and modern amenities. The more expensive ones have flat-screen TVs, quiet air-conditioning, and more stylish decor. They all open onto a lush garden, which has a small, inviting pool area. The on-site restaurant is great for breakfast.

Outside of Chetumal

On the road to the like-named ruins, ★ **Explorean Kohunlich** (toll-free Mex. tel. 800/504-5000, www.theexplorean.com, US$225-352 s/d bungalow) is a luxurious resort with 40 deluxe bungalows set on 30 hectares (74 acres) of tropical forest. Each has gleaming stone floors, high *palapa* ceilings, elegant furnishings, and privacy walls for sunbathing. Two suites also have plunge pools. The main building houses a fine restaurant, a full-service spa, and a lap pool that overlooks the jungle (you can see the ruins at Kohunlich from here). Excursions like rappelling in the jungle, kayaking through a crocodile reserve, or mountain biking through forgotten forests and ruins are included.

INFORMATION AND SERVICES

Tourist Information

Near the waterfront, the **city tourist office** (Av. 5 de Mayo at Carmen Ochoa de Merino, tel. 983/835-0860, 8:30am-4:30pm Mon.-Fri.) has a decent selection of brochures and maps. There also is a **tourist information booth** in the main bus terminal (Av. Insurgentes at Av. de los Héroes, 9am-8pm daily).

Emergency Services

About two kilometers (1.2 miles) from the center of town, **Hospital General de Chetumal** (Avs. Andrés Quintana Roo at Juan José Isiordia, tel. 983/832-8194, 24 hours) is the city's main hospital.

For meds, try **Farmacia Similares** (Av. de los Héroes near Calle Plutarco Elias, tel. 983/833-2232, 8am-9pm daily) or its **sister store** (Calle Cristóbal Colón btwn Avs. Belice and de los Héroes, tel. 983/833-2331), which is open 24 hours.

The **police** can be reached by dialing toll-free 066.

Money

HSBC (Av. Othon Blanco btwn Av. 5 de Mayo and Av. de los Héroes, 9am-5pm Mon.-Fri.) and **Banorte** (Av. de los Héroes btwn Lázaro Cárdenas and Plutarco Elias, 9am-4pm Mon.-Fri.) are both conveniently located downtown. There also is an ATM at the **main bus station** (Av. Insurgentes at Av. de los Héroes, 9am-8pm daily).

Media and Communications

The **post office** (Av. Plutarco Elias Calles btwn Avs. 5 de Mayo and 16 de Septiembre, 8am-4pm Mon.-Fri., 9am-1pm Sat.) is just a block from the main drag. For Internet access, there is a string of **Internet cafés** across from

Chetumal Bus Schedule

Departures from Chetumal's **main bus terminal** (Av. Insurgentes at Av. de los Héroes, tel. 983/832-5110) are for first-class service, though some second-class buses stop here as well; tickets for either service can be purchased downtown, in the **second-class bus terminal** (Av. Belice at Av. Cristóbal Colón). Destinations from the main bus terminal include:

Destination	Price	Duration	Schedule
Bacalar	US$2.50-2.75	50 minutes	every 30-60 minutes 1:15am-11:45pm
Cancún	US$18.25-30	5.5-6.5 hours	every 30-90 minutes 12:15am-11:45pm
Mahahual	US$6.25	2.5 hours	5:40am and 4:10pm or take Xcalak bus (Mercado Nuevo terminal only)
Mérida	US$34.25	5.5-6 hours	7:30am, 1:30pm, 5pm, and 11:30pm
Playa del Carmen	US$13-29.50	4.5-5.5 hours	take any Cancún bus
Tulum	US$13.50-20.50	3.5-4 hours	take any Cancún bus

Buses for **Belize City** (US$11.50, 3 hours), **Corozal** (US$3, 1 hour), and **Orangewalk** (US$4, 2 hours) leave the **Mercado Nuevo** (Av. de los Héroes at Circuito Segundo, no phone) 18 times daily 4:30am-6:30pm. Some pass the main ADO terminal en route. Buses bound for **Xcalak** (US$7.75, 4-5 hours) also leave from here at 5:40am and 4:10pm.

Buses to the **Zona Libre** (US$2, 30 minutes) leave the **Minibus terminal** (Av. Primo de Verdad at Av. Miguel Hidalgo, no phone) every 15 minutes 6:30am-8pm.

the Mercado Ignacio Manuel Altamirano (Efraín Aguilar btwn Avs. Belice and de los Héroes); most charge US$1 per hour and are open 7am-midnight daily.

Immigration
The **immigration office** (Av. México s/n, tel. 983/834-5046, 9am-1pm Mon.-Fri.) is located half a block from the border with Belize. Heading south on Avenida México, it's on your left-hand side.

Laundry and Storage
Though catering primarily to hotels and restaurants, **Lavandería Industrial** (Av. Mahatma Ghandi near Av. 16 de Septiembre, tel. 983/129-2458, 8am-8pm daily) also takes small loads at US$1.35 per kilo (2.2 pounds). There is no signage, so listen for the huge dryers and look for huge piles of tablecloths.

Conveniently located in the main bus station, **Lockers, Revistas y Novedades Laudy** (Av. Insurgentes at Av. de los Héroes, 8am-8pm daily) stores bags for US$0.65 per hour.

GETTING THERE AND AROUND
Chetumal is a relatively large city, but the parts most travelers are interested in are all within easy walking distance—mostly along Avenida de los Héroes and El Malecón. The exception is the main bus terminal and Mercado Nuevo, both of which are 10-12 grubby blocks from the center. A cab to either terminal, or anywhere around downtown, costs US$2-3.

Air
The **Chetumal International Airport** (CTM, tel. 983/832-6625) receives only a few

flights each day. Airlines serving it include **Interjet** (toll-free Mex. tel. 800/011-2345, toll-free U.S. tel. 866/285-9525, www.interjet.com.mx) and the air taxi service **Avioquintana** (tel. 998/734-1975, www.avioquintana.com).

Bus

All first-class buses leave from the **main bus terminal** (Av. Insurgentes at Av. de los Héroes, tel. 983/832-5110), though most second-class buses also stop here on the way in or out of town.

The **second-class bus station** (Avs. Belice and Cristóbal Colón, tel. 983/832-0639) is located just west of the Museo de la Cultura Maya; tickets for first-class buses also can be purchased here if you want to buy your tickets in advance but don't want to make the trek to the main terminal.

Two other terminals—the **Minibus terminal** (Av. Primo de Verdad at Av. Miguel Hidalgo, no phone) and **Mercado Nuevo** (Av. de los Héroes and Circuito Segundo, no phone)—have service to Bacalar, Xcalak, the Zona Libre, and to destinations in Belize.

Combi

Combis and *taxi colectivos* (US$2-3, every 30 minutes) run between Chetumal and Bacalar daily. You can catch either on Avenida Independencia at Calle Héroes de Chapultepec.

Car

The highways in this area are now all paved and well maintained. Car rental agencies in town include **Continental Rent-a-Car** (Av. de los Héroes near Av. Mahatma Gandhi, tel. 983/832-2411, www.continentalcar.com.mx, 8am-8pm daily) and **Europcar** (Chetumal Noor Hotel, Blvd. Bahía at Ave. José Maria, tel. 983/833-9959, www.europcar.com, 8am-8pm daily).

Taxi

Taxis can be flagged down easily in downtown Chetumal. Few are metered, so be sure to agree on a price before you set off toward your destination.

Water Taxi

San Pedro Water Jets Express (Blvd. Bahía near Av. Independencia, tel. 983/833-3201, www.sanpedrowatertaxi.com) offers service to two destinations in Belize: San Pedro (US$60) and Caye Caulker (US$65). The boat leaves Chetumal at 3pm; it returns at 7am from Caye Caulker and 8am from San Pedro. Service varies monthly—be sure to check the website for the most updated information.

Around Chetumal

The area around Chetumal has a number of worthwhile attractions, all the better because so few travelers linger here.

CALDERITAS

Located just seven kilometers (4 miles) north of Chetumal, Calderitas is a bayside town known for its **seafood restaurants** (8am-6pm daily, US$4-10)—most along the waterfront across from the main plaza—and its **public beaches.** During the week it's a mellow scene, but on weekends locals descend upon the town for a day of R&R and some revelry, too.

Boat rides can be arranged at many of the bayside establishments to explore **Chetumal Bay** (US$150, up to 8 people) in search of manatees, which were once abundant in these waters, or to visit **Isla Tamalcab** (US$40, up to 8 people), an uninhabited island with white-sand beaches and good snorkeling, and home to spider monkeys and *tepescuintles* (pacas in English).

If you want to stay overnight, the best place in town is **Yax Há Resort & Explorer** (Av.

Oxtankah Archaeological Zone

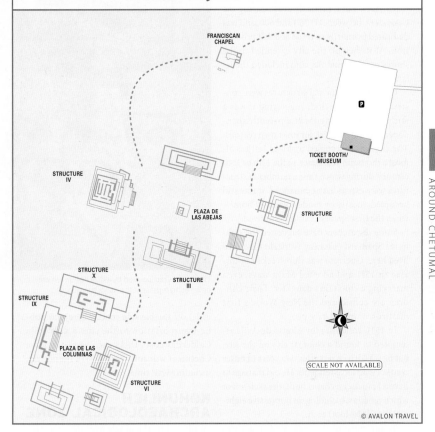

FRANCISCAN
CHAPEL

P

TICKET BOOTH/
MUSEUM

STRUCTURE
IV

PLAZA DE
LAS ABEJAS

STRUCTURE
I

STRUCTURE
X

STRUCTURE
III

STRUCTURE
IX

PLAZA DE LAS
COLUMNAS

STRUCTURE
VI

SCALE NOT AVAILABLE

© AVALON TRAVEL

Yucatán 415, tel. 983/834-4127, www.yaxhare-sort.com, US$8 pp camping, US$19-27 per RV, US$38.50 s/d with a/c, US$54-69 s/d with a/c and kitchenette). Located on the waterfront, it offers everything from camp- and RV sites to bungalows. The bungalows themselves range from one-room units with air-conditioning, satellite TV, and minifridges to two-bedroom units with fully equipped kitchens; all have porches with chairs that overlook the bay. There also is a pool and a restaurant on-site.

Getting There

Calderitas is a quick bus ride from down-town Chetumal. *Combis* leave from Avenida Cristóbal Colón, behind the Museo de la Cultura Maya, roughly every half hour 6am-9pm daily (US$0.65, 15 minutes). If you've got a **car,** head east out of Chetumal on Boulevard Bahía, which becomes the main drag in Calderitas. Alternatively (though less scenic), take Avenida Insurgentes east until you get to the turnoff, and follow the signs from there.

OXTANKAH ARCHAEOLOGICAL ZONE

Oxtankah (8am-5pm daily, US$4) is a small archaeological site whose name means Between Branches, so called by early archae-ologists after the many trees growing amid, and on top of, the structures. Relatively little is known about Oxtankah—including its true name—but it probably arose during the Classic era, between AD 300 and 600, and was dedicated primarily to trade and salt production. At its height, the city extended to the shores of Chetumal Bay and included the island of Tamalcab.

Oxtankah's principal structures were constructed in this period, suggesting it was a fairly robust city, but it was apparently abandoned around AD 600, for unknown reasons. The city was reoccupied by Maya settlers almost a thousand years later, in the 14th or 15th century, during which time a number of structures were expanded or enhanced. It was still occupied, mostly by modest earthen homes, when the first Spanish explorers arrived.

Some researchers have suggested the infamous Spaniard castaway Gonzalo Guerrero lived here; Guerrero was shipwrecked in this area in 1511 and adopted Maya ways, even marrying a chieftain's daughter. Their children are considered the New World's first mestizos, or mixed-race people.

In 1531, conquistador Alonso de Avila attempted to found a colonial city on the site, but he was driven out after two years of bitter conflict with local residents. He did manage to have a Franciscan chapel built, the skeleton of which remains, including an impressive eight-meter-tall (26-foot) arch.

Today, most of the excavated structures in Oxtankah surround two plazas: **Abejas** (Bees) plaza, the city's main ceremonial and elite residential center, and the somewhat smaller **Columnas** (Columns) plaza, whose large palace probably served an administrative function. Architecturally, the structures are more closely related to those of the Petén region (present-day Guatemala) than to Yucatecan ones, suggesting a close relationship with that area. There's a small **museum** on-site; signage is in Spanish only.

Getting There

Oxtankah is located seven kilometers (4 miles) north of Calderitas, about one kilometer (0.6

The famous red-painted masks at Kohunlich are believed to represent the Maya sun god.

mile) off the bayside road. There's no public transportation to the site; a **cab** from Calderitas costs US$3 each way; one from Chetumal will run about US$18 round-trip, including wait time.

KOHUNLICH ARCHAEOLOGICAL ZONE

Swallowed by the jungle over the centuries, **Kohunlich** (8am-5pm daily, US$4.50) was first discovered in 1912 by American explorer Raymond Merwin, but it was not until the 1960s that excavation of the site began in earnest. Today, the ruins are in harmony with the surrounding vegetation; wandering through it, you'll be rewarded with more than 200 structures, stelae, and uncovered mounds that have trees growing out of them and moss spreading over their stones—a beautiful sight. Most date to the Late Preclassic (AD 100-200) through the Classic (AD 600-900) periods.

Kohunlich's most famous and compelling structure is the **Temple of the Masks.** Constructed in AD 500, it features six

Kohunlich Archaeological Zone

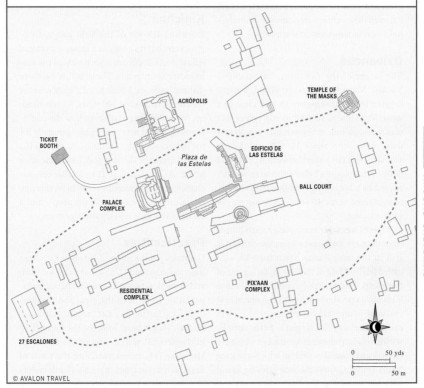

- ACRÓPOLIS
- TEMPLE OF THE MASKS
- TICKET BOOTH
- EDIFICIO DE LAS ESTELAS
- Plaza de las Estelas
- BALL COURT
- PALACE COMPLEX
- RESIDENTIAL COMPLEX
- PIX'AAN COMPLEX
- 27 ESCALONES

© AVALON TRAVEL

0   50 yds
0   50 m

two-meter-tall (6.6-foot) stucco masks, believed to be representations of the Maya sun god, with star-incised eyes, mustaches, and nose plugs. Intriguingly, each is slightly different, leading some to speculate that they also represent successive members of the ruling dynasty; it would not have been unusual for the city's elite to draw an overt connection between themselves and a high god.

Southwest of the Temple of the Masks is **27 Escalones,** the largest and most impressive residential area in Kohunlich. Built on a cliff with a spectacular bird's-eye view of the jungle, it is one of the largest palaces in the Maya world, reached by climbing its namesake 27 steps. As you walk through the site, keep an eye out for *aguadas* (cisterns) that once were part of a complex system of Kohunlich's reservoirs.

Getting There

Kohunlich is located about 60 kilometers (37 miles) west of Chetumal. By **car,** take Highway 186 west and turn south (left) at the sign to Kohunlich. An 8.5-kilometer (5.3-mile) paved road leads straight to the site. There is no public transportation to the site.

DZIBANCHÉ AND KINICHNÁ ARCHAEOLOGICAL ZONES

If the crowds at Chichén Itzá and Tulum get you down, these picturesque twin ruins may be the antidote you need. Dzibanché and its smaller neighbor, Kinichná, see very few visitors—it's not uncommon to have them to yourself, in fact—and feature modest-size temples in varying states of restoration. (A great many structures aren't excavated at all, but even they—abrupt tree-covered mounds—hold a certain mystery and appeal.)

Dzibanché

The larger of the two sites, Dzibanché is Yucatec Maya for Etched in Wood, a name created by archaeologists in reference to a wood lintel inscribed with hieroglyphics that was found in one of the primary temples. A date on the lintel reads AD 618, and the site seems to have flourished between AD 300 and 800. Archaeologists believe this area was occupied by a sprawling, widely dispersed city that covered some 40 square kilometers (25 square miles).

The site has three main plazas, each higher than the next. Dzibanché's namesake lintel is still in the temple atop **Structure VI,** also called the Building of the Lintels, facing one of the plazas. Unfortunately, climbing Structure VI is no longer allowed, but it's just one of several large pyramids here, the rest of which you can clamber up. The largest is **Structure II,** with an ornate temple at its summit where archaeologists found a tomb of a high-ranking leader (judging from the rich offering found with his remains). The steep stairways and lofty upper temples here are reminiscent of Tikal and other temples in the Petén area of present-day Guatemala, suggesting a strong connection between the two regions.

Kinichná

Kinichná (House of the Sun) has just one structure, but it's a biggie: a massive pyramid whose summit affords a great view of the surrounding countryside. The structure has three distinct levels, each built in a different era over the course of around 400 years. As you climb up, it's fascinating to observe how the craftsmanship and artistry changed—generally for the better—over the centuries. At the top is a stucco image of the sun god, hence the site's name. As in Structure II in Dzibanché, archaeologists uncovered a tomb here, this one containing the remains of two people and a cache of fine jade jewelry and figurines.

Practicalities

Dzibanché and Kinichná are open 8am-5pm daily; admission is US$4 and valid for both archaeological zones. There is no public transportation to or from the area, and precious little local traffic, so a **car** (or tour van) is essential. To get here, look for the turnoff 50 kilometers (31 miles) west of Chetumal on Highway 186, before reaching the town of Francisco Villa; from there it's 15 kilometers (9 miles) north down a bumpy dirt road. You'll reach Kinichná first, then Dzibanché about 2 kilometers (1.2 miles) later.

Chichén Itzá

Look for ★ to find recommended
sights, activities, dining, and lodging.

Highlights

★ **Chichén Itzá Archaeological Zone:**
Voted one of the New Seven Wonders of the
World, the Yucatán's most famous ruin is all
about hyperbole: the iconic star-aligned pyramid, the gigantic Maya ball court, even the crush
of bikini-clad day-trippers from Cancún. Be sure
to arrive early to enjoy this singular ancient city
(page 270).

★ **Iglesia y Ex-Convento San
Bernardino de Siena:** Located in a quiet
corner of Valladolid, this elegant church has
a spacious esplanade and beautiful interior, a
small museum, plus a natural cenote inside the
convent walls (page 285).

★ **Ek' Balam Archaeological Zone:** A
stunning stucco frieze with angel-like figures and
a huge "monster mouth" is the highlight of this
small, serene site near Valladolid. A nearby cenote makes for a cool après-ruins swim (page 295).

★ **Flamingo Tours:** The world's largest
and pinkest flamingos congregate by the thousands—even tens of thousands—in the man-
grove-fringed estuaries near Río Lagartos. Boat
tours bring you up close to these most peculiar
of birds, plus dozens of other species along the
way (page 300).

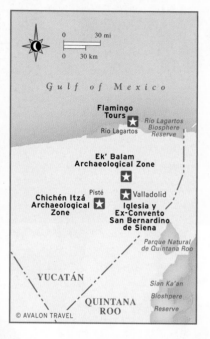

For many travelers, Chichén Itzá is the Eiffel Tower of the Yucatán Peninsula—you can't possibly go home without visiting it.

And for good reason: Chichén Itzá was selected as one of the New Seven Wonders of the World and boasts some of Mexico's most recognizable ancient structures, including its four-sided main pyramid and the Maya world's largest ball court. But that's just the beginning, believe it or not, of things to do in this area. The nearby ruins of Ek' Balam are less crowded than Chichén Itzá and feature an exquisitely preserved stucco frieze. To the north, the coastal town of Río Lagartos is famous for its flamingo reserve and bird-watching tours. Lastly, Valladolid is a lovely but oft-overlooked colonial town, with beautiful and historic churches, nearby cenotes (even one in town), and plenty of options for lodging and eating—definitely consider basing yourself there. Throughout the area, look for cenotes to explore and admire, or even to take a refreshing dip.

PLANNING YOUR TIME

Chichén Itzá can be visited in a full day; a half day will do if you just want the highlights. There are myriad tours to the site, but having your own car allows you to beat the crowds (hint: arrive early) and to make side trips to nearby cenotes and villages. Chichén Itzá also has a worthwhile sound and light show, which you can attend the night before or after you visit the ruins. Ek' Balam is a much smaller site—budget a few hours, including visits to neighboring cenotes. Bird-watching tours at Río Lagartos typically leave in the early morning or late afternoon—consider staying a night there to avoid driving in the dark. Otherwise, Valladolid is a logical base, with interesting sights, good accommodations, and a central location.

Previous: palm grove; Uayma's remarkable main church. **Above:** Valladolid doorway.

Chichén Itzá

Chichén Itzá is one of the finest archaeological sites in Mexico, and in all of Mesoamerica. It is also one of the most visited. Located just two hours from both Cancún and Mérida, the site is often inundated by tour groups. That fact should not dissuade independent travelers from visiting—crowded or not, Chichén Itzá is a truly magnificent ruin and a must-see on any archaeology tour of the Yucatán. That said, you can make the most of your visit by arriving right when the gates open, so you can see the big stuff first and be exploring the outer areas by the time the tour buses start to roll in.

ORIENTATION

Chichén Itzá is located in the middle of the Yucatán Peninsula, about 200 kilometers (124 miles) from Cancún and 120 kilometers (74 miles) from Mérida, making it a doable but longish day trip from either. Just two kilometers (1.2 miles) from the ruins sits Pisté, a one-road town that's strangely underdeveloped considering its proximity to such an important and heavily visited site. The hotels and restaurants here are unremarkable, and there's not much to do or see in town. There are several higher-end options near and on the road to the ruins. Another option is to stay in Valladolid, just 42 kilometers (26 miles) away—an easy jaunt.

★ CHICHÉN ITZÁ ARCHAEOLOGICAL ZONE

Chichén Itzá (8am-5pm daily, US$14, US$13 sound and light show only) is a monumental archaeological site, remarkable for both its size and scope. The ruins include impressive palaces, temples, and altars, as well as the largest-known ball court in the Maya world. One of the most widely recognized (and heavily visited) ruins in the world, it was declared a World Heritage Site by UNESCO in 1988 and one of the New Seven Wonders of the World in 2007. In 2012, Instituto Nacional de Antropología e Historia (INAH) partnered with Google to photograph—by bicycle—the site for Google Street View maps.

History

What we call Chichén Itzá surely had another name when it was founded. The name means Mouth of the Well of the Itzá, but the Itzá, an illiterate and seminomadic group of uncertain origin, didn't arrive here until the 12th century. Before the Itzá, the area was controlled—or at least greatly influenced—by Toltec migrants who arrived from central Mexico around AD 1000. Most of Chichén's most notable structures, including its famous four-sided pyramid, and images like the reclining *chac-mool,* bear a striking resemblance to structures and images found at Tula, the ancient Toltec capital, in the state of Hidalgo. Before the Toltecs, the area was populated by Maya, evidenced by the Puuc- and Chenes-style design of the earliest structures here, such as the Nunnery and Casa Colorada.

The three major influences—Maya, Toltec, and Itzá—are indisputable, but the exact chronology and circumstances of those groups' interaction (or lack thereof) is one of the most hotly contested issues in Maya archaeology. Part of the difficulty in understanding Chichén Itzá more fully is that its occupants created very few stelae and left few Long Count dates on their monuments. In this way Chichén Itzá is different from virtually every other ancient city in the Yucatán. It's ironic, actually, that Chichén Itzá is the most widely recognized "Maya" ruin considering it was so deeply influenced by non-Maya cultures, and its history and architecture are so atypical of the region.

Chichén Itzá's influence ebbed and flowed over its many centuries of existence and occupation. It first peaked in the mid-9th century,

Chichén Itzá

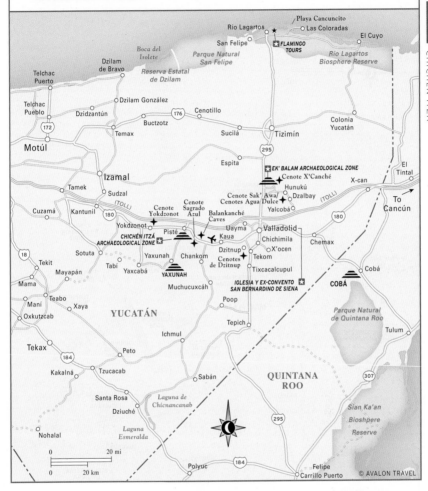

© AVALON TRAVEL

or Late Classic period, when it eclipsed Cobá as the dominant power in the northern Yucatán region. The effects of a widespread collapse of Maya cities to the south (like Calakmul, Tikal, and Palenque) reached Chichén Itzá in the late 900s, and it too collapsed abruptly. The city rose again under Toltec and later Itzá influence, but went into its final decline after an internal dispute led to the rise of Mayapán, which would come to control much of the Yucatán Peninsula.

Chichén Itzá was all but abandoned by the early 1200s, though it remained an important religious pilgrimage site even after the arrival of the Spanish.

El Castillo

The most dramatic structure in Chichén Itzá is El Castillo (The Castle), also known as the Temple of Kukulcán. At 24 meters (79 feet), it's the tallest structure on the site, and certainly the most recognizable. Dating to around AD

Chichén Itzá Archaeological Zone

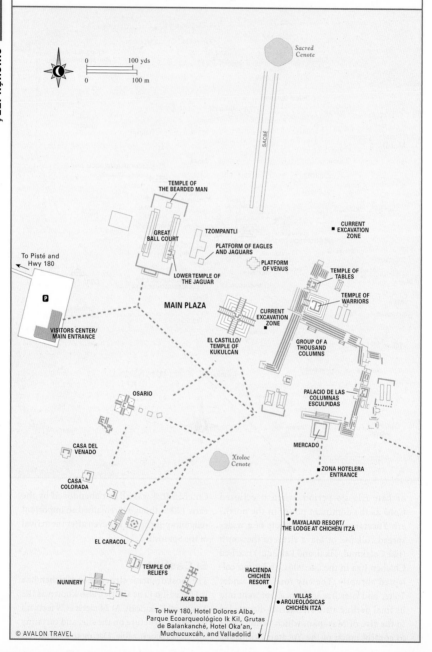

0 100 yds
0 100 m

Sacred Cenote

SACBÉ

TEMPLE OF THE BEARDED MAN

GREAT BALL COURT

TZOMPANTLI

PLATFORM OF EAGLES AND JAGUARS

PLATFORM OF VENUS

CURRENT EXCAVATION ZONE

TEMPLE OF TABLES

TEMPLE OF WARRIORS

To Pisté and Hwy 180

P

VISITORS CENTER/ MAIN ENTRANCE

LOWER TEMPLE OF THE JAGUAR

MAIN PLAZA

CURRENT EXCAVATION ZONE

EL CASTILLO/ TEMPLE OF KUKULCAN

GROUP OF A THOUSAND COLUMNS

OSARIO

PALACIO DE LAS COLUMNAS ESCULPIDAS

CASA DEL VENADO

MERCADO

CASA COLORADA

Xtoloc Cenote

ZONA HOTELERA ENTRANCE

EL CARACOL

MAYALAND RESORT/ THE LODGE AT CHICHÉN ITZÁ

TEMPLE OF RELIEFS

NUNNERY

HACIENDA CHICHEN RESORT

AKAB DZIB

VILLAS ARQUEOLÓGICAS CHICHÉN ITZÁ

To Hwy 180, Hotel Dolores Alba, Parque Ecoarqueológico Ik Kil, Grutas de Balankanché, Hotel Oka'an, Muchucuxcáh, and Valladolid

© AVALON TRAVEL

850, El Castillo was built according to strict astronomical guidelines. There are nine levels, which, divided by the central staircase, make for 18 platforms, the number of months in the Maya calendar. Each of the four sides has 91 steps, which, added together along with the platform on top, total 365—one for each day of the year. And there are 52 inset panels on each face of the structure, equal to the number of years in each cycle of the Calendar Round.

On the spring and autumn equinoxes (March 21 and September 22), the afternoon sun lights up a bright zigzag strip on the outside wall of the north staircase as well as the giant serpent heads at the base, giving the appearance of a serpent slithering down the steps. Chichén Itzá is mobbed during those periods, especially by spiritual-minded folks seeking communion with the ancient Maya. The effect also occurs in the days just before and after the equinox, and there are significantly fewer people blocking the view.

Climbing El Castillo used to be a given for any visit to Chichén Itzá, and the views from its top level are breathtaking. However, an elderly tourist died in 2005 after tumbling from near the top of the pyramid to the ground. The accident, combined with longtime warnings from archaeologists that the structure was being irreparably eroded by the hundreds of thousands of visitors who climbed it yearly, prompted officials to close it off. Pyramids at other sites have been restricted as well, and it's looking more and more like a standard policy at Maya archaeological zones.

Deep inside El Castillo and accessed by way of a steep, narrow staircase are several chambers; inside one is a red-painted, jade-studded bench in the figure of a jaguar, which may have served as a throne of sorts. You used to be able to climb the stairs to see the chambers and throne—a fascinating, albeit humid and highly claustrophobic affair—but access was closed at the same time climbing the pyramid was prohibited.

Great Ball Court

Chichén Itzá's famous Great Ball Court is the largest ball court in Mesoamerica by a wide margin. The playing field is 135 meters (443 feet) by 65 meters (213 feet), with two parallel walls 8 meters high (26 feet) and scoring rings in impossibly high perches in the center. The players would've had to hit a 12-pound rubber ball through the rings using only their elbows, wrists, and hips (they wore heavy padding). The game likely lasted for hours; at the game's end, the captain of one team—or even

Chichén Itzá's main pyramid rises 24 meters (79 feet) high, and is precisely oriented to the sun and stars.

the whole team—was apparently sacrificed, possibly by decapitation. There's disagreement about *which* team got the axe, however. Some say it was the losers—otherwise, the game's best players would constantly be wiped out. Some argue that it was the winners, and that being sacrificed would have been the ultimate honor. Of course, it's likely the game varied from city to city and evolved over the many centuries it was played. Along the walls, reliefs depict the ball game and sacrifices.

On the outside of the ball court, the **Lower Temple of the Jaguar** has incredibly fine relief carvings depicting the Maya creation myth. An upper temple is off-limits to visitors, but is decorated with a variety of carvings and remnants of what were likely colorful murals.

The Platforms

As you make your way from the ball court to the Temple of Warriors, you'll pass the gruesome **Tzompantli** (Wall of Skulls). A low T-shaped platform, it is decorated on all sides with row upon row of carved skulls, most with eyes staring out of the large sockets. Among the skulls are images of warriors holding the heads of decapitated victims, skeletons intertwined with snakes, and eagles eating human hearts (a common image in Toltec design, further evidence of their presence here). It is presumed that ceremonies performed on this platform culminated in a sacrificial death for the victim, the head then left on display, perhaps with others already in place. It's estimated that the platform was built AD 1050-1200. Nearby, the **Platform of Venus** and **Platform of Eagles and Jaguars** are smaller square structures, each with low stairways on all four sides, which were likely used for ritualistic music and dancing.

Sacred Cenote

This natural well is 300 meters (984 feet) north of the main structures, along the remains of a *sacbé* (raised stone road) constructed during the Classic period. Almost 60 meters (197 feet) in diameter and 30 meters (98.4 feet) down to the surface of the water, it was a place for sacrifices, mostly to Chaac, the god of rain, who was believed to live in its depths. The cenote has been dredged and scoured by divers numerous times, beginning as early as 1900, and the remains of scores of victims, mostly children and young adults, have been recovered, as well as innumerable jade and stone artifacts. (Most are now displayed at the Museo Nacional de Antropología in Mexico City.) On the edge of the cenote is a ruined sweat bath, probably used for purification rituals before sacrificial ceremonies. The name Chichén Itzá (Mouth of the Well of the Itzá) is surely derived from this deeply sacred cenote, and it remained an important Maya pilgrimage site well into the Spanish conquest.

Temple of Warriors and Group of a Thousand Columns

The Temple of Warriors is where some of the distinctive reclining *chac-mool* figures are found. However, its name comes from the rectangular monoliths in front, which are carved on all sides with images of warriors. (Some are also prisoners, their hands tied behind their backs.) This temple is also closed to entry, and it can be hard to appreciate the fading images from the rope perimeter. You may be able to get a closer look from the temple's south side, where you can easily make out the figures' expressions and dress (though access is sometimes blocked there as well). The south side is impressive for its facade, too, where a series of well-preserved human and animal figures adorn the lower portion, while above, human faces emerge from serpents' mouths, framed by eagle profiles, with masks of Chaac, the hook-nosed god of rain, on the corners.

The aptly named Group of a Thousand Columns is adjacent to the Temple of Warriors. Its perfectly aligned cylindrical columns likely held up a grand roof structure.

Across the plaza, the **Palacio de las Columnas Esculpidas** (Palace of Sculptured Columns) also has cylindrical columns, but with intricate carvings, suggesting this was the ceremonial center of this portion of the complex. Continuing through the trees, you'll reach the **Mercado** (market). The name is purely speculative, though it's easy to imagine a breezy bustling market here, protected from the sun under a wood and *palapa* roof built atop the structure's remarkably high columns.

Osario, El Caracol, and the Nunnery

From the market, bear left (away from El Castillo, just visible through the trees) until you meet the path leading to the site's southern entrance. You'll pass the **Osario** (ossuary), also known as the Tomb of the High Priest. Like a miniature version of El Castillo, the pyramid at one time had four stairways on each side and a temple at the crest. From the top platform, a vertical passageway leads into a chamber where seven tombs were discovered, along with numerous copper and jade artifacts indicating the deceased were of special importance (and hence the temple's name). Continuing on, you'll pass two more large structures, **Casa del Venado** (House of the Deer) and **Casa Colorada** (Red House).

The highlight of this portion of Chichén Itzá is **El Caracol** (The Snail Shell), also known as the Observatory, and perhaps the most graceful structure at Chichén Itzá. A two-tiered circular structure is set atop a broad rectangular platform, with window slits facing south and west, and another aligned according to the path of the moon during the spring equinoxes. Ancient astronomers used structures like this one to track celestial events and patterns—the orbits of the Moon and Venus, and the coming of solar and lunar eclipses, for example—with uncanny accuracy.

Beyond El Caracol is the **Nunnery,** so-named by Spanish explorers who thought it looked like convents back home. Judging from its size, location, and many rooms, the Nunnery was probably an administrative palace. Its exuberant facades show strong Chenes influence, another example of the blending of styles in Chichén Itzá.

Sound and Light Show

Recently revamped, the site puts on a nightly high-tech sound and light show at 7pm in the winter (Oct.-Apr.) and at 8pm in the summer (May-Sept.). Tickets cost US$13 and are separate from the general admission to the ruins. The sound and light show is presented in Spanish, but for an additional US$3.50, you can rent headphones with a recorded English-language translation of the program.

Practicalities

The grounds are open 8am-5pm daily. Admission is US$14 per adult, US$0.50 for children under 12; it must be paid in two parts—the state fee and the federal fee—at separate windows. The fee does not include entrance to the sound and light show (US$13). Additionally, US$4 is charged to enter with a video camera; parking is US$2.50.

Guides can be hired at the entrance according to fixed and clearly marked prices: US$45 for a two-hour tour in Spanish, US$60 in English, French, Italian, or German. Prices are per group, which can include up to eight people. Tips are customary and not included in the price. The visitors center has restrooms, an ATM, free luggage storage, a café, a bookstore, a gift shop, and an information center.

MAYALAND PLANETARIUM

Mayaland Resort (Zona Hotelera, Carr. Mérida-Valladolid Km. 120, toll-free Mex. tel. 800/719-5465, toll-free U.S. tel. 877/240-5864, www.mayaland.com, US$9) offers half-hour shows about Maya astronomy and scientific advances at a modern planetarium on the resort's grounds. Built in 2013, the planetarium replicates the shape of Chichén Itzá's famous Caracol structure, itself believed to be an observatory and located just steps from the resort's rear entrance. A planetarium show is part of several pricey all-day Chichén Itzá package tours from Cancún or Mérida, including a "Be Maya" tour that also has Maya cuisine and numerology components. Independent travelers can see the show

Chichén Itzá: Sold!

The great Chichén Itzá archaeological zone was actually, until very recently, private property. One of the New Seven Wonders of the World, one of Mexico's most popular tourist attractions, one of the most important ancient cities in the Americas, a site still sacred to Maya and New Agers alike—was also a piece of real estate, owned by the Barbachanos, one of Mexico's wealthiest families. But after a long and increasingly bitter dispute over control and ownership of the land, the Mexican government and the Barbachanos agreed on terms—and a price—and the land became property of the Mexican state in 2010.

Chichén Itzá was, of course, indigenous land when Spanish conquistadores arrived. It was later included in Spanish land grants and used for many years for farming and ranching. The ruins were visited by explorers John Stephens and Frederick Catherwood, but it was largely ignored until American explorer and amateur archaeologist Edward Thompson purchased it in 1894. Thompson, who had excavated other Maya sites, found and removed dozens of artifacts, shipping most to Harvard's Peabody Museum. Thompson nearly lost the land after being accused of stealing Mexican treasures, and eventually sold it to the elder Barbachano in 1944.

Over the years, the Barbachanos created the Mayaland Resort and Hacienda Chichén. They later purchased Uxmal ruins and built hotels there as well. The arrangement was mostly agreeable, with the government and family splitting ticket revenue, and the Barbachanos were adept hoteliers, even hosting a string of celebrity visitors, from European royalty to Saudi sheiks.

The elder Barbachano died in the 1960s, leaving the property to his children and grandchildren. Not long after, the first grumblings were heard: Many Mexicans felt cultural treasures like Chichén Itzá ought not be owned by private families, and local Maya argued it was rightfully theirs. The Mexican government passed a law in 1972 making the ruins (though not the land they sit on) property of the state. Maya vendors stormed the property more than once, demanding greater access for their wares.

By the early 2000s, the Mexican government was exploring the possibility of expropriating the land. The Barbachanos, perhaps sensing the writing on the wall, finally negotiated a sale. The elder Barbachano had once said he'd sell Chichén Itza for US$250 million. In the end, his heirs sold the land for around $220 million pesos, or US$17.6 million. The Mayaland Resort and the Haciendas at Chichén Itzá and Uxmal remain open; there's even a special entrance from Hacienda Chichén directly into the ruins. With over a million visitors to Chichén Itzá alone per year, and growing, the family that once owned the ruins still has a strong and lucrative stake in its future.

for US$9; showtimes vary, and schedule and tickets are available at the resort.

GRUTAS DE BALANKANCHÉ

Six kilometers (3.7 miles) east of Chichén Itzá are the **Balankanché Caves** (9am-5pm daily, US$7.50). Excavated in 1959 by *National Geographic* archaeologist Dr. E. Wyllys Andrews, the artifacts and ceremonial sites found here gave researchers a better understanding of ancient Maya cosmology, especially related to the notion of *Xibalba* (the underworld). Nowadays, the caves are just a step above a tourist trap—a wide path

meandering 500 meters (0.3 mile) down a tunnel with urns and other artifacts supposedly set up in their original locations. Wires and colored lights illuminate the path, but the recorded narration does nothing of the sort—it's so garbled you can hardly understand it, no matter what language it's in.

Entry times are fixed according to language: English at 11am, 1pm, and 3pm; Spanish at 9am, noon, 2pm, and 4pm; and French at 10am. A minimum of six visitors is needed for the 45-minute tour to depart. It's worth a visit if you're traveling with kids. Be sure to wear walking shoes—the path can be slippery in places.

PARQUE ECOARQUEOLÓGICO IK KIL

Three kilometers (1.9 miles) east of Pisté, the centerpiece of the **Parque Ecoarqueológico Ik Kil** (Carr. Mérida-Cancún Km. 122, tel. 985/851-0002, cenote_ikkil@hotmail.com, 8am-6pm daily Apr.-Oct., 8am-5pm daily Nov.-Mar., US$4.50) is the immense, perfectly round **Cenote Sagrado Azul,** with a partial stone roof. Although the cenote is real, the alterations to its natural state—supported walls, a set of stairs leading you in, a waterfall—make it feel pretty artificial. While not representative of the typical cenote experience, this is a good option if you are traveling with small children and need a spot to cool off. Lockers are available for US$2.50. The cenote and on-site restaurant (breakfast US$7, lunch buffet US$9.50) get packed with tour groups 12:30pm-2:30pm; try visiting outside those times for a mellower experience. Better yet, stay at one of the on-site bungalows (US$75 s/d with a/c).

FOOD

Eating options are pretty limited in Pisté but improve somewhat if you have a car and can get to and from the large hotels.

Restaurante Las Mestizas (Calle 15 s/n, tel. 985/851-0069, 7am-9pm daily, US$5-12) is the best sit-down place to eat in Pisté, with an airy, colonial-style interior and tasty good-sized portions. Problem is that it's no secret—expect a bustling dining room; if there's a wait list, it typically moves fast. The food is classic Yucatecan fare, from *panuchos* to *pollo pibil.*

Popular with locals, ★ **La Gran Chaya** (Calle 15 s/n, no phone, 7am-10:30pm daily, US$2.50-5), located across from the town church, is a hole-in-the-wall eatery with bright plastic tables and chairs set up in front. Meals range from egg plates to piping hot *salbutes.* Be sure to order an *agua* or *licuados*—frothy cold drinks made with a variety of fresh fruits—to wash it all down.

Set in a 16th-century hacienda, the ★ **Hacienda Chichén Resort's restaurant** (Zona Hotelera, Carr. Mérida-Valladolid Km. 120, tel. 985/851-0045, 7am-10pm daily, US$12-25) is a soothing place to eat after a long day at the ruins. The menu is varied—Yucatecan specialties, pastas, sandwiches—and on the occasional evening, a trio plays regional music. Much of the featured produce is grown in its beautiful organic garden.

If you can stomach the tour groups, the lunch buffet at **Mayaland Resort** (Zona

patio dining at Las Mestizas in Pisté

Pisté

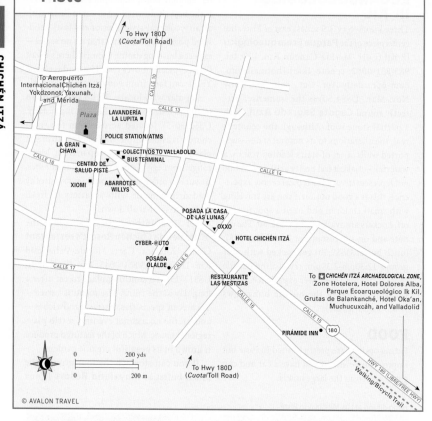

To Hwy 180D
(*Cuota*/Toll Road)

CALLE 10

To Aeropuerto
Internacional Chichén Itzá,
Yokdzonot, Yaxunah,
and Mérida

Plaza

CALLE 13

LAVANDERÍA
LA LUPITA ■

POLICE STATION/ATMS

CALLE 16

LA GRAN
CHAYA ■

■ COLECTIVOS TO VALLADOLID
▼ BUS TERMINAL

CENTRO DE
SALUD PISTÉ ▼

XIOMI ■

ABARROTES
WILLYS

CALLE 14

POSADA LA CASA
DE LAS LUNAS ▼
▼ OXXO

■ HOTEL CHICHÉN ITZÁ

CYBER-@UTO ▼

CALLE 6

POSADA
OLALDE ●

CALLE 17

RESTAURANTE ▼
LAS MESTIZAS

CALLE 16

To ✦ *CHICHÉN ITZÁ ARCHAEOLOGICAL ZONE*,
Zone Hotelera, Hotel Dolores Alba,
Parque Ecoarqueológico Ik Kil,
Grutas de Balankanché, Hotel Oka'an,
Muchucuxcáh, and Valladolid

CALLE 15

PIRÁMIDE INN ● (180)

0   200 yds
0   200 m

To Hwy 180D
(*Cuota*/Toll Road)

HWY 180 (LIBRE/FREE HWY)

Walking/Bicycle Trail

© AVALON TRAVEL

Hotelera, Carr. Mérida-Valladolid Km. 120, tel. 985/851-0100, noon-4:30pm daily, US$11) offers a variety of hot and cold dishes that will definitely fill you up. Live music, ballet *folklórico* shows, and outdoor seating are nice touches. After your meal, visitors are welcome to use one of the hotel pools too.

For groceries, **Abarrotes Willy's** (Calle 15 s/n, 7am-10pm daily) has the best selection of foodstuffs in town.

ACCOMMODATIONS

A handful of upscale hotels make up the small Zona Hotelera on the east side of Chichén Itzá, complete with its own entrance to the ruins. Nearby, in the town of Pisté, there are also a

few budget and mid-range options. Be sure to reserve early during the spring and fall equinoxes. All the options below (except Ik Kil) have Wi-Fi available, though often in the reception area only. Book rooms online for the lowest rates.

Under US$50

On the eastern end of Pisté toward the ruins, **Pirámide Inn** (Calle 15 at Calle 20, tel. 985/851-0115, www.chichen.com, US$32 s/d with a/c, US$4 pp camping) is a low, sprawling hotel with large rooms that are clean though a bit dark. The decor is distinctly 1970s den, with some rooms sporting bubblegum paint jobs and lacquered brick walls.

The air conditioners appear to be from the same era, and can be loud. Cement seating frames a pool in a pleasant fruit tree garden. Backpackers can **camp** (US$4 pp) here, with access to the pool and cleanish shared bathrooms—BYO gear.

Posada Olalde (Calle 6 at Calle 17, tel. 985/851-0086, US$22 s/d) has a dozen simple rooms with fans and bathrooms that are showing some wear and tear. Rooms share a long porch facing a leafy courtyard. The access road is easy to miss—look for it just west of (and on the opposite side of the street from) the OXXO mini-mart. There's street parking only. Wi-Fi is available in the rooms.

The best deal around, ★ Posada La Casa de las Lunas (Calle 15 s/n, tel. 985/851-0289, posada.laslunas@gmail.com, US$16 s/d, US$19-22 s/d with a/c) has modern, spic-and-span rooms with thick beds, tile bathrooms, and silent air-conditioning. All share a covered porch that faces a tidy courtyard; each has Wi-Fi. If every peso counts, consider the fan-only rooms; just be aware that they have cold water-only bathrooms. There's off-street parking too, and a pool is in the works. Look for the entrance just west of the OXXO convenience store.

US$50-100

Hotel Dolores Alba Chichén Itzá (Carr. Mérida-Cancún Km. 122, tel. 985/858-1555, www.doloresalba.com, US$53 s with a/c, US$56 d with a/c) is in a choice location just three kilometers (1.9 miles) east of the ruins, one kilometer (0.6 mile) from the Balankanché Caves, and across the street from the Parque Ecoarqueológico Ik Kil. Rooms are dated, for sure, but they're spotless and have good beds; the simple tile work on the walls spiffs up the decor a bit. The hotel has two large swimming pools—the one in back has a mostly natural stone bottom, with channels reminiscent of an ocean reef. Other pluses include a pleasant outdoor restaurant (7am-10pm daily, US$5-10) and free shuttle service to the ruins during the day (though not back). Full breakfast is included in the rate.

Part of the Mayaland conglomerate, **Hotel Chichén Itzá** (Calle 15 s/n, tel. 985/851-0022, www.mayaland.com, US$61-85 s/d with a/c) is one of the nicest hotels in downtown Pisté, featuring rooms with a king or two queen beds and comfortable furnishings, large modern bathrooms, and simple Mexican decor. The less-expensive rooms face the street and can be noisy, while the top-floor ones are larger and overlook the hotel's attractive garden and pool area. There's a cavernous restaurant (7am-10pm daily) that's often packed with tour groups.

Villas Arqueológicas Chichén Itzá (Zona Hotelera, Carr. Mérida-Valladolid Km. 120, tel. 985/851-0187, toll-free Mex. tel. 800/557-7755, www.villasarqueologicas.com.mx, US$63 s/d with a/c, US$116 suite with a/c) is a pleasant two-story hotel with a mellow ambience. Boxy but nice rooms are set around a lush courtyard with an inviting L-shaped pool. There's a library/TV room with comfy couches and a variety of reading material—from romance novels to archaeology books—and a decent restaurant on-site too. Very tall folks should note that alcove walls bracket the ends of the beds.

Set in a lush forest, ★ **Parque Ecoarqueológico Ik Kil** (Carr. Mérida-Cancún Km. 122, tel. 985/851-0002, US$75 s/d with a/c) offers 14 modern and ultra-comfortable bungalows. All are spacious and have whirlpool tubs and comfortable beds; a handful of the units sport pullout sofas too. Silent air-conditioning and a private porch make it all the better. Guests get unlimited use of the on-site cenote, including after hours. It's a fantastic value, especially for those traveling with kids.

US$100-150

A holistic retreat center in a forest setting, **Hotel Oka'an** (Carr. Mérida-Cancún Km. 122, tel. 985/105-8402, www.hotelokaan.com, US$105-122 s/d with a/c, US$146 suite with a/c) beckons with a full spa, yoga workshops, and the occasional spiritual ceremony. Ample standard rooms are bright and tasteful in a pastel sort of way, with modern bathrooms and private balconies. Larger and more luxurious bungalows have decorative stone butterflies and turtles detailing the floors and earthy contemporary architecture, plus private terraces. There's also a pleasant open-air restaurant (8am-10pm daily, US$7.50-10), though service is hit or miss. For post-ruin lounging, an infinity pool cascades into smaller shaded basins, but don't miss the killer view from the *mirador* terrace—Chichén Itzá's El Castillo pops up over the (arduously manicured) treeline. Look for the road marquis just west of the Hotel Dolores Alba and continue 1.5 kilometers (0.9 mile) on an unpaved road; it's a US$8 taxi ride from Pisté.

Over US$150

Once the headquarters for the Carnegie Institute's Chichén Itzá expedition, the ★ **Hacienda Chichén Resort** (Zona Hotelera, Carr. Mérida-Valladolid Km. 120, tel. 985/851-0045, toll-free U.S. tel. 877/631-4005, www.haciendachichen.com, US$179-199 s/d with a/c, US$215-299 suite with a/c) is now a tranquil hotel set on lush tropical grounds. Newer units are quite comfortable, with tile floors, exposed beam ceilings, and wood furnishings. Many of the older units

occupy the original cottages used by archaeologists who conducted their first excavations of Chichén Itzá—enticing in theory, though the cinder-block walls and pervasive mustiness diminish the charm. Still, the latter are usually booked solid. Be sure to wander the grounds with an eye for the original hacienda (stone blocks from the ruins are incorporated into the main building) and narrow-gauge railroad tracks that were used to transport artifacts from Chichén Itzá. There's also a gorgeous pool, full-service spa (11am-7pm daily), and a fine dining room. Only some of the rooms have Wi-Fi.

The Lodge at Chichén Itzá (Zona Hotelera, Carr. Mérida-Valladolid Km. 120, tel. 998/887-9162, toll-free Mex. tel. 800/719-5465, toll-free U.S. tel. 877/240-5864, www.mayaland.com, US$187-195 s/d with a/c, US$250-690 suite with a/c) is part of the larger Mayaland Resort, which is literally at the rear entrance to the ruins; visitors must pass through the resort (and two of its gift shops) to get to the ticket booth. The grounds are gorgeous: 100 acres of tamed tropical jungle featuring walking and horseback riding trails, a full-service spa, three restaurants, and three pools. The Lodge's *palapa*-roofed bungalows are pleasant, with stained-glass windows,

the entrance to Hacienda Chichén Resort

hardwood furniture, and terraces with rocking chairs. Lodge accommodations are typically reserved for independent travelers, and their location—including a separate access road and parking lot—is fairly removed from Mayaland proper, where groups are handled. Still, you're bound to encounter various loud flocks of guests during your stay, especially in the reception area or restaurant, diminishing the charm for some.

INFORMATION AND SERVICES

There is no tourist office in Pisté; hotel receptionists are sometimes helpful—depends who you get—as are other travelers. Pisté also doesn't have a bank, but there are two local ATMs: one inside the OXXO market, the other in Chichén Itzá's visitors center. At the time of research, HSBC and Santander ATMs were being added to the Palacio Municipal.

Emergency Services

The **police** have an office (tel. 985/851-0365) in the Palacio Municipal, facing the town church. An officer is on duty 24 hours a day, and there's usually one waving through traffic near the plaza. **Centro de Salud Pisté** (Calle 15 s/n, no phone, 7am-1pm and 5pm-7pm Mon.-Fri., 8am-8pm Sat.-Sun.) is one of two clinics in town. For anything serious, you're better off going to Mérida or Cancún. **Farmacia Similares** (Calle 15 s/n, no phone 7am-10pm Mon.-Sat., 9am-9pm Sun.) is just east of the main plaza.

Media and Communications

Xiomi (Calle 16 s/n, 10am-10pm daily, US$0.80/hour) is a reliable Internet café located behind Abarrotes Willy's supermarket. If it's full, try **Ciber-@uto** (Calle 4A, 9am-7pm daily, US$1/hour), a combination Internet café and car wash run out of a family home. Look for it off the road that parallels the main drag, across from the cemetery.

Laundry

Lavandería La Lupita (Calle 10 near Calle 13, 8am-8pm Mon.-Sat.) charges US$1.80 per kilo (2.2 pounds) to wash and dry clothes; they'll do same-day service if you drop your load off first thing in the morning.

GETTING THERE AND AROUND
Bus

Pisté's small **bus terminal** (Calle 15 s/n, 8:30am-5:30pm daily, cash only) is just

A cool dip makes for a great ending to a long day of ruin hopping.

southeast of the Palacio Municipal and about 2.5 kilometers (1.6 miles) from the entrance to Chichén Itzá. There is also a **ticket office** in the gift shop at the ruins (tel. 985/851-0377, 9am-5pm daily). (The visitors center at Chichén Itzá also has **free luggage storage,** which makes it easy to catch a bus right after visiting the ruins.)

All first-class departures leave from Chichén Itzá only. Second-class departure times listed here are for the terminal in Pisté. Second-class buses coming and going between 8am and 5:30pm stop at both the terminal and the parking lot at the ruins. If planning to catch a second-class bus at the ruins, keep in mind that buses headed toward Cancún stop at the ruins slightly after the listed times, while those bound for Mérida pass by slightly earlier. Most bus service to and from Pisté and Chichén Itzá is on Oriente, ADO's second-class line, but the few first-class buses are worth the extra cost.

- Cancún: One daily first-class bus (US$19.85, 3.5 hours) at 4:30pm; second-class buses (US$10.35, 4-4.5 hours) every 30-60 minutes 12:30am-9:30pm.

- Cobá: For the town and archaeological site (US$5.25, 2.5 hours), take the second-class Tulum bus at 12:25am, 7:30am, or 1pm; the first-class buses do not stop there.

- Mérida: One first-class bus (US$11.15, 2 hours) leaves at 4:15pm; second-class buses (US$5.75, 2.5 hours) leave every 30-60 minutes 6am-11:30pm.

- Playa del Carmen: One first-class bus (US$28.75, 3.5 hours) leaves at 4:30pm; second-class buses (US$10.76, 4 hours) leave at 12:25am, 7:35am, and 1:05pm.

- Tulum: First-class buses (US$14.75, 2.5 hours) leave at 8:25am and 4:30pm;

second-class departures (US$7.50, 3.5 hours) at 12:25, 7:30am, and 1pm.

- Valladolid: First-class buses (US$6.50, 50 minutes) leave at 8:25am, 11:10am, and 4:30pm; second-class service (US$2, 1 hour) leaves every 30-60 minutes 12:25am-10:30pm.

White *colectivos* (US$2, 40 minutes) leave for Valladolid every 30 minutes 7am-6pm from in front of the bus terminal.

Car

Chichén Itzá lies adjacent to Highway 180, 40 kilometers (25 miles) west of Valladolid, 120 kilometers (75 miles) east of Mérida, and 200 kilometers (124 miles) west of Cancún. For drivers, the quickest way to get there is via the *cuota,* a large modern freeway extending from Cancún most of the way to Mérida, with a well-marked exit for Chichén Itzá and Pisté. There's a price for speed and convenience, though: The toll from Mérida is US$6, and a whopping US$22.30 from Cancún. You can also take the old *carretera libre* (free highway) all or part of the way; it's in reasonably good condition but takes much longer, mainly because you pass through numerous small villages and seemingly innumerable *topes* (speed bumps).

Air

Aeropuerto Internacional Chichén Itzá is 16 kilometers (9.9 miles) east of Pisté, near the town of Kaua. Inaugurated in April 2000, it is one of the most modern airports in the country, with an 1,800-meter (5,900-foot) runway capable of receiving 747 jets. Although it initially received dozens of regular and charter flights, its license was suspended in 2001. Today it stands virtually empty, receiving only a smattering of charters, mostly from Cancún, Cozumel, and Chetumal, though rumors of restarting service crop up from time to time.

Villages Near Chichén Itzá

Around Chichén Itzá and Pisté are several small, mostly indigenous villages. They're a short distance on the map, but worlds apart from the buses, hotels, and sheer mass of tourists at the archaeological site. In some villages, travelers can visit off-the-beaten-track ruins, take tours—including visiting local families—and swim in cenotes; you can even stay the night in simple lodges and at least one foreign-operated hotel. Time permitting, a visit to one of these towns can be an excellent complement to the shock and awe of Chichén Itzá.

YOKDZONOT

Located 15 kilometers (9.3 miles) west from Pisté along the *libre*, the village of Yokdzonot has one of the area's loveliest cenotes that's not on a tour bus circuit: **Cenote Yokdzonot** (Calle 20 btwn Calles 27 and 29, tel. 999/149-9315, 9am-5pm daily, US$3.75 adult, US$2 child under 10). Run by a Maya cooperative of mostly women, the cenote is an open pool 40 meters (131 feet) deep, with trees casting shadows across brilliant teal water, tree roots dangling like ropes down the limestone walls,

and mojarra fish glinting in the sunlight. For US$3.25, visitors can zipline across the cenote or rappel 20 meters (66 feet) down into it. Camping is available on-site for US$15.75 per person, which includes a four-person tent with bedding, and a restaurant (US$4-8) serves all meals.

As a bonus for staying the night (or if you ask nicely after closing time), you can watch bats funnel out at dusk, and March-June, the swallows departing at dawn. The coop also offers bicycle tours of nearby cenotes (90 minutes, US$3.75). The highway sign for the cenote is easily missed; go south from the highway on the dirt road just west of the domed cement plaza, aiming for the cell phone tower. Taxis from Pisté charge US$6, or you can take a westbound second-class bus (US$0.80) and walk 300 meters (984 feet) to the cenote.

To overnight in a bed in Yokdzonot, follow the blue "ecohotel" signs north across the highway to **Yucatán Mayan Retreat** (aka Eco-Hotel Yokdzonot, tel. 984/140-4338, www.yucatanmayanretreat.webs.com,

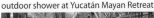
outdoor shower at Yucatán Mayan Retreat

US$12.50 pp camping with equipment, US$32 s/d with shared bath, US$44 suite with a/c), a forested oasis with a clutch of comfortable *cabañas*, each with flat-screen TV and fridge, a spotless outdoor guest kitchen, and an aboveground plunge pool. Wi-Fi is available. If you arrive without a reservation, stop at the caretaker's house for information—a bubblegum pink house at the bottom of the access road to the hotel.

YAXUNAH

The small Maya village of Yaxunah is just 32 kilometers (20 miles) south of Pisté; it has three little-visited sights that make for a worthwhile afternoon of exploring.

Yaxunah ruins (free) is set just beyond the country road leading to its namesake village. Visitors literally drive onto the site—as in pick a pyramid and park your car—and are welcome to explore it; there are no facilities here. Instead, surrounded by farmland, there are several small pyramids, including one with rounded walls, lots of platforms, and one large stone mound covered in trees (presumably a temple). Yaxunah was first settled around 750-500 BC. Around AD 400-500, the royal family was evidently tortured and murdered, their bodies (11 in all, including several children) thrown haphazardly into a tomb now designated Burial B. The city was conquered by Cobá in AD 600, and its population grew rapidly; most of Yaxunah's primary structures date from that time. Also built was a 100-kilometer (62-mile) sacbé (raised road) between the two cities, one of the longest yet discovered. Chichén Itzá conquered Yaxunah around AD 900, but apparently did not occupy it. Yaxunah's population eventually dispersed, and the city was effectively abandoned around AD 1150.

Yaxunah Centro Cultural (one block from central plaza, www.yaxunahcentrocultural.org, 9am-7pm daily, US$1.75) is the pride and joy of this Maya village. A modern building, it has an engaging mural celebrating Maya history and the people's relationship with the land. Inside is a one-room museum with interesting exhibits on the Yaxunah ruins, including a site map, dioramas, pottery fragments, and a re-creation of one of the tombs found there. The museum also houses exhibits on current-day Maya, their culture, and some of their important religious ceremonies. Outside, visitors can explore the botanical garden, which features plants used in everyday Maya life; signage includes plant names plus their uses. All information is in English and Spanish. Occasionally, the Centro Cultural hosts folkloric dance performances; check the website for more information.

Yaxunah Cenote (one block from central plaza, 9am-7pm daily, US$1.75) is a refreshing swimming hole surrounded by tall shade trees. A sturdy staircase leads visitors to the clear water, where they can cool off after a day of exploring. Picnic tables are available for BYO snacks and drinks. It's located across from and managed by Yaxunah Centro Cultural.

The village of Yaxunah is located 32 kilometers (20 miles) south of Pisté. To get there, head south on Calle 22. You'll pass the village of Popola, and 6.5 kilometers (4 miles) later, the Yaxunah ruins will appear. The namesake town is 1.5 kilometers (0.9 mile) west of there.

MUCHUCUXCÁH

The village of Muchucuxcáh is a pleasant place to be based if you're interested in experiencing life in a typical Maya village. Travelers can stay at the **Centro de Turismo Comunitario de Muchucuxcáh** (tel. 985/808-1789), a cooperative started by a local nonprofit, **El Hombre Sobre La Tierra** (tel. 999/927-0719, http://elhombresobrelatierra.org). The Centro has eight typical *palapas* (US$9.50 pp) in a forest setting; each has hammocks (no beds here), mosquito nets, fans, and 24-hour electricity. Bathrooms are shared but quite clean. There's a big swimming pool on-site—perfect after a day of exploring—and three traditional Maya **meals** (US$19 pp/day) are prepared fresh for guests and served in a pleasant thatch-roofed dining room. The Centro also offers guided hikes, excursions to cenotes, and village tours; Maya cooking lessons and hammock weaving instruction also are available.

Muchucuxcáh is located 35 kilometers (22 miles) south of Pisté. To get to the village, take the *libre* (free highway) east for about 13 kilometers (8 miles), then take a right onto the turnoff to Chankom. Continue on that road, past two villages, until you arrive at Muchucuxcáh. With only five streets in town, the Centro is impossible to miss. Private transportation to and from Pisté, Valladolid, Mérida, and Cancún also can be arranged.

Valladolid

Valladolid draws tourists because of its mellow colonial atmosphere and its central location: 30 minutes from the archaeological zones of Chichén Itzá and Ek' Balam, an hour from the ruins at Cobá and the flamingo reserve in Río Lagartos, and two hours from Mérida, Cancún, and Tulum. It's an easy bus or car ride to any of these destinations, restaurants and hotels are reasonably priced, and you have the advantage of staying in a colonial Mexican town. If you're en route to one of the regional sites or simply want to have a small-city experience, consider spending a night here—you're sure to be happily surprised.

HISTORY

The site of several Maya revolts against the Spanish, Valladolid was conquered in 1543 by Francisco de Montejo, cousin of the like-named Spaniard who founded Mérida. It was once the Maya city of Zací. Montejo brutalized its inhabitants and crushed their temples, building large churches and homes in their place. It is perhaps not surprising, then, that the Caste War started in Valladolid, and that the city played an important role in the beginning of the Mexican Revolution. Today, Valladolid is a charming colonial town with a rich history and strong Maya presence.

ORIENTATION

Valladolid is easy to get around. It's laid out in a grid pattern with even-numbered streets running north to south, odd-numbered streets running east to west. The central plaza at the center of the city is bordered by Calles 39, 40, 41, and 42.

SIGHTS
★ Iglesia y Ex-Convento San Bernardino de Siena

Located at the end of the Calzada de los Frailes, the **Iglesia y Ex-Convento San Bernardino de Siena** (Calle 41-A, tel. 985/856-2160, 8am-noon and 5pm-8pm daily) is one of Valladolid's most attractive structures. Built by Franciscan missionaries between 1552 and 1560, the church is entered through a series of arches, and the facade, covered in a checkerboard-like stucco pattern, rises into a squat tower with turrets. Inside, there are original 16th-century frescoes, catacombs, and crypts. Mass is held at 7am and 7pm Monday-Friday; at 7am, 8:30am, and 7pm Saturday; and at 7am, 8am, 9am, 10am, 5pm, 6pm, 7pm, and 8:30pm Sunday.

Annexed to the church is the ex-convent (9am-6pm daily, US$2, free on Sun.). Its rooms radiate from a center courtyard that features, uniquely, a cenote. Called Sis-Há (Cold Water), the cenote helped the monks be self-reliant. In 2004, an Instituto Nacional de Antropología e Historia (INAH)-funded exploration of the cenote resulted in the discovery of 164 muskets, bayonets, spears, and one cannon. The arms were thrown into the cenote between 1847 and 1848; they are believed to have been sent by the British via Jamaica. The arms were used when the monastery was turned into a fortress during the Caste War. A small exhibit room displays some of these weapons as well as photos and descriptions of the INAH exploration.

Valladolid

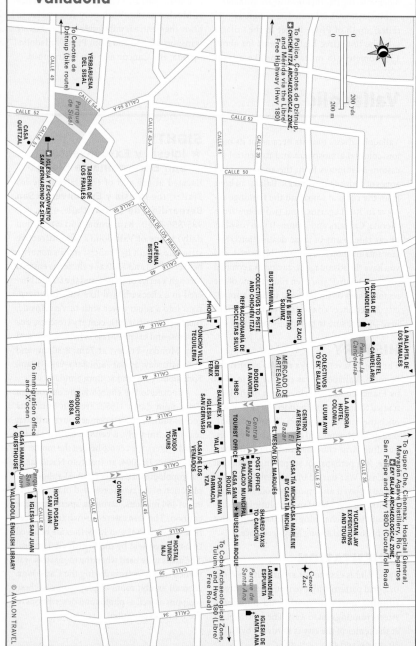

0   200 yds
0   200 m

CALLE 49
CALLE 52
CALLE 51
CALLE 54-A
CALLE 54-A
CALLE 43-A
CALLE 41
CALLE 39
CALLE 52
CALLE 50
CALLE 50
CALZADA DE LOS FRAILES
CALLE 48
CALLE 46
CALLE 44
CALLE 47
CALLE 42
CALLE 40
CALLE 45
CALLE 47
CALLE 38
CALLE 49
CALLE 43
CALLE 37
CALLE 35
CALLE 36
CALLE 34

To Police, Cenotes de Dzitnup,
CHICHÉN ITZÁ ARCHAEOLOGICAL ZONE,
and Mérida via the Libre/
Free Highway (Hwy 180)

To Cenotes de
Dzitnup (bike route)

YERBABUENA
DEL SISAL

CASA
QUETZAL

Parque
de Sisal

IGLESIA Y EX-CONVENTO
SAN BERNARDINO DE SIENA

TABERNA DE
LOS FRAILES

CAFÉNA
BISTRO

PHONET

PONCHO VILLA
TEQUILERIA

COLECTIVOS TO PISTÉ
AND CHICHEN ITZA

BUS TERMINAL

REFRACCIONARIA DE
BICICLETAS SILVA

CAFÉ & BISTRO
SQUIMZ

HOTEL ZACI

CIBER
FENIX

IGLESIA DE
SAN GERVASIO

BANAMEX

BODEGA
LA FAVORITA

HSBC

Central
Plaza

TOURIST OFFICE

MERCADO DE
ARTESANIAS

IGLESIA DE
LA CANDELARIA

HOSTEL
CANDELARIA

Parque la
Candelaria

COLECTIVOS
TO EK' BALAM

LA PALAPITA DE
LOS TAMALES

LA AURORA
HOTEL
COLONIAL

LUUM AYNI

CENTRO
ARTESANAL ZACI

El
Bazar

CASA TÍA MICHA/CASA MARLENE

EL MESÓN DEL MARQUÉS

YUCATAN JAY
EXPEDITIONS
AND TOURS

To immigration office
and X'ocen

PRODUCTOS
SOSA

MEXICO
TOURS

CASA DE LOS
VENADOS

YALAT

PORTAL MAYA

FARMACIA
YZA

POST OFFICE

BANCOMER

PALACIO MUNICIPAL

CASA SAN
ROQUE

MUSEO SAN ROQUE

SHARED TAXIS
TO CANCÚN

CASA HAMACA
GUESTHOUSE

Parque
San Juan

IGLESIA SAN JUAN

VALLADOLID ENGLISH LIBRARY

CONATO

HOTEL POSADA
SAN JUAN

HOSTAL
TUNICH
NAJ

LAVANDERIA
ESPUMITA

Cenote
Zaci

Parque de
Santa Ana

IGLESIA DE
SANTA ANA

To Cobá Archaeological Zone,
Tulum, and Hwy 180 (Libre/
Free Road)

To Super Che, Cinemax, Hospital General,
Mayapan Agave Distillery, Río Lagartos,
San Felipe and Hwy 180D (Cuota/Toll Road)

EK BALAM ARCHAEOLOGICAL ZONE

© AVALON TRAVEL

Casa de los Venados

If you have even a passing interest in Mexican folk art—or an infatuation with exquisite colonial buildings—make sure to visit the **Casa de los Venados** (House of the Deer, Calle 40 btwn Calles 41 and 43, tel. 985/856-2289, www.casadelosvenados.com, 10am tour daily, US$5 donation requested). After an architectural award-winning remodel of this 17th-century house, the American couple who own it had so many visitors stopping by to see their extensive art collection that they now welcome visitors for tours of their mansion home and their incredible 3,000-piece collection—the largest Mexican folk art collection not owned by a museum. The pieces span John and Dorianne Venator's 50-plus years of seeking out and commissioning *catrinas,* clay sculptures, wood carvings, paintings, and other decorative objects created by some of the most talented contemporary artisans from across Mexico, and the work usually incorporates religious, indigenous, or cultural themes. The museum is a labor of love, with all donations benefiting a local volunteer-run medical clinic and the Lions Club.

Iglesia de San Gervasio

Overlooking the central plaza, the **San Gervasio Church** (Calle 41 at Calle 42, no phone) has a sober Franciscan style. It was originally built in 1545 but in 1705 was deemed profane and ordered demolished by the local bishop as the result of a political rivalry that involved the storming of the church, the desanctifying of its altar, and the death of four politicians. (The incident is now known as *El Crimen de los Alcaldes,* or The Mayors' Crime.) The church was rebuilt a year later, but its orientation changed so that the new altar would not be in the same position as the prior—indeed, the Iglesia de San Gervasio is one of the only colonial-era churches in the Yucatán whose facade faces north instead of west.

Museo San Roque

A long, high-ceilinged room—this used to be a church—the **San Roque Museum** (Calle 41 btwn Calles 38 and 40, no phone, 8am-8pm Mon.-Fri., 9am-6pm Sat.-Sun., free) needs a serious updating but is still a worthwhile stop, with historical exhibits on Valladolid, many focusing on the Caste War and the beginning of the Mexican Revolution. Try not to be freaked out by the mannequins. Signage is in Spanish only.

Valladolid's central plaza

Palacio Municipal

On the 2nd floor of the **city hall** (7am-7pm daily, free) is a large balcony overlooking the central plaza, with four large paintings by local artist Manuel Lizama. The paintings depict events in Valladolid's history: pre-Hispanic communities, the city's founding, the Caste War, and the Mexican Revolution. It's not spectacular, but still interesting.

Cenote Zaci

Right in the middle of town, **Cenote Zaci** (Calle 36 btwn Calles 37 and 39, no phone, 8am-6pm daily, US$1.50 adult, US$1.25 child under 13) is a dark natural pool at the bottom of a huge cavern, with a bank of trees on one side and a path looping down from the entrance above. It's often pooh-poohed as inferior to cenotes at Dzitnup, but it's a perfectly peaceful and attractive spot, and a lot quicker and easier to get to. You may find leaves and pollen floating on the water's surface, but it's still great for swimming. To have the cenote to yourself, go midweek, or better yet right after closing time, entering through the restaurant (you can use their bathroom to change) instead of the main gates.

Mayapán Agave Distillery

Along Valladolid's northern ring road, two kilometers (1.2 miles) south of the Cancún toll highway, the artisanal **Mayapán Agave Distillery** (Libremiento Nte. Km. 7, tel. 985/858-0246, www.mayapan.mx, 9am-6pm Mon.-Sat., US$3) leads visitors on half-hour tours that take in its agave fields and warehouse-size facility, detailing the traditional steps used to ferment, mash by horse-drawn mill, and distill the agave plant into liquor. They can't call it tequila because it's not made in Jalisco, but your taste buds might not be so finicky. Tours conclude with three different tastings and a subtle nudge toward the gift shop. English tours are available.

Cenotes de Dzitnup

Four kilometers (2.5 miles) west of Valladolid on Highway 180 is the small community of Dzitnup, home to two appealing underground cenotes. Both make for a unique and refreshing swim—and on warm days you may find them somewhat crowded. Both share a ticket kiosk and a large parking lot. Many small *artesanía* stands sit at the entrance, and you'll be aggressively pursued by children offering to watch your car or sell you knickknacks.

Although the two are across the street from each other, **Cenote Xkeken** (no phone, 8am-7pm daily, US$3.75 adult, US$2 under 17, video cameras US$2.50) has been open longer and is better known; many postcards and travel guides call it "Cenote Dzitnup." After a reasonably easy descent underground (in a few places you must bend over because of a low ceiling; there's a hanging rope to help), you'll come to a circular pond of clear, cool water. It's a pretty, albeit damp, place, with a high dome ceiling that has one small opening at the top letting in a ray of sun and dangling green vines. Often an errant bird can be seen swooping low over the water before heading to the sun and sky through the tiny opening. Stalactites and at least one large stalagmite adorn the ceiling and cenote floor.

At **Cenote Samula** (no phone, 8am-5pm daily, US$3.75 adult, US$2 under 17, video cameras US$2.50), tree roots dangle impressively from the cavern roof all the way down to the water. You enter through a narrow tunnel, which opens onto a set of stairs that zigzag down to the water. Fearless kids jump from the stairs into the clear turquoise water below.

Many people ride bikes here, following a paved path that runs parallel to the highway. A cab to the cenotes runs about US$5.

Tours

MexiGo Tours (Calle 43 btwn Calles 40 and 42, tel. 985/856-0777, www.mexigotours.com, 8:30am-8pm) is highly recommended for group **tours** to take in local and regional attractions. Popular trips include visits to archaeological sites, cenotes, and caves, and outings to spot wildlife like flamingos, howler monkeys, and even bat-eating snakes. Tours range from US$35 to US$85, depending on the

Adopt a Work of Art

Much of Mexico's finest colonial art is not found in a museum or big-city gallery, but rather in the churches, rectories, and nunneries in small towns and out-of-the-way villages. The Yucatán Peninsula is no exception, with a church in virtually every town, some dating to the 17th century or earlier, many boasting surprisingly rich artwork. But such artwork—including gilded altarpieces, gorgeous murals, and ornate stone or tile facades—can be very difficult to preserve, much less restore to their original glory. Enter **Adopte una Obra de Arte** (Adopt a Work of Art, www.adopteunaobradearte.com), a nonprofit organization dedicated to preserving and restoring Mexico's rich colonial and religious art, usually in collaboration with experts from the national anthropology institute, or INAH; it also works to educate residents and visitors about the works' history and significance. The nonprofit's Yucatán chapter opened in 1992 and has restored religious artwork in towns and cities throughout the region. The project makes exploring the region all the more interesting, with stunning art in places you might least expect. Here are a few highlights:

VALLADOLID: La Capilla de la Virgin de la Candelaria. Adopte helped restore this large church's exterior, main altar, pulpit, and numerous small statues and paintings in the latter. Much of the interior had been repainted previously but rather poorly; the present condition is thought to closely resemble the original design.

UAYMA: Templo y Ex-convent de Santo Domingo. Located 15 kilometers (9.3 miles) northwest of Valladolid, this 17th-century church was nearly destroyed during the Caste War. It stood roofless and decrepit until 2003, when Adopte began a yearlong restoration. The vibrant color and fantastic flower-adorned facade make this one of the Yucatan's most unique churches.

TABI: Iglesia de Tabi. The church in this one-street town, located 50 kilometers (31 miles) southwest of Pisté, has one of the region's finest baroque altarpieces, rescued from near-collapse and beautifully restored by Adopte. Even more remarkable is the camarín, a small chamber behind the main altar, completely blanketed in gilded woodwork, murals, and fine paintings.

distance and length of each; they often include breakfast, lunch, and transportation, but not site entrance fees. A minimum of three people is required for excursions.

Yucatan Jay Expeditions and Tours (Calle 38 btwn Calles 35 and 37, cell. tel. 986/103-3452, hours vary) specializes in tours focused on spotting birds locally and regionally. (There are 543 species of birds registered in the entire peninsula—a true hot spot for birders or those interested in birding.) Tours are led by experienced guides with an obvious passion for their work. Many tours also combine stops in traditional Maya villages as well as at cenotes.

ENTERTAINMENT AND EVENTS

Taking the cue from Mérida's successful weekly celebrations, Sundays here now feature a year-round cultural event called **Domingo Vallisoletano.** From 10am until about 8:30pm, the city closes the streets around the central plaza for artisan expositions, *trova* balladeers, folkloric dancing, and programs for kids. The tourist office also leads free hour-long tours of the area around the plaza at 11am, 1pm, and 4pm, though you may want to confirm these times.

Viernes de Trova is another popular event hosted by the municipality. Every other Friday in Parque de los Héroes (Calle 41 at Calle 38), musical groups perform trova on an open-air stage, starting at 8:30pm. Grab a seat and some munchies and enjoy the show.

Every January 27-February 2, Valladolid celebrates its patron saint, La Vírgen de la Candelaria, in the **Expo-Feria Valladolid.** It's a blowout outdoor festival, where you'll see bullfights, rodeos, musical entertainment, and lots of food stands selling local delicacies and heart-stopping goodies. Venues vary; ask at the tourist office or your hotel for details.

If you need a movie fix, head to **Cinemex** (Plaza Bella, Calle 42 s/n, tel. 985/257-6969, toll-free Mex. tel. 800/710-8888, www.cinemex.com, US$3), where the latest Hollywood and Mexican films are screened. Look for it on the road headed north toward Ek' Balam.

Momentos Sagrados Mayas (Sacred Maya Moments, X'ocen, tel. 999/924-4465, US$9.50) is a popular 80-minute show celebrating the traditional and daily lives of the living Maya people; over 300 people from villages around the Yucatán perform dances, rituals, and scenes from everyday life. The show is presented on an open-air stage in the community of X'ocen, located about 14 kilometers (8.5 miles) south of Valladolid. It typically runs on Sundays at 4pm January-March.

SHOPPING

Calzada de los Frailes, the charming colonial street that connects the Iglesia San Bernardino de Siena with central Valladolid, is dotted with boutique shops selling mostly high-end goods—in other words, window shopping at its best! You'll find traditional *jipi* hat makers, folk art shops, custom leather wear, and even an artisanal chocolate shop. Most stores are open 10am-8pm daily.

A tranquil courtyard of workshops and stores, the **Centro Artesanal Zaci** (Calle 39 btwn Calles 40 and 42, no phone, 7am-10pm daily) showcases the work of Maya women from Valladolid and nearby villages who make and sell their *huipiles* and hand-stitched blouses on-site. For a wider selection, the **Mercado de Artesanías** (Calle 39 at Calle 44, 8am-8pm Mon.-Sat., 8am-2pm Sun.) has a decent variety of *guayaberas*, embroidered *huipiles*, hammocks, and other popular handicrafts; haggling is par for the course.

If you're interested in high-end Mexican handicrafts and art, **Yalat** (Calle 41 btwn Calles 40 and 42, tel. 985/856-1969, 9am-8pm daily) is worth a stop. It's pricey, but the quality and variety of items are excellent. There's also a leafy garden toward the back, where artisanal products like chocolate, coffee, and honey are sold.

A family-owned business still chugging away after more than 100 years, the unassuming shop of distiller **Productos Sosa** (Calle 42 btwn Calles 47 and 49, tel. 985/856-2142, 8:30am-1:30pm and 4pm-7:30pm Mon.-Fri., 8:30am-2:30pm Sat.) sells smooth sugar cane liquors infused with ingredients like mint or anise with honey.

Poncho Villa Tequileria (Calle 41 btwn Calles 44 and 46, no phone, tequileriaponchovilla@hotmail.com, 9am-8pm daily) is a small shop specializing in tequila and mescal. A family-owned and run business, staff members are very knowledgeable and often give historical overviews of each liquor. Free *degustaciónes* (tastings) are part of a visit; you'll be introduced to a range of bottles—from mixers to the finest produced. Most folks leave with at least a bottle or two (US$7-250).

FOOD
Yucatecan and Mexican

Near the Iglesia y Ex-Convento San Bernardino de Siena, the low lighting, attentive service, and open-air *palapa* dining room at **Taberna de los Frailes** (Calle 49 at Calle 41A, tel. 985/856-0689, www.tabernadelosfrailes.com, 1pm-11pm daily, US$8-16) set an elegant backdrop for a crowd-pleasing menu of creative Yucatecan mainstays, seafood cocktails, and a few vegetarian entrées. Its upscale bar has some sofa seating and a terrace area shaded by a profuse canopy of passion fruit. The restaurant's proximity to the monastery cenote can draw the odd mosquito; ask the staff for repellent if you need it.

★ **Yerbabuena del Sisal** (Calle 54-A btwn Calles 45 and 49, tel. 985/856-1406, 8am-5pm Tues.-Sun., US$3.50-5) is a whimsical place offering fresh Mexican dishes with a good variety of vegetarian options. Entrées range from tortas (Mexican-style sandwiches) and chilaquiles (tortilla and egg dish) to veggie burgers and stuffed peppers. For a breeze, head to the back where tables are set up in a small outdoor garden patio.

Though doing a brisk business in takeout, **La Palapita de los Tamales** (Calle 42 at Calle 33, no phone, 1pm-4pm and 6pm-10pm Mon.-Fri., US$1.50-4) is a great little sit-down restaurant selling Yucatecan-style tamales. The chef heats the tamales over an open-fire stove at the entrance. Among the most popular are the *chachawa* (chicken and egg tamale served in a tomato sauce), *espelón* (pork, beans, and egg tamale wrapped in a banana leaf), and *colados* (strained corn dough tamales). Seating is in a pleasant garden setting.

El Bazar (central plaza, Calle 39 at Calle 40, US$1.50-4) is a local food court with a dozen or so inexpensive eateries selling mostly premade Yucatecan specialties. Hours are variable, but all are open for breakfast and lunch. Food is hit or miss—take a look at the offerings and decide which looks the freshest. (If anything, avoid the tamales.) Better yet, order something off the menu that hasn't been sitting around, like scrambled eggs or *salbutes*.

Other Specialties

Located next to the bus station, ★ **Café & Bistro Squimz** (Calle 39 near Calle 46, tel. 985/856-4156, www.squimz.com.mx, 7am-11pm daily, US$3-6) is well worth a stop even if you're not on your way out of town. Big breakfasts and sandwiches are the specialties, though the coffee drinks and to-die-for milkshakes shouldn't be overlooked. If you've got a sweet tooth, try the homemade flan napolitano.

Bohemia is alive and well at **Conato** (Calle 40 btwn Calles 45 and 47, tel. 985/856-2586, 5:30pm-2:30am Wed.-Mon., US$3.25-7), where religious iconography and images of Frida Kahlo clutter a dining room of family-style wooden tables set off by a colonial tile floor. Yucatecan-influenced chicken dishes, fresh salads, and serviceable pasta dishes have creative visual flourishes, and the govinda dessert crepes laced with cream and chocolate are almost too pretty to eat. Open until late, it's also a sociable place for drinks or coffee.

Cafeína Bistro (Calzada de los Frailes near Calle 48, tel. 985/856-2654, 8am-2am daily, US$4-7) is a locals' favorite serving up thin-crust pizza, pasta dishes, salads, and even chicken wings in a dimly lit pub-like setting. If you're hungry, try the Yuc-Mex pizza with homemade sausage, cheese, avocado, and pico de gallo (fresh tomato-based topping with cilantro, onion, and serrano chile)—it packs an unexpected punch. Drink specials, from beer to milkshakes, are often offered.

Groceries

Luum Ayni (Calle 37 btwn Calles 40 and 42, tel. 985/107-6379, www.luumayni.com, 10am-4pm Tues.-Sat.) is a small shop selling artisanal honey, jams, and bread, all from a local permaculture center. Every Saturday, a wider selection of organic produce and products is sold.

Bodega La Favorita (Calle 39 btwn Calles 42 and 44, 7am-10pm daily) is a small grocery store with a decent selection of fresh and canned foods. If you have a car, head to the better stocked **Super Che** (Plaza Bella, Calle 42 s/n, 7am-10pm daily), which is on the northern end of town, on the road headed toward Ek' Balam.

ACCOMMODATIONS

Valladolid offers a good selection of simple and mid-range hotels. Most are convenient to the central plaza. All have free Wi-Fi and, except for the hostel, provide parking.

Under US$50

Fan-cooled dormitories at ★ **Hostel Candelaria** (Parque la Candelaria, Calle 35 btwn Calles 42 and 44, tel. 985/856-2267, www.hostelvalladolidyucatan.com, US$10.50 dorm, US$24 s/d with shared bath, US$28 s/d) have 10-14 beds sharing one bathroom, with a low-ceilinged women-only dorm and a roomier mixed dorm. What the dorms lack in space is more than made up for by a sprawling back garden thick with papaya trees and hibiscus, shading an al fresco kitchen and eating area and hammocks tucked in nooks with personal reading lights. Inside the colonial building, you'll find another kitchen, free computers, lockers—including some for charging electronics—and a TV room. Socialize with other travelers over the free breakfast, then rent a bicycle to tour the local cenotes.

Hostal Tunich Naj (Calle 38 btwn Calles 43 and 45, tel. 985/856-0873, valladolidhosting@yahoo.com, US$11 dorm, US$25 s/d, US$32 s/d with a/c) is a small hostel with a colonial feel. Dorms are spacious and breezy with bunks, good mattresses, and lockers. Shared bathrooms are clean and have great water pressure. There's also an outdoor kitchen for guests to use; more common spaces are in the works. If you opt for a private room, ask for one away from the street—it can get noisy, especially at night. Wi-Fi is available and continental breakfast is included.

La Aurora Hotel Colonial (Calle 42 btwn Calles 35 and 37, tel. 985/856-1219, www.hotellaaurora.com, US$36/40 s/d with a/c) is a charming place with two floors of rooms opening onto a sunny courtyard with a pool. Units are basic but very comfortable with good beds, modern bathrooms, flat-screen TVs, and Wi-Fi. Original talavera tile floors, loads of bromeliads, and ironwork lanterns help create a colonial ambience. For a treat, head to the roof, where a whirpool tub, bar, and views of the city make it hard to leave.

Set around a grassy courtyard, **Hotel Zaci** (Calle 44 btwn Calles 37 and 39, tel. 985/856-2167, www.hotelzaci.blogspot.com, US$30-38 s/d with a/c) offers well-kept ground-floor rooms with decorative details like stenciling and ironwork furnishings. The top two floors contain remodeled "premier" rooms, which boast flat-screen TVs, updated decor, and nicer linens; there's also better light on the upper floors. A small, clean pool is a nice plus. On-site parking is available too.

US$50-100

★ **Casa Quetzal** (Calle 51 btwn Calles 50 and 52, tel. 985/856-4796, www.casa-quetzal.com, US$91-110 s/d with a/c, US$116 suite with a/c) is a charming, well-run bed-and-breakfast near the San Bernardino de Siena church. Large, attractive, high-ceilinged rooms surround a pretty garden and swimming pool, while a community kitchen and reading room featuring Oaxacan folk art lend a homey feel. All rooms have hammocks, air-conditioning, Wi-Fi, and cable TV. Free yoga classes are offered daily. The hotel is somewhat removed from the central plaza, but the 10-minute walk there—along the iconic Calzada de los Frailes—is a pleasure itself.

A converted 17th-century casona, **El Mesón del Marqués** (central plaza, Calle 39 btwn Calles 40 and 42, tel. 985/856-2073, www.mesondelmarques.com, US$67-80 s/d standard with a/c, US$77-89 s/d superior with a/c, US$130-169 suite with a/c) has lush courtyards, a gurgling fountain, arches upon arches, and a verdant garden with an egg-shaped pool. Rooms are divided into three categories: standard, superior, and suite. The first two have rustic wood furnishings and ironwork headboards—standards are smaller and have older air-conditioners and TVs. Suites are spacious and sleek, with lots of natural light as well as private terraces. All have Wi-Fi.

Casa San Roque (Calle 41 btwn Calles 38 and 40, tel. 985/856-2642, www.casasanroquevalladolid.com, US$54/63 s/d with a/c) is a six-room hotel with modern rooms that have a colonial feel. All have gleaming tile floors, heavy wood furnishings, and splashes of bright colors; the bathrooms are sleek and spotless. There's a pleasant outdoor sitting area where breakfast is served. A refreshing pool is a welcome sight after a long day of sightseeing. Best of all, Casa San Roque is just one block from the central plaza.

US$100-150

★ **Hotel Posada San Juan** (Parque San Juan, Calle 40 at Calle 49, tel. 985/856-0129, www.posadasanjuan.com, US$110 s/d with a/c) is a gorgeously renovated 19th-century mansion located just a few blocks south of the central plaza. The eight rooms are elegant but homey with high-end furnishings, Mexican folk art, and custom-designed talavera tile

Valladolid Bus Schedule

Departures from Valladolid's **bus station** (Calle 39 at Calle 46, tel. 985/856-3448) include:

Destination	Price	Duration	Schedule
Cancún	US$9.75-12	2.25 hrs	8 departures
Chichén Itzá/Pisté	US$4-5.25	50 mins	every 30-60 mins
Chiquilá (Isla Holbox)	US$5.75	3.5 hrs	2:30am
Cobá	US$3	1 hr	8:30am, 9:30am, 2:45pm
Izamal	US$3.25	2 hrs	12:50pm
Mérida	US$9.75-11	2.25 hrs	19 departures
Playa del Carmen	US$12	2.5-3.5 hrs	7 departures
Tizimín	US$2	1 hr	every 30-75 mins
Tulum	US$7	1.5 hrs	5 departures

floors. Bathrooms bring the outside in with skylights, exposed stone walls, rainshower heads, and tropical plants. A full breakfast buffet is served on the wide and breezy veranda with views of the garden and pool. Service is genuinely friendly, and families are very welcome.

Casa Hamaca Guesthouse (Parque San Juan, Calle 49 at Calle 40, tel. 985/100-4270, www.casahamaca.com, US$110-150 s/d with a/c) faces a quiet church plaza about five blocks south of the main square, making it peaceful and convenient. A lush garden and small pool add to the tranquility, and the guesthouse is spacious and bright. The eight rooms vary in size and decor, though all have dramatic murals. There's an outdoor restaurant (7am-10pm daily), where a hearty complimentary breakfast is served. Massages, Maya cleansings, and other treatments can be arranged, as can rewarding volunteer opportunities or Spanish classes. Casa Hamaca is wheelchair accessible and family friendly too.

Just steps from the central plaza are the combined hotels of **Casa Tía Micha** and **Casa Marlene by Casa Tía Micha** (Calle 39 btwn Calles 38 and 40, tel. 985/856-0499, www.casatiamicha.com, US$98-115 s/d with a/c, US$115-140 suite with a/c). Both are

comfortable, but the feel is very colonial meets grandma—not bad, just unexpected. Think stately wooden doors, talavera tile floors, and vintage furniture alongside wall stenciling, porcelain knickknacks, and rocking chairs. There's a refreshing pool on-site and Wi-Fi—both pluses. A full breakfast is served in the tranquil fruit tree garden, near the old *pozo* (well).

INFORMATION AND SERVICES
Tourist Information

Try your best at prying some useful information from Valladolid's **tourist office** (Palacio Municipal, Calle 40 at Calle 41, tel. 985/856-2529, ext. 114, 8am-9pm Mon.-Sat., 8am-2pm Sun.). At the very least, you should be able to get a map or two, and English is spoken.

Valladolid English Library (Parque San Juan, Calle 49 at Calle 40, tel. 985/100-4270, 9am-1pm Mon.-Sat.) is a lending library with over 2,500 books on the shelves. Visitors will find everything from children's books and beach fiction to Mesoamerican history books and "how-to" reads. Every third Tuesday of the month, there's also a speaker series on areas of interest as varied as public safety, Reiki, and Mayan medicine.

Emergency Services

If you need medical assistance, the modern new **Hospital General** (Av. Chan Yokdzonot, tel. 985/856-2883, 24 hours) is located 4.5 kilometers (2.8 miles) south of the *cuota* highway; for meds only, **Farmacia Yza** (Calle 41 near Calle 40, tel. 985/856-4018, 7am-11pm Mon.-Sat., 8am-10pm Sun.) is just off the central plaza. The **police** (Parque Bacalar, Calle 41 s/n, 24 hours) can be reached at 985/856-2100 or toll-free at 066.

Money

On or near the central plaza, **HSBC** (Calle 41 btwn Calles 42 and 44, 9am-5pm Mon.-Fri., 9am-3pm Sat.), **Banamex** (Calle 41 btwn Calles 42 and 44, 9am-4pm Mon.-Fri.), and **Bancomer** (Calle 40 btwn Calles 39 and 41, 8:30am-4pm Mon.-Fri.) all have ATMs. **Note:** Bancomer charges an exorbitant US$6 for ATM withdrawals by foreign cards.

Media and Communications

A tiny **post office** (Calle 40 btwn Calles 39 and 41, 8am-4:30pm Mon.-Fri., 8am-1pm Sat.) sits on the central plaza. There's free Wi-Fi in the central plaza, and we assume that the signal's strongest where the laptop-toting teens congregate in front of the Palacio Municipal. For computer access, try **Phonet** (Calle 46 at Calle 41, 7am-midnight daily, US$0.70/hour). If it's full, head a block down to **Ciber Fenix** (Calle 41 btwn Calles 44 and 46, 8am-11pm daily), which charges the same per hour.

Immigration

The **immigration office** (Carretera Valladolid-Felipe Carrillo Puerto Km. 2.5, tel. 985/856-2075, 9am-1pm Mon.-Fri.) is located about three kilometers (1.9 miles) south of Valladolid on the road to Chichimilá.

Laundry

The bustling **Lavandería Espumita** (Calle 39 btwn Calles 34 and 36 at Calle 33, no phone, 8am-8pm Mon.-Sat., 8am-1pm Sun.) charges US$0.75 per kilo (2.2 pounds).

GETTING THERE AND AROUND

Bus

Valladolid's **bus terminal** (Calle 39 at Calle 46, tel. 985/856-3448) is an easy walk from the central plaza, or if you have a lot of bags, a cheap taxi ride.

Taxi

Taxis are relatively easy to flag down, especially around the central plaza, and typically cost US$1.50-2 around town.

Colectivos (shared vans and taxis) to Pisté and Chichén Itzá (US$2, 40 minutes) depart approximately every 30 minutes from Calle 39 near the ADO bus terminal, and those for Mérida (US$11.25, 2.5 hours) leave from the terminal. Shared taxis for Cancún (US$11, 2.5 hours) congregate at Calle 38 between Calles 39 and 41 3am-10pm daily.

Car

If you arrive from the toll highway (*cuota*), you'll enter town via Calle 42 (and return on Calle 40). It's a sobering US$17.25 toll driving in from Cancún, US$10 from Mérida (Kantunil), and US$4.25 to Chichén Itzá (Pisté). In the center, eastbound Calle 41 and westbound Calle 39 access the free highway (*libre*).

To rent a car in town, **Portal Maya** (Calle 41 btwn Calles 38 and 40, tel. 985/856-2513, portalmaya@hotmail.com, 9am-1:30pm and 4pm-8pm Mon.-Sat.) is your lone option; economy cars typically run US$40-47 with insurance included. Custom tours also can be arranged.

Bicycle

Bikes can be rented at **Refraccionaría de Bicicletas Silva** (Calle 44 btwn Calles 39 and 41, tel. 985/856-3667, 8:30am-7pm daily) for US$0.65 per hour or US$4.50 per day. For a variety of bikes to choose from, including tandems, go to **MexiGo Tours** (Calle 43 btwn Calles 40 and 42, tel. 985/856-0777, www.mexigotours.com, 8:30am-8pm); bikes rent for US$1-2 per hour or US$5-12.50 per day.

Ek' Balam

Ek' Balam, Maya for Black Jaguar, is a unique and fascinating archaeological site whose significance has only recently been revealed and appreciated. Serious restoration of Ek' Balam didn't begin until the mid-1990s, and it was then that an incredibly well-preserved stucco frieze was discovered, hidden under an innocuous stone facade near the top of the site's main pyramid. The discovery rocketed Ek' Balam into preeminence, first among Maya scholars and more slowly among travelers in the Yucatán, once the frieze was excavated and opened to the public. Much remains a mystery about Ek' Balam, but archaeologists believe it was founded around 300 BC and became an important commercial center, its influence peaking in AD 700-1100.

Ek' Balam sees a fraction of the tourists that visit other Maya sites, despite being in close proximity to Valladolid, Cancún, and Mérida. The site is small enough that even an hour is enough to appreciate its treasures; even better, it's a tranquil place that doesn't get besieged by mammoth tour groups.

ORIENTATION

Ek' Balam is located 30 kilometers (19 miles) north of Valladolid, off Highway 295. Ek' Balam **village** is two kilometers (1.2 miles) west, with two good options for accommodations and one restaurant; for other alternatives and traveler services, head to Valladolid.

★ EK' BALAM ARCHAEOLOGICAL ZONE

Entering **Ek' Balam** (8am-5pm daily, US$11.50), you'll pass through a low thick wall and an elegant corbeled arch. Walls are rare in Maya cities, and were most commonly used for defense, as in the cases of Becán and Tulum. Ek' Balam's low thick walls would not have slowed marauding rivals, however, and so they most likely served to enforce social divisions, with some areas off-limits (but not out of view!) to all but the elite. They may also have been decorative—the city possessed great aesthetic flair, as the entry arch and the famous stucco frieze demonstrate.

Acrópolis and El Trono

The highlight of Ek' Balam is an artful and remarkably pristine stucco frieze known as **El Trono** (The Throne), located under a protective *palapa* roof two-thirds of the way up Ek' Balam's main pyramid, the **Acrópolis.** A steep stairway leads up the center of the pyramid, and a platform to the left of the stairs provides visitors a close-up view of El Trono.

About 85 percent of El Trono is the original stucco. Often structures like this would have been painted blue or red, but not so here. In fact, shortly after it was built, El Trono was sealed behind a stone wall 50-60 centimeters (19-24 inches) thick. It remained there untouched until the 1990s, when restoration workers accidentally—and fortuitously—dislodged one of the protective stones, revealing the hidden chamber beneath.

The tall, winged figures immediately catch your eye, as they appear so much like angels. In fact, they are high priests. Notice that one is deformed—his left arm is longer than the right and has only four fingers. The Maya considered birth defects to be a sign of divinity, and the priest depicted here may have risen to his position precisely because of his deformation.

Directly over the door is a seated figure (unfortunately, the head is missing). This represents Ukit Kan Le'k Tok', one of Ek' Balam's former rulers, described in inscriptions as the "king of kings," and the person for whom El Trono was built and dedicated. A tomb was discovered in the chamber behind the frieze, containing thousands of jade, gold, obsidian, and ceramic artifacts left as offerings to this powerful leader. The small face at the

Ek' Balam Archaeological Zone

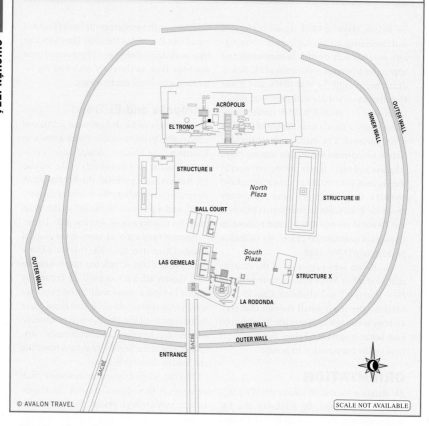

ACRÓPOLIS

EL TRONO

INNER WALL

OUTER WALL

STRUCTURE II

North Plaza

STRUCTURE III

BALL COURT

South Plaza

LAS GEMELAS

STRUCTURE X

LA RODONDA

INNER WALL

OUTER WALL

OUTER WALL

SACBÉ

SACBÉ

ENTRANCE

© AVALON TRAVEL

SCALE NOT AVAILABLE

king-figure's navel represents a rival whom he defeated in war.

Viewed as a whole, the frieze is unmistakably a Chenes-style monster mouth: a huge stylized mask in which the doorway represents the gaping mouth of a high god. The pointed upper and lower teeth are easy to spot, as are the spiral eyes. Monster mouths are never mundane, but this one is especially elaborate: Notice how two beautifully crafted figures straddle the lower eyelids, while hoisting the upper lids with their shoulders. At least five more figures, plus lattice patterns and other designs, adorn the rest of the mask.

Before heading down, climb the rest of the way to the top of the Acrópolis for a panoramic vista. At 32 meters (105 feet) high and 158 meters (515 feet) wide, the Acrópolis is bigger than Chichén Itzá's main pyramid, and in fact is one of the largest Maya pyramids ever built, a detail that's often overlooked amid the excitement surrounding El Trono. The scene from atop is memorable; with the exception of the odd telephone and radio tower, and the site's visitors center, the view of the broad Yucatecan landscape is probably not all that different than the one Maya priests and kings enjoyed from this very same vantage point more than a thousand years ago.

South Plaza

Descending the pyramid, you can see that Ek' Balam is a fairly small site, with two midsize plazas (north and south), a ball court in the middle, and its main structures crowded together.

On the south side of the south plaza stands **La Rodonda,** or the Oval Palace. A squat midsize structure, La Rodonda has an eclectic array of overlapping lines and curves, stairs, and terraces. It underwent numerous iterations, as did virtually all Maya temples, but the result here was especially eclectic. Archaeologists suspect La Rodonda was used for astronomical observations, and the discovery of several richly adorned tombs suggest it had a ceremonial purpose as well.

Flanking La Redonda are **Las Gemelas** (The Twins), known as Structure 17. As the plaque indicates, these identical structures are perhaps the best example of Ek' Balam's particular architectural style. Having perfected the use of stucco, Ek' Balam's builders did not concern themselves with precise masonry, as the stones would be covered in a thick stucco cap. However, stucco proved much less resilient to erosion, and centuries later the structures here appear shabbier than even much older ones, like in Campeche's Río Bec region, where stucco was less common and stone blocks were more carefully cut and fitted. Recent excavations have focused on these two buildings, where intriguing freehand marks and paintings—perhaps akin to graffiti today—have been discovered.

Practicalities

Guides can be hired at the entrance to the ruins (US$50, 1-1.5 hours, available in Spanish or English). French- and Italian-speaking guides are sometimes available. Additionally, US$4 is charged to enter with a video camera; parking is free.

CENOTE X'CANCHÉ

A short distance from the Ek' Balam archaeological site, **Cenote X'Canché** (cell tel. 985/100-9815, www.ekbalam.com.mx,

9am-3:30pm daily, US$2) is an excellent community-run ecotourism project, and a must-do add-on to a ruins visit. From Ek' Balam's parking area, a dirt road winds 1.5 kilometers (0.9 mile) through low dense forest to the cenote, which is 14 meters (46 feet) deep and nearly circular, with sheer walls and tree roots descending picturesquely to cool, clean water. A wooden staircase leads to the water's edge, great for swimming. It's a pleasant shaded walk in, though many visitors rent bikes (US$6 for 3 hours) or take advantage of the on-site bike taxis (US$6.25 pp roundtrip). Facilities include restrooms, shower and changing areas, a restaurant, *palapa*-shaded hammocks for reading and hanging out, and comfortable overnight accommodations in simple cabins (US$28 s/d/t) or in campsites (US$6.25 pp). Rappelling from the cenote edge or ziplining across it can each be arranged for an additional fee (US$5-25, half price child under 12); there are also admission packages (US$19) that include those activities plus bicycle rental.

CENOTE SAK' AWA

Cenote Sak' Awa (no phone, 11am-sunset daily, US$3.75) makes for a rewarding postruins visit if you have a car. The trip there is an adventure in itself—a back road from Ek' Balam through the Mayan villages of Hunukú and Dzalbay (remarkably big signage leads visitors through the countryside to the cenote). You'll pass men on bikes loaded down with wood or crops, women balancing jugs of water on their heads, and skinny dogs running after your car. Once there, a 350-meter (0.2 mile) trail leads to the entrance—a hole in the ground with a rickety staircase leading down. As your eyes adjust, you'll see you're headed to an island in a perfectly round cavern—a donut hole, of sorts—surrounded by crystal clear teal water. Openings in the cavern roof let in light and long tree roots. The water itself is refreshing and cool—perfect on a hot afternoon. You'll see small catfish and turtles swimming past, with an occasional swallow swooping down from above to skim the surface of the water. It's an eerily gorgeous site with few visitors, so you're likely to have it to yourself. Facilities include changing rooms and a questionable toilet. It's located 15 kilometers (9.3 miles) east of Ek' Balam.

CENOTES AGUA DULCE

Absolutely gorgeous but occasionally overrun by organized tour groups are the **Cenotes Agua Dulce** (tel. 985/856-2200, 8am-5:30pm daily, US$2.50-4.50 à la carte cenotes, US$13.25 all cenotes). It is made up of four separate cenotes: **Agua Dulce, Palomitas, Las Cavernas,** and **El Oasis.** The first two are classic cenotes—deep underground pools of turquoise water surrounded by stalagmites and stalactites; they're reached by long staircases starting at ground level and leading down into the earth several dozen meters. The second two are not for swimming—one is dry (so is actually a cavern, not a cenote), and the other is too shallow to swim in. They are worth a visit if you can avoid the tour groups, which typically stop here on Mondays and Fridays. There's a restaurant on-site serving buffet lunch (US$7), changing areas, and bathrooms. Life vests are included. It's located just north of the village of Yalcobá,

about 20 kilometers (12.4 miles) from Ek' Balam and 24 kilometers (15 miles) from Valladolid.

FOOD AND ACCOMMODATIONS

In the Maya village near the ruins, ★ **Genesis Retreat Ek' Balam** (cell tel. 985/101-0277, www.genesisretreat.com, US$45 s/d with shared bath, US$45 with shared bath and a/c, US$65-73 s/d, US$77 s/d/t/q) has nine rooms and *cabañas* set on a leafy enclosed property, all different in style. Each faces a natural bio-filtered pool in a jungle garden. Morning pastries and coffee are included in the rate; full breakfasts (US$8.50) and three-course dinners (US$12) are available to guests only. There's true environmental commitment at work here: Recycled materials were used in its construction, its 101-hectare (250-acre) organic farm provides most of the produce for its meals, and there's a solar hot-water system and extensive greywater reuse on the property. The hardworking Canadian owner also offers tours of the village and local artisan workshops, and is involved in a number of educational projects around town. Be aware that a number of friendly

Cenote Sak' Awa

pooches lounge about the property—fine if you like dogs, but not everyone's thing.

Dolcemente Ek' Balam (tel. 999/913-9670, vacanzadolce@gmail.com, US$38 s/d, US$47 s/d with a/c) doesn't compete with Genesis for Zen or eco-ambience; it's simply a comfortable hotel. Spacious rooms have tile floors, decent beds, private hot-water bathrooms, and fans (except for two rooms with air-conditioning). Upstairs units have higher ceilings and better ventilation—making them worth requesting—and all look onto the hotel's somewhat unkempt garden. The on-site restaurant (10am-11pm Tues.-Sun., US$8-14) serves up solid Italian food, including fresh handmade ravioli, fettuccini, and other pasta. Meals are served in a large, tasteful dining room.

Cenote X'Canché (cell tel. 985/100-9815, www.ekbalam.com.mx, US$28 s/d/t) rents three well-built and solar-powered *palapa cabañas* near the cenote, each with queen bed and a hammock (plus mosquito nets). The windows have good screens, and there's hot water and a fan. There also are campsites (US$6.25 pp)—BYO gear. A three-course lunch or dinner at its restaurant costs US$8; breakfast is US$7.

GETTING THERE AND AROUND
Car

From Valladolid, drive north on Highway 295 toward Tizimín for about 17 kilometers (10.5 miles), past the town of Temozón, to a well-marked right-hand turnoff to Ek' Balam. From there, drive another 11 kilometers (6.8 miles) to an intersection: Turn left to reach the village and accommodations, or continue straight to reach the archaeological site.

Taxi

Colectivo (shared) taxis from Valladolid to the village of Ek' Balam leave from a stop on Calle 44 between Calles 35 and 37 (US$3.25); mornings have the most frequent departures. Otherwise, a private taxi costs about US$15 for up to four people. If you're planning on visiting the ruins only, you can often negotiate with the driver to wait there for a couple of hours and bring you back for around US$25.

the lush grounds at Genesis Retreat Ek' Balam

Río Lagartos and San Felipe

A little more than 100 kilometers (62 miles) north of Valladolid, the Reserva de la Bíosfera de Ría Lagartos (Biosphere Reserve of Ría Lagartos) is justly famous for the huge colonies of flamingos that nest and feed there. Designated a biosphere reserve in 1999, it covers over 63,000 hectares (155,700 acres); beyond flamingos, the reserve also is home to 395 other bird species. Río Lagartos is the nearest town to the reserve. Most tour operators offering excursions into the reserve are based here; travelers also will find small inns and basic restaurants. San Felipe is just west of Río Lagartos and makes for a pleasant afternoon visit. If you have a car, consider staying in Río Lagartos and driving to San Felipe for a post-tour meal.

Río Lagartos overlooks a massive estuary and national park.

RÍO LAGARTOS

Every year tens of thousands of pink and cerise *Phoenicopterus ruber ruber* flamingos come to Río Lagartos to feed and nest in the salt flats at the end of the long coastal lagoon, or *ría,* extending east of town. It's also a favorite haunt of plovers, white egrets, herons, cormorants, hawks, and pelicans (not to mention bird-watchers).

Río Lagartos itself is an isolated community that wouldn't really merit a visit were it not for the flamingo and bird-watching tours. The population is a mix of longtime local families and an ever-fluctuating supply of itinerant workers, many from as far away as Chiapas and Veracruz. Most come to work at the nearby Las Coloradas salt factory (salt has been harvested along the Gulf coast since pre-Hispanic times, and remains one of its most important exports today); some say the constant ebb and flow of semipermanent workers partly explains why Río Lagartos exhibits so little community spirit.

Sights
★ **FLAMINGO TOURS**

It's possible to see flamingos in Río Lagartos year-round, but the highest concentration is present April-July and October-February. The earlier period is brooding season, and visitors are not allowed to approach the nesting area lest parent flamingos (skittish by nature) accidentally knock their lone eggs out of the nests; you can still visit the feeding area, however. During the latter period, you'll likely see juvenile flamingos beginning to color. Flamingos are gray or white when they hatch and gradually grow pink from beta carotene in their diet, mostly from algae and brine shrimp. At three months, the black feathers along their wings begin to grow.

Tours are offered 6am-5pm daily, but early morning is the best time to go. It takes almost 45 minutes to get to the flamingo sites, and leaving early lets you see more birds along the way. The water is also calmer in the morning. Binoculars aren't absolutely necessary but nice to have; bring your own or ask to borrow a pair.

Located on the west side of town, **Río Lagartos Adventures** (Ría Maya Restaurant, Calle 19 at Calle 14, cell. tel. 986/100-8390, www.riolagartosnaturetours.com) is the most experienced and recommended tour operator, with English- and Italian-speaking guides. Standard trips last two hours and include short stops at a spot called Las Salinas, where you can take a mineral-rich mud bath, and at the beach opposite town, where you wash it all off (US$90 for up to 6 people). Visitors wanting more time can book a three-hour tour that goes deeper into the mangroves or stays longer on the beach (US$119 for up to 6 people). Evening boat tours to spot crocodiles in the reserve also can be arranged (US$90 for up to 6 people). Tours do not include US$2.50 admission per person to enter the reserve. If you call ahead, guides will combine small groups so visitors can split the cost of the tour.

Another option is to take a flamingo tour with the local cooperative (cell. tel. 986/107-3082). It's effectively the same boat trip for less (US$55 for up to 6 people). The main differences are that the boats tend to be older and less comfortable; also, guides typically aren't bilingual. Crocodile tours as well as fishing trips also can be arranged. Look for the coop's kiosk on the waterfront, just south of Hotel Villa de Pescadores.

BALNEARIO CHIQUILÁ

On the eastern end of town, **Balneario Chiquilá** (free) is a freshwater swimming hole just steps from the estuary. It's a popular spot for locals—on any given day, you'll find kids splashing and cannon-balling into the refreshing clear water. Small palapas provide shade and a place to chill out once you've cooled off. Nearby, there's a lookout tower with views of the estuary. There's also an **open-air restaurant** (9am-7pm daily, US$4-8) serving fresh fish plates and classic Mexican dishes. On the far end of the parking lot, look for the wooden boardwalk leading through a mangrove forest to two springs surrounded by lush vegetation; swimming is not permitted.

PLAYA CANCUNCITO

If you're aching for beach time, Playa Cancuncito provides an easy fix. A windswept beach with tawny sand and calm teal waters, it's a perfect place for beachcombing or just sitting back with a paperback novel. Be

flamingos in flight

sure to bring your own snacks and plenty of water—there's nothing here but surf and sand. If you have a car, follow the road signs to the town of Las Coloradas; you'll hit Cancuncito immediately after you've crossed the bridge (and before you arrive at Las Coloradas). You also can hire a boat to take you (US$20 for up to 6 people); ask at your hotel or at the local cooperative (cell. tel. 986/107-3082) about arranging the boat trip.

Food

Spy on pelicans at the dockside **Restaurante Isla Contoy** (end of Calle 19, tel. 986/862-0000, 8am-8pm daily, US$6-9). It's a good spot for breakfast—specials mostly include eggs, beans, and coffee—and the lunch and dinner menu has mostly seafood, including *filete,* shrimp cocktail, and ceviche.

For super-fresh fish, try no-frills **Restaurant Las Gaviotas** (waterfront btwn Calles 12 and 14, 9am-7pm daily, US$7-11). A family affair, the catch arrives daily and the fisherman's wife cooks it up and adds a few sides.

Accommodations

Hotel Punta Ponto (waterfront at Calle 19, tel. 986/862-0509, US$28-38 s/d with a/c) is a basic hotel with small, clean rooms that have air-conditioning and minifridges. All are on the 2nd story of the owner's home and open onto a wide veranda with sweeping views of the estuary. There are plenty of outdoor chairs and tables, making it a perfect place to relax after a day of exploring and bird-watching. Breakfast is included in the rate.

★ **Hotel Villa de Pescadores** (waterfront at Calle 14, tel. 986/106-9579, www.hotelriolagartos.com.mx, US$48-52 s/d with a/c) has 14 rooms with spectacular views of the estuary and the Gulf of Mexico beyond. Each is clean and spacious and has a private balcony or terrace. All have quiet air-conditioners and satellite TV (flat screens in some). Be sure to head to the roof to get a bird's-eye view of the town and its surroundings waters. Breakfast is included in the rate and served at the on-site restaurant. Wi-Fi is available too.

Facing the central park, **Hotel Tabasco Río** (Calle 12 at Calle 13, tel. 986/862-0116, www.tabascoriohotel.com, US$44-56 s/d with a/c, US$62 suite with a/c) has modern rooms with TVs and fridges, orange accent walls, and updated bathrooms, all illuminated by fluorescent lights that shudder and flicker to life. Two mini-suites have contemporary efficiency kitchens that could use a deep-cleaning. There's a sunny atrium, and Wi-Fi is available. Ask for a quieter room away from the street.

Information and Services

There is no tourist office in Río Lagartos, but the folks at Río Lagartos Adventures are knowledgeable and happy to help. Nor is there a bank or ATM, or immediate plans for either. For medical attention, head to Valladolid.

Getting There and Around

Noreste has bus service from Río Lagartos from its **terminal** a few blocks from Restaurante Isla Contoy (end of Calle 19). Departures for San Felipe (US$0.50, 15 minutes) continue to Tizimín (US$2, 1.5 hours, 10 departures, 5:30am-5:15pm); three buses continue to Mérida (US$9, 4.5 hours, 5:30am, 6:30am, and 3:30pm), or you can connect in Tizimín. Note that the last bus to Tizimín usually arrives too late to catch the last connecting bus to Mérida.

Noreste also provides **second-class bus service** from Mérida (Calle 67 btwn Calles 50 and 52, US$9, 4 hours, 5:30pm daily) as well as from Tizimín (Calle 47 btwn Calles 46 and 48, tel. 986/863-2034, US$2, 1.5 hours, 8 departures, 4am-7:45pm).

Río Lagartos is at the end of Highway 295, about 100 kilometers (62 miles) north of Valladolid by car. From the free or toll highways, follow signs toward Tizimín, but skip the center by taking the western bypass road just before it—follow the Mérida/Highway 176 signs. Continue on the bypass road for 12 kilometers (7.5 miles) until it rejoins the Río Lagartos/Highway 295 route.

SAN FELIPE

While Río Lagartos is somewhat downtrodden, San Felipe has well-maintained streets and sidewalks, brightly painted houses—including many made from wood on the main drag of Calle 10—and a clean, attractive waterfront promenade. It makes for a nice afternoon side trip from Río Lagartos to take in what life is like in a typical fishing village.

If you need a bit more action than people watching, San Felipe has excellent sportfishing, especially for flat-water targets like tarpon, snook, bonefish, and permit. **Yucatán Fly Fishing Adventures** (toll-free U.S. tel. 800/552-2729, www.yucatanflyfishing.com) offers recommended day trips as well as multiday tours from here.

Another reason to travel to San Felipe is ★ **Restaurant El Popular Vaselina** (Calle 9 at Calle 12, tel. 986/862-2083, 8am-7pm daily, US$5-8). A big thatch-roofed restaurant, it's known throughout the peninsula for its excellent, super-fresh seafood. Try the ceviche—it's usually an appetizer, but the servings here are big enough to make a meal, and then some. Fronting San Felipe's pleasant promenade, the tables have nice views of and breezes off the water. Service is friendly and prompt.

Information and Services

San Felipe has no bank, ATM, or tourist office. A small **medical clinic** is on Calle 15 at Calle 10-A, but is open limited hours only.

Getting There and Around

The **Noreste bus terminal** is on the main street entering town, but may be closed if there's no imminent arrival or departure. Check Río Lagartos for departure times; buses from there stop in San Felipe about 15 minutes later en route to Tizimín (US$2.50, 1 hour) or Mérida (US$9.50, 4.5 hours).

Second-class buses head to San Felipe daily from Mérida's Noreste terminal (Calle 67 btwn Calles 50 and 52, US$9.50, 3.5 hours, 5:30pm) as well as from Tizimín's Noreste terminal (Calle 47 btwn Calles 46 and 48, tel. 986/863-2034, US$2.50, 2 hours, 8 departures, 4am-7:45pm).

If you're driving, the well-signed cutoff to San Felipe is a few kilometers (less than 2 miles) before entering Río Lagartos.

TIZIMÍN

There's no real reason to stop in Tizimín, a busy, nondescript town, unless you're switching buses or staying the night on your way to or from Río Lagartos.

San Felipe's sleepy main avenue

Food and Accommodations

Just a couple of blocks from the bus station, **Hotel 49** (Calle 49 btwn Calles 46 and 48, tel. 986/863-2136, www.hotel49.com, US$32 s/d with a/c) is a solid option if you're stuck in Tizimín. The tile-floored rooms are surprisingly clean and well kept, and cable TV, free Wi-Fi, and a tidy little café make it even better. There's lots of secure parking in a central courtyard shaded by what looks like an enormous sail from a boat.

Pizza Messina's (central park, Calle 53 at Calles 50, tel. 986/863-6940, www.messinaspizza.com, 11am-midnight daily, US$3.75-6) is a 40-year stalwart serving up tasty pizza pies, cold and hot subs, and pasta dishes. In the evening, take your eats to a bench outside to admire the dramatically lit Iglesia de los Santos Reyes, or take a seat at a booth and enjoy the arctic air-conditioning.

Getting There and Around

Tizimín's shiny **ADO/Oriente terminal** (Calle 46 btwn Calles 45 and 47, tel. 986/863-2424) makes for a pleasant and comfortable stopover. Departures include:

- Cancún: US$7-9, 3 hours, 5 departures, 5:15am-6pm

- Mérida: US$7, 3 hours, 5:30am, 11am, and 4pm

- Valladolid: US$1.50, 1 hour, 8 departures, 4:30am-8:15pm

The **Noreste terminal** (Calle 47 btwn Calles 46 and 48, tel. 986/863-2034) is around the corner and has second-class service to:

- Chiquilá: US$5, 2.5 hours, 11am, 1pm, and 2:15pm

Restaurant El Popular Vaselina is a San Felipe institution.

- Río Lagartos and San Felipe: US$2-2.50, 1.5-2 hours, 8 departures, 4am-7:45pm

Noreste also has first-class service to Cancún (US$7, 3 hours, 5:30am and 6:45am) and Mérida (US$7, 3 hours, 6 departures, 5:30am-6:30pm).

For faster and more frequent service to Mérida, shared air-conditioned vans called *colectivos* (US$4, 2 hours) depart approximately every 75 minutes—or when full—5:30am-2:30pm from the corner of Calles 47 and 46. They arrive next to Mérida's Noreste terminal.

Mérida, the Puuc Route, and Campeche

Look for ★ to find recommended
sights, activities, dining, and lodging.

Highlights

★ **Museo Regional de Antropología "Palacio Cantón":** It's no surprise that a state brimming with ancient ruins would have an anthropology museum as outstanding as this one, with fascinating displays on Maya art, astronomy, architecture, mathematics, all housed in one of Mérida's finest colonial mansions (page 313).

★ **Domingo en Mérida:** Every Sunday, locals and tourists alike throng to Mérida's main plaza to munch on street food, watch dance performances, and share in the pleasure of simply being there, while a long stretch of Paseo de Montejo is closed to traffic (page 318).

★ **Convento de San Antonio de Padua:** Izamal's famous church-convent is awesome for its size—only the Vatican has a bigger church atrium—but troubling for having been built atop one of the Maya's most sacred sites; some of the pilfered stones are still visible in the convent's thick walls (page 353).

★ **Uxmal Archaeological Zone:** From the soaring Pyramid of the Magician to the stately Governor's Palace, Uxmal is one of the most remarkable of all Maya ruins. Plan on spending more than a day—Uxmal has a nighttime light show and a slew of caves, villages, and smaller ruins nearby (page 361).

★ **Cenotes de Cuzamá:** It's hard to say what's more fun—clattering down colonial-era rails on a horse-drawn trolley through abandoned henequen fields, or climbing down a rickety ladder through a crack in the earth to swim in the cool iridescent waters of ancient cenotes (page 383).

★ **The City Walls:** Built three centuries ago to ward off marauding pirates, the massive

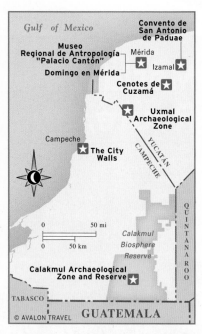

stone walls and imposing bastions that encircle Campeche City's colonial center have been converted into picturesque elevated walkways and first-rate museums (page 395).

★ **Calakmul Archaeological Zone and Reserve:** Deep in a nature reserve, Calakmul is home to toucans, monkeys, and even pumas and jaguars, if you're lucky enough to spot them. And the ancient Maya city here covers 70 square kilometers (27 square miles) and has 6,000 structures, including one of the largest pyramids the Maya ever built (page 414).

If there's a heart of the Yucatán Peninsula, surely it's Mérida and its rich surroundings.

Mérida is one of Mexico's finest colonial cities, with spectacular museums and galleries, daily performances and cultural events, and a genuinely warm and welcoming population. On Sundays, the city center (and many surrounding blocks) are closed to traffic and open to families, street performances, and food carts. Outside of Mérida is Izamal, another lovely colonial town, known for its historic church and the mustard-yellow hue of many homes and buildings. Also reachable in a day are the coastal towns of Progreso, a nice beach getaway, and Celestún, where you can tour a nearby flamingo reserve. South of Mérida is the utterly amazing Puuc Route, home to must-see Maya ruins like Uxmal and Kabah, plus small villages, gaping caves, and cool cenotes. Farther still is the oft-overlooked state of Campeche; its capital, Campeche City, rivals Mérida for its colorful city center and historical attractions. The city was plagued by pirate attacks, and walls and forts built for defense have been put to use as museums and galleries. Meanwhile, southern Campeche boasts incredible (and little-visited) Maya ruins, including Calakmul, located deep in a nature reserve teeming with wildlife.

PLANNING YOUR TIME

This chapter covers a lot of ground—the more time you can budget here, the better! Merida is well worth 3-4 full days, and is especially lively on Sundays. Plan on a day trip to the Gulf coast beaches at Progreso and another jaunt (possibly overnight) to Izamal and surroundings. The Puuc Route also brims with attractions; there are daylong tours from Mérida, but you can easily fill 2-3 full days visiting Maya ruins, colonial villages, and unique caves and cenotes. West of Mérida, the flamingo reserve at Celestún is best visited in the early morning or early evening. And from there is the state of Campeche—budget two days for Campeche City, a colonial gem with nearby ruins and haciendas, and another 2-3 days for the majestic archaeological sites and nature reserves in the Río Bec region. Bus service is limited outside the cities; having your own car is highly recommended.

Previous: Campeche's forts now house memorable museums; Becan ruins in southern Campeche.
Above: doorway in Campeche City.

Mérida, the Puuc Route, and Campeche

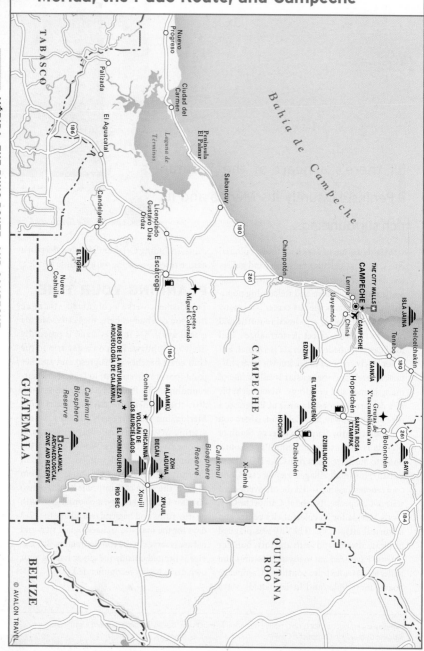

© AVALON TRAVEL

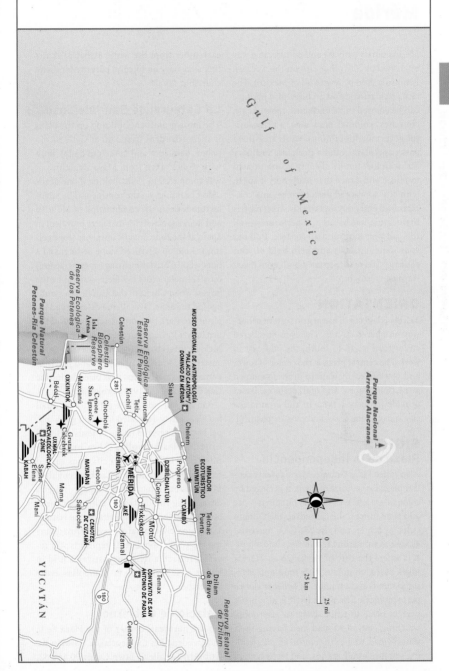

Gulf of Mexico

Parque Nacional
Arrecife Alacranes

YUCATÁN

Reserva Ecológica
de los Petenes

Parque Natural
Petenes-Ría Celestún

Reserva Ecológica
Estatal El Palmar

MUSEO REGIONAL DE ANTROPOLOGÍA
"PALACIO CANTÓN" Y
DOMINGO EN MÉRIDA

Reserva Estatal
de Dzilam

Isla
Arena
Celestún
Biosphere
Reserve

Celestún

Sisal

Chelem

Progreso

Chicxulub
Puerto

Telchac
Puerto

Dzilam
de Bravo

Temax

Cenotillo

Bécal

OXKINTOK

Maxcanú

Chocholá
San Ignacio
Cenote

Kinchil

Tetiz

Hunucmá

Umán

Calcehtok

Gruttas

UXMAL
ARCHAEOLOGICAL
ZONE

KABAH

Santa
Elena

Mani

Mama

MAYAPAN

Tecoh

Sacalum

CENOTES
DE CUZAMÁ

Izamal

CONVENTO DE SAN
ANTONIO DE PADUA

MÉRIDA

AKE

Tixkokob

Motul

Conkal

DZIBILCHALTÚN

X'CAMBÓ

MIRADOR
ECOTURÍSTICO
UAYMITÚN

281

180

180

0   25 km

0   25 mi

Mérida

Mérida bursts with art and culture, in a way unrivaled by any other city on the Yucatán Peninsula (and by few in all of Mexico). The city's rich artistic and architectural heritage can be enjoyed in its museums, monuments, churches, colonial mansions, and beautiful government buildings, while tree-lined parks and plazas offer a peek into ordinary Mexican life. But it's the city's commitment to music and dance that really sets it apart, with city-sponsored performances and concerts held every day and weekly street parties that feature live bands and performers—all this, all year long, and all for free. Pull out your dancing shoes and grab hold of your camera—you're sure to need both even if you stay just one night.

ORIENTATION

Mérida is laid out in a neat grid pattern of one-way numbered streets. The even-numbered streets run north to south, the odd east to west. The central plaza is the center of town, and you can easily walk to most downtown attractions, shops, and marketplaces. Buses provide frequent service in and around the city and outlying areas, and cabs are plentiful.

SIGHTS
Plaza de la Independencia

Also called Plaza Grande, Mérida's leafy central plaza is the heart of town; it is ringed by colonial-era and 19th-century buildings—city and state offices, the cathedral, the Olimpo cultural center, and the MACAY museum, as well as numerous restaurants and shops. It is where the core of Domingo en Mérida takes place, complete with food and *artesanía* stands and a number of *ballet folklórico* performances. The plaza itself is also just a perfect place to while away an afternoon, watching *guayabera*-clad men having their shoes shined, women in colorful *huipiles* tending small sidewalk stands, and teens texting

each other from the white S-shaped chairs that were once an integral part of Méridiano courtship rituals.

La Catedral de San Ildefonso

The most prominent building on the plaza is the **cathedral** (Calle 60 at Calle 61, no phone, 6am-1pm and 4pm-7pm daily). Built with stones taken from Maya structures, it was completed in 1598, making it one of the oldest buildings on the continent. The architecture reflects the combination of Moorish and Renaissance styles that were prevalent in Spain at the time. Inside, immense stone columns hold up a latticed stone ceiling, and a huge wood Christ measuring 8 meters (26 feet) on a 12-meter cross (39 feet)—said to be the largest wood Christ in the Americas—stands behind the altar. Overall, the exterior and interior are stark in comparison to some of the ornately adorned churches in other parts of Mexico; this is partly owing to the traditional austerity of Franciscan design, and partly to damage and looting that took place during the Caste War and the 1910 Revolution.

On the left side of the cathedral, a small but elaborately decorated iron and glass chapel houses a revered image of Jesus called **El Cristo de las Ampollas** (The Christ of the Blisters). The original crucifix was carved from a tree in Ichmul that had been engulfed in flames but remained undamaged; later a devastating fire destroyed Ichmul's church but only left blister-like welts on the statues. Unfortunately, the statue was destroyed during the revolution, but its replica is still revered. In fact, a religious festival is held in honor of El Cristo de las Ampollas every September.

Palacio de Gobierno

On the northeast corner of the Plaza de la Independencia is the neoclassic **Palacio de Gobierno** (Calle 61 btwn Calles 60 and 62,

Mérida

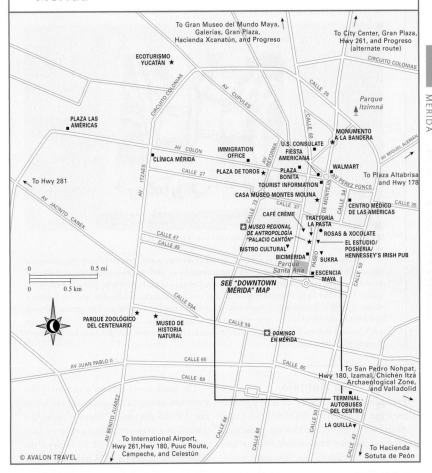

8am-10pm daily, free), the seat of government offices for the state of Yucatán. Inaugurated in 1892, it contains several impressive abstract murals by the famous Mérida-born artist Fernando Castro Pacheco. Created between 1971 and 1974 and showcased along the staircase and in the upper galleries, these works depict the history of the region—from the time of the ancient Maya to modern-day Mexico. Restoration of these works was completed in 2004 under the supervision of Pacheco himself by four professional restoration artists from the Centro de Restauración de Bellas Artes in Mexico City.

On the west side of the Plaza de la Independencia is the **Palacio Municipal** (Calle 62 btwn Calles 61 and 62), which serves as Mérida's city hall. Dating to 1735, this architectural beauty is two stories of arch upon arch with a four-sided clock tower. It boasts the oldest coat of arms of the city of Mérida—look for it at the bottom of the main staircase.

Sign Language

In colonial times, Mérida's street signs had both words and pictures.

As you navigate through the numbered streets of Mérida, you'll soon begin noticing whimsical street signs—carved pictures of animals, household items, and people—adorning street corners. These signs pay homage to Mérida's past when, because of the high illiteracy rate, the city hung painted wooden signs of familiar figures so that every inhabitant could find an address. Typically, these signs directly related to establishments or sights nearby: a pair of nuns to signal a convent, a violin to indicate an instrument maker, a bull to direct people to the Plaza de Toros (bullring). Look around and you'll not only get a flavor of where things were in Mérida's past, but also where they might still be today.

Museo Casa Montejo

Facing the southern edge of the central plaza is the **Casa de Montejo** (Calle 63 btwn Calles 60 and 62, tel. 999/923-0633, www.casasdeculturabanamex.com/museocasamontejo, 10am-7pm Tues.-Sat., 10am-2pm Sun., free), which was constructed between 1543 and 1549 by Maya slaves. The portico originally was the only decoration on the facade; note the intricate carvings of Spaniards with their feet firmly planted on the heads of Maya—a lasting reminder of Spanish tyranny. Originally the home of Francisco de Montejo "El Adelantado" (The Older), it was eventually bequeathed to Francisco de Montejo "El Mozo" (The Younger). Thirteen generations of Montejos lived in the house until it was sold to Simón Peón y Peón in 1839. Peón's descendants subsequently lived in the house until it was sold to Banamex in 1980.

The bank now takes up a section of the structure, but in 2010 a section of the house just off the enormous interior courtyard opened as a museum. Inside are several ornate rooms, decorated in 19th-century style. Highlights include a 1678 painting of the (third) reconstruction of the Santiago de Guatemala Cathedral and a grand dining room with formal wood-paneled doors and walls. The dining room's segmented ceiling is painted with sky and plant murals that give the illusion of being on an outdoor terrace. Beyond these rooms, there's a gallery with rotating exhibits, and interactive computer stations that utilize talking deer and stiff-looking conquistadors to narrate history lessons.

Interpretive signage is in both English and Spanish. Free guided tours in Spanish also are offered Tuesday-Saturday at 11am, 1pm, and

5pm, Sunday at 11am and 1pm only. The air-conditioning inside the entire museum hovers around subzero, and the bathrooms are spacious, spotless, and handy if you're sightseeing around the plaza.

★ Museo Regional de Antropología "Palacio Cantón"

The **Museum of Anthropology "Canton Palace"** (Paseo de Montejo at Calle 43, tel. 999/923-0557, www.palaciocanton.inah.gob.mx, 8am-5pm Tues.-Sun., US$3.25) houses the finest collections of Maya artifacts in the Yucatán Peninsula, spanning from the Preclassic to present-day eras. Only the Museo Nacional de Antropología in Mexico City is better, though there's no shortage of wow-power in Mérida: The collection ranges from ornately painted ceramic jars to massive funerary urns, from delicate jewelry and ritual items made of jade, obsidian, and seashells to imposing stone monoliths covered in hieroglyphics. There are also detailed descriptions of the Maya calendar and advancements in astronomy, architecture, and agriculture, all in Spanish and English.

The museum itself is housed in one of Mérida's ornate mansions, most of which were built during the henequen boom in the early 20th century. Designed by Italian architect Enrico Deserti—the same architect who built the Teatro Peón Contreras—it was originally the home of the former governor of Yucatán, General Francisco Cantón Rosado. It served as the official state residence from 1948 to 1960, and eventually, in 1977, the mansion became the city's Museo Regional de Antropología.

Museo Macay

The **Museo Fernando García Ponce-Macay** (Museo Macay, Pasaje Revolución btwn Calles 58 and 60, tel. 999/928-3258, www.macay.org, 10am-6pm daily, free) is a first-class modern art museum boasting an impressive collection of Yucatecan art, including paintings by its namesake Fernando García Ponce, Gabriel Ramírez Aznar, and Fernando Castro Pacheco (who painted the arresting murals in the Palacio de Gobierno).

The museum occupies the beautiful 16th-century **Palacio Arzobispal** (Palace of the Archbishop), which is next to the cathedral; the passageway between the two is administered by the Museo Macay and often features sculpture exhibits. Construction on the sprawling Palace of the Archbishop began in 1573 under the direction of Fray Diego de

Palacio Cantón in Mérida

Downtown Mérida

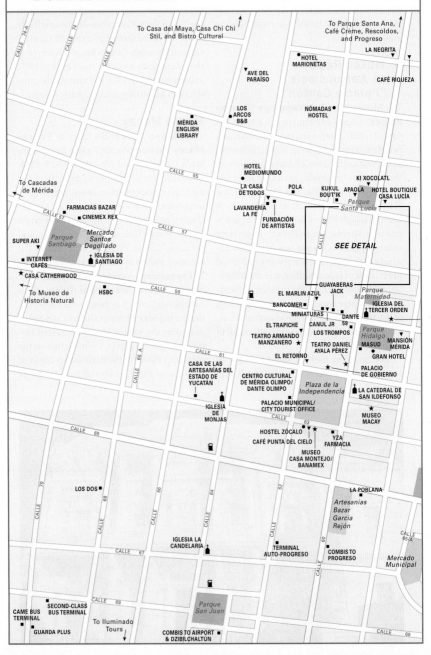

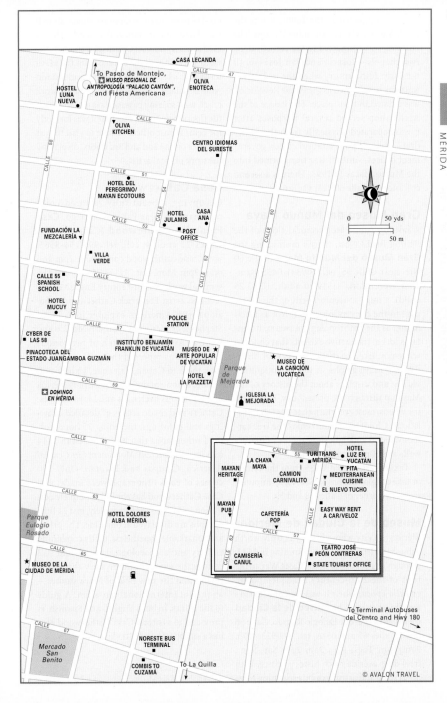

CASA LECANDA

To Paseo de Montejo,
MUSEO REGIONAL DE
ANTROPOLOGÍA "PALACIO CANTÓN",
and Fiesta Americana

HOSTEL
LUNA
NUEVA

OLIVA
ENOTECA

CALLE 47

OLIVA
KITCHEN

CALLE 49

CENTRO IDIOMAS
DEL SURESTE

CALLE 51

HOTEL DEL
PEREGRINO/
MAYAN ECOTOURS

CALLE 54

CALLE 58

CASA
ANA

HOTEL
JULAMIS

CALLE 53

POST
OFFICE

CALLE 50

FUNDACIÓN LA
MEZCALERÍA

VILLA
VERDE

CALLE 52

CALLE 55
SPANISH
SCHOOL

CALLE 56

CALLE 55

HOTEL
MUCUY

CALLE 57

POLICE
STATION

CYBER DE
LAS 58

PINACOTECA DEL
ESTADO JUANGAMBOA GUZMÁN

INSTITUTO BENJAMÍN
FRANKLIN DE YUCATÁN

MUSEO DE ★
ARTE POPULAR
DE YUCATÁN

MUSEO DE
LA CANCIÓN
YUCATECA

Parque
de
Mejorada

CALLE 59

HOTEL
LA PIAZZETA

DOMINGO
EN MÉRIDA

IGLESIA LA
MEJORADA

CALLE 61

CALLE 63

Parque
Eulogio
Rosado

HOTEL DOLORES
ALBA MÉRIDA

CALLE 65

MUSEO DE LA ★
CIUDAD DE MÉRIDA

CALLE 67

Mercado
San
Benito

NORESTE BUS
TERMINAL

COMBIS TO
CUZAMÁ

To La Quilla

To Terminal Autobuses
del Centro and Hwy 180

0   50 yds
0   50 m

MAYAN
HERITAGE

LA CHAYA
MAYA

CALLE 55

TURITRANS-
MÉRIDA

HOTEL
LUZ EN
YUCATÁN

PITA
MEDITERRANEAN
CUISINE

CAMION
CARNIVALITO

EL NUEVO TUCHO

CALLE 60

MAYAN
PUB

CAFETERÍA
POP

EASY WAY RENT
A CAR/VELOZ

CALLE 57

CALLE 62

CAMISERÍA
CANUL

TEATRO JOSÉ
PEÓN CONTRERAS

STATE TOURIST OFFICE

© AVALON TRAVEL

Landa. Completed in the 1600s, it was the residence of several of Yucatán's bishops. The building was connected to the cathedral via two chapels—Rosario and San José—until the early 20th century when the pedestrian walkway now known as the Pasaje Revolución was created in their place. The Palace of the Archbishop served several purposes after it was separated physically from the cathedral—military post, cultural center, government offices—until it was transformed into the Museo Macay in 1993. There is a second entrance on Calle 60 near Calle 63.

Gran Museo del Mundo Maya

A not-too-subtle architectural clone of the Beijing Bird's Nest, there's no missing the **Gran Museo del Mundo Maya** (Calle 60 Nte. near Calle 55, tel. 999/341-0435, 8am-5pm Wed.-Mon., US$9.50 adult, US$3.25 child), a huge museum north of the center next to the convention center. Not as fascinating as the anthropology museum, it contains lots of interactive exhibits that children will enjoy, like one that converts your birthday into Maya glyphs, as well as antiquities, videos, and displays about the history of the Maya up through the present day. Except for the videos, most everything has English translations. Children will also enjoy the free cartoony sound and light show on the museum's walls at 8:30pm Friday-Sunday.

Taxis charge about US$5 from the center, or take a Siglo XXI bus (US$0.45, 25 minutes) from the corner of Calles 58 and 59.

Museo de la Ciudad de Mérida

Mérida is a city whose history is truly worth a museum, from its bloody founding in 1542, through its near defeat in the Caste War, to the turn-of-the-20th-century henequen boom, or *bella época,* when it was one of Mexico's wealthiest cities. The **Museo de la Ciudad de Mérida** (Parque Eulogio Rosado, Calle 56 btwn Calles 65 and 65-A, tel. 999/923-4273, 9am-6pm Tues.-Fri., 9am-2pm Sat.-Sun., free) does Mérida's rich history justice, with interesting and artful exhibits spanning from

pre-Hispanic to contemporary times, all well translated and of manageable depth. There's even some sly humor: One display suggests the word Yucatán may have come from the Maya term *Yuk ak katan,* or "I don't understand your language." The museum is itself a work of art, with soaring passageways and stunning tile floors, belying the fact that it was formerly the central post office. Be sure to visit the art galleries on the 2nd and 3rd floors, displaying the work of local artists.

Casa Catherwood

Occupying a beautifully restored colonial mansion near Parque Santiago, **Casa Frederick Catherwood** (Calle 59 btwn Calles 72 and 74, cell. tel. 999/154-5565, www.casa-catherwood.com, 10am-2pm and 6pm-9pm Mon.-Sat., US$3.25) honors the seminal work of 19th-century English architect and artist Frederick Catherwood, who, along with American explorer John Lloyd Stephens, crisscrossed southern Mexico and Central America in search of mysterious ancient ruins reported there. Their travels took them to Copán, Palenque, Uxmal, and Tulum, among many other sites, plus Mérida and numerous haciendas and Maya villages. Catherwood made scores of detailed drawings and paintings, including 25 hand-colored lithographs that he published in 1844 as *Views of Ancient Monuments in Central America, Chiapas and Yucatán.* Only 300 copies of each lithograph were made, and Casa Catherwood has the only complete collection in Mexico; unfortunately, just 24 lithographs are displayed at one time. The prints are remarkable nonetheless, deftly combining artistry and archaeological detail, and still convey the wonder and mystery that made them—and the new field of Maya studies—an instant international sensation. A guide to the prints, in both English and Spanish, is provided to visitors. Casa Catherwood also has a small café and gift shop.

Museo de Arte Popular de Yucatán

Housed in a restored *casona* (large colonial home), the **Museo de Arte Popular de Yucatán** (Casa Molina, Calle 50A btwn Calles 57 and 59, tel. 999/928-5263, 10am-5pm Tues.-Sat., 10am-3pm Sun., free) boasts a gorgeous collection of Mexican folk art created by master artisans. An entire room is dedicated to Yucatecan artisanry, though you'll find a magnificent range of ceramics, textiles, cardboard, and wood items from throughout the country. A modest gift shop also sells some beautiful works of folk art.

Other Museums

The **Museo de la Canción Yucateca** (Calle 57 at Calle 48, tel. 999/923-7224, 9am-5pm Tues.-Fri., 9am-3pm Sat.-Sun., US$1.25, free Sun.) focuses on the development of Yucatecan music and its artists. Divided into five areas, the first provides a historical overview of the region's music, from its beginnings in the late 1800s to present day. The remaining exhibits pay homage to Yucatán's most famous composers, singers, and musicians and contain portraits, instruments, and some personal belongings. Signage is in Spanish, but you can ask for English interpretive handouts. At the time of research, a new building for this museum was being constructed just east of Parque Hidalgo.

The **Pinacoteca del Estado Juan Gamboa Guzmán** (Calle 59 btwn Calles 58 and 60, tel. 999/924-5233, 9am-5pm Tues.-Sat., 10am-5pm Sun., free) is located in an annex to an abandoned Jesuit church, known as the Tercera Orden. It houses mostly religious works of art from the colonial period, though it also has a handful of paintings by the famous Yucatecan artist Juan Gamboa Guzmán and bronze statutes by Enrique Gottidiener, an influential Mexican artist who lived and died in Mérida. The building itself is beautiful to wander in, and if you're lucky, you'll be able to sneak a peek into the dilapidated church itself.

A stately mansion with a garden terrace popular for weddings, the **Casa Museo Montes Molina** (Paseo de Montejo btwn Calles 33 and 35, tel. 999/925-5999, www.laquintamm.com, 9am-5pm Mon.-Fri., 9am-1pm Sat., US$3.75 adult, US$2.50 child) is a unique experience in that it's still intermittently lived in by the octogenarian descendant of sisal hacienda owners. It's a working household, not a static relic, and visitors can ogle the French-influenced architecture and Tiffany stained-glass doors upstairs as well as the servants' quarters downstairs. The 40-minute tours are given in English at 9am, 11am, and 3pm Monday-Friday, and 9am and 11am Saturday; in Spanish, tours are at 10am, noon, 2pm, and 4pm Monday-Friday, and 10am and noon Saturday.

Although the six permanent exhibits at the **Museo de Historia Natural** (Calle 59 btwn Calles 84 and 84-A, tel. 999/924-0994, 9am-3pm Tues.-Sun., free) look as if they haven't been updated since their inauguration in the 1980s, the museum does a decent job of explaining the basics of the solar system and the development of the Earth. Documentaries are screened every Sunday at noon. Signage is in Spanish only.

Parque Zoológico del Centenario

Referred to as "El Centenario" by locals, the **city zoo** (Av. Itzáes at Calle 59, tel. 999/928-5815, www.merida.gob.mx/centenario, 8am-5pm Tues.-Sun., free) is a popular spot for families, especially on weekends. It has kiddie rides, playgrounds, and an overwhelming number of concession stands. The zoo also has a decent selection of animals, but the cramped quarters can be upsetting. On Sunday, magicians, clowns, puppets, and theater groups come out to entertain children and their parents.

ENTERTAINMENT AND EVENTS

As one of Mexico's colonial shining stars, Mérida is the region's cultural supernova. With free nightly performances, theaters, art

Mérida's Weekly Cultural Events

SUNDAY (DOMINGO EN MÉRIDA)

- **Bici-Ruta:** 5 kilometers (3.1 miles) of streets in the historic center are open to bicyclists and pedestrians only (8:30am-noon); rent bicycles in front of the Palacio Municipal and along Paseo de Montejo (US$2/hour)

- **Plaza de la Independencia:** handicrafts market and outdoor food stands (9am-9pm)

- **Parque Santa Lucía:** folk art bazaar and salsa dancing (11am-3pm)

- **Palacio Municipal:** regional dance performance (1pm)

MONDAY

- **Palacio Municipal:** regional dance performance (9pm)

TUESDAY

- **Parque Santiago:** live big-band music and dancing (8:30pm)

- **Centro Cultural de Mérida Olimpo:** trova (classical guitar and ballads) performance (8:30pm)

WEDNESDAY

- **Cementerio General:** guided tour of famous people buried in Mérida's main cemetery (8pm)

galleries, cinemas, and a planetarium, there is something for everyone. For up-to-date information on monthly events, check out the free tourism magazines and brochures; the most helpful include *Yucatán Today, Explore Yucatán,* and the *Cartelera Cultural* (www.merida.gob.mx/turismo/contenido/cultura/eventos.htm).

★ Domingo en Mérida

Sunday is a wonderful day in Mérida. Everyone puts on their Sunday best and comes to the city center, where the streets are closed to traffic. *Artesanía* vendors set up stalls, and pushcarts do a lively business selling *tortas* (sandwiches), *elote* (corn on the cob), drinks, and sweets. Be sure to catch one of the many free performances throughout the day. The most popular is folkloric dancing presented in front of the Palacio Municipal, often featuring the city's remarkably skilled youth dance troupe. Another worthwhile event is the **Bici-Ruta**

(www.merida.gob.mx/biciruta, 9am-noon), a 5-kilometer (6.2-mile) route, including a section of Paseo de Montejo, where the road is closed to make room for bicycling; it's popular with local families, but visitors can easily rent bikes (US$2/hour) and join in—look for the bike rental stand in front of the Palacio Municipal or go to **Bicimérida** (Paseo de Montejo at Calle 45, tel. 999/287-3538, 9am-10pm Mon.-Fri., 8am-7pm Sat., 7am-3pm Sun.).

Nightlife

Over three dozen organic, artisan, and Fair Trade mezcals stock the shelves at the hopping **Fundación La Mezcalería** (Calle 56 btwn Calles 53 and 55, tel. 999/121-0411, 8pm-2:30am Wed.-Sun.), where a 20-something crowd chats and sips inexpensive cocktails in an artsy lounge peppered with vintage sofas, mismatched tables, and modular plastic chairs. Folks start shimmying to the DJ around 10:30pm or so.

THURSDAY

- **Parque Zoológico del Centenario:** live music and dancing, mostly mambo, salsa, and chachachá (4pm)

- **Parque Santa Lucía:** regional dance, music, and spoken-word performances (9pm)

- **Calle 60 from Plaza de la Independencia to Calle 53:** *En El Corazón de Mérida* (In the Heart of Mérida), with Calle 60 closed for live bands, dancing, and outdoor eating (8pm-11pm)

FRIDAY

- **Catedral de San Ildefonso:** reenactment of ancient Maya ball game (8pm)

- **Calle 60 from Plaza de la Independencia to Calle 53:** *En El Corazón de Mérida* (8pm-11pm)

SATURDAY

- **Calle 60 from Plaza de la Independencia to Calle 53:** *En El Corazón de Mérida* (8pm-2am)

- **Paseo de Montejo at Calle 47:** Noche Mexicana—food stalls, handicrafts booths, live music, and dance performances (8pm-11pm)

La Negrita (Calle 62 at Calle 49, tel. 999/187-7615, noon-10pm daily) is a longtime cantina—it opened in 1918—that got a total refresh. What was once a men-only dive bar is now an everyone-welcome pub. The look is old-school Yucatán meets hipster Mérida. And the drinks are kind of the same: Tecate meets artisanal mezcal and local microbrews. Botanas (appetizers) come with each round of drinks, plus there's happy hour every day (5pm-8pm) and live music on weekends.

Though the Dubliner owner laments that he can only stock Guinness in cans, **Hennessy's Irish Pub** (Paseo de Montejo btwn Calles 41 and 43, tel. 999/923-8993, www.hennessysirishpub.mx, noon-midnight Sun.-Wed., noon-2am Thurs.-Sat.) is spot-on as the best melting pot in town. A grand colonial building plastered with memorabilia from the Emerald Isle, it's a friendly place to meet the locals (and not just expats) over darts, billiards, or a sturdy helping of bangers and mash. Live music, trivia nights, and movie screenings entertain throughout the week.

Reggae, rock, and *trova* figure prominently in **La Casa de Todos** (aka Peña, Calle 64 at Calle 55, tel. 999/221-8852, 9pm-2am most days), a small bar known for its live music and leftist leanings. Drinks and light vegetarian fare are served; opening hours and cover charge vary with the act, but most start around 10pm.

Live rock, reggae, and jazz are featured at the **Mayan Pub** (Calle 62 btwn Calles 55 and 57, tel. 999/923-1271, 7pm-3am Wed.-Sun.), a boho restaurant-bar set in a renovated colonial home. Head to the leafy garden for the best seats in the house.

Live Caribbean rhythms get people spinning at **Mambocafé** (Plaza Las Américas mall, Calle 56-A at Av. Colón, tel. 999/987-8787, 9pm-3am Wed.-Sat., US$7 cover). Yes, it's in a mall, and yes, it's a chain, but that doesn't stop Mambocafé from being one of the hottest salsa spots in town.

El Nuevo Tucho (Calle 60 btwn Calles 55 and 57, tel. 999/924-2323, noon-9:30pm daily, US$5-10) is a good introduction to the *salon familiar*, a family-friendly bar where locals head for regional food, drink, and entertainment like comedy acts, live music, and *ballet folklórico*. Performances typically start at 3:30pm, at which point you shouldn't expect much conversation—speakers blast away any possibility of interaction. In fact, pointing at the menu may be more effective than shouting out your order.

Music and Dance

Music is heard all over Mérida, and dancing is a way of life. Informal and free concerts and other entertainment are regularly presented for Mérida's residents and visitors at parks and plazas throughout the city. Every Thursday, Friday, and Saturday night, Calle 60 is closed from the central plaza past Parque Santa Lucía, restaurants bring out tables and chairs, and live bands play salsa and merengue, encouraging dancing in the streets. Sunday features traditional music and dance performances in the center of town. In fact, all the regularly scheduled events throughout the week involve music and dancing in some way, whether to watch or to join in.

Theater

Built during Mérida's boom in the early 1900s, the ornately beautiful **Teatro José Peón Contreras** (Calle 60 at Calle 57, tel. 999/923-7354, 9am-9pm daily, US$5-20) mostly hosts music concerts and dance performances, including those by the resident **Orquesta Sinfónica de Yucatán** (www.sinfonicadeyucatan.com.mx) September-December. For a listing of events, stop by the box office or check at the tourist information center next door. During the day when there aren't rehearsals, you can take a look around the theater if the staff isn't busy cleaning it.

Teatro Armando Manzanero (Calle 62 btwn Calles 59 and 61, tel. 999/924-9990, 10am-9pm Tues.-Sun.) is an art-deco venue housing a main theater and two smaller ones.

It's an artsy place with top-notch programming year-round—productions vary from modern dance performances to international film festivals.

Teatro Daniel Ayala Pérez (Calle 60 btwn Calles 59 and 61, tel. 999/928-6863, 9am-9pm Tues.-Sun.) is a cavernous modern theater that is used mainly for dramatic performances. Ticket prices range US$3-10.

Cultural Centers

Centro Cultural de Mérida Olimpo (Calle 61 at Calle 62, tel. 999/942-0000, ext. 80121, 10am-10pm Tues.-Sun.) is a cultural center housed in an award-winning building. There are modern exhibition halls, a research library, a planetarium, and theaters where films are screened and concerts are held. The programming is chock-full each month—check the bulletin board at the entrance for listings.

A collectively run cultural center popular with locals, **La Quilla** (Calle 69 btwn Calles 44 and 46, www.laquilla.blogspot.com, 4pm-8pm Wed.-Thurs., 6pm-midnight Fri.-Sat., 1pm-7pm Sun.) is the place to catch a free independent film; groove to punk, hip-hop, reggae, metal, and ska shows on the back patio; or just kick back with a beer on a sofa and take in the current art exhibit.

Fundación de Artistas (Calle 55 btwn Calles 62 and 64, tel. 999/923-5905, www.fundaciondeartistas.org, 11am-7pm Tues.-Sun.) is a nonprofit organization dedicated to supporting local and international artists—painters, musicians, chefs—through exhibits, concerts, workshops, even an on-again-off-again café. Stop by to see what's on deck while you're in town. The renovated *casona* (large colonial home) itself is an interesting and beautiful place to wander through.

Cinema

If you want to get your Hollywood fix, there are lots of movie theaters in Mérida. As elsewhere in Mexico, movies are discounted all day Wednesday, and most theaters have discount matinees. Check the local paper, *El*

Bird-watching is popular throughout the Yucatán Peninsula.

alternative art films and also hosts international film festivals.

Festivals and Events

Since 2001, the city of Mérida has hosted the annual **Festival de Aves Toh** (Toh Bird Festival, tel. 999/988-4437, www.festivalavesyucatan.com), offering a myriad of bird-related activities March-November (think bird-watching tours, photo contests, conferences, and workshops). The festival culminates in a weekend-long "Bird-a-thon Xoc Ch'ich" in late November-early December, when bird-watchers from around the world gather in teams to observe (or at least get a glimpse of) and count as many of the 465 bird species registered in the state as possible (543 species are registered in the entire peninsula). It's a well-attended event and one that welcomes amateurs and experts alike. It's a great way to see the state and, of course, learn about its birds too.

Mérida also plays host to the international modern dance festival **de Danza Oc' Ohtic.** Since 1994, professional dance companies from all over the world come to perform, often creating such a buzz that there are enormous lines to see the shows. The festival typically takes place during the first two weeks of December—with ticket prices around US$5-10, it's hard to resist.

La Noche Blanca (8pm-2am, free) is a citywide celebration of the arts, when galleries, concert halls, museums, and theaters open their doors to the general public and introduce them to different forms of art. Typically held in May and December, 50 venues and organizations typically participate. The city provides complimentary shuttle service to all the locales, and itself sponsors concerts and dance performances in city parks and public buildings too.

The monthlong **Festival de la Ciudad** is held every January to commemorate the founding of the city of Mérida. Started in 2005, the festival brings hundreds of artists from around the world to share their works of art, dance, music, drama, film, and

Diario de Yucatán (www.yucatan.com.mx/seccion/cines), for schedules.

Facing Parque Santiago, **Cinemex Rex** (Calle 57 btwn Calles 70 and 72, toll-free Mex. tel. 800/710-8888, US$2.25) shows U.S. and Mexican films on its two screens.

The major shopping malls all have modern megaplexes, most with both regular and VIP (also called *platino*) theaters; the latter cost a bit more but feature reclining leather seats, a food and drink menu, even waiter service. Gran Plaza (Calle 50 Diagonal 460) and Galerías (Calle 60 299-A, near the Periférico) have **Cinemex** (toll-free Mex. tel. 800/710-8888; www.cinemex.com, US$3 regular, US$4.50 VIP), while Plaza Altabrisa (Calle Correa Rachó) and Plaza Las Américas (Calle 56-A at Av. Colón) have **Cinépolis** (toll-free Mex. tel. 800/120-0220, www.cinepolis.com, US$3 regular, US$5 VIP), though Las Américas does not have VIP screens.

Teatro Armando Manzanero (Calle 62 btwn Calles 59 and 61, tel. 999/924-9990, 10am-9pm Tues.-Sun.) occasionally shows literature. Events and workshops are held in Mérida's historic buildings and parks. For a list of scheduled events, stop by one of the tourist offices.

Another arts explosion, the **Festival Anual de las Artes Otoño Cultural** lasts for a month during September and October, with dance, *trova*, theater, and literary events that are mostly free. Stop by one of the tourist offices for more information about featured events.

SHOPPING

If there is any place in the Yucatán Peninsula where you are certain to find something that you absolutely cannot resist, it's Mérida. From small family-run stores to rambling *artesanía* markets, Mérida attracts the treasures of the region: hammocks, *guayaberas, huipiles,* handcrafted toys, ceramic figurines, *jipi* hats, and Maya replicas.

Markets

The **Mercado Lucas de Galvez** (Calle 67 btwn Calles 56 and 58, 8am-8pm daily)—better known as the **Mercado Municipal**—is a city block-wide building bustling with vendors of all sorts. It's an experience all its own. The 1st floor—with its myriad colors and layers of scents—is where the main action is: rows of neatly stacked fruits and vegetables, flowers of all sorts, beef and pork parts (you're sure to see heads, hooves, and stomachs), mounds of herbs and spices, incense and religious icons, children's toys, rows of women's shoes, stand upon stand of gold jewelry—just about anything you're looking for (and aren't) is here. The 2nd floor is quieter and focused on *artesanía: guayaberas*, handwoven hammocks, sandals, and *huipiles* from the Yucatán, plus folk art from other parts of the country. And if you get hungry and have a strong stomach, there are dozens of restaurants serving cheap local fare on both floors. Next door is a newer (though half-empty) market, the **Mercado San Benito** (Calle 54 btwn Calles 67 and 69, 10:30am-8pm Mon.-Fri.), with vendors selling more of the same.

Near the Mercado Municipal, the **Artesanías Bazar García Rejón** (Calle 60 at Calle 65, 9am-8pm daily) is a market devoted entirely to local arts and crafts. There's a good selection of sandals, clothing, hammocks, and other regional items. Remember to bargain—most items have been marked up in anticipation of the custom.

A boho **open-air market** (Calle 60 btwn Calles 57 and 59, sunset-11pm Fri.-Sat.) is often set up on weekend evenings alongside Parque Maternidad. Handmade jewelry, batik, feather art, and clothing from Chiapas are the top sellers.

Each Sunday, an **Artesanía Bazaar** is held at Parque Santa Lucía (11am-3pm) as part of the weekly city-sponsored Domingo en Mérida. Booths wind through the park and are packed with all sorts of tchotchkes, local crafts, and tempting *antojitos*. Live Yucatecan music features in the early afternoon, and chairs are set up so that you can take it all in.

Artesanía

Casa de las Artesanías del Estado de Yucatán (Calle 63 btwn Calles 64 and 66, tel. 999/928-6676, 8:30am-9pm Mon.-Sat., 10am-5pm Sun.) is a state-owned arts and crafts shop run out of a converted convent. Some of the items are worthwhile, especially the clothing and woodwork, but a great deal of kitsch has crept into this once-superb shop. Definitely have a look around—just head to the register once you hit the coconut monkeys.

El Estudio (Paseo de Montejo btwn Calles 41 and 43, cell. tel. 999/239-0401, 10am-8pm Mon.-Thurs., 10am-10pm Fri.-Sat.) is a boutique specializing in high-end handicrafts from around Mexico. This is a perfect place to find a special gift—hand-stitched pillowcases from Oaxaca, lucha libre dolls from Mexico City, hand-blown margarita glasses from Guadalajara. Credit cards are accepted, fortunately.

The quirky **Miniaturas** (Calle 59 btwn Calles 60 and 62, tel. 999/928-6503, 10am-2pm and 4pm-8pm Mon.-Sat.) is packed with a huge collection of *tiny* arts and crafts from every Mexican state. Be sure to check out the whimsical papier-mâché catrinas (skeletons).

Yucatán is renowned for producing some of the best hammocks in Mexico, and in Mérida, they're just about everywhere you look. If you want a sure thing, head to **La Poblana** (Calle 65 btwn Calles 58 and 60, tel. 999/928-6093, 8:30am-6pm Mon.-Fri., 8:30am-5pm Sat.), a mom-and-pop shop specializing in hammocks of all colors, lengths, and materials.

Posheria (Paseo de Montejo btwn Calles 41 and 43, tel. 999/221-8756, 7am-1pm and 5pm-10pm daily) specializes in *pox* (pronounced pohsh), a traditional—and strong—liquor made from sugarcane and corn. Originally used in religious ceremonies among the Maya populations in Chiapas, it quickly grew to be a social drink in and beyond those communities. This shop sells a variety of artisanal pox; tasting is offered. Chiapanecan coffee is served too.

Traditional Clothing

Although you'll be able to find traditional clothing in Mérida's markets, there are several stores with excellent selections that are pricey but also better quality.

If you're on the search for the perfect *huipil* or *terno*, try **Escencia Maya** (Parque Santa Ana, Calle 47 btwn Calles 58 and 60, tel. 999/923-0040, 8am-10pm Mon.-Sat., 8am-4pm Sun.), **Masud** (Parque Hidalgo, Calle 60 btwn Calles 59 and 61, tel. 999/923-7269, 9am-7pm Mon.-Sat.), and **Camisería Canul** (Calle 62 btwn Calles 57 and 59, tel. 999/923-0158, 9am-8pm Mon.-Sat., 10am-2pm Sun.).

If a fine *guayabera* (traditional men's shirt) is what you're looking for, head to **Fábrica de Guayaberas Jack** (Calle 59 btwn Calles 60 and 62, tel. 999/928-6002, 10am-8:30pm Mon.-Sat., 10am-2:30pm Sun.) and **Canul Jr.** (Calle 59 btwn Calles 60 and 62, tel. 999/923-1811, 9am-8pm Mon.-Sat., 10am-1pm Sun.). Custom-made *guayaberas* (who doesn't need a *guayabera* with lightning bolts?) can be made in about a week for off-the-rack prices.

Kukul Bout'ik (Calle 55 btwn Calles 60 and 62, tel. 999/923-2240, noon-8pm Mon.-Tues., 11am-10pm Wed.-Sat., 10am-9pm Sun.) specializes in luxury clothing and home goods that celebrate Mexican indigenous artistry. You'll find traditional *huipiles* and hand-woven bags sitting side by side with Tzotzil-stitched Docksider and whimsical pillowcases made from the sansevieria plant.

Traditional panama hats (also called *jipi* hats because they're made of jipijapa palm leaves) can be found at **Fábrica de Guayaberas Jack** (Calle 59 btwn Calles 60 and 62, tel. 999/928-6002, 10am-8:30pm Mon.-Sat., 10am-2:30pm Sun.) or **Casa de las Artesanías del Estado de Yucatán** (Calle 63 btwn Calles 64 and 66, tel. 999/928-6676, 8:30am-9pm Mon.-Sat., 10am-5pm Sun.). Not cheap, *finos* (the most supple) can run as high as US$90.

Bookstores

Next to the Palacio Municipal, **Dante Olimpo** (Calle 61 near Calle 62, tel. 999/928-2611, 8am-10:30pm daily) has an excellent selection of reading material in English. It has one sister store downtown: **Dante 59** (Calle 59 btwn Calles 60 and 62, tel. 999/928-3674, 8am-9:30pm Mon.-Sat., 10am-6pm Sun.).

The **Mérida English Library** (Calle 53 btwn Calles 66 and 68, tel. 999/924-8401, www.meridaenglishlibrary.com, 9am-1pm and 6:30pm-9:30pm Mon., 9am-1pm Tues.-Sat.) has a huge selection of English-language books. It's mostly set up for long-term visitors—only registered members can check out books—but tourists can read books in the library's quiet reading area, buy books from the for-sale rack, and join weekly programs and get-togethers, including monthly socials, English-Spanish conversation exchanges, AA meetings (in English), and House and Garden tours—call or check the website for current schedules. There is also an excellent bulletin board with postings of tours, short- and long-term housing, and items for sale, plus a children's room.

Malls

Gran Plaza (Calle 50 Diagonal 460, tel. 999/944-7658, 10am-9:30pm daily) is the city's largest and fanciest mall, with dozens of upper-end stores and a multiplex movie theater.

Located a short distance past Gran Plaza, **Galerías** (Calle 60 near the Periférico, www. galerias.com, 11am-8:30pm daily) is another modern, upscale mall that features an ice skating rink.

City Center (Periférico at Calle 32, 10am-10pm daily) is a newer upscale mall; its restaurants and bars draw locals in the evening.

Plaza Altabrisa (Calle Correa Rachó, tel. 999/167-9719, www.plazaaltabrisa.com, 11am-8:30pm daily) is located in the northeast part of town and has a Cinépolis VIP, among other shops and attractions.

Plaza Las Américas (Calle 56-A at Av. Colón, 10am-9:30pm daily) is a standard mall with a JCPenney, lots of ATMs, and a Cinépolis movie theater (no VIP).

SPORTS AND RECREATION
Bullfights

If you're interested in what makes bullfighting so popular in Mexico, catch a *corrida* (literally, a running) at the **Plaza de Toros Mérida** (Calle 72 at Calle 33, US$8-25). Unless you want to work on your tan, opt for the premium *sombra* (shade) seats—the extra charge is worth every bead of sweat you save. Tickets are available at the bullring's box office the day of the event—the cost depends on the experience of the bullfighter and the location of the seat. Look around the Plaza de la Independencia for posters advertising the next *corrida*.

Golf

Just a 20-minute drive north of Mérida is the **Club de Golf Yucatán** (Carr. Mérida-Progreso Km. 14.5, tel. 999/922-0071, www. golfyucatan.com, 6:30am-6pm daily). At the far end of an upscale gated community, the 18-hole, par-72 golf course is open to the public and costs US$85 per round. Equipment rentals are available. Reserve a day or two in advance for weekends.

FOOD

Mérida has a rich selection of restaurants, from great hole-in-the-wall joints to award-winning restaurants. Yucatecan and Mexican cuisine predominates, but you'll also find good alternatives around town.

Yucatecan and Mexican

The popular and reasonably priced ★ **La Chaya Maya** (Calle 55 btwn Calles 60 and 62, tel. 999/928-4780, 8am-11pm daily, US$6-9) might stop you from eating elsewhere for the remainder of your stay. Tall wooden doors frame a columned colonial courtyard, and you can dine under the ceiling fans or in one of two dignified dining rooms. Every dish is beautifully presented, from the *papadzules* to the *los tres mosqueteros yucatecos* (three Yucatecan musketeers) crepes. While you're waiting for your meal, you can watch traditionally dressed women make handmade tortillas.

One of a handful of trendy restaurants on Parque Santa Lucía, ★ **Apaola** (Calle 60 at Calle 55, tel. 999/923-1979, 1pm-midnight Mon.-Sat., 2pm-10pm Sun., US$15-30) serves up a fierce fusion of Oaxacan, Yucatecan, and other traditional Mexican dishes. The presentation is gourmet all the way, with flourishes of color and unexpected artistic flair. The mezcal cocktails also are inventive and created to pair with your meal. Best of all, there's plenty of seating outdoors—perfect on a Thursday evening when the city sponsors free music and dance performances at the park. Reservations are highly recommended.

El Trapiche (Calle 62 btwn Calles 59 and 61, 7:30am-11pm daily, US$3-7) is a convenient and solid option for Yucatecan eats. Located just a block from the central plaza, its menu is rife with all the standards: *salbutes, panuchos, pollo pibil, poc-chuc,* and so on. For those who need a break from Yucatecan dishes, there's a good variety of pizzas too. The dining room is far from fancy—wood tables, fluorescent lighting, and a view of cars racing past.

With funky 1970s decor and a retro mural on the back wall, **Cafetería Pop** (Calle 57 btwn Calles 60 and 62, tel. 999/928-6163, www.cafeteriapop.com, 7am-midnight Mon.-Sat., 8am-midnight Sun., US$4-8) seems like a total hipster diner but, in fact, has just maintained its look since it opened in 1971. Friendly waiters serve simple Mexican food in this all-welcoming place—you'll find everything from *guayabera*-clad locals talking politics, to five-year-old tourists munching on cornflakes. Breakfast specials are particularly tasty.

A popular chain, **Los Trompos** (Calle 60 at Calle 59, tel. 999/926-4654, www.lostrompos.com.mx, 7:30am-1am Sun.-Thurs., 7am-2am Fri.-Sat., US$2-14) draws the meat- and cheese-loving crowds with tasty fast-food items like pizza *pastoreña* (with pineapple and spit-grilled pork) and *poc-chuc* tacos, though there's a pricier full menu as well. The decor is upscale coffee shop, with a classy stone wall and historical photos of Mérida framed on the walls.

Parque Santa Ana (Calle 60 at Calle 47) and **Parque Santiago** (Calle 59 at Calle 72) also have reliable *cocinas económicas* (mom-and-pop eateries) serving up Yucatecan fare. Most meals run around $2-4 and come quick and hot to your plastic table. Order a cold beer or a pitcher of freshly made lemonade to wash it down. These eateries are typically open 9am-9pm daily.

Italian and Mediterranean

★ **Oliva Enoteca** (Calle 47 and Calle 54, tel. 999/923-3081, www.olivamerida.com, 1pm-5pm and 7pm-midnight Mon.-Sat., US$7-25) is a small upscale Italian restaurant serving gorgeous antipasto plates, homemade pastas, and meat/chicken/fish entrées that make you wish you had room for them all. If you like seafood, start your meal with the grilled octopus with roasted kale and beets—it's perfection on a plate. A second, larger restaurant, **Oliva Kitchen** (Calle 56 at Calle 49, tel. 999/923-2248, noon-4pm and 7pm-11pm Mon.-Sat., US$5-11) gives its little sister a run for her money.

With sidewalk tables along the wide boulevard of tree-lined Paseo de Montejo, **Trattoría La Pasta** (Paseo de Montejo btwn Calles 39 and 41, tel. 999/157-8986, www.trattorialapasta.com, noon-5pm and 7:30pm-midnight Mon.-Sat., US$7-10) is a convivial and casual spot for delectable fresh pastas,

a lunchtime platter at La Chaya Maya restaurant

salads, and Tuscan-style pizza. (The owner/ chef hails from Pisa, and credits his grandmother on most of the recipes.) There's a good selection of wine and beer and a few rich desserts like panna cotta.

Everything's made from scratch at the Mediterranean bistro **Rescoldos** (Calle 62 btwn Calles 41 and 43, tel. 999/286-1028, www.rescoldosbistro.com, 6pm-11pm Wed.-Sat., US$5-8). And from the spanakopita, vegetarian moussaka, and falafel to the pastas, wood-fired calzones, and thincrust pizzas (try the smoked salmon), it's tough to go wrong here. Start the evening with a white sangria on the back garden terrace and save room for a homemade gelato or tiramisu.

Pita Mediterranean Cuisine (Calle 55 btwn Calle 58 and 60, tel. 999/923-1592, 7am-11pm Mon.-Sat., 7am-2pm Sun., US$5-14) is a small restaurant specializing in delicious Lebanese/Israeli fare—falafel plates, tabbouleh, hummus, shawarma, and pita wraps. Classic Mexican breakfasts also are served each morning. Service is quick and friendly. Head to the back patio for a table with a breeze.

Other Specialties

Great for breakfast or a lazy lunch, ★ **Bistro Cultural** (Calle 66 btwn Calles 41 and 43, tel. 999/923-2013, 8:30am-5:30pm Mon.-Fri., 8:30am-4:30pm Sat.-Sun., US$4-7) serves French cuisine in an artsy bohemian space and on a shady patio. The menu changes daily but includes items like crepes, quiche, tartelettes, and colorful salads; many of the vegetables used are harvested from the restaurant's own organic gardens. Save room—there's often an enticing lineup of French pastries too.

Fresh seafood's the draw at **Marlin Azul** (Calle 62 btwn Calles 57 and 59, tel. 999/224-3052, 8:30am-4:30pm Mon.-Sat., US$5-8), a low-key locals' favorite with a long counter and a few tables. Street noise and loud music may battle for dominance, but the excellent ceviches, shrimp fajitas, and fish fillets stuffed with shrimp and octopus have kept this place buzzing for over 20 years.

Ave del Paraíso (Calle 66 btwn Calles 49 and 53, tel. 999/289-2249, noon-3pm and 6pm-10pm Mon.-Fri., US$6-9) is a hopping Thai food restaurant on a quiet Mérida street. The menu features classics like lemongrass soup, green papaya salad, and grilled meat satays, but the real reason to come here is the curry. Red, green, yellow, Panang-style, and the special house blend—the dishes are spicy, fragrant, and absolutely mouthwatering. Come early to guarantee a seat without a wait.

A sophisticated lounge and bistro nestled in one of the most upscale hotels in town, **Mansión Mérida** (Parque Hidalgo, Calle 59 btwn Calles 58 and 60, tel. 999/924-4642, www.mansionmerida.com, 7am-midnight daily, US$6-12) channels French café culture. Order a sparkling wine cocktail and imbibe under spreading white umbrellas in the Parque Hidalgo, or snack on a focaccia sandwich inside while surrounded by murals inspired by Toulouse-Lautrec and other modernists. Jazz combos and the occasional 1980s cover band play 9pm-11pm Saturday.

Cafés

Sukra (Paseo de Montejo btwn Calles 43 and 44, tel. 999/923-4453, www.sukracafe.com, 8am-7pm Tues.-Sat., 8am-2pm Sun., US$4-7) is a popular café with outdoor seating on swanky Paseo de Montejo. Menu items vary from omelets and taco plates to sandwiches and big salads. Weekday lunch specials include an entrée, fruit drink, coffee, and dessert for just US$5. There's also live music every Sunday starting at 10am—a perfect way to kick off the day.

If you need a patisserie fix, linger in the garden patio of French-run **Café Crème** (Calle 41 at Calle 60, tel. 999/278-5073, 8:30am-5:30pm Mon.-Fri., 8:30am-2pm Sat., US$3.75-5) for exquisite quiches, cheese plates, pâtés, and strong espresso, plus complimentary chocolates after your food. Be forewarned: Its pastries and croissants sell out by around 11am.

On the main plaza right next to the Casa de Montejo, the calming and icily air-conditioned **Café Punta del Cielo** (Calle 63 btwn Calles 60 and 62, tel. 999/923-1134, 7am-10:30pm daily) is a well-located respite from the daytime heat and *centro* traffic. Browse the local papers over a panino sandwich or just recharge with a frozen coffee.

Café Riqueza (Calle 60 at Calle 49, tel. 999/928-2864, 8am-8pm Mon.-Fri., 8am-5pm Sat.) is a tiny place offering fantastic coffee drinks made from beans grown in Chiapas and Veracruz. Order a cold cappuccino to go or enjoy a flavored coffee at one of the three tables. Ground coffee and beans are also sold for US$12-17.50 per kilogram (2.2 pounds).

Sweets

Ki Xocolatl (Parque Santa Lucía, Calle 55 btwn Calles 60 and 62, tel. 999/920-5869, www.ki-xocolatl.com, 9am-11pm Mon.-Sat., 9am-6pm Sun.) specializes in high-end artisanal chocolates made from 100 percent Mexican ingredients: organic cacao from Chiapas and Tabasco, organic vanilla from Veracruz, and sugarcane from Yucatán. Chocolates can be purchased by the piece, by the kilo, or in artful packaging—any which way, these chocolates are especially addicting. Wi-Fi facilitates lingering.

El Retorno (Calle 62 btwn Calles 59 and 61, tel. 999/928-5634, www.panificadoraelretorno.com, 6am-9pm daily, US$0.40-2.50) is one of the city's most reliable bakery chains, with one shop half a block from the Plaza de la Independencia. You'll find cookies, cakes, and breads of all tastes and shapes.

Just steps from Parque Santa Lucía, **Pola** (Calle 55 btwn Calles 62 and 64, noon-10pm daily, US$1.50-3) serves up delicious, creamy, homemade gelato. Flavors change daily but include chai, peanut butter cup, bitter orange, and yes, chocolate and strawberry too. An artsy room with benches and small tables makes it easy to linger (and oh-so-tempting to get a second—or third—scoop).

Groceries

Facing Parque Santiago, **Super Aki** (Calle 72 at Calle 59, 6:30am-10:30pm daily) is a full grocery store offering canned goods, produce, fresh meats, dairy products, and more.

The **Mercado Municipal** (Calle 67 btwn Calles 56 and 58, 8am-8pm daily) is a rambling two-story market offering every fruit, vegetable, and meat sold in the region. Upstairs, there are about a dozen cheap eateries—not the cleanest, but the bustling shoppers and yelling vendors are definitely an experience; *comidas corridas* (two-course meals with a drink) cost US$2-5, and you can also order cheap tacos, *tortas,* and tamales.

For fresh fruits, vegetables, and meats without the hustle and bustle of the larger Mercado Municipal, try **Mercado Santos Degollado** (Calle 57 btwn Calles 70 and 72, 6am-2pm daily). On Parque Santiago, this market gives you a taste of how the locals shop with its myriad fruit and vegetable stands, *tortillerías,* shoe repair shops, and flower sellers. Stay for a meal—the handful of small restaurants are known citywide for their excellent seafood tacos and *tortas.* Prices run US$2-6 for a full meal.

If you're looking for a megastore, there's a **Walmart** (Paseo de Montejo at Av. Pérez Ponce, tel. 999/926-0106, 7am-11pm daily) across the street from the Fiesta Americana hotel.

ACCOMMODATIONS

Mérida has a profusion of charming inns and bed-and-breakfasts, suited to all tastes and budgets. Many are in restored *casonas* (large colonial home) or colonial-era buildings, giving visitors a taste of a Mérida long ago. Most listed here have fewer than 10 rooms, so it's best to call ahead or reserve online. All have Wi-Fi.

Under US$25

★ **Nómadas Hostel** (Calle 62 at Calle 51, tel. 999/924-5223, www.nomadastravel.com, US$11.25 dorm, US$17 s with shared bath, US$25 d with shared bath, US$31-34 s/d,

Haciendas Turned Hotels

After lying abandoned for decades or even centuries, the Yucatán Peninsula's old henequen haciendas are returning to—and sometimes surpassing—their former colonial glory. Many have been restored as unique and super-deluxe hotels, making great use of the thick walls, high ceilings, and lush grounds. They're not cheap, but the setting and service are unforgettable. Here are a few of the best near Mérida.

Once a sisal-producing hacienda, **La Hacienda Xcanatún** (Carr. Mérida-Progreso Km. 12, tel. 999/930-2140, www.xcanatun.com, US$275-350 s/d with a/c) boasts 18 beautifully restored suites set in winding tropical gardens. Rooms have Lebanese-style floors, hand-carved furnishings, Mexican and Far Eastern antiques, and original oil paintings. Most also enjoy private sitting areas and whirlpool tubs. There's a full-service spa, two pools, and a gourmet restaurant on-site.

Hacienda San José Pachul (Carr. Tetiz-Kinchil Km. 41, tel. 999/125-5230, www.haciendasanjosepachul.com, US$175-195 s/d with a/c) is a completely renovated hacienda with two gorgeous guestrooms—a modern one with floor-to-ceiling windows and a private garden, and a colonial-style one with 5.5-meter (18-foot) ceilings and a private sitting room. Both are stylish and comfortable; they include king-size beds, luxurious linens, a music system, flat-screen TVs, and Wi-Fi. Guests also are given a local cell phone to use, for free, during their stay (local calls only). There's a gourmet restaurant and pool on-site too. It's located 36 kilometers (22 miles) east of Mérida, toward Celestún.

US$37 s/d with a/c) is one of the most popular hostels in town, and with good reason: Dorms are clean and comfortable, and there's also a spacious women-only room. All bunks have an individual light, fan, and locker, and the community bathrooms are well maintained. Continental breakfast is included, and guests have access to a clean, fully equipped kitchen and a great pool too. The hostel also offers free salsa lessons, yoga, and cooking classes; there's even live trova music Monday-Friday nights. It can get a bit crowded in the busy season, but all in all it's a great place for backpackers.

On the central plaza, **Hostel Zócalo** (Calle 63 btwn Calles 60 and 62, tel. 999/930-9562, www.hostalzocalo.com, US$10 dorm, US$18 s/d with shared bath, US$24 s/d with private bath) is a rambling, fan-cooled place with private rooms tucked in here and there, dorm rooms spread throughout, and lots of common space. If you're angling for a private room, the ones with balconies have amazing views over the main plaza, though they share bathrooms. The six-bed dorms—one just for women—are comfortable and have good, firm mattresses. A big buffet breakfast is included in the rate, and there's a common kitchen too.

Children are very welcome—great for families traveling on a tight budget.

Hostel Luna Nueva (Calle 49 at Calle 56A, tel. 999/923-0482, www.lunanuevahostel.com, US$8.50 dorm, US$27-29 s/d with a/c) is a bright and airy place with one co-ed dorm and three private rooms. The dorm is spacious so easily accommodates eight bunk beds with thin mattresses and a sitting area; the shared bathrooms are single sex (they're stinky but clean—chalk it up to old plumbing). Private rooms are comfortable, with firm beds, heavy wood furnishings, cable TV, and very welcome air-conditioning. There's Wi-Fi throughout the building plus two guest computers. There's no common kitchen, which is a bummer, but a small on-site café sells cheap eats.

Casa Chi Chi Stil (Calle 66 btwn Calles 43 and 45, cell. tel. 999/396-4136, chichistil@libero.it, US$15 s/d with shared bath, US$17 s/d) is a small budget hotel with four basic rooms—think good beds, decent linens, a couple fluorescent lights, a fan, and a door. Two share a Jack and Jill bathroom, which is convenient, especially in the middle of the night. There's a small plunge pool and cozy outdoor

Hacienda Temozón (Hwy. 261 Km. 182, tel. 999/923-8089, www.thehaciendas.com, US$450-590 s/d with a/c) has 28 elegant rooms and suites. Each has 5-7-meter (16.4- to 23-foot) ceilings, gleaming tile floors, luxurious amenities, and modern furnishings; suites have al fresco bathtubs. Outside, the manicured grounds feature walking trails, a pool, and a tennis court. There also are three on-site cenotes. The original machinery used to process henequen sits at the entrance to the full-service spa—a nice touch.

Hacienda Santa Rosa (off Hwy. 180, tel. 999/923-1923, www.haciendasantarosa.com, US$228-590 s/d with a/c) is as classy as Temozón though less grand: 11 luxurious rooms, beautifully maintained but smallish grounds, a pool with shade trees, and an outdoor spa. The main attractions here are privacy and personalized service. You won't find the bells and whistles of other haciendas, but you'll enjoy a restful and ultra-comfortable stay.

A 400-year-old estate, **Hacienda San Pedro Nohpat** (off Hwy. 180, tel. 999/988-0542, www.haciendaholidays.com, US$95-125 s/d with a/c) offers three suites, each decorated in a mishmash of styles. All have modern amenities like quiet air conditioners, satellite TV, and minifridges. The grounds are well kept and include a pool, hot tub, and comfy indoor and outdoor lounges. A full breakfast is included in the rate too. Best of all, it's just one kilometer (0.6 mile) from Mérida's city limits.

seating areas. A super-clean, fully equipped common kitchen is a huge plus. There's Wi-Fi too. Weekly and monthly rates are available.

US$25-50

Hotel Mucuy (Calle 57 btwn Calles 56 and 58, tel. 999/928-5193, www.hotelmucuy.com, US$28 s/d with fan, US$30 s/d with a/c) is a motel-like building behind a colonial facade. Rooms open onto a sunny, verdant courtyard with a tile pool that's fed by a splashing cascade. The units are simple but spotless with hot-water bathrooms; most have twin beds with flower bedspreads and slatted windows. The owner, Doña Ofelia, is a true delight and has earned many repeat guests since the hotel opened in 1974. Rates include 12 hours of parking in a lot across the street.

Facing Parque Mejorada, **Hotel La Piazzeta** (Calle 50 btwn Calles 57 and 59, tel. 999/923-3909, www.hotellapiazzettamerida.com, US$42-62 s/d with a/c) has 10 rooms with shabby chic flair, modern bathrooms, and lots of natural light. All have pillow-top beds—you've come to sleep, after all—and a couple have small balconies with views of the park. Rates include a big breakfast at the

hotel's hip Mediterranean restaurant. There's a rooftop lounge and Wi-Fi throughout the hotel; guest bikes are available for free too.

Hotel Dolores Alba Mérida (Calle 63 btwn Calles 52 and 54, tel. 999/928-5650, www.doloresalba.com, US$41-44 colonial s/d with a/c, US$53-56 modern s/d with a/c) is a huge hotel with rooms in two sections: the "colonial" side with older, simpler rooms located in the original building, and a "modern" side with larger rooms, plasma TVs, and sliding glass doors overlooking the pool. All are well-kept, with tiled floors (and even tiled headboards), firm beds, cable TV, and in-room telephones. There's an elevator too. In the courtyard, lounge chairs surround a terrific outdoor swimming pool—heaven on a hot Mérida day. The hotel's only drawback is its location in the middle of a busy commercial area; it's safe, but can be pretty loud and hectic. On-site parking and a (just so-so) breakfast buffet are included.

★ **Casa Ana** (Calle 52 btwn Calles 51 and 53, tel. 999/924-0005, www.casaana.com, US$50 s/d with a/c) is a good option if you want a smaller place and don't mind the long walk to the central plaza. There are five rooms, all large and airy with simple, colorful decor. All face a lush interior garden with a small pool and an outdoor *palapa* lounge. There's also a pleasant outdoor dining area where breakfast is served (included in the rate); additional meals also can be arranged with advance notice. Wi-Fi is available in all the rooms and common areas. The longtime owner, Ana, is a wealth of information and a gracious host.

Located on Parque Hidalgo, **Gran Hotel** (Calle 60 at Calle 59, tel. 999/924-7730, www. granhoteldemerida.com.mx, US$37-48 s/d with a/c, US$70 suite with a/c) is a gorgeous neoclassic building, with Corinthian columns, beautiful tile floors, and a soaring atrium filled with comfortable armchairs and low tables. Opened in 1901, the hotel has elegant, though somewhat aged, accommodations with *tiny* bathrooms; all have ironwork headboards, heavy wood furnishings, phones, and cable TV. Be sure to look at a few rooms before deciding: Some have no windows and others have industrial carpeting. Free parking is available two blocks away.

US$50-75

Charming and irreverent, ★ **Hotel Luz en Yucatán** (Calle 55 btwn Calles 58 and 60, tel. 999/924-0035, www.luzenyucatan. com, US$54-64 s/d with a/c, US$74-104 s/d with kitchen and a/c) is like no other hotel in Mérida—or the whole region, for that matter. For starters, its prices are sliding scale—the website asks you to describe yourself as "exceedingly," "moderately," or "not at all" successful and gives rates accordingly (they vary by US$5), and they don't require deposits since "real life is sufficiently punitive." Some of the smaller rooms are a bit dark, but the others—especially the studios, one-bedrooms, and suite—are a great value, with full kitchens, patios, and plenty of space and natural light. All have bright whimsical decor, plus modern TVs, air conditioners, and other amenities. A small pool and garden and free parking seal the deal—it's a great choice.

The adults-only **Hotel Julamis** (Calle 53 at Calle 54, tel. 999/924-1818, www.hoteljulamis.com, US$59-81 s/d with a/c, US$99 two-bdrm house with a/c) is set in a 200-year-old house with tin star lamps in the hallways, rooms with original tile floors, and vibrant bursts of fuchsia bougainvillea. Some rooms have astounding room murals that look like silk wallpaper; all are outfitted with luxurious amenities. An intimate courtyard draped by hanging vines is the setting for

one of many colonial-style hotels and B&Bs in Mérida

a gourmet breakfast, prepared by chef and owner Alexander Rudin. Upstairs, a terrace with whirpool tub, lounge beds, and a guest-only bar gazes out over the city. There's street parking only, but it's not difficult. A fully equipped two-bedroom house, in the same style, also is available for rent next door.

Hotel del Peregrino (Calle 51 btwn Calles 54 and 56, tel. 999/924-3007, www.hoteldelperegrino.com, US$60 s/d with a/c) occupies a gorgeous colonial home with high ceilings and original tile floors. Rooms are uniform in style with mustard-yellow walls, dark wood furnishings, and smart TVs. Continental-plus breakfast—fruit, yogurt, pastries, and pancakes—is served in the central patio, and a fully equipped open-air kitchen is also available to guests. Best of all, there's a rooftop terrace with nice views of the city and an outdoor whirpool tub. Guests also can use the nearby pool at the Nómadas Hostel. Wi-Fi is available throughout the hotel and there's also a guest computer.

Hotel MedioMundo (Calle 55 btwn Calles 64 and 66, tel. 999/924-5472, www.hotelmediomundo.com, US$68-72 s/d with fan, US$76-80 s/d with a/c) is a hacienda-style guesthouse with high blue-painted walls and two courtyards—one with a lush garden and fountain, the other with a small swimming pool and shaded tables. Ten spacious rooms have deep beds, large spotless bathrooms, and very spare decor, save the exuberant tile floors that date to the original construction. Continental breakfast is included; no children under eight are permitted. Wi-Fi is available.

Hotel Marionetas (Calle 49 btwn Calles 62 and 64, tel. 999/928-3377, www.hotelmarionetas.com, US$68-76 s/d with a/c, US$93 suite with kitchenette and a/c) gets its name from the building's former tenant—a well-known puppet theater company. The eight spacious rooms and one suite are all slightly different, whether in the color of the walls or the design of the tile floors. Decor is attractive and streamlined, making the most of select items—an ornate wood-framed mirror in one room, a wrought-iron vanity in another.

There's a sunny inner courtyard, small pool, and a pleasant on-site restaurant.

US$75-100

★ **Casa del Maya** (Calle 66 btwn Calles 45 and 47, tel. 999/181-1880, US$90-95 s/d with a/c) is a colonial-style bed-and-breakfast, offering a perfect combination of comfort and service. Six spacious rooms are set in three sections around the property; all have pillow-top mattresses, luxurious linens, handcrafted furniture, and high-end folk art. They also enjoy rainshower heads, flat-screen TVs, and strong Wi-Fi. There's a lap pool in the middle of the property and plenty of cozy spots in the leafy garden to relax. A full gourmet breakfast, complete with to-die-for cinnamon rolls, fresh fruit, yogurt, and an ever-changing entrée, is served under a large palapa. The affable owners, Jordy and Steve, are a fountain of information on area sites; they also happily make reservations for tours, restaurants, and spa services.

Cascadas de Mérida (Calle 57 btwn Calles 74-A and 76, tel. 999/923-8484, www.cascadasdemerida.com, US$86 s with a/c, US$94 d with a/c) gets its name from artificial *cascadas* (waterfalls) built cleverly into the hotel's stone retaining wall; the sound of gurgling water drowns out street noise, and the glass-walled showers have a bright outdoorsy feel (yet are totally private). The four rooms are comfortable and modern, with stone walls, skylights, and attractive Mexican and Guatemalan furnishings, plus cable TV and air-conditioning. Though not a colonial structure, the hotel has a sunny backyard with a large pool surrounded by hammocks and leafy plants. A bountiful breakfast is included, and the friendly proprietors have a wealth of local expertise.

Virtually every inch of wall space at **Los Arcos Bed & Breakfast** (Calle 66 btwn Calles 49 and 53, tel. 999/928-0214, www.losarcosmerida.com, US$85-95 s/d with a/c) is filled with artwork, some from Mexico, some from Africa, some painted by the owners themselves. Add potted houseplants, a

MÉRIDA, THE PUUC ROUTE, AND CAMPECHE

MÉRIDA

small swimming pool, and some dogs, and you've got this unique, eclectic guesthouse. The rooms—there are only two—are comfy, with high ceilings, big bathrooms, cable TV, and CD players. There's no on-site parking, but street parking is plentiful. A big breakfast is included; no children under 17 are allowed.

Across from Santa Lucía park, **Hotel Boutique Casa Lucía** (Calle 60 btwn Calles 53 and 55, tel. 999/928-0740, www.casalucia. com.mx, US$85-99 s/d with a/c, US$113 suite with a/c) is an elegant hotel built in a restored 19th-century mansion. Rooms are spacious and sumptuous with deep beds, high-thread-count linens, and marble bathrooms; exposed wood beams, oil paintings, and antique furnishings are nice touches. The large interior courtyard has a well-kept pool and *palapa* lounge—a fine place to cool off after a day of sightseeing. Room service and on-site parking is available.

Over US$100

Villa Verde (Calle 56 btwn Calles 53 and 55, tel. 999/290-7759, www.villaverdemerida.com, US$130 s/d with a/c) is a gorgeously renovated colonial mansion with a large waterfall pool, lots of common areas for lounging, and little extras like guest cocktail hour every evening and gourmet breakfast every morning. Rooms are spacious and elegant with original mosaic tile floors, six-meter-high (20-foot) ceilings and modern art. The owners, Robert and Michael, are genuinely welcoming and share suggestions for area sights and hot spots around town. Their friendly pets lounge around the property—totally fine if you like furry creatures, but not everyone's thing.

The serene seven-room ★ **Casa Lecanda** (Calle 47 btwn Calles 54 and 56, tel. 999/928-0112, www.casalecanda.com, US$230-270 s/d with a/c, US$310 suite with a/c) comprises two sections: three front patio rooms in a classic 1800s courtyard house with three-meter-high (10-foot) ceilings and original wooden ceiling beams, and a newer section of stylish garden suites or balcony rooms with wooden terraces at the back. In between, a grand ceiba tree overlooks a central pool, and guests can lounge in the outside seating and hammocks of dramatic entryways and breezy archway patios. Throughout the hotel are exquisite tile floors, and all rooms have plasma TVs, beds with carved wooden headboards and down comforters, and roomy semi-open bathrooms. Rates include continental breakfast, dinner is available by advance request, and parking is available. Service is excellent.

Fashioned from two 19th-century *casonas,* **Rosas & Xocolate** (Paseo de Montejo at Calle 41, tel. 999/924-2992, www.rosasandxocolate. com, US$245-275 s/d with a/c, US$388-695 suite with a/c) pampers guests like no other place in town. Cedar cabinetry, luxurious fabrics, and fluffy comforters are soothing, and double-paned windows repel street noise. Bathe with chocolate soap in a magnificent open-air bathtub (in all rooms), or swan around the full spa, small pool, and good-sized gym. Full breakfast is included and served in its fusion cuisine restaurant; a jazz ensemble serenades the chic Moon Lounge terrace Wednesday-Saturday. Ground-floor water features are lovely, though at night the hotel keeps it so *romántico* (read: dark) that it's amazing there aren't frequent unplanned plunges. Parking is included.

INFORMATION AND SERVICES
Tourist Information

When you get to Mérida, pick up a copy of *Yucatán Today* or *Explore Yucatán,* two of the most helpful tourist magazines in Mexico. Published monthly and distributed free at hotels, shops, and tourist offices, the magazines have maps, suggested itineraries, short articles, and lists of upcoming events. While focusing on Mérida, both also cover Progreso, the Puuc Route, Izamal, Chichén Itzá, and Valladolid.

The city and state tourism boards— **Información Turística del Ayuntamiento** and **Departamento de Turismo del Estado de Yucatán,** respectively—both offer a wide selection of maps, brochures, and usually someone who speaks English. In general, however, the staff at the state office is much more helpful for specific questions and any information not found in the brochures. The two offices are located two blocks apart: next to the Teatro José Peón Contreras (Calle 60 btwn Calles 55 and 57, tel. 999/924-9290, www.merida.gob.mx, 8am-8pm daily), and just inside the Palacio de Gobierno (central plaza, Calle 61 at Calle 60, tel. 999/930-3101, www.yucatan.travel, 8am-9pm Mon.-Sat., 8am-8pm Sun.).

Other convenient city tourist offices are located in the Palacio Municipal (central plaza, Calle 62 btwn Calles 61 and 63, tel. 999/942-0000, ext. 80119, 8am-8pm daily), a sidewalk kiosk on Paseo de Montejo (at Av. Colón, 8am-8pm daily), and at a booth in the arrivals *(llegadas)* area of the CAME first-class bus terminal (Calle 70 btwn Calles 69 and 71, 9am-7:30pm daily).

Emergency Services

Considered the best hospital in town, **Clínica de Mérida** (Av. Itzáes 242, Col. García Ginerés, tel. 999/924-1800, www.clinicademerida.com.mx) is a state-of-the-art facility with 24-hour emergency service. A close second is the **Centro Médico de las Américas** (CMA, Calle 54 near Calle 33-A, tel. 999/926-2111, www.centromedicodelasamericas.com.mx, 24 hours). For meds, head to the well-stocked **Yza Farmacia** (central plaza, Calle 63 btwn Calles 60 and 62, tel. 999/924-9510, 24 hours), which delivers. If you're staying closer to Parque Santiago, **Farmacias Bazar** (Calle 57 btwn Calles 70 and 72, tel. 999/928-5454, 8am-9pm Mon.-Sat., 8am-2pm Sun.) is another good option. The **police station** (Calle 57 btwn Calles 52 and 54, tel. 999/942-0060, toll-free Mex. tel. 066) is open 24 hours.

Money

You'll have no problem accessing your money in Mérida. Virtually every bank in town—and there are a lot of them—has a 24-hour ATM that happily accepts foreign debit cards. Many convenience stores also have cash machines. Most banks will exchange U.S. dollars and euros, and a few will change other currencies.

You can also try changing cash at a *casa de cambio* (currency-exchange office) or at the front desk of any upscale hotel, but the rates at either are rarely good.

Most of the banks and ATMs are on or near the Plaza de la Independencia and along Calle 59. Among many others are **Banamex** (Casa de Montejo, Calle 63 btwn Calles 60 and 62, 9am-4pm Mon.-Fri., 10am-2pm Sat.), **HSBC** (Calle 59 btwn Calles 68 and 70, 9am-5pm Mon.-Fri.), and **Bancomer** (Calle 59 at Calle 62, 8:30am-4pm Mon.-Fri.).

Media and Communications

The **post office** is located on Calle 53 between Calles 52 and 54 (8am-2pm Mon.-Fri.). Internet cafés can be a bit sparse. The most central is the student-packed **Cyber de las 58** (Calle 58 btwn Calles 57 and 59, 7am-9pm Mon.-Fri., 8am-6pm Sat., US$1/hour). If you're down by Parque Santiago, there are several **side-by-side cybercafes** on Calle 59 just past the park, all charging around US$0.75 per hour and open 8:30am-10:30pm every day. Most central parks have free Wi-Fi. (The central plaza even has outlets beside many of the benches so you can recharge your phone or tablet while feeding the pigeons.)

If you're hankering for English-language magazines, you'll find a decent selection at **Sanborn's** (Fiesta Americana, Paseo de Montejo at Av. Colón, 7:30am-1am daily).

Immigration and Consulates

The **immigration office** (Av. Colón btwn Calles 8 and 10, Col. García Ginerés, tel. 999/925-4553, 9am-1pm Mon.-Fri.) is four long blocks west of the Fiesta Americana.

Many European countries have closed their Mérida consulates and moved their offices to Cancún. Some countries still maintain honorary consulates, often in private homes or offices; services vary from emergency-only assistance to basic passport and visa matters. Call ahead to see if these consulates can help you or if you're better off going to Cancún. For a listing of consulates in the region, see the Essentials chapter.

Laundry and Storage

Reliable and centrally situated, **Lavandería La Fe** (Calle 64 at Calle 55, tel. 999/924-4531, 8am-7:30pm Mon.-Fri., 8am-5pm Sat.) charges US$4.50 for the first three kilos (6.6 pounds) and US$1-2 each additional kilo. Clothes are typically ready the same day if you drop them off early; pickup and delivery service is available for US$5.

Many hotels will store luggage for guests, even those checking out, for free on request. If yours doesn't, **Guarda Plus** (Calle 70 btwn Calles 69 and 71, 6am-9:30pm daily) is across from the CAME bus station and stores bags for US$0.45-1.25 per hour per bag, depending on the size. There is no daily rate, unfortunately.

Language and Instruction

Centro Idiomas del Sureste (CIS, Calle 52 btwn Calles 49 and 51, tel. 999/923-0954, www.cisyucatan.com.mx) offers all levels of Spanish instruction, with class sizes varying from one to eight students. Courses last at least one week and start every Monday. Students also can get intensive language training that's focused on an area of interest—CIS is a favorite with Spanish teachers and Maya scholars because of it. Homestays and area excursions are integral parts of the program too.

Plastered with arthouse movie posters and jazzed up in candy colors, the **Calle 55 Spanish School** (Calle 55 btwn Calles 56 and 58, tel. 999/274-3130, www.calle-55.com) has a sunny colonial courtyard building in the center of town. Group offerings range 4-20 hours per week; individual instruction is also available. Homestays, hotel bookings, and apartment rentals can be arranged too. The school is run by a vivacious Mexican French couple.

Instituto Benjamín Franklin de Yucatán (Calle 57 near Calle 54, tel. 999/928-0097, www.benjaminfranklin.com.mx) offers Spanish grammar and conversation classes as well as Mexican history, culture, and socioeconomic courses. An entrance exam is given to determine individual language ability so that students are placed in the appropriate level. Area field trips also are offered, as are homestays.

Los Dos (Calle 68 btwn Calles 65 and 67, tel. 999/928-1116, www.los-dos.com) is a popular cooking school, specializing in Yucatecan cuisine. Run by David Sterling, a Manhattan transplant and accomplished chef, classes are fun and informative and held in his gorgeous colonial home. The popular Taste of Yucatán course (US$200 pp, minimum 6 people, 8:30am-4pm) starts at Los Dos with pastries and coffee and a short introduction to Maya and modern Yucatecan cuisine. Then it's off to the market with David to buy fresh vegetables, fish, meat, chiles, cilantro, corn dough for tortilla chips or tamales—anything and everything you'll need. Back at the kitchen, you don a Los Dos apron (yours to keep) and prepare a midday snack. Afterward, the real cooking begins—depending on what you found at the market, it may include *cochinita pibil, pollo pibil,* tamales, *panuchos,* or other Yucatecan classics. The class ends with a grand white-tablecloth meal featuring your creations, plus complimentary wine and beer. Three-day, weeklong, and private courses also can be arranged. Reserve at least 72 hours in advance, as the schedule fills up fast.

GETTING THERE
Air

Mérida's **Manuel Crescencio Rejón International Airport** (MID, Av. Itzáes/Hwy. 180, tel. 999/940-6090) is located seven kilometers (4.3 miles) southwest of the town center. The airport has several car rental agencies and a 24-hour ATM.

The following airlines serve Mérida's International Airport:

- **Aeroméxico** (airport tel. 999/946-1530, toll-free Mex. tel. 800/237-6639, www.aeromexico.com)

- **Interjet** (toll-free Mex. tel. 800/011-2345, toll-free U.S. tel. 866/285-9525, www.interjet.com.mx)

- **United Airlines** (toll-free Mex. tel. 800/900-5000, toll-free U.S. tel. 800/864-8331, www.united.com)

- **Viva Aerobus** (toll-free U.S. tel. 888/935-9848, www.vivaaerobus.com)
- **Volaris** (toll-free U.S. tel. 855/865-2747, www.volaris.mx)

Bus

Mérida has several bus stations. The first-class station is known by the acronym **CAME** (pronounced KAH-meh, Calle 70 btwn Calles 69 and 71, tel. 999/924-0830, toll-free Mex. tel. 800/702-8000, www.ado.com.mx) and has ADO, ADO-GL, OCC, and ADO Platino service. Most of your bus travel, especially long distance, will be from here. There's another first-class bus station in Plaza Bonita, known as **Fiesta Americana** (Av. Colón at Calle 60, tel. 999/920-5523) because of its location behind the same-named hotel. Service is limited but includes nonstop service to Cancún International Airport, Cancún, and Playa del Carmen.

Buses from the **second-class bus terminal** (Calle 69 btwn Calles 68 and 70, tel. 999/924-8391), around the corner from CAME, serve many of the same destinations but make more stops at small towns along the way. Buses tend to be dumpier, the trips longer, and the price marginally lower—better to stick with first-class service whenever possible. That said, the Sunday Puuc Route Tour bus leaves from here as do buses to Chiquilá, for those headed to Isla Holbox.

Terminal Noreste (Calle 67 btwn Calles 50 and 52, Noreste tel. 999/924-6355, Oriente tel. 999/928-6230, Líneas Unidas tel. 999/924-7865) is the base for regional bus lines. Most tourists using this terminal are headed to Río Lagartos to see the flamingos, or to Cuzamá to visit the cenotes; other destinations include Mayapán, Maní, Izamal, and Isla Holbox (via Chiquilá).

Terminal Auto-Progreso (Calle 62 btwn Calles 65 and 67, tel. 999/928-3965, www.autoprogreso.com) primarily serves Progreso (US$1.20/2.15 one-way/round-trip, 50 minutes), with departures every 15 minutes 4am-10pm.

Terminal Autobuses del Centro (Calle 65 btwn Calles 46 and 48, tel. 999/923-9962) provides service to Aké archaeological zone (US$1.60, 1 hour) at 5:30am, 8:40am, 4pm, and 7pm.

Car

Good highways approach Mérida from all directions. Be prepared for one-way streets, and avoid arriving on Sunday, when a large area in the center of town is closed to vehicles. If you don't know the city, it can be a real headache to drive to your hotel, since many are downtown. If you're **arriving via Highway 180,** note that it becomes Calle 65 and hits the busy Mercado Municipal area at Calle 56—it's less congested if you bypass this area by jogging right on Calle 52 and then left onto Calle 61 to reach the center.

The *periférico* is a wide, paved traffic loop that circumscribes the city, making it possible to bypass the congested downtown streets if you're headed from Chichén Itzá to Celestún, for example.

Parking is restricted in the center, with yellow-and-red curbs marking prohibited areas, though this is relaxed between 9pm and 7am Monday-Saturday and all day Sunday. Street parking is easier to find the farther you go from the Plaza de la Independencia. The city government has a map of public lots at www.merida.gob.mx/transporte/ubicacion.html; most charge US$0.75-1 per hour. Be sure to check a lot's opening time if you park overnight and need to leave early in the morning.

Highway 180 is a modern toll highway (*carretera cuota*) that runs from Mérida to Cancún and Playa del Carmen. It begins 16 kilometers (9.9 miles) east of Mérida at Kantunil; from Mérida take Highway 180 toward Valladolid. Tolls are steep—US$6 to Chichén Itzá, US$10 to Valladolid, US$23 to Playa del Carmen, and US$26 to Cancún—but the road is in great condition, with rest stops, gas stations, and clearly marked exits; it's also nearly empty since most bus and trucking companies choose to take the *libre* (free road), which runs parallel to the highway. Although the *libre* is

Driving Distances from Downtown Mérida

LOCATION	DISTANCE	LOCATION	DISTANCE
Airport	7 km (4 mi)	Mahahual	389 km (241 mi)
Campeche City	253 km (158 mi)	Palenque	555 km (346 mi)
Cancún	320 km (199 mi)	Playa del Carmen	288 km (178 mi)
Celestún	86 km (52 mi)	Progreso	33 km (20 mi)
Chetumal	416 km (258 mi)	Río Lagartos	263 km (165 mi)
Chichén Itzá	120 km (75 mi)	Ticul	84 km (50 mi)
Cobá	232 km (145 mi)	Tulum	274 km (171 mi)
Dzibilchaltún	16 km (10 mi)	Uxmal	80 km (50 mi)
Ek' Balam	179 km (111 mi)	Valladolid	160 km (100 mi)
Izamal	72 km (44 mi)	Xpujil	476 km (295 mi)

slower and teeming with speed bumps, it takes drivers through small villages and past fields of henequen and corn—sights worth seeing if you're not in a rush.

GETTING AROUND

The best way to see Mérida is on foot. Granted, some of the sidewalks are narrow and the traffic can be thick, but the city is a pleasure to wander. Look for street names, which are usually found at intersections, high up on building corners.

To and From the Airport

Taxis charge a fixed US$14 from the airport to town, while the reverse trip costs approximately US$8—agree on a price beforehand. There is no airport bus per se, but vans marked UMAN leave every 10 minutes from Parque San Juan (Calle 69 btwn Calles 62 and 64) and pass the airport entrance road (US$0.45, 25 minutes). Be sure to ask the driver to let you off at *el aeropuerto;* it's a 500-meter (0.3-mile) walk from the stop to the terminal. From the airport, you can walk to Avenida Itzáes and catch an UMAN van to Parque San Juan—there is a bus stop just to your right when you reach the main road. Or wait for a 79-Aviación bus (US$0.45, 30 minutes) in front of the Budget office just outside the terminal—they pass less frequently (every 15-20 minutes), but you don't have to walk so far. Bus No. 79 goes to Parque San Juan as well, passing the first- and second-class bus terminals along the way. Note that the UMAN vans don't have much room for luggage—if you are loaded down, consider springing for a cab.

Bus

The most useful city buses are the ones that go between downtown and points along Paseo de Montejo. Downtown, catch an "Itzamná" bus on Calle 59 between Calles 56 and 58 (US$0.45). You can take the same bus all along Paseo de Montejo in either direction.

Taxi

Cabs can be hailed on the street or at taxi stands at most neighborhoods parks. For late-night service, most hotels, restaurants, bars, and nightclubs can call one for you, upon request. Most taxis aren't metered, so establish your fare in advance; expect to pay US$3-4 in the downtown area, and US$5-6 as far as the *periférico,* while a ride to the airport runs around US$8. If you happen to get into a cab with a taximetro (meter), the minimum fare is US$1.25.

Mérida Bus Schedule

The first-class bus station **CAME** (Calle 70 btwn. Calles 69 and 71, tel. 999/924-0830, toll-free Mex. tel. 800/702-8000, www.ado.com.mx) serves most major destinations, including:

Destination	Price	Duration	Schedule
Campeche	US$12.75-16	2.5 hrs	48 departures
Cancún	US$20-36	4.5 hrs	34 departures
Cancún airport	US$36-40	4-4.5 hrs	5:15am, 8:15am, 11am, and 10:55pm from Fiesta Americana terminal
Chetumal	US$26	5.5-6 hrs	7:30am, 1pm, 6pm
Chichén Itzá/Pisté	US$8	2 hrs	8:30am and 9:15am or take 2nd-class bus
Mexico City	US$100-118	19-20 hrs	7 departures
Palenque	US$36	7.5-9 hrs	8:30am, 7:45pm, and 10pm
Playa del Carmen	US$26-28	4-6 hrs	14 departures
Tulum	US$19	4 hrs	10:40am, 12:40pm, 5:40pm, and 8:15pm
Valladolid	US$9.75-11	2.5 hrs	19 departures

The **second-class bus terminal** (Calle 69 btwn. Calles 68 and 70, tel. 999/924-8391) serves nearer destinations, including:

Destination	Price	Duration	Schedule
Chichén Itzá/Pisté	US$5	2 hrs	hourly
Chiquilá	US$14	5.5 hrs	11:30pm; or connect
Puuc Route	US$11.25	8-8.5 hrs	8am Sunday (round-trip)
Santa Elena	US$3.25	1.75 hrs	6am and 9am
Ticul	US$4.75	1.5 hrs	hourly
Uxmal	US$3	1.25 hrs	8 departures
Valladolid	US$7.50	3 hrs	hourly

Terminal Noreste (Calle 67 btwn. Calles 50 and 52, Noreste tel. 999/924-6355, Oriente tel. 999/928-6230, Líneas Unidas tel. 999/924-7865) has several small bus lines serving destinations, including:

Destination	Price	Duration	Schedule
Celestún	US$3.50	2.5 hrs	hourly
Cuzamá (combi)	US$1.50	1 hr	every 15 mins
Izamal	US$2	1.5 hrs	hourly
Maní	US$2.75	2.5 hrs	hourly
Mayapán Ruins	US$2	1.5 hrs	hourly
Río Lagartos & San Felipe	US$10	3.5-4 hrs	5:30pm
Tizimín	US$6-7.50	2.5-4 hrs	6 departures

Bike

Bicimérida (Paseo de Montejo at Calle 45, tel. 999/287-3538, 9am-10pm Mon.-Fri., 8am-7pm Sat., 7am-3pm Sun.) rents bikes for US$2 per hour or US$3.25 per two hours. Most bikes have baskets and come with locks, upon request (no helmets though).

Car

Mérida has a slew of car rental agencies, and rental rates fluctuate with the season—expect a spike during Christmas and other holidays—and how many days you're renting. Non-holiday base rates average US$50 per day for a basic car, including tax and insurance.

Several international companies have offices at the Fiesta Americana hotel: **Europcar** (tel. 999/925-3548, toll-free Mex. tel. 800/201-2084, www.europcar.com), **National** (tel. 999/920-7722, toll-free Mex. tel. 877/222-9058, www.nationalcar.com), and **Payless Car Rental** (tel. 999/925-8283, www.paylesscar.com). Remember, you'll get better rates online, even last minute, than you will simply walking in.

Recommended local agencies include **Easy Way Rent a Car** (Calle 60 btwn Calles 55 and 57, tel. 999/930-9500, toll-free U.S./Can. tel. 877/640-3279, www.easywayrentacar.com, 7am-11pm daily) and **Veloz** (Calle 60 btwn Calles 55 and 57, tel. 999/928-0373, toll-free Mex. tel. 800/712-1375, www.velozrentacar.mx, 8am-8pm Mon.-Sat., 8am-3pm Sun.).

Tours

There is a *lot* to see and do in and around Mérida: Maya ruins, colonial churches, cenotes, caves, bird-watching, mountain biking, snorkeling, rappelling, and more. Guided tours are a practical way—and in a few cases, the only way—to see and do it all. But don't feel bound by set trips: Small tour companies often customize outings to fit travelers' particular interests and stamina. You just have to ask.

CITY TOURS

Bus tours of the city are a good way to get your bearings straight, and to get a sense of which places in Mérida you'd like to return to (and which not). There are two bus operators that provide a good lay of the land.

Camión Carnavalito (aka Gua Gua, Calle 55 between Calles 60 and 62, tel. 999/927-6119, US$7.50 adult, US$4.50 child) offers a two-hour driving tour of the city on an open-air school bus. The route includes the historic center and outlying neighborhoods. Tours leave at 10am, 1pm, 4pm, and 7pm Monday-Saturday, and 1pm and 3pm Sunday. Guides speak both English and Spanish. Look for the multicolored bus on Calle 55 in front of Parque Santa Lucía.

Turibus (Paseo de Montejo at Av. Colón, tel. 999/920-7636, 9am-9pm daily, US$9.50 adult, US$5 child under 12, multiday passes available) operates a fleet of apple-red double-decker buses that have all-day hop-on, hop-off service along a preset route; the stops include the central plaza, Museum of Anthropology, Itzimná church and park, Gran Plaza mall, and Monumento a la Bandera. Buses pass any given stop approximately every 55 minutes; tickets can be purchased onboard. Multilingual recorded explanations of various historic buildings and points of interest are played along the way.

Mérida's narrow streets were originally designed for *calesas* (horse-drawn buggies), and you can still ride one through the historic center where mansions with carved facades, stone gargoyles, and wrought-iron fences still stand (although some much better than others). Sunday is the best day to hire a *calesa,* as many streets are closed to vehicular traffic and the rest are relatively quiet; other days, you'll have to share the streets with the exhaust from passing cars. The easiest places to hire a *calesa* are at the Plaza de la Independencia or in front of the Hotel Fiesta Americana (Paseo de Montejo at Av. Colón). Drivers are typically at both sites 8am-midnight daily. Tours last 30-90 minutes and range US$20-40. Be sure to agree upon a price before sitting down for the ride.

The **city tourist office** (Palacio Municipal, Calle 62 btwn Calles 61 and 63, tel. 999/942-0000, ext. 80119) offers a free walking tour Monday-Saturday at 9:30am in English and Spanish. The tour lasts 1.5 hours and focuses on the buildings around the Plaza de la Independencia. To sign up, stop by the tourism office at 9:15am the morning you'd like to take the tour.

REGIONAL TOURS

Tour options vary widely, from large tour buses hitting must-see destinations like Chichén Itzá, Uxmal, and Celestún, to personalized outings to little-visited places, or exploring specific themes, like Maya culture or local wildlife. Prices vary as well, from US$35 for day trips, to weeklong expeditions costing a grand or more, depending on the number of people on the tour. No matter what your preference, be sure to ask about extra costs, like admission to the ruins and whether trips include guide service or simply transportation.

Ecoturismo Yucatán (Calle 3 btwn Calles 32-A and 34, tel. 999/920-2772, www.ecoyuc. com) offers excellent outdoors tours to flamingo sanctuaries and cenotes as well as to haciendas and archaeological sites; many excursions involve biking and kayaking too. The agency is known for customized 7- to 15-day tours that range as far as Campeche's Río Bec

region and Akumal on the Caribbean coast. **Mayan Heritage** (Calle 62 btwn Calles 55 and 57, tel. 999/924-8283, www.mayanheritage.com.mx) offers similar organized and custom excursions.

Iluminado Tours (Calle 66 No. 588 btwn Calles 73 and 75, tel. 999/924-3176, www.iluminado-tours.com) specializes in multiday tours that combine visits to places like Ek' Balam and Izamal with an emphasis on Maya spirituality and personal enlightenment. Check the website for offerings even farther afield, including the Sacred Maya tours of southern Campeche and Chiapas. Iluminado is run by a Canadian expat in association with local experts, including a former director of Chichén Itzá.

Mayan Ecotours (Calle 51 btwn Calles 54 and 56, tel. 999/987-3710, www.mayanecotours.com) offers a range of general and specialized tours, from swimming in cenotes or kayaking in mangrove forests to visiting archaeological sites or Maya families. Lunch at a restaurant or hacienda is included in many tours, and multilingual guides are available.

Turitransmérida (Calle 55 btwn Calles 60 and 62, tel. 999/924-1199, www.turitransmerida.com.mx) may be Mérida's largest tour operator, with a fleet of buses and various excursions offered daily. The quality of tours is decent, and the agency is known for its punctuality and professionalism, but groups can be up to 40 people in high season.

Celestún

Celestún is a small fishing village on the northwest shoulder of the Yucatán Peninsula; it sits on the mainland side of a 22-kilometer-long (13.6-mile) inlet-estuary known as the Ría Celestún, which is located in the Celestún Biosphere Reserve. The shallow, super-salty waters are an ideal breeding and feeding area for *Phoenicopterus ruber ruber,* the largest and pinkest of the world's five flamingo species and Celestún's primary attraction. The

reserve (which is home to myriad other bird species as well) has helped to make this inlet one of Mexico's best bird-watching areas and is known by bird enthusiasts worldwide.

Though tourism is growing, Celestún's coastal waters teem with fish and octopus, and catching them is still the main industry of locals here. The town has about 7,000 permanent residents, but 10,000 fishermen ply the coast from here to Río Lagartos during octopus season (August-December). Celestún is also an important salt-extraction area, producing 21,000 tons of salt every year. Salt production has been a vital industry since AD 600, and fishing goes back even further, of course.

If you're not a hard-core bird-watcher, a trip to the flamingo reserve is about the only reason to come to Celestún, and the town is just close enough to Mérida (96 kilometers/60 miles) to make day trips possible. Numerous operators offer tours here from Mérida, or you can do it yourself relatively easily by bus—either way, it's a pretty long day. If you have some time and a car, staying a night or even two lets you visit the reserve pressure-free, check out some additional area tours, and have some beach time.

RESERVA ECOLÓGICA DE LOS PETENES

The **Flamingo Reserve (Petenes Ecological Reserve)** is one of just a few breeding areas in the Northern Hemisphere for the American flamingo; it is home to the species' largest colony—up to 35,000 flamingos in the November-February mating season. Hundreds of other birds and waterfowl nest in the wetlands and mangrove forests—about 300 of the 509 identified bird species in the Yucatán Peninsula can be spied here. It's not unusual to see a blue heron or an anhinga perched on a tree stump with wings outstretched, drying in the sun.

One reason for the diversity of birdlife is the diversity of habitat, which includes mangrove forests, coastal dunes, savannas, low deciduous forest, hummocks (small islands of mangroves in the wetlands), seashore, and, of course, the Celestún estuaries.

Flamingo Tours

A standard flamingo tour unfolds in three parts: a visit to the flamingo feeding grounds, followed by a short ride through the mangroves, and then a stop to go swimming in an *ojo de agua* (literally, an "eye of water," the common term for a freshwater spring).

Because the sites are relatively far apart, you spend quite a lot of time motoring from one place to the next. In a 90-minute trip, you'll spend 20-30 minutes observing the flamingos, and somewhat less at the other spots. It doesn't sound like much, but the boat ride itself is pleasant enough, and most people find the stops sufficient. If you want more time with the flamingos—especially if the flock is at its height—private guides are the most flexible. With either the state guide service or the fishermen's cooperative, you'll have to get everyone in the boat (and the guide) to agree to adjust the schedule.

The **Parador Turístico Cultur** (no phone, 8am-5pm daily) is the rather inelegant name for the pier and visitors center where the state-sponsored guide service is based. It is three kilometers (1.9 miles) from Celestún, on the west side of the highway bridge spanning the *ría*. From there, you can book a complete tour (US$75, 1 hour, up to 6 people); there's also an additional US$2.25 per person park fee. The people at the ticket counter won't necessarily offer to put small groups together, but you can do so yourself by simply asking around; arrive around 10am (that's the 8am bus from Mérida) for the best chance at forming a group. Guide service is available in Spanish and English.

Celestún's **fishermen's cooperative** (no phone, 8am-4pm daily) also offers flamingo tours, leaving from the beach at the end of Calle 11. Trips from here are basically the same, though longer, as you first have to motor down the coast to the entrance of the estuary. Tours cost US$100 (2 hours, up to 9 people). If you end up waiting more than an hour for a group to develop, captains often will take smaller groups at a reduced cost.

Another cooperative, **Manglares de Dzinitún** (tel. 999/232-5915) offers a more active two-hour tour (US$30 pp) where you walk a short distance through a mangrove canal on a wooden boardwalk and then canoe or kayak out to see the flamingos (you can paddle your own kayak, but guides row the canoe). Boats drop off at a different location, and you're met comfort food for breakfast—think big plates of pancakes and eggs—and switches to pizza pies and burgers at night. For a change of pace, try the pizza with banana slices and pineapple. Almost best of all, it's open early and late.

The **Mercado Municipal** (central plaza, 7am-6pm daily) has a decent selection of fruits, veggies, bread, and other foodstuffs. There are also several cheap taco stands near the entrance.

ACCOMMODATIONS
Under US$50
Right on the beach, **Hotel Gutiérrez** (Calle 12 at Calle 13, tel. 988/916-2648, US$25 s/d, US$32 s/d with a/c) is a basic hotel with good beds and recently upgraded bathrooms. The beach is kept clean and the staff is accommodating. It also has a nice little restaurant on-site—perfect for a leisurely breakfast with a view. Wi-Fi is available, but spotty, in the rooms.

Hotel María del Carmen (Calle 12 btwn Calles 13 and 15, tel. 988/916-2170, US$29 s/d with fan, US$35 s/d with a/c and TV) is a budget hotel on a well-tended stretch of beach; it's run by a family that lives in the adjoining building. The good news is that the rooms are simple and clean with strong Wi-Fi. Each has two double beds, hammock hooks, and a balcony or terrace; most have ocean views. The downer is that the rooms are showing their age—threadbare linens, corroded sink handles, old air-conditioning units. For the rate and location, though, it's a decent value.

US$50-100
One kilometer (0.6 mile) north of town, the tranquil ★ **Celeste Vida Guest House** (Calle 12 s/n, tel. 988/916-2536, www.hotelcelestevida.com, US$95 studio, US$130 apartment) has it all. Decorated with colorful traditional fabrics, its three fan-cooled units—two kitchenette studios and an apartment with a full kitchen—harvest the ocean breeze, and there's a huge guest kitchen and barbecue to boot. Grab a novel from the book library and a cold beer from the fridge and

Celeste Vida Guest House

with bicycles to use for an easy ride back to your starting point.

FOOD
On the inland side of the main drag, **Restaurante Chivirico** (Calle 12 at Calle 11, tel. 988/916-2001, 11:30am-6:30pm daily, US$6-10) is a locals' favorite for super-fresh seafood, and is well worth the sacrifice in ocean view. The specialty is fish fillet stuffed with shrimp, but the ceviche and *pescado entero* (whole fish) are also tasty.

★ **La Palapa** (Calle 12 btwn Calles 11 and 13, tel. 988/916-2063, 11am-6pm daily, US$7-12) is the most popular and reliable restaurant in Celestún, serving tasty seafood plus various chicken and beef dishes, all beneath a soaring *palapa* roof with a view of the ocean. Service, facilities, and cleanliness are impeccable. Tour groups often eat here, but the dining area is large enough to give everyone space.

On the central plaza, **El Lobo** (Calle 10 at Calle 13, no phone, 8am-11am and 7pm-midnight Tues.-Sun., US$3-8) serves up classic laze under a *palapa* by the water's edge, or borrow a kayak or bicycle and go exploring. The Canadian owners are an excellent source of local information. Wi-Fi is available, and *mototaxis* charge US$2 from town. There's a two-night minimum.

Over US$100

Ten kilometers (6.2 miles) north of town, **Hotel Xixim** (Antigua Carr. a Sisal Km. 10, tel. 988/916-2100, www.hotelxixim.com, US$230-280 s/d, US$350 master suite) features 32 *palapa*-roofed bungalows nestled in a cluster of coastal dunes. Bungalows are decorated in a modern beachy way, feature luxe amenities, and have French doors opening onto ample patios with hammocks. (Master suites have two terraces, a living room, and a private plunge pool.) The grounds feature two pools, an immense shade *palapa*, an observation tower, and, of course, the beach—scenic, unmanicured, and loaded with seashells—all a short walk away. Please note: There's no air-conditioning, which some guests find irksome given the rates, but most take it in stride (along with the mosquitoes and geckos). Amenities include Wi-Fi (in the common areas), a yoga studio, and a modern restaurant specializing in Mexican dishes (US$10-15).

INFORMATION AND SERVICES

Celestún's **Centro de Salud** (Calle 5 btwn Calles 8 and 10, no phone, 7am-noon and 1pm-4pm Mon.-Fri.) is a basic health clinic. While emergency service is provided, serious injuries should be treated in Mérida. For medications, try **Farmacia Celestún** (central plaza, tel. 988/916-2106, 8am-11pm daily), facing the central park. The **police** (tel. 988/957-0200, 24 hours) are also on the central park, stationed in the Palacio Municipal (city hall).

Celestún has no banks, but there's a 24-hour ATM outside the **Palacio del Gobierno** and a second inside **Super**

Willy's (7am-10pm daily). Both are located on the central plaza, where there are also two Internet cafés that charge US$0.75 per hour: **Cyberline** (10am-2pm and 5pm-9pm daily) and **Jackuukutki.com** (10am-11pm daily).

GETTING THERE AND AROUND
Bus

Buses to Celestún leave from Mérida's Terminal Noreste every hour (except 7am) 5am-8pm daily (US$3, 2 hours). Assuming you're coming for the flamingo tours, the driver usually stops at the *parador* (staging area) before going the rest of the way into town. In Celestún, the small bus terminal (tel. 988/916-2067) is at the southeast corner of the central park. There are buses to Mérida (US$3, 2 hours, hourly 5am-8pm) in addition to various intermediate towns.

Car

From Mérida, take Avenida Aviación past the airport and toward the town of Umán. In Umán, you'll come to a tangled four-way intersection in the center of town, packed with cars, bicycle taxis, pedestrians, and an overworked traffic cop. Bear right at two consecutive forks—at the church and then at the market—then turn right again onto Calle 25, just a few blocks later. There are street signs for Celestún, but they can be easy to miss. Calle 25 leads out of town toward Kinchil, then connects to Highway 281 toward the coast.

Triciclos and *Mototaxis*

You can walk just about anywhere in Celestún, although when it's hot you may prefer to take a bicycle taxi, or *triciclo.* A ride in town costs around US$1, or for US$1.50 you can get a ride to the Parador Turístico where flamingo trips start, about three kilometers (1.9 miles) back down the highway. With baggage, your best bet is a *mototaxi* (US$2).

Progreso

On the Gulf of Mexico, Progreso is Mérida's closest access to the sea, an easy 33-kilometer (20.5-mile) drive from the city on Highway 261. Méridianos—as many as 150,000 during July and August weekends—flock here in summer to escape the intense heat and sticky humidity. Cruise ships also land here 2-3 times a week, disgorging several thousand passengers each. With tourists in town, Progreso comes to life; the restaurants are all open, the shops are bustling, and the beaches are filled with families enjoying the surf and sea. It's no Riviera Maya, but does the trick if you're burning up in Mérida.

The city was founded in 1856 and rose to prominence in the halcyon days of the henequen industry; henequen barons built grand estates east of town, and huge ships were a regular feature of the town waterfront. (Progreso's wharf was "only" two kilometers (1.2 miles) long then—less than a third its current length—but already an engineering marvel.) With the collapse of the henequen industry, Progreso's glimmer faded significantly; the port remained active, but the town took on a dumpy industrial aspect that persisted for decades.

Progreso has made a number of renovations in an attempt to brighten its image and entice day-trippers and cruise ship passengers to spend more time in town. The effort has paid off, especially along the waterfront, which has an attractive walkway and clean beach. It has also developed into a popular destination for Canadian snowbirds. One thing the town can't fix, however, is the frequent and sometimes powerful coastal wind, which buffets the entire northern coast and sometimes makes sunbathing a bit like being in a sandblaster. It's not all bad though: You can always take kiteboarding lessons to harvest the winds.

SIGHTS
Playa Central

Travelers arriving from the Caribbean side of the peninsula will find the Gulf coast rather underwhelming. The sand is coarser, and the water doesn't have the brilliant shades of blue that make the Quintana Roo coast justly famous. But the beach at Progreso is still fairly broad and clean and will do just fine, especially when the mercury rises inland. The water stays shallow a long way out and is relatively calm, although expect some chop during the stormy season (June-October) and know that the wind never really dies down. The beach is dotted with *palapa*-roofed sun shelters; across the street is a line of restaurants and cafés.

Street vendors rent **beach chairs with umbrellas** (US$10/day) on the beachfront road near Calle 76. There also are **bathrooms** (US$0.35), **showers** (US$0.65), and **changing areas** (US$0.35) here too.

El Muelle

At the turn of the 20th century, Progreso's two-kilometer-long (1.2-mile) pier was the longest stone wharf in the world. It had to be—the Yucatán Peninsula sits on a long limestone shelf that drops ever so gradually into the Gulf, making this and most of its bays extremely shallow. In fact, some scientists conjecture that at one time Yucatán, Cuba, and Florida were all one long extension of land.

Despite the length of Progreso's pier, it sat in only six meters (19.7 feet) of water, which proved insufficient for larger container ships. The activity on the pier declined greatly after a second pier was built in 1968 in the Yucalpetén harbor, six kilometers (3.7 miles) west of town. Progreso's pier continued to receive ships—mostly cruise ships and those that came to pick up exports such as honey, cement, fish, salt, and steel. In an effort to accommodate them and to attract more, the

Progreso

Gulf of Mexico

Playa Central

EL MUELLE ★

CRUISE SHIP TERMINAL

Malecón

CALLE 19

TOURIST INFORMATION
LE SAINT BONNET
PLAYA LINDA HOTEL
BEACH RENTALS/ RESTROOM
FLAMINGOS
SHARK RESTAURANT
Parque de la Paz

CALLE 21

CALLE 23

To Zocalo Beach Hostal →

CALLE 25

TOURIST OFFICE EL FARO ★
MERCADO MUNICIPAL
PLAZA DEL MAR/ CINES PROGRESO/ ADO

CALLE 27

To Chicxulub Puerto →

AUTO-PROGRESO TERMINAL
BANAMEX
FARMACIA YZA

COMBIS TO CHICXULUB PUERTO AND YUCALPETÉN
VANS TO MÉRIDA
CIBER ZONE
LAVANDERÍA
FARMACIAS SIMILARES
EL TACONAZO
HOTEL SAN MIGUEL

CALLE 29

SUPER SAN FRANCISCO DE ASIS
BANORTE
Plaza Central
POST OFFICE

CALLE 31

CALLE 33

CALLE 86
CALLE 84
CALLE 82
CALLE 80
CALLE 78
CALLE 76
CALLE 74
CALLE 72
CALLE 70
CALLE 68
CALLE 66
CALLE 64
CALLE 62

CENTRO MÉDICO AMERICANO

CALLE 35

CALLE 37

CALLE 39

261   261

To Chicxulub Puerto, Uaymitún Reserve, Xcambó Archaeological Zone, Telchac Puerto, and Dzilam de Bravo

To Yucalpetén, Hwy 261, Casa de Piedra, Dzibalchaltún Archaeological Zone, and Mérida

SCALE NOT AVAILABLE

© AVALON TRAVEL

pier was lengthened and now extends an amazing seven kilometers (4.3 miles) into the Gulf. A fleet of trucks and buses ferry cruise shippers and cargo back and forth. The public used to be able to walk to the end of the pier, but it's no longer allowed due to heightened security measures.

El Faro

Built between 1885 and 1891 on the site of an earlier lighthouse, today's 40-meter (131-foot) *faro* (lighthouse) was originally lit with kerosene. It was converted to electricity in 1923; a 1,000-watt lightbulb and a backup generator ensure there's always light to lead

sailors through the shallow Gulf waters into Progreso. It's not officially open to tourists, but lighthouse buffs may be able to finagle a visit by asking for permission at the tourist office.

Parque Nacional Arrecife Alacranes

A United Nations-designated biosphere reserve, **Parque Nacional Arrecife Alacranes** (http://arrecifealacranes.conanp. gob.mx) is made up of five islands (Desterrada, Desertora, Pájaros, Pérez, Chica) located 125 kilometers (78 miles) north of Progreso in the Gulf of Mexico. Covering nearly 300 square kilometers (116 square miles)—the islands themselves make up only a fraction of that figure—the reserve is a haven for a variety of marine birds, turtles, lobsters, conch, sharks, and other species that are at risk of extinction. Unfortunately, there are no organized tours to the park—lack of interest combined with the high cost of fuel make trips too expensive to be profitable for tour operators. If you're interested in a private tour, contact the Comisión Nacional de Áreas Naturales Protegidas (CONANP), the national park's office in Mérida (Calle 18 at Av. Pérez Ponce, tel. 999/938-0709), which can help recommend reputable tour operators to the park.

ENTERTAINMENT AND SHOPPING

Cines Progreso (Plaza del Mar, Calle 27 btwn Calles 76 and 78, tel. 969/934-4176, US$3.50) shows U.S. and Mexican films on its two screens in the evening. On Wednesday, tickets are two for one.

For Mexican folk art and crafts, check out the open-air *artesanía* **market** on the boardwalk whenever there's a cruise ship in town, typically Monday and Wednesday.

SPORTS AND RECREATION

You can rent personal watercraft, kayaks, and other gear from small kiosks on the beach, including in front of **El Viejo y El Mar restaurant** (Calle 19 at Calle 78). There, the equipment is available roughly 10am-4:30pm daily; ask in the restaurant if you don't find anyone on the beach.

To soar above the surf, enlist world-ranked Jessica Winkler of **Kite Beach Yucatan** (tel. 999/910-8721, www.kitebeachyucatan.com) for private or group kiteboarding classes at all levels. A private three-day beginner's class runs US$550; more advanced lessons and tours also are available.

Yuckite (tel. 999/279-0255, www.yuckite. com) offers kiteboarding classes ($44/hour private, US$25/hour group) as well as magnificent stand-up paddling tours (US$14-27 pp, plus US$13 for guide) to some of the region's most beautiful mangroves and lagoons.

FOOD
Restaurants

Besides the usual Yucatecan favorites, **Le Saint Bonnet** (Calle 19 at Calle 78, tel. 969/935-2299, 8am-10pm Sun.-Thurs., 8am-midnight Fri.-Sat., US$6-12) serves a big array

a view of *el faro* (the lighthouse) in Progreso

of seafood, sandwiches, and international dishes. The filling breakfasts are especially good and include fruit salad and excellent coffee. Staffers pop windows into the ocean-view panes when the wind picks up, and there's a kids' play structure and trampoline in the back to occupy the little ones.

Shark Restaurant (Calle 19 near Calle 72, tel. 969/935-2116, 10am-6pm daily, US$6-10) specializes in seafood *carpacho*—a version of carpaccio made from thinly sliced fish, octopus, or conch served in an olive oil, vinegar, and white wine sauce. It's also the only waterfront restaurant with tables on the beach, for sea breezes, picture-perfect views, and direct access to the sand and surf.

For cheap nighttime eats, head to **El Taconazo** (Calle 80 near central park, tel. 969/935-6405, 6pm-11pm daily), a hole-in-the-wall serving great tacos *al pastor*.

Just minutes from Progreso, ★ **Casa de Piedra** (Carr. Mérida-Progreso Km. 12, www.xcanatun.com, tel. 999/930-2140, 7:30am-11pm Mon.-Wed., 7:30am-midnight Thurs.-Sat., 7:30am-9pm Sun., US$15-22), offers an exquisite fusion of Caribbean and Yucatecan dishes. Housed within Hacienda Xcanatún, diners enjoy meals in an elegant dining room or on the romantic patio, with live music

Thursday-Sunday. It's a great choice, especially if you're craving something a little different. Reserve ahead, especially on weekends.

Groceries

The **Mercado Municipal** (Calle 80 btwn Calles 25 and 27, 8am-3pm daily, food stalls close between 5pm and 8pm) is where locals shop for their daily needs, from fruits, veggies, and fresh meats to clothes, toiletries, and other personal items. There are a handful of eateries offering cheap meals and snacks too.

Super San Francisco de Asis (Calle 80 btwn Calles 29 and 31, 7am-10pm daily) is a large modern supermarket in the middle of town.

ACCOMMODATIONS

Progreso has a growing but still limited selection of decent accommodations. Finding a room can be hard in July and August as well as during Semana Santa—be sure to make reservations. All the options below offer free Wi-Fi.

Zocalo Beach Hostal (Calle 21 at Calle 54, cell. tel. 969/103-0294, US$11 dorm, US$17/22 s/d with shared bath, US$30-33 s/d) has soaring ceilings, original colonial floors, an enormous upstairs ocean-view veranda, and probably a few years' worth of carpentry

Grab some fresh fruit at Progreso's colorful market.

work to keep the owners occupied. Many rooms dazzle with whimsical colors, though the haphazard subdivision of the building would make an architect cringe. Dorms are co-ed and have twin beds and strong fans; private rooms are clean and simple, though some have frosted glass doors (not exactly private). There's a well-equipped common kitchen, and the beach is just a block away. Rates include a full breakfast. Ask about the home's colorful history of boarding mariners and miscreants.

One of the best budget options in town, ★ **Hotel San Miguel** (Calle 78 btwn Calle 29 and 31, tel. 969/935-1357, sanmiguelhotel@ hotmail.com, US$25 s/d, US$31 s/d with a/c) offers modern and clean rooms near the central plaza. Each has air-conditioning, Wi-Fi, a minifridge, and cable TV. Best of all, it's just a few blocks' walk to the beach. No parking is available, but there's plenty of street parking in this town.

Playa Linda Hotel (Calle 76 btwn Calles 19 and 21, tel. 969/103-9214, www.playalinda-yucatan.com, US$31-47 s/d with a/c, US$50-63 suite with a/c) has compact rooms with attractive cherrywood furniture and good light. Ample suites have efficiency kitchens but no utensils, and some have balconies overlooking the sea. The only drawback with its location is that it has no parking.

INFORMATION AND SERVICES
Tourist Information

The **tourist office** (Calle 80 at Calle 25, tel. 969/935-5972, ext. 18, 8am-8pm Mon.-Fri., 9am-2pm Sat.) gives friendly and capable assistance from its bustling office in the Casa de Cultura. When there are cruise ships in port, a staffer mans an **information kiosk** (Calle 80 at the beach, no phone, 9am-1:30pm) on the boardwalk.

Emergency Services

Centro Médico Americano (Calle 33 btwn Calles 80 and 82, tel. 969/935-0951) is the best hospital in Progreso, with a 24-hour emergency room. For medications, head to **Farmacia Yza** (Calle 78 at Calle 29, tel. 969/935-0684, 24 hours) or across the street to **Farmacias Similares** (Calle 29 btwn Calles 78 and 80, tel. 969/934-4205, 7am-9pm Mon.-Sat., 8am-8pm Sun.). The **police station** (tel. 969/935-0026, 24 hours) is located just west of Progreso in the town of Yucalpetén.

Money

A block apart, **Banamex** (Calle 80 btwn Calles 27 and 29, 9am-4pm Mon.-Sat.) and **Banorte** (Calle 80 at Calle 31, 8:30am-4pm Mon.-Fri.) have reliable ATMs and will exchange foreign cash.

Media and Communications

Send snail mail at Progreso's **post office** (Calle 31 btwn Calles 78 and 80, 8am-4pm Mon.-Fri., 9am-noon Sat.), just east of Parque Independencia, or use the electronic variety at **Ciber Zone** (Calle 29 near Calle 80, no phone, 9am-9pm daily, US$0.65/hour).

Laundry

Lavandería (Calle 29 btwn Calles 76 and 78, no phone, 8am-2pm and 4pm-7pm Mon.-Sat.) charges US$0.70 per kilo (2.2 pounds), with a three-kilo (6.6-pound) minimum. Service is typically next-day.

GETTING THERE AND AROUND
Bus

From Mérida, buses leave the **Auto-Progreso** terminal on Calle 62 between Calles 65 and 67 every 15 minutes 4am-10pm (US$1.20/2.15 one-way/round-trip, 50 minutes). You'll be dropped off at the Progreso **bus station** (Calle 29 btwn Calles 80 and 82, tel. 999/900-4796, www.autoprogreso.com), a few blocks from the center of town. The return schedule is every 15 minutes 5am-9pm. Auto-Progreso also organizes **day trips** to attractions such as Uxmal (US$49 pp) and Chichén Itzá (US$49 pp) using air-conditioned vans or small buses. Entrance fees and bilingual guide are included. Though geared at cruise ship visitors, tours are open to all. Email in

Dzibilchaltún Archaeological Zone

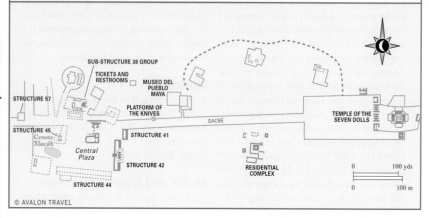

SUB-STRUCTURE 38 GROUP

TICKETS AND
RESTROOMS

MUSEO DEL
PUEBLO
MAYA

STRUCTURE 57

PLATFORM OF
THE KNIVES

SACBÉ

TEMPLE OF THE
SEVEN DOLLS

STRUCTURE 45

Cenote
Xlacáh

STRUCTURE 41

Central
Plaza

STRUCTURE 42

RESIDENTIAL
COMPLEX

STRUCTURE 44

0   100 yds

0   100 m

© AVALON TRAVEL

advance (or stop by the night before) to see if you can join an existing trip.

Vans (US$1) also shuttle between Mérida and Progreso, leaving Mérida every 15 minutes or so from a small station at Calle 60 between Calles 65 and 67; in Progreso, the station is on Calle 80 between Calles 29 and 31, with the last bus to Mérida leaving at 8:30pm.

For destinations a short distance east or west of Progreso, go to the corner of Calles 82 and 29, where you'll find a small parking lot filled with *combis* (Volkswagen minivans) headed to towns like Chicxulub Puerto and Uaymitún. *Combis* leave about every 10 minutes and cost US$0.50. To reach destinations farther along the coastal road, travelers must puddle jump from town to town, changing combis at the end of each route.

There's no first-class ADO service to or from Progreso, but you can buy advance tickets for departures from Mérida at the local office of **ADO** (Plaza del Mar mall, Calle 27 btwn Calles 76 and 78, tel. 969/935-2433, 8:30am-8pm Mon.-Fri., 10am-6pm Sat.-Sun.).

Car

From downtown Mérida, drive north on either Paseo de Montejo or Calle 60. The two streets eventually merge and become Highway 261, which leads directly to Progreso. To go east or west of Progreso by car, head south from town on Highway 261 until you hit the turnoffs.

DZIBILCHALTÚN ARCHAEOLOGICAL ZONE

A short detour off the highway between Mérida and Progreso is the archaeologically significant but somewhat underwhelming Maya ruin of **Dzibilchaltún** (Hwy. 261 Km. 15, 8am-5pm daily, US$7.75). Recognized as the oldest continuously used Maya ceremonial and administrative center on the peninsula, Dzibilchaltún (dzee-beel-chawl-TOON) was inhabited from as early as 1000 BC clear up to the arrival of the Spanish. The **Temple of the Seven Dolls** is the only known Maya temple with windows, and its orientation suggests it was used for astronomical observations—during the fall and spring equinoxes, the sun rises directly through the temple doors. The temple is named for a set of small clay figures that were found inside during its excavation. The ruins of a 16th-century church, built by the Spanish, also sit on the site.

The seven dolls and other artifacts are displayed in the site's exceptional **Museo del Pueblo Maya** (8am-4pm Tues.-Sun.). It focuses on the history of Dzibilchaltún as well as the area's cultural and economic development; signage is in Spanish and English. A 350-meter-long (1,148-foot) ecological path links the museum to the ruins. Along the way, trees and plants are labeled, and small *palapa*-roofed billboards have information on local flora and fauna.

Don't forget a swimsuit so you can cool off in the blue waters of its **Cenote Xlakáh** (8am-3:30pm Tues.-Sun.), an open pool speckled with lily pads.

Getting There and Around

Dzibilchaltún is located 16 kilometers (10 miles) north of Mérida. If driving, follow Highway 261 north toward Progreso for 12 kilometers (7.4 miles), where a road sign indicates the exit for the ruins. Follow this road east for about 4 kilometers (2.5 miles), past a village and directly to Dzibilchaltún. If taking public transportation from Mérida, vans (US$0.85, 30 minutes) leave frequently from the *combi* stop near Parque Maternidad on Calle 58 between Calles 57 and 59.

East of Progreso

The area east of Progreso has seen little tourist interest or development, though change is slowly coming. The coastal highway passes through quiet port towns like Chicxulub Puerto, Telchac Puerto, and Dzilam de Bravo. The beaches are less developed than those at Progreso, and strong winds make them more popular among windsurfers and kitesurfers than sunbathers. There's a modest archaeological site and small flamingo reserve, but little else in the way of sights. Hotels and restaurants also are limited, but a growing number of private homes, many owned by Canadian expats, dot the coastline (and can be rented via www.vrbo.com and similar sites).

RESERVA UAYMITÚN

About 16 kilometers (10 miles) east of Progreso, the coastal road wanders behind a long string of upscale houses and past fishing villages to the small town of Uaymitún (why-mih-TOON), home of the **Mirador Ecoturístico Uaymitún** (Uaymitún

Flamingos and other wildlife can often be spotted from an observation tower near Uaymitún.

East of Progreso

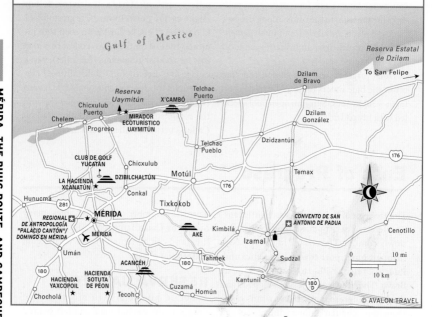

© AVALON TRAVEL

Ecotouristic Viewpoint, Carr. Chicxulub-Telchac Puerto Km. 15, tel. 999/942-1900, 8am-5pm daily, free). Well worth a stop, it's a high wooden platform overlooking a protected part of the extensive marshland that runs just inland along much of the Gulf coast. Thousands of flamingos come here to feed, and with binoculars you can get a decent look at these beautiful, peculiar birds in their natural habitat. If you're lucky, some may come closer to the platform. May-November is the best time to see flamingos, but there are a variety of bird species that can be seen year-round from the *mirador*. Binoculars can be rented at the information booth for US$1.

Tip: Another spot to see flamingos is along the road to X'Cambó ruins; the road cuts across the marshland, where the birds sometimes feed.

X'CAMBÓ ARCHAEOLOGICAL ZONE

Six kilometers (3.7 miles) inland from Telchac Puerto, on the road to Tixkokob, are the Maya ruins of **X'Cambó** (Carr. Dzemul-X'Cambó Km. 14, 8am-5pm daily, US$3.50). Sometimes referred to as Xtampu, the name means either Place of the Crabs or Place of the Crocodiles. X'Cambó was inhabited as early as 150 BC and was a major salt and salted-fish distribution center for the Maya cities of Izamal, Chichén Itzá, and Uxmal. It enjoyed the wealth that came from these commodities—the 600 skeletons that were unearthed during its excavation showed no signs of disease and had jewel-encrusted teeth, an indication of status. Archaeologists also discovered ceramics from distant Maya cities in Belize and Guatemala.

Today, the site is somewhat underwhelming, with various low-lying structures surrounding two plazas. None have surface ornamentation, though the tallest—the Pyramid of the Cross—affords a view of the

Chicxulub Crater

In 1978, a scientist using magnetic scanning and gravitational maps to scout for oil-drilling sites for Mexico's state-owned oil company noticed two huge arcs, one in the Gulf of Mexico, the other on the northern Yucatán Peninsula, which together appeared to form a circle. He immediately suspected it was a meteor crater, but was unable to secure core samples from PEMEX to back up the claim. A short time later, but unaware of the Gulf of Mexico findings, several scientists proposed a radical theory—that a meteor impact had caused the well-documented but unexplained mass extinctions, including of the dinosaurs, around 65 million years ago; they cited numerous pieces of suggestive evidence, but lacked the "smoking gun": a crater big enough to suggest such a cataclysmic event.

Amazingly, it wasn't until 1990, and thanks to a newspaper reporter, that the parties became aware of one another; core samples and other analyses—from satellite mapping to studying the configuration of cenotes along the crater's edge—have all but confirmed the theory. Researchers believe the meteorite was at least 10 kilometers (6.2 miles) across, and that it plowed into the Earth at around 72,000 kilometers per hour (44,740 mph). The impact gouged a crater 180 kilometers (112 miles) across and 2.5 kilometers (1.6 miles) deep, generating temperatures three times those on the surface of the sun. It caused the entire planet to tremble, volcanoes to erupt, and mega-tsunamis thousands of feet high to ricochet across the oceans. Millions of tons of pulverized rock and noxious gases formed a thick cloud that plunged the Earth into darkness for years, possibly decades. The lack of sunlight and other ecologic trauma led to the demise of more than 70 percent of all living things on the planet, including the dinosaurs, which in turn ushered in the age of mammals and humankind.

The crater—the largest yet discovered on Earth—is named after the closest settlement to its center: a dusty northern Yucatán Peninsula town called Chicxulub. Say what you will about Chicxulub's charm, or lack thereof, but it bears the unique distinction of being where life as we know it began.

coast. The site also has a small Catholic chapel, which was built on a small Maya structure using stones from the site. It was erected where the Virgin Mary is said to have appeared to local villagers; a festival in her honor is held here every May 30.

Accommodations

Just before the turnoff to X'Cambó, **Yucatán Beach** (Carr. Chicxulub-Telchac Puerto Km. 27.5, tel. 999/271-0413, www.yucatanbeach. com.mx, US$94/157 weekday/weekend) offers eight modern villas—four beachfront and four just steps from the beach. Each has three bedrooms and three full bathrooms—big enough for 10 people—plus a fully equipped kitchen, hot tub, and free use of the resort's kayaks. There's a pool, self-service laundry on-site, a mini-mart, Wi-Fi (in reception), and a restaurant too. Although it's pretty isolated, this makes a great place to base yourself, especially if you're looking for some R&R and are traveling with your family or a group of friends.

TELCHAC PUERTO

Continuing along the coast east from Chicxulub Puerto, the road parallels the sea for 75 kilometers (47 miles) to Dzilam de Bravo. Along the way are several small villages, all tuned in to life on the sea, with upmarket rental houses dotting the landscape in between. The largest of these villages is Telchac Puerto, about 40 kilometers (25 miles) east of Progreso.

Sights

Laguna Rosada is the large shallow lagoon directly behind town, and boatmen offer none-too-thrilling trips from a small embarcadero between the main plaza and marina. A more rewarding option is to head nine kilometers (5.6 miles) east to the village of **San**

Crisanto (www.sancrisanto.org), where paddling tours of the nearby mangroves, with a stop for swimming, are just US$2.50 per person (tel. 991/110-5371, 9am-5pm daily).

Food

Restaurante Los Tiburones (Calle 20 btwn Calles 19 and 21, near the town pier, tel. 991/917-4000, 7am-10pm daily, US$4-8) serves up fresh seafood dishes—from ceviches to *pulpo en su tinta*—all at reasonable prices. Meals come with a generous selection of complimentary appetizers. Open early, so traditional Mexican breakfasts are also a hit (be sure to order a glass of freshly squeezed OJ).

For more options, head to the central plaza, where there are a handful of **seafood restaurants** (8am-6pm daily, US$3-7).

Accommodations

Two blocks from the ocean, **Libros y Sueños** (Calle 23 btwn Calles 30 and 32, tel. 991/917-4125, US$19 s/d with fan) offers seven very basic rooms with tile floors, whitewashed walls, and cement bed frames. Though all have fans, try to nab a room on the 2nd floor to catch the evening breeze. Wi-Fi is available in the lobby. It also has an English-language bookstore that's well stocked with cheap paperback novels.

Hotel Reef Yucatán (Carr. Progreso-Telchac Puerto Km. 32, tel. 999/941-9494, www.reefyucatan.com, US$84/143 s/d with a/c) is an all-inclusive resort just outside of Telchac Puerto. Rooms are remarkably charmless—white tile floors, a bed or two, a TV, dark-brown furnishings, and not much more. The main restaurant also feels more like a high school cafeteria than a resort, with its plastic chairs, fluorescent lights, and lines of tray-toting guests. However, the beach is one of the finest on this coast—wide, clean, and overlooking the emerald ocean. There also are two well-kept pools, tennis courts, a mini-golf course, and a kids' club—not bad, given the price. Another good option is a day pass (US$50 adult, US$26-29 child, 9am-6pm),

which includes breakfast, lunch, open bar, and use of all the facilities.

Getting There and Around

From Progreso, catch a *combi* from the corner lot at Calles 82 and 29 to Chicxulub Puerto, where there's onward service to Telchac Puerto; there's no direct transportation from Progreso.

Having your own car is by far the easiest and surest way to see this quiet stretch of coast. From Mérida, take Highway 261 north toward the coast; as you approach Progreso, follow signs east (or right) to Telchac Puerto.

The most convenient way to get around town is to catch a bike or motorcycle taxi (US$0.50).

DZILAM DE BRAVO

At the end of the line is the quiet fishing town of Dzilam de Bravo, where legend has it that the pirate Jean Lafitte is buried. The real draw here, though, is miles of pristine coastline and mangrove forests east of town, teeming with birds and wildlife and dotted with lonely beaches and freshwater upwellings that make for a refreshing swim.

Practicalities

A number of small restaurants near the main plaza (9am-6pm daily, US$4-10) serve standard meals—seafood is recommended, of course.

If you're driving, you can reach (or leave) Dzilam de Bravo via the coastal highway from Progreso, or by zigzagging through small inland villages to/from Izamal or Mérida. A handful of buses and *colectivos* cover the same routes, albeit slowly and infrequently.

Reserva Estatal de Dzilam and Parque Natural San Felipe

Extending east of Dzilam de Bravo nearly to the town of San Felipe are two state nature preserves: the modest **Dzilam State Reserve** and the much larger **San Felipe Natural Park** (tel. 999/930-3380, www.sedmua.yucatan.gob.mx). Together they cover nearly a thousand square kilometers (386 square miles) of coastal wetlands, mangrove forests, and a narrow *tierra firme* (dry land) buffer. The reserves are home to four types of protected mangroves—red, black, white, and *botoncillo*—and numerous bird and animal species, from pelicans to crocodiles to spider monkeys. The area is also notable for a number of freshwater upwellings known as *bocas* (which literally translates as mouths; they're also known as *ojos de agua*, or eyes of water); some are ensconced in mangroves, others bubble up right in the middle of the ocean, making for unique ecosystems and in some cases refreshing swimming holes. The largest and most famous—Xbuya Ha—spews an impressive 3,500 liters (925 gallons) of freshwater per minute.

Sayachuleb (Calle 9 btwn Calles 2 and 2-A, next to the lighthouse, tel. 999/275-9072, www.dzilamdebravoyucatanecoturismo.blogspot.mx) is a local fishermen's cooperative that offers 2-5-hour tours into the reserves by motorboat or kayak, visiting various *bocas*, tangled waterways, and isolated beaches; fishing, bird-watching, and even camping can be incorporated into most trips. You can also ask around the pier or main plaza for local guides.

Izamal

North of Highway 180, between Mérida and Chichén Itzá, Izamal is a fine old colonial city with a beautiful and famous convent, friendly residents, and a fascinating history. Most tourists arrive here on a tour bus, visit the convent and the city center for an hour or so, and then motor off again. But Izamal is a great place for independent travelers to stay a night or two, soaking in the atmosphere and rich history of this classic Yucatecan town.

The first thing you notice about Izamal is the color: Virtually all the buildings and facades in Izamal are painted a rich mustard yellow, as is the convent. And Izamal has not one but two large tree-filled plazas—Parque Zamná and Parque Crescencio Carrillo y Ancona (named after an Izamal-born dramatist)—which form the heart of the city. It is a very walkable city, and part of the pleasure of Izamal is simply wandering about its narrow streets, discovering picturesque facades, stone churches, artistic workshops, and even Maya pyramids.

HISTORY

Pope John Paul II visited Izamal in August 1993, instantly transforming the city and cathedral into places of high Catholic importance. But it has been an important religious site since the time of the ancient Maya—it was one of three major pilgrimage sites in pre-Columbian Yucatán, along with Chichén Itzá and San Gervasio on Isla Cozumel. Spanish priests and colonizers recognized the area's importance and lost little time constructing a magnificent convent and church atop one of the largest existing Maya pyramids, even using the same stones as building materials. Fray Diego de Landa, who would later gain notoriety for burning dozens of Maya codices, oversaw the church.

SIGHTS
★ Convento de San Antonio de Padua

The most imposing structure in this small town is the mustard-colored **Convento de San Antonio de Padua** (Parque Crescencio Carrillo y Ancona, 6am-8pm daily, free). Completed in 1562 under the direction of Fray Diego de Landa, the convent was built upon—and used many of the stones of—what was once the immense Maya temple Pap Hol Chac. If you look closely, you'll even see some Maya glyphs in the church walls themselves. A 7,806-square-meter (84,023-square-foot) grassy atrium enclosed by 75 arches sits at the front of this beautiful complex. It's the

Izamal

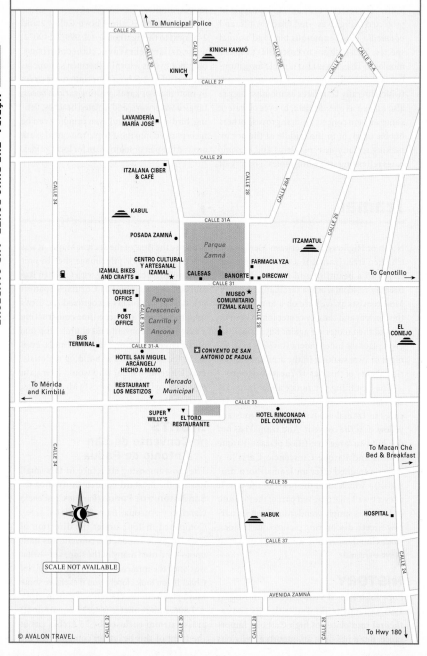

To Municipal Police

CALLE 25

CALLE 30
CALLE 28

KINICH KAKMÓ

KINICH

CALLE 27

CALLE 26B
CALLE 26
CALLE 26-A

LAVANDERÍA
MARÍA JOSÉ

CALLE 34

CALLE 29

ITZALANA CIBER
& CAFÉ

CALLE 28

CALLE 26A

KABUL

CALLE 31A

POSADA ZAMNÁ

Parque
Zamná

CALLE 26

ITZAMATUL

CENTRO CULTURAL
Y ARTESANAL
IZAMAL

FARMACIA YZA

IZAMAL BIKES
AND CRAFTS

CALESAS   BANORTE   DIRECWAY

To Cenotillo

CALLE 31

TOURIST
OFFICE

POST
OFFICE

Parque
Crescencio
Carrillo y
Ancona

CALLE 30A

MUSEO
COMUNITARIO
ITZMAL KAUIL

CALLE 28

BUS
TERMINAL

CALLE 31-A

EL
CONEJO

HOTEL SAN MIGUEL
ARCÁNGEL/
HECHO A MANO

CONVENTO DE SAN
ANTONIO DE PADUA

To Mérida
and Kimbilá

RESTAURANT
LOS MESTIZOS

Mercado
Municipal

CALLE 33

SUPER
WILLY'S

EL TORO
RESTAURANTE

HOTEL RINCONADA
DEL CONVENTO

To Macan Ché
Bed & Breakfast

CALLE 34

CALLE 35

HABUK

HOSPITAL

CALLE 37

CALLE 24

SCALE NOT AVAILABLE

AVENIDA ZAMNÁ

© AVALON TRAVEL

CALLE 32

CALLE 30

CALLE 28

CALLE 26

To Hwy 180

Cenotes Off the Beaten Path

Avid swimmers and admirers of cenotes may want to check out some of these less-visited sites.

- Often declared one of the most lovely cenotes on the peninsula, the semi-open **Cenote Kankirixché** (9am-6pm daily, free-US$1.25, depending on season) contains turquoise water striped with ropy tree roots, stalagmites, and stalactites. It's located south of Mérida, about eight kilometers (5 miles) east off Highway 261, between Abala and Mukuyché.

- **Cenote X-Batun** and **Cenote Dzonbacal,** also known as **Cenotes San Antonio Mulix** (9am-6pm daily, US$3.25) for a nearby hacienda, are contrasting sister cenotes. X-Batun is a long sunny pool at the foot of a vine-draped cliff, while Dzonbacal is ensconced in a tree-covered cavern, reached by steep stairs. The cenotes are near Umán, 50 kilometers (31 miles) south of Merida.

- About 48 kilometers (30 miles) east of Izamal, the village of **Cenotillo** (Little Cenote) boasts almost 150 cenotes nearby; popular ones include Kaipech, Xayín, and Yook Chac (9am-6pm daily). Stop by the Palacio Municipal to inquire about finding a local guide.

Cenote Kankirixché is an unexpectedly beautiful place to cool off.

- In the small town and former henequen estate of **Sabacché,** a local cooperative maintains two cenotes, a restaurant, *cabaña* and tent lodging, and also rents out bicycles and snorkeling equipment. Of the two cenotes, the semi-open **Calcuch** (9am-6pm daily, US$4) is the lovelier, with a dramatic circular stairway that descends 14 meters (46 feet). The town is located between Cuzamá and San Isidro Ochil.

- A smaller developed cenote with a restaurant and children's wading pools, stalactites bristle from the roof of the illuminated **Cenote San Ignacio** (www.cenotesanignacio.com, 9am-6pm daily, US$6), and visitors can splash in its 6-meter-deep (19.7-foot) waters. The cenote is situated in Chocholá, south of Mérida along Highway 180 to Campeche.

largest open-air atrium in the Americas and, many claim, the second-largest in the world (the largest being at St. Peter's in the Vatican). There's a reasonably interesting **sound and light show** Tuesday, Thursday, and Saturday at 8:30pm (US$6, 30 minutes); an hour earlier in winter.

There are also two small **exhibitions** (10am-1pm and 3pm-6pm Tues.-Sat., 9am-5pm Sun., US$0.40 each) on-site. One commemorates Pope John Paul II's 1993 visit, though it's not a terribly interesting collection—lots of photos and random facts. Another pays homage to Nuestra Señora de Izamal, the Yucatán's religious patroness. This statue of the Virgin Mary has reportedly performed several miracles, and religious followers from around the Yucatán often make pilgrimages to see her; you may see some of them climbing the steps of the convent on their knees.

Archaeological Zones

Kinich Kakmó (also known as Kinich Kak Moo, Calle 28 btwn Calles 25 and 27, 8am-5pm daily, free) is one of numerous Maya ruins in Izamal proper. While the others are relatively modest, Kinich Kakmó is a whopping 195 meters (640 feet) long, 173 meters (568 feet) wide, and 34 meters (112 feet) high, making it the largest pyramid in the state of Yucatán, and the third- to fifth-largest in Mexico, depending on how you define "large." Built between AD 250 and 600, the pyramid was dedicated to the sun god, or Fire Macaw, and was the principal structure of a massive plaza that extended over much of present-day Izamal. Interestingly, it was once a deeply important site for Maya shamans and worshippers, just as Izamal's Convento de San Antonio de Padua has become for Mexican Catholics today. Kinich Kakmó is not as fully restored as pyramids like El Castillo in Chichén Itzá, but it is still worth a climb, especially for the views of the city and surroundings. On a clear day, you can even see Chichén Itzá, 50 kilometers (31 miles) to the east.

Other smaller pyramids that can be visited include **Itzamatul** (Calle 26 at Calle 31, 8am-5pm daily, free), which affords a fine view of the city and Kinich Kakmó; **El Conejo** (Calle 22 btwn Calles 31 and 33, 8am-5pm daily, free); and **Habuk** (Calle 28 btwn Calles 35 and 37, 8am-5pm daily, free).

Museums

Located in a gorgeously renovated 16th-century home, the **Centro Cultural y Artesanal Izamal** (Parque Crescencio Carrillo y Ancona, Calle 31 btwn Calles 30 and 32, tel. 988/954-1012, www.centroculturalizamal.org.mx, 9am-7pm Mon.-Sat., 10am-5pm Sun., US$1.75) has a spectacular museum of Mexican folk art. Works displayed were created by the country's grand master artisans and include pieces in clay, wood, paper, and handwoven fabrics. There's an entire room dedicated to Yucatecan *artesanía* too. A gift shop sells beautiful—if pricey—crafts from the region; sales directly benefit the indigenous cooperative that creates them. Wandering around the property, you'll also find an exhibit on the henequen haciendas, a small café, and the Maya ruin of Kabul, which dates to the 6th century (closed at the time of research).

The **Museo Comunitario Itzmal Kauil** (Calle 30 s/n, kitty-corner from Banorte ATM, tel. 995/940-0032, 9am-1pm and 4pm-5pm daily, free) is a small museum with modest displays on Izamal's ancient, colonial, and modern-day history. Displays are all in Spanish.

Artisan Workshops

There are several artisan workshops where passersby can stop in, watch how a particular piece of folk art is made, and, of course, buy

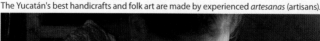

The Yucatán's best handicrafts and folk art are made by experienced *artesanas* (artisans).

something straight from the artist. Wandering around town, you'll see signs for tin workers, hammock weavers, woodworkers, and jewelry makers. Most of the workshops are run out of people's homes, so opening hours are pretty casual—don't be shy about knocking if the shop appears closed—at worst, you'll be told when to come back. Free city maps listing the location of many of the workshops are distributed at the tourist office and the Centro Cultural y Artesanal Izamal.

SHOPPING

Hecho a Mano (Calle 31-A btwn Calles 30 and 30-A, tel. 988/954-0344, 11am-2pm and 4pm-7pm daily) is a small folk-art boutique owned and operated by the collector-photographer team Hector Garza and Jeanne Hunt. The pieces and photos are beautiful and museum quality, with prices that often match. If you're looking for a special gift or simply like window-shopping, you'll enjoy a stop here.

If you're in the market for local folk art, head to one of the many **artisan workshops** around town, where you can buy items that you watched being made; free city maps listing workshop locations are distributed at the tourist office and the Centro Cultural y Artesanal Izamal. Another good option is browsing the *artesanía* tables set up in Parque Crescencio Carrillo y Ancona. Most days, vendors set up display tables in the park 8am-3pm.

The nearby town of Kimbilá is known as the place to go for fine *guayaberas* and *huipiles* at wholesale prices; in fact, many of the shops in Mérida stock up there. Go to the town's central plaza to check out some well-stocked mom-and-pop shops. From Izamal, head west on Calle 31 for about 10 kilometers (6.2 miles); in the village of Citilcum, turn left onto Calle 20 and continue for 2 kilometers (1.2 miles). You'll end up in Kimbilá's central plaza.

FOOD

The most upscale place in town, ★ **Kinich** (Calle 27 btwn Calles 28 and 30, tel. 988/954-0489, noon-9pm daily, US$8-16) is a breezy *palapa*-roofed restaurant that serves regional dishes, including excellent *poc-chuc* (marinated grilled pork). And if you've never seen tortillas being made, check out the tiny *palapa* in back, where you'll find women sitting around a small fire, patting and cooking tortillas into shape for your meal. Kinich is located a block from the like-named ruins.

Next to the *mercado*, **Restaurant Los Mestizos** (Calle 33 near Calle 30, tel. 988/954-0289, 7:30am-11pm daily, US$5-12) is jam-packed with heavy wood tables and decked out in garish pink walls, orange table coverings, and a profusion of streamers hanging from the ceiling. Regardless of the loud decor, Los Mestizos is actually a pretty quiet place for a cool drink and a plate of regional food.

Just half a block away, **El Toro Restaurante** (Calle 33 btwn Calles 30 and 32, tel. 988/954-1169, 8am-11pm daily, US$5-8) offers a similar menu—try the *salbutes, papadzules,* or quesadillas day or night. Wi-Fi is also available.

Mercado Municipal (facing Parque Crescencio Carrillo y Ancona) is where you'll find fresh produce, dairy, and meats. Shops are open 6am-2pm daily, and some stay open as late as 8pm Monday-Saturday.

Behind the market, next to El Toro restaurant, **Super Willy's** supermarket is open 7am-10:30pm daily.

ACCOMMODATIONS

Lodging is somewhat limited in Izamal. Many visitors arrive on large tour buses and stay just long enough to visit the convent and climb the pyramid at Kinich Kakmó. Staying a night or two, though, gives travelers the freedom to wander the quiet streets, stop in artisan workshops, and enjoy the lifestyle of this slow-paced town. All the options listed here have Wi-Fi available.

The grounds at ★ **Macan Ché Bed & Breakfast** (Calle 22 btwn Calles 33 and 35, tel. 988/954-0287, www.macanche.com, US$48 s/d, US$58-70 s/d with a/c, US$140 house with a/c) overflow with tropical plants and local fruit trees, while the bungalows are decorated according to individual themes—Santa Fe, Casa Maya, Catherwood—and newer suites have luxurious bathtubs and dramatic murals. Most rooms have patios and a hammock, perfect for whiling away a lazy afternoon. Ditto for the small pool, which has a natural stone bottom. An excellent full breakfast is included and served in a pleasant open-air dining area; dinner is available—and highly recommended—but must be reserved in advance. For longer stays, ask about the on-site house rentals. Spa services, yoga, and cooking classes can also be arranged.

Hotel Rinconada del Convento (Calle 33 btwn Calles 28 and 30, tel. 988/954-0151, www.hotelizamal.com, US$56-75 s/d with a/c) is a good value in a great location. Its name means "kitty-corner from the convent," an apt description for this rambling remodeled home facing the convent. There are 11 comfortable though lackluster rooms, all with air-conditioning, cable TV, Wi-Fi, and minifridges. The difference in the rates boils down to the decor and view—the less expensive rooms have old-school heavy wood furnishings and no view, while the others have sleek modern decor and partial views of the convent. The highlight here is the common space—a beautiful terraced garden, a well-maintained lap pool, and a tile-roofed patio overlooking it all.

Hotel San Miguel Arcángel (Calle 31-A btwn Calles 30 and 30-A, tel. 988/954-0109, www.sanmiguelhotel.com.mx, US$41 s/d with a/c) is a good option if you want to be in the center of town, literally. If you don't mind the sound of traffic in the morning or bird cacophony in the evening, the balcony rooms have terrific views of Parque Crescencio Carrillo y Ancona and the San Antonio de Padua convent. Rooms have high ceilings, tile floors, and, of course, some have those balconies. There are cozy sitting areas and a patio with tables where continental breakfast is served. A hot tub in back is a nice plus.

Cheap and central, **Posada Zamná** (Calle 33 btwn Calles 31 and 31-A, tel. 988/954-0758, US$22 s/d with a/c) may blind you with its startlingly white walls and floor tiling, but once your eyes adjust you'll find basic hotel rooms with firm beds, spotless bathrooms (though no toilet seats), flat-screen TVs, and quiet air-conditioning. There's a nice seating area, and Parque Zamná is just outside.

the open-air dining room at Macan Ché

INFORMATION AND SERVICES

Tourist Information

The **tourist office** (Parque Crescencio Carrillo y Ancona, tel. 988/954-1096, 8am-2pm and 5pm-9pm Mon.-Sat., 9am-2pm Sun.) is in the Palacio Municipal. There are plenty of brochures and maps; staffers often speak English.

Emergency Services

Izamal's public **hospital** (Calle 24 btwn Calles 35 and 37, tel. 988/954-0241) has a 24-hour emergency room. The telephone is answered only 8am-8pm; after hours, go directly to the clinic. **Farmacia Yza** (Calle 28 at Calle 31, tel. 988/954-0600, 24 hours) faces the east side of Parque Zamná. The **tourist police** in Izamal may be the friendliest in the Yucatán Peninsula, and sometimes flag down travelers simply to offer assistance (no tip expected). One or more officers are usually stationed at intersections around the center. The **municipal police** are located at the former train station, the *ex-estación de tren* (Calle 30 at Calle 19, tel. 988/954-0505, toll-free Mex. tel. 066, 24 hours).

Money

There's no bank in town, though **Banorte** (Calle 28 at Calle 31) has a 24-hour ATM, and there's another cash machine inside **Super Willy's** (Calle 33 btwn Calles 30 and 32, 7am-10:30pm).

Media and Communications

The **post office** (8am-1pm Mon.-Sat.) is on Calle 30-A, inside the Palacio del Gobierno. Parque Zamná and Parque Crescencio Carrillo y Ancona have Wi-Fi al fresco, and Internet cafés **Itzalana Ciber & Café** (Calle 30 at Calle 29, 10am-2pm and 5pm-10pm Mon.-Sat., 9am-1pm Sun., US$0.75/hour) and pricier **Direcway** (Calle 31 btwn Calles 26 and 28, 8am-10pm daily, US$1.25/hour) have computers indoors.

Pay phones are oddly hard to find in Izamal. There is one affixed to a corner wall in the Mercado Municipal, on the south side of Parque Crescencio Carrillo y Ancona, and a rather battered one at the Pemex station at Calles 31 and 34.

Laundry

Lavandería María José (Calle 30 btwn Calles 27 and 29, tel. 988/954-0037, 8am-8pm Mon.-Sat.) charges US$0.60 per kilo (2.2 pounds), with a three-kilo (6.6-pound) minimum. Clothes are typically ready within 2-3 hours.

HACIENDA AND RUINS AKÉ

A visit to the Maya ruins of **Aké** (8am-5pm daily, US$2.75) makes for a good excursion from Izamal. Believed to have been occupied from the Late Preclassic until the Postclassic period, Aké reached its height of influence sometime between AD 600 and 1200; it was abandoned around 1450. The city was the nucleus of many sacbés (raised roads), including one 32 kilometers (20 miles) long that connected it to Izamal. However, at some point a wall was built around the site, suggesting that alliances must have soured. The village was also the backdrop for a fierce battle in 1528 between the Maya and Francisco de Montejo "El Mozo" (The Younger).

Entering the site, two restored structures sit on a large open plaza. Structure 1, also known as the Estructura de las Pilastras (Structure of the Pilasters, or pillars) is the more striking of the two. A rectangular platform 104 meters (341 feet) long, 36.5 meters (120 feet) wide, and 8.5 meters (28 feet) high, its stairs are actually large blocks of stone—some up to 1.8 meters (6 feet) long. But its most unusual feature is a phalanx of 35 stacked square columns (approximately 4.6 meters/15 feet high) that must have supported an enormous roof. Between Structure 1 and the entrance is the site's tallest building, Structure 2, which can be climbed from the plaza side for treetop views of the surrounding area.

Next door, the **Hacienda de San Lorenzo de Aké** (tel. 999/923-0493, www.ruinasdeake.

com, 8am-5pm Mon.-Fri, US$12.50, tour by reservation) is a 19th-century mansion and henequen production facility that still makes sisal twine. Hour-and-a-half-long tours feature a short film (in English or Spanish) about the hacienda and visits to the desfibradora (henequen mill) and the cordelería (rope factory), where workers spin bales of fiber into twine. A blazing-yellow chapel lords above the hacienda from what looks like a hill, but upon closer inspection turns out to be Maya stonework.

To get here from Izamal, take Highway 180 west to the signed turnoff at Kilometer 41 and continue north 11 kilometers (6.8 miles). The site also is accessible from the Izamal-Tixkokob road, though it's not signed well. By public transportation it's easiest from Mérida; second-class buses (US$1.50, 1 hour) leave from the **Terminal Autobuses del Centro** (Calle 65 btwn Calles 46 and 48, tel. 999/923-9962) at 5:30am, 8:40am, 4pm, and 7:10pm, returning at 2pm and 4pm.

GETTING THERE AND AROUND

Izamal is served by first- and second-class buses, though having a car will allow you to visit the outlying areas like Kimbilá. The town itself is quite easy to navigate on foot: The bus terminal, major sights, and a handful of hotels and restaurants are all within easy walking distance.

Bus

Izamal's **bus terminal** is one block west of the Palacio Municipal, at the end of Calle 31-A. All bus services are second-class routes with **Oriente** (tel. 988/954-0107).

- Cancún: US$9.50, 5 hours, 6:10am, 2:30pm, and 4:30pm
- Mérida: US$1.75, 1.5 hours, 16 departures, 4:45am-7:30pm
- Tizimín: US$5.50, 2.5 hours, 7:30am and 6:15pm
- Valladolid: US$3.75, 2 hours, take any Cancún bus

Car

Driving on the *cuota* (toll road), there are well-marked turnoffs to Izamal at Kilometer 68, coming from either Cancún or Mérida. Arriving on the *libre* (free road), follow the signs headed north at Kantunil. For a more scenic route from Mérida, follow Calle 65 out of town and across the *periférico*. Using rural roads, you'll pass through the town of Tixcocob, and can make side jaunts to the Aké ruins and Hacienda San José Cholul.

Bicycle

Izamal Bikes and Crafts (Parque Crescencio Carrillo y Ancona, Calle 31 btwn Calles 30 and 32, tel. 988/954-1172, www.izamalbikesandcrafts.com, 8am-2pm and 4pm-8pm Mon.-Sat.) rents retro bikes in a variety of sizes. Rentals run US$2 per hour.

Tours

All day long you'll find a queue of *calesas* or *victorias* parked along the long northern wall of the convent offering **horse-carriage tours.** Ostensibly for tourists—a scenic 30-60-minute tour around town runs US$10-16, depending on its duration—these tiny horse-pulled buggies also do an active business carrying local families from place to place.

The Puuc Route

You can easily spend two full days (or more) in the region south of Mérida, with its rich concentration of Maya ruins, caves, and small appealing towns. The Puuc ruins are the main attraction, of course, from the stunning size and accomplishment of Uxmal to the fantastic artistry of smaller sites like Labná and Kabah. The route also includes the Loltún caves, a great introduction to the Yucatán's vast underground world.

GETTING THERE AND AROUND

Bus

On Sunday only, an ATS bus headed for the Puuc Route leaves Mérida's second-class bus terminal at 8am, spends 30 minutes apiece at Sayil, Labná, and Xlapak, 50 minutes at Kabah, and two hours at Uxmal, before returning to Mérida around 4:30pm (US$11.25, entry fees not included). Merida tour agencies are a possible option too, if you don't want to rent a car.

There are also ordinary buses to Uxmal (US$3, 1.25 hours, 8 departures, 6am-5pm) that leave from Mérida's second-class bus terminal; there's also service to the nearby towns of Ticul and Santa Elena. Returning to Mérida, you can flag down a second-class bus on the highway at the Uxmal turnoff, but they only pass every hour or so.

Car

If you're driving, Highway 261 leads to the Puuc Route. From Mérida, the drive to Uxmal takes about one hour; from Campeche City allow two hours.

★ UXMAL ARCHAEOLOGICAL ZONE

The massive scale, elegant structures, and intricate decoration of **Uxmal** (8am-5pm daily, US$13 including sound and light show,

US$3.75 show only) make it one of the most memorable Maya ruins in the Yucatán, and a perennial favorite for casual visitors and Maya-buffs alike. It was the greatest of the Maya cities in the Puuc region, and contains some of the best—and best-preserved—examples of Puuc-style architecture. And though Uxmal is located just 80 kilometers (50 miles) from Mérida, it doesn't get the crush of visitors (or vendors) that sites like Chichén Itzá and Tulum do, making a visit here all the more enjoyable.

History

Some believe Uxmal was founded by Maya from Guatemala's Petén region in the 6th century. Others contend it dates back even further, perhaps to the Preclassic period. Unlike most of northern Yucatán, the Puuc region has good soils, allowing for greater population density than other areas. Uxmal emerged as the dominant city-state between AD 850 and 900, when the Pyramid of the Magician, the Great Pyramid, and the Nunnery were built, and is believed to have been the hub of a district of about 160 square kilometers (62 square miles) encompassing many sites, including the lesser sites in the area: Kabah, Sayil, Labná, and Xlapak. However, in the mid-10th century Uxmal was abruptly abandoned, probably after being defeated by armies from Chichén Itzá and as part of a pan-Maya collapse around that time. During the Postclassic era, the Xiu clan based in the nearby town of Maní spuriously claimed to be descended from Uxmal's rulers and occupied the ruins. All that said, however, relatively few stelae have been found at Uxmal, so less is known about the ruling dynasties here than at other major sites.

The Maya word *uxmal* (oosh-MAHL) means "thrice built." The name notwithstanding, it is believed that Uxmal was built five times, each time over top of the last. Puuc architecture is one of the major achievements of

The Puuc Route

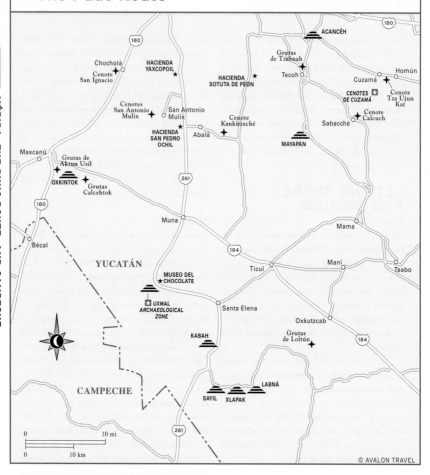

ACANCÉH

Grutas
de Tzabnah

Chocholá   HACIENDA
Cenote   YAXCOPOIL   Tecoh   Cuzamá   Homún
San Ignacio   HACIENDA   Cenote
                SOTUTA DE PÉON   CENOTES   Tza Ujun
                                         DE CUZAMÁ   Kat
Cenotes   San Antonio   Cenote
San Antonio   Mulix   Calcuch
Mulix   Cenote
          HACIENDA   Kankirixché   Sabacché
          SAN PEDRO   Abalá
          OCHIL   MAYAPÁN
Maxcanú
     Grutas de
     Aktun Usil
     OXKINTOK
          Grutas
          Calcehtok

180   Mama

Bécal   Maní

          YUCATÁN   Muna   184   Ticul   Teabo

          MUSEO DEL   Santa Elena
          CHOCOLATE

          UXMAL
          ARCHAEOLOGICAL
          ZONE

          KABAH   Grutas
                    de Loltún   184
                              Oxkutzcab

                         LABNÁ

CAMPECHE   SAYIL   XLAPAK

0   10 mi

0   10 km

261

© AVALON TRAVEL

Mesoamerica, whose hallmarks include un-adorned lower levels, heavily decorated upper friezes, boot-shaped vault stones, thin squares of limestone veneer, and rows of pseudo-columns. The constant threat of drought also inspired the Maya to adorn their structures with hundreds of stone masks and carvings representing the rain god, Chaac, easily identified by his prominent hooked nose. Unlike most Maya centers in Yucatán, Uxmal was not built around a cenote, since there are none in this arid part of the peninsula. Rainwater

was collected in *aguadas* (natural holes in the ground) as well as in manufactured *chultúnes* (cisterns) built into the ground, sometimes right inside a house or under a patio.

Pyramid of the Magician

Passing through the visitors center and up a slow-sloping pathway, the first structure you reach is Uxmal's tallest and among its most distinctive. The Pyramid of the Magician stands 38 meters (125 feet) high and has a distinctive elliptical base, rather than the square

Uxmal Archaeological Zone

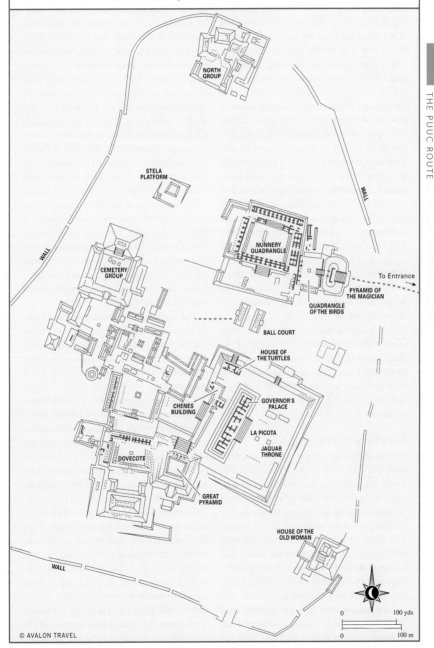

NORTH
GROUP

STELA
PLATFORM

WALL

WALL

NUNNERY
QUADRANGLE

CEMETERY
GROUP

To Entrance

PYRAMID OF
THE MAGICIAN

QUADRANGLE
OF THE BIRDS

BALL COURT

HOUSE OF
THE TURTLES

CHENES
BUILDING

GOVERNOR'S
PALACE

LA PICOTA

JAGUAR
THRONE

DOVECOTE

GREAT
PYRAMID

HOUSE OF THE
OLD WOMAN

WALL

0   100 yds

0   100 m

© AVALON TRAVEL

or rectangular base of most pyramids. The softly curved edges combined with its impressive height and girth lend the temple a striking elegance. You will approach the Pyramid of the Magician from the back, but the other (west) side is by far the most ornate. There, a staircase rises at an imposing 60-degree angle, lined by the hooked-nose masks representing Chaac, the rain god. Three-quarters of the way up, a huge monster-mouth facade—borrowed from Chenes-style construction from present-day Campeche—surrounds a temple door. At the top is a two-story rectangular temple, with crosshatch panels beside the doors. You'll have to take our word for it, though, as tourists are no longer allowed to climb the pyramid, nor those at many other ruins. The restrictions are to prevent undue erosion, as well as accidents (of which there have been many, including a fatal tumble by a tourist at Chichén Itzá in 2005).

Before leaving, take note of the small but attractive plaza on the Pyramid of the Magician's west side. It's known as the **Quadrangle of the Birds,** so named for the birds carved into the upper frieze of the small building opposite the Pyramid of the Magician. And there are more than just birds, including Puuc-style decorative columns, faux thatching (or bird feathers?), and crescent-moon edging, all in remarkably good condition.

Nunnery Quadrangle

The Nunnery Quadrangle is the huge courtyard directly west of the Pyramid of the Magician. Covering an area 60 by 45 meters (197 by 148 feet), the (almost) square is bounded on each side by long buildings. The buildings contain numerous small rooms, and reminded the first Spanish explorers of nunneries in Spain, hence the name. The buildings evidently were built in a single concentrated effort at the end of the 9th century, shortly before the city's collapse.

The combination of a plain lower level topped by an ornate frieze—a staple of Puuc architecture—can be seen in all four buildings

of the Nunnery Quadrangle. The west building has the most ornate frieze. Notice the stacked Chaac masks at either end and, working toward the center, geometric spirals that represent clouds (note that the Maya glyph for cloud has a similar design). Interspersed are panels with lattice patterns, also typical of Puuc design; here they are especially fine, embedded with flowers. The niche over the center door contains the figure of the God of the Underworld (God N, to archaeologists), with the body of a turtle, sitting under a canopy of feathers. The designers of Uxmal were obsessed with the male phallus, and figures at the ends of the facade are disrobed, with rather prodigious members that appear scarred or tattooed (ouch!). A large phallus also once stood in the center of the Nunnery Quadrangle, but it has since disappeared. Finally, notice the two long, feathered snakes that weave (and interweave) the length of the frieze. From the mouth of one emerges a human face, a way of emphasizing the divine origin of Uxmal's leaders.

The north building is the largest and highest of the four, affording great views of the entire site from its broad platform. The frieze contains exquisite Chaac masks, with finely curved incisor teeth and distinct upper and lower eyelids.

To many observers, the east building is the most refined in its design and execution. Simple latticework is broken by triangular forms over the doors. On closer look, you can see the forms are in fact an inverted stack of two-headed feathered serpents. Above them are shields depicting owls, which the Maya associated with warfare and sacrifice.

The south building has a vaulted arch, giving access to and from the quadrangle. High on its sloped walls, look for red handprints, left from the original construction. Notice, too, the carvings of thatched huts, or *na,* over each of the doors. In fact, you can see such images in numerous temples in this region, and beyond. The precise meaning of the huts is unclear—they may have represented the newborn universe, as in some Maya creation myths—but like the handprints in the archway, they lend a powerful humanity to these ancient ruins, not least because the very same *na* remain a fixture of Maya communities today.

Governor's Palace

An archway leads out of the Nunnery Quadrangle across a grassy esplanade and past Uxmal's modest **ball court.** Bearing left, you'll climb a large platform to the Governor's Palace. At the top of the steps, pause a moment to appreciate the scope of this complex, considered by some to be the height of Puuc architecture. The platform you just climbed is artificial—it was built by hand out of piled stone, and measures a mind-boggling 187 meters (613.5 feet) long, 170 meters (558 feet) wide, and 8-10 meters (26-33 feet) high. On top of it are a number of structures, the most notable being the Governor's Palace, which measures 98 meters (321.5 feet) long and 12 meters (39 feet) wide (and it's built on still another 7-meter/23-foot-high platform). The upper frieze has lattice patterns, feathered serpents, and over 100 Chaac masks; in all, it took some 15,000 individual stone pieces to create it. Over the center door was the face—now gone—of a god, probably Lord Chaac,

surrounded by feather headdress, featuring Chaac masks. Two arrow-shaped corbel arches originally allowed passage from one side to the other, but were later plugged, perhaps to create more rooms or to stabilize the structure. The high-vaulted interior rooms are musty and unpleasant, but do walk around the north end, where, at the corners, near the ground, some excellent carved pieces can be examined close-up.

On the small platform in front of the palace, a throne in the shape of a two-headed **jaguar** was uncovered by John Stephens in 1841, and remains today. Such thrones were a common symbol of Maya authority—a similar one was found in Palenque and a single-headed one deep inside El Castillo at Chichén Itzá. Stephens tried to take the artifact with him but, lucky for us, found it "too heavy to carry away." He evidently never thought to look beneath it—there, archaeologists found a cache of nearly a thousand extremely fine jade, obsidian, and ceramic items.

Also on this platform is the **House of the Turtles,** a simple but elegant structure measuring 11 by 30 meters (36 by 98 feet). The lower half is very plain, but the upper part is decorated with a frieze of columns, topped by a cornice adorned by a series of turtles.

Uxmal is one of the Maya world's most impressive ruins and a perennial traveler's favorite.

The Maya associated turtles and other wetland creatures with rain and fertility, and this structure, like so much else in Uxmal, was probably used for ceremonies to bring rain. Inside is a sunny courtyard, and from the north side is a fine view of the ball court, with the Nunnery Quadrangle and the Pyramid of the Magician beyond.

The Great Pyramid

Behind the Governor's Palace is the Great Pyramid, a more typical Maya pyramid, standing 30 meters (98 feet) on a series of terraces. You can see that it predates the Governor's Palace, as the latter's platform partially overlaps the pyramid's northeast corner. At the top—you can still climb this one—a small temple contains an impressively large but partially buried Chaac mask. The temple's exterior is adorned with latticework and, most notably, panels depicting macaws.

Dovecote

Beside the Great Pyramid, excavation continues on a part of Uxmal known as the Dovecote. The name derives from the patchwork of niches in the roof comb of the complex's most prominent feature, a high wall separating two of the three large plazas identified here. In addition to its ornate roof comb, the wall contains a beautiful vaulted arch and several vaulted rooms on its lower level. Its facade once had large figures molded from stucco; they've long since been destroyed or removed, but several protruding stone struts remain. The struts would have supported the fragile stucco figures, and are, in a modest way, an insight into these silent structures and the people who built them. The ruins did not spring ready-made from the ground, but were built by regular people who faced the same challenges modern designers do, like: How do we keep all these decorations from falling off?

Sound and Light Show

Every evening a sound and light show is presented at the ruins overlooking the awe-inspiring Nunnery Quadrangle. Different structures are lit up as an accompaniment to the Maya lore that is played over loudspeakers (in Spanish) and through headsets (English, French, German, and Italian; US$2.50 rental). It's well worth checking out, especially if you've never seen a show like this. Simply being at the archaeological site at night, with the ancient stone structures looming around you and the occasional flash of lightning in the distance, is undeniably impressive. You can't help but cast your mind back to ancient times, to imagine living in this mysterious city on a warm dark night gazing at the stars, the same ones we see today.

Practicalities

The ruins and museum are open 8am-5pm daily; the sound and light show takes place at 7pm in the winter (Oct.-Apr.) and at 8pm in the summer (May-Sept.). General admission to the ruins and sound and light show is US$13. It's possible to go to the sound and light show the night before you visit the ruins for the single general admission price, but you must inform the ticket seller before buying a ticket. You will buy part of the general admission ticket—not the show-only ticket—to get into the show, and then pay the remainder the following day to enter the ruins. Don't lose your ticket from the show, as you must present it the next morning. Parking is US$2 per car; use of a video camera is US$3.50. If you only plan to see the show and not visit the ruins, admission is US$3.75. (Unfortunately, there are no reduced or refunded tickets if you don't go to the sound and light show.)

Guides to the ruins charge fixed prices and can be hired right at the entrance. Tours last around 90 minutes and cost US$38 in Spanish or US$44 for English, Italian, French, or German (8 people maximum on any tour).

In addition to the museum and gift shops, the visitors center has an ATM, snack bar, and postal drop box.

Food and Accommodations

Two large upper-end hotels (each with a restaurant) are near the entrance of Uxmal.

Hacienda Uxmal once housed Uxmal's first archaeologists.

Smaller and more affordable lodging and food can be had in the nearby towns of Santa Elena, Ticul, and Oxkutzcab.

Hacienda Uxmal (Carr. Mérida-Campeche Km. 78, tel. 997/976-2012, toll-free Mex. tel. 800/719-5465, toll-free U.S. tel. 877/240-5864, www.mayaland.com, US$119-218 s/d with a/c) was originally the residence of the archaeologists that first excavated Uxmal. Today, it is a colonial-style hotel sitting on manicured grounds with jogging trails and a nice pool. The rooms are classically Yucatecan in style, with striking *talavera* tile floors, marble bathrooms, heavy carved furniture, and ironwork beds. Past guests include Queen Elizabeth II, the Shah of Iran, Henry Kissinger, and Jacqueline Kennedy Onassis.

Directly across from the ruins is **The Lodge at Uxmal** (Carr. Mérida-Campeche Km. 78, tel. 998/887-2495, toll-free Mex. tel. 800/719-5465, toll-free U.S. tel. 877/240-5864, www.mayaland.com, US$374-433 s/d with a/c). It's a very comfortable boutique hotel with a great location, but with nightly

rates starting at almost US$400, it is simply overpriced. Check the website for discounts or hope there's a tour group at Hacienda Uxmal, when independent travelers get free upgrades to this location. Wi-Fi is available.

Just steps from Uxmal's entrance, the **Coole Chepa Chi** (The Lodge at Uxmal, tel. 997/976-2030, 7am-10pm daily, US$10-25) is a convenient restaurant for a post-ruins or pre-sound-and-light-show meal. The kitchen serves up a good variety of international dishes—from Mexican to Italian to just plain sandwiches. If you're really hungry, opt for the Yucatecan buffet, available at every meal for just US$9.

MUSEO DEL CHOCOLATE

Located across from Uxmal, the **Museum of Chocolate** (Hwy. 261 Km. 78, tel. 999/289-9914, www.choco-storymexico.com, 9am-7:30pm daily, US$7.50 adult, US$5.75 child 6-12) pulls back the curtain on chocolate, its role in Maya culture, and its development in the world market. Organized by historical periods, the museum is set in a series of Maya thatch huts; as visitors travel between them, they progress through the history of chocolate too. Along the way, visitors can watch a Maya ritual offering to the rain god, Chaac, as well as a chocolate-making demonstration where you can taste a drink. (Unfortunately, there's also a small zoo of regional animals—you'll pass jaguars, spider monkeys, and other creatures in tiny cages.) Signage is in both English and Spanish. A small café sells panino sandwiches and—surprise!—chocolate, though not as many decadent treats as one might hope.

KABAH ARCHAEOLOGICAL ZONE

Kabah (8am-5pm daily, US$3) is located 22 kilometers (13.7 miles) southeast of Uxmal, on the other side of the small town of Santa Elena. Kabah's major temples were constructed in AD 850-900, though the area was probably first settled as far back as 300 BC-AD 250. The site spans many square kilometers, though only the ceremonial center

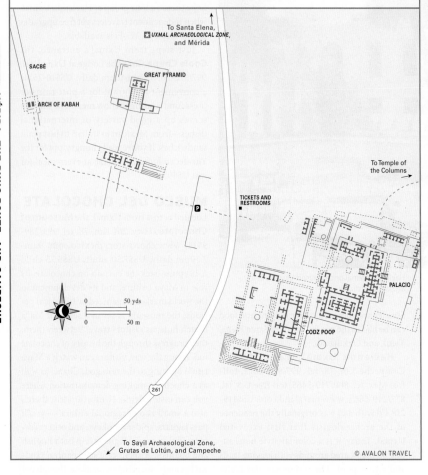

Kabah Archaeological Zone

To Santa Elena,
★ UXMAL ARCHAEOLOGICAL ZONE,
and Mérida

SACBÉ

GREAT PYRAMID

⊞ ARCH OF KABAH

To Temple of
the Columns →

P

TICKETS AND
RESTROOMS

PALACIO

CODZ POOP

0   50 yds
0   50 m

261

To Sayil Archaeological Zone,
Grutas de Loltún, and Campeche

© AVALON TRAVEL

has been cleared and restored. The highway cuts right through the ancient city, so there are ruins on either side. The main points of interest are on the east side of the road, where the ticket booth is located.

Codz Poop

From the entrance, walk parallel to the road to the southernmost structure. A short but very steep staircase leads to a raised platform and to Codz Poop, Kabah's most ornate building and one of the most arresting structures on the Puuc Route. Dedicated to the rain god, Chaac, and measuring nearly 45 meters (148 feet) long and 6 meters (19.7 feet) high, the temple's entire west facade is covered in some 250 Chaac masks, with the typical googly eyes and long hooked nose. Even the steps into the doorways are modified Chaac noses. Looking closely, you can see how each mask is made of the same set of pieces, and can imagine a Maya manufacturing line, with carvers churning out scores of eyelids, pupils, and teeth, and others assembling the masks on the temple.

The rear side of Codz Poop is nearly as impressive, with huge stucco figures set against a latticework frieze. Be sure to peek at the side panels of the main door, where impressive bas-reliefs depict battle scenes.

Palacio and Temple of the Columns

A path from Codz Poop leads to the raised platform where the Palacio (Palace) stands. A broken set of stairs leads to the top, though climbing it is not allowed. The Palacio displays more typical Puuc architecture, with ornate friezes atop unadorned lower facades.

Around the northern edge of the Palacio, a path leads through the trees to the mildly interesting Temple of the Columns. The name says it all, as the facade is covered in attached decorative columns. Two *chultúnes* that used to collect and store water flank the path just as you reach the temple—be careful not to tumble in! Archaeologists recently announced the discovery of pottery, *metates* (grinding stones), and hearths from a kitchen used to prepare food for the city's rulers.

Arch of Kabah and Great Pyramid

On the other side of the road (and through the parking area), a path leads 200 meters (656 feet) to the impressive Arch of Kabah. The six-meter-high (19.7-foot) arch dates to AD 670-770 and marked one end of a grand *sacbé*, or raised stone-paved road, that extended 30 kilometers (19 miles) from Kabah to Uxmal and is still traceable today. For the first 15 kilometers (9.3 miles), from Kabah to the settlement of Nohpat, the road runs perfectly straight, before veering slightly to reach Uxmal. North of the path leading to the arch is the Great Pyramid, the largest structure in Kabah. Yet to be excavated and off-limits to climbing, it remains for now an impressively huge mound covered in grass and trees.

SAYIL ARCHAEOLOGICAL ZONE

Sayil (8am-5pm daily, US$3) is even more spread out than Kabah, but the long leafy paths between monuments are part of the pleasure of visiting this site. Archaeologists believe the area was settled as early as the 2nd or 3rd century AD, though virtually all of its major structures were built in the short period between the end of the 8th century and middle of the 10th. Sayil's population most likely peaked at around 10,000 people, with another 7,000 living in outlying areas.

Sayil is located just seven kilometers (4.3 miles) from Kabah; coming from Kabah on Highway 261, look for the well-marked left-hand turnoff.

Sayil Archaeological Zone

← To Kabah Archaeological Zone,
Santa Elena, and 🅿 UXMAL
ARCHAEOLOGICAL ZONE

To Labná
Archaeological
Zone and Grutas
de Loltún →

TICKETS AND
RESTROOMS

P

CHULTÚN

STELA 4
STELA 3

GRAN
PALACIO

TEMPLE OF THE
HIEROGLYPHIC
JAMBS

EL
MIRADOR

YUM KEEP

0   200 yds

0   200 m

BALL COURT

PALACIO
SUR

© AVALON TRAVEL

Gran Palacio

The path from the parking and ticket area leads past several deeply decayed stelae to the Great Palace, also called Palacio Norte. As the on-site plaque makes clear, the structure contains more than 90 rooms and may have housed up to 350 people; the west side is better preserved than the east. Although the palace appears to be three stories, in fact each level is supported by a core of piled stone, as opposed to the story below it—an example of how Maya architects were accomplished illusionists. Visitors aren't allowed to climb to the upper levels, but you can still appreciate the craftsmanship of the palace's 2nd-floor frieze; most notable are curious "Diving Gods" over the doorways, their upturned legs easily discerned. Tulum and Cobá have similar figures, which may represent the God of Maize (God E, to archaeologists). The corners have imposing Chaac masks, and decorative columns help unify the nearly 60-meter-long (197-foot) building.

El Mirador

A path leads south from the palace to El Mirador, a small temple whose name means The Lookout. Built atop a crumbling pyramid, the structure has five rooms and a high-reaching roof comb. Though substantially collapsed, the structure is still impressive for its height and the complexity of its comb.

Yum Keep

Continuing another 50 meters (164 feet) past El Mirador, the path leads to Yum Keep, or the Stela of the Phallus. Kabah's spiritual leaders, like those of Uxmal and other cities, were obsessed with the male phallus. Here, a rather poorly executed stone panel depicts an ancient Dirk Diggler, his face and hands still partly visible, and an enormous penis hanging to his knees.

Other Structures

Sayil's remaining structures aren't terribly impressive as such, but the walk there, with sunlight filtering through the foliage overhead, is rewarding. To see them, follow the path that forks off the main one between the Palacio and El Mirador. First, you'll come upon the Temple of the Hieroglyphic Jambs, which is not nearly as interesting as its name might suggest. The structure is literally buried in the forest floor, with only the roof and a small portion of the carved doorways visible. The path continues 500 meters (0.3 mile) to the much-decayed Palacio Sur, with columns, broken Chaac masks, and other figures discernable on the southern frieze. Beside the complex is Sayil's ball court, also in significant disrepair.

XLAPAK ARCHAEOLOGICAL ZONE

Xlapak (8am-5pm daily, free) is the smallest of the Puuc Route ruins, a Late Classic site that may have originally been part of nearby Labná. Because it has just one restored building, organized tours and independent travelers often skip Xlapak to have more time at the larger sites. That said, Xlapak's lone structure is an attractive one, with ornate facades on both sides and some very well-preserved Chaac masks. The path through the site is well maintained and shady too—a good place to spot birds and other wildlife.

LABNÁ ARCHAEOLOGICAL ZONE

Labná (8am-5pm daily, US$3) is for many people the best of the four smaller Puuc ruins. Rising to prominence in the Classic period, Labná likely had a peak population of 3,000-plus residents, judging from the numerous chultúnes (underground water cisterns) found at the site—more than 60 at last count. Like so many Classic period cities, the apex of its development—around AD 600-750—was followed in short order by abrupt collapse and abandonment in the 9th century.

El Palacio

Labná's impressive main palace is the first structure you come to after passing through the ticket area. As the plaque there explains,

Labná Archaeological Zone

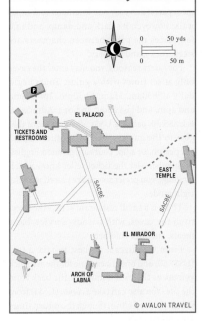

0   50 yds

0   50 m

P

EL PALACIO

TICKETS AND RESTROOMS

EAST TEMPLE

SACBÉ

SACBÉ

EL MIRADOR

ARCH OF LABNA

© AVALON TRAVEL

gaping mouth. Some argue the presence of the plumed snake—shown here "giving birth" to the man emerging from its mouth—suggests strong influence from central Mexico, where the Quetzalcoatl (aka Kukulcán, the feathered snake) was widely worshipped.

Arch of Labná

From the Palacio, a *sacbé* (raised road) leads across a plaza of high flowing grass to the south side of the site and its most famous structure, the Arch of Labná. It's an exquisitely constructed portal vault, with a smooth elliptical ceiling, forming a spacious three- by six-meter (10- by 20-foot) passageway—one of the largest and finest arches known in the Maya world. In its heyday, the arch most likely served as an elegant passageway between residential and administrative structures, both reserved for Labná's elite. Both sides of the arch are decorated, one with deep-relief spirals and checkerboard patterns (associated with clouds and rain) and the other with two *na*, or thatched Maya huts. The doors of the huts were used as niches, probably to display important figures, and red and blue paint is still visible there. Remarkably, only the arch's stairs and the roof comb required significant restoration. The rest has stood, as is, for over a thousand years.

El Mirador

Opposite the arch, a squat temple sits at the peak of a high, steep pile of rocks. Atop the temple, an impressive roof comb soars even higher. This is El Mirador, the building that explorer John Lloyd Stephens called "the most curious and extraordinary structure" he'd seen in his travels through the Maya world. Stone struts suggest the roof comb was once adorned with a complex array of stucco figures, including a huge statue over the center door. Stephens reported only "scattered arms and legs" remained at his visit, more than a century and a half ago; today only the legs of a single figure remain.

the structure underwent at least 12 different constructions and has 67 rooms distributed over two main levels and seven patios. It stretches 135 meters (443 feet) and stands on an even larger artificial platform. The west end (left, as you face it) probably housed Labná's ruling family, while the east side contained *metates* (stones used for grinding corn) and was therefore most likely used by their servants.

Take time to appreciate the palace's fantastic frieze. Many familiar elements are especially embellished here: The noses and eyes of the Chaac masks are turned upward as if peering into the sky, and the latticework is more complex than simple X-patterns seen elsewhere. On one corner, right of the central stairs, a human face can be seen emerging from the mouth of a feathered snake. It seems to have been a late modification: Notice how the hooked nose of the prior mask was turned around to make room for the snake's

GRUTAS DE LOLTÚN

Seven kilometers (4.3 miles) southwest of Oxkutzcab, the **Loltún caves** are the largest known caves in Yucatán. This vast underground network served ancient people as a source of water and pottery clay—ceramics and carved reliefs dating from 1600 BC have been discovered here. It eventually developed into an important pilgrimage and ceremonial space for Maya (caves typically represented fertility and the entrance to Xibalba, the underworld). Researchers working in Loltún also uncovered bones belonging to mastodons and other extinct mammals that date to 9000 BC. While some argue that early hunters dragged these animals to the caves, it has yet to be proven. For now, stone tools dating to 5000-3000 BC mark the earliest sign of humans in Loltún.

Visiting the Caves

A route through the caverns has been wired for colored lights, which are turned on as groups descend into the site. Loltún means "stone flower" in Maya, and you'll see many carvings of small flowers. One of the more intriguing sights is dozens of handprints on the cavern walls, either in silhouette or negative outline, whose meaning remains a mystery. Early Maya also placed stone cisterns (*chultúnes*) under the dripping stalactites to catch "virgin water," important in ceremonies honoring Chaac, the rain god. But the most important archaeological find here is the relief dubbed The Warrior, which is carved on a rock face just outside the Nahkab entrance to Loltún. Strangely, it appears to follow the Izapan style of Kaminaljuyú, the enormous Preclassic city near Guatemala City. Toward the end of the hour-long tour, you come to an opening in the roof of an enormous two-story-high cavern. The sun pours into the room, creating dust-flecked shafts of golden light. The gnarled trunk of a towering tree grows from the floor of the cave, reaching hundreds of feet up through the sunny opening, and flocks of birds twitter and flit in and around the green leafy vines that dangle freely into the immense chamber from above.

Practicalities

Wear good walking shoes in the caves. For the most part it's an easy one-kilometer (0.6-mile) walk; however, it's dark and damp, and in a few places the paths between chambers are steep, rocky, and slippery.

For safety reasons, you may enter the caves only at set times with a guide. Tours begin daily at 9:30am, 11am, 12:30pm, 2pm, 3pm, and 4pm, and last about an hour. Admission is US$5.50, parking US$1.50, but none of that goes to the guides—budget another US$2-3 per person for a tip. Tours are given in English or Spanish—let the ticket seller know which language you prefer so you are paired with the right guide.

There is a small restaurant across the street from the caves, with friendly service, basic meals, and nice cold beer.

From Oxkutzcab, it's best to take a taxi (US$7.50) and organize a time for them to pick you up, as there's not much traffic back from the site. You also can take a *combi* (US$1) from the market to Loltún, though the return times are unpredictable.

TICUL

Northeast of Santa Elena, the pleasant town of Ticul is a pottery and shoemaking center. Like Santa Elena, Ticul is a good place to base yourself if you think you'll want more than one day along the Puuc Route. You'll avoid the long drive back to Mérida after the first day of ruins and can get an early start the next day. Note that many businesses close 2pm-5pm.

Sights

Ticul's elaborate, high-domed 18th-century church, **Templo de San Antonio de Padua** (Calle 25A btwn Calles 24 and 26), has a beautiful stained-glass window over an arched doorway framed by simple columns. Other than those flourishes, the structure possesses the unadorned austerity typical of so many Franciscan churches in this region. Next to it is a Franciscan monastery built 200 years earlier. Both are on the central plaza—impossible to miss.

Ticul

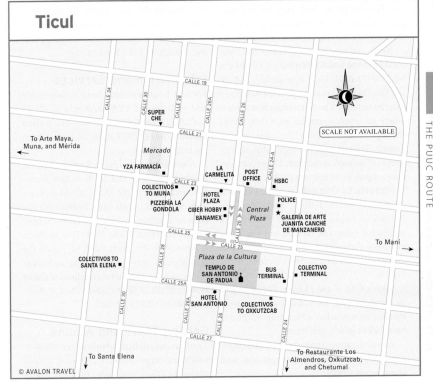

The **Galería de Arte Juanita Canché de Manzanero** (central plaza, tel. 997/972-0701, 9am-1pm and 7pm-9pm Mon.-Fri., 4pm-9pm Sat.-Sun.) is a modest gallery with photos, paintings, and occasional music or dance performances. It is named for the mother of famed Mexican crooner Armando Manzanero, who wrote and performed hundreds of songs, including "Somos Novios" and "Voy a Apagar la Luz." Manzanero was born in Mérida, but his mother is a native of Ticul.

Shopping

The hills and riverbeds around Ticul have great clay, and the town has long been famous for its pottery. By far, the most highly regarded studio here is **Arte Maya** (Calle 23 btwn Calles 46 and 46-A, tel. 997/973-7034, 8am-8pm daily), on the highway toward Muna. The family-run studio was founded by the late Wilbert González and now operates as an art school and pottery store. The shop specializes in high-quality reproductions of classic Maya art, using laboriously prepared clay and all-natural paint made from local soils and minerals. The artists typically model their work from photographs of pieces found during archaeological excavations—the finished products are by no means cheap, but they are remarkable in their faithfulness to the originals. Short tours (in Spanish) are given on request, and if someone is working, you are usually free to watch.

Food

Facing the central plaza, **La Carmelita** (Calle 23 at Calle 26, tel. 997/972-0515, 9:30am-6pm daily, US$2-5) is a mom-and-pop restaurant serving good no-frills Yucatecan dishes to a loyal clientele. The fish plates and shrimp cocktails are particularly popular, and with good reason—they're fresh and tasty, a rarity this far from the coast.

Near the southern entrance to town, **Restaurante Los Almendros** (Calle 24 s/n, tel. 997/972-0021, 10am-8pm daily, US$4-15) is a Ticul institution and one of the best *típico* eateries in town. The restaurant claims this is where *poc-chuc*, a popular meat dish served throughout the Yucatán Peninsula, was invented. True or not, the food here, mostly Maya-influenced, is excellent. Diners can also take a dip in its swimming pool.

Pizzería La Gondola (Calle 23 at Calle 26-A, tel. 997/972-0112, 8am-1pm and 5:30pm-midnight daily, US$4-9) may have somewhat reluctant service, but the pizza and pasta dishes are well prepared and make for a good alternative to Mexican food, if you need it.

Super Che (Calle 21 btwn Calles 28 and 30, no phone, 7am-10pm daily) is a large, well-stocked supermarket with produce, canned food, baked goods, and more.

Across the street, the town *mercado* (6am-2pm daily) has fresh fruits, vegetables, and cheap lunch stands.

Accommodations

Centrally located across from the town church, **Hotel San Antonio** (Calle 25-A at Calle 26, tel. 997/972-1893, hotelsan-antonioticul@hotmail.com, US$16 s with a/c, US$21 d with a/c, US$34 suite with a/c) is a pleasant and comfortable place to stay. Rooms fall into two categories: basic units have small balconies, cable TV, in-room phones, and aging air conditioners, and spacious suites have similar, updated amenities. There's a good, inexpensive restaurant on-site too. Parking and Wi-Fi are available.

Hotel Plaza (Calle 23 btwn Calles 26 and 26-A, tel. 997/972-0484, www.hotelplazayucatan.com, US$25-31 s/d with a/c), located on the central plaza, is a good choice with spotless, simple tile-floor rooms that open onto a breezy interior courtyard with lots of seating. Beds are decent and have bright bedspreads

that liven up the stark rooms. All units have cable TV and in-room telephones. Breakfast is included in the rate, and there's secure parking, though it's a few blocks away.

Information and Services

For a 24-hour pharmacy, head to the reliable and well-stocked **YZA Farmacia** (Calle 23 at Calle 28, tel. 997/972-1080). The **police station** (tel. 997/972-0210, 24 hours) is on the central plaza.

Also on the central plaza, **Banamex** (Calle 26 btwn Calles 23 and 24, 9am-4pm Mon.-Fri.) and **HSBC** (Calle 23 at Calle 24-A, 9am-5pm Mon.-Fri.) both have 24-hour ATMs; Banamex exchanges dollars and euros as well. The **post office** (Calle 23 at Calle 26, 8am-4:30pm Mon.-Fri., 8am-noon Sat.) is on the central plaza, near the entrance to the Palacio Municipal. For Internet access, head to **Ciber Hobby** (Calle 26 btwn Calles 23 and 25, 9am-10pm daily, US$0.65/hour).

Getting There and Around

Ticul has a small **bus terminal** (tel. 997/972-0162) and large *colectivo* terminal, almost across the street from each other on Calle 24 behind the church and central plaza. A number of smaller terminals nearby have *colectivo* service to nearby towns.

The bus terminal has service to Mérida (US$4.75, 1.5 hours, 7am), though *colectivos* are the fastest and cheapest service to Mérida (US$3, 1 hour, 4am-7:30pm). Vans leave whenever full (usually every half hour); buy a ticket at the counter, where you also select a numbered seat assignment.

Colectivos to nearby villages use separate terminals, including to Santa Elena (US$0.75, 20 minutes, board on Calle 30 btwn Calles 25 and 25-A), Muna (US$1, 15 minutes, board on Calle 23 btwn Calles 26-A and 28), and Oxkutzcab (US$1, 30 minutes, board on Calle 25-A btwn Calles 24 and 26). *Colectivos* leave whenever they fill up, typically every 30-60 minutes, roughly 7am-8pm.

You also can get from town to town quite affordably by taxi, and that is recommended at night when *colectivo* service is reduced or nil. A taxi from Ticul to Santa Elena, for example, costs US$4.50.

SANTA ELENA

This peaceful community lies smack-dab in the middle of the Puuc Route, just 16 kilometers (9.9 miles) southeast of Uxmal and seven kilometers (4.3 miles) north of Kabah, the first of the smaller sites. It's a pleasant and convenient base for exploring the entire region, with three fine lodging options, a couple of good restaurants, and an impressive church.

Sights

Long before reaching Santa Elena, you can see its imposing **Iglesia de San Mateo** rising like a misplaced airplane hangar on a distant hilltop. (Some say it was built atop a Maya ruin—not at all uncommon—but you can see from the town's central plaza that it's simply a rocky hill.) A huge, pinkish stone box standing 35 meters (115 feet) high, 50 meters (164 feet) long, and 20 meters (66 feet) wide, the church has almost no exterior adornment. The cavernous nave is also austere, with thick white walls and wood pews. The exceptions are the ornate wooden altar and large wooden *retablos* (hand-carved religious scenes depicted in ornate boxes) along the walls. Be sure to ask the church attendant (he's usually hanging out in the nave) to let you up to the roof, reached via a rickety spiral staircase. Near the top is the organ platform (sans organ) with a dizzying view down into the nave. The roof affords an awesome vista of the surrounding countryside.

A small **museum** (9am-6:30pm daily, US$0.75) alongside the church has detailed and somewhat disturbing displays of the mummified remains of four children who died in the 1800s and were buried in the church floor (a common practice) and uncovered during renovations in 1980. Twelve bodies were discovered; five were reburied, three were taken by authorities and never returned, and four are displayed in glass cases here. The tiny corpses may have been children of German transplants brought during the French occupation that died (or were killed) during the Caste War. The museum also has a replica Maya tomb under glass in the floor of the same room. (Notice a theme?) It shows a skeleton and common burial items, like a stone axe and ceramic dishes, thought to be needed in the next world. Photos, a painted Maya doorway, a few pre-Hispanic and colonial items, and henequen-related information round out the displays.

Food

In the evening, visitors inevitably migrate to ★ **The Pickled Onion** (Hwy. 261 at Ticul road, cell. tel. 997/111-7922, www.thepickledonionyucatan.com, 7:30am-9:15pm daily, US$4-9), a labor of love by a hospitable English Canadian expat. You can munch on excellent Yucatecan dishes like the melt-in-your-mouth *poc-chuc*; try the excellent beef meatballs with almonds, raisins, and mint; or order a box lunch (US$6.25 including bottle of water) to take ruin-hopping—a great idea, as there are so few places to eat along the Puuc Route. Look for the restaurant set up off the main road, halfway between the Flycatcher Inn and Sacbe Boutique Inn.

On the main road to the ruins, the *palapa*-roofed **Restaurant El Chac-Mool** (Calle 18 No. 211-B, no phone, 8am-9pm daily, US$4-10) serves basic Yucatecan specialties, sandwiches, and a smattering of vegetarian options. The food is unremarkable—sometimes reheated, sometimes freshly made—but it's reliable. Service is friendly but sluggish, so it's best to save this place for a post-ruins visit.

Accommodations

★ **The Pickled Onion** (Hwy. 261 at Ticul road, cell. tel. 997/111-7922, www.thepickledonionyucatan.com, US$40-55 s/d) has eight freestanding *palapa*-roofed units (the largest accommodates 5 people) with outdoor sitting areas, mosaic-tiled bathrooms, minifridges, coffeemakers, and well-screened windows. There's a refreshing pool and an outdoor hammock lounge for relaxing after a day of ruin-hopping. A hearty continental breakfast is served on a leafy patio reserved for guests only, while the on-site restaurant is popular with visitors from beyond the hotel walls. Wi-Fi is available too.

★ **The Flycatcher Inn** (southern end of town, off Hwy. 261, tel. 997/978-5350, www. flycatcherinn.com, US$60-85 s/d with a/c, including full breakfast) is a tranquil bed-and-breakfast set on lush tropical grounds. The seven guest rooms have cheerful Mexican folk art, handmade ironwork furniture, and sunny patios. The owners, Kristine Ellingson and Santiago Domínguez, are well versed in the region's sights and history, and often help guests plan their itineraries over breakfast. (There are suggested itineraries, and tons more info, on the Flycatcher's website.) The property includes some 10 hectares (25 acres) of pristine forest behind the hotel—so pristine, in fact, that the owners discovered a small Maya ruin there dating to around AD 1000. You can see it, along with myriad trees, butterflies, and birds, along a short nature trail. Wi-Fi is available. No children under six are allowed.

Set on seven hectares (17 acres) of low forest, **La Nueva Altia** (Hwy. 261 Km. 159, cell. tel. 998/106-6822, www.nuevaaltia.com, US$53-60 s/d) has several two-story bungalows with an airy room on each floor. Units are simple but very comfortable with whitewashed walls, good beds, and large private balconies/terraces. There's a small pool as well as a large *palapa* common space where breakfast is served (and Wi-Fi can be had). The grounds are entirely solar-powered, and wastewater is recycled too. A popular spot for workshops, the hotel has a New Agey feel—drum circles, Maya ceremonies, meditation spaces, and an octagonal-shaped holistic center (in honor of the star with the "purest vibration" in the Maya calendar). A little unusual if you're staying as an independent traveler, but not a deal breaker.

breakfast time at The Pickled Onion

Across the highway, **Sacbe Boutique Inn** (Hwy. 261 Km. 159, tel. 997/978-5158, sacbebungalows@gmail.com, US$35 s/d) has eight recently upgraded cement-block bungalows, all with private bath, high-thread-count linens, sturdy mosquito screens, porches, and Wi-Fi. The grounds are lush and well maintained; there's a playground, obstacle course, pool, and even a stable for the owner's horses. Continental breakfast is included in the rate. It's popular with tour groups.

Information and Services

There is almost nothing in the way of traveler services in this town; it's still very much a small Yucatecan village despite the popularity of the area. **The Pickled Onion** (Hwy. 261 at Ticul road, cell. tel. 997/111-7922, 7:30am-9pm daily) has Wi-Fi available for free to its patrons, and there's an **Internet café** (Calle 18 at Calle 19, 2nd Floor, 8am-10pm daily, US$0.80/hour) near the church. The nearest **ATMs** are at the Uxmal ruins and in Ticul.

Getting There and Around

Like almost everywhere on the Puuc Route, Santa Elena is easiest to reach and negotiate if you have a car. That said, many people do visit by bus and do just fine. Second-class buses between Campeche and Mérida pass in both directions on Highway 261, a block from the Flycatcher Inn and right in front of The Pickled Onion, Sacbe Boutique Inn, and La Nueva Altia.

Buses to Campeche (US$7, 3 hours) and Mérida (US$3.25, 1.5 hours) pass through Santa Elena approximately every two hours, 6:30am-8pm. Lodgings have the most current schedules. Buses to Mérida can drop you off at Uxmal, a 20-minute trip (US$1).

All the Santa Elena hotels listed are along Highway 261, on the southern outskirts of town. Headed south from Uxmal, do not enter Santa Elena proper; instead, continue on the highway 1-2 kilometers (0.6-1.2 miles) and look for the hotel signs. From Ticul, cut through town to the highway—the Flycatcher Inn is directly across the road, The Pickled Onion is at the junction, and Sacbe Boutique Inn and La Nueva Altia are to the left about a kilometer (0.6 mile) away. The nearest **gas stations** are in Ticul and Muna, though you can buy small amounts of gas from private homes in Santa Elena; ask at your hotel for one close by.

OXKUTZCAB

Oxkutzcab is conveniently located near the Loltún caves and the Puuc Route. It's a small village that is surrounded by extremely fertile land—it is known as the orange capital of the Yucatán Peninsula, and a huge citrus processing plant nearby employs many area residents. As you approach town, be sure to look for the orange groves alongside the high healthy fields of corn, bananas, and coconut palms.

Sights and Events

Oxkutzcab's **central plaza** is bordered by a large Franciscan church, the **Templo y Ex-Convento de San Francisco,** and an attractive arched building that holds municipal offices. The plaza itself has concrete benches, a gazebo, and a painted plaster statue of a woman carrying a load of oranges on her head.

Leonardo Paz is an accomplished painter and muralist and an Oxkutzcab native son. He painted the beautiful long **mural** above the market and several smaller works around town. In the plaza, look on the back side of the

Sacbe Boutique Inn has colorful palapa-roofed cabins.

gazebo to see paintings depicting the War of the Castes and the infamous *auto de fé*, when in 1562 Franciscan priest Fray Diego de Landa burned scores of irreplaceable Maya codices and sculptures.

Facing the town church, **Mercado 20 de Noviembre** (6am-4pm daily) is worth wandering into. Paz's colorful mural mirrors the scene just below it, with indigenous women sitting in front of huge piles of fruit and packing boxes stacked in every free space. Most memorable is the incredible assortment of citrus fruits, including oranges, limes, grapefruit, bright pink *pitayas,* and tiny yellow *nanzim.* The best market days are Tuesday, Thursday, and Sunday.

Oxkutzcab's two-week **Orange Festival** is celebrated in late October or early November and is renowned throughout Yucatán. Definitely stop by if you are in the area, and be sure to make a hotel reservation if you want to stay overnight during the festivities.

Food and Accommodations

Just seven kilometers (4.3 miles) from the Loltún caves, **Hotel Puuc** (Calle 55 at Calle 44, tel. 997/975-0103, www.oxkutzcab-hotelpuuc.com, US$20-26 s/d with fan, US$23-29 s/d with a/c, US$33 suite, US$36 suite with a/c) offers over three dozen spacious and clean rooms with cable TV, including seven suites with king-size bed, sofa bed, and minifridge. There's plenty of parking, a large shaded pool, free Wi-Fi, and a good restaurant on-site. The friendly owners also know a lot about area ruins, churches, and caves—be sure to ask for advice if you need it.

Restaurante Labná (Hotel Puuc, Calle 55 at Calle 44, tel. 997/975-0103, 7am-4pm Mon.-Sat., US$3-7) serves regional food in a simple, brightly decorated dining area. Menu items include Yucatecan-style chicken and pork plus Mexican standards such as quesadillas and grilled beef.

For more options, head to the central plaza, where a few simple eateries serve up Yucatecan specialties.

Information and Services

For meds, **Farmacia María del Carmen** (Calle 51 at Calle 52, tel. 997/975-2793, 7am-11pm Mon.-Sat., 7am-3pm Sun.) is across from the market. For cash, **Banamex** (Calle 50 btwn Calles 51 and 53, 9am-4pm Mon.-Fri.), on the central plaza, has an ATM and exchanges foreign currencies. Check your email next door at the well-named **Ciber Ox** (Calle 50 btwn Calles 51 and 53, 8am-11pm daily, US$0.80/hour).

Getting There and Around

Oxkutzcab's **main bus terminal** (tel. 997/975-0308, Calle 51 at Calle 56) has second-class bus service to Mérida (US$3.75, 2 hours, hourly 5:30am-11pm), with stops along the way in Umán, Muna, and Ticul.

You can catch *colectivos* to Ticul (US$1.20, 30 minutes) every 10-15 minutes 6am-8:30pm daily, from the corner of Calles 51 and 54.

To get to the Loltún caves, flag down a *combi* outside Hotel Puuc (US$1).

NORTHWEST OF THE PUUC ROUTE
Hacienda Yaxcopoil

Just off Highway 261 between Mérida and Uxmal, **Hacienda Yaxcopoil** (Hwy. 261, 33 kilometers/20.5 miles south of Mérida, tel. 999/900-1193, www.yaxcopoil.com, 8am-6pm Mon.-Sat., 9am-5pm Sun., US$4.75) was one of dozens of huge henequen (a type of cactus, sometimes referred to as sisal) estates that dotted the Yucatán Peninsula. Built in the 17th century, Yaxcopoil (yawsh-ko-po-EEL) grew to encompass 11,000 hectares (27,181 acres), reaching its zenith during World War I, when rope made from the thorny, fibrous henequen plant was in great demand. A visit to the hacienda today leaves a bit to be desired—consistent guide service or written descriptions, for starters—but you can stroll through the grand old rooms, where antique furniture, old photos, and original tile floors give a sense of the life the *patrones* (landowners) enjoyed. You can even spend the night in the guesthouse, complete with kitchen and

Fray Diego de Landa

Just north of Oxkutzcab, the town of Maní has a quiet, peaceful atmosphere that belies a wrenching history. It was here, in 1562, that Friar Diego de Landa conducted a now-infamous *auto de fé*, in which he burned at least two dozen irreplaceable Maya codices and thousands of painted vases and other items, because he deemed them works of the devil. He accused numerous Maya religious leaders and laypeople of idolatry, and ordered them tortured, publicly humiliated, and imprisoned. The act was outrageous, even by Spanish colonial standards, and Landa was shipped back to Spain to face the Council of the Indies, the colonial authority, for conducting an illegal inquisition. He was eventually absolved—a panel of inspectors found he had broken no laws—but not before Landa came to regret his act, at least somewhat. Confined to a convent awaiting judgment, he set about writing down all he could remember about the Maya.

It was no minor undertaking: Landa spoke Yucatec Maya fluently and had lived, traveled, and preached throughout the Yucatán for 13 years before his expulsion. In all, Landa spent close to a decade completing *An Account of the Things of Yucatán*. He returned to Mérida in 1571 as the newly appointed Bishop of Yucatán, and died there in 1579. Landa's manuscript was largely forgotten until being rediscovered in 1863. Among other things, the manuscript contains a crude alphabet (or more precisely, a syllabary), which has proved invaluable to the modern-day decoding of the Maya hieroglyphics. Ironically, the very man who destroyed so much of the Maya's written history also provided the key for future researchers to unlock what remained.

outdoor patio (US$80 s/d). But don't leave without visiting the machine room out back, which you may have to ask to be unlocked. There, huge machinery once used to extract fiber from the henequen leaves and bind it into bales still stands. The high brick chimney is from the days of steam power (notice the narrow tubes running underfoot), while the massive diesel engine was added in 1913 and used until the hacienda stopped production in 1984.

Admission to Yaxcopoil is a bit much considering how little formal information there is, but if you speak any Spanish, definitely chat up whoever is there—many staffers either worked the hacienda, or their parents or grandparents did, and many have interesting stories. The history of henequen production—the grandeur of the estates, the cruel exploitation of indigenous workers, the political and economic influence wielded by hacienda owners—is as fascinating as it is little understood.

Hacienda San Pedro Ochil

Best visited for a meal before or after a day trip from Mérida, the terrace restaurant at 17th-century **Hacienda San Pedro Ochil** (Hwy. 261 Km. 176.5, tel. 999/924-7465, www.haciendaochil.com, 10am-6pm daily, US$7-15) serves traditional Yucatecan dishes, including an excellent *cochinita pibil* (marinated pork). You can wander the decaying old hacienda grounds, but frustratingly, there's no swimming in its cenote—there's a pool built in front of it (!) and another shaded stone pool for a dip. Pass on the henequen museum—it's mostly an advertisement for a chain of upscale hacienda hotels. There's a US$3 admission if you want to poke around or swim without eating.

Muna

This small town is home to many of the people who work at or around the Uxmal archaeological site. For travelers, there's not much reason to stop, and now that the highway loops around it, many people don't make it into town. But Muna does have a 17th-century Franciscan church—**Templo de la Virgen de la Asunción**—that's notable for its facade, which is adorned with lacy belfries that glow a mellow gold in the late afternoon. People are friendly, and the shady plaza has a number of fruit stands. This is also a good place to fill

Oxkintok Archaeological Zone

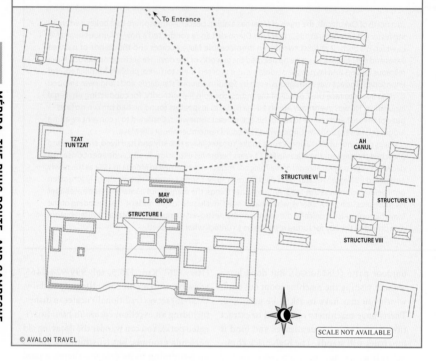

To Entrance

TZAT TUN TZAT

AH CANUL

STRUCTURE VI

STRUCTURE VII

MAY GROUP

STRUCTURE I

STRUCTURE VIII

SCALE NOT AVAILABLE

© AVALON TRAVEL

your gas tank (the Pemex gas station is on the central plaza).

There is no bus station in Muna, so buses and *colectivos* stop at the northwest corner of the plaza, near the church. There is usually a bus representative hanging around nearby selling tickets. Transportation to Mérida (US$1.75, 1 hour) leaves frequently 5:30am-midnight. Buses to Uxmal (US$1, 25 minutes) leave at 9am, 2pm, 4pm, and 7pm; taxis charge US$7.

Oxkintok Archaeological Zone

Though seldom visited, **Oxkintok** (8am-5pm daily, US$3) is a large, well-maintained site that's both scenic and archaeologically significant, with palaces, temples, and plazas scattered amid trees and high grass. Though not awe-inducing like other sites, it's the sort of place that makes spending an extra day

or two on the Puuc Route so rewarding, especially combined with a visit to the nearby Calcehtok caves.

Oxkintok (Three Stone Suns) is notable for having a very early Long Count date, found on a stone lintel, corresponding to the year AD 475, and evidence suggests the site was occupied as early as the 3rd century BC. It was a powerful, and at times dominant, commercial center during much of the Classic period, before experiencing a rapid and mysterious decline in the 9th century—the latest dated inscription is from AD 859.

Oxkintok's most famous feature, however, is a small structure known as **Tzat tun tzat,** or El Laberinto (The Labyrinth). Located behind the cluster of structures to your right as you enter the site, and unique in Maya construction, Tzat tun tzat has more than a dozen chambers interwoven over three levels and connected by narrow tunnels, stairways, gates, and vaulted passages. Archaeologists are unsure of the building's exact significance, though it seems likely to have been related to myths of journeying from Earth to the lower and upper worlds, and may have been used as a tomb or for symbolic rituals. Unfortunately, visitors are no longer permitted to enter the structure, so you have to forge your own theories from outside.

To the left of the entrance is a larger cluster of structures called **Ah Canul,** where a number of columns, incised with human forms, can be seen in various states of disrepair. The figures represent gods, warriors, and local elite, and may have been a precursor to warrior columns found in sites like Chichén Itzá and Mayapán.

Oxkintok has undergone sporadic exploration and investigation, including visits by Stephens and Catherwood in 1842 and pioneering Mayanist Tatiana Proskouriakoff (who studied the warrior columns), and more recent research focusing on the remains of a surprisingly extensive urban center, covering as much as eight square kilometers (3 square miles). Tombs have been found in a number of the structures, though sadly many artifacts have been lost to looters.

To reach Oxkintok by car, follow the signs eastbound from Highway 180, or westbound on Highway 184. There's no regular public transport there, though you may be able to get a cab or motorcycle taxi from the towns of Maxcanú or Calcehtok. Consider combining a visit here with a tour of the Calcehtok Caves.

Grutas Aktun Usil

Located two kilometers (1.2 miles) south of Oxkintok ruins is the remarkable and little-visited **Aktun Usil Caves.** According to INAH (Mexico's National Institute of Anthropology and History), it was an ancient Maya ritual site, where calendars related to agricultural and societal cycles were created as early as AD 750. Today, visitors can visit its three main chambers with a guide. The first features a 12-meter-high (39-foot) ceiling with an impressive display of Maya hieroglyphs and cave paintings of turtles and frogs honoring Chaac, the god of rain. The second room has mammoth stalagmites and stalactites, *chultúnes* (natural stone cisterns used to collect water), rock carvings, and even stone masks wedged into crevices. The final chamber is the smallest but in some ways the most human—several handprints, in silhouette, can be easily seen on the ceiling above, and

MÉRIDA, THE PUUC ROUTE, AND CAMPECHE
THE PUUC ROUTE

the little-visited Oxkintok ruins

fragments of bones, pottery, and stone phalluses are strewn on the cave floor below.

Aktun Usil is still considered sacred to the local Maya. Though visitors could access the cave on their own—it's relatively easy to clamber in, and there's natural light through several openings above—they must enter with a local guide. This is so certain customs are properly followed, such as asking the cave "permission" to enter and passing copal incense over visitors to purify them before entering. Tours typically cost US$30-55 (1-1.5 hours for up to 4 people). Victor Chim (cell. tel. 997/113-3910) is a recommended bilingual local guide with extensive knowledge of the cave and the surrounding ruins; most official Oxkintok guides also can lead tours to the site.

Grutas de Calcehtok

The **Calcehtok Caves (aka Grutas de Xpukil,** tel. 999/276-8122, 9:30am-3:30pm Mon.-Fri., 8am-5pm Sat.-Sun.) are part of the Yucatán's second-largest cave system (only Loltún is larger) and certainly among the most adventurous to visit. Up to four kilometers (2.5 miles) of the cave can be explored, during which you squeeze through narrow gaps, teeter along slippery pathways, and crawl and clamber through muddy passageways. Along the way are huge chambers filled with stalactites and stalagmites, and tiny rooms where archaeologists have found human bones and other remains of pre-Hispanic Maya ceremonies. Calcehtok's caves are definitely less commercialized than others—you don't need any technical experience, but be prepared to get dirty.

Guides typically wait for visitors at the crest of a short path leading from the parking lot toward the cave entrance. (If no one is there, it means they are with other visitors, and you can either wait or come back later. *Never* enter this or any other cave without a guide.) Various tours are available, ranging from one hour to several, depending on how deep into the cave you want to go. Prices vary accordingly, but start at roughly US$14 per hour (up to 4 people). Before going in,

agree with the guide how long the tour will last and how far into the cave you will get. If you have a flashlight, bring it as a backup. Tennis shoes or boots are best, although Tevas should be fine. Some visitors also wear dust masks to avoid possible infection from fungus on bat guano.

To get here, follow the signs on Highway 184 until you reach a turnoff that leads to a small parking lot.

RUTA DE LOS CONVENTOS

Located along or just off Highway 18, a route dotted with notable colonial convents in small towns, these sights are easily reached by car and make for interesting stops between Mérida and the Puuc Route. Note that most churches are closed approximately 1pm-4pm. Oxkutzcab or Ticul are the best nearby towns to spend the night if you can't pack it all in on a day trip. Driving from the *periférico* in Mérida, you'll be following signs for Kanasín.

Acancéh Archaeological Zone

With a name that translates to "the moan of the deer," the official **Acancéh archaeological zone** (8am-5pm daily, US$3) consists of two main parts: a large pyramid and secondary temple right in the center of the town of Acancéh, and a second, somewhat smaller structure called El Palacio de Estucos (Palace of the Stuccos) a few blocks away. In reality, the majority of the remains of this ancient city are scattered throughout town; most are on private property—backyards, front yards, under houses, and so on—and it is either impossible or impractical to excavate them. Still, archaeologists believe the area was settled as early as 300 BC but didn't reach its peak until AD 400-600. Curiously, Acancéh's structures show strong influences from Petén (northern Guatemala) as well as Teotihuacán in central Mexico, both quite distant.

As you drive through town, the pyramid is impossible to miss, facing a large dirt lot (Acancéh's central plaza, actually). A small kiosk at the corner is where you buy your ticket, and a guide may accompany you up the pyramid (no fee, but a small tip is appreciated). At the top, under a protective tin roof, are a series of large stucco masks; unfortunately, the actual faces are missing or significantly deteriorated. They surely depict important gods, but archaeologists have been unable to identify most of them.

If you've got a car, the guide likely will lead you to the Palacio de los Estucos on his bike. A large, complex palace, it shows a blending of architectural styles, including, for example, both curved and squared corners. On the uppermost level is a long frieze of impressive stucco designs (hence the structure's name) in the shapes of birds, a ram, and a man-jaguar, among others. Be sure to ask your guide to point out the lintel of one of the top-level doorways, which is made of a deeply grooved *metate,* used for grinding corn. Too worn down for its original purpose, it was reused in the construction here. Not only resourceful, it lends a certain human touch to the structure.

★ Cenotes de Cuzamá

A tour of the cenotes at Chunkanán, better known as the **Cenotes de Cuzamá** (cell. tel. 999/103-6447, 8am-5pm daily, US$22/ trolley, up to 4 people), is a favorite non-archaeological outing from Mérida. When the henequen plantations were functioning, the harvest was stacked on small trolleys that were pulled by horses over long networks of lightweight rails. Here, local residents have put their trolleys back to use, outfitting the carts to hold four passengers and offering horse-drawn tours to three beautiful cenotes along the rail line. The trip to the cenotes is half the fun—there is only one set of rails and an unspoken etiquette as to which driver has to pull over, which entails unloading the passengers and hoisting the cart off the tracks before the other trolley clatters past. With a few starts and stops, you make it to the cenotes. The first, Cenote Chacsinicche, is the largest and easiest to

get into, with concrete stairs leading to a cavernous pool. The second two, Cenotes Chan-Ucil and Bolonchoojol, are more challenging—in both you have to negotiate a slippery ladder from the cavern roof down to the water. Wear Tevas or sneakers. The effort is worth it, however, for the sublime experience of swimming in the crystalline water with sunbeams and tree roots angling down through the roof. The whole trip is 18 kilometers (11 miles) round-trip and takes about three hours with a half-hour stop at each cenote. *Tábanos* (horseflies) are the only annoyance, buzzing around the horse and cart. They have a nasty bite, so be careful not to let one land on you. Look for the big parking lot on the right-hand side of the road as you approach from the village of Chunkanán.

In the same small village, **Sac Nicté** (tel. 999/923-7598, www.sacnictemx.blogspot. com, US$75 for up to 4 people) is a compound of three Maya-style *palapa*-roofed *cabañas* that together have a kitchen, dining area, hot-water bathroom, space for four hammocks, plus a pool. There are no beds. Authentic Mayan meals can be delivered "fresh and smoky" to your door, and several guided tours—including a moonlight visit to the cenotes or visits to other regional cenotes—can be arranged by the compound's owner.

The entrance to the cenotes is in the village of Chunkanán, just over three kilometers (1.9 miles) from the larger town of Cuzamá. To get there by public transport, catch a Cuzamá-bound *colectivo* outside Mérida's Terminal Noreste (US$1.20, 45 minutes, every 30 minutes 5:30am-8pm, last return bus at 7:15pm), then hop a *triciclo,* or bicycle taxi, to the cenotes (US$1.75 each way).

Cenote Tza Ujun Kat

One kilometer (0.6 mile) west of Cuzamá in the town of Homún (across from the cemetery) lies the **Cenote Tza Ujun Kat** (9am-sunset daily, US$1). Visited mostly by locals, it's a large clear-blue swimming hole that's accessible by a short cement stairway. An opening in the cavern roof allows shafts of light to beam in during the late afternoon—an inspiring view and a great photo op to boot. This is a good alternative if you want to go to a cenote but don't have the time to take the tour in Cuzamá. There are a few other lovely cenotes nearby; ask here for directions or a guide.

Grutas de Tzabnah

Located just outside of the village of Tecoh, the **Tzabnah caves** (10am-5pm Mon.-Fri., 8am-5pm Sat.-Sun., US$6.25) are something of a mixed bag: A 1.5-hour guided tour leads you past a dozen crystalline underground cenotes, but some of the walls and limestone formations are marred with spray paint. The payoff is a 50-meter (164-foot) crawl to the last and largest cenote, which has beams of sunlight entering from two holes in the roof and makes for a refreshing swim.

Hacienda Sotuta de Péon

A visit to the 19th-century **Hacienda Sotuta de Péon** (off Hwy. 184, tel. 999/941-6441, tours 10am and 1pm daily, US$29.50 adult, US$14.75 child) is one of the most popular day trips from Mérida. It comprises a 2.5-hour tour of a working henequen plantation where visitors can see the process from start to finish. The bilingual guides give visitors an excellent crash course in the economic and social history of the region. Mule-drawn trolleys take you through the fields of "green gold," and there's a splendid and dramatically lit cenote cavern for swimming. The premises include a good restaurant and luxurious *cabañas* if you want to spend the night (US$171-238 s/d with a/c). This is one of the priciest hacienda tours you'll find, and it caters to large groups, though its proximity to town is a bonus.

By car, the hacienda is about 45 minutes from Mérida, leaving the city via Calle 42 Sur, or 50 minutes via Highway 184 by way of Tecoh; both routes are well signed. If you don't have a car, the hacienda charges US$17 per person (half price for children) for round-trip transportation.

Mayapán Archaeological Zone

Mayapán (8am-5pm daily, US$2.50) is thought by some to have been one of the most important cities in the pre-Hispanic Maya world, although you'd never know from the trickle of visitors the site gets nowadays. Mayapán is not on any tour itinerary, and independent travelers tend to skip it going to or from the "main" Puuc sites farther south. While not as grand as Uxmal or Chichén Itzá, it rarely disappoints the people who do stop. Mayapán is a compact, immaculately maintained site with two primary pyramids, an observatory, a cenote, and excellent fresco paintings and stucco masks. It was founded around AD 1000 after the powerful Cocom dynasty left Chichén Itzá to establish the region's capital here. (Chichén Itzá was subsequently abandoned except as a place for religious worship and pilgrimages.) Mayapán dominated northern Yucatán until almost the mid-15th century, when it was abruptly abandoned, perhaps because of an internal revolt. The first indigenous people met by the Spanish newcomers still called themselves *maya uinic* (Maya men) in reference to their former capital, and it is from there that modern use of the word Maya emerged. Unfortunately, there are few explanatory plaques on-site.

Second-class buses from Mérida's Terminal Noreste pass the ruins' entrance in both directions (US$1.75, 1.5 hours, hourly 5:30am-8pm); take the bus headed to the town of Telchaquillo and let the driver know you'd like to get off at Mayapán ruins (not Mayapán town, which is in an entirely different area and bus route!).

Maní

The town of Maní is best known as the site of Fray Diego de Landa's egregious 1562 *auto de fé*, an inquisition that destroyed many of the most precious objects of Maya culture. Prior to that, it was the nucleus of the powerful Xiu dynasty, whose leader converted to Christianity and allied himself with the Spanish. Today, a visit to the municipal building across from

Mayapán Archaeological Zone

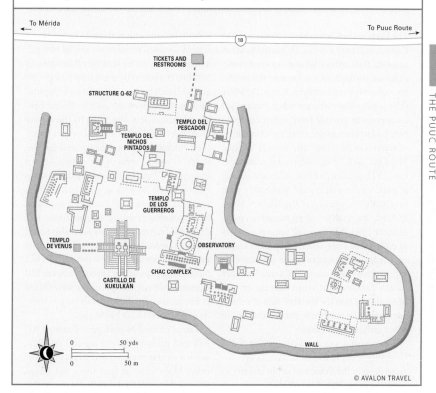

To Mérida

To Puuc Route

18

TICKETS AND
RESTROOMS

STRUCTURE Q-62

TEMPLO DEL
PESCADOR

TEMPLO DEL
NICHOS
PINTADOS

TEMPLO
DE LOS
GUERREROS

TEMPLO
DE VENUS

OBSERVATORY

CHAC COMPLEX

CASTILLO DE
KUKULKÁN

0   50 yds

0   50 m

WALL

© AVALON TRAVEL

the church reveals some of the carved Maya stones repurposed and incorporated into it.

Built on the site of a Maya temple using many of the former building's stones, the beautiful 1549 **Ex-Convento de San Miguel Arcángel** (9am-noon and 4pm-7pm Wed.-Sun.) is one of the oldest monasteries in the Yucatán. The church contains an intricate three-tiered *retablo* surrounded by frescoes, including one of Michael, the town's patron saint, vanquishing the devil, and another of the stigmata of St. Francis of Assisi. The grassy area in front of the church was where Fray de Landa's infamous burning of Maya codices and precious items took place.

★ **Restaurante El Príncipe Tutul-Xiu** (Calle 26 btwn Calles 25 and 27, tel. 997/978-4257, 11am-6pm daily, US$5-7) has a devoted following from around Yucatán that keeps it busy on weekends. A series of connected palapas with basketry lighting and a profusion of Maya-themed stone decor are the backdrop for the tender and delectable *poc-chuc* that keeps customers coming. Servings are ample and come with *cebollas asadas* (grilled onions), *frijol colado* (spicy black bean sauce), and handmade tortillas.

Colectivos to Oxkutzcab (US$0.50, 15 minutes) depart from the corner of Calles 26 (the main road) and 25, and there are hourly local buses to Merida (US$3, 2 hours).

The Chenes Region

The Maya of the Chenes region (today, central Campeche) chose a decidedly hostile location to found their cities. Hot and dry conditions, common throughout the Yucatán Peninsula, are especially persistent here. Worse, the water table is quite low—whereas other Maya relied on cenotes to provide fresh water, residents here had to venture deep into caves in search of water. (In fact, the word *chen* is Yucatec Maya for "well," and modern-day communities like Hopelchén and Bolonchén are named, in part, for the well around which they were originally founded.) Yet the Chenes Maya thrived, not only founding numerous magnificent cities, but devising innovative ways to collect and store water. They also created an ornate architectural style that quickly spread across the peninsula; Chenes "monster mouth" facades, which turn the exterior wall of a building into the fantastic face of a deity, are among the most recognizable features in Maya archaeological sites.

Chenes sites are no easier to visit today than they were to live in millennia ago, located deep in the forest and as hot and dry as ever. They may be too far off the beaten path for average visitors, but for ruin hounds the isolation is divine.

EDZNÁ ARCHAEOLOGICAL ZONE

Edzná (8am-5pm daily, US$3.25, US$8 sound and light show only) is the nearest major archaeological site to Campeche City, and makes for an excellent day trip. Agencies in Campeche offer van service to Edzná, with or without a guide, which can be convenient if your time is short or you don't want to risk missing the bus home. Guides at the site charge around US$30 for 1.5-hour tours of the ruins in either Spanish or English.

History

Nestled in a fertile valley between low mountains, the area is thought to have been settled by small farmers as early as 600 BC, and its earliest lasting structures built around 300 BC. It eventually grew into a large city and regional power, supporting a population in the tens of thousands. Edzná's regional influence is illustrated by the variety of architectural styles and influences found there, including Petén, Chenes, and Río Bec styles, as well as some of the earliest-known examples of Puuc architecture. Edzná is also notable for its network of water canals, measuring 22 kilometers (13.7 miles) in all, which helped control flooding, irrigate fields, and drain fields. Archaeologists have also found some 70 *chultúnes* (underground reservoirs) used to collect and store water for Edzná's burgeoning population. Several scenes in Mel Gibson's 2006 release *Apocalypto* were filmed at Edzná, the actual temples serving as backdrop for models built by the crew.

Edzná entered its peak period around AD 600 and prospered until around AD 900, when it went into a rapid decline, as did many other Maya cities at that time. But Edzná managed to avoid total collapse—probably thanks to its consistently rich agricultural resources—and remained an important population center as late as AD 1450, when it was finally abandoned. Early researchers postulated that Edzná meant House of Grimaces and was a reference to a series of masks that decorated the comb of the Temple of Five Stories. Now archaeologists believe the name means Home of the Itzás, a reference to settlers who emigrated from central Mexico well after the Maya collapse of the 9th and 10th centuries and reoccupied many of the fallen cities. If so, the city's original name has been lost to history.

Gran Plaza

Coming from the entrance, a path deposits you on the northwest corner of a huge grassy

Edzná Archaeological Zone

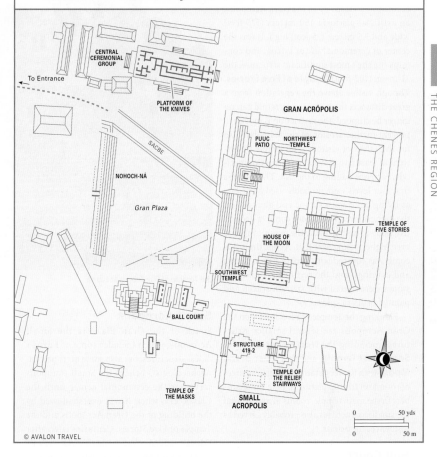

To Entrance

CENTRAL CEREMONIAL GROUP

PLATFORM OF THE KNIVES

GRAN ACRÓPOLIS

SACBE

NOHOCH-NÁ

Gran Plaza

PUUC PATIO

NORTHWEST TEMPLE

TEMPLE OF FIVE STORIES

HOUSE OF THE MOON

SOUTHWEST TEMPLE

BALL COURT

STRUCTURE 419-2

TEMPLE OF THE RELIEF STAIRWAYS

TEMPLE OF THE MASKS

SMALL ACROPLIS

0   50 yds

0   50 m

© AVALON TRAVEL

courtyard known as the Gran Plaza. To your left is the **Platform of the Knives,** on top of which are the much-decayed remains of several fine residences, most likely used by Edzná's elite. The platform's name comes from a small offering of flint knives found by archaeologists in one of the structures. To your right is the narrow end of another platform, this one called **Nohoch-Ná** (Big House) that extends an impressive 125 meters (410 feet) along the Gran Plaza's western edge. Atop are bases for what were once four long halls,

probably used for administrative functions like collecting tributes or mediating conflicts. High stairs run the entire length and most likely doubled as bleachers for events and ceremonies held in the Gran Plaza itself. Visitors often stand at the top of this structure and clap their hands once—the sound can be heard throughout the site, like thunder, bouncing off the walls of structures. An impressive architectural feat, and one that elicits images of speeches made to ancient Maya crowds in the plaza below.

Gran Acrópolis

On the east side of the Gran Plaza, a wide bank of stairs leads up to the Gran Acrópolis, an artificial platform 160 meters (525 feet) wide and 7.5 meters (25 feet) high. It was the center of ceremonial life at Edzná, and contains the site's most significant structure, the 31-meter (102-foot) **Temple of Five Stories.** Though visible above the vegetation from a great distance, the imposing pyramid can no longer be climbed; the restriction is mostly to prevent further erosion of the stairs but also for the safety of visitors. The temple underwent at least five distinct construction periods, each one adding to the last. The temple's first four levels were probably used by priests as living quarters; a shrine and altar are on the highest level, with a roof comb (a decorative element built to make the pyramid appear even higher) rising over that. At one time, this comb was covered with ornate stucco masks and carvings, and the rest of the building's stones were coated with smooth stucco and painted brilliant colors.

Flanking the Temple of Five Stories on the Gran Acrópolis are several smaller structures, including the **Northwest Temple, Southwest Temple,** and the **House of the Moon,** with its steep stairs leading to vestiges of rooms on the top platform. Like the chambers in the main temple, rooms in and around the smaller structures also probably served as residences for priests.

Ball Court

Dividing the two areas is the ball court, with a north-south pitch, and ramps and scoring rings (barely visible here) on the east and west sides. This orientation, common in Maya ball courts, emphasized the religious significance attached to the game, casting it as sunrise versus sunset, light versus dark, good versus evil. Royalty would have likely watched the game from rooms on top of the two ramps, while commoners would have crowded around the ends, if they were allowed to watch at all.

the Temple of Five Stories at Edzná

Small Acropolis

South of the Gran Plaza is the Small Acropolis, which includes some of Edzná's oldest structures, but also some of its newest. Archaeologists believe the Small Acropolis served as the ceremonial center until the Classic era, when it was overshadowed by the building of the Gran Acrópolis and the Temple of Five Stories. Centuries later, after Edzná's sudden collapse and slow recovery, its new residents once again began construction projects in this area of the city. The **Temple of the Relief Stairways,** built in the Late Classic or Early Postclassic era, is the largest such structure. Its name comes from the curious use of *stelae* (carved monoliths) left over from Edzná's glory days to build the new temple's staircase; this may have been a deliberate insult to the fallen kings, but a simpler explanation is that the newcomers were illiterate and short on stones.

At the south edge of the Small Acropolis, the **Temple of the Masks** contains Edzná's best-preserved stucco decorations. The carved stone masks at the temple's east and west ends represent the sun god's face in its dawn (young) and dusk (old) incarnations, respectively. The faces have scarifications on the cheeks, large ear ornaments, and teeth filed to a point—all characteristics of the Maya nobility. Traces of the original red paint remain.

Sound and Light Show

Friday and Saturday nights (7pm winter, 8pm summer, US$8), there's a decent sound and light show, which involves walking through the site itself—a real treat at night.

Food and Accommodations

Four kilometers (2.5 miles) from Edzná, **Hacienda y Glamping La Carlotta** (Carr. Noh-yaxché Km. 21, tel. 981/872-8455, www. glamping.com, US$122 s/d with a/c, US$140 glamping with a/c) has 10 stand-alone suites that face a sunny, well-tended pool. Each is spacious and upscale, with canopy beds, comfy sitting areas, and bathrooms that are so big, they could almost serve as a second guest room. All have satellite TV and Wi-Fi. A short walk away is the "glamping" section— a Taj Mahal-sized tent, with wood floors, a full living room, rugs, lamps, and flat-screen TV as well as the requisite traveling trunks

and globe (à la Hollywood safari). There's also a canopy bed, running water, a clawfoot tub, and a flush toilet. Oh, and air-conditioning. Did we mention this is a tent? An on-site restaurant provides à la carte meals—necessary since there aren't really any other options nearby.

Getting There

If you're driving from Campeche, take Highway 180 east to Chencoyil, then go east on Highway 261 to Cayal, where you turn right and continue to the Edzná site. (The signage is very good.) The 60-kilometer (37-mile) drive takes about one hour. If you don't have a car, second-class bus service (US$2.50, 1 hour) is available from Campeche, leaving every 30 minutes 7am-7pm from Calle Chihuahua, one block east of the Mercado Municipal. Look for buses headed to Bonfil. Ask the driver to drop you at the *desvío* Edzná (turnoff to Edzná); it's about 200 meters (656 feet) from there to the entrance.

EL TABASQUEÑO ARCHAEOLOGICAL ZONE

Dating to the Classic period, **El Tabasqueño** (aka Xtabás, 8am-5pm daily, free) reached its peak between AD 750 and 900. It is a small

glamping (camping but more glamorous) near Edzná

site, with the excavated structures facing a rectangular plaza. The most notable is the one-story **Structure 1,** often called the Temple Palace; the facade has an impressive monster-mouth doorway, the corners of which are flanked by two rows of eight Chaac masks, a classic Chenes feature. The rest of the structure consists of eight rooms, a temple, and a central staircase. To the southwest stands a 3.5-meter (11.5-foot) **tower.** The site is down a well-signed two-kilometer (1.2-mile) gravel road that begins from Highway 269 a few kilometers south of Pakchén.

HOCHOB ARCHAEOLOGICAL ZONE

Meaning Place of the Corn Cobs, **Hochob** (8am-5pm daily, US$2.25) sits on a 30-meter-high (98-foot) rise, the top of which was flattened to build part of the city. It consists of three plazas, though only one has been significantly excavated. Fortunately, it is in that plaza that the most stunning of the site's buildings is found: **Structure 1,** or the Main Palace, consisting of just three rooms, has a wildly ornate facade with open-mouth serpents and masks, all representative of Itzamná, the creator deity. The doorway is a classic monster-mouth mask, with fangs, piercing eyes, and enormous earflaps. It is flanked by cascades of Chaac masks, hooked nose and all, on the corners. **Structure 5,** on the same plaza, has two temples, the easternmost one sporting the remains of a roof comb. As you walk through the site, notice the *chultúnes* (natural stone cisterns) that were used to collect water in ancient times.

To arrive, take Highway 269 south past Dzibalchén to the town of Chencoh, where a 3.5-kilometer (2.2-mile) paved road leads to the site. There's no sign going southbound; turn right at the Pemex station.

DZIBILNOCAC ARCHAEOLOGICAL ZONE

Unlike the other Chenes sites, **Dzibilnocac** (8am-5pm daily, free) sits in a flat, wide-open space. With a name meaning Painted Vault or Great Painted Turtle, it dates to 500-50 BC, though it reached its height between AD 300 and 900. It is a fairly large site measuring 1.32 square kilometers (0.8 square mile), with several groups of structures consisting of pyramids, administrative buildings, and dwellings. Most of the site is unexcavated, however, so only a small portion can be visited. In that area, the most impressive building is **Structure A1,** the Palace-Temple, a raised platform with three Río Bec-style towers, each set on rounded bases. Only one tower, however, is significantly well preserved; it is covered in intricate monster masks with representations of Chaac on the corners.

Getting There

Dzibilnocac is located 400 meters (0.2 mile) east of the town of Iturbide, 18 kilometers (11 miles) north of Highway 269 after you hit the town of Dzibalchén. There's second-class bus service from Campeche City via Hopelchén (3 hours, US$5.50); just be sure to leave Campeche early so you have time to get back (there are no hotels in Iturbide).

SANTA ROSA XTAMPAK ARCHAEOLOGICAL ZONE

Like many Maya cities in the Yucatán Peninsula, **Santa Rosa Xtampak** (8am-5pm daily, US$2.25) reached its heyday around AD 600-850, and archaeologists believe that this old city was once the heart of the Chenes empire. It had more than 60 *chultúnes* (underground water reservoirs), suggesting a population of more than 10,000 people. Its main structure, the **Palace,** is one of the most architecturally complex buildings in the Maya world, with three floors, 11 staircases, and 44 rooms. The site has scores of structures, though only a half dozen or so have been extricated from the thick trees and brush. Opposite the palace is a **residential structure** with a beautiful monster-mouth entrance, a classic feature of Chenes sites. Farther down the path, the huge **Cuartel** hulks, in semi-collapse, amid the trees.

John Stephens visited Xtampak in 1842, but

Santa Rosa Xtampak Archaeological Zone

SCALE NOT AVAILABLE

PALACE

LA CASA COLORADA

Central Plaza

CUARTEL

© AVALON TRAVEL

large population of Mennonites living in the area. The plaza's often filled with Mennonites in their distinctive garb, the men in matching black bib overalls and straw cowboy hats and the women in pioneer frocks and bonnets.

Sights

Otherwise unadorned, the 1667 **Iglesia San Antonio de Padua** (main plaza) boasts an intricately carved and painted Baroque altar—one of the oldest in the Yucatán Peninsula—that's lined with gold and silver and segmented by corkscrew columns.

Just outside of town, the **Tohcok Archaeological Zone** (aka Tacob Archaeological Zone, 8am-5pm daily, free) is a small Late Classic site that peaked about AD 600-750. It contains approximately 40 structures spread throughout some five hectares (12 acres), though only a few have been restored. Even so, the ones on view are worth a look for the Puuc-style columns, vaulted rooms, and the newly restored frieze of the rain god Chaac. The voluble caretaker loves to show off his beloved ruins; he can guide you to a *chultún* (subterranean cistern) on the other side of the road, and show you the jumble of carved stones that have yet to be reassembled. Signed as Tacob, the ruins are along Highway 261, 3.5 kilometers (2.2 miles) northwest of Hopelchén. Yellow-and-white school buses putter between the ruins and the town plaza every half hour 8am-6pm and charge US$0.50. Walking also is an easy, and pleasant, option.

Food and Accommodations

On the main plaza, **Hotel Los Arcos** (Calle 23 s/n, cell. tel. 996/100-8782, US$12/16 s/d, US$18/22 s/d with a/c) is a cheap sleep with older beds, hammock hooks, and bathrooms that could use some extra Soft Scrub. Management may be in cahoots with the airlines in charging à la carte—air-conditioning costs an extra US$6, and it's another US$3 for a room with TV. There's a small lobby **restaurant** (7am-3pm daily, US$3-6) serving gut-busting meat-and-vegetable platters that are a hit with the local Mennonites.

major excavation didn't begin until the mid-1990s, and continues today. For that reason, much of the palace is off-limits, as are other structures, but if you're there when workers are present, it offers a unique opportunity to see the difficult and dirty process of archaeology in action.

Getting There

Santa Rosa Xtampak lies 45 kilometers (28 miles) down a paved road off Highway 261. It's another 137 kilometers (85 miles) from the turnoff to Campeche City. If this is a stopover between Campeche and Mérida—or even a side trip from the Puuc Route—start early. Driving from Campeche, take Highway 261 past Hopelchén to the marked turnoff just north of town.

HOPELCHÉN

Maya for Place of the Five Wells, Hopelchén is notable as the municipal seat for the Chenes region and as the main market town for the

Information and Services

There's a small **tourism office** (Calle 23 s/n, 8am-3pm daily) in the Casa de Cultura one block north of the main plaza, and a **Bancomer** (Calle 20 s/n, 8:30am-4pm Mon.-Fri.) with a 24-hour ATM, just off the plaza itself.

Getting There

From Campeche's second-class terminal, buses (US$3.75, 1.5 hours) leave hourly 5am-6:30pm and return until 7:30pm, though there's no 6pm Campeche-bound bus. Faster vans to Campeche (US$3.25, 1.25 hours) leave every 30 minutes from beside the church.

The town's **bus terminal** (Calle 16 btwn Calles 17 and 19), at the Mercado Municipal, has second-class service to Mérida (US$6, 2.5 hours, 6 departures, 5am-6:30pm), Campeche (US$3.50, 1.5 hours, 10 departures, 3:30am-5:30pm), and Xpujil (US$7, 3 hours, 8pm).

GRUTAS DE X'TACUMBILXUNA'AN

With a name meaning Hidden Lady, the **X'tacumbilxuna'an caves** (aka Great Well of Bolonchén, 10am-5pm Tues.-Sun., US$3.25) is named after a Maya legend that recalls how Earth hid its daughter, Water, underground to prevent her from being found by her lover, Man. The cave system was "discovered" by John L. Stephens and Frederick Catherwood in 1841 and made famous by the latter's lithograph, which shows locals hauling pails of water up a long wood ladder to the surface (so much for the hiding spot, Lady). Today, a portion of the cave has been outfitted for visitors, with steps and smooth walkways; snazzy lighting highlights some of the spectacular stalagmites and stalactites along the way, and guides narrate points of interest.

Getting There

The Grutas de X'tacumbilxuna'an are located three kilometers (1.9 miles) north of the town of Bolonchén de Rejón, off Highway 261. If you're busing it, take a second-class bus from Hopelchén to Mérida (US$1.25, 30 minutes) and ask to be dropped off at the turnoff to the cave; the entrance is about half a kilometer (0.3 mile) from the highway. A pedestrian-only path makes it an easy and pleasant walk.

KANKI ARCHAEOLOGICAL ZONE

Kanki (8am-5pm daily, free) is a modest but decently excavated site located in a hilly area of northern Campeche state and surrounded by farm lands. Its builders took advantage of the hills to construct interconnected structures and patios over different levels. The site's primary structure, designated Structure 1, is a two-level palace surrounded by 10 courtyards. The structure most likely served ceremonial and administrative purposes, and perhaps as a residence for royalty. Kanki's architecture is mainly Puuc, with corbelled vaults, long passages with multiple doorways, and buildings that feature plain lower sections and highly decorative upper friezes and roof combs. Much of Kanki's decorative features have collapsed, thanks to time and vegetation, but remnants of Chaac masks and other designs can be spotted. Kanki was first settled around AD 500, reached its peak around AD 600 to 650, declined, and was eventually abandoned around AD 900. The site's original name is unknown; Kanki is Yucatec Maya for Place of Chultunes, a reference to the numerous stone water basins (chultúnes) found there.

Getting There

To get to Kanki, take Highway 180 to the town of Tenabo. At the exit, go east, following the signs to the ruins for about 15 kilometers (9.3 miles). You'll be traveling on a country road, passing corn and squash fields along the way. The last 1.5 kilometers (0.9 mile) is on a well-maintained dirt road.

Isla Jaina Archaeological Zone

About 96 kilometers (59 miles) north of Campeche City is the swampy offshore island of Jaina. Meaning House in the Water, this island site holds the largest-known Maya burial ground on the Yucatán Peninsula; more than 1,000 interments have been found on it. According to the archaeologist Sylvanus Morley, who discovered the site in 1943, Jaina was used by the Maya elite—probably Puuc nobility—beginning in AD 652. Bodies were carried in long, colorful processions to this island and were interred in burial jars in crouched positions, their skin often stained red—a symbol of eternal life—and bodies wrapped in either a straw mat or white cloth. Some were found with a jade stone in their mouths. Plates with food, jewelry, weapons, tools, and other precious items were placed on the heads of the dead to accompany them to the afterlife. Small figurines (10-25 centimeters/4-10 inches tall) also were buried, resting on the deceased's folded arms. These finely crafted ceramic sculptures now are considered masterpieces of Mesoamerican art. They portray the buried in ritual costumes, like those of warriors and ball players, and are frozen in ritual positions, including as captives being tortured. These tiny sculptures also often doubled as rattles, with clay balls rolling around the hollow interiors.

The island is off-limits to all but INAH-approved researchers, but it contains two structure groups that have been extensively restored: **Zacpool** on the southeastern side of the island, and **Zayasol** on the northwestern side. They are each composed of pyramids, temple platforms, and dwellings—all made of limestone clay covered in stone. Interestingly, to build these structures the Maya raised the low elevation of the island by building platforms made of *sascab* (limestone material), brought from the mainland in canoes.

The next best thing to visiting the island is checking out the small but spectacular collection of Isla Jaina figurines and burial art at the **Museo Arqueológico del Camino Real** (9:30am-5:30pm Wed.-Mon., 9:30am-4pm Tues., US$2.25). Located next to the main church in the town of Hecelchakán, this modest museum also has a fine set of Maya stelae and columns in the garden. Hecelchakán is located about 70 kilometers (43 miles) north of Campeche on Highway 180 toward Mérida.

Campeche City

Campeche City is a gorgeous, historically rich city with a meticulously restored city center, fascinating sights, and an UNESCO World Heritage designation to boot. Long considered a lesser version of Mérida, Campeche City has truly come into its own, with much-improved lodging and eating options, and a warm tourist-friendly atmosphere. The city's unique network of walls, bastions, and forts—built centuries ago to ward off pirates—have been cleverly repurposed as museums and galleries. And the compact city center is ideal for exploring, with its colorful facades, historic churches, cobblestone streets (some pedestrian only), and a leafy central plaza that's frequently used for free performances and events.

HISTORY

Campeche is a Spanish corruption of "Ah Kim Pech," the name of the Maya town that occupied the same spot. Ah Kim Pech was an important indigenous commercial center, serving as a gateway between the Yucatán Peninsula and central Mexico. Spanish explorers first arrived here by ship in 1517; recognizing its strategic location, they immediately set out to control it themselves. The Maya were not pleased, and dealt the would-be conquerors one demoralizing defeat after another. In fact, the Maya kicked serious Spanish arse for the next 23 years; it wasn't until October 4, 1540, that Spanish soldiers led by Francisco de Montejo finally conquered Ah Kim Pech and founded the city of Campeche. Before long,

Campeche City

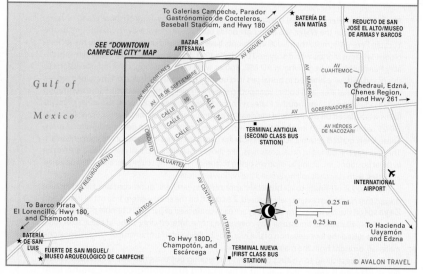

To Galerias Campeche, Parador
Gastrónomico de Cocteleros,
Baseball Stadium, and Hwy 180

BATERÍA DE
SAN MATÍAS

REDUCTO DE SAN
JOSÉ EL ALTO/MUSEO
DE ARMAS Y BARCOS

*SEE "DOWNTOWN
CAMPECHE CITY" MAP*

BAZAR
ARTESANAL

AV MIGUEL ALEMAN

AV CUAHTEMOC

Gulf of

AV MADERO

AV
CUAHTEMOC

To Chedraui, Edzná,
Chenes Region,
and Hwy 261 →

Mexico

AV RUIZ CORTINES

AV 16 DE SEPTIEMBRE

CALLE 10
CALLE 12
CALLE 14

CALLE 53

AV GOBERNADORES

TERMINAL ANTIGUA
(SECOND CLASS BUS
STATION)

AV HÉROES
DE NACOZARI

BALUARTES

CIRCUITO

AV RESURGIMIENTO

AV CENTRAL

AV MATEOS

INTERNATIONAL
AIRPORT

To Barco Pirata
El Lorencillo, Hwy 180,
and Champotón

BATERÍA
DE SAN
LUIS

FUERTE DE SAN MIGUEL/
MUSEO ARQUEOLÓGICO DE CAMPECHE

To Hwy 180D,
Champotón, and
Escárcega

AV TRUEBA

TERMINAL NUEVA
(FIRST CLASS BUS
STATION)

To Hacienda
Uayamón
and Edzna

0   0.25 mi
0   0.25 km

© AVALON TRAVEL

the city was once again a major port and trade center, though for Spanish galleons instead of Maya canoes. Among other exports was *palo de Campeche* (Campeche wood), a tropical wood used to make fabric dyes—highly valued in Europe and elsewhere.

The Spanish had their favor returned, however, in the form of marauding pirates. Many were supported by Spain's archenemies, England and France, and were attracted by the easy pickings at Campeche's ports and busy shipping lanes. For nearly 200 years—until Campeche's defensive walls were finally completed—the people of Campeche endured nearly constant harassment and assault from ne'er-do-wells and scalawags. The city was destroyed on several occasions, including February 9, 1663, when pirates killed scores of men, women, and children in the worst massacre in the city's history. Another infamous assault was led by Laurent Graff, also known as Lorencillo, who attacked Campeche with an army of 700 men on July 6, 1685. They didn't stop with just sacking the city; they also took dozens of prisoners and demanded the city

leaders pay an exorbitant ransom. After two months of occupation, the city hadn't paid—it didn't have the money—so the pirates planned a mass execution. After the first round of killings, a city representative talked the pirates out of the plan, and even out of the city.

The ordeal prompted the Spanish crown to build fortifications, which would eventually bring relative peace and protection to Campeche. A solid stone and mortar wall was built around the city, eight meters (26 feet) high and three meters (10 feet) thick. There were gates on each of the four sides; two of them—Puerta del Mar (Sea Gate) and Puerta de la Tierra (Land Gate)—are still used. Nine *baluartes* (bastions) were erected in strategic locations, in order to best defend the city from attacks of any kind. Part of the wall extended into the sea and was outfitted with a huge gate, which was opened to let merchants in, but could be quickly closed against any pirates in close pursuit. Although isolated attacks continued until 1717, the walls served their purpose, bringing the reign of pirate terror to an end.

Campeche City walls

SIGHTS

Bright pastel facades and cobblestoned streets make Campeche's city center one of the most beautiful in the whole peninsula.

★ The City Walls

Campeche's imposing walls, bastions, and forts lend a wonderful old-world ambience to the city. Most contain museums, and exploring them is a great way to spend an afternoon, or a whole day. Five of the seven bastions surrounding the city center can be visited, as can two forts on the city's edges. The city and Instituto Nacional de Antropología e Historia (INAH, National Institute of Anthropology and History) are in ongoing discussions about the feasibility of reconstructing more sections.

Built in 1690, **Baluarte Nuestra Señora de la Soledad** (Calle 8 at Calle 57, 8:30am-5pm Tues.-Sun., US$2.50) is the largest of the city's bastions and home to a small but very worthwhile museum. The **Museo de la Arquitectura Maya** has a superb collection of stelae and other artifacts from the Río

Bec, Chenes, and Puuc regions, accompanied by modern displays and explanations in both Spanish and English. With just four rooms, it offers a primer on Maya writing, sculpture, and architectural styles without being overwhelming. Outside the entrance are more stelae and a ramp leading to the top of the wall.

At the corner of Calle 55 and Calle 8, don't overlook the detailed **bronze model of the walled city** by artist Pablo Rafael López Artasánchez; it depicts what Campeche looked like when it was encircled by walls. Residents of the historic center like to stroll by and point out where their houses are.

Puerta de Tierra (Calle 59 at Calle 18, 8am-9pm Mon.-Wed., 8am-5pm Thurs.-Fri., 9am-7pm Sat.-Sun., US$1) was one of two heavily fortified gates into the city; today it is the only original section of the city's wall in existence. The entrance fee allows you to climb onto the eight-meter (26-foot) wall, where a narrow causeway makes for a memorable stroll to **Baluarte San Juan** (Calle 63 at Calle 18) on one end and **Baluarte San Francisco** (Calle 57 at Calle 18) on the other. From above, you'll get a (low-flying) bird's-eye view of the city center, including gorgeous facades with only ruins and overgrown lots behind them. Baluarte San Francisco also has a small **pirate museum** (9am-4pm, free), with detailed information on the region's most famous pirates.

The Puerta de la Tierra is also where the **Espectáculo de Luz y Sonido** (8pm Thurs.-Sun., US$3.25 adult, US$1.50 child) is held during the summer months. A 90-minute sound and light show, it's a retelling of Campeche's violent past with flashing lights, blasting speakers, some firecrackers, and a sword fight or two atop the wall. It's kind of corny but lots of fun for kids. Audio translation is available for an additional US$2.

The first of the nine bastions to be built, **Baluarte San Carlos** (Calle 8 btwn Calles 63 and 65, 8am-8pm Mon.-Sat., 10am-6pm Sun., US$1.75) houses yet another small museum. Though still called the **Museo de la Ciudad** (City Museum), its exhibits focus

Downtown Campeche City

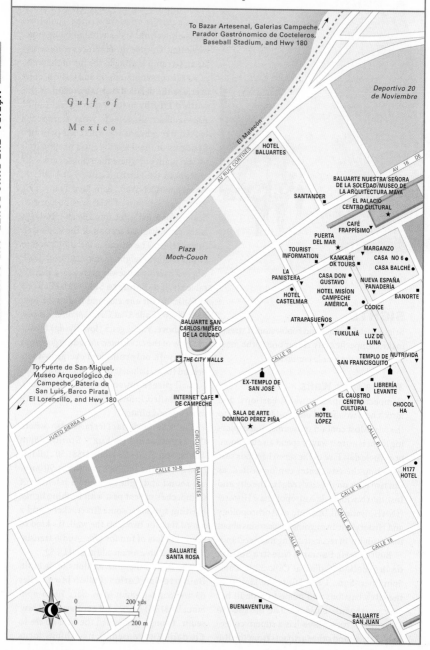

To Bazar Artesenal, Galerias Campeche,
Parador Gastrónomico de Cocteleros,
Baseball Stadium, and Hwy 180

Deportivo 20
de Noviembre

Gulf of

Mexico

El Malecón

AV RUIZ CORTINES

AV 16 DE

HOTEL
BALUARTES

BALUARTE NUESTRA SEÑORA
DE LA SOLEDAD/MUSEO DE
LA ARQUITECTURA MAYA

SANTANDER

EL PALACIO
CENTRO CULTURAL

CAFÉ
FRAPPISIMO

PUERTA
DEL MAR

Plaza
Moch-Couoh

TOURIST
INFORMATION

MARGANZO

KANKABI'
OK TOURS

CASA NO 6

CASA BALCHÉ

LA
PANISTERA

CASA DON
GUSTAVO

NUEVA ESPAÑA
PANADERÍA

HOTEL
CASTELMAR

HOTEL MISIÓN
CAMPECHE
AMÉRICA

BANORTE

CÓDICE

ATRAPASUEÑOS

BALUARTE SAN
CARLOS/MUSEO
DE LA CIUDAD

TUKULNÁ

LUZ DE
LUNA

THE CITY WALLS

CALLE 10

TEMPLO DE
SAN FRANCISQUITO

NUTRIVIDA

To Fuerte de San Miguel,
Museo Arqueológico de
Campeche, Batería de
San Luis, Barco Pirata
El Lorencillo, and Hwy 180

EX-TEMPLO DE
SAN JOSÉ

LIBRERÍA
LEVANTE

EL CAUSTRO
CENTRO
CULTURAL

CHOCOL
HA

INTERNET CAFE
DE CAMPECHE

JUSTO SIERRA M

SALA DE ARTE
DOMINGO PÉREZ PIÑA

CALLE 12

HOTEL
LÓPEZ

CALLE 61

CIRCUITO

CALLE 10-B

BALUARTES

CALLE 14

H177
HOTEL

CALLE 63

BALUARTE
SANTA ROSA

CALLE 65

CALLE 16

0   200 yds
0   200 m

BUENAVENTURA

BALUARTE
SAN JUAN

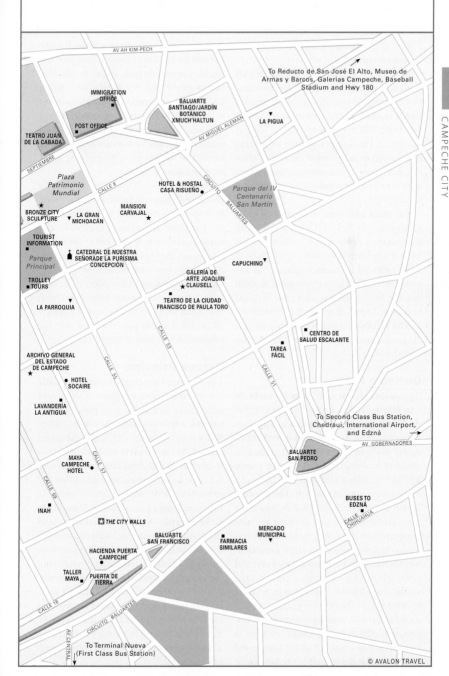

AV AH KIM-PECH

To Reducto de San José El Alto, Museo de
Armas y Barcos, Galerias Campeche, Baseball
Stadium and Hwy 180

IMMIGRATION
OFFICE

BALUARTE
SANTIAGO/JARDÍN
BOTÁNICO
XMUCH'HALTUN

LA PIGUA

POST OFFICE

AV. MIGUEL ALEMÁN

TEATRO JUAN
DE LA CABADA

SEPTIEMBRE

Plaza
Patrimonio
Mundial

CALLE 8

HOTEL & HOSTAL
CASA RISUEÑO

CIRCUITO BALUARTES

Parque del IV
Centenario
San Martín

BRONZE CITY
SCULPTURE

LA GRAN
MICHOACÁN

MANSION
CARVAJAL

TOURIST
INFORMATION

Parque
Principal

CATEDRAL DE NUESTRA
SEÑORA DE LA PURÍSIMA
CONCEPCIÓN

CAPUCHINO

GALERÍA DE
ARTE JOAQUIN
CLAUSELL

TROLLEY
TOURS

LA PARROQUIA

TEATRO DE LA CIUDAD
FRANCISCO DE PAULA TORO

CENTRO DE
SALUD ESCALANTE

TAREA
FÁCIL

ARCHIVO GENERAL
DEL ESTADO
DE CAMPECHE

CALLE 53

CALLE 52

HOTEL
SOCAIRE

CALLE 51

LAVANDERÍA
LA ANTIGUA

To Second Class Bus Station,
Chedraui, International Airport,
and Edzná

AV. GOBERNADORES

MAYA
CAMPECHE
HOTEL

CALLE 57

BALUARTE
SAN PEDRO

CALLE 59

BUSES TO
EDZNÁ

INAH

CALLE CHIHUAHUA

THE CITY WALLS

BALUARTE
SAN FRANCISCO

FARMACIA
SIMILARES

MERCADO
MUNICIPAL

HACIENDA PUERTA
CAMPECHE

TALLER
MAYA

PUERTA DE
TIERRA

CALLE 18

CIRCUITO BALUARTES

AV. CENTRAL

To Terminal Nueva
(First Class Bus Station)

© AVALON TRAVEL

on Campeche's archaeological sites, including dioramas and high-quality videos about the Maya. There also is a small section on the history of chocolate. Signage and videos are in Spanish only.

Built in the early 1700s, **Baluarte San Pedro** (Calle 16 at Calle 51) has had several incarnations—a stronghold, barracks, INAH research center, arts and crafts market, and a folk art museum. At the time of research, it stood empty, waiting for its next role. As you walk by, look at the coat of arms above the door, which features the two keys of heaven and the papal crown, the symbol of Saint Peter.

Baluarte Santiago (Calle 49-C at Calle 8, 9am-5pm daily, US$1) was completed in 1704, nearly a century after the first fort was built. It was torn down in the early 1900s to make room for government offices, but was reconstructed at the same location in 1955, bearing little resemblance to the original building. Today, this tiny fort houses the **Jardín Botánico Xmuch'haltun,** a botanical garden boasting more than 200 varieties of native plant species.

Outlying Forts

If you go to only one sight, make it **Fuerte de San Miguel** and its **Museo Arqueológico de Campeche** (Av. Escencia s/n, 8am-5pm Tues.-Sun., US$3), about 2.5 kilometers (1.6 miles) south of the center. Built at the end of the 18th century, the fort sits atop a large hill and includes a moat, drawbridge, and a breathtaking view of the Gulf. The museum here is the real highlight though, housing a truly fantastic collection of Maya artifacts from around the state, including several pieces from the ruins at Isla Jaina, a spectacular jade funeral mask found at Calakmul, and urns decorated with tapirs, monkeys, and turtles from Río Bec. Signage is in Spanish; look for the cardboard information sheets in each exhibit hall. If using public transportation, take a Playa Bonita/Lerma bus from in front of the post office (US$0.35). The bus will drop you off at the turnoff to the fort, which

is about another 500 meters (0.3 mile) up a steep hill. A taxi from the center of town costs around US$3.

Below the Fuerte de San Miguel is the **Batería de San Luis** (Avenida Resurgimiento s/n, 8am-6pm daily, free), a small fortification that is empty save one exhibit on Captain Pedro Sainz de Baranda y Borreiro, a native of Campeche and a naval commander who in 1835 became the governor of Yucatán. It's used as military offices, so there are some security hurdles for visitors; go in the morning to ask for permission to enter.

On the other side of town, the **Reducto de San José El Alto** (Av. Francisco Morazán s/n, 8am-5pm Tues.-Sun., free) is a well-renovated fort complete with cannons, thick walls, and a spectacular view of the Gulf of Mexico. It also houses the **Museo de Armas y Barcos,** a one-room maritime museum where you'll find model ships and a few colonial-era artifacts. Signage is in Spanish only. To get here, take a San José El Alto bus from the market (US$0.35); it'll drop you off a block from the entrance. A taxi costs around US$3.

Parque Principal

The **Parque Principal** (Calle 10 at Calle 55), or central plaza, is a pleasant, shady spot to rest your feet, and a good place to begin and end a tour of Campeche's many sights. Better yet, on Saturday and Sunday the streets around the central plaza are blocked to traffic and fill up with food carts and small vendors, and local families come out to chat and stroll about. In the evening, one or two *lotería* (Mexican bingo) games start up (6pm-11pm, US$0.05/card)—tourists are welcome—and the municipal band gives a classic oompah concert in the central kiosk, blaring forth on trumpets, clarinets, tubas, and cymbals with the energy of a great orchestra. In addition, at 8pm every evening (except Monday), a spectacular sound and light show is projected onto the former Palacio Municipal (city hall); it celebrates Campeche's history and riches in a magnificent display of lights, colors, imagery, and music.

The Ex-Templo de San José once served as a lighthouse.

El Palacio Centro Cultural

Named after the gorgeously renovated building it occupies—the former Palacio Municipal (city hall)—**El Palacio Centro Cultural** (central park, Calle 8 btwn Calles 55 and 57, tel. 981/811-0366, 10am-7pm Tues.-Sun., free) is more a city museum than a cultural center. Three extensive exhibit halls describe different parts of the city's early history: its fortifications, commerce, and boats. Beyond the well-maintained antiquities and bilingual signage are hands-on multimedia exhibits, engaging movies (Spanish only, unfortunately), and even a simulation of an Atlantic boat crossing (visitors actually step onto a replica of a galleon—take hold of your seat, you'll hit stormy weather and be chased by pirates). This is a fascinating, educational, and must-see stop.

Churches

On the east side of the plaza is **Catedral de Nuestra Señora de la Purísima Concepción** (Calle 55 btwn Calles 8 and 10, 6:30am-9pm daily), the city's cathedral and one of the oldest churches on the Yucatán Peninsula. Construction was ordered by Francisco de Montejo in 1540 and completed in 1760 (and you thought it took the contractor a long time to finish your deck!). However, it wasn't until 1895 that the church was proclaimed the town's cathedral by Pope Léon XIII. Architecturally, the building is notable as having one of the only baroque facades in the Yucatán Peninsula; its towers also remain among the highest structures in the city.

Built by the Jesuits in 1756, the **Ex-Templo de San José** (Calle 10 at Calle 63, hours vary) is a beautiful structure, decorated with an impressive blue and yellow tile facade. The history of the building is as varied as that of the city of Campeche: It has gone from being a church to a lighthouse (check out the weather vane) to a library to a warehouse to—today—an art exhibition space. It is owned and administered by the Instituto Campechano, the neighboring university, which has been around as long as the church. Take a look inside when it's open for events.

Templo de San Francisquito (Calle 12 at Calle 59, 8am-7pm daily) was built by the Franciscan Order in the mid-17th century to replace the church and cloister that had been destroyed by successive pirate invasions—and to protect against future ones. As a result, the exterior is stark with thick stone walls, while the interior is graced by intricate baroque altarpieces that are covered in phytomorphic reliefs. Today, the cloister houses the **El Claustro Centro Cultural** (Calle 12 btwn Calles 59 and 61, tel. 981/816-2957, 8:30am-9pm Mon.-Fri.), one of the city's cultural centers.

Galleries

The **Galería de Arte Joaquín Clausell** (Calle 12 btwn Calles 51 and 53, tel. 981/811-3653, 8:30am-3pm and 4pm-8pm, free) and the **Sala de Arte Domingo Pérez Piña** (Calle 12 at Calle 65, tel. 981/816-6056, 8am-8pm Tues.-Sat., free) are small galleries featuring a rotation of artwork by regional artists.

Peek into the state archive building,

the **Archivo General del Estado de Campeche** (Calle 12 btwn Calles 57 and 59, tel. 981/816-0939, 8am-3pm Mon.-Fri., free) to see its latest art or historical exhibit. Shows are usually compiled by INAH or ICC, the national and state history and cultural institutes, and can be quite good.

Ex-Templo de San José (Calle 10 at Calle 63, hours vary, free) and the **El Claustro Centro Cultural** (Calle 12 btwn Calles 59 and 61, tel. 981/816-2957, 8:30am-9pm Mon.-Fri., free) also have art and cultural exhibits periodically.

Notable Architecture

Mansión Carvajal (Calle 10 btwn Calles 51 and 53, tel. 981/811-3384, 8am-3pm Mon.-Fri., free) is a 19th-century mansion that has been restored to its original elegance. Built at the beginning of the 1800s, it originally was the home of the wealthy Carvajal family, who owned the Uayamón hacienda. By the late 1900s, however, it had been converted twice—once into a hotel, later into a dance hall. Today, it houses state government offices. Open to the public, it is well worth a quick visit to get a sense of the opulence the upper classes enjoyed during the 19th century. Check out the Moorish-style architecture, art nouveau staircase with Carrera marble steps, Tuscan columns, and iron balustrade.

Steps from the central plaza, a very mini Vegas-style **water fountain** (Plaza Patrimonio Mundial, Calle 8 btwn Calles 55 and 53) is timed to "dance" to classical beats and multicolored lights. Performances are every night 7pm-9pm (hourly, 20 minutes, free). Buy a *paleta* (popsicle) from a local vendor, scout out a spot on a park bench, and enjoy the show.

ENTERTAINMENT AND EVENTS

One of the best resources for free cultural events is the monthly *Cartelera Cultural* (www.culturacampeche.com), a guide available at the state tourist office, El Claustro Centro Cultural, and other locations around town.

El Pregonero

While exploring Campeche City's historic center, you're sure to encounter life-size bronze sculptures of everyday Campechanos. They are the work of acclaimed sculptor Antonio Miguel Horn, who also has exhibited in New York, Philadelphia, and elsewhere. There are five sculptures in all, each depicting a character from a classic Campechano song by Zoila Quijano McGregor: a fisherman, an old woman, a street vendor, a bread maker, and "el pregonero"—the town crier—installed in the city center's main plazas and walkways. Simple yet resonant, the pieces were commissioned in 2010, during Mexico's bicentennial celebrations, as a reminder of simpler lives and yesteryear's pursuits, amid the hubbub of today's modern world.

Weekends and Evenings in the Parque Principal

Every weekend, the city streets around the central plaza are closed to cars, restaurants place their tables outdoors, food and trinket vendors set up stalls, and bingo games get going in front of the cathedral for US$0.05 per game. Both evenings, the city hosts cultural events—typically, a concert or other live music performances—and people fill the park benches to enjoy the show.

Every evening (except Monday), the city sponsors a spectacular **sound and light show** (central plaza, 8pm Tues.-Sun., free). Called *Celebramos Campeche* (Celebrate Campeche), it is a multimedia presentation projected onto the facade of the former Palacio Municipal (city hall). The show is a brilliant display of Campeche's origins and riches, beginning with the ancient Maya and the state's remarkable biodiversity, continuing with the Spanish conquest and life in the New World, and ending with today's popular celebrations including Day of the Dead and Carnaval. It is a breathtaking show and well worth your while. Arrive early for a good seat.

Nightlife

Campeche is not known for its nightlife. In the colonial center, most people either have drinks at the outdoor cafés and bars on Calle 59 or go to the central plaza to watch free music performances. If you feel like dancing or are looking for a change of scenery, head south on the Malecón, where you'll find a handful of discos and bars about one kilometer (0.6 mile) from the center of town.

Theater

The **Teatro de la Ciudad Francisco de Paula Toro** (Calle 12 btwn Calles 51 and 53, tel. 981/811-3653, US$5-30) was commissioned by the commander-in-chief of Campeche, Don Francisco de Paula Toro, a Cuban immigrant who eventually became the governor of Yucatán. It was built during the middle of a cholera epidemic, against the wishes of the clergy, who wanted the funds to be funneled to the church instead. Nevertheless, the theater was inaugurated in September 1834, and it quickly became the center of cultural activity in Campeche. Today, the theater remains an important part of city life, hosting dance, dramatic, and musical performances throughout the year. It's open only when there is a scheduled event; stop by or call to see if there is anything showing while you're in town.

The **Teatro Juan de la Cabada** (Av. 16 de Septiembre at Calle 53, tel. 981/811-0008, US$5-30) is the city's modern theater space; it offers a wide range of dramatic, dance, and musical programming. Like the Teatro de la Ciudad, the box office is only open when there is a scheduled performance.

Cultural Centers

A restored mansion, **Centro Cultural Casa No. 6** (central park, Calle 57 btwn Calles 8 and 10, tel. 981/816-1782, 9am-9pm daily, US$1.25) exhibits how the Campechano upper crust lived in the 19th century; rooms transport visitors back with period furnishings and art. Once you've seen the house, visit the center's artsy gift shop and bookstore.

El Claustro Centro Cultural (Calle 12 btwn Calles 59 and 61, tel. 981/816-2957, 8:30am-9pm Mon.-Fri.) organizes numerous arts and cultural events throughout the year; check out the bulletin boards at the entrance for the schedule. Notably, it's located inside the former cloister of the Templo de San Francisquito.

Cinema

Located inside the Galerias Campeche mall, **Cinépolis VIP** (Malecón at Calle Dársena, toll-free Mex. tel. 800/120-0220, www.cinepolis.com, US$5) is a swanky movie theater featuring reclining leather seats, a food and drink menu, even waiter service.

Festivals and Events

Held every February, **Carnaval** is Campeche's blowout party of the year. Typically lasting over two weeks, it features musical performances, dances, the crowning of the king and queen, costume parties, even a "funerary" parade where an effigy of a pirate is burned and thrown into the Gulf of Mexico. If you plan to be in town during the festivities, it's definitely worth making hotel reservations well in advance.

The **Festival del Centro Histórico de Campeche** is a major festival when musicians, dance troupes, and artists perform or exhibit their work in and around the city. Each year, organizers select one Mexican state and one foreign country to be the focus of the event's programming. Most of the events take place in the central plaza, including the kickoff concert. It lasts the entire month of December, and festivalgoers enjoy the added bonus of checking out local handicrafts as well as tasting Campeche's culinary treats, both sold at street-side stands.

Every December, Campeche hosts the **Festival de Jazz.** Lasting approximately two weeks, it attracts musicians from all over the world. Call or stop by the state tourism office for details on scheduled events and concerts.

SHOPPING

Shopping in Campeche is a limited sport. Most shops are geared toward local needs, so you'll find lots of paper stores, teen clothing boutiques, and shoe shops. Stores that are geared toward tourists often specialize in kitsch, offering a smattering of T-shirts, ashtrays, and key chains.

Tukulná (Calle 10 btwn Calles 59 and 61, tel. 981/816-9088, 8am-8pm daily) is a state-run shop specializing in Campechano handicrafts created by local artisans. You'll find everything from handmade clothing to rocking chairs. In the back, there's also a re-creation of a Maya home as well as a *jipi* hat cave, complete with awkward-looking mannequins.

An official boutique of the **Instituto Nacional de Antropología e Historia** (INAH, Calle 59 btwn Calles 14 and 16, no phone, 8am-5pm daily), this shop sells breathtaking true-to-life replicas of Maya figurines, vases, and jewelry. In fact, they're so good, pieces come with their own papers authenticating they're copies (apparently, travelers were being stopped by customs officials believing they were exporting Maya relics). You'll also find quality T-shirts and hats with the INAH logo, books on archaeological sites, and even some Maya-inspired tchotchkes like key chains and playing cards.

Taller Maya (Calle 59 btwn Calles 16 and 18, tel. 981/811-5703, www.tallermaya.org, 9am-7pm Mon.-Sat.) is a nonprofit project that sells everyday items created by a collaboration between Maya artisans and contemporary Mexican designers. Think clothing and handbags, duvet covers and pillowcases, all with Maya designs. Or artisanal soaps, made with organic honey. Even modern jewelry using colorful beans or jade—both important to the Maya. Prices are higher than normal but reflect fair wages paid to all the artists.

For guayaberas, huipiles, and other traditional wear, head to **Códice** (Calle 59 at Calle 10, tel. 981/816-7359, www.glyphs.com. mx, 8am-9:30pm Mon.-Sat., 9am-9pm Sun.). You'll find high-quality clothing, mostly in linen and cotton here. There's also a small but good selection of shoes and handbags, most incorporating local designs and styles.

Bazar Artesanal (Malecón btwn Calles 49 and 51, cell. tel. 981/127-1036, 10:30am-8:30pm Mon.-Fri., 10:30am-6:30pm Sat.-Sun.) is a modern handicraft market across from the Malecón. Artisans sell their work directly to customers here; light haggling is welcome.

Librería Levante (Calle 12 btwn Calles 59 and 61, tel. 981/816-5473, 9am-8pm Mon.-Fri., 9am-5pm Sat., 9am-3pm Sun.) carries a few English-language titles, including guidebooks, books on the Maya, and children's books. Maps and *artesanía* are also sold.

Galerias Campeche (Malecón at Calle Dársena, tel. 981/815-1593, 9am-9pm daily) is a swanky mall on the north side of town. There's nothing unexpected here—you'll find big department stores, international boutique chains, a food court, and movie theater. Almost best of all is the knockout air-conditioning.

SPORTS AND RECREATION
El Malecón

Campeche's Malecón (promenade) stretches for three kilometers (1.9 miles) along the Gulf of Mexico; after years of neglect, it was rescued with the addition of fresh pavement, monuments, and benches. It's especially popular in the mornings and evenings, when you'll share the pathway with dog-walkers, in-line skaters, and couples out for a brisk stroll. You can join the walkers or, better yet, rent a bike in town for a couple of hours to explore it. The only downers are that the adjacent avenue can get busy, and the piers used by fishing boats can get kind of smelly, but those don't take away from the fun of being out and about.

Baseball

The **Piratas de Campeche** (www.piratasde-campeche.mx) is one of 16 teams that make up Mexico's professional baseball league, the Liga Mexicana de Béisbol (www.milb.com). You can catch a ball game on the north side of town at the **Estadio Nelson Barrera**

Romellón (Filiberto Qui Farfán No. 2, Col. Camino Real, US$3-10) April-August.

FOOD

Campeche has a smattering of cozy cafés and classy Mexican and international restaurants. Not sure what you feel like eating? Take a stroll down Calle 59, a pedestrian-only street with a wide variety of restaurants and cafés, most with outdoor seating.

Mexican and Campechano

Open 24 hours, the diner-style ★ **La Parroquia** (Calle 55 btwn Calles 10 and 12, tel. 981/816-2530, US$3-12) is always busy. You'll find good Campechano dishes, traditional Mexican meals, and a TV tuned to soap operas or a soccer game. The daily special (US$5.50) includes a main dish, beans, rice, dessert, and a large drink. Free Wi-Fi is available too.

Luz de Luna (Calle 59 btwn Calles 10 and 12, cell. tel. 981/811-0624, 8am-midnight daily, US$5-9) serves Mexican dishes and international options geared toward travelers pining for comfort food. Breakfasts include French toast or *chilaquiles,* and dinner is mobbed with folks happily munching on fajitas, pastas, and seafood. The shoebox dining room is plastered in folk art, with carved and painted wood chairs and festive tin star lighting; the food is served on gorgeous handmade plates.

Fans and loud TVs blast from every corner of **Capuchino** (Circuito Baluartes btwn Calles 12 and 14, tel. 981/811-3137, 10am-6pm daily, US$4-6), which specializes in heaping servings of traditional Campechano dishes at good prices. It's popular with local families—there's a kids play structure on the back patio—and most servings can probably satiate two.

Seafood

★ **Marganzo** (Calle 8 btwn Calles 57 and 59, tel. 981/811-3898, 7am-11pm daily, US$4-12) screams tourist trap—the staff sports name tags and traditional dress—but it's hard to beat for tasty food and reasonable prices. Seafood is the specialty—*pampano relleno de mariscos* (white fish filled with seafood) is a favorite among regulars—but the *pollo pibil* and other meat dishes don't disappoint. Servings are large and come with a tableful of complimentary appetizers.

Considered one of the best eateries in town, **La Pigua** (Av. Miguel Alemán btwn Calles 49-A and 49-B, tel. 981/811-3365, www.

Campeche's Malecón

lapigua.com.mx, 1pm-9pm daily, US$9-23) is an upscale restaurant and popular lunchtime stop for professionals and couples. The food is pricey but excellent—coconut shrimp with apple chutney is the specialty—and the service is first rate. Reservations are recommended, especially for dinner.

For fresh seafood right on the water, head to the **Parador Gastrónomico de Cocteleros** (Malecón at Calle Adriano Chino Wong, 11am-7pm daily, US$5-10). A total locals scene, you'll find a string of palapa-roofed restaurants, all looking the same and pretty much selling the same menu: shrimp cocktail, oyster empanadas, grilled and fried fish, ceviche—anything seafood-related, you'll likely find here. They're located near the baseball stadium, about four kilometers (2.5 miles) north of the colonial center.

Vegetarian

Hung with swarms of its eponymous dream catchers, German-owned **Atrapasueños** (Calle 10 btwn Calles 59 and 61, tel. 981/816-5000, 8am-8pm Mon.-Sat., US$3-7) makes super-fresh and tasty dishes like vegetable lasagna and hearty soups, accompanied by its homemade whole-wheat bread. Earthy it is: Tables are fashioned from split tree trunks, and yoga classes take place in the back room most evenings. Look for the driftwood sign that says "Comida Vegetariana."

Nutrivida (Calle 12 btwn Calles 57 and 59, 8am-8:30pm Mon.-Fri., 8am-2pm Sat., US$2-4) is a popular joint offering great soy-based meals, lots of veggie burgers, yogurt, and fruit dishes. Locals pop in for lunch to pick up speedily prepared burgers and lard-free tamales.

Cafés

★ **Chocol Ha** (Calle 59 btwn Calles 12 and 14, tel. 981/811-7893, 5:30pm-11pm Mon.-Thurs., 5:30pm-midnight Fri.-Sat.) delights with a menu of both sweet and savory crepes like *chaya* with cheese or spicy mango, and fabulous chocolate drinks made with chile, vanilla, mint, and other tasty ingredients.

Tabascan cacao is processed and made into chocolate on-site; ask for the schedule if you'd like to visit during production times. A grassy back patio has soft lighting, and there's Wi-Fi throughout.

The best espresso drinks and desserts in town await you at the swanky **Café Frappísimo** (Calle 8 btwn Calles 55 and 57, tel. 981/811-1140, 8am-11pm Mon.-Fri., 8am-midnight Sat.-Sun., US$1.50-4), an air-conditioned café where young professionals ooh and ah over the frappes, baguette sandwiches, and pastries, and linger for conversation. It's located next to El Palacio Centro Cultural, with a view of its interior courtyard on one side and a colonial street on the other. Wi-Fi is available.

Sweets

La Panistera (Calle 8 near Calle 61, no phone, 8:30am-9pm Mon.-Sat., US$0.75-3) tempts passersby with the smells of freshly baked goodies wafting out to the sidewalk. Step in and your mouth will water just by the sight: chocolate croissants, raspberry macaroons, lemon tarts, cinnamon buns, brioche, country bread, pesto focaccia, and more. Coffee drinks and small tables make it easy to linger.

La Nueva España Panadería y Pastelería (Calle 59 at Calle 10, 7am-9:30pm daily, US$0.50-2) sells regional egg breads and sweet breads. Be there at 7am or 4pm to get the goods hot and fresh.

Just north of the central plaza, **La Gran Michoacán** (Calle 8 btwn Calles 53 and 55, 8am-10pm daily, US$1-3) offers a good variety of refreshing treats—homemade popsicles, ice cream, and fruit juices.

Groceries

For the freshest fruits and vegetables, check out the **Mercado Municipal** (Circuito Baluartes Este at Calle 57, 5am-4pm daily), which is located just outside of the colonial center, across from Baluarte San Francisco.

Located on the road to Edzná, **Chedraui** (Calle Central s/n, 7am-10pm daily) is a large and well-stocked supermarket selling the usual food and household items; it also has a bakery and pharmacy on-site.

ACCOMMODATIONS

Campeche's city center has vastly improved its hotel offerings in the past few years. Where before, bright exteriors gave way to poorly maintained interiors, today you'll often find modern hotels and upgraded colonial-style inns.

Under US$25

If there's such a thing as an upscale hostel, ★ **Casa Balché** (central plaza, Calle 57 btwn Calles 8 and 10, tel. 981/811-0087, www.casabalche.com, US$17.50 dorm, US$25/50 s/d with shared bath) is it. A modern living room—complete with wood beams, exposed stone walls, checkerboard floors, and stylish furniture—serves as the reception and common space. It has a spectacular view of the central plaza below. The two dorms are airy and bright and have three bunk beds apiece; guests enjoy thick mattresses, individual reading lights, blindingly white linens, and handcrafted throw pillows (no lockers, though). There's also a well-equipped common kitchen that has a long table for family-style eating. Breakfast is not included, though for an extra US$1.50, that's thrown in too.

Hotel & Hostal Casa Risueño (Calle 10 btwn Calles 49 and 51, tel. 981/816-8231, hospedajerisueno@gmail.com, US$9.50 dorm, US$21/23 s/d, US$25/28 s/d with a/c) has gender-separated dorms with four bunk beds, fans, lockers, and a smattering of natural light. Private rooms are simple affairs with exterior windows and (in some) wheezy air conditioners. All the rooms are very clean though also very cramped. The best feature about the place is a tranquil rooftop garden terrace—the only place to hang out besides the rooms. Wi-Fi and cable TV are available for US$2.50 extra (private rooms only).

US$25-50

A colonial-style hotel, ★ **Maya Campeche**

Hotel (Calle 57 btwn Calles 14 and 16, tel. 981/816-8053, www.mayacampechehotel.com, US$42/47 s/d with a/c) offers cozy rooms in the heart of the city; all have high ceilings, stenciled walls, and ironwork furnishings. Some are a bit dark—reminiscent of large closets, actually—but quiet air-conditioning, flat-screen TVs, Wi-Fi, and spotless bathrooms make that easy to overlook. A rooftop lounge makes a great place to watch the sun set over the city.

Hotel López (Calle 12 btwn Calles 61 and 63, tel. 981/816-3344, www.hotellopez-campeche.com.mx, US$42 s/d with a/c) has somewhat sterile and sparse rooms, but details like artwork and arched doorways disappear once the lights are out, while quiet air-conditioning and firm beds last all night long. All units have hot water and cable TV; there's Wi-Fi, a small pool, and free parking too. If you're after comfort and value, this is a fine choice.

US$50-100

★ **Hotel Socaire** (Calle 57 btwn Calles 12 and 14, tel. 981/811-2130, www.hotelsocaire.com.mx, US$72-82 s/d with a/c, US$113-144 suite with a/c) is a beautifully restored colonial hotel in the heart of the town. Rooms, though simple in decor, have original tile floors, high ceilings, and exposed stone walls. Beds are thick and linens are luxurious; bathrooms are modern and the air-conditioning is quiet. Some suites have private whirlpool tubs too. Common areas include outdoor lounges, a pool, and an artsy café. Wi-Fi is available too.

Contemporary design won't break the bank at **H177 Hotel** (Calle 14 btwn Calles 59 and 61, tel. 981/816-4463, www.h177hotel.com, US$49/56 s/d with a/c, US$70 suite with a/c), where minimalist rooms with stone accent walls boast flat-screen TVs, rainshower heads, and good beds with duvets and lots of comfy pillows. If rooms have windows—they're interior and frosted glass—you'll want to use air-conditioning so it doesn't get too humid. Rooftop suites open onto a terrace, where there's also a large common area for lounging. There's also a plunge pool in the center courtyard. Hall lights spring to life on motion sensors, like your own private disco. Wi-Fi is available.

Hotel Castelmar (Calle 61 btwn Calles 8 and 10, tel. 981/811-1204, toll-free Mex. tel. 800/010-1515, www.castelmarhotel.com, US$72/78 s/d with a/c, US$91 suite with a/c), a former military barracks built in 1880, charms guests with its original tile floors, double-high ceilings, and dramatic wall hangings of oversized rosaries and bells. Public areas are especially pleasant, with heavy wooden rocking chairs in the lobby, a lovely lap pool stocked with fluffy towels, and lots of places to lounge under the wood-beamed arcades. Rooms themselves are simple and a bit dark but very comfortable. Still not sold? There's free parking and Wi-Fi, and breakfast is available (US$4-7) on the courtyard patio.

Hotel Misión Campeche América (Calle 10 btwn Calles 59 and 61, tel. 981/816-4588, www.hotelesmision.com.mx, US$73 s/d with a/c) occupies a pleasant three-story mansion with breezy corridors and high-ceilinged rooms. All the rooms have been recently re-modeled; each has cheerful green accent stripes, plush duvets and pillowy headboards (that, randomly, hang well above head level). The best rooms include numbers 117 and 118, which look onto a quiet interior courtyard, and rooms 101-103, which are spacious and have street views. Wi-Fi and parking is available.

A high-rise hotel fronting the Malecón, **Hotel Baluartes** (Av. 16 de Septiembre at Av. Ruíz Cortinez, tel. 981/816-3911, toll-free Mex. tel. 800/667-1444, www.baluartes.com. mx, US$80-98 s with a/c, US$88-112 d with a/c, US$168-202 suite with a/c) offers comfortable rooms with air-conditioning and cable TV. All are recently remodeled in a minimalist modular style that will please admirers of Mondrian. The oceanfront rooms have superb views (and cost the same as those facing the parking lot), and some city-facing rooms feature a great tableau of the cathedral by night. Wi-Fi and parking are available, and there's also a huge pool on-site.

Hotel Socaire is one of many colonial-style hotels in Campeche City.

Over US$100

Casa Don Gustavo (Calle 59 btwn Calles 8 and 10, tel. 981/816-8090, toll-free Mex. tel. 800/839-0959, www.casadongustavo.com, US$185 s/d with a/c, US$212-238 suite with a/c) is an 18th-century time travel fantasy. A family-run boutique hotel, the *casona* encompasses 10 luxurious suites—all but one with king bed—with original French-style furniture, wooden ceiling beams, and crystal chandeliers, plus modern bathrooms with bidets. Two balcony rooms overlook the pedestrian-only street. Outdoor spaces include a small swimming pool, a garden with swaying palms, and a rooftop whirpool tub with a view of the cathedral. Make sure to scout out the lookout tower where the former owner would watch for ships coming into port. Continental breakfast is included, though its restaurant also serves full breakfast, lunch, and dinner. Wi-Fi and parking are available.

★ **Hacienda Puerta Campeche** (Calle 59 at Calle 18, tel. 981/816-7508, www.starwood-hotels.com, US$460 s/d with a/c, US$540-600

Travel back in time at Casa Don Gustavo.

suite with a/c) is, hands down, the most luxurious hotel in town. Several adjoining 17th-century houses were gutted and transformed into this intimate 15-room hotel. The guest rooms feature pillow-top beds, 18-foot ceilings, large marble bathrooms, and artful decorations. But the swimming pool is the hotel's most memorable feature: It weaves through several enclosed rooms of the original houses, complete with doorways and brightly painted walls. There's also a gourmet garden-side restaurant and a rooftop lounge. Outside of high season, rates drop by 40 percent or more. Wi-Fi and some street parking are available.

Outside of Town
Hacienda Uayamón (Carr. China-Edzná Km. 20, tel. 981/813-0530, www.starwoodhotels.com, US$530 s/d with a/c, US$590 suite with a/c) is a renovated 18th-century hacienda located just 20 kilometers (12.4 miles) from Campeche City. It features 12 freestanding units, each with elegant furnishings, private terraces, and luxe amenities. The grounds are gorgeous, and several unused buildings have been left in a state of semi-disrepair to create a more authentic ambience. The pool is ensconced within the two remaining walls of the once-elegant ballroom; the dining room's large picture window looks out over former henequen fields. The restaurant (US$10-25) serves a variety of international fare; reservations are required for non-guests. Rates drop considerably outside of the high season—check the website for special offers.

INFORMATION AND SERVICES
Tourist Information
The **city tourist office** (Calle 55 btwn Calles 8 and 10, tel. 981/811-3989, 9am-2pm and 3pm-9pm daily) sits in the kiosk in the central plaza. It has plenty of maps and brochures that often prove more helpful than the staffers. If it's busy, head to its **second office** (Calle 8 btwn Calles 59 and 61, no phone, same hours) in a small stand-alone building, just two blocks away. The state also has an informative, and very useful, tourism website: www.campeche.travel.

Emergency Services
Campeche City's main hospital is the **Centro de Salud Escalante** (Calle 49 at Calle 14, tel. 981/816-2409, 24 hours). For prescriptions, bustling **Farmacia Similares** (Circuito Baluartes at Calle 55, tel. 981/816-1787, 24 hours) has good prices. To reach the police, dial 066 from any phone.

Money
There are lots of banks in the city center that have ATMs, though only a few also have currency-exchange services. Convenient ones with both include **Banorte** (central plaza, Calle 57 at Calle 10, 9am-4pm Mon.-Fri.) and **Santander** (Av 16 de Septiembre at Calle 59, 9am-6pm Mon.-Fri., 10am-2pm Sat.).

Media and Communications
The **post office** (Av. 16 de Septiembre at Calle 53, 8am-4pm Mon.-Fri., 8am-noon

Sat.) is in the Palacio Federal. Centrally located Internet cafés include **Tarea Fácil** (Calle 49 btwn Calles 14 and 16, 9am-11pm daily, US$0.65/hour) and **Internet Café de Campeche** (Calle 65 btwn Calles 10 and 12, 9am-10pm Mon.-Sat., noon-8pm Sun., US$0.50/hour).

There are three big newspapers covering Campeche: *Tribuna de Campeche* (www.tribunacampeche.com), *Novedades Campeche* (www.novedadesdecampeche. com.mx), and *El Sur de Campeche* (www. elsur.mx). All are available at most newsstands in the capital and statewide.

Immigration
The **immigration office** (Av. 16 de Septiembre at Calle 53, 1st Floor, tel. 981/816-0369, 9am-1pm Mon.-Fri.) is located in the same building as the post office.

Laundry
Lavandería La Antigua (Calle 57 btwn Calles 12 and 14, tel. 981/811-6900, 8am-4:45pm Mon.-Sat., US$1/kilo [2.2 pounds]) offers same-day service if you drop off your laundry early.

Language and Instruction
The **Universidad Autónoma de Campeche's Centro de Español y Maya** (Av. Agustín Melgar s/n, tel. 981/811-9800, ext. 75200, www.cem.uacam.mx) offers long-term Spanish language classes to foreigners. The group classes aren't very intensive—only four hours per week during a six-month semester—but they include cultural outings and activities. Homestays also can be arranged.

GETTING THERE
Campeche City is on the Gulf coast, 190 kilometers (118 miles) southwest of Mérida, and is a natural stopover on your way to (or from) the states of Chiapas or Tabasco.

Air
Aeropuerto Internacional de Campeche Alberto Acuña Ongay (CPE, Carr. Campeche-Chiná), Campeche's modest airport, lies about two kilometers (1.2 miles) northeast of the city. Frequent "China" buses (US$0.35) from the market drop off at the roundabout in front of the airport entrance; it's a five-minute walk to the terminal. To get there by taxi costs US$12 and takes 15 minutes; from the airport, taxis charge US$25.

Campeche City only has service to/from Mexico City on **Aeroméxico** (toll-free Mex. tel. 800/237-6639, www.aeromexico.com) and **Interjet** (toll-free Mex. tel. 800/011-2345, toll-free U.S. tel. 866/285-9525, www. interjet.com.mx).

Bus
Campeche's **first-class ADO station** (Av. Central at Av. Casa de Justicia, tel. 981/811-9910, toll-free Mex. tel. 800/702-8000, www. ado.com.mx), known as *la terminal nueva* (the new terminal), is located on the outskirts of town. Advance tickets also can be purchased at the local office of **ADO** (Malecón at Calle Dársena, no phone, 9am-7pm daily) in the Galerias Campeche, a modern shopping mall near the Reducto de San José El Alto fort.

Campeche also has a **second-class station** (Av. Gobernadores at Calle Chile, tel. 981/816-3445), known as *la terminal antigua* (the old terminal) or the "ex-ADO." It's located a few blocks from the colonial center. For the Edzná archaeological site, buses (US$2.50, 1 hour) leave about every 30 minutes 7am-7pm from Calle Chihuahua, one block east of the Mercado Municipal. Look for buses headed to Bonfil.

Car
Two good highways link Campeche City and Mérida. Highway 180 is known as the *vía corta* (the short route) and goes north from Campeche through Hecelchakán, Bécal, and Umán. Highway 261 is known as the *vía larga* (the long route) because it veers east through Hopelchén and then north through Santa Elena and the Puuc region. Their monikers notwithstanding, driving time is about the same (2-2.5 hours). If you're driving to

Campeche Bus Schedule

Campeche's **first-class bus station** (tel. 981/811-9910, toll-free Mex. tel. 800/702-8000, www.ado.com.mx) is located on Avenida Central at Avenida Casa de Justicia—a bit too far to walk with bags, but under 10 minutes in a taxi. Many buses here are *de paso* (mid-route), which means they have limited space and may depart up to 15 minutes early or late. Tickets on *de paso* buses can only be purchased same-day, so get to the terminal at least a half hour early to be sure to snag a seat:

Destination	Price	Duration	Schedule
Cancún	US$36-44	7-8 hrs	7 departures, 6:55am-11:30pm
Chetumal	US$28	6.5 hrs	2pm
Mérida	US$11-16	2.5 hrs	56 departures
Mexico City	US$90-109	16.5-17.5 hrs	8 departures
Palenque	US$24	4.5-6.5 hrs	12:30am, 11am, and 10:15pm
Xpujil	US$20	4.5 hrs	2pm

Campeche's **second-class bus station** (Av. Gobernadores at Calle Chile, tel. 981/816-3445) is several long noisy blocks beyond the city walls; it's also known as the "ex-ADO" terminal:

Destination	Price	Duration	Schedule
Dzibalchén	US$5.50	3 hrs	hourly
Hopelchén	US$3.50	1.5 hrs	hourly
Santa Elena	US$7.50	3 hrs	6am and 9:15am
Uxmal ruins	US$8	3.5 hrs	Take Santa Elena bus
Xpujil	US$11	6 hrs	8:15am and 6:30pm

Uxmal and the Puuc region (and aren't planning to stop at Edzná), take Highway 180 to Hecelchakán and cut across to Highway 261. With fewer towns to pass through, you'll save about 45 minutes.

From Campeche south to Champotón, you can take Highway 180-Cuota (toll road) or Highway 180-Libre (free road). The former is a wide, fast highway and costs US$4.25; the latter goes nearer the ocean (but not always right alongside it) and passes through several small towns with their ubiquitous speed bumps. At Champotón, you can continue on Highway 180 to Ciudad del Carmen and on to Tabasco state, or take Highway 261 farther south to Escárcega, where you turn right for Palenque and the highlands of Chiapas or left for Calakmul and, eventually, the Caribbean coast.

GETTING AROUND

Campeche's city center is small and very easy to navigate on foot, but unless you have a bike or rental car, you will need a taxi or local bus to get to and from the bus terminals, airport, and some of the outlying sights.

Bus

To get to the first-class ADO bus station, take an S.E.P./Av. Central bus or minivan (US$0.35, every 15 minutes) from in front of the market on Calle 18 at Calle 53; the trip takes about 20 minutes. For the second-class terminal, catch one that says Terminal Sur. To get to the Fuerte de San Miguel and the Museo de Cultura Maya, take a Lerma/Playa Bonita bus (US$0.35, every 30 minutes) from Calle 55 at Circuito Baluartes (on the market side) or from the front of the post office on Avenida 16 de Septiembre (also known as Circuito Baluartes) at Calle 53; ask the driver to let you off about 2.5 kilometers (1.6 miles) south of town, at *la subida* San Miguel (the climb to San Miguel). From there, it's a tough 0.5-kilometer (0.3-mile) climb to the fort. To get to the Reducto de San José El Alto and the Museo de Armas y Barcos, take a San José El Alto bus from the market (US$0.35, every 30 minutes); it'll drop you off a block from the entrance.

Taxi

Cabs are relatively easy to flag down around town, and there are taxi stands next to the cathedral, near the market, and in front of both bus terminals. Your hotel should also be able to call one for you; if not, try **Radio Taxi Gaviotas** (tel. 981/815-3036). Fares around town are US$2 during the day, US$4 after 11pm (or if you call them). A cab to the airport will run about US$12. Be sure to confirm the price before getting in.

Car

Payless Car Rental (tel. 981/823-4111, toll-free U.S. tel. 800/729-5377, www.paylesscarrental.com) and **Europcar** (tel. 981/823-4083,

www.europcar.com) have offices at the airport, and **Easy Way Rent a Car** (Hotel Misión Campeche América, Calle 10 btwn Calles 59 and 61, tel. 981/811-2236, toll-free Mex. tel. 800/327-9929, toll-free U.S./Can. tel. 877/846-3279, www.easywayrentacar.com, 8:30am-9:30pm daily) is located in the center. Compact cars with air-conditioning start around US$50 per day.

Bicycle

Bikes can be a fun way to see the Malecón and the outlying sights. **Buenaventura** (Av. Circuito Baluartes btwn Calles 14 and 16, tel. 981/144-3388, www.viajesbuenaventura.com.mx, 9am-8pm Mon.-Sat.) rents well-maintained bikes, including helmet and lock, at US$2 for the first hour and US$1.25 per hour afterward. Bring ID. **Kankabi' Ok Tours** (Calle 59 btwn Calles 8 and 10, tel. 981/811-2792, www.kankabiok.com, 9am-1pm and 5pm-9pm Mon.-Sat., 5pm-9pm Sun.) also rents bicycles by the hour (US$1.25-2) or day (US$9.50).

Tours

Trolley tours of Campeche's city center, historic neighborhoods, and its outlying forts are offered by **Tranvía de la Ciudad** (hourly

Board a trolley for a tour of town.

9am-1pm and 5pm-8pm daily, US$6.25, child under 10 free). Each tour lasts 45 minutes with commentary in Spanish only. Trolleys leave from the central plaza on weekdays and from the Plaza Patrimonio Mundial (Calle 8 btwn Calles 55 and 53) on weekends.

Fun for kids, **Barco Pirata El Lorencillo** (tel. 981/829-0696, noon and 4pm Tues.-Sun., US$9.50 adult, US$5 child) is a one-hour boat ride along the coast, with information on Campeche's history of piracy as well as a full-blown pirate show as the main event. Drinks and snacks are sold onboard. Catch the boat at El Faro del Moro restaurant on Avenida Resurgimiento at the southern edge of town.

With a minimum of two people, **Kankabi' Ok Tours** (Calle 59 btwn Calles 8 and 10, tel. 981/811-2792, www.kankabiok.com, 9am-1pm and 5pm-9pm Mon.-Sat., 5pm-9pm Sun.) can organize transportation or guided tours to regional sights, from half-day jaunts to Edzná to daylong excursions to the Chenes region sites of Hochob and Dzibilnocac. Kayaking tours in nearby mangrove forests and bike tours of Campeche City are also offered.

South of Campeche City

The coast south of Campeche City is rarely visited by foreign travelers—it's mostly a local affair dotted with fishing villages. From Campeche City, the route south via Escárcega is the fastest way to reach Calakmul and the Río Bec region.

CHAMPOTÓN

Seafood lovers get a faraway look in their eyes when talking about Champotón, a seaside town between Campeche and Escárcega that's renowned for its *coctelerías* (seafood cocktail restaurants). Situated along the mouth of the Río Champotón, its bay was the site of an infamous 1517 battle where Spaniard Francisco Hernández de Córdova was routed by Maya leader Moch Couoh, giving rise to the name Bahia de la Mala Pelea (Bay of the Bad Fight).

Sports and Recreation

Eighteen kilometers (11 miles) south of town, **La Mar Campeche** (Carr. Champotón-Cd. del Carmen Km. 120, tel. 982/813-4909 ext. 2977, www.lamarcampeche.com.mx, 9am-6pm daily) offers snorkeling, scuba diving, stand-up paddling, and kayaking excursions. One-tank boat dives to see shipwrecks, including equipment, lunch, and a bilingual dive master, cost US$75. It's located within the Aak-Bal Golf & Beach Resort.

Food and Accommodations

On the coastal road running through town, **Pelícanos** (Av. Carlos Sansores Pérez btwn Calles 11 and 13, tel. 982/828-1418, www. restaurantpelicanos.blogspot.mx, 7:30am-7pm daily, US$5-11) serves up super-fresh seafood dishes every day of the week. Don't underestimate the size of those free appetizers—you needn't order any of your own. Air-conditioning and tablecloths are nice pluses.

Bahía de Tortugas (Av. Carlos Sansores Pérez btwn Calles 31 and 33, tel. 982/118-9725, 8am-11:30pm daily, US$6-12) is a reliable beachfront restaurant, with *palapa* shade, plastic chairs and tables in the sand, and the surf just steps away. The menu is classic Mexican beach eats—seafood, finger foods, and ice cold drinks. It's a great place to stop, especially if you're looking for a bit of R&R on the beach. There's a pool on-site too.

Most folks come to town just to eat at the *coctelerías*. If you're driving, the best place to go is just north of town, where there are a handful of waterfront *palapas* open approximately 6am-8pm. The *cocteles* start at US$4, and you can swim along the sandy shoreline. To sample the local catch in town, try the busy **market** (Av. Revolución btwn Calles 32 and 34, 6am-11pm) between the bus terminal and the lighthouse.

One of the best options in town, **Hotel Aaktun Kay** (Calle 30 btwn Calle 28-B and Av. Revolución, tel. 982/828-1800, US$28/38 s/d with a/c) is a modern hotel with rooms opening onto a courtyard with a well-maintained pool. Each room has good beds, flat-screen TVs, quiet air-conditioning, Wi-Fi, and almost best of all, an ample terrace overlooking the bay. Service is genuinely friendly too.

Information and Services

ATMs can be found inside the ADO bus terminal and at **Banamex** (Calle 29, off the main plaza, 9am-4pm Mon.-Fri.), which also changes money. Across the street from Banamex, **Papelería Champotón Centro** (Calle 29, 8am-2pm and 5pm-8pm Mon.-Sat., 9am-1pm Sun., US$0.80/hour) has two computers with Internet access.

Getting There

On the main road, first- and second-class buses service the **ADO terminal** (Av. Revolución at Calle 32, tel. 982/828-0003). Daily first-class departures include:

• Campeche: US$4.75-6, 1 hour, 14 departures 12:30am-10:30pm (second-class every 30 minutes, US$2.25)

• Mérida: US$14-16.25, 3.5-4 hours, 14 departures 12:30am-10:30pm

• Xpujil: US$16, 4 hours, 3:05pm (second-class 6:20am, 9:42am, and 11:27pm, US$10)

CENOTES MIGUEL COLORADO

If you're driving, the ecotourism project of **Cenotes Miguel Colorado** (cell. tel. 982/108-5669, 7am-5pm daily, US$6.25) makes a worthy detour between Champotón and Escárcega. Located in the small *ejido* of Miguel Colorado, the main attraction here is Cenote Agua Azul, an open pool buffered by tall limestone cliffs and thick forest. The admission fee includes two blood-pumping zipline rides, each 244 meters (800 feet) across and 85 meters (279 feet) above the water, and kayaking through and swimming in the cenote's deep blue waters. The water's clearest in April when the trees shed their leaves and let more light through.

An undulating trail winds around Cenote Agua Azul to Cenote Los Patos, where migratory birds gather in the mornings, including noisy Canada geese in December. Throughout the forest canopy, it's easy to see (and hear)

Ceviche is a classic dish in Champotón.

the resident spider and howler monkeys, and wildlife watchers should arrange a visit at dusk, when thousands of bats swarm and ascend in a vortex from a crater named K41.

Food is available on-site, made by local women.

Getting There

The town and project are well signed from Highway 261. Go 10 kilometers (6.2 miles) east on a road with sneaky potholes, then left another 3 kilometers (1.9 miles) from the "cenote" sign in town.

ESCÁRCEGA

Escárcega is a dreary town at the junction of Highways 186 and 261. For tourists it is mainly a gas stop as they head east to the archaeological sites in the Río Bec area (154 kilometers/95 miles) or north to Campeche City (150 kilometers/93 miles), or a place to change buses.

Food and Accommodations

If you get stuck in town, **Hotel Escárcega** (Av. Justo Sierra Méndez No. 87, tel. 982/824-0187, hotelescarcega@hotmail.com, US$16 s/d, US$28 s/d with a/c) is short on personality— think cheap, basic rooms with threadbare linens—but it'll do for a night, especially if you're on a tight budget.

The rooms are remarkably better at **Global Express Hotel Escárcega** (Carr. Escárcega-Villahermosa Km. 152, tel. 982/824-0424, www.globalescarcega.freshcreator.com, US$50-53 s/d with a/c). Each unit is modern in design with quiet air-conditioning, flat-screen cable TVs, and Wi-Fi. There's a small pool and continental breakfast too. Located at the entrance to town, across from the PEMEX station, it's easy to spot but can be noisy with traffic, especially early in the morning.

For eats, there are a number of small family-run restaurants near the main bus station (Highway 261 and Av. Justo Sierra Méndez).

Information and Services

Near the second-class bus terminal, **Bancomer** (Calle 27 s/n, 9am-4pm Mon.-Fri.) has an ATM; there's another ATM in the ADO bus terminal.

Getting There

The **ADO bus terminal** (Hwy. 261 at Av. Justo Sierra Méndez, tel. 982/824-0144) is located on the north side of town, on the road to Campeche City. Always arrive a half hour early—service here is *de paso* (mid-route), which means seats are limited and buses may come 15 minutes early or late.

Daily departures include:

- Cancún: US$27-41, 9-11 hours, 7 departures 12:25am-11:35pm

- Campeche: US$11-12, 2 hours, 9 departures 2am-11:55pm

- Chetumal: US$15-18, 3.5-4.5 hours, 9 departures 12:25am-10:10pm

- Mérida: US$17.50-22, 4.5 hours, 8 departures 2am-11:55pm

- Palenque: US$15, 3 hours, midnight, 1am, 5:30am, 12:50pm

- Xpujil: US$7-11, 2.5 hours, 4:20pm, 8:10pm

The ADO buses don't stop en route, but those from the **second-class bus terminal** (Av. Justo Sierra Méndez at Calle 31, tel. 982/824-0498) can drop you at the Calakmul turnoff (US$4.50, 1.5 hours) or the hotels just west of Xpujil (US$7, 2.5 hours); departures are at 8am, 11:20am, 1:40pm, 5pm, and 10:40pm.

Note: The gas stations here are the last eastbound until Xpujil.

Río Bec Region

Campeche's Río Bec region is located in the southern part of the state, cut lengthwise by Highway 186. It's flanked by the tiny towns of Xpujil and Escárcega, and filled with the remarkable—and remarkably untouristed—Río Bec archaeological sites. The earliest occupation of the Río Bec area occurred between 1000 and 300 BC, though the height of construction was much later, between AD 550 and 830. At the end of the 9th century, however, Maya cities across the region suddenly collapsed, and their populations dispersed. By the time of the Spanish conquest, the once-glorious cities were almost completely abandoned. The Río Bec sites were rediscovered early in the 20th century by chicle tappers and are still being explored and excavated today. Indeed, this area has been the source of many of the most noteworthy archaeological discoveries of the last decades.

Today, you'll find the massive Calakmul ruins, the mother of Río Bec sites, and possibly of the Maya world. It boasts the largest Maya pyramid, the most number of stelae of any Maya ruin, and possibly the greatest number of total structures (they are still being mapped and counted). If that weren't enough reason to visit, Calakmul is located deep in a nature reserve, and it's common to spot monkeys and tropical birds in the thick tree cover.

Farther along Highway 186 are several smaller sites that, while lacking the sheer size and scale of Calakmul, are no less compelling. Balamkú is near the turnoff to Calakmul; Chicanná, Becán, and Xpujil are closer to the village of Xpujil (the only town of any size in the area); and El Hormiguero is down a rough dirt road. The Río Bec archaeological zone is currently off-limits to independent visitors, but tours can be arranged.

Most share the distinctive Río Bec architectural style, with its meticulous stonework and high steeple-like towers. There's no doubt that this area is the next Puuc Route, but for now you can have these stunning sites practically to yourself.

★ CALAKMUL ARCHAEOLOGICAL ZONE AND RESERVE

A UNESCO World Heritage Site, **Calakmul** (8am-5pm daily, US$3.25) may be the remains of the largest city-state in Maya history, home to as many as 60,000 people—and thousands more under its sphere of influence—and the seat of immense military, cultural, and economic power. Calakmul boasts the largest Maya pyramid yet discovered, looming nearly 60 meters (197 feet) above the forest floor. A whopping 6,750 structures have been mapped, and thousands more remain covered in thick brush and forest. Nine jade funeral masks and some 120 stelae have been found here, more than at any other Maya site. Another measure of Calakmul's influence can be found in the stelae of other Maya cities, in which Calakmul appears more often than any other.

History

Calakmul was originally called Kaan (Kingdom of the Serpent Head). The Maya name Calakmul (Two Adjacent Mounds) was coined by a Maya-speaking botanist and explorer who spotted the site's two most prominent pyramids from an airplane while surveying for chicle in 1931. However, the site went unexplored for over 50 years, even as archaeologists discovered numerous references in the inscriptions of Palenque, Tikal, and other cities to a powerful but as-yet-unknown kingdom. The first major excavation of Calakmul began in 1985, and the importance of the long-lost city quickly emerged.

Much remains unknown about Calakmul, however. It's clear that the city was enormous, with more than 6,000 structures spread over 70 square kilometers (27 square miles).

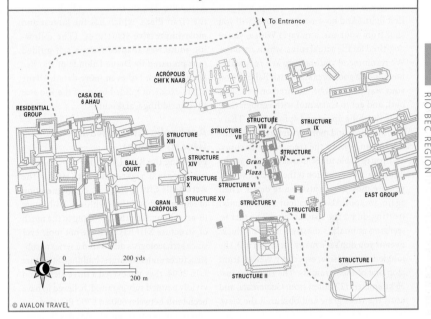

Calakmul Archaeological Zone

To Entrance

ACRÓPOLIS CHII'K NAAB

CASA DEL 6 AHAU

RESIDENTIAL GROUP

STRUCTURE XIII

STRUCTURE VII

STRUCTURE VIII

STRUCTURE IX

STRUCTURE XIV

STRUCTURE IV

Gran Plaza

BALL COURT

STRUCTURE X

STRUCTURE XV

STRUCTURE VI

STRUCTURE V

EAST GROUP

GRAN ACRÓPOLIS

STRUCTURE III

0 200 yds

0 200 m

STRUCTURE II

STRUCTURE I

© AVALON TRAVEL

Around 60,000 people lived here at the city's peak, possibly the largest Maya city ever. It was also a very old city, first settled in the 6th century BC, with many of its major structures erected by AD 250. The size of Calakmul's structures is attributable, in part, to the Maya custom of adding new temples and layers over and atop existing structures to mark significant dates or political changes. Over the centuries, they added up to create some of the Maya world's largest pyramids.

Calakmul emerged as a major power in the Classic era; the greatest number of stelae found here are dated between AD 431 and 790. The city used its military and economic power to forge many strategic alliances (usually skewed to Calakmul's advantage), and waged fierce battle with those kingdoms with whom it couldn't come to terms. Calakmul attacked Palenque in AD 599 and 611, and then Tikal in 657, under the leadership of king Yukom the Great. That ruler's son, known as Jaguar Paw, attacked Tikal again in 695 but was defeated, and his capture is glorified in inscriptions at Tikal. After that ignominious loss, Calakmul went into steady decline, a precursor to the widespread collapse of Classic-era Maya cities over the next two centuries.

Visiting the Ruins

Calakmul is deep in the Calakmul Biosphere Reserve, a dense protected forest teeming with animal life. Look for howler and spider monkeys, toucans, parrots, and other assorted birds and rodents as you wander the site, as well as on the winding 60-kilometer (37-mile) road from the highway to the entrance. (Be aware that mosquitoes can be voracious during the rainy season, or after any heavy rain; wear long clothes and bring heavy-duty insect repellent.) The reserve is home to five of Mexico's six wildcat species, including jaguars and pumas, and every so often visitors are treated to a glimpse of one.

Everyone will tell you that in order to see wildlife, you need to visit Calakmul early in the morning. But think about it: Even if you leave Xpujil at 5am—ouch—you don't get into the core of the reserve until 6:30am, well past first light. (And how many creatures will you spot from your car, anyway?) Worse, you're dog-tired for the actual ruins, which are huge. We recommend you wake up at a reasonable hour, have a good breakfast, visit Balamkú on your way in (you'll be too tired on your way out), and get to Calakmul with enough time to be finishing up around 4pm or 5pm. That's the time birds and monkeys return from feeding to hang out in the trees near the ruins, and you're liable to see just as many as in the morning. The exception is the big cats, which, yes, are most active just before dawn. Then again, we spotted a puma (our one and only) trotting down the road at 5pm! The fact is, spotting animals is mostly a matter of luck. Even if you don't see many (or any at all), the jungle is impressive, especially viewed from atop one of the pyramids. The ruins are just 35 kilometers (22 miles) from Guatemala, and until the trees grew and obscured the view, on a clear day you could spot the El Mirador ruins, just across the border.

From the entrance, a path leads about a kilometer (0.6 mile) through the forest before splitting into long, medium, and short routes. The long route loops past two smaller complexes and begins in earnest in the Gran Acrópolis. The short route leads directly to the Gran Plaza, which has the largest and most impressive structures. (The following route was adapted from a self-guided tour prepared by Diane Lalonde of Río Bec Dreams hotel. For even more detail, Diane offers excellent guided tours of the Río Bec sites, including Calakmul.)

Acrópolis Chii`k Naab (North Group)

Following the Ruta Larga (long route) path, you'll pass a right-hand turnoff for the **Acrópolis Chii`k Naab.** A conglomeration of 68 mapped buildings within a 2.4-hectare (6-acre) boundary, this grouping to the north of Structure XIII has been the hot topic ever since archaeologists discovered a series of sub-structures under its largest building, Structure I. In 2004, they uncovered a three-tiered and vividly painted sub-pyramid, believed to have been built between 600 and 700 BC, that was covered in pristine murals. Besides their excellent state of preservation, what makes these frescoes so important to Mayanists is that they depict the lives of the common people, not the nobles, gods, or spiritual representations

Calakmul ruins in Campeche are nestled deep in a biosphere reserve.

that comprise the subject matter of all other known Maya murals. The tableaux have been pored over by academics anxious to learn more about the people's daily lives in that period, including what kind of food they ate and the clothes they wore.

At the time of research, the archaeology team forecast that the structure would soon open to the public. Many locals, however, point out that they've been saying that for years.

Gran Acrópolis

Continue on the path to another turnoff, this one to the **Residential Group,** aka **Casa del 6 Ahau,** an elegant complex of rooms most likely used by one of Calakmul's elite extended families. The rooms' walls have niches and holes, which were surely used to hold wooden doors, curtain rods, or beams supporting the thatched roof. Rooms vary in size, some facing a central patio, others reached by narrow corridors, and it's easy to imagine a nuanced domestic scene unfolding here, with royal leaders coming and going, and children playing in the patio watched by elder grandparents sitting in their doorways. The kingly name "6 Ahau" was inscribed on a vault here, though nothing more of that ruler is known.

The path leads over a small rise to the Gran Acrópolis. **Structure XX** will be on your right, with its small maze of rooms and columns. Continuing counterclockwise (keeping the structures to your right), you'll pass **Structures XVI, XVII,** and **XV,** all with huge deteriorating stelae at their bases. The next one, **Structure X,** has somewhat better-preserved stelae, including **Stela 75,** which purportedly marks the birth of Yukom the Great, Calakmul's most accomplished leader, in AD 600. The stairway of Structure X is crumbling, but an older stairway—preserved beneath the outer one, a consequence of the Maya habit of draping new structures upon existing ones—has been exposed and is easily climbed.

Continue across the acropolis's center through Calakmul's modest **ball court,** which was built from stones gathered from an older building that was destroyed. At the north end of the ball court is a remarkably well-preserved stela depicting a ball player. An inscription on the stela suggests the ball court was constructed in AD 751.

At the north end of the Gran Acrópolis is **Structure XIII.** Impressive in its own right, Structure XIII is also notable for being one of the best places to get a photograph of Structure II (the big one). Getting to the top is a little tricky: Climb the stairs and go to the far left. There, you can clamber up the end of a broken wall, and then another, to reach the third level. Go back to the center and cut through one of the doorways, where a narrow ledge zigzags to the top.

Gran Plaza

Descending Structure XIII, bear left to **Structure XIV,** a rare "two-sided" temple with stairways on either side of the structure. It dates to the Late Classic era and has stelae marking the year of the temple's construction, AD 740. Climb up and over Structure XIV—or take the path around—and continue beneath the trees to the Gran Plaza. As in the Gran Acrópolis, make a counterclockwise loop through this large plaza, keeping the buildings to your right.

The first one you pass is **Structure VI,** a large pyramid-like temple with two reasonably well-preserved stelae at its summit; some of the original red paint is still visible. The structure's precise orientation suggests it was used for astronomical purposes, primarily observations of the sun; it is aligned with Structure IV, on the opposite side of the plaza, allowing Maya astronomers to mark the yearly equinoxes and solstices.

Continuing on, you'll encounter **Structure V,** a small square temple surrounded by well-preserved stelae. Dates on the stelae are from the 7th century, and the glyphs and images commemorate accomplishments of Yukom the Great and his father, Scroll-Serpent.

And then there's the big one: **Structure II,** also known as the Great Pyramid. It forms the southern edge of the Gran Plaza, rising 53 meters (174 feet) over a hefty two-hectare (5-acre)

The Maya Collapse

Something went terribly wrong for the Maya between the years AD 800 and 900. Hundreds of Classic Maya cities were abandoned, monarchies disappeared, and the population fell by millions, mainly due to death and plummeting birthrates. The collapse was widespread but was most dramatic in the Southern Lowlands, a swath of tropical forest stretching from the Gulf of Mexico to Honduras and including once-glorious cities such as Palenque, Tikal, and Copán. (Archaeologists first suspected a collapse after noticing a sudden drop-off in inscriptions; it has been confirmed through excavations of peasant dwellings from before and after that period.)

There are many theories for the collapse, varying from climate change and epidemic diseases to foreign invasion and peasant revolt. In his carefully argued book *The Fall of the Ancient Maya* (Thames and Hudson, 2002), archaeologist and professor of anthropology at Pennsylvania State University David Webster suggests it was a series of conditions, rather than a single event, that led to the collapse.

To a certain degree, it was the very success of Maya cities during the Classic era that set the stage for their demise. Webster points to a population boom just before the collapse, which would have left agricultural lands dangerously depleted just as demand spiked. Classic-era farming techniques were ill-suited to meet the challenge; in particular, the lack of draft animals kept productivity low, meaning Maya farmers could not generate large surpluses of corn and other food. (Even if they could, storage was difficult given the hot, humid climate.) The lack of animals also limited how far away farmers could cultivate land and still be able to transport their crops to the city center; as a result, available land was overused. As Webster puts it, "too many farmers [growing] too many crops on too much of the landscape left the Classic Maya world acutely vulnerable to an environmental catastrophe, such as drought or crop disease."

Certain kingdoms reached their tipping point before others (prompting some to launch 11th-hour military campaigns against weakened rivals), but few escaped the wave of malnutrition, disease, lower birthrates, and outright starvation that seems to have swept across the Maya world in the 9th century. Kings and nobility would have faced increasing unrest and insurrection—after

footprint. It's the largest Maya pyramid yet discovered, and the highest in the Yucatán Peninsula. Unlike sites such as Chichén Itzá, where the most impressive structures were built relatively late, Structure II dates to the very beginning of Calakmul's rise to power, in the Preclassic period. The huge stoic masks flanking the central staircase were covered by subsequent additions, and were discovered only recently. Structure II has proved a treasure trove of Maya artifacts: Several exquisite jade funeral masks have been found in elaborate tombs housed in temples at the top of the structure—a total of nine such masks have been found in Calakmul, more than any other site, and one is displayed in the Museo Arqueológico de Campeche (the rest are in the Museo Nacional de Antropología in Mexico City). More recently, archaeologists discovered a perfectly preserved temple deep

in Structure II's core (à la Rosalia Temple in Copán, Honduras) with a large stucco frieze. The temple is still being excavated and is off-limits to the public, but in time visitors may be allowed to view this inner sanctum via a short tunnel about halfway up the main stairway. Climbing Structure II is a must for most visitors, though it's no easy task—use the right-hand staircase, as it's in the best condition.

Continuing around the Gran Plaza, **Structure IV** is the oldest building in the group, and one of the oldest in the city. Its core sections—others were added in later years—date to between 300 BC and AD 250. **Structure VII** completes the loop around the plaza; it was here that one of Calakmul's most recognizable jade masks was found. Climb Structure VII for one last look, over the treetops, of Structure II in all its glory. And if you're there in the late afternoon, you may

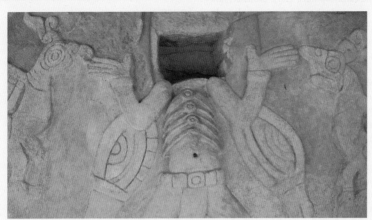

Decapitated figures at Mayan sites often symbolize death or calamity.

all, their legitimacy was based on their ability to induce the gods to bestow rain, fertility, and prosperity—further destabilizing the social structure and food supply.

The collapse was not universal, of course, and the fall of lowland powers gave other city-states an opportunity to expand and gain influence. But the Maya world was dramatically and permanently changed by it; the grand cities built by the Classic-era Maya were abandoned to the jungle, most never to be reoccupied, and, as Webster notes, "Cortés and his little army almost starved in 1525 while crossing a wilderness that had supported millions of people seven centuries earlier."

spot a family of howler monkeys that gathers in the Gran Plaza's trees.

From the Gran Plaza, a path cuts between Structures IV and VII and back to the entrance and parking lot. For those who can't get enough, two more structures await your exploration: **Structure I,** another huge pyramid, is visible from Structure II, though it remains almost completely ensconced in dark-green vegetation. To get there, look for a path on the east side of Structure II. From Structure I, another path leads to **Structure III,** a Petén-style structure and the principal temple in the East Group, the oldest part of the city. Structure III is unique for apparently having never been altered; two jade masks were found in tombs here. From the East Group, a path leads back to the Gran Plaza.

Museo de Naturaleza y Arqueología de Calakmul

A fine addition to the Calakmul experience, the new solar-powered **Museo de Naturaleza y Arqueología de Calakmul** (8am-4pm daily, free), 20 kilometers (12.4 miles) from the highway turnoff, contains four spacious exhibition rooms dedicated to the geology, biodiversity, and archaeology of the area. Some interpretive materials are in English. And until the anxiously awaited Chii`k Naab murals open to the public, the museum is the best place to visualize them through its replica of the staired pyramid and the magnificent murals. Welcome amenities here include bathrooms that are a million times nicer than those at the ruins.

Food and Accommodations

The Calakmul area has little in the way of lodging and eating options. Those available, however, span the budget spectrum, which makes staying near the ruins possible for everyone.

Just past the gate at the turnoff to Calakmul ruins, **Hotel Puerta Calakmul** (turnoff at Carr. Escárcega-Chetumal Km. 98, tel. 998/892-2624, www.puertacalakmul.com.mx, US$160 s/d) has 15 spacious cabins in a wooded area near the highway (read: You'll hear both late-night trucks and early morning songbirds). The cabins are comfortable but nowhere near luxe, especially given the rate; think good beds, mosquito nets, painted cement floors, murals, and outdoor terraces with hammocks. The restaurant (US$8-22), though pricey, is very pleasant with leaf-shaped tables and a high bank of windows. There's a small pool on-site and Wi-Fi too. Continental breakfast is included.

In the nearby village of Conhuás, **Restaurant La Selva** (Carr. Escárcega-Chetumal, tel. 983/733-8706, US$21 s/d), is a popular roadside diner that slings enormous combo plates and rents a half dozen *palapa*-roofed *cabañas* in town. It's a basic setup, with torn window screens and private cement bathrooms lacking toilet seats, but that's made up for by the mosquito nets, the good beds, and warm blankets (it can get chilly at night). If you have gear, you can camp in front of the restaurant for US$4 per person—a cold-water bathroom is available. Look for it 2.5 kilometers (1.6 miles) west of the Calakmul turnoff.

Seven kilometers (4.3 miles) down the road to Calakmul, **Campamento Yaax'che** (turnoff at Carr. Escárcega-Chetumal Km. 98, tel. 983/871-6064, www.ecoturismocalakmul.com, US$11 pp camping) is one of the few honest-to-goodness campgrounds you'll find just about anywhere in the region. Campsites are scattered in a pleasant wooded area, and tents with all the necessary equipment (including airbeds) are included. There are compost toilets and barrels of water for bathing. There's also a simple eatery (6am-10pm daily, US$3-5) that serves up good, basic meals from its wood-burning stove. Several tours of the reserve also are offered by experienced guides. Its central office is in Xpujil, next to the ADO bus station.

Tours

Ka'an Expeditions (Av. Calakmul s/n, tel. 983/871-6000, www.kaanexpeditions.com, noon-8pm Tues.-Sun.) offers fantastic tours of Calakmul that highlight Maya history and culture as well as the reserve's mind-boggling variety of flora and fauna. Day tours from Xpujil (US$75 pp, minimum 2 people) include lunch and entrance fees, and adventurous multiday camping trips also can be organized. Guides are bilingual certified naturalists.

For more information about visiting the ruins and the biosphere reserve, including a listing of private guides, check out **www.visitcalakmul.com.**

Getting There

Calakmul is a solid two-hour drive from Xpujil. From the turnoff on Highway 186, it's 60 kilometers (37 miles) down a paved but narrow and winding road to the archaeological zone, turning twice to circumvent the new museum. Drive carefully and be ready to stop or pull over for other cars, animals, and (most commonly) large families of dim-witted ocellated turkeys in the road. And get your wallet out: There's a US$3.50 per car and US$1.75 per person toll to use the road, which is on ejido land; another US$4 charge to enter the biosphere reserve at Kilometer 20; and a US$3.25 ruins entrance fee. Ouch! Also, if you've hired a cab, be sure it has the necessary permits to enter the biosphere reserve. If not, it will only be able to take you as far as the entrance to the reserve; at that point, a shuttle is available to take visitors to the site for US$50 (1-4 people).

Note: Visitors are not permitted to enter the biosphere reserve after 2:30pm.

BALAMKÚ ARCHAEOLOGICAL ZONE

For years, archaeologists and the area's few tourists paid scant attention to little old **Balamkú** (8am-5pm daily, US$2.50), preferring instead to focus on Calakmul, Becán, and

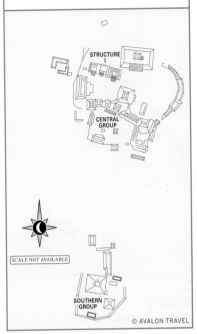

Balamkú Archaeological Zone

STRUCTURE I

CENTRAL GROUP

SCALE NOT AVAILABLE

SOUTHERN GROUP

© AVALON TRAVEL

THE FRIEZE

Balamkú's frieze depicts a rich scene of gods, animals, and men quite different from those appearing at surrounding sites. Some 20 meters (66 feet) long and in remarkably good condition, including a great deal of original color, the frieze has four frames. At the center of each is an animal—a toad and two crocodiles are discernible, the fourth has decomposed. Toads and crocodiles (both amphibious) represented fertility to the Maya, especially in this arid region. Above the animal figures—in the case of the toad, emerging from its gaping upturned mouth—are kings, sitting cross-legged on jaguar-skin cushions and surrounded by lilies, another sign of fertility. The implication is that the king, too, is endowed with powers of rebirth and prosperity, and will deliver them to his subjects. The frames are separated by jaguars with reptile heads. Two are bound like prisoners, and were likely meant to evoke war, ritual sacrifice, and the middle world between life and death.

The cardinal directions figure prominently in Maya mythology, and Maya artisans had to develop ways of portraying the four directions in two-dimensional forms. In Balamkú's frieze, the bottom of each frame has a mask portraying Cauac, the snaggle-toothed Earth Monster. The end masks are in profile and represent north and south. The center masks both face forward; however, the one beneath the toad is pictured with a serpent devouring a bird, a symbol for west. Epigraphers, who decipher ancient writing, believe such devices would have been readily understood by most Maya observers, even illiterate commoners, and visitors from far-off cities and kingdoms.

The chamber where the frieze was found has been carefully reconstructed to protect the fragile stucco and preserve the appearance of the surrounding structure and plaza—from the outside you can hardly tell anything is there. It is accessible through a side door that is kept locked—ask someone at the entrance, or the attendant at the site, to open the door for a peek inside.

the grander sites of this region. But in 1990 archaeologists uncovered an incredibly well-preserved 20-meter (66-foot) **stucco frieze** inside a ruined pyramid here, and Balamkú instantly became a must-see on the southern Campeche Maya route. In fact, relatively little has been excavated here, so there's not much to see beyond the frieze.

History

Balamkú (House of the Jaguar) shows signs of occupation as early as 300 BC. It reached its peak in the Early Classic era (AD 300-600) before collapsing, along with so many other Maya cities, toward the end of the first millennium. The frieze was built around AD 550-650 and is located in one of three bases that make up **Structure I,** in the site's central group. The frieze had been deliberately covered, probably in the course of enlarging the pyramid.

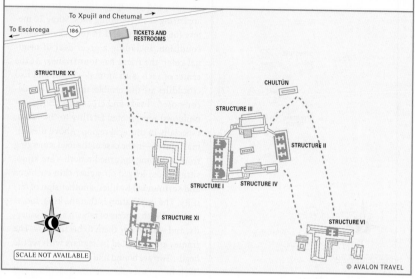

Chicanná Archaeological Zone

To Xpujil and Chetumal →

To Escárcega ← 186

TICKETS AND RESTROOMS

STRUCTURE XX

CHULTÚN

STRUCTURE III

STRUCTURE II

STRUCTURE I   STRUCTURE IV

STRUCTURE XI

STRUCTURE VI

SCALE NOT AVAILABLE

© AVALON TRAVEL

Getting There

Balamkú is located just off Highway 186, about five kilometers (3.1 miles) west of the turnoff to Calakmul.

CHICANNÁ ARCHAEOLOGICAL ZONE

The name **Chicanná** (8am-5pm daily, US$2.75), meaning House of the Serpent Mouth, is a reference to the site's most impressive feature: huge stone jaws framing the doorway of the main palace. The ornate design, commonly called a "monster mouth," is a classic feature of Chenes-style architecture, and Chicanná's is one of the best around. But the site also contains elements of Río Bec architecture, another example of the mixing of styles common in this region.

If you visit Chicanná in the afternoon, keep your eyes peeled for families of keel-billed toucans and the similar-looking collared aracari—a real treat. In the trees, look for rodents and small mammals, including the gray fox.

History

Despite its ominous name, archaeologists believe Chicanná was a retreat used by the elite of Becán, which is just two kilometers (1.2 miles) west and connected by an ancient roadway. Dating to the Late Preclassic period, it reached its apogee between AD 500 and 700. By AD 1100, however, it had been abandoned.

Structures XX and XI

From the entrance, you'll first pass **Structure XX,** a small but exquisitely designed temple-residence. Its main doorway is framed by a monster mouth, and gives way to a foyer-type room and, farther in, a twin staircase leading to the upper level. The upper facade also has a monster-mouth doorway and, to either side, columns of masks representing Chaac, the hook-nosed god of rain. The elegance of this structure and others, plus details like the small rosettes on the 1st floor (with little human faces in the middle!) are a primary reason Chicanná is thought to have been a royal retreat. Continuing along the path, you'll pass a turnoff to **Structure XI,** the oldest in the group, dating to AD 300, before reaching Chicanná's Central Plaza.

Central Plaza

The first building you reach in the Central Plaza is **Structure I,** whose two tall, steeply pitched towers are typical of Río Bec style. Opposite is **Structure II,** with its spectacular monster-mouth facade framing the doorway. The two spiral features above the door are the eyes; similar spirals to each side are the ears, and the teeth are quite obvious, above the door and protruding up from the patio like a snake with a mean underbite. A section of red glyphs can be seen to the right of the door. Left of the main entrance, a smaller door is topped with a stone decoration in the form of a *na,* the traditional thatched hut used by ancient Maya and still common today. The exact meaning of the image here (and seen at Uxmal, Labná, and other ruins) is unclear, though a thatched hut—with a three-stone hearth inside it—represents the beginning of the universe in some Maya creation myths.

Completing the Central Plaza are **Structures III** and **IV,** both multiroom buildings, while newly excavated **Structure VI,** with a dramatic windowed roof comb and red paint visible on its back side, stands a short distance southeast of the plaza. Look for a footpath between Structures II and IV leading there.

Getting There

Chicanná is located 8.8 kilometers (5.5 miles) west of Xpujil on Highway 186. The site is just 500 meters (0.3 mile) from the highway turnoff.

BECÁN ARCHAEOLOGICAL ZONE

East of Chicanná on Highway 186 is the turnoff to **Becán** (8am-5pm daily, US$2.75). The largest of the Río Bec sites (save Calakmul, of course), Becán is a fascinating site, especially if you enjoy climbing and clambering around.

History

The area around Becán was settled as early as 600 BC but did not rise to greatness until more than 1,000 years later, in part because it dwelled under the ever-present shadow of Calakmul. When Calakmul went into decline at the turn of the 8th century, Becán quickly emerged as one of the most important commercial and political centers of the Río Bec region. The sheer size of its pyramids and other structures suggests it commanded a labor force of many thousands.

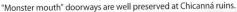

"Monster mouth" doorways are well preserved at Chicanná ruins.

Becán Archaeological Zone

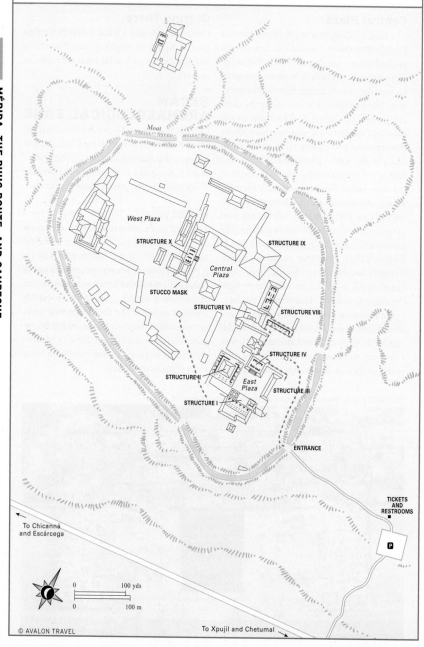

Moat

West Plaza

STRUCTURE X

STRUCTURE IX

Central Plaza

STUCCO MASK

STRUCTURE VI

STRUCTURE VIII

STRUCTURE IV

STRUCTURE II

East Plaza

STRUCTURE III

STRUCTURE I

ENTRANCE

TICKETS AND RESTROOMS

P

To Chicanná and Escárcega

0   100 yds
0   100 m

© AVALON TRAVEL

To Xpujil and Chetumal

The Moat

The name Becán means "ravine formed by water," no doubt a reference to the huge dry moat that forms a half moon around the site. Measuring an impressive 15 meters (49 feet) wide and 4 meters (13 feet) deep, the moat was most likely used for defense, and is one of very few such structures found in Mesoamerica.

Central Plaza

A pathway from the ticket booth leads through the trees, across the moat, and to the back side of **Structure IV,** which has a profusion of decorative elements and openings. As tempting as it will be to clamber up it, there is much better access from the other side, at the end of your visit. Instead, continue through Becán's unique corbelled alley—a long covered passageway that functioned as a public street. It contains small niches that likely held images of deities, and where passersby might have paused to make small offerings.

Emerging onto the Central Plaza, the massive pyramids, **Structures VIII** and **IX,** loom to your right in the northeast corner of the plaza. Both can be climbed, and afford spectacular views of the countryside. Structure IX, at 30 meters (98 feet) high, is the tallest structure at Becán; at the top is a platform

with a huge mask on one end and a shield-image on the other.

At the west end of the Central Plaza is **Structure X.** Though not as imposing as the two pyramids, many visitors find this one the site's most fascinating. Walking around the back, or west, side, you'll see that the structure contains several large central chambers (12 in all) and innumerable smaller rooms, spread over several levels and connected by way of winding staircases and passageways; there's even a hidden 2nd-floor patio on the south end. While many Maya structures gained complexity as new rooms and levels were added, Structure X's elegant design suggests it was planned from the start. The rooms are clearly residences, and some archaeologists speculate Structure X was a dormitory, of sorts, possibly for Becán's religious leaders.

Be sure not to miss the beautiful and extremely well-preserved stucco mask on Structure X's southern exterior wall. Only recently uncovered, the mask may depict the sun god Kinichná. It has much of its original red paint and is protected by a pane of glass. The **ball court** lies adjacent to the southern end of Structure X.

the view between Becán's massive twin pyramids

East Plaza

A short path leads through trees along the edge of the site to the East Plaza. The long imposing palace you see is **Structure I.** Its twin towers are much decayed, but still have remains of the impossibly steep staircases typical of the Río Bec style. The stairs on the southeast side are the least perilous. Below, two levels of vaulted rooms are clearly more luxurious than the austere cells in Structure X; it's not hard to imagine Becán's elite occupying these grand, roomy chambers.

Structure I's back wall forms one side of the East Plaza. On the opposite side is **Structure IV,** the same building you encountered entering the site, albeit from the other side. Structure IV's staircase is well preserved, and a rope makes it even more climbable. At the top, look for narrow doorways on either side of the platform leading to spiral staircases down to musty rooms and passages in the structure's interior.

Back on the East Plaza, a staircase at the northeast corner (between Structures III and IV) leads down to the path you take to exit the site.

Getting There

Bécan is located five kilometers (3.1 miles) east of Chicanná and seven kilometers (4.3 miles) west of Xpujil. The turnoff is well marked, and an access road of several hundred meters brings you to the entrance area.

XPUJIL ARCHAEOLOGICAL ZONE

Xpujil (8am-5pm daily, US$2.85) is a small but well-preserved site. It dates to 400 BC, though it reached its height between AD 500 and 750. **Structure I,** built in classic Río Bec style, is the most famous of the few structures that have been excavated here. It has three towers—a central one flanked by two smaller ones—and several false staircases. (It is unusual because of the number of towers—most temples in the region only have two.) On the back of the central tower, check out what's left of two huge, stylized masks.

Notably, Structure I also has 12 rooms that are oriented toward the cardinal points; the building itself is aligned with Structure VIII at the Becán ruins, 10 kilometers (6.2 miles) away. The remaining buildings, **Structures II, III,** and **IV,** are believed to have been aristocratic residences.

Getting There

The well-marked Xpujil ruins are located on the western edge of the like-named town, right next to the highway.

EL HORMIGUERO ARCHAEOLOGICAL ZONE

Spanish for The Anthill, **El Hormiguero** (8am-5pm daily, free) reached its height between AD 730 and 830. It is a site that few people visit, mostly because of the difficulty of arriving. Although only a few structures have been excavated, those that have been uncovered are dramatic (and worth the trip!). It is most notable for **Structure II,** a 50-meter-long (164-foot) building in the Southern Group with two tall towers flanking an enormous monster-mouth doorway. From there, a path leads visitors directly to the Central Group, where **Structure V**—and its imposing monster-mouth entrance—looms before visitors. With unexcavated mounds everywhere you look, the site really fires the imagination.

Getting There

Located 22 kilometers (13.7 miles) south of Xpujil town, Hormiguero was, until recently, almost impossible to access without a heavy-duty four-wheel-drive vehicle and a lot of time. The road has improved significantly, and though it is still no autobahn, just about any car can jostle through as long as you go slowly and it hasn't rained. Expect to startle the caretaker—he rarely sees visitors.

RÍO BEC ARCHAEOLOGICAL ZONE

The namesake site of this region is made up of 70 scattered groups (2,000 mapped mounds) and is currently being excavated.

Xpujil Archaeological Zone

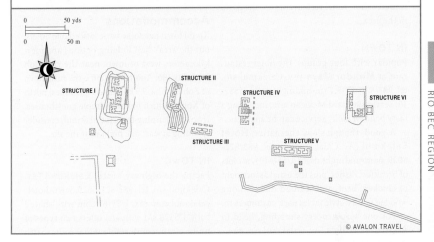

The architecture follows the region's dominant style, with high steep towers and tight-fitting stonework. A lack of a central plaza and no evidence of a larger settlement, however, suggest that Río Bec was a getaway of sorts for the elite. It is believed that each group of structures functioned like a colonial-era hacienda, occupied by a privileged family and a small staff.

Getting There

Unfortunately, Río Bec is quite difficult to visit. You must have permission to enter the area, and the access road is rutted and overgrown; after a rain, it can be impossible to pass. The proprietors of Río Bec Dreams hotel can arrange a tour of Río Bec in the drier months, generally between early February and early May, but a few days' advance notice is required.

VOLCÁN DE LOS MURCIÉLAGOS

At about Kilometer 107 on Highway 186, there is a small turnoff on the north side, just big enough to pull your car off the road. From there, walk a couple of hundred meters through the trees and up a small hill to a huge sinkhole, at the bottom of which is a narrow cave opening. At dusk every night, an estimated three million small black bats emerge from this cave in an endless whirling rush. Known locally as the volcán de los murciélagos (volcano of the bats), it is an incredible spectacle and like no other. At the height, you can feel the wind from their collective wings and winding upward flight—a few may even crash into you or stop for a rest on your pant leg. (No worries—they're harmless to humans, feeding mostly on insects.)

If driving near the cave at dusk, heed the yellow bat signs on the highway and slow down so you don't hit them. Better yet, pull over and watch the bats darkening the sky.

XPUJIL TOWN AND AROUND

A small, dusty village with one traffic light, Xpujil is the only place in the Río Bec region with basic services for tourists. Not a particularly pleasant town, it's a convenient place to stay if you don't have a car. If you do have a rental, it's worth staying outside of town and coming in to fill your gas tank.

Food

The restaurant selection in and around Xpujil is pretty slim. Hotel restaurants are the go-to in the area.

IN TOWN

Popular with tour groups, the hotel restaurant at **Mirador Maya** (Av. Calakmul s/n, tel. 983/871-6005, 7am-midnight daily, US$7-10) serves standard Mexican fare, including a tasty *pollo en mole*. Service can be apathetic.

A good, though slow, alternative, **Hotel Calakmul** (Av. Calakmul s/n, tel. 983/871-6029, 6am-midnight daily, US$6-10) has lots of breakfast dishes, plus the usual assortment of chicken, beef, and seafood dishes. Long wooden family-style tables pack customers in.

For one-stop grocery shopping, head to **Abarrotes Willy's** (Av. Calakmul s/n, 8am-10pm daily).

OUTSIDE OF TOWN

★ **Río Bec Dreams** (Carr. Escárcega-Chetumal Km. 141, no phone, www.riobecdreams.com, 7:30am-9pm daily, US$7-12.50) offers the area's best meals. The international menu includes an unexpected variety of dishes—think hummus with pita bread, Niçoise salad, chicken curry, and chili con carne; count on excellent preparation, hearty portions, and friendly service. Box breakfasts and lunches also are available with advance notice, and are highly recommended for a long day at the ruins.

Chicanná Ecovillage Resort (Carr. Escárcega-Chetumal Km. 144, tel. 983/871-6075, www.chicannaecovillageresort.com, 7am-10pm daily, US$8-20) has a reliable though overpriced restaurant, with a large international menu.

In Zoh Laguna, the **Museo Deocundo Acopa Lezama** (Calle Caobas at Calle Zapote, 5pm-10pm daily, US$6-12) doubles as a popular pizzeria. Other options in town include the recommended guesthouses: **Cabañas El Viajero** (Calle Caobas s/n, cell. tel. 983/101-6949, 7am-9pm), which offers full meals for just US$4; and the *palapa* restaurant at **Cabañas Mercedes** (Calle Zapote s/n, tel. 983/871-6029, 7am-9pm, US$6-7).

Accommodations

Xpujil town has some basic, affordable hotels, but the area's best lodging options are a few kilometers west of town, near the ruins on Highway 186. Another option is the rural town of Zoh Laguna, 9.5 kilometers (5.9 miles) north of Xpujil, which has two simple guesthouses. If you're planning to visit Calakmul, consider spending at least one night near the site.

IN TOWN

Facing the highway, **Hotel Calakmul** (Av. Calakmul s/n, tel. 983/871-6029, www.hotelcalakmul.com.mx, US$16 cabin with shared bath, US$28 s/d with a/c) offers two types of units: clean, comfortable motel rooms with air-conditioning, cable TV, and fuzzy blankets featuring unicorns and tigers; and tiny wood cabins with firm beds, mosquito nets, and fans that share bathrooms. There's a well-tended—and well-advertised—pool (it's the only one in town). An on-site restaurant plus Wi-Fi makes this a decent place to stay.

In a pinch, head to **Mirador Maya** (Av. Calakmul s/n, tel. 983/871-6005, www.hotelmiradormaya.com, US$22 s/d cabin, US$35 s/d cabin with a/c, US$28/40 s/d with a/c), which looks like a Girl Scout camp transplanted from an alpine lake to a grubby lot in Xpujil. The cabins themselves are dark with high A-frame ceilings, but have fairly large bathrooms, hot water, and a picket fence porch. Mosquito nets aren't provided, so double-check the screens. The main building has two air-conditioned motel rooms, which are significantly more comfortable, with satellite TV, tiled bathrooms, and decent beds, though there are no blankets if you turn on the air-conditioning. Wi-Fi is available.

OUTSIDE OF TOWN

★ **Río Bec Dreams** (Carr. Escárcega-Chetumal Km. 141, no phone, www.riobecdreams.com, US$58 s/d jungalow, US$68-78 s/d cabin) has four lovely

License, Please

There are numerous military and police checkpoints in southern Campeche, especially east of Xpujil near the border with Quintana Roo. You also may encounter them on the Carretera Fronteriza outside Palenque, and on coastal roads in the Costa Maya. Checkpoints are typically announced by orange pylons placed down the center lane and large signs flanked by uniformed soldiers or officers. Drug smugglers and illegal immigrants are the main targets, and most tourists are waved through. The etiquette is to roll through slowly, coming to a full stop only if the soldier or officer signals you to do so. If you are stopped, you may be asked for your passport, driver's license, or vehicle registration, and the trunk of your car may be searched, even the contents of your bags (though this is fairly rare). Friendly cooperation—and not having anything illegal—is the best way to get through these checkpoints as quickly as possible.

"jungalows"—bungalows in the jungle—with private bathrooms, good screens, and details like hand-painted sinks, high-thread-count linens, coffee machines, and purified water. There also are three spacious palapa-roofed cabins with screened-in porches that have equally charming decor and amenities. Well-maintained paths connect the units to a plunge pool and a great on-site restaurant. All in all, this is a very comfortable place to stay. The Canadian and British owners are extremely knowledgeable about the region, and give highly recommended tours of the area's ruins too. Wi-Fi is available. Look for the hotel's sign and flags near the bus stop 12 kilometers (7.4 miles) west of Xpujil. Cash only.

Across from the like-named ruins, **Chicanná Ecovillage Resort** (Carr. Escárcega-Chetumal Km. 144, tel. 983/871-6075, www.chicannaecovillageresort.com, US$70 s/d) offers one- and two-story stucco villas that sit on manicured grounds; rooms are spacious, with Maya-theme decor and modern amenities except air-conditioning. All have a terrace or balcony, plus there's an inviting pool. The hotel isn't perfect—some of the beds are saggy and the restaurant is overpriced—but given the challenges of running a high-end hotel in this neck of the woods, it's a real oasis. Some English is spoken. Wi-Fi is available in reception.

In Zoh Laguna, **Cabañas El Viajero** (Calle Caobas s/n, cell. tel. 983/101-6949, US$10/20 s/d with fan, US$25 s/d with a/c) has six rooms

with tile platform beds, cable TV, and hot-water bathrooms without toilet seats. More basic wooden *cabañas* have fans and large cement bathrooms, but there are wall gaps and no bed nets. Around the corner, the old-time stalwart **Cabañas Mercedes** (Calle Zapote s/n, tel. 983/114-9933, US$13/16 s/d with fan) offers one- and two-queen-bed *cabañas* with ceiling fans, thin beds, brightly painted walls, and well-screened windows trimmed with frilly curtains.

Information and Services

Xpujil Hospital Integral (Av. Siluituc btwn Calles Balakbal and Becán, tel. 983/871-6100) is a basic clinic with 24-hour emergency service. For meds, **Farmacia del Centro** (Av. Calakmul, tel. 983/871-6285, 24 hours) is next to the Abarrotes Willy's grocery store.

For cash, there's a **24-hour ATM** (Av. Halaltún btwn Calles Balakbal and Becán) outside of the Palacio Municipal (city hall), and another inside **Abarrotes Willy's** (Av. Calakmul s/n, 8am-10pm daily).

For Internet, **Internet Mundo Maya** (Av. Calakmul s/n, 8am-10:30pm Sun.-Thurs., 8am-5pm Fri., US$0.50/hour) is conveniently located next to the bus station.

In Zoh Laguna, the **Museo Deocundo Acopa Lezama** (Calle Caobas at Calle Zapote, approximately 5pm-10pm daily, free) houses an interesting collection of historical town photos while also doubling as a pizzeria and Internet café (US$0.75/hour).

Getting There and Around

Having a rental car is all but essential to enjoy the ruins here. Without one, you'll either spend a lot of time waiting for rides or a lot of money on taxi service, or both. Hitching is possible to and from Calakmul but not a sure thing.

BUS

The bus station is on the main drag in the center of town. You can catch buses east to Chetumal (US$7-9, 2 hours, 6:45pm and 8:45pm) and to Cancún (US$23-33, 7-8 hours, 11:45am and 8:45pm), with stops in Tulum (US$17-24, 4-5 hours) and Playa del Carmen (US$19-28, 6-7 hours). Westbound, there's service to Campeche (US$20, 4.5 hours, 12:45pm) and Escárcega (US$7-11, 2 hours, 5 departures daily 1:30am-11pm). *Colectivos* to Chetumal (US$7, 1.5 hours) also leave frequently from beside Abarrotes Willy's; if you're in a rush, you can throw down US$35-40 and commandeer the whole vehicle.

CAR

There are three gas stations to choose from—two as you head east from town and one just to the west.

TAXI

If you don't have a car, your best bet is to take a cab to the ruins. You can either call one from the **main taxi cooperative** (983/871-6101) or stop by the taxi stand next to the town's one traffic light. Round-trip transportation costs US$60-70 for 1-4 people to Calakmul and Balamkú or to Kohunlich and Dzibanché, or around US$30-40 for 1-4 people to Chicanná, Becán, and Xpujil.

Palenque

Highlights

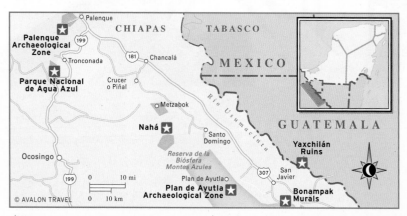

★ **Palenque Archaeological Zone:** One of the most important Maya sites, Palenque also happens to be among the most beautiful, with graceful structures and well-preserved carvings and hieroglyphics. And unlike so many other ruins, it's got a terrific museum too (page 435).

★ **Parque Nacional de Agua Azul:** Pictures don't do justice to this remarkable natural phenomenon: Luminescent blue water tumbles over a series of powerful waterfalls and gathers in calm clear pools, perfect for swimming. It's a great day trip from Palenque, but plan on going midweek—this place definitely draws a crowd (page 453).

★ **Nahá:** Deep in the rainforest, this Lacandón Maya village isn't easy to reach, but it's all the more rewarding when you do. Visitors sleep in simple cabins, explore pristine lakes and forest trails, and experience ancient Maya ceremonies, all in a welcoming but unadulterated atmosphere (page 455).

★ **Plan de Ayutla Archaeological Zone:** Climb to the tops of twin pyramids to discover wondrous semi-excavated temples, some with high peaked ceilings, others with ancient glyphs painted on their walls. Best of all, there's not a soul in sight (page 459).

★ **Bonampak Murals:** Inside a temple halfway up Bonampak's main staircase are some of the finest and best-preserved Maya murals yet discovered. In brilliant colors they tell of the ascension of a boy king, jungle warfare, and ritual bloodletting (page 466).

★ **Yaxchilán Ruins:** Perched on a leafy riverbank, Yaxchilán exudes a regal bearing, as if waiting assuredly for its glory days to return. When you're not admiring the gorgeous carvings and complex layout, keep an eye out for huge crocodiles sunning themselves on the riverbank and howler monkeys swinging in the trees (page 468).

Trrue, Palenque and the state of Chiapas are not technically part of the Yucatán Peninsula (in fact, they don't even share a border). But the two regions' history and culture are so deeply intertwined,

it's impossible to truly understand one without knowledge of the other.

The main connection is Mayan, of course, from pre-Hispanic times to the present. Much of what archaeologists know about the ancient Maya throughout Mesoamerica stems from work conducted at Palenque, from early advances in deciphering Maya writing to the discovery of the tomb of Lord Pakal. Palenque is also, quite simply, a masterpiece of Maya construction, a must-see for its elegant structures and artful inscriptions.

Palenque and the Yucatán are bound by modern Maya society as well. The Lacandón Maya of central Chiapas are direct descendants of Yucatec Maya who fled into the rainforest to escape Spanish conquest. Today they continue to speak Yucatec Maya, even as they've adapted to a vastly different environment and circumstances. And like the Yucatán, Palenque's marquee attraction is just the beginning of what a visitor can see and do

there. Popular day trips include visiting additional (and excellent) ruins like Yaxchilán and Bonampak, and a series of scenic waterfalls along the peculiarly turquoise Tulijá River; longer excursions include visiting remote Lacandón villages, nestled deep in the rainforest.

PLANNING YOUR TIME

It's worth budgeting a full day to visit the archaeological site at Palenque; although it isn't terribly big, it's a place many enjoying lingering over, and the on-site museum is highly recommended. The popular day trips from town—visiting Yaxchilán and Bonampak, or the waterfalls—each require a full day; a trip to the remote Lacandón villages requires at least two days and a night, preferably more. If time is short, there's a much more accessible Lacandón community near Bonampak ruins, but it is also significantly more commercialized.

Previous: The last leg of the trip to Yaxchilán ruins is by motorized canoe; Tropical vegetation surrounds the cabins at Misol-Há. **Above:** Palenque's tower is unique in Maya architecture.

Palenque

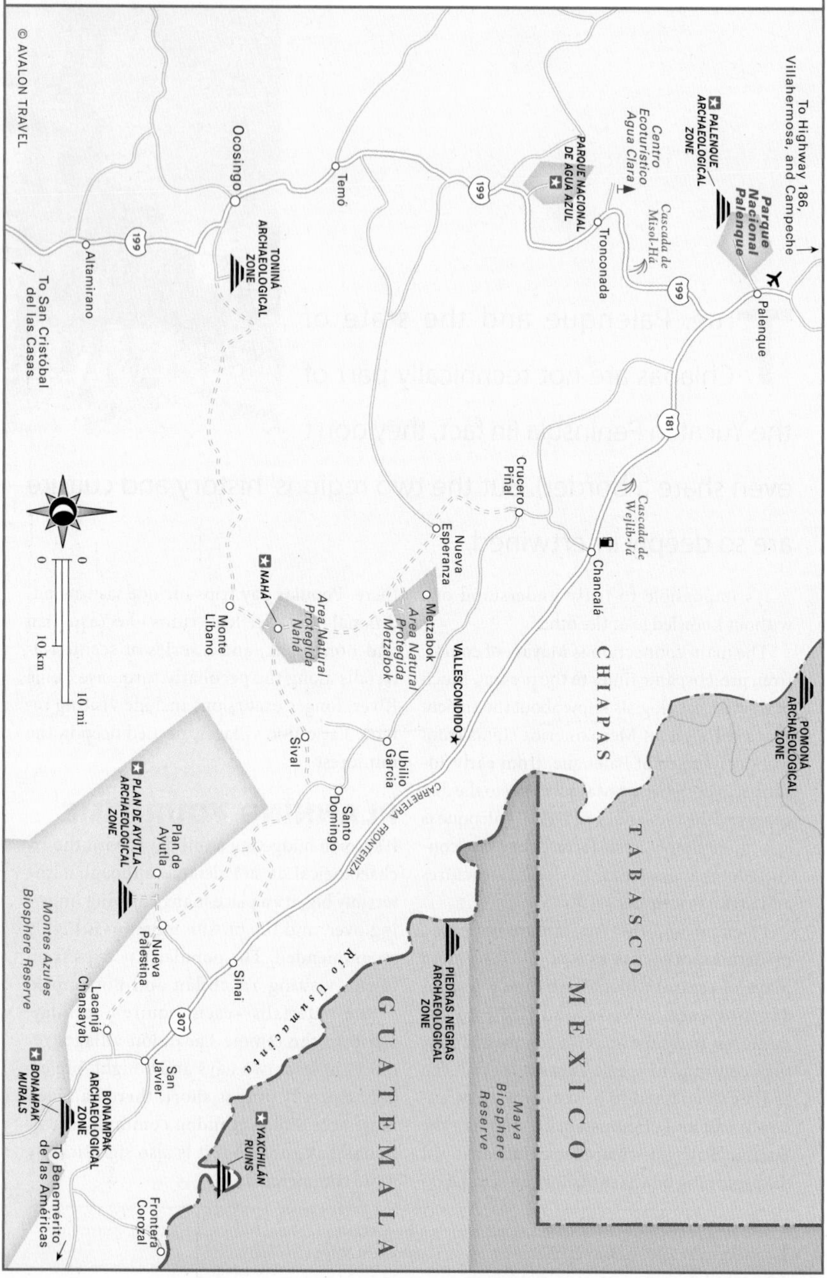

© AVALON TRAVEL

To Highway 186,
Villahermosa, and Campeche

PALENQUE
ARCHAEOLOGICAL
ZONE

Centro
Ecoturístico
Agua Clara

PARQUE NACIONAL
DE AGUA AZUL

199

Parque
Nacional
Palenque

Cascada de
Misol-Há

Troncanada

Palenque

199

181

Ocosingo

Temó

TONINÁ
ARCHAEOLOGICAL
ZONE

199

Altamirano

To San Cristóbal
del las Casas

Crucero
Piñal

Cascada de
Wejlib-Já

Chancalá

C H I A P A S

Nueva
Esperanza

Metzabok

Área Natural
Protegida
Metzabok

VALLESCONDIDO

NAHÁ

Área Natural
Protegida
Nahá

Monte
Líbano

Sival

Ubilio
García

Santo
Domingo

CARRETERA FRONTERIZA

POMONA
ARCHAEOLOGICAL
ZONE

T A B A S C O

M E X I C O

PLAN DE AYUTLA
ARCHAEOLOGICAL
ZONE

Plan de
Ayutla

Nueva
Palestina

Sinaí

Lacanjá
Chansayab

Montes Azules
Biosphere Reserve

307

San
Javier

BONAMPAK MURALS

BONAMPAK
ARCHAEOLOGICAL
ZONE

To Benemérito
de las Américas

Frontera
Corozal

YAXCHILÁN
RUINS

R í o   U s u m a c i n t a

PIEDRAS NEGRAS
ARCHAEOLOGICAL
ZONE

G U A T E M A L A

Maya
Biosphere
Reserve

0   10 km

0   10 mi

Palenque Archaeological Zone and Town

The town of Santo Domingo de Palenque, usually just called Palenque, is eight kilometers (5 miles) from the Palenque archaeological zone. The town itself is rather grubby and nondescript, but it bulges at the seams with tourists here to visit the ruins. Avenida Juárez is the main drag, where you'll find the bus terminal, tour agencies, and other services, plus a number of no-frills hotels. Many travelers find the leafy neighborhood of La Cañada and the hotels along the road to the ruins to be more pleasant spots to spend the night, though they cost a bit more. There's a small central plaza at one end of Avenida Juárez, and a large sculpture of a Maya warrior's head (and the turnoff to the ruins) at the other.

★ PALENQUE ARCHAEOLOGICAL ZONE

Palenque (8am-5pm daily, US$4) is a must-see on any itinerary of Maya ruins. It is a relatively small site—by no means as large as Chichén Itzá or Tikal—but considered by many to be the Mona Lisa of Maya ruins, with a particularly graceful design and construction. Its setting, on a lush green shelf at the edge of the Sierra de Chiapas forest, perfectly complements its elegant design and ornate carvings. And unlike many archaeological sites, Palenque's museum is terrific, with a small but exquisite collection of stone, ceramic, and stucco artifacts accompanied by well-written explanations.

History

The word Palenque, Spanish for fortification, is a rough translation of the Ch'ol Maya term Otolum (Strong Houses); that's how local residents described the mysterious stone ruins to Spanish explorers at the time of the conquest. The ancient city's true original name

was Lakam Ha, or Big Water, surely a reference to the many springs and streams found in the area. It was the capital of a city-state known as B'aak (Bone Kingdom).

Scholars have been able to decipher enough Maya glyphs to construct a reasonable genealogy of the Palenque kings, from the rule of Chaacal I (AD 501) to the demise of Kuk (AD 783). But it was the period from AD 615 to 702, during the glorious reigns of Pakal the Great and his eldest son, Kan Balam, that Palenque grew from a minor city to an important economic and political center.

Palenque's most distinguished leader, Pakal the Great (properly called K'inich Janaab' Pakal, or Great Sun Shield, but also referred to as Lord Pakal or Pakal II) was born in AD 603 and ascended to the throne in AD 615, when he was just 12 years old. Pakal lived to be 81 years old—remarkable for that time—and during his long rule expanded Palenque's influence throughout the western Maya lowlands. He built the Temple of the Inscriptions to house his own elaborate tomb, and commissioned many of the most notable structures and artwork in the palace.

Pakal was succeeded by his eldest son, Kan Balam (Serpent Jaguar, also written as Chan Balam), who was noteworthy for having six digits on his hands and feet. (To maintain the royal bloodline, Maya rulers often took relatives as wives, eventually leading to birth defects. Pakal himself had a clubfoot, and some archaeologists believe his mother and father were siblings. Likewise, Pakal may have married his sister, leading to his son's defects.) Kan Balam reigned for 18 years and built the temples of the Cross, Foliated Cross, and Sun to prove the preordination of his rule.

When Kan Balam died in AD 702, his younger brother, Kan Xul, took the reins of power. His rule was Palenque's apogee in

Palenque Archaeological Zone

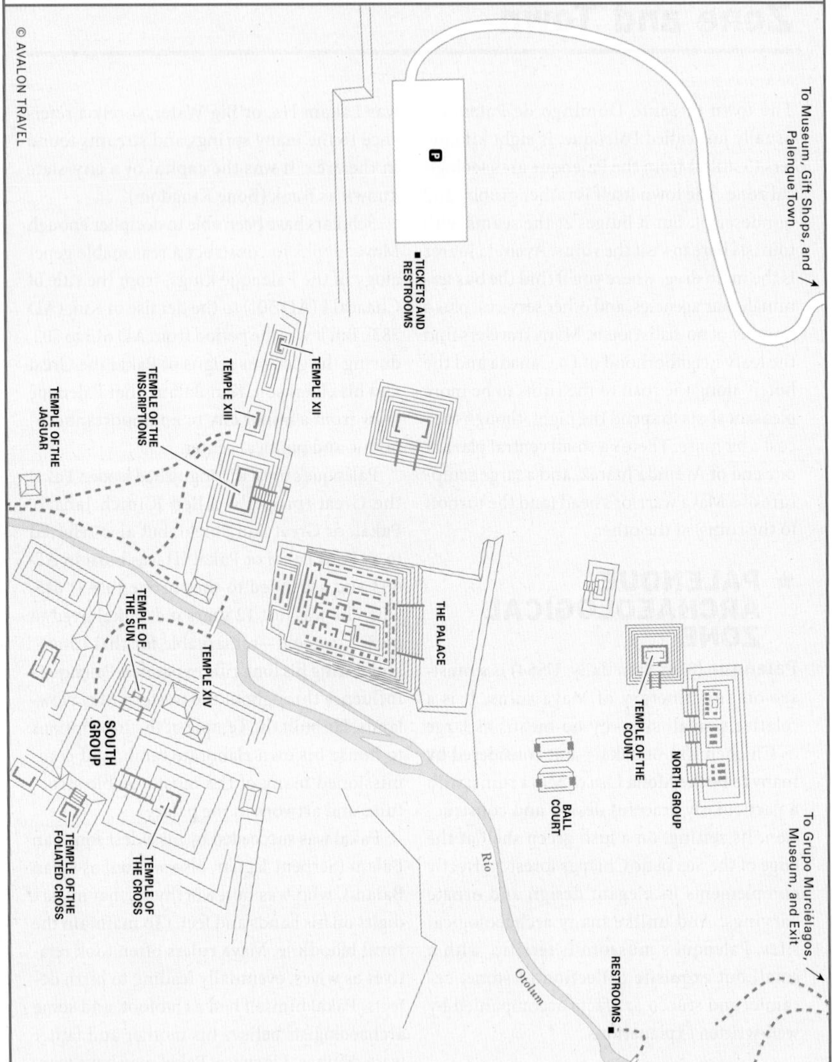

© AVALON TRAVEL

P

TICKETS AND
RESTROOMS

To Museum, Gift Shops, and
Palenque Town

TEMPLE OF THE
JAGUAR

TEMPLE OF THE
INSCRIPTIONS

TEMPLE XIII

TEMPLE XII

TEMPLE OF
THE SUN

TEMPLE XIV

SOUTH
GROUP

TEMPLE OF THE
FOLIATED CROSS

TEMPLE OF
THE CROSS

THE PALACE

TEMPLE OF THE
COUNT

NORTH GROUP

BALL
COURT

RESTROOMS

To Grupo Murciélagos,
Museum, and Exit

Río

Otulum

Baño de
la Reina

0   60 yds

0   60 m

terms of population—over 50,000 by some estimates—and political power, controlling a region that extended nearly from the Sierra Madre to the Gulf of Mexico. But the glory was not to last; in AD 711, Palenque attacked its longtime rival, Toniná, but was unexpectedly defeated by the much smaller kingdom. Palenque's king was captured and killed—described in victorious carvings and texts in Toniná—leaving Palenque in disarray, with no supreme ruler for over a decade. A new king named K'inich Akal Mo' Nab'—presumably a descendant of the Pakal dynasty, but it's uncertain—emerged in AD 722, and was succeeded by his son and grandson. Several new structures were commissioned under their reigns, and Palenque appeared to be on the rise once again. However, the historical record abruptly ends in AD 799, after which the city underwent a rapid and lasting decline, part of a widespread Maya collapse during that period.

The first detailed account of Palenque by Europeans was made by a Spanish army captain, Antonio del Río, who passed through in March 1785. (Two centuries earlier, Hernán Cortés came within a few dozen kilometers of the ruins but apparently never knew they were there.) Del Río drew maps and plans and eventually received a royal order to excavate the site for a year. But the Spaniard's "excavation" was amateur and brutish and led to the destruction of a number of structures. Captain del Río also broadcast wild and fantastic assumptions about the beginnings of the Maya. It wasn't long before Europeans envisioned Palenque as the lost city of Atlantis or a sister civilization to the ancient Egyptians. A true picture of Palenque didn't emerge until the mid-1800s, when the American diplomat John L. Stephens and English artist Frederick Catherwood visited the site and wrote and drew realistic and detailed accounts of what they saw.

For detailed reports and photos of current and past archaeological digs in Palenque, check out www.mesoweb.com/palenque.

Temples XII and XIII

Through the entrance you follow a short road and a few steps up to Palenque's main plaza. The first two temples on your right are Temple XII and XIII, and are known as Funerary Corridor for their deathly ornamentation and content.

Temple XII is also known as **Temple of the Skull,** so named for the stucco relief of a rabbit skull, visible at the base of one of

Palenque's palace

the pillars on the upper temple and probably representing a god of the underworld. (Unfortunately, you can't climb the stairs to get a better look.) In the 1990s, archaeologists uncovered a passageway leading from that same upper patio to a sarcophagus deep in the structure's interior, just as was famously discovered in the site's Temple of the Inscriptions. Inside the tomb were the remains of a leader, as yet unidentified, plus several other bodies, most likely the leader's servants. Alas, the passage and tomb are also off-limits to visitors.

To the left is **Temple XIII,** which also contains a recently discovered crypt. Dubbed the **Tomb of the Red Queen,** the three-room chamber has a large stone sarcophagus in which archaeologists discovered the remains of a woman. The woman had been interred with a jade mask, a rich collection of jade jewelry, pearls, obsidian knives, and bone needles, and was covered in cinnabar powder, a prized red pigment, hence the evocative name. The woman's identity hasn't been determined, thanks to the lack of inscriptions of any kind. Because of its similarities to the tomb of Pakal the Great, Palenque's most influential leader, archaeologists originally suspected the remains were of his mother; however, DNA tests found no commonalities between the skeletons. It is now believed the remains are of Pakal's wife, Tz'ak-bu Ajaw. The remains of the Red Queen were removed and reinterred in a different location to better preserve them. Visitors can see the tomb and sarcophagus (which is itself painted red) through a passageway near the bottom of the stairs. This is not the original entryway, however; it was created to study—and now showcase—the inner tomb. The original entry has not yet been discovered.

Temple of the Inscriptions

Just beyond Temple XIII is the **Temple of the Inscriptions,** a 24-meter-high (79-foot) pyramid and Palenque's most famous structure. Its name derives from the magnificent glyph-covered tablets found in the spacious temple at its summit, which tell the ancestral history of the Palenque rulers. It was toward the rear of that lofty gallery that Mexican archaeologist Alberto Ruz L'Huillier first uncovered, in 1949, a secret stairway cleverly hidden under a stone slab. The stairs were intentionally jammed with rubble and debris, clearly to prevent access to whatever lay beneath.

It took Ruz three years to excavate the stairway, which descended in several sections all the way to ground level. At the foot of the stairs, Ruz found another sealed passage, in front of which were clay dishes filled with red pigment, jade earplugs, beads, a large oblong pearl, and the skeletons of six sacrificial victims. A final large stone door was removed, and on June 15, 1952, Ruz made what many consider to be the greatest discovery of Maya archaeology: the untouched crypt of K'inich Janaab' Pakal, or Pakal the Great.

The centerpiece of the chamber is the massive sarcophagus, hewn from a single stone and topped by a flat four-meter-long (13-foot), five-ton slab of stone. The slab is beautifully carved with the figure of Pakal in death, surrounded by monsters, serpents, sun and shell signs, and many more glyphs that recount death and its passage. The walls of the chamber are decorated with various gods, from which scientists have deduced a tremendous amount about the Palencanos' theology.

Working slowly to preserve everything in its pristine state, Ruz didn't open the lid of the sarcophagus for six months. It then took a week of difficult work in the stifling, dust-choked room to finally lift the five-ton slab. On November 28, 1952, the scientists had their first peek inside. In the large rectangular sarcophagus they found another, body-shaped sarcophagus, within which was Pakal's skeleton, with precious jewelry and special accoutrements to accompany him on his journey into the next world. A jade mosaic mask covered the face, under which his teeth had been painted red. (The mask was exhibited at the Museo Nacional de Antropología in Mexico City until December 24, 1985, when it was stolen along with several other precious

Maya Funerary Rites

From ancient times to today, across cultures and continents, funeral rites have played an important role in virtually all human societies. The Maya were (and are) no exception, with elaborate practices and beliefs associated with death, laying the dead to rest, and what occurs in the afterlife. Although modern religion has extinguished many traditional practices, especially related to death and burial, remnants still remain in Maya communities of today.

Ancient Maya believed that most people who died had to travel through a dark and perilous underworld known as Xibalba. Those who died in battle, by sacrifice or suicide, or as infants were spared the trip, but everyone else needed supplies: Bodies were often buried with corn in their mouths (for nourishment), with a jade or other precious stone in their mouth (for currency), and with objects like whistles or figurines (for guidance or protection); a body might also be buried with a personal tool or possession, possibly to help identify the deceased in the afterlife. Early Maya tended to bury their dead in a fetal position or inside large urns; later, it was more common to extend the body with the head facing north or west.

Common people were usually buried in graves dug right into the floor of their homes. (In fact, looking for human remains beneath a structure is one way archaeologists determine if it was a residence or not.) Royalty were afforded far more elaborate rites, including the construction of massive vaults and pyramids in their honor. The tombs of royalty were often filled with precious items, including jade masks, fine pottery, elaborate tools and weapons, beads, jewelry, and platters of food and drink. In some cases, the nobleperson's attendants were sacrificed and buried at their sides. Remains have also been found in cenotes (sacrificial victims, most likely) and in caves (where ritual burials may have taken place).

Of course, failing to follow such rites can be a sign of social unrest. Archaeologists have discovered tombs filled with a jumble of various bodies, sometimes decapitated or mutilated—these may be unlucky royalty, killed by rivals or in peasant uprisings, whose haphazard burial would have been a deliberate insult.

Today, many Maya follow primarily Catholic (or evangelical Christian) mores, including burial in graveyards, overseen by church leaders. Yet certain traditional practices remain, including sacrificing animals, ritual cleansings, and the role of shamans, harkening back to pre-Hispanic times.

historical artifacts. The mask was recovered in an abandoned house in Acapulco in 1989, mostly undamaged.)

The excavation of the Temple of the Inscriptions forced a revision of archaeologists' conception and understanding of the ancient Maya. It was long believed that the pyramids had served a single function: to provide a platform for ceremonial temples and rituals to be closer to the heavens. But the discovery of Pakal's tomb revealed that pyramids were used as tombs for revered leaders as well, and numerous other such temple-crypts have since been discovered.

The Temple of the Inscriptions and the passageway to Pakal's tomb have been closed for several years, as erosion caused by hundreds of thousands of visitors became increasingly severe. In fact, access to major structures has been restricted at many Maya sites, including Uxmal, Chichén Itzá, and Tulum, with no sign of reopening.

El Panchán (The Palace)

Palenque's palace is one of the Maya world's most compelling and impressive complexes. Built atop a platform 10 meters (33 feet) high and covering an area larger than a city block, it is composed of 13 vaulted "houses," four enclosed patios, and three spacious underground arcades. It was built in phases over the course of nearly four centuries, and served as both residential quarters for the city's elite and as an exclusive administrative and ceremonial center. The iconic tower is unique in Maya architecture—only a handful of minor tower like structures even compare—and archaeologists have speculated that it was built to provide a ceremonial observation point of the winter solstice (December 22), when the sun appears to drop directly into the Temple of the Inscriptions. It may also have been used to make astronomical calculations, an important part of Maya religious rites, or was simply a watchtower. Unfortunately, the top of the tower had collapsed by the time it was rediscovered, so the structure's original height and appearance—and therefore function—could only be guessed from the pattern of rubble.

Two sunken patios on the palace's northern half are each dedicated to a different purpose. The Patio of the Captives, in the northeast corner, contains large stone panels depicting important prisoners captured in war; notice how each has his hand on the opposite shoulder, a common gesture of submission. In the northwest corner, the smaller Patio of Warrior Chiefs is believed to have served as a meeting place for military leaders. Pillars facing into this patio have remnants of stucco moldings depicting figures in elaborate militaristic regalia.

The southern half of the palace is more residential and ceremonial in nature, with enclosed rooms and small tidy patios. In the southwest corner, two holes marked with notched stones probably served as toilets, and are connected to a surprisingly sophisticated drainage and plumbing system built beneath the stone floors. It still works too—after heavy rain, maintenance workers sweep standing water into the holes to drain it out. Also look for a narrow flight of stairs leading down into a maze of underground rooms that likely served as royal sleeping quarters.

Dividing the southwest and southeast sections is the palace's most notable temple, the Casa de Ascensión de Poder (House of Enthronement). It was here that Palenque's supreme *ahau* (high lords or kings) were officially throned, likely in elaborate ceremonies attended by a small cadre of religious, military, and political leaders. On the western exterior wall is the Oval Tablet, which depicts the city's best-known ruler, Pakal the Great, receiving the insignias of power from his mother in AD 615. Also look for paintings of flowers on the same wall—they're originals.

Even the palace's exterior facades are fascinating, and easy to miss while exploring the labyrinthine interior. The West Gallery, atop a long bank of stairs facing the main plaza, has six stout pillars, four of which are still decorated with large stucco reliefs. A plaque at one end describes what's depicted there, including a man holding a serpent and dancing with a woman dressed in a traditional *huipil,* and an incarnation of Chaac, the god of rain, decapitating captives. The East Gallery has similarly elaborate relief carvings, including several circular frames that probably contained images of assorted gods (but which were destroyed or looted long ago). A vaulted archway leads back into the Patio of the Captives.

South Group

Across a small stream from the Temple of the Inscriptions and the palace, the South Group, also known as the Crosses Group, rises from an elevated bluff. The group contains three temples, all built during the reign of Kan Balam, the son and heir of Pakal the Great.

The largest and most prominent structure in the group is the **Temple of the Cross,** standing atop a nine-level pyramid-like base and crowned by a grand roof comb. Inside the upper structure—unfortunately you are not permitted to climb the stairs—is a shrine where archaeologists discovered a remarkable relief carving relating the ascension of Kan Balam to the throne and his place among a long line of rulers. In the carving, Kan Balam is pictured with his father, Pakal the Great, on either side of an ornate "world tree," a stylized cross symbolizing a sacred ceiba tree, which in Maya cosmology joins the corporal world to the mythic upper and lower realms. Pakal is dressed in funerary clothes, suggesting he has already died, and indeed the text describes Kan Balam visiting his deceased father to receive the accoutrements of power. The two figures are flanked by extensive hieroglyphic text telling of ancestors, gods, and former rulers, meant to legitimize Kan Balam's claim to power. Side panels depict Kan Balam wearing the full paraphernalia of royalty after his accession, as well as a wizened figure archaeologists classify as God-L, a lord of the underworld, shown smoking a cigar and wearing an owl-feather headdress. Archaeologists also discovered a major tomb at the base of the Temple of the Cross, containing the headless body of an official, perhaps the governor of a neighboring city, and hundreds of pieces of jade. They also found a collection of extremely fine ceramic figurines and incense burners, many of which are on display in the museum.

On the South Group's east side, a winding path leads up a steep incline to the **Temple of the Foliated Cross.** The structure is much deteriorated, but notable for the large keyhole-shaped niches in the corners of its upper facade. And like the Temple of the Sun, the enclosed gallery contains a terrific relief carving depicting Kan Balam assuming kingly power and duties from his deceased father, this time in the form of a bloodletting tool. The cross between them is adorned with corn leaves, hence the temple's name, symbolizing life and the birth of mankind, and a striking forward-facing deity representing rebirth.

The **Temple of the Sun** is the smallest of the three temples, but in many ways the best

preserved. Built atop a modest platform on the grouping's west side—climbing is prohibited here as well—its pillars, facade, and roof comb have elaborate stucco decoration. Although you can't see it from below, the temple contains yet another relief carving depicting Kan Balam and Pakal the Great at the former's enthronement. Instead of a cross between them, however, there is a disk like shield, held up by two kneeling deities and representing the sun and warfare.

The Ball Court and North Group

A large grassy plaza on the palace's north side is flanked by several structures. Closest to the palace is Palenque's ball court, notable for its I-shaped playing area and believed to have doubled as a site for ritual sacrifices. Perpendicular to the ball court is the North Group, made up of five temples, most quite deteriorated. Temple II is the best preserved, a sturdy stone structure crowning a terraced platform; at the foot of the stairs is a well-preserved stucco molding depicting Tláloc, a deity most likely introduced to the Maya by emissaries from the great central Mexican city of Teotihuacán, near present-day Mexico City. Finally, the Temple of the Count is a similarly

Many consider Palenque to be the most beautiful Maya archaeological zone.

stout structure atop a supporting pyramid, so-named for Jean-Frédéric Waldeck, an eccentric French count who lived there in the early 1830s and whose embellished drawings and wild speculations fostered lasting misconceptions of the Maya, especially regarding an alleged connection to ancient Egypt.

A well-marked path leads from the palace, past the ball court, and down a steep hillside to the main road. Along the way you'll pass the **Grupo Murciélagos** (Bats Group), a maze of low foundations that most likely served as elite residential quarters, and **Baño de la Reina** (Queen's Bath), a scenic waterfall and pool; swimming is no longer permitted, however. This is a good way to exit the ruins (assuming you came by *combi*), as the path emerges from the trees not far from Palenque's museum.

Museum

After you see the ruins, be sure to leave time to visit Palenque's **museum** (no phone, 8am-5pm Tues.-Sun.), which contains a truly incredible collection of stucco and stone artifacts found at Palenque, including ornate incense burners and perfectly preserved relief carvings and hieroglyphic panels, with excellent explanations in both Spanish and English. It's not a huge museum—an hour should suffice—but absolutely worth visiting, and for many people a highlight of their visit to Palenque. An exhibit called "The Tomb of Pakal" includes a life-size reproduction of the sarcophagus and elaborately carved lid, installed in an exact replica of the crypt made of Plexiglas so you can see through to appreciate its unique design. (It's more effective than it sounds.) Professionally produced videos and wall displays describe the tomb's discovery and explain the symbols and imagery found within.

Admission to the museum is included with admission to the ruins—be sure to hang on to your ticket! **Note:** Although the ruins are open daily, the museum is closed on Monday.

Practicalities

The archaeological site is open 8am-5pm daily (US$4, last entry at 4:30pm). The museum is open 8am-5pm Tuesday-Sunday only. Guides can be hired at the entrance to the ruins; official trained guides charge US$65 for a two-hour tour in English or in Spanish, or you can test your luck with one of the freelance guides hanging out near the entrance, who charge US$20-25 for a somewhat shorter tour, and who typically speak Spanish only.

Palenque is technically part of a national park, and there's a park-service gate a kilometer (0.6 mile) or so before reaching the ruins; admission is US$2 per person. There is parking at the ruins, although on busy days drivers end up parking well down the access road.

It is possible to enter the archaeological site at a smaller gate just past the museum, but from there it's a steep uphill walk to the main structures. A better idea, if you're arriving by *combi*, is to enter at the main gate and exit through the lower one, where it's just a short walk to the museum.

SIGHTS

Aluxes Ecoparque Palenque (Carr. Ruínas Km. 2.6, tel. 916/345-5180, www.ecoparque-palenque.com, 9am-4:45pm daily, US$6.25 adult, US$3.75 child) is an ecopark located partway between the Palenque town and the ruins. Though aimed at school groups, it makes for an interesting visit, with paths leading through several acres of protected forest. The ecopark helps support the foundation's animal rehabilitation program, so there's a chance to see jaguars, alligators, and other animals. Guided bird-watching and nighttime tours are also offered.

SHOPPING

Two **gift shops** (8am-5pm Tues.-Sun.) next to Palenque's **museum** have reasonably good selections of books and locally produced *artesanía*. Otherwise, shops line the main streets of Palenque selling postcards, T-shirts, and arts and crafts—good if you're running short on time or happen to be in the market for something a little kitschy.

Palenque Town

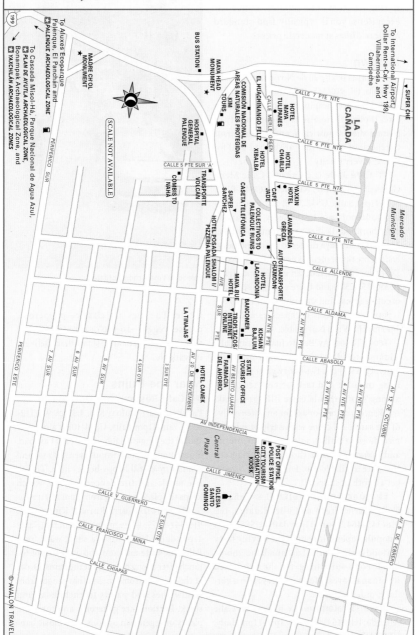

To International Airport,
Dollar Rent-a-Car, Hwy 199,
Villahermosa, and
Campeche

199
To Aluxes Ecoparque
Palenque, El Panchán and
+ PALENQUE ARCHAEOLOGICAL ZONE

To Cascada Misol-Há, Parque Nacional de Agua Azul,
Palenque, El Panchán and
+ PLAN DE AYUTLA ARCHAEOLOGICAL ZONE,
Bonampak Archaeological Zone, and
+ YAXCHILÁN ARCHAEOLOGICAL ZONES

MADRE CH'OL
MONUMENT

BUS STATION

MAYA HEAD
MONUMENT

KIM
TOURS

COMISIÓN NACIONAL DE
ÁREAS NATURALES PROTEGIDAS

HOSPITAL
GENERAL
PALENQUE

(SCALE NOT AVAILABLE)

EL HUACHINANGO FELIZ

HOTEL
MAYA
TULIPANES

CALLE MERLE GREEN

HOTEL
XIBALBA

CALLE 5 PTE SUR 'A'

TRANSPORTE
VOLCÁN

COMBIS TO
NAHÁ

SUPER
SÁNCHEZ

COLECTIVOS TO
PALENQUE RUINS

CASETA TELEFÓNICA

HOTEL POSADA SHALOM I/
PIZZERÍA PALENQUE

HOTEL
LACANDONIA

MAYA BUÉ
HOTEL

TROPI-TACOS/
INTERNET
ONLINE

LA TINAJAS

1 AVE
SUR
PTE

AV 20 DE NOVIEMBRE

BANCOMER

KICHAN
BAJLUM

FARMACIA
DEL AHORRO

HOTEL CANEK

SUPER CHÉ

LA
CAÑADA

CALLE 7 PTE NTE

CALLE 6 PTE NTE

HOTEL
CHABLIS

CALLE 5 PTE NTE

CAFÉ
JADE

YAXKIN
HOTEL

LAVANDERÍA
GRECIA

CALLE 4 PTE NTE

AUTOTRANSPORTE
CHAMOÁN

CALLE ALLENDE

CALLE ALDAMA

1 AV NTE PTE

2 AV NTE PTE

CALLE ABASOLO

AV BENITO JUÁREZ

STATE
TOURIST OFFICE

3 AV NTE PTE

4 AV NTE PTE

5 AV NTE PTE

Mercado
Municipal

AV 12 DE OCTUBRE

AV INDEPENDENCIA

Central
Plaza

CALLE JIMÉNEZ

IGLESIA
SANTO
DOMINGO

POST OFFICE
POLICE STATION
CITY TOURISM
INFORMATION
KIOSK

CALLE V GUERRERO

2 SUR OTE

3 SUR OTE

4 SUR OTE

5 AV SUR

6 AV SUR

7 AV SUR

PERIFÉRICO SUR

PERIFÉRICO ESTE

CALLE FRANCISCO J MINA

CALLE CHIAPAS

AV 5 DE FEBRERO

© AVALON TRAVEL

FOOD

Palenque has a large but not particularly inspiring selection of restaurants. With a few exceptions, you'll typically find standard Mexican dishes at moderate prices.

In Town

Las Tinajas (Calle 20 de Noviembre at Calle Abasolo, tel. 916/345-4970, 7am-11pm daily, US$5-12) serves heaping portions of Mexican fare, though there also is a good variety of pasta dishes, sandwiches, and salads. *Jarras* (pitchers) of fruit drinks are a good deal for the very, very thirsty.

★ **Café Jade** (La Cañada, Calle Merle Green at Calle 5 Pte. Nte., tel. 916/345-0102, 7am-11pm daily, US$2.75-6) is a modern indoor/outdoor café in the leafy La Cañada neighborhood. Dishes vary from traditional Mexican and Maya dishes to pasta and burgers; the breakfast menu is especially extensive. Daily specials include an entrée and drink (US$2.75-4.50), and there's a great selection of coffee drinks and smoothies too. This place is popular with locals, backpackers, and ladies who lunch. Wi-Fi is available.

Tropi Tacos (Av. Benito Juárez near Calle Aldama, tel. 916/345-0254, 7am-midnight daily, US$3-5) is a two-story eatery specializing in quick and tasty street tacos. Pick among standard à la carte fillings—steak, chicken, *al pastor*—or ask for an *ordén* of five of the same. All come with a trio of salsas—*pico de gallo* (mild), *salsa verde* (medium), and *tomate con chile* (hot). Vegetarian options are available too. For the best breeze, get a booth upstairs.

El Huachinago Feliz (La Cañada, Calle Merle Green at Calle Hidalgo, tel. 916/345-4642, 9am-11pm daily, US$5-10) is a popular open-air restaurant serving tasty seafood dishes in the La Cañada neighborhood. For a sure thing, try the fish baked in banana leaves. Meals are served in a verdant, quiet setting.

Pizzería Palenque (Av. Juárez near Calle Allende, tel. 916/345-0332, 1pm-11pm daily, US$8-15) offers decent pizza pies in a breezy

Palenque's main thoroughfare

locale. The pies are classic—pepperoni, cheese, veggie—so you're sure to find one that's appealing, or at least familiar. Delivery is available.

Near the Ruins

★ **Café Restaurante Don Mucho** (El Panchán, Carr. Ruínas Km. 4.5, tel. 916/112-8338, 7am-11pm daily, US$4-10) is a popular spot in the jungle neighborhood of El Panchán. Homemade pastas, wood-oven pizzas, and *comida típica* fill happy bellies here. There's live music and fire dancers nightly, which keeps the place hopping from 8pm to 11pm.

Mayabell (Carr. Ruínas Km. 6, tel. 916/341-6977, www.mayabell.com.mx, 7am-11pm daily, US$4-10) is a short walk from Palenque's site museum and a great spot for lunch after a long morning at the ruins. Order at the counter from a menu that ranges from sandwiches and pastas to enchiladas and steak. Portions are generous, and there are plenty of vegetarian options. Live music happens every night 8pm-10pm too.

Groceries

Super Che (Av. Velasco Suárez at Hwy. 199, no phone, 7am-10pm daily) is the name given to "small" Chedraui supermarkets, though by any other standard this is a huge store, with fruits, veggies, canned goods, nonperishables, and even an in-house bakery. For basic groceries closer to the center of town, try **Super Sánchez** (Av. Juárez near Av. 20 de Noviembre, no phone, 7am-10pm daily).

ACCOMMODATIONS

Hotels in Palenque proper tend to be barebones, adequate for a night or two but not especially charming. The advantage is having easy access to the bus terminal and tour agencies, plus banks, Internet, and restaurants. In the northwest corner of town, a neighborhood called **La Cañada** has better lodging options in a more serene setting, but is somewhat removed from the conveniences in town. There are also several pleasant mid- and high-end resorts on the road to the ruins, and a neighborhood called **El Panchán**, nestled in the forest, with (mostly) basic accommodations and a distinctly bohemian air. Getting back and forth to town can be somewhat inconvenient if you don't have a car, especially at night after *combi* service ends; then again, the laidback atmosphere may convince you there's not much reason to go into town anyway.

In Town
UNDER US$25

Hotel Canek (Av. 20 de Noviembre near Calle Abasolo, tel. 916/345-0150, www.hotelcanek.com, US$6.50 dorm, US$19 s/d, US$25-29 s/d with a/c) offers big clean rooms with hot-water bathrooms, cable TV, and Wi-Fi too. The dorm has twins and queen-size beds—no bunks here—and include sheets and towel. There are no lockers, but small safes at the reception desk are assigned to each guest to store their valuables. A rooftop palapa with hammocks and chairs makes for a breezy common space and arguably the best view in town.

Yaxkin Hostel (La Cañada, Calle Merle Green at Calle 5 Pte. Nte., tel. 916/345-0102, www.yaxkinhostels.com, US$9.75 dorm, US$22 s/d with shared bath, US$38-41 s/d with a/c) is a rambling place in a lovely garden setting. It's a place of contrasts: Some rooms are very pleasant and airy, while others are little more than a cement box with a window; bugs are an issue, but then again, it is basically in the jungle; the kitchen is small and poorly equipped but there's a great café onsite; and there's Wi-Fi but you can only get a signal in the reception area. Service, too, is hit or miss. If there's availability, take a look at a few rooms before deciding. In a pinch, it'll do.

Don't be put off by the shabby entrance at ★ **Hotel Posada Shalom I** (Av. Juárez btwn Calles Allende and Aldama, tel. 916/345-0944, www.hotelposadashalom.com, US$19 s/d, US$25 s/d with a/c). Inside, rooms are small but recently renovated with good beds, nice linens, plasma TVs, and modern bathrooms. Most have windows that open onto an interior hallway, so units are dark but quiet. Wi-Fi is available too. Best of all, it's conveniently located in the middle of town—close to shuttles, restaurants, and the central park.

US$25-50

★ **Hotel Xibalba** (La Cañada, Calle Merle Green 9, tel. 916/345-0411, www.hotelxibalba.com, US$47 s/d with a/c) is one of Palenque's best small hotels, with airy and well-maintained rooms in the leafy Cañada neighborhood. All units have air-conditioning, fans, Wi-Fi, and small flat-screen TVs; those in the main building are spacious with simple pastel decor. A second building has a high Maya-esque entryway and smaller rooms that have a certain coziness and isolation that some guests prefer. The upper floors in both buildings get better light and are worth requesting. There's a decent café on-site too.

Hotel Lacandonia (Calle Allende at Av. Hidalgo, tel. 916/345-0057, www.lacandonia-hotel.com, US$38 s with a/c, US$44 d with a/c) faces a busy and somewhat grubby street corner, but is surprisingly comfortable. Rooms have good mattresses, with iron-lattice headboards and matching vanities. All have air-conditioning, Wi-Fi, and cable TV, and those facing Avenida Hidalgo have small balconies as well. The upside to the location is that *combis* to the ruins are across the street, and those to Agua Azul/Misol-Há and Bonampak/Yaxchilán just around the corner.

Maya Rue Hotel (Calle Aldama btwn Av. Benito Juárez and Calle 5 de Mayo, tel. 916/345-0743, hotelmayarue@gmail.com, US$32 s/d with a/c) is a three-story walk-up hotel in the center of town. Rooms have an urban industrial feel—lots of cement, white-washed walls, and black-and-white photos—but are comfortable at heart, each with a good bed, hot-water bathroom, flat-screen TV, air-conditioning, and good Wi-Fi. If you don't have much luggage, ask for a room on the top floor, all of which have high ceilings and nice views of the surrounding hills.

OVER US$50

Hotel Maya Tulipanes (La Cañada, Calle Merle Green 6, tel. 916/345-0201, toll-free Mex. tel. 800/714-4710, www.mayatulipanes.com. mx, US$72 s/d with a/c) is a large, modern hotel in La Cañada. The 74 rooms are a bit plain Jane but perfectly comfortable. Amenities include air-conditioning, cable TV, in-room telephones, and Wi-Fi. The hotel also has a small pool, a restaurant, and parking. Tour groups often stay here, but it doesn't seem to affect the service independent guests receive, other than some hustle and bustle at breakfast.

Hotel Chablis (La Cañada, Calle Merle Green 7, tel. 916/345-0870, toll-free Mex. tel. 800/714-4710, www.hotelchablis.com, US$92 s/d with a/c) is a step up from the Maya Tulipanes (in fact, they're owned by the same company). It's a smaller hotel—51 rooms—and more luxe in style. Still, the amenities are the same: cable TV, air-conditioning, and Wi-Fi—even a small pool (with whirlpool tub) and a restaurant. It also caters to independent travelers, which may be important to some. It's a fine choice, budget permitting.

Near the Ruins
UNDER US$25

★ **Margarita and Ed** (El Panchán, Carr. Ruínas Km. 4.5, tel. 916/348-6990, US$17 s/d *cabañas*, US$20 s/d, US$32 s/d with a/c) is perfect for budget travelers who want a jungle setting but like modern comforts. Three brick buildings with wide verandas house the rooms; units are spotless, with gleaming tile floors, upgraded bathrooms, firm beds, and reliable fans or air-conditioning. They have niceties like flower bedspreads and buy-by-the-dozen paintings. A couple of rustic *cabañas* also are available near the entrance.

Jungle Palace (El Panchán, Carr. Ruínas Km. 4.5, tel. 916/101-7036, www.elpanchan. com, US$7.50/11 s/d with shared bath, US$14/16 s/d) is a *cabaña* hotel offering 18 basic units in the middle of the jungle neighborhood of El Panchán. Units are hit or miss: Some have gleaming tile floors and decent beds, while others have holes in the screens and paint chipping off the walls. Try to get one on the 2nd floor with a private porch—overall, these seem to be the pick of the litter. That, and during the rainy season the nearby river often overflows, flooding the ground-floor units.

Though its cabins are grim, **El Jaguar** (El Panchán, Carr. Ruínas Km. 4.5, tel. 916/101-7036, www.elpanchan.com, US$2 pp camping) is the only place to camp in El Panchán. If you have your own gear, head here. Be sure to wear your flips-flops in the shared bathrooms though—they need a serious scrub down.

US$25-50

If El Panchán isn't quite your scene but you'd like to stay nearby, **Kin Balam Cabañas** (Carr. Ruínas Km. 4.5, tel. 916/345-1826, www.kin-balam.com, US$29 s/d with shared bath, US$43-49 s/d) may be just the fix. Located just across the highway, it has several stand-alone cabins that open onto a well-tended pool. Each has a thatch roof, big windows with mosquito screens, firm beds, and good linens. Bathrooms, whether en suite or shared, are clean and have hot water. Though not as alluring as sleeping in the thick of the jungle, the *cabañas* are modern and comfortable, and the cleared grounds offer spectacular stargazing.

Mayabell (Carr. Ruínas Km. 6, tel. 916/341-6977, www.mayabell.com.mx, US$1.25-5 pp hammock, US$5 pp camping, US$19 trailer spot, US$19/25 s/d with shared bath, US$28/54 s/d, US$41/69 s/d with a/c, US$225 2-bdrm apartment with a/c) is a great option for budget and mid-range travelers. A string of open-air *palapas* serve for tents and hammocks, while RVs park on a grassy area near the entrance. *Cabañas* are surprisingly pleasant, with low comfortable beds, small shady patios, and a creek burbling nearby; ones with private bath are a bit more spacious and modern in style. There's a large swimming pool, which hits the spot on hot muggy days, and an affordable restaurant that has live music every night too.

OVER US$50

Chan-Kah Resort Village (Carr. Ruínas Km. 3, tel. 916/345-0762, www.chan-kah.com.mx, US$82 s/d with a/c, US$270 master suite with a/c) is made up of spacious casitas in a manicured jungle setting. They're somewhat dated in style but are comfortable nonetheless with large bathrooms, shaded patios with chairs, and amenities like strong air-conditioning, flat-screen TVs, and Wi-Fi. The resort's huge stone-bottom pool and restaurant-bar area are oddly out of place, but units at the rear of the property (Nos. 71 through 83) and a smaller second pool exude the natural peacefulness of the surroundings.

Piedra de Agua (Carr. Ruínas Km. 2.5, tel. 916/345-0842, www.palenque.piedradeagua.com, US$130 s/d) is an upscale hotel set on a small leafy property. Rooms are elegant with tropical wood furnishings, colorful folk art, and mosaic tile floors. Each has a spacious patio with a palapa roof and an outdoor tub. There's Wi-Fi in all the rooms though no air-conditioning—a deal breaker for some, especially considering the nightly rate (it also makes for a slightly musty smell). The grounds include a lap pool, spa, and a welcoming lounge near reception.

★ **Boutique Hotel Quinta Chanabnal** (Carr. Ruínas Km. 2.2, tel. 916/345-5320, www.quintachanabnal.com, US$177-330 suite with a/c, US$415 master suite with a/c) provides modern luxury in a setting designed to evoke ancient Maya times. There are just

Cozy screened cabins at Kin Balam give visitors the feeling of sleeping outdoors.

Detour: Comalcalco

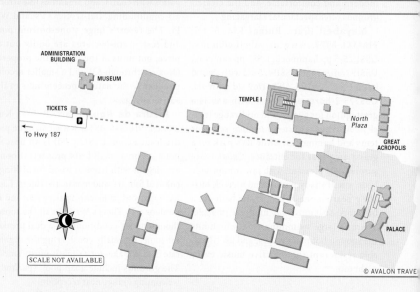

ADMINISTRATION BUILDING

MUSEUM

TICKETS

P

← To Hwy 187

TEMPLE I

North Plaza

GREAT ACROPOLIS

PALACE

SCALE NOT AVAILABLE

© AVALON TRAVE

Like Chiapas, the state of Tabasco is not technically part of the Yucatán Peninsula, but can make a quick and rewarding detour if you've got the time. An hour beyond the state capital, Villahermosa, are the Maya ruins of Comalcalco, notable for being constructed of adobe-like brick instead of stone. Comalcalco also is the heart of chocolate country—visiting working plantations to learn how cacao is grown and processed makes for a worthwhile day trip.

Comalcalco archaeological zone (8am-5pm daily, US$3.25) is located in a lush agricultural setting a short distance from a like-named town. The site's earliest structures date to around AD 250 and consist of large mounds made from dirt mixed with crushed oyster shells for strength

eight guest suites, all huge, with high ceilings, warm furnishings and colors, and amenities like in-room safes, stocked mini fridges, flatscreen TVs, and Wi-Fi. Meanwhile, the leafy grounds and common areas feature Maya images and design, from glyphs painted on the walls to impressive replicas of stone temples and reliefs—all designed by the Italian owner. A mosaic-tiled pool nestled in the forest is in itself a treat; hearing howler monkeys above and spotting green parrots flying past is almost magical. A guest-only restaurant, serving gourmet meals, is on-site too. Continental breakfast is included.

INFORMATION AND SERVICES
Tourist Information

The **state tourist office** (Av. Juárez at Abasolo, no phone, www.turismochiapas.gob.mx, 9am-9pm daily) hands out decent maps and can answer basic questions. The **city tourism office** (8am-3pm and 6pm-8pm Mon.-Fri.) has a tiny kiosk on the central plaza; service is hit or miss.

Emergency Services

The **Hospital General Palenque** (Av. Juárez s/n, tel. 916/345-0733, 24 hours) is one block east of the bus station. For meds, try and cohesion. Around AD 500-700, distinctive bricks were developed as an alternative to stone, which is rare and difficult to quarry in Tabasco's swampy environment. The bricks were made of a mixture of dirt and crushed oyster shells then fired in kilns; they were then used to cover and expand the earlier packed-dirt temples, and in some cases were incised with designs, including animals, humans, glyphs, and patterns.

Temple 1, the immense structure on the left as you walk in from the entrance, has the best remaining example of the stucco high relief that once covered most of the structures. Look for the animal figures along the pyramid's southeast corner as well as a molded skull about halfway up the main stairway. Opposite Temple 1, the **Great Acropolis** is 80 meters (262 feet) long and has a stucco mask of Kinich Ahau, the sun god. To the right, walk up a hill to the **palace,** which reveals a panoramic view of the countryside, including unexcavated mounds and a chocolate plantation in the distance.

A small but very interesting **museum** has several artifacts as well as a few human skeletons found by workers while excavating the site. The museum is at the entrance to the site.

About half a kilometer (0.3 mile) beyond the road to the ruins, **Hacienda Cholula** (Carr. Comalcalco-Paraíso, tel. 933/334-3815, fcholula_tabasco@yahoo.com.mx, 9am-5pm daily, US$3.50) offers an interesting hour-long guided tour of its cacao plantation. You'll stroll through the orchard, then visit the factory where the cacao seeds are processed and turned into chocolate candies.

Two blocks from the central plaza, **Hacienda La Luz** (Calle Leandro Rovirosa Wade s/n, tel. 999/337-1122, www.haciendalaluz.mx, US$5) offers a similar "choco tour" at 9am, 11am, 1pm, and 3pm Tuesday-Sunday. There's also a small museum with displays of antique machinery once used to process cacao seeds into chocolate. Chocolate making workshops are also offered.

PRACTICALITIES

In Villahermosa, **Autotransportes Comalli Plus** (Calle Reforma at Calle Bravo) and **Transportes Torruco** (Calle Reforma at Calle La Arboleda) provide *combi* service to and from Comalcalco; their terminals are a block apart near the ADO bus station. Vans run every 20 minutes 4:30am-9pm daily (US$2.25, 45 minutes).

To get to the ruins, take any bus headed north on Carretera Comalcalco-Paraíso (US$0.50, 10 minutes). From the highway drop-off, it's about a 10-minute walk to the entrance of the ruins. Hacienda Cholula is about 500 meters (0.3 mile) farther down the main road. A cab from town to either place costs about US$3-4.

Farmacia del Ahorro (Av. Juárez at Calle Abasolo, tel. 916/345-5014, 7am-10pm daily), which is well stocked. The **police station** (Av. Independencia near Hidalgo, tel. 916/345-0405, toll-free Mex. tel. 066, 24 hours) is in the Palacio Municipal.

Money

Located on Avenida Juárez, **Bancomer** (8:30am-4pm Mon.-Fri., 9am-4pm Sat.) and **Banamex** (9am-4pm Mon.-Fri.) have 24-hour ATMs. There's also a Santander ATM in the bus station (Carr. 199 at Av. Juárez).

Media and Communications

The **post office** (Av. Independencia at Calle Bravo) is open 8am-8pm Monday-Friday and 8am-noon Saturday. **Internet Online** (Av. Juárez btwn Calles Aldama and Abasolo, 7:30am-9:30pm daily) is one of myriad Internet cafés in town, charging US$1 per hour. In El Panchán, **Café Restaurante Don Mucho** has Wi-Fi for US$1.75 per hour; BYO tablet or laptop.

Laundry and Storage

Lavandería Grecia (Av. Hidalgo near Calle Allende, no phone, 7am-8pm daily) charges US$0.75 per kilo (2.2 pounds) for next-day service and US$1.25 for same-day service if you drop off your clothes early.

In El Panchán, **Jungle Palace Lavandería** (El Panchán, Carr. Ruínas Km. 4.5, 7am-3pm Mon.-Sat.) provides laundry service for US$2 per three kilograms (6.6 pounds).

There's **luggage storage** at the bus station (Hwy. 199 at Av. Juárez, tel. 916/345-1344, 7am-11pm daily) for US$0.40-1.25 per bag per hour.

GETTING THERE

Air

The tiny **Palenque International Airport** (PQM, Hwy. 199 Km. 24.5, tel. 916/345-1692) is located about five kilometers (3.1 miles) north of town. At the time of research, **Interjet** (toll-free Mex. tel. 800/011-2345, toll-free U.S. tel. 866/285-9525, www.interjet.com.mx) was the only airline with regularly scheduled flights into the airport, twice a week.

Bus

The **ADO bus terminal** (Hwy. 199 at Av. Juárez, tel. 916/345-1344) is located at the entrance town, across from the Maya Head monument. Destinations include:

- Campeche: US$24, 5-5.5 hours, 2:10am, 8am, 9pm, and 11pm

- Cancún: US$55-65, 12.5-13 hours, 12:25am, 8:50pm, 9:45pm, and 11:30pm

- Mérida: US$36, 7.5-8 hours, 2:10am, 8am, 9pm, and 11pm

- Mexico City: US$50, 14-15 hours, 6:30pm

- Villahermosa: US$9.50-11, 2.5 hours, 18 departures, 5am-10pm

- Villahermosa Airport: US$18, 2-2.5 hours, 5 departures, 7am-8:30pm

Combi

Autotransporte Chamoan (Av. Miguel Hidalgo btwn Calles 4 and Allende, cell. tel. 916/348-4684) provides *combi* service to destinations in the Río Usumacinta valley, including to Nueva Palestina (US$3.25, 2 hours), the Lacandón community of Lacanjá Chansayab

(US$7.50, 2.5 hours); Crucero Bonampak (US$7.50, 2.5 hours), where you can catch another *combi* to Bonampak ruins; and finally to Frontera Corozal (US$7.50, 3 hours), where you can catch boats to Yaxchilán ruins. *Combis* leave hourly from Palenque (8am-4pm daily) and Frontera Corozal (4am-4pm).

Car

Dollar Rent-a-Car (Palenque International Airport, Hwy. 199 Km. 24.5, cell. tel. 916/112-3811, toll-free Mex. tel. 800/365-1111, www.dollarmexico.com.mx, 8am-1pm and 3pm-6pm Mon.-Sat., 8am-4pm Sun.) is the only car rental agency in Palenque. (Otherwise, the nearest rental agency is in Villahermosa, 150 kilometers [93 miles] away.) To save yourself a trip to the airport, call in advance to have your rental delivered to your hotel. A couple of tips: Stick to driving during daylight hours; security has improved immensely in this area, but the occasional robbery does occur, almost always after dark. Also, fill your gas tank whenever you can, as gas stations are few and far between. In a pinch, look for roadside gasoline stands, which typically sell gas in semitransparent jugs of 5, 10, or 20 liters.

GETTING AROUND

Palenque town is easy to navigate on foot. To get to the ruins or accommodations outside of town, though, you'll either have to take a *colectivo* or a taxi.

Colectivo

Local shuttle companies provide *colectivo* service to and from the ruins (US$1.25, every 10-15 minutes, 6am-6pm daily). You can board at their terminals in town, at the Maya Head monument, or anywhere along the road to the ruins. Be aware that if you buy your ticket at the terminal, the cashier may try to sell you a round-trip ticket. Don't bother—this saves no money and no time; instead, it means you'll have to wait for a *colectivo* from that specific company when you're ready to leave.

Taxi

A taxi between town and the ruins costs around US$5. Within the town limit (the *periférico*), a cab ride costs US$2. To the airport, a cab ride is around US$7.50.

Travel Agencies

Lots of travel agencies want your business in this town. Prices vary according to the level of service: The least expensive typically include transport only—no guides or entrance fees. For more, the tour may include entrance fees, guide service, and even meals. Definitely ask what's included before booking. The most popular trips are to Misol-Há and Agua Azul (US$14-16 pp, noon-6:30pm); to Bonampak and Yaxchilán ruins (US$41-47 pp, 6am-7pm); and two-day excursions to Bonampak, Yaxchilán, and the Lacandón forest (US$82-85 pp, including meals and lodging). You can also do a combination trip, such as a morning tour of Palenque ruins followed by an afternoon at Misol-Há and Agua Azul (US$22 pp, 8am-6:30pm).

Tour operators also offer convenient "drop-off" tours so you don't have to backtrack to Palenque. These include spending the morning at Misol-Há and Agua Azul, then continuing to San Cristóbal de las Casas (US$22 pp); or, if you're headed to Guatemala, spending the day visiting Bonampak and Yaxchilán, spending the night near the border, and the next morning taking a 30-minute boat ride to Betel, Guatemala, where a shuttle takes you to Flores (US$85 pp, including all transport, meals, and lodging).

In town, **Kim Tours** (across from the bus station, Av. Juárez s/n, tel. 916/345-0336, www.kimtourspalenque.com, 9am-7pm daily) and **Kichan Bajlun** (Av. Juárez btwn Calles Aldama and Abasolo, tel. 916/345-2452, www.kichanbajlum.com, 7:30am-9pm daily) are reliable agencies. In El Panchán, **El Mono Blanco del Panchán** (El Panchán, Carr. Ruínas Km. 4.5, 7am-10pm daily) has a travel agency that books the same tours, at the same prices, as those offered in town. Look for it near the entrance to the neighborhood.

Along the Río Tulijá

There's no mistaking the Río Tulijá, a ribbon of luminescent turquoise water wending through farmland and dense tropical forest, visible from parts of Highway 199 between Palenque and Ocosingo. Known to local Maya as Yaks-Ha (Blue Water), the river was described by Chiapanecan poet Elva Macías as "a peacock dragging its watery tail," and you'd be forgiven if at first glance you thought it was the result of contamination or a mineral dissolved in the water. In fact, the water is not only clean but perfectly transparent, and the unusual color is the result of sunlight reflecting off the limestone riverbed. (For that reason, the effect isn't visible all year; during rainy season—roughly August-January—sediment washes into the river and turns the water a turbid brown.)

ORIENTATION

There are two especially impressive sights along the Río Tulijá: **Misol-Há** (a high beautiful waterfall) and **Agua Azul** (a series of powerful waterfalls). Both are reached by way of access roads (2-4 kilometers/1.2-2.5 miles long) that are well marked on Highway 199. Tour operators in Palenque offer popular and affordable tours to the falls, typically spending 30-60 minutes at Misol-Há and 2-3 hours at Agua Azul before returning to Palenque. You also can visit them independently, preferably by car, as there's little public transport along the access roads.

A third spot—a large, lovely pool called Agua Clara—used to be included on tours in this area. However, members of the local *ejido* (land cooperatives) have maintained roadblocks there for several years, charging an exorbitant fee for vehicles (especially tour vans) to pass. Eventually tour groups simply stopped going there; negotiations are said to be ongoing. Independent travelers may still encounter the roadblock; simply pay the asking fee and continue on. Ask tour operators in Palenque for the latest information.

CASCADA DE MISOL-HÁ

Maya for waterfall, **Misol-Há** (Hwy. 199 Km. 18, cell. tel. 555/151-3377, www.misol-ha.com, 7am-6pm daily, US$1.25 admission, US$0.75 toll) is definitely that, and a beautiful one, falling some 30 meters (98 feet) from an overhanging semicircular cliff down into a broad shimmering pool. The water doesn't appear blue here—the pool is too deep—but it's a gorgeous sight nonetheless, and fantastic for swimming, especially on hot afternoons. (Unfortunately, most tours stop here in the morning, before you've had a chance to get hot and sweaty!) There's a fairly deep cave on the far side, but getting there is the most memorable part—by way of a slippery path along the base of the cliff and behind the falls, buffeted by mist from the falling water.

Food and Accommodations

Misol-Há has a dozen wood *cabañas* (US$18-33 s/d, US$33-40 1- or 2-bdrm cabin with kitchenette) built in a stand of thick trees within earshot of the crashing waterfall. Surprisingly well outfitted, all have hot-water bathrooms, fans, and one or two queen beds; larger units have separate bedrooms, fully equipped kitchenettes, and dining areas. Best of all, you have the falls all to yourself in the early morning and late afternoon. The admission fee, but not the toll, is included in the rate.

A modern welcome center includes a large **restaurant** (7am-10pm daily, US$4-10), bathrooms, Wi-Fi, and parking. From there, it's just 50 meters (164 feet) to the falls.

Getting There

The turnoff to Misol-Há is about 21 kilometers (13 miles) south of Palenque, and the welcome center and falls are about 2 kilometers (1.2 miles) from the highway turnoff. To get here by *combi* from Palenque, **Transporte Volcán** (Av. Juárez at Calle 5a Pte. Sur A, no phone) provides service to and from the turnoff every 20 minutes 4am-6pm daily (US$1.85, 30 minutes). From the turnoff, it's about a 20-minute walk to the falls. All visitors, whether arriving by vehicle or foot, must pay a US$0.75 toll to use the road to the falls.

the impressive falls of Misol-Há

★ PARQUE NACIONAL DE AGUA AZUL

The churning cascades and serene pools of **Agua Azul National Park** (Hwy. 199 Km. 58, 7am-6pm daily, US$2.50) are reason enough to visit, but the blue-teal color of the water is what makes it especially impressive. The Tulijá is quite powerful here (having been joined upstream by another river, the Río Shumuljá) and tumbles down several kilometers of stair-stepped limestone, variously splintering and rejoining, and forming hundreds of waterfalls in the process. Between the falls—which range from just a few feet to several stories high—are pools of water where the water's teal hue can be appreciated. Several of the largest pools have been shored up to allow swimming and wading, and various *miradores* (vista points) afford fine views of the falls from above and below.

A wide paved path leads from the parking area up alongside the falls, with smaller trails leading to the observation points and designated swimming areas. Unfortunately, there are also myriad stalls crammed along the pathway, hawking food, T-shirts, artesanía, souvenirs, and more. The first several hundred meters have the most shops—also the largest falls and most accessible pools,

not coincidentally. However, even on busy days (it's a madhouse during Christmas and Semana Santa), the park's upper section remains much quieter and less crowded, and a number of scenic pools are great for cooling off. The upper section starts about a kilometer (0.6 mile) from the entrance, where the path turns to dirt. Even farther, about an hour's hike, is El Cañon (The Canyon), where the valley narrows and a number of additional falls are located.

Be cautious when swimming or wading in Agua Azul, as the current is deceptively strong in many places, even those that look placid. Drownings have occurred, and there are relatively few signs warning of the danger. There also are restroom and changing areas (US$0.75) available.

Food and Accommodations

There are several **mom-and-pop restaurants** (7am-7pm daily, US$3-8) along the path leading visitors past the different waterfalls and swimming areas. They sell basic Mexican eats—quesadillas, empanadas, tacos, etc.—and freshly made juices too.

Posada La Cascadita (tel. 916/111-6834, US$16 s/d) is a five-room motel about halfway up the waterfalls path. It's set in a clearing

Parque Nacional de Agua Azul has a series of frothy white waterfalls interrupted by tranquil turquoise pools.

behind a like-named restaurant. Rooms are clean and brightly painted; each has two decent beds, a fan, plus private bathroom (no toilet seats though). It's a perfectly comfortable, albeit no-frills, place to spend the night. (Best of all, you can enjoy the waterfalls after hours, with no tourists or vendors.) Look for the sign next to the wood building housing CONANP (Comisión Nacional de Áreas Naturales Protegidas), one of the only solid structures along the path of tchotchke stands and open-air restaurants.

If you have your own gear, there are 20 **campsites** (US$3.25 pp) alongside the river, near the parking lot as you enter the site. Most of the sites have cement floors and a palapa cover. Shared bathrooms are a bit grim, but will do for a night or two (wear flip-flops).

For availability, ask at nearby Cabañas Los Almendros.

Getting There

Agua Azul is located off Highway 199, about 60 kilometers (37 miles) south of Palenque. The entrance is about 4 kilometers (2.5 miles) down a windy road from a well-marked turn-off on the highway. To get here by combi from Palenque, **Transporte Volcán** (Av. Juárez at Calle 5a Pte. Sur A, no phone) provides service to and from the turnoff every 20 minutes 4am-6pm daily (US$2.50, 1-1.5 hours). Taxis (US$1.25) are often waiting at the turnoff to ferry passengers who arrive by *combi*; otherwise, it's an hour's walk down, and an even longer walk back up. **Note:** There are two tolls to use the road, each US$1 per vehicle.

Villages Along the Carretera Fronteriza

The Carretera Fronteriza (Border Highway) runs from Palenque southeast along the Río Usumacinta and the Guatemalan border to the town of Frontera Corozal; from there it loops down and west again, eventually reaching the city of Comitán in central Chiapas.

The first section, between Palenque and Frontera Corozal, is covered here, including a variety of villages, detours, and roadside attractions, roughly in the order you'd encounter them driving from Palenque. Some make for a quick stop, others an extended side trip; some have food and lodging, others do not.

A number of agencies in Palenque offer transportation through this region, hitting the major destinations, and are recommended for their convenience and reasonable prices. Alternatively, *colectivos* ply the Carretera Fronteriza throughout the day, and a rental car is very handy for places off the main road, as bus service to those areas can be very slow and unpredictable.

CASCADA WEJLIB-JÁ

Ch'ol Maya for falling water, **Wejlib-Já** (tel. 916/596-0303, 8am-7pm, US$1.50) is a large waterfall and swimming area that's popular among locals and a reasonably worthwhile stop for travelers looking for a place to cool off. From the parking area, a path follows the riverbank past several swimming holes and waterside picnic tables. (There's also a simple eatery near the entrance.) It's a short distance farther to the falls, a thick rope of water lumbering through a limestone notch and crashing into a large pool 20 meters (66 feet) below. There's a zipline (US$2.50) across it, and a path winds around to the bottom where you can swim as well. The falls are most powerful in September and October, at the end of the rainy season, but the water is clearer during the dry months.

Getting There

A huge sign marks the turnoff to Wejlib-Já, about 30 kilometers (19 miles) from Palenque.

From there, it's 500 meters (0.3 mile) by dirt road to the entrance.

VALLESCONDIDO

More a roadside business than a village, ★ **Vallescondido** (Carr. Fronteriza del Sur Km. 61, cell. tel. 916/100-0399, busil_h@hotmail.com) is arguably the best lodging and food between Palenque and Frontera Corozal. A fresh, well-prepared buffet breakfast (7am-10am daily, US$7.50 pp) includes eggs, beans, coffee and juice, fresh fruit, handmade tortillas, and more, served in an open-air dining area beneath a thick forest canopy. It can get crowded—lots of tour groups stop here on the way to Bonampak and Yaxchilán—but makes a great pit stop nonetheless. Lunch and dinner also are served upon request (US$12).

Vallescondido's handful of *cabañas* (US$85 s/d, US$113 for up to 5 guests) are on the opposite side of the highway, near the owners' ranch house. Fourteen units share several one-story buildings with long, wide porches. Each has good beds with luxurious linens, high sloped ceilings, and oversized windows; bathrooms are tucked behind attractive stone walls—truly a sight for sore eyes after a long day at the ruins. There's a beautiful creek that runs through the property; it's a popular spot for guests to cool off. Service is friendly, though there's no official reception desk. If the restaurant is closed, try knocking on the door of the main ranch house. Full breakfast is included in the rate.

Getting There

Vallescondido is located between Chancalá and the military checkpoint at the turnoff to Nueva Palestina. It's easy to spot if you pass before 10am, as there's always a collection of cars and tour buses pulled off along the shoulder in front. Otherwise, there are huge road signs as you approach, so you're sure not to miss it.

★ NAHÁ

The remote Lacandón village of Nahá is situated beside a beautiful lake and surrounded by hills covered in a lush rainforest. About 70 Lacandón Maya families live there, surviving in much the same way their predecessors did generations ago, mostly by fishing and small-scale farming. Tourists are a fairly new development here, and are received with cordial reserve befitting this resourceful and reclusive indigenous group. (Christian missionaries have not enjoyed a warm welcome, however.) As the Lacandón village of Lacanjá Chansayab, near the Bonampak ruins, grows exceedingly touristy, a small but steady number of travelers are making the far more difficult trip to Nahá (and the even smaller and less-visited sister village of Metzabok) in search of more "authentic" Lacandón culture and community.

Sights

Nahá is a good place to observe and learn about Lacandón culture and lifestyle, while Metzabok has somewhat richer outdoor opportunities. A highlight for many visitors is a ritual ceremony with **Don Antonio** (tel. 555/150-5953, US$12.50 pp, advance notice required), an octogenarian spiritual leader and successor to the great now-deceased Lacandón shaman Chan K'in Viejo. The village also has a modest **museum** (open by appointment, US$1.25) with photos and artifacts explaining Lacandón history, beliefs, and practices. Signage is in Spanish, with some English translations.

Centro Ecoturístico Nahá Canan K'ax (tel. 555/150-5953, www.nahaecoturismo.com, US$22-42 for up to 4 people) offers various nature outings. Excursions include a short (2 kilometers/1.2 miles) **nature trail** that leads from the village to Laguna Nahá. There it's possible to **canoe** on the lake, whose reed-filled shallows and curving tree-shaded banks offer fine bird-watching. There's also a **waterfall** within walking distance, and numerous opportunities to see and learn more about the rich rainforest flora, such as medicinal plants.

Food and Accommodations

Centro Ecoturístico Nahá Canan K'ax (tel. 555/150-5953, www.nahaecoturismo.com, US$19-28 s/d with shared bath, US$47-54 s/d) offers simple but surprisingly comfortable thatch-roofed cabins on a grassy plot. Each has one or two decent beds (including a few king-size ones), mosquito nets, colorful linens, and 24-hour electricity. There are hooks for hammocks too. Reservations are recommended. There also is space for camping (US$4 pp), provided you bring your own gear.

A small *comedor* (US$3.50-6) serves traditional Lacandón and Mexican meals alongside a gurgling creek.

Getting There

COMBI

Transportes Pajchiltic (Calle 3 Sur Ote. near Calle 5 Pte. Sur, US$3.75, 4 hours) provides daily combi (public van) service from Palenque to Nahá with seven departures 9:30am-1pm. The return is less frequent, departing Nahá at 1am and 11am. Be sure to buy your ticket in advance and arrive early to claim a seat; combis fill up fast. Also keep in mind that departure and arrival times are estimates at best, and some combis are canceled altogether—plan accordingly.

CAR

Driving to Nahá on your own is a difficult but not impossible task, and affords more flexibility to come and go. A truck is definitely preferable, but it's doable in a midsize rental car as long as the road is dry. Whatever you're driving, be sure your tank is full and you have a spare tire, and leave early to have plenty of daylight.

Nahá is about 100 kilometers (62 miles) from Palenque. To get there, head east on Carretera Fronteriza del Sur for 44 kilometers (27 miles) to the town of La Reforma. Turn right and continue another 14 kilometers (8.7 miles) to an intersection known as Crucero Piñal, where a sign directs you to the right again. The road is paved to there and for another 3.5 kilometers (2 miles) beyond, before turning to gravel and eventually dirt. In the village of Piedrón (3.5 kilometers/2 miles after the pavement ends), continue straight to the fork; from there the road is easy to follow but increasingly rough, passing through small settlements and the town of Nueva Esperanza. Forty kilometers (25 miles) from La Reforma is a well-marked turnoff to Metzabok (6 kilometers/3.7 miles); it's another 18 rutted kilometers (11 miles) to reach Nahá. Budget at least three hours for the trip.

METZABOK

Metzabok is a quiet Lacandón community of just 20 families, who live in simple wood homes in a region of numerous lakes and waterways. The community is situated on the edge of **Laguna Tzibana**, whose name means "painted house" in Lacandón Maya, and is most likely a reference to prehistoric paintings visible along the lake's edge. (The word Metzabok comes from the god of the Maya ball game, though it's unclear why the name was used here.) Laguna Tzibana is connected by a natural canal to Laguna Metzabok, a much larger lake and the source of several of the rainforest's streams and rivers. The entire region is protected as part of a federal nature reserve, and is home to a rich array of plants, birds, and mammals.

Metzabok's residents are less accustomed to outsiders and generally more reserved than Nahá's, making it harder (but not impossible) to experience Lacandón life and culture. By the same token, the surrounding rainforest and waterways are even more pristine, and excursions longer and more varied.

There are no public telephones, Internet, or other services in Metzabok, and cabins and meal service are available with advance notice only. The tourism contact person in Metzabok is **Enrique Valenzuela** (tel. 916/345-0967); alternatively, visit the Palenque office of the **Comisión Nacional de Áreas Naturales Protegidas** (National Commission of Protected Natural Areas, La Cañada, Prolongación Av. Juárez 1085, tel. 916/345-0967, metzabok_05@yahoo.com.

mx, 9am-6pm Mon.-Fri.), which oversees the reserve and tourism there.

Sights

Since it's surrounded by water, it's no surprise that the best way to enjoy Metzabok's sights is by boat. Local men and boys give paddling tours, whose length and price depends on what you see and how many people are in the group.

Basic tours (US$25-40, 1.5-3 hours) typically begin by paddling across Laguna Tzibana to a set of red *pinturas rupestras* (prehistoric pictograms) on a sheer stone wall right on the edge of the lake. Though streaked and faded, various designs are discernible, including handprints, deities, birds, and monkeys. Nearby, a small **cave** has a clutch of ceremonial artifacts, including incense holders, urns, and even a human skull, though it's unclear how old they are.

A short paddle from the paintings is an **unexcavated archaeological site,** also near the water's edge; very little is known about the history or origins of the site, though it's quite extensive, including numerous mounds and foundations and at least one large pyramid-like structure. The thick forest cover makes it difficult to appreciate, but clambering over and around the tree cover also adds to the appeal and mystery of this ancient site.

Looming over Laguna Tzibana is a high round **butte;** tours often include climbing a winding trail to the top, where a *mirador* (vista point) offers all-embracing views of the lagoons and verdant forest beyond.

Longer excursions (US$60-80, 5 hours) include all of the above, plus paddling into **Laguna Metzabok,** where there is another set of prehistoric paintings (in multiple colors), a large cave, and additional opportunities for short walks in the forest.

Food and Accommodations

Near the entrance of town, several small thatched-roof *cabañas* (tel. 916/345-0967, US$38) are available for rent, each with two queen beds, hammock hooks, and private bathroom. They're reasonably comfortable, though far from luxurious—don't be startled by insects or even the occasional mouse, as the units are shuttered between visitors, sometimes for long periods of time. Advance notice is required to be sure the key is available and the cabins tidied up.

There are no restaurants in town, but **home-cooked meals** (US$3-6) can be

Ancient pictograms in Metzabok show human and animal figures.

prepared by a local family or community member. As with the cabins, advance notice is required to allow time to buy necessary supplies.

Getting There
COMBI

There is no reliable combi service to Metzabok. Combis to Nahá from Palenque typically drop off passengers at the turnoff, which is about six hilly kilometers (3.7 miles) from town; if there are enough people headed to Metzabok, though, the driver will take a detour to town. To return to Palenque, travelers need to be at the Metzabok turnoff at midnight or 10am to catch the combi from Nahá—not a good plan, especially in the middle of the night. A better option is to take an inbound combi to Nahá (seven combis pass the turnoff between 12:30pm and 4:30pm) and spend some time there before catching a bus back to Palenque. That way, if the bus is late or canceled, you're in town instead of at a lonely crossroads.

CAR

Metzabok is some 80 kilometers (50 miles) from Palenque, half by dirt road. To get there, head east on Carretera Fronteriza del Sur for 44 kilometers (27 miles) to the town of La Reforma. Turn right and continue another 14 kilometers (8.7 miles) to an intersection known as Crucero Piñal, where a sign directs you to the right again. The road is paved to there and for another 3.5 kilometers (2 miles) beyond, before turning to gravel and eventually dirt. In the village of Piedrón (3.5 kilometers/2 miles after the pavement ends), continue straight to the fork; from there the road is easy to follow but increasingly rough, passing through small settlements and the town of Nueva Esperanza. Forty kilometers (25 miles) from La Reforma is a well-marked turnoff to Metzabok (6 kilometers/3.7 miles). Budget at least two hours for the trip.

NUEVA PALESTINA

Wide dusty streets and an unusually large central square make this Tzeltal Maya village seem even sleepier than it already is. The best reason to make a detour to Nueva Palestina, located 11 kilometers (6.8 miles) south of the main highway by paved road, is to visit Plan de Ayutla archaeological zone, a fascinating and little-visited site that researchers believe may be the remains of a long-sought Classic-era city. Other local sights, including a large natural swimming hole and a frothing waterfall, wouldn't really merit a special trip themselves, but can be nice places to cool off after visiting the ruins.

Nueva Palestina has limited services. You'll find a handful of shops, including mini-marts, a pharmacy, and an Internet café, around the main square and on the wide avenues leading into and away from town.

Sights
POZA PO'OP CHAN

As if the English connotation weren't concerning enough, Po'op Chan is Tzeltal Maya for Serpent in the Water—not the most enticing name for a swimming hole! Nevertheless, this large aqua-blue *poza* (pool) makes for a pleasant and cooling swim, and at 70 meters (230 feet) across is even big enough to navigate by kayak. A platform at the downstream end of the pool makes getting in easy, and there are several tables along the bank for having a picnic lunch.

Poza Po'op Chan is located in the rear of **Campamento Po'op Chan** (cell. tel. 555/004-7135, campamentopoopchan@yahoo. com, 8:30am-6pm daily), which charges US$1.25 admission and rents inflatable kayaks for US$2 per hour. A trail connects Po'op Chan and Cascada Las Golondrinas, a mild and pleasant walk of about three kilometers (1.9 miles).

CASCADA LAS GOLONDRINAS (CH'EN ULICH)

This sloping multipart falls gets its name— Swallows Waterfall—from a cave behind the main curtain of water that's a favorite nesting area for the loud, energetic birds. A low wooden footbridge extends across the river at the foot of the main cascade, making for a cool and misty vista point. Several small pools are popular for swimming and wading. At the entrance are several *palapa* umbrellas with small tables beneath them, plus bathrooms and a modest eatery.

The turnoff to the falls is about two kilometers (1.2 miles) north of Nueva Palestina (before entering town, if you're coming from the highway); from there it's another kilometer (0.6 mile) down a dirt road to the parking area and entrance. You can also walk to the falls on a trail from **Campamento Po'op Chan** (tel. 555/004-7135, campamentopoopchan@ yahoo.com), about three kilometers (1.9 miles) each way. Admission is US$1.25, and it's open 8:30am-6pm daily.

SENDERO RÍO CEDRO

For a more challenging excursion, Sendero Río Cedro (Cedar River Trail) connects Nueva Palestina to the Lacandón village of Lacanjá Chansayab, a 6-8-hour hike that ranges from cornfields to pristine rainforest of the Montes Azules Biosphere Reserve, passes waterfalls and massive ceiba trees, and heads across numerous waterways. **Camping** is possible at Campamento Río Cedro, a small Lacandón settlement about two hours from Nueva Palestina, where local guides lead short side trips into the forest and to nearby lagoons. From there to Lacanjá Chansayab is another 4-6 hours, mostly through dense rainforest and across the namesake Río Cedro. The trail splits and fades in numerous places, making a private guide all but essential. Consider hiring a guide for the whole trip; ask for recommendations in one of the lodges in Nueva Palestina or Lacanjá Chansayab.

★ PLAN DE AYUTLA ARCHAEOLOGICAL ZONE

For all the attention paid to must-see archaeological sites like Palenque and Yaxchilán, the **ruins of Plan de Ayutla** rank as one of the most fascinating and memorable in the region and the state. Seven kilometers (4.3 miles) outside Nueva Palestina and way off the beaten path, the ruins consist of twin pyramids ensconced in trees and vegetation and crowned by a complex of remarkably well-preserved structures that are a thrill to explore and clamber about. What's more, there is growing evidence that these are the remains of the ancient Maya city of Sak Tz'i', whose location has been one of the enduring archaeological mysteries of the Río Usumacinta and Lacandón region.

For decades, archaeologists have known of Sak Tz'i' (Tzeltal Maya for White Dog) from inscriptions at Piedras Negras and Bonampak, but could never find the city's location or remains. The city seems to have played the role of ancient swing voter (or "catalyzing agent" in archaeological parlance), never a major player itself, yet capable of tipping the balance of power among the dominant cities through strategic alliances. This role is suggested in part by military defeats at the hands of various rivals, including Piedras Negras in AD 628, Yaxchilán and Bonampak in AD 726—possibly the battle portrayed in Bonampak's famous murals—and Toniná even later. But Sak Tz'i' may have had the last laugh: As the major powers collapsed one by one around the turn of the 9th century, Sak Tz'i' held on until at least AD 864, making it one of the last significant Maya cities to fall.

The buildings atop the pyramid on the left (as you enter the site) are larger and more elaborate, including several multiroom "palace structures," with original stucco and paint still visible, and two temples with stunning 10-meter (33-foot) vaulted ceilings. Together they form a grand multilevel complex that probably served as residential quarters for the city's elite, and today makes for fun exploring. The structures on the other pyramid are smaller—probably related to administrative functions—but no less impressive. In particular, a small but artful building dubbed Temple of the Inscription has faint hieroglyphic text on two sides, while a nearby structure has a distinctive temple-within-a-temple design, similar to structures found at Palenque.

Several plazas occupy the space between the acropolises and contain various structures. One, designated Structure 39, is a ball court—at 65 meters (213 feet) long, it's the largest ball court in the region, even bigger than the ones at Palenque and Toniná. Archaeologists have also uncovered an ancient theater, complete with bleacher-style seating, and, most remarkably, what appears to be a royal bath, complete with drainage and ceramic water basins. Baths are extremely rare in Mesoamerican archaeology—in Mexico, only three others have been identified (two of those are also in Chiapas, at Palenque and Toniná, while the third is at Teotihuacán, near Mexico City). There's clearly much more to be learned and excavated at Plan de Ayutla; the city covered around 24 hectares (60 acres) and contains over 70 structures.

To get to the ruins, continue on the main road past Nueva Palestina for 4.25 kilometers (2.6 miles), looking for a smaller unmarked road just before a bridge and curve. Turn left there and go another 3 kilometers (1.9 miles) to where the road makes a curious S-curve beneath a stand of trees—there are no signs, but you can't miss the twin pyramids looming on either side of the road. The archaeological site is technically on private property, and you may be asked to pay an admission fee of US$2.25 per person.

Food and Accommodations

Campamento Po'op Chan (cell. tel. 555/004-7135, campamentopoopchan@ yahoo.com, US$15 pp with shared bath) has simple wood cabins built on stilts overlooking a small stream, utilizing so-so shared toilets and showers. Cabins are reasonably clean and comfortable, each with two double beds, a patio, and mosquito screens for walls. Large holes in the screens—not to mention gaps in the floorboards—make insect repellent a good idea, especially in the rainy/buggy season.

The *campamento* receives mostly groups, which typically bring their own food supplies.

Ask at reception about arranging meals at Po'op Chan; otherwise, there are several simple eateries in town.

Getting There

The turnoff to Nueva Palestina is at Kilometer 107, right where a major military checkpoint is located. From there, it's 11 kilometers (6.8 miles) into town, all paved. The road turns to dirt on the opposite side of town.

Autotransporte Chamoan (in Palenque, Av. Miguel Hidalgo btwn Calles 4 and Allende, cell. tel. 916/348-4684) provides daily *combi* service from Palenque to Nuevo Palestina (US$3.25, 2 hours) at 11:30am and 12:30pm. To return, *combis* leave the small terminal facing the main square at 4am and 5am. A taxi from the central plaza to Campamento Po'op Chan (or returning from the *campamento* to town) is US$2.50. Or take a taxi to the highway turnoff (US$4), where you can flag down a *combi* headed either direction.

LACANJÁ CHANSAYAB

For many years, the Lacandón village of Lacanjá Chansayab was a true off-the-beaten-path destination—an adventuresome jaunt into the *selva Lacandona* (Lacandón jungle) that was occasionally added to still-nascent tours of Yaxchilán and Bonampak. How things have changed. Today, Lacanjá Chansayab more closely resembles a summer camp than it does an indigenous village, with virtually every family engaged in tourism, mainly in the form of cookie-cutter *campamentos* (rustic lodging) and tours along well-worn forest trails. Competition seems to have quickly overpowered most sense of community spirit among local residents. A visit here can still be rewarding—the rainforest remains impressive, and nighttime is quiet and reflective—but it's not the sublime eco-cultural encounter many expect.

Sights and Activities

Every *campamento* offers **guided walks,** or *caminatas,* through the rainforest to nearby sights, typically lasting 3-4 hours and costing

US$16-30 (up to 10 people). Popular excursions include **Ruínas Lacanjá,** a minimally excavated archaeological site ensconced in lush rainforest, with a small main temple with traces of the original red paint still visible and several inscribed panels and stelae; and **Cascadas Las Golondrinas,** a scenic waterfall made up of four different cascades pouring over a long cliff. The latter is easy enough to reach on your own, following a 2.5-kilometer (1.5-mile) trail accessed through Parador Sak Nok' (US$2.25 pp).

Level II to Level IV **rafting trips** (US$45-52 pp) down the Río Lacanjá also are offered by **Campamento Río Lacanjá** (tel. 967/631-7498, toll-free Mex. tel. 800/397-5072, www.ecochiapas.com/lacanja) and **Topche Ecolodge** (no phone, www.ecolodgetopche.com). Most trips include a two-hour hike back to town, with stops at Lacanjá ruins and Cascadas **Las Golondrinas**.

Food

All the *campamentos* have small **restaurants** (7am-9pm daily), which are open to guests and nonguests alike. All serve standard Mexican meals at moderate prices (US$4-6), typically in open-air dining rooms.

Accommodations

★ **Campamento Río Lacanjá** (tel. 967/631-7498, toll-free Mex. tel. 800/397-5072, www.ecochiapas.com/lacanja, US$32/38 s/d with shared bath, US$50/56 s/d) is the most atmospheric of the *campamentos* in Lacanjá Chansayab. The complex includes 13 simple wood cabins with mosquito nets over the beds and small porches with hammocks, built in a shady grove alongside a small river. Spotless bathrooms and showers are in a central building. To get here, turn left at the village center and continue to the end of the road. There's an open-air restaurant on-site too.

Topche Ecolodge (no phone, www.ecolodgetopche.com, US$28 s/d with shared bath, US$38 s/d), 0.5 kilometer (0.3 mile) west of the main intersection, is run by the amiable Don Enrique Chankin Paniagua and family. The shared-bath units are cheap but pretty grim, with plywood walls and grubby cement floors. The private units are more appealing, with tile floors and high sloped ceilings. The family operates a pleasant restaurant adjacent to the cabins. Wi-Fi (US$2/hour) is available in common areas too.

Campamento Ya'aj Che (tel. 934/115-9211, campamento_yaajche@hotmail.com, US$9 pp with shared bath, US$30/42 s/d),

Simple family-style dining is the norm in Lacanjá Chansayab.

just south of the main intersection, has simple wood cabins with corrugated metal roofs and shared bathrooms located within earshot of a gurgling stream. Boxy private units are more comfortable, with private bathrooms and tile floors, but lack the outdoorsy ambience.

Posada Los Tulipanes (tel. 934/115-9211, US$41 s/d) is a five-room hotel in the center of town. Each room is simple and clean with two queen beds, en suite bathrooms, garish bedspreads, red mosquito nets, and pink walls. All that's missing are velvet paintings. Rooms share a long porch with hammocks. Look for it across from the medical clinic.

Information and Services

There's **Wi-Fi** (US$2/hour) at **Topche Ecolodge** (no phone, www.ecolodgetopche. com). The village also has a very basic medical **clinic,** but medical issues of any severity ought to be handled in Palenque or Villahermosa.

Getting There

The well-marked turnoff to Lacanjá Chansayab is at the roadside town of San Javier, about 130 kilometers (81 miles) from Palenque. Bear right there, and again at a second intersection about a kilometer (0.6 mile) later. Continue for 8 kilometers (5 miles) to the village center.

Autotransporte Chamoan (in Palenque, Av. Miguel Hidalgo btwn Calles 4 and Allende, cell. tel. 916/348-4684) provides daily combi service from Palenque to Lacanjá Chansayab (US$7.50, 2.5 hours) on vans headed to Frontera Corozal. At least they're supposed to drive passengers all the way into the village, provided you inform the driver in advance. If for some reason you are dropped in San Javier on the highway, a taxi to the village costs US$2-3.

FRONTERA COROZAL

This quiet community along the banks of the Río Usumacinta is the jumping-off point for visiting the Yaxchilán archaeological site, a terrific Maya ruin located about 25 kilometers (15.5 miles) downriver. It's also a convenient border crossing into Guatemala, just across the river, and you may be asked to show your passport (and pay a small fee) at a checkpoint at the entrance of town, even if you intend to remain in Mexico. The town itself is quite new, founded in 1976 by Ch'ol Maya émigrés from northern Chiapas, along with a small number of Lacandón and Tzeltal families.

Many *cabañas* in Lacanjá Chansayab are built alongside the river.

Relations are far from perfect, but locals take pride in their town's multicultural origins.

Sights

Museo Comunitario Frontera Corozal (7am-2pm daily, free) is a well-organized one-room museum, with exhibits on the history of the community, local flora and fauna, and archaeological discoveries, including the museum's pièce de résistance: two three-meter (10-foot), three-ton stelae found in the surrounding forest, carefully restored, and installed here. Signage is in Spanish only.

Food

Escudo Jaguar (tel. 919/153-5637, www.escudojaguar.com) and **Centro Turístico Nueva Alianza** (cell. tel. 919/209-2456, www.hotelnuevaalianza.com) both have open-air **restaurants** (7am-8pm daily, US$5-10) serving decent regional fare in large *palapa*-covered dining areas. They cater to tour groups so can get pretty busy, especially for lunch.

Imperio del Maya (no phone, 7am-2pm daily, US$3-7) serves up simple but reliable Mexican food in a spacious and airy dining room. It typically offers a *comida corrida* (lunch special) that includes soup, main dish, and drink for US$5. Look for it on the main drag, **next to the Yaxchilán ticket booth.**

Accommodations

Right on the river, **Escudo Jaguar** (tel. 919/153-5637, www.escudojaguar.com, US$6.25 pp camping, US$19-24 s/d with shared bath, US$36-54 s/d) is a longtime favorite for tour groups. It has several comfortable thatch-roofed *cabañas* on a manicured plot of land. All have strong ceiling fans, mosquito nets, and 24-hour electricity. Smaller units share clean single-sex bathrooms; larger ones have en suite bathrooms and private patios with hammocks. Camping is available on a flat, grassy area with lots of shade trees (BYO gear). Wi-Fi (US$1.25/hour) is available at the on-site restaurant.

Centro Turístico Nueva Alianza (cell. tel. 919/209-2456, www.hotelnuevaalianza.com, US$9.50 s/d with shared bath, US$32 s/d) is set on an atmospheric property with an expansive lawn and tall shade trees. It has several pleasant wood cabins with palapa roofs, all with tile bathrooms and a spacious porch with hammocks, table, and chairs. Units that share bathrooms also share a building with walls that don't quite reach the thatch-roofed ceiling (knock on wood your neighbors don't

Nueva Alianza *cabaña*

snore). These rooms are quite simple—a bed with mosquito net, cement floors, a fan, and a lightbulb. For the price though, they're pretty good. Free Wi-Fi is available in the common areas too.

Information and Services

There is no bank or ATM in town, and no one accepts credit cards; bring enough cash to get you through your stay. **Escudo Jaguar** (tel. 919/153-5637, www.escudojaguar.com) offers Wi-Fi to hotel guests and diners for US$1.25 per hour; all others can usually plead their case (if not, just buy a soda and you should get the all-clear).

The **immigration office** (no phone, 8:30am-5:30pm daily) is on the main drag, across from the Yaxchilán ticket booth.

Getting There and Around
COMBI

From Palenque, **Autotransporte Chamoan** (Av. Miguel Hidalgo btwn Calles 4 and Allende, cell. tel. 916/348-4684) provides *combi* service to Frontera Corozal (US$7.50, 3 hours) hourly 8am-4pm daily. The bus stops in front of the Yaxchilán ruins ticket booth, a short distance from the river dock, where you can catch a boat to the ruins. The same *combis* return to Palenque hourly 4am-4pm daily. If arriving by car, prepare to pay a US$1.25 toll to enter town.

CAR

From Palenque, follow the Carretera Fronteriza for 162 kilometers (100 miles) to Crucero Corozal, a well-marked turnoff. From there, it's another 22 kilometers (13.7 miles) to town. Once there, all vehicles must pay a US$1.25 toll to enter.

Driving between Palenque and Frontera Corozal used to be unsafe due to armed robberies. The situation has improved immensely, however, and the entire 185-kilometer (115-mile) stretch is considered safe. However, for the sake of caution, it is recommended to drive during daylight hours only.

BOAT

The **boat cooperative** (Guatemala tel. 502/5369-6769) that goes to Yaxchilán archaeological zone also provides one-way transportation to Betel, Guatemala (US$40 for 1-3 people, US$50 for 4, US$60 for 5-7, US$75 for 7-10, 40 minutes), where buses to Flores, outside the archaeological site of Tikal, depart daily at around 11am, 1pm, 3pm, and 5pm (US$11, 4 hours). Remember to pass Mexican **immigration** (no phone, 8:30am-5:30pm daily) in Frontera Corozal before departing; the building is across the street from the Yaxchilán ticket booth, on the main drag. Guatemalan immigration is in Betel.

Bonampak Archaeological Zone

Bonampak (8am-5pm daily, US$3.25) is a modest site overall, but home to some of the best ancient Maya murals ever discovered. The famous murals adorn the interior walls of a small temple built innocuously on the staircase of the city's main acropolis; painted in brilliant teal, red, and other colors, they depict sacrifices, ritual bloodletting, and violent battle scenes. The images shattered previous assumptions about the Maya, who had been portrayed by many researchers as a peace-loving civilization, in sharp contrast to Central Mexican indigenous groups and, of course, the Spanish colonizers.

HISTORY

Located in a fertile valley, the ruins are near a small tributary of the Río Lacanjá, with protective hills to one side. The earliest evidence of human occupation at Bonampak are ceramics dated to AD 100, and it reached its apogee in the Late Classic era (AD 600-800).

Bonampak Archaeological Zone

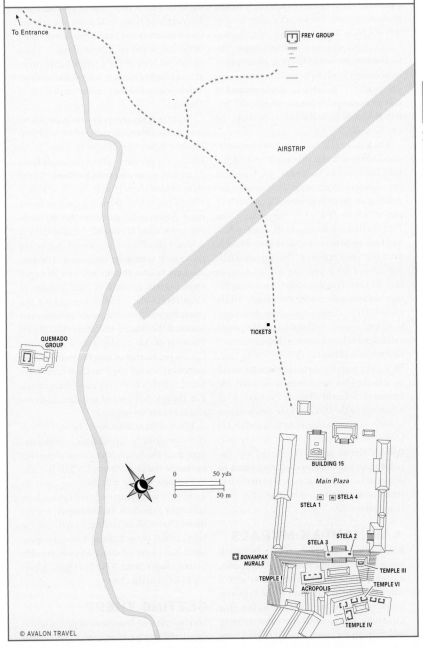

To Entrance

FREY GROUP

AIRSTRIP

QUEMADO
GROUP

TICKETS

0   50 yds
0   50 m

BUILDING 15

Main Plaza

STELA 4

STELA 1

STELA 2

STELA 3

BONAMPAK
MURALS

TEMPLE III

TEMPLE I

TEMPLE VI

ACROPOLIS

TEMPLE IV

© AVALON TRAVEL

Bonampak had a close and surprisingly amicable relationship with the nearby city of Yaxchilán, just 20 kilometers (12.4 miles) to the southeast. Bonampak's most notable leader, Chaan-Muan, was married to the sister of Yaxchilán's great king Shield Jaguar. The brothers-in-law joined forces in a war against an unknown third city in the 7th century, possibly Sak Tz'i'. The battle is commemorated in part of Bonampak's famous murals and lintels. Relatively little else is known about the city, however.

Much more ink, however, has been dedicated to the scandal that arose around the site's discovery in the 1940s. An American conscientious objector (or draft dodger, depending on the telling) named Karl Frey was part of a team headed by filmmaker Giles Healy to find and document the ruins, which had been reported to archaeologists 40 years prior but never explored. The two had a falling out and the expedition was abandoned; later, in 1946, Frey succeeded in reaching the site, but evidently missed the murals. Healy made the trip several months later, discovered the murals—even the local Lacandón people seemed not to have known of their existence—and made headlines with his startling find. Frey spent years trying to convince the world he was the true discoverer, to no avail. He formed part of an ill-advised exploration team organized by the Mexican Fine Arts Institute in 1949—a joint Carnegie Institute and INAH (national anthropology institute) exploration had already gone and returned with detailed maps and drawings—during which he drowned in the Río Lacanjá, reportedly trying to save a fellow team member after their canoe capsized.

★ BONAMPAK MURALS

Bonampak's murals are housed in **Temple I**, which stands on a low level of the **Acropolis**, a large stepped structure that backs onto a jungle-covered hill. In front of the Acropolis is a plaza with low buildings around the other three sides. Researchers believe that the story told through the murals should be read from left to right, from Room 1 to Room 3. The setting of Room 1's mural is the palace, where the child-heir is presented to the court and 336 days later is the focal point of a celebration with actors and musicians. Room 2 is set in the jungle and on a flight of stairs. These murals tell the story of a jungle battle, probably in honor of the heir, led by Chaan-Muan. This is considered the greatest battle scene in Maya art.

Next the scene moves to a staircase, where the captives are ritually tortured while Chaan-Muan watches from above. In Room 3, the setting is a pyramid, where costumed lords dance and a captive awaits his death. To the side, noblewomen ritually let their blood, while a pot-bellied dwarf is presented to the court. Anthropologists believe that the child-heir never ruled Bonampak, because there is evidence that the site was abandoned before the murals were even completed. The murals have faded with time and were damaged when the first researchers used kerosene to clean them—the kerosene brought out the colors but weakened the paints' adhesion and hastened the flaking and decay. The Museo Nacional de Antropología, in Mexico City, has a reproduction of how the murals likely looked in their full glory, and lesser copies are found in Tuxtla Gutiérrez and Villahermosa. But, though they are old and damaged, you still can't beat the originals.

When visiting Bonampak, be sure to look at the beautifully carved scenes on the underside of the lintels (the slab of stone that forms the top of a doorway). Their location makes them easy to miss, but they are truly some of the best Maya relief carvings you'll see outside of a museum. In Bonampak, Lintel I shows Chaan-Muan holding a captive by the hair; Lintel II shows Itzanaaj B'alam doing the same; and Lintel III shows a figure, possibly Chaan-Muan's father, Knot Eye Jaguar, spearing a victim in the chest.

GETTING THERE

Most people visit Bonampak as part of an all-day round-trip package from Palenque that also includes visiting Yaxchilán archaeological site. The "tour" usually includes just transportation—no guide service, though the drivers are often quite knowledgeable. This is a very practical option, even for those who eschew packages of any sort, because visiting both ruins in a day requires keeping a tight schedule, which is impossible if you're traveling by *combi.*

A rental car is quicker, but you still get pinched for things that are included in the tour price (not to mention gas and the rental itself): Independent travelers must pay a toll (US$1.75), at the highway turnoff, to use the road approaching Bonampak. From there, a local cooperative controls the 10-kilometer (6.2-mile) access road to the ruins and charges US$5 per person (3 or more passengers) or US$12.50 per shuttle (fewer than 3 passengers) for round-trip shuttle service to the ruins. Anyone not arriving by tour must take a shuttle, whether arriving by public transportation or car, though small discounts are available for students and seniors. Your best shot at sharing a ride is to be at the shuttle stop between 1pm and 3pm, when tour groups from Yaxchilán are arriving.

Combi

From Palenque, *combis* operated by **Autotransporte Chamoan** (Av. Miguel Hidalgo btwn Calles 4 and Allende, cell. tel. 916/348-4684) leave for Frontera Corozal hourly 8am-4pm daily; be sure to ask the driver to drop you at Crucero Bonampak (Bonampak turnoff, US$7.50, 2.5 hours), which is a kilometer (0.6 mile) off the main road and not an automatic stop. From there, you must take a local van (US$5 pp, 3 or more passengers; US$12.50 fewer than 3 passengers) to the ruins.

Car

About 130 kilometers (81 miles) southeast of Palenque in the town of San Javier are large signs and a prominent intersection marking the turnoff to Bonampak. Turn right and go a short distance farther to a second intersection, known as Crucero Bonampak (Bonampak turnoff); a US$1.75 toll must be paid here. It's another 10 kilometers (6.2 miles) to the ruins, but private cars aren't allowed past; instead you must park and take a local shuttle round-trip (US$5 pp, 3 or more passengers; US$12.50 fewer than 3 passengers). There's a parking lot (free, at least) from where the shuttle departs.

Combis are a good way to visit Bonampak, Yaxchilán, and nearby villages.

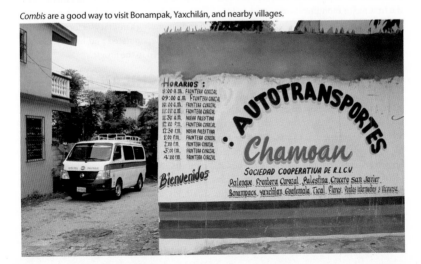

Yaxchilán Archaeological Zone

Yaxchilán (8am-5pm daily, US$3.75) lies on the Río Usumacinta, Mexico's largest river and the border between Mexico and Guatemala. Archaeologists have found at least 35 stelae, 60 carved lintels, 21 altars, and five stairways covered with hieroglyphs here—a treasure trove for epigraphers. Yaxchilán's rulers were obsessed with venerating their dynasty as well as legitimizing their rule, and endowed a major monument-carving operation to achieve these goals. In fact, it was Yaxchilán's hieroglyphs that provided much of the raw material that led to the deciphering of the Maya writing system. **Note:** Tickets should be purchased at the ticket booth on the main drag in Frontera Corozal. While there is a ticket counter at the ruins themselves, it's often unmanned. Visitors arriving without a ticket risk not being allowed into the site.

HISTORY

Yaxchilán was a powerful city-state during the Classic era, ruled by the Jaguar dynasty, which traced its roots to AD 320 and a ruler named Yat B'alam (Jaguar Penis). The earliest recorded date at the site is from AD 435, and the first major monuments appeared early in the 6th century.

Yaxchilán's greatest ruler was Izamnaaj B'alam, or Shield Jaguar, who was born in AD 647 and ruled for more than six decades (AD 681-742), a remarkable feat for a man whose life expectancy would have been less than 40 years. He undertook numerous construction projects, including the construction of Structure 23 on the main plaza. Dedicated to his wife Lady Xoc, it is the only Maya temple known to have been built specifically in honor of a woman. (Palenque's Temple XIII, in which archaeologists excavated the so-called Tomb of the Red Queen, may be another, but that is not confirmed.) But the construction and dedication of Structure 23 may have had more to do with politics than enlightenment; Shield

Jaguar took a second wife late in life and named the son from that union, Bird Jaguar, heir to the throne. Structure 23, which shows Lady Xoc conducting various noble rituals, may have been a way of appeasing her powerful family.

Curiously, Bird Jaguar was not crowned until AD 752, a full 10 years after his father's death. Archaeologists interpret this as a sign of tepid political support for the young monarch; as further evidence, they point to Bird Jaguar's obsessive self-aggrandizement once he finally did assume the throne, as if he were desperate to legitimize his position. Bird Jaguar built numerous buildings, most notably Structure 33, and seems to have commissioned a stelae or relief carving to commemorate his every accomplishment, including military victories, bloodletting ceremonies, the sacrifice of important captives, and even winning a ball game match. Bird Jaguar was the beginning of the end for the Jaguar dynasty, which lasted until about AD 800. Its last ruler, Ta-Skull, Bird Jaguar's grandson, is credited with just two small, rather poorly constructed temples (Structures 3 and 64), which contain the latest known date inscription at Yaxchilán, AD 808, commemorating a military victory. Yaxchilán gradually depopulated and by AD 900 had been returned to the jungle.

★ YAXCHILÁN RUINS

A steep path leads up from the boat pier to Yaxchilán's on-site ticket booth, which is often unmanned. (Be sure to buy your ticket in Frontera Corozal or risk not being allowed in! Look for the ticket booth in Frontera Corozal on the main street as you approach the river.) Entering the site, the main road leads to the Main Plaza, with the Great Acropolis a long steep flight of stairs above. But instead of following the main path, consider taking the small path that cuts to your right up the hill to the **Little Acropolis.** It's a steep climb, but

Yaxchilán Archaeological Zone

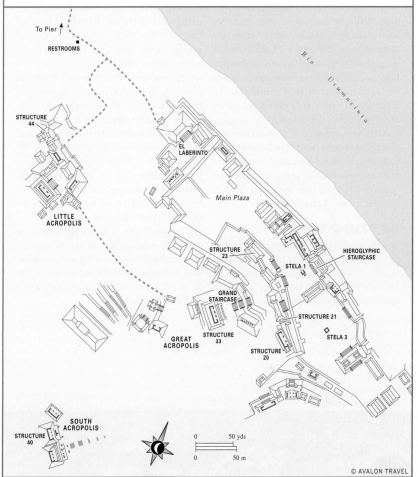

© AVALON TRAVEL

once there, the rest of your visit is downhill. The most important structure in this complex is Structure 44, which was built by Shield Jaguar in celebration of his military successes.

Continue on the path to reach the **Great Acropolis** from the back side. It's a pleasant walk, and you may spot howler monkeys in the trees along the way. Around front, you'll be at the top of a long flight of stone stairs and in front of one of Yaxchilán's most notable structures, **Structure 33,** with its intricate

facade and soaring roof comb. Built by Bird Jaguar to celebrate himself—who else?—it includes incredibly fine lintels (the slab of stone that forms the top of a doorway) and panels depicting the ruler's accomplishments, including summoning his deceased ancestors in the midst of a ball game.

Descending the stairs, you'll reach the **Main Plaza,** a long rectangular plaza built alongside the riverbank, framed by numerous structures and dotted with large stelae.

Structure 20 and **Structure 21** are to the right of the staircase as you reach the bottom; built by Shield Jaguar and Bird Jaguar, respectively, both have lintels portraying rituals related to the birth of heirs. On the other side of the staircase, **Structure 23** is the famous temple built by Shield Jaguar and dedicated to Lady Xoc. This is where archaeologists discovered exquisitely carved panels portraying the noblewoman performing rituals, including drawing a thorny twine through her tongue.

At the west end of the Main Plaza is a complex called **El Laberinto** (The Labyrinth), so named for its maze of vaulted passageways and chambers; it likely served as residential quarters. The main path leads back through the trees to the boat landing.

GETTING THERE

Yaxchilán is located 25 kilometers (15.5 miles) down the Río Usumacinta from the town of Frontera Corozal, and can only be reached by *lancha* (a long, colorful, canoe-like boat with a sun cover and powerful outboard motor). The 45- to 60-minute ride leaves from a pier at the end of the main road, where a number of co-operatives and private outfits compete for arriving tourists. The first boats leave Frontera Corozal at 7am, the last at 3pm. Be sure to buy your admission ticket to the ruins at the booth as you approach the pier.

The boat trip is definitely part of the fun of visiting this remote site, zipping down the river in a long colorful *lancha* with Guatemala on one side and Mexico on the other, with the chance to see birds, howler monkeys, and beefy crocodiles sunning themselves on the riverbank. Round-trip prices are fairly uniform and depend on the size of your group: US$50 for 1-3 passengers, US$60 for 4, US$82 for 5-7, and US$100 for 8-10. The price includes two hours at the site; you can stay longer, but you'll have to tip the boatman (even better, throw in a Coke and something to eat as well). **Tip:** If you're looking to share a boat, wait in front of the Yaxchilán ticket booth in Frontera Corozal. Tour groups typically arrive between 8am and 9am.

Yaxchilán crocodile

Background

The Landscape

The history of the Yucatán Peninsula is deeply intertwined with its unique geology and ecology. From the ancient Maya to modern-day tourism, the land and its resources have shaped the course of Yucatecan events. And the Yucatán, in turn, has helped shape the course of Mexican history, from being the stage upon which the early Spanish conquest was conducted to helping rescue a moribund Mexican economy in the 1980s. An understanding of the Yucatán Peninsula's land, ecology, culture, and politics is vital to understanding the region today.

GEOGRAPHY

The Yucatán Peninsula spans some 113,000 square kilometers (70,215 square miles) in southeastern Mexico, and is made up of three states: Yucatán, Campeche, and Quintana Roo. It has more than 1,600 kilometers (994 miles) of shoreline, with the Caribbean Sea to the east and the Gulf of Mexico to the north and west. To the southwest are the Mexican states of Tabasco and Chiapas, and directly south are the countries of Belize and Guatemala.

Geologically, the Yucatán Peninsula is a flat shelf of limestone, a porous rock that acts like a huge sponge. Rainfall is absorbed into the ground and delivered to natural stone-lined sinks and underground rivers. The result is that the Yucatán has virtually no surface water, neither rivers nor lakes. It also has very few hills. The geology changes as you move south, and the first sizable river—the Río Hondo—forms a natural boundary between Belize and Mexico.

The Coast

The northern and western coasts are bordered by the emerald waters of the Gulf of Mexico. Just inland, the land is dotted with lagoons, sandbars, and swamps. The east coast is edged by the turquoise Caribbean, and the glorious islands of Isla Cozumel, Isla Mujeres, and Isla Contoy lie just offshore. Along the coast runs the Mesoamerican Reef, the second-longest coral reef in the world.

Cenotes

Over the course of millennia, water that seeped below the Yucatán's porous limestone shelf eroded a vast network of underground rivers and caves. When a cave's ceiling wears thin, it may eventually cave in, exposing the water below. The Maya called such sinkholes *dzo'not,* which Spanish explorers recorded as *cenotes.* Most cenotes are extremely deep, and interconnected by way of underground channels. A cenote's surface may be near ground level, but more often it is much farther down, as much as 90 meters (295 feet) below ground level. In those cases, the Maya gathered water by carving stairs into the slick limestone walls or by hanging long ladders into abysmal hollows that led to underground lakes.

Estuaries

The Yucatán's countless estuaries, or *rías* in Spanish (not to be confused with *ríos,* or rivers), play host to hundreds of bird species. The most recognized estuary dweller in the region is the American flamingo, the largest and pinkest of the flamingo species. But a variety of other birds live, at least part of the year, in these estuaries too. Typical birds spotted include the blue-winged teal, northern shoveler, and lesser scaup, as well as wading birds like the heron, snowy egret, and white ibis. Río Lagartos and Celestún are the best-known and most-visited estuaries in the

---

Yucatán Peninsula, but those in Sian Ka'an Biosphere Reserve, Isla Holbox, and Xcalak also are vibrant and accessible.

CLIMATE

The weather in the Yucatán falls into a rainy season (May-October) and a dry season (November-April). Travelers to the region in the dry season will experience warm days, occasional brief storms called *nortes,* and plenty of tourists. In the rainy season, expect spectacular storms and hot, muggy days. The region is infamous for its heat and humidity in May and June, which hovers around 90°F *and* 90 percent humidity.

Hurricane season runs July-November, with most activity occurring mid-August-mid-October. Cloudy conditions and scattered showers are common during this period, occasionally developing into tropical storms. Hurricanes are still relatively rare, but their effects are wide-reaching—even if a storm isn't predicted to hit the Yucatán, it may send plenty of heavy rain and surf that direction. If a hurricane *is* bearing down, don't try to tough it out; cut short your trip or head inland immediately.

ENVIRONMENTAL ISSUES
Hurricanes

Evidence that global warming may cause an increase in the number and/or intensity of Atlantic hurricanes has serious implications for the Yucatán Peninsula, already known to be within Hurricane Alley. The region has weathered countless storms, but something was different about Hurricanes Wilma (2005) and Dean (2007)—both storms broke records for intensity and caused major structural damage, but they also reshaped the shoreline in a way not seen before. Cancún's beaches were especially hard hit, the sand stripped away in many places to expose the hardened limestone beneath. Elsewhere, unusually thick deposits of sand on the coral reef and inland mangroves wiped out large portions of both important ecosystems.

Overdevelopment

Runaway construction along the Riviera Maya has a host of interconnected environmental impacts, some well-known, others poorly understood (and surely many that have yet to be identified). An obvious impact is the destruction of mangrove swamps, which extend along much of the coast a short distance inland from

It's no wonder why Bacalar is also known as the Lake of Seven Colors.

the beach. Well known for supporting wild-life, mangroves also help buffer the effects of hurricane-related surge and currents, and are an important source of nutrients for coral and other sealife, as water from the wetlands drains into the ocean. Although protected by federal law, mangroves have been a primary victim of massive development projects.

Mangroves are emblematic of a more general characteristic of the Riviera Maya: highly porous earth and a weblike underground watershed. Contamination is extremely difficult to clean up or even contain, as it spreads quickly in multiple directions via underground currents, including into the ocean. This is damaging not only to the environment but also to local communities—and the resorts themselves—which draw drinking water from the same system.

And those local communities are growing even faster than the resorts—by some estimates, resorts require an average of five employees for every guest room. Multiply that by the number of resorts operating and being built, and it's no surprise that the region's population is booming. In that sense, development is doubly dangerous: increasing the risk of contamination while simultaneously spurring demand for the very resource it most threatens.

Deforestation

Among the top concerns of environmentalists in Mexico is deforestation, which has accelerated with Mexico's burgeoning population. Slash-and-burn farming is still widely practiced in remote areas, with or without regulation. In an effort to protect the land, environmentalists are searching for alternative sources of income for locals. One is to train them to become guides by teaching them about the flora and fauna of the region as well as how to speak English. While not solving the problem, it does place an economic value on the forest itself and provides an incentive for preserving it.

Another focus is the plight of the palm tree. The palm is an important part of the cultural and practical lifestyle of the indigenous people of Quintana Roo—it is used for thatch roofing and to construct lobster traps. However, the palms used—*Thrinax radiata* and *Coccothrinax readii*—are becoming increasingly rare.

Plants and Animals

Quintana Roo's forests are home to mangroves, bamboo, and swamp cypresses. Ferns, vines, and flowers creep from tree to tree and create a dense growth. The southern part of the Yucatán Peninsula, with its classic tropical rainforest, hosts tall mahoganies, *campeche zapote,* and *kapok*—all covered with wild jungle vines. On topmost limbs, orchids and air ferns reach for the sun.

Many animals found nowhere else in Mexico inhabit the Yucatán Peninsula's expansive flatlands and thick jungles. Spotting them can be difficult, though with patience and a skilled guide, not impossible.

TREES
Palms

A wide variety of palm trees and their relatives grow on the peninsula—tall, short, fruited, and even oil-producing varieties. Though similar, palms have distinct characteristics:

- Queen palms are often used for landscaping and bear a sweet fruit.
- Thatch palms are called *chit* by Maya, who use the fronds extensively for roof thatch.
- Coconut palms—the ones often seen on the beach—produce oil, food, drink, and shelter and are valued by locals as a nutritious food source and cash crop.

Other Trees

The ceiba (also called *kapok*) is a sacred tree for the Maya. Considered the link between the underworld, the material world, and the heavens, this huge tree is revered and left undisturbed—even if it sprouts in the middle of a fertile cornfield.

When visiting in the summer, you can't miss the beautiful *framboyanes* (royal poinciana). When in bloom, its wide-spreading branches become covered in clusters of brilliant orange-red flowers. These trees often line sidewalks and plazas, and when clustered together present a dazzling show.

FLOWERS

While wandering through jungle regions, you'll see numerous flowering plants. Here in their natural environment, these plants thrive in a way unknown to windowsills at home: Crotons exhibit wild colors, pothos grow 30-centimeter (11.8-inch) leaves, the philodendron splits every leaf in gargantuan glory, and common morning glory creeps and climbs effortlessly over bushes and trees. You'll also be introduced to less well-known residents of this semitropical world: the exotic white and red ginger, plumeria (sometimes called frangipani) with its wonderful fragrance and myriad colors, and hibiscus and bougainvillea, which bloom in an array of bright hues.

Orchids

Orchids can be found on the highest limbs of the tallest trees, especially in the state of Quintana Roo. Of the 71 species reported in the Yucatán Peninsula, 80 percent are epiphytic, attached to host trees and deriving moisture and nutrients from the air and rain. Orchids grow in myriad sizes and shapes: tiny buttons spanning the length of a half-meter-long (2-foot) branch, large-petaled blossoms with ruffled edges, or intense tiger-striped miniatures.

Ceiba trees are sacred to the Maya.

- Royal palms are tall with smooth trunks.
- Henequen is a cousin to the palm tree; from its fiber come twine, rope, matting, and other products. Because of its abundance, new uses for it are constantly sought.

Fruit Trees

Quintana Roo grows sweet and sour oranges, limes, and grapefruit. Avocado is abundant, and the papaya tree is practically a weed. The *mamey* tree grows full and tall (15-20 meters/49-65 feet), providing not only welcome shade but also an avocado-shaped fruit, brown on the outside with a vivid, salmon-pink flesh that tastes like a sweet yam. The *guaya* is another unusual fruit tree and a member of the lychee nut family. This rangy evergreen thrives on sea air and is commonly seen along the coast. Its small, green, leathery pods grow in clumps like grapes and contain a sweet, yellowish, jellylike flesh—tasty! The calabash tree provides gourds used for containers by Maya.

MAMMALS
Nine-Banded Armadillos

The size of a small dog and sporting a thick coat of armor, this peculiar creature gets its name from the nine bands (or external "joints") that circle its midsection and give the little tank some flexibility. The armadillo's keen sense of smell can detect insects and grubs—its primary food source—up to 15 centimeters (6 inches) underground, and its sharp claws make digging for them easy. An armadillo also digs underground burrows, into which it may carry a full bushel of grass to make its nest, where it will sleep through the hot day and emerge at night. Unlike armadillos that roll up into a tight ball when threatened, this species will race to its burrow, arch its back, and wedge in so that it cannot be pulled out. The Yucatán Peninsula is a favored habitat for its scant rainfall; too much rain floods the burrow and can drown young armadillos.

Giant Anteaters

A cousin of the armadillo, this extraordinary animal measures two meters (6.6 feet) from the tip of its tubular snout to the end of its bushy tail. Its coarse coat is colored shades of brown-gray; the hindquarters are darker in tone, while a contrasting wedge-shaped pattern of black and white decorates the throat and shoulders. Characterized by an elongated head, long tubular mouth, and extended tongue (but no teeth), it can weigh up to 39 kilograms (86 pounds). The anteater walks on the knuckles of its paws, allowing its claws to remain tucked under while it looks for food. Giant anteaters are found in forests and swampy areas in Mexico and throughout Central and South America.

Tapirs

South American tapirs are found from the southern part of Mexico to southern Brazil. A stout-bodied animal, it has short legs and a tail, small eyes, and rounded ears. The nose and upper lip extend into a short but very mobile proboscis. Tapirs usually live near streams or rivers, which they use for daily bathing and as an escape from predators, especially jaguars and humans. Shy and placid, these nocturnal animals have a definite home range, wearing a path between the jungle and their feeding area. If attacked, the tapir lowers its head and blindly crashes off through the forest; they've been known to collide with trees and knock themselves out in their chaotic attempt to flee.

Peccaries

Next to deer, peccaries are the most widely hunted game on the Yucatán Peninsula. Two species of peccaries are found here: the collared javelina peccary and the white-lipped peccary. The feisty collared javelina stands 50 centimeters (20 inches) at the shoulder and can be one meter (3.3 feet) long, weighing as much as 30 kilograms (66 pounds). It is black and white with a narrow, semicircular collar of white hair on the shoulders. The name javelina (which means spear in Spanish) comes from the two tusks that protrude from its mouth. A related species, the white-lipped peccary, is reddish brown to black and has an area of white around its mouth. Larger than the javelina, it can grow to 105 centimeters (41 inches) long and is found deep in tropical rainforests living in herds of 100 or more. Peccaries often are compared to the wild pigs found in Europe, but in fact they belong to entirely different families.

Felines

Seven species of cats are found in North America, four in the tropics. One of them—the jaguar—is heavy chested with sturdy, muscled forelegs. It has small, rounded ears and its tail is relatively short. Its color varies from tan and white to pure black. The male can weigh 65-115 kilograms (143-254 pounds), females 45-85 kilograms (99-187 pounds). The largest of the cats on the peninsula, the jaguar is about the same size as a leopard. Other cats found here are the ocelot and puma. In tropical forests of the past, the large cats were the only predators capable of controlling the populations of hoofed game such as deer, peccaries, and tapirs. If hunting is poor and times are tough, the jaguar will go into rivers and scoop up fish with its large paws. The river is also one of the jaguar's favorite spots for hunting tapirs, when the latter come to drink.

Monkeys

The jungles of Mexico are home to three species of monkeys: spider, howler, and black howler. Intelligent and endearing, these creatures are prime targets for the pet trade. They have been so hunted, in fact, that today all three are in danger of extinction. Experts estimate that for every monkey sold, three die during transportation and distribution. In an effort to protect these creatures, the Mexican government has prohibited their capture or trade. Tropical monkeys are most active at sunrise and sundown. If you go to Cobá or Punta Laguna Spider Monkey Reserve, keep your ears perked and your eyes peeled. You may see—or at least hear—a few monkeys. If possible, consider waking early or staying late to increase your chances of spotting a few. Other places to see spider and howler monkeys are Calakmul and Yaxchilán archaeological sites.

SEALIFE
Coral Reefs

The spectacular coral reefs that grace the peninsula's east coast are made up of millions of tiny carnivorous organisms called polyps. Individual polyps can be less than a centimeter (0.4 inch) long or up to 15 centimeters (6 inches) in diameter. Related to the jellyfish and sea anemone, coral polyps capture prey with tiny tentacles that deliver a deadly sting.

Reef-building polyps have limestone exoskeletons, which they create by extracting calcium from the seawater. Reefs are formed as generation after generation of polyps attach themselves to and atop each other. Different species attach in different ways, resulting in the many shapes and sizes of ocean reefs: delicate lace, trees with reaching branches, pleated mushrooms, stovepipes, petaled flowers, fans, domes, heads of cabbage, and stalks of broccoli. Though made up of individual polyps, coral structures function like a single organism, sharing nutrients through a central gastrovascular system. Even in ideal conditions, most coral grows no more than five centimeters (two inches) per year.

Fish

The Yucatán's barrier reef is home to myriad fish species, including parrot fish, candy bass, moray eels, spotted scorpion fish, turquoise angelfish, fairy basslets, flame fish, and gargantuan manta rays. Several species of shark also thrive in the waters off Quintana Roo, though they're not considered a serious threat to swimmers and divers. Sport fish—sailfish, marlin, and bluefin tuna—also inhabit the outer Caribbean waters.

Inland, anglers will find hard-fighting bonefish and pompano in the area's lagoons, and snorkelers and divers will find several species of blind fish in the crystal clear waters of cenotes. These fish live out their existence in dark underground rivers and lakes and have no use for eyes.

Sea Turtles

Tens of thousands of sea turtles of various species once nested on the coastal beaches of Quintana Roo. As the coast became populated, turtles were severely overhunted for their eggs, meat, and shell, and their numbers began to fall. Hotel and resort developments have hastened the decline, as there are fewer and fewer patches of untrammeled sand in which turtles can dig nests and lay their eggs. The Mexican government and various ecological organizations are trying hard to save the dwindling turtle population. Turtle eggs are dug up and reburied in sand on safe beaches; or when the hatchlings break through their shells, they are brought to a beach and allowed to rush toward the sea in hopes of imprinting a sense of belonging there so that they will later return to the spot. In some cases the hatchlings are scooped up and placed in tanks

The Yucatán's Biosphere Reserves

Mexico is one of the most biodiverse places on the planet—in league with places like Brazil, Congo, and Indonesia. It boasts deserts, rainforests, mountains, and coral reefs, and over 200,000 species of plants and animals, half of which exist nowhere else. Mexico has set aside nearly 10 percent of its national territory as protected areas of various kinds. These include biosphere reserves, a United Nations-certified designation, that have at least 10,000 hectares (24,771 acres) of protected habitat and a pristine core with no human disturbance or settlements. Mexico has a whopping 40 biosphere reserves—only the United States, Russia, and Spain have more. Six are in the Yucatán Peninsula (described below), and there are another eight in Chiapas, including two near Palenque.

Sian Ka'an: Yucatec Maya for "Birthplace of the Sky," Sian Ka'an covers over a half million hectares (1.2 million acres) of coastal forest, wetlands, and shallow bays and is home to turtles, dolphins, and innumerable birds. Tours are available from Tulum, including visiting Maya sites within the reserve.

Ría Lagartos: Accessible from the Gulf coast town of Río Lagartos, the like-named ría (estuary) is best known as a flamingo reserve, but is also home to hundreds of bird species (many rare or endemic) plus turtles and other reptiles.

Ría Celestún: Another well-known flamingo reserve, Ría Celestún is rich with birds, reptiles, and wetland and coastal vegetation of all kinds. Tours are available from the town of Celestún; it also is a popular day trip from Mérida.

to grow larger before being released into the open sea. The government is also enforcing tough penalties for people who take turtle eggs or capture, kill, or sell these creatures once they hatch.

Manatees

The manatee—sometimes called the sea cow—is a gentle, inquisitive giant. They are closely related to dugongs, and more distantly to elephants, aardvarks, and hyraxes. Newborns weigh 30-35 kilograms (66-77 pounds), while adults can measure four meters (13 feet) in length and weigh nearly 1,600 kilograms (3,500 pounds). Shaped like an Idaho potato, manatees have coarse pinkish-gray skin, tiny sunken eyes, a flattened tail and flipper-like forelimbs (including toenails), and prehensile lips covered in sensitive whiskers. The manatee is the only aquatic mammal that's completely vegetarian, eating an astounding 10 percent of its body weight every day in aquatic grass and vegetation; it's unique among all mammals for constantly growing new teeth to replace those worn down by its voracious feeding.

Large numbers of them once roamed the shallow inlets, bays, and estuaries of the Caribbean; their images are frequently seen in the art of the ancient Maya, who hunted them for food. Today, though posing no threat to humans or other animals, and ecologically important for their ability to clear waterways of oxygen-choking vegetation, manatees are endangered in the Yucatán and elsewhere. The population has been reduced by the encroachment of people in their habitats along the river ways and shorelines. Ever-growing numbers of motorboats also inflict deadly gashes on these surface-feeding creatures. Nowadays it is very rare to spot one; the most sightings are reported in Punta Allen and Bahía de la Ascensión.

BIRDS

Since a major part of the Yucatán Peninsula is still undeveloped and covered with trees and brush, it isn't surprising to find exotic, rarely seen birds across the landscape. The Mexican government is beginning to realize the great value in this and is making efforts to protect nesting grounds. In addition to the

Calakmul: Located in southern Campeche, this biosphere reserve spans 723,000 hectares (1.8 million acres) of tropical rainforest and teems with animals such as spider monkeys, howler monkeys, jaguars, and toucans. The reserve's namesake is the massive Maya ruin at its heart, home to some of the largest known pyramids in Mesoamerica. It's accessible from Campeche's Río Bec region.

Banco Chinchorro: One of the largest coral atolls in the world, Chinchorro Bank is 30 kilometers (19 miles) off the southern Quintana Roo coast. Notoriously treacherous for colonial-era ships, today it's a diving and snorkeling paradise, with rich coral and marinelife. Tours are available from Mahahual or Xcalak.

Arrecifes Alacranes: Over a hundred kilometers (62 miles) out to sea from the Gulf coast town of Progreso, the circular coral atoll known as Arrecifes Alacranes (Scorpion Reef) is Yucatán state's only major coral reef. Birds populate the small sandy islands, and there's a century-old lighthouse. No regular tours are available, however.

American flamingos are the largest and pinkest flamingos in the world.

growing number of nature reserves, some of the best bird-watching locales are the archaeological zones. At dawn and dusk, when most of the visitors are absent, the trees that surround the ancient structures come alive with birdsong. Of all the ruins, Cobá—with its marsh-rimmed lakes, nearby cornfields, and relatively tall, humid forest—is a particularly good site for bird-watching. One of the more impressive birds to look for here is the keel-billed toucan, often seen perched high on a bare limb in the early hours of the morning. Others include *chachalacas* (held in reverence by the Maya), screeching parrots, and, occasionally, the ocellated turkey.

Flamingos

The wetlands along the Yucatán's northern coast are shallow and murky and bordered in many places by thick mangrove forests. The water content is unusually high in salt and other minerals—the ancient Maya gathered salt here, and several salt factories still operate. A formidable habitat for most creatures, it's ideal for *Phoenicopterus ruber ruber*—the American flamingo, the largest and pinkest of the world's five flamingo species. Nearly 30,000 of the peculiar birds nest here, feeding on algae and other tiny organisms that thrive in the salty water. Flamingos are actually born white, but they turn pink from the carotene in the algae they eat.

For years, flamingos only nested around Río Lagartos, near the peninsula's northeastern tip. But in 1988, Hurricane Gilbert destroyed their nesting grounds—not to mention the town of Río Lagartos—and forced the birds to relocate. They are now found all along the north coast, including at three major feeding and reproduction grounds: Río Lagartos, Celestún, and Uaymitún. Though in smaller numbers, they also can be found on Isla Holbox.

The best way to observe flamingos is on a boat tour at sunrise, when the birds are most active, turning their heads upside down and dragging their beaks along the bottom of the shallow water to suck in the mud that contains their food. (In the morning, you should see dozens of other birds too, such as storks, herons, and kingfishers.) If you go in the spring, you may see the male flamingos performing their strange mating dance—craning their necks, clucking loudly, and generally strutting their stuff.

Although flamingos live in the region year-round, you'll see the highest numbers at Río Lagartos in the spring and summer and at Celestún in the winter. Uaymitún has a pretty steady population but has no boat tours—instead you observe the birds through binoculars from a raised platform. No matter when you go, make as little noise as possible and ask your guide to keep his distance. Flamingos are nervous and easily spooked into flying away en masse. While the exodus would no doubt be an impressive sight, it may cause the birds to abandon the site altogether.

Quetzals

Though the ancient Maya made abundant use of the dazzling quetzal feathers for ceremonial costumes and headdresses, they hunted other fowl for food; nevertheless, the quetzal is the only known bird from the pre-Columbian era and is now almost extinct. Today, they are still found (though rarely) in the high cloud forests of Chiapas and Central America, where they thrive on the constant moisture.

REPTILES

Although reptiles thrive in Yucatán's warm, sunny environment, humans are their worst enemy. In the past, some species were greatly reduced in number—hunted for their unusual skin. Although hunting them is now illegal, black marketers still take their toll on the species.

Caymans

The cayman is a member of the crocodilian order. Its habits and appearance are similar to those of crocodiles, with the main difference being in its underskin: The cayman's skin is reinforced with bony plates on the belly, making it useless for the leather market. (Alligators and crocodiles, with smooth belly skin and sides, have been hunted almost to extinction in some parts of the world because of the value of their skin.)

iguana

Several species of cayman frequent the brackish inlet waters near the estuaries of Río Lagartos (literally, River of Lizards); though seen less frequently, they also inhabit mangroves on the Caribbean coast. A large cayman can be 2.5 meters (8.2 feet) long and very dark gray-green and broad-snouted with eyelids that look swollen and wrinkled. Some cayman species have eyelids that look like a pair of blunt horns. They are quicker than alligators and have longer, sharper teeth. Skilled hunters, cayman are quick in water and on land, and will attack a person if cornered. The best advice is to give caymans a wide berth if spotted.

Iguanas

This group of American lizards—Iguanidae family—includes various large plant-eaters seen frequently in Quintana Roo. Iguanas grow to be one meter (3.3 feet) long and have a blunt head and long flat tail. Bands of black and gray circle its body, and a serrated column reaches down the middle of its back almost to the tail. The young iguana is bright emerald-green and often supplements its diet by eating insects and larvae.

The lizard's forelimbs hold the front half of its body up off the ground while its two back limbs are kept relaxed and splayed alongside its hindquarters. When the iguana is frightened, however, its hind legs do everything they're supposed to, and the iguana crashes quickly (though clumsily) into the brush searching for its burrow and safety. This reptile is not aggressive—it mostly enjoys basking in the bright sunshine along the Caribbean—but if cornered it will bite and use its tail in self-defense.

From centuries past, recorded references attest to the iguana's medicinal value, which partly explains the active trade of live iguana in the marketplaces. Iguana stew is believed to cure or relieve various human ailments.

Other Lizards

You'll see a great variety of other lizards on the peninsula; some are brightly striped in various shades of green and yellow, and others are earth-toned and blend in with the gray and beige limestone that dots the landscape. Skinny as wisps of thread running on hind legs, or chunky and waddling with armor-like skin, the range is endless and fascinating.

Be sure to look for the black anole, which changes colors to match its environment, either when danger is imminent or as subterfuge to fool the insects on which it feeds. At mating time, the male anole puffs out its bright-red throat-fan so that all female lizards will see it.

Coral Snakes

Two species of coral snakes, which are related to the cobra, are found in the southern part of the Yucatán Peninsula. They have prominent rings around their bodies in the same sequence of red, black, yellow, or white and grow to 1-1.5 meters (3.3-4.9 feet). Their bodies are slender, with no pronounced distinction between the head and neck.

Coral snakes spend the day in mossy clumps under rocks or logs, emerging only at night. Though the bite of a coral snake can kill within 24 hours, chances of the average tourist being bitten by a coral (or any other) snake are slim.

Tropical Rattlesnakes

The tropical rattlesnake (*cascabel* in Spanish) is the deadliest and most treacherous species of rattler. It differs slightly from other species by having vividly contrasting neckbands. It grows 2-2.5 meters (6.6-8.2 feet) long and is found mainly in the higher and drier areas of the tropics. Contrary to popular myth, this serpent doesn't always rattle a warning of its impending strike.

INSECTS AND ARACHNIDS

Air-breathing invertebrates are unavoidable in any tropical locale. Some are annoying (gnats and no-see-ums), some are dangerous (black widows, bird spiders, and scorpions), and others can cause pain when they bite (red ants); but many are beautiful (butterflies and moths), and *all* are fascinating.

Butterflies and Moths

The Yucatán has an incredible abundance of beautiful moths and butterflies, some 40,000 species in all. Hikers might see the magnificent blue morpho, orange-barred sulphur, copperhead, cloudless sulphur, malachite, admiral, calico, ruddy dagger-wing, tropical buckeye, and emperor. The famous monarch is also a visitor during its annual migration from the northeastern United States. It usually makes a stopover on Quintana Roo's east coast on its way south to the Central American mountains where it spends the winter. The huge black witch moth—males can have a wingspan of 18 centimeters (7 inches) and are sometimes mistaken for bats—is called *mariposa de la muerte* ("butterfly of death" in Spanish) or *ma ha na* (Yucatec Maya for "enter the home"), stemming from a common belief that if the moth enters the home of a sick person, that person will soon die.

Spiders and Scorpions

The Yucatán has some scary-looking spiders and scorpions (*arañas* and *alacranes*), but none is particularly dangerous. The Yucatán rust rump tarantula is surely the most striking, a hairy medium-size tarantula with long legs and a distinctive orange or rust-colored rear. Like most tarantulas, they are nocturnal and fairly timid, with females spending much of their time in burrows in the ground, and males roaming around incessantly looking for them. Its bite is harmless, but that doesn't mean you should handle one: When threatened, tarantulas can shake off a cloud of tiny hairs, which are highly irritating if inhaled.

The Yucatán's long black scorpions—up to 10 centimeters (4 inches)!—have a painful sting that can cause swelling, and for some people shortness of breath, but is not deadly. Like tarantulas, scorpions avoid human contact and are therefore rare to see; that said, it's always a good idea to shake out shoes and beach towels before using them, just in case.

Bees

The Yucatán's most famous bee—of numerous species found here—is the aptly named Yucatán bee, also known as the Maya bee. The small stingless insect produces a particularly sweet honey that was prized by the ancient Maya, and was one of the most widely traded commodities in the Maya world. (Some researchers say the Descending God figure at Tulum and other archaeological sites is the god of bees.) The ancient Maya were expert beekeepers, a tradition that lives on today, albeit much reduced thanks in part to the availability of cheap standard honey. Yucatán honey (harvested using more modern methods) is still sold in Mexico and abroad, mostly online and in organic and specialty stores.

Traditional Maya beekeeping techniques are still used today.

History

ACROSS THE BERING LAND BRIDGE

People and animals from Asia crossed the Bering land bridge into North America in the Pleistocene epoch about 50,000 years ago, when sea levels were much lower. As early as 10,000 BC, Ice Age humans hunted woolly mammoth and other large animals roaming the cool, moist landscape of central Mexico. The earliest traces of humans in the Yucatán Peninsula are obsidian spear points and stone tools dating to 9,000 BC. The Loltún caves in the state of Yucatán contained a cache of mammoth bones, which are thought to have been dragged there by a roving band of hunters. As the region dried out and large game disappeared in the next millennia, tools of a more settled way of life appeared, such as grinding stones for preparing seeds and plant fibers.

ANCIENT CIVILIZATION

Between 7,000 and 2,000 BC, society evolved from hunting and gathering to farming; corn, squash, and beans were independently cultivated in widely separated areas in Mexico. Archaeologists believe that the earliest people who we can call Maya, or proto-Maya, inhabited the Pacific coast of Chiapas and Guatemala. These tribes lived in villages that held more than 1,000 inhabitants apiece; beautiful painted and incised ceramic jars for food storage have been found from this region and time period. After 1,000 BC this way of life spread south to the highlands site of Kaminaljuyú (now part of Guatemala City) and, through the next millennium, to the rest of the Maya world. Meanwhile, in what are now the Mexican states of Veracruz and Tabasco, another culture, the Olmecs, was developing what is now considered Mesoamerica's first civilization. Its influence was felt throughout Mexico and Central America. Archaeologists believe that before the Olmecs disappeared around 300 BC, they contributed two crucial cultural advances to the Maya: the Long Count calendar and the hieroglyphic writing system.

BACKGROUND
HISTORY

Yaxchilán ruins

LATE PRECLASSIC PERIOD

During the Late Preclassic era (300 BC-AD 250), the Pacific coastal plain saw the rise of a Maya culture in Izapa near Tapachula, Chiapas. The Izapans worshipped gods that were precursors of the Classic Maya pantheon and commemorated religious and historical events in bas-relief carvings that emphasized costume and finery.

During the same period, the northern Guatemalan highlands were booming with construction; this was the heyday of Kaminaljuyú, which grew to enormous size, with more than 120 temple-mounds and numerous stelae. The earliest calendar inscription that researchers are able to read comes from a monument found at El Baúl to the southwest of Kaminaljuyú; it has been translated as AD 36.

In the Petén jungle region just north of the highlands, the dominant culture was the Chicanel, whose hallmarks are elaborate temple-pyramids lined with enormous stucco god-masks (as in Kohunlich). The recently excavated Petén sites of Nakbé and El Mirador are the most spectacular Chicanel cities yet found. El Mirador contains a 70-meter-tall (230-foot) temple-pyramid complex that is the tallest ancient structure in Mesoamerica. Despite the obvious prosperity of this region, there is almost no evidence of Long Count dates or writing systems in either the Petén jungle or the Yucatán Peninsula just to the north.

EARLY CLASSIC PERIOD

The great efflorescence of the southern Maya world stopped at the end of the Early Classic period (AD 250-600). Kaminaljuyú and other cities were abandoned; researchers believe that the area was invaded by Teotihuacano warriors extending the reach of their Valley of Mexico-based empire. On the Yucatán Peninsula, there is evidence of Teotihuacano occupation at the Río Bec site of Becán and at Acanceh near Mérida. You can see Teotihuacano-style costumes and gods in carvings at the great Petén city of Tikal and at Copán in Honduras. By AD 600, the Teotihuacano empire had collapsed, and the stage was set for the Classic Maya eras.

LATE CLASSIC PERIOD

The Maya heartland of the Late Classic period (AD 600-925) extended from Copán in Honduras through Tikal in Guatemala and ended at Palenque in Chiapas. The

Maya stelae commemorate political, religious, and funerary events.

Early Civilizations and Maya Timeline

- **Paleoindian:** before 7000 BC
- **Archaic:** 7000-2000 BC
- **Early Preclassic:** 2000-1000 BC
- **Middle Preclassic:** 1000-300 BC
- **Late Preclassic:** 300 BC-AD 250
- **Early Classic:** AD 250-600
- **Late Classic:** AD 600-925
- **Early Postclassic:** AD 925-1200
- **Late Postclassic:** AD 1200-1530

development of these city-states, which also included Yaxchilán and Bonampak, almost always followed the same pattern. Early in this era, a new and vigorous breed of rulers founded a series of dynasties bent on deifying themselves and their ancestors. All the arts and sciences of the Maya world, from architecture to astronomy, were focused on this goal. The Long Count calendar and the hieroglyphic writing system were the most crucial tools in this effort, as the rulers needed to recount the stories of their dynasties and of their own glorious careers.

During the Late Classic era, painting, sculpture, and carving reached their climax; objects such as Lord Pakal's sarcophagus lid from Palenque are now recognized as among the finest pieces of world art. Royal monuments stood at the center of large and bustling cities. Cobá and Dzibilchaltún each probably contained 50,000 inhabitants, and there was vigorous intercity trade. Each Classic city-state reached its apogee at a different time; the southern cities peaked first, with the northern Puuc region cities following close behind.

By AD 925, nearly all the city-states had collapsed and were left in a state of near-abandonment. The Classic Maya decline is one of the great enigmas of Mesoamerican archaeology. There are a myriad of theories—disease,

invasion, peasant revolt—but many researchers now believe the collapse was caused by a combination of factors, including overpopulation, environmental degradation, and a series of devastating droughts. With the abandonment of the cities, the cultural advances disappeared as well. The last Long Count date was recorded in AD 909, and many religious customs and beliefs were never seen again.

EARLY POSTCLASSIC PERIOD

After the Puuc region was abandoned—almost certainly because of a foreign invasion—the center of Maya power moved east to Chichén. During this Early Postclassic era (AD 925-1200), the Toltec influence took hold, marking the end of the most artistic era and the birth of a new militaristic society built around a blend of ceremonialism, civic and social organization, and conquest. Chichén was the great power of northern Yucatán. Competing city-states either submitted to its warriors or, like the Puuc cities and Cobá, were destroyed.

LATE POSTCLASSIC PERIOD

After Chichén's fall in AD 1224—probably due to an invasion—a heretofore lowly tribe calling themselves the Itzá became the Late Postclassic (AD 1200-1530) masters of Yucatecan power politics. Kukulcán II of Chichén founded Mayapán in AD 1263-1283. After his death and the abandonment of Chichén, an aggressive Itzá lineage named the Cocom seized power and used Mayapán as a base to take over northern Yucatán. They succeeded through wars using Tabascan mercenaries and intermarrying with other powerful lineages. Foreign lineage heads were forced to live in Mayapán where they could easily be controlled. At its height, the city covered 6.5 square kilometers (4 square miles) within a defensive wall that contained more than 15,000 inhabitants. Architecturally, Mayapán leaves much to be desired; the city plan was haphazard, and its greatest monument was a sloppy, smaller copy of Chichén's Pyramid of Kukulcán.

The Cocom ruled for 250 years until AD 1441-1461, when an upstart Uxmal-based lineage named the Xiu rebelled and slaughtered the Cocom. Mayapán was abandoned and Yucatán's city-states were weakened in a series of bloody intramural wars that left them hopelessly divided when the conquistadors arrived. By the time of that conquest, culture was once again being imported from outside the Maya world. Putún Maya seafaring traders brought new styles of art and religious beliefs back from their trips to central Mexico. Their influence can be seen in the Mixtec-style frescoes at Tulum on the Quintana Roo coast.

SPANISH ARRIVAL AND CONQUEST

After Columbus's arrival in the New World, other adventurers traveling the same seas soon found the Yucatán Peninsula. In 1519, 34-year-old Hernán Cortés set out from Cuba—against the wishes of the Spanish governor—with 11 ships, 120 sailors, and 550 soldiers to search for slaves, a lucrative business. His search began on the Yucatán coast but eventually encompassed most of present-day Mexico. However, it took many decades and many lives for Spanish conquistadors to quell the Maya's resistance and cunning, despite a major advantage in military technology, including horses, gunpowder, and metal swords and armor. Francisco de Montejo, who took part in Cortés's earlier expedition into central Mexico, spent 1528-1535 trying to conquer the Yucatán, first from the east at Tulum and later from the west near Campeche and Tabasco, but was driven out each time. Montejo's son, also named Francisco de Montejo "El Mozo" (The Younger), took up the effort and eventually founded the city of Mérida in 1542 and Campeche in 1546. From those strongholds, the Spanish conquest slowly spread across the peninsula.

Economic and religious oppression were central to the conquest, too. The Xiu indigenous group proved an important ally to the Spanish after its leader converted to Christianity. And in 1562, a friar named Diego de Landa, upon learning his converts still practiced certain Maya ceremonies, became enraged and ordered the torture and imprisonment of numerous Maya spiritual leaders. He also gathered all the religious artifacts and Maya texts—which he said contained "superstitions and the devil's lies"—and had them burned. It was a staggering loss—at least 27 codices—and one that Landa later seemed to regret and attempted to reconcile by writing a detailed record of Maya customs, mathematics, and writing.

The Caste War

By the 1840s, the brutalized and subjugated Maya organized a revolt against Euro-Mexican colonizers. Called the Caste War, this savage war saw Maya taking revenge on every white man, woman, and child by means of murder and rape. European survivors made their way to the last Spanish strongholds of Mérida and Campeche. The governments of the two cities appealed for help to Spain, France, and the United States. No one answered the call. It was soon apparent that the remaining two cities would be wiped out.

But just as Mérida's leaders were preparing to evacuate the city, the Maya abruptly picked up their weapons and left. The reason was an unusually early appearance of flying ants, a sign of coming rain and to the Maya an all-important signal to begin planting corn. Despite the suffering visited upon them over three centuries of Spanish conquest, the Maya warriors, who were also farmers, simply could not risk missing the planting season. They turned their backs on certain victory and returned to their villages to tend their fields.

The unexpected reprieve allowed time for thousands of troops to arrive from Cuba, Mexico City, and the United States, and vengeance was merciless. Maya were killed indiscriminately. Some were taken prisoner and sold to Cuba as slaves; others left their villages and hid in the jungles—in some cases, for decades. Between 1846 and 1850, the population of the Yucatán Peninsula was reduced from 500,000 to 300,000. Quintana Roo along the Caribbean coast was considered a dangerous no-man's-land for almost another 100 years.

Growing Maya Power

Many Maya Indians escaped slaughter during the Caste War by fleeing to the isolated coastal forests of present-day Quintana Roo. A large number regrouped under the cult of the "Talking Cross"—an actual wooden cross that, with the help of a priest and a ventriloquist, spoke to the beleaguered indigenous fighters, urging them to continue fighting. Followers called themselves *Cruzob* (People of the Cross) and made a stronghold in the town of Chan Santa Cruz, today Carrillo Puerto. Research (and common sense) suggests the Maya knew full well that a human voice was responsible for the "talking," but that many believed it was inspired by God.

Close to the border with British Honduras (now Belize), the leaders of Chan Santa Cruz began selling timber to the British and were given weapons in return. Simultaneously (roughly 1855-1857), internal strife weakened the relations between Campeche and Mérida, and their mutual defense as well. Maya leaders took advantage of the conflict and attacked Fort Bacalar, eventually gaining control of the entire southern Caribbean coast.

Up until that time, indigenous soldiers simply killed the people they captured, but starting in 1858 they took lessons from the colonials and began to keep whites for slave labor. Women were put to work doing household chores and some became concubines, while men were forced to work the fields and build new constructions. (The main church in Carrillo Puerto was built largely by white slaves.)

For the next 40 years, the Maya people and soldiers based in and around Chan Santa Cruz kept the east coast of the Yucatán for themselves, and a shaky truce with the Mexican government endured. The native people were economically independent, self-governing, and, with no roads in or out of the region, almost totally isolated. They were not at war as long as everyone left them alone.

The Last Stand

Only when President Porfirio Díaz took power in 1877 did the Mexican federal government begin to think seriously about the Yucatán Peninsula. Through the years, Quintana Roo's isolation and the strength of the Maya in their treacherous jungle had foiled repeated efforts by Mexican soldiers to capture the region. The army's expeditions were infrequent, but it rankled Díaz that a relatively small and modestly armed Maya force had been able to keep the Mexican army at bay for so long. An assault in 1901, under the command of General Ignacio Bravo, broke the government's losing streak. The general captured a village, laid railroad tracks, and built a walled fort. Supplies arriving by rail kept the fort stocked, but the indigenous defenders responded by holding the fort under siege for an entire year. Reinforcements finally came from the capital and the Maya were forced to retreat, first from the fort and then from many of their villages and strongholds. A period of brutal Mexican occupation followed, lasting until 1915, yet Maya partisans still didn't give up. They conducted guerrilla raids from the tangled coastal forest until the Mexican army, frustrated and demoralized, pulled out and returned Quintana Roo to the Maya.

Beginning in 1917 and lasting to 1920, however, influenza and smallpox swept through the Maya-held territories, killing hundreds of thousands of Maya. In 1920, with the last of their army severely diminished and foreign gum-tappers creeping into former Maya territories, indigenous leaders entered into a negotiated settlement with the Mexican federal government. The final treaties were signed in 1936, erasing the last vestiges of Maya national sovereignty in the region.

LAND REFORMS

Beginning in 1875, international demand for twine and rope made from henequen, a type of agave cactus that thrives in northern Yucatán, brought prosperity to Mérida, the state capital. Beautiful mansions were built by entrepreneurs who led the good life, sending their children to school in Europe and cruising with their wives to New Orleans in search of new luxuries and entertainment. Port towns were developed on the Gulf coast, and a two-kilometer (1.2-mile) wharf in Progreso was built to accommodate the large ships that came for sisal (hemp from the henequen plant).

The only thing that didn't change was the lifestyle of indigenous people, who provided most of the labor on colonial haciendas. Henequen plants have incredibly hard, sharp spines and at certain times emit a horrendous stench. Maya workers labored long, hard hours, living in constant debt to the hacienda store.

Prosperity helped bring the Yucatán to the attention of the world. But in 1908, an American journalist named John Kenneth Turner stirred things up when he documented the difficult lives of the indigenous plantation workers and the accompanying opulence enjoyed by the owners. The report set a series of reforms into motion. Carrillo Puerto, the first socialist governor of Mérida, helped native workers set up a labor union, educational center, and political club that served to organize and focus resistance to the powerful hacienda system. Carrillo made numerous agrarian reforms, including decreeing that abandoned haciendas could be appropriated by the government. With his power and popularity growing, conservatives saw only one way to stop him. In 1923, Carrillo Puerto was assassinated.

By then, though, the Mexican Revolution had been won and reforms were being made throughout the country, including redistribution of land and mandatory education. Mexico entered its golden years, a 40-year period of sustained and substantial growth dubbed The Mexican Miracle, all the more miraculous because it took place in defiance of the worldwide Great Depression. In the late 1930s, President Lázaro Cárdenas undertook a massive nationalization program, claiming the major electricity, oil, and other companies for the state, and created state-run companies like PEMEX, the oil conglomerate still in existence today. In the Yucatán, Cárdenas usurped large parts of hacienda lands—as much as half of the Yucatán's total arable land, by some accounts, most dedicated to the growing of henequen—and redistributed them to poor farmers.

THE PRI YEARS

The economic prosperity allowed the ruling Institutional Revolutionary Party (PRI) to consolidate power, and before long it held every major office in the federal government, and most state governments as well. The Mexican Miracle had not ameliorated all social inequalities—and in fact had exacerbated some—but the PRI grew increasingly intolerant of dissent. Deeply corrupt, the party—and by extension the state—resorted to brutal and increasingly blatant repression to silence detractors. The most notorious example was the gunning down of scores of student demonstrators—some say up to 250—by security forces in 1968 in Mexico City's Tlatelolco Plaza. The massacre took place at night; by morning the plaza was cleared of bodies and scrubbed of blood, and the government simply denied that it ever happened.

The oil crisis that struck the United States in the early 1970s was at first a boon for Mexico, whose coffers were filled with money from pricey oil exports. But a failure to diversify the economy left Mexico vulnerable; as oil prices stabilized, the peso began to devalue. It had fallen as much as 500 percent by 1982, prompting then-president López Portillo to nationalize Mexico's banks. Foreign investment quickly dried up, and the 1980s were dubbed La Década Perdida (The Lost Decade) for Mexico and much of Latin America, a time of severe economic stagnation and crisis. In September 1985, a magnitude-8.1 earthquake struck Mexico City, killing 9,000 people and leaving 100,000 more homeless. It seemed Mexico had hit its nadir.

Yet it was during this same period that Cancún began to take off as a major vacation destination, drawing tourism and much-needed foreign dollars into the Mexican economy. The crises were not over—the implementation of the North American Free Trade Agreement (NAFTA) in 1994 was met simultaneously by a massive devaluation of the peso and an armed uprising by a peasant army called the Zapatistas in the state of Chiapas—but Mexico's economy regained some of its footing. A series of electoral reforms implemented in the late 1980s and through the 1990s paved the way for the historic 2000 presidential election, in which an opposition candidate—former Coca-Cola executive Vicente Fox of the right-of-center Partido de Acción Nacional (PAN)—defeated the PRI, ending the latter's 70-year reign of power. Fox was succeeded in 2006 by another PAN member, Felipe Calderón Hinojosa, in an election in which the PRI finished a distant third.

President Calderón campaigned on a promise to expand Mexico's job market and encourage foreign investment, including for new tourism projects in the Yucatán and elsewhere. But it was another pledge—to break up the drug trade and the cartels that controlled it—that consumed his entire presidency and plunged parts of Mexico into a spasm of violence unlike any since the revolution.

THE DRUG WARS

"The Drug War," as it is generally called, has its roots in the insatiable demand for drugs in the United States. Mexican drug cartels gained strength as operations in Colombia and the Caribbean were choked off in the 1990s; drug production in Mexico itself has also grown, especially methamphetamines. Mexican cartels traditionally operated within strictly defined territories—such as the Gulf cartel, the Sinaloa cartel, the Juárez cartel—and did so largely with impunity, thanks to corruption in the police and PRI-controlled local governments. The arrangement, though illicit, kept violence to a minimum as cartels kept to themselves and politicians and police turned a blind eye.

In 2006, encouraged by the United States, President Calderón dispatched the Mexican military to various northern cities to break up the cartels and their distribution networks. They achieved some initial success, but the broader effect was to disrupt the longtime balance of power. As control of routes and territories wavered, violence between rival cartels erupted with shocking speed and ferocity, with frequent shoot-outs and a gruesome cycle of attacks and reprisals. The official death toll is a staggering 60,000 people, though some estimates put it at double that. The vast majority of victims were gang-affiliated, though at least 2,000 police, soldiers, journalists, politicians, and even children were killed; 27,000 people are still classified as "missing." It's notable that virtually all the weapons used in the drug war were smuggled there from the United States.

MEXICO TODAY

In 2012, Mexico's national soccer team won its first Olympic gold medal, defeating heavily favored Brazil at the London games. It was a small blessing perhaps, but one that lifted the country's collective spirit. The election in 2012 of PRI candidate Enrique Peña Nieto seemed to signal an end to the drug war; Peña Nieto has focused on addressing drug abuse, unemployment, and corruption on a local level, and drug-related violence has diminished markedly. The Mexican military made several high-profile arrests, including the notorious cartel leader Joaquin "El Chapo" Guzmán Loera in Mazatlán in February 2014. (A year later, El Chapo escaped his maximum security prison via a sophisticated mile-long tunnel, adding to his fame and embarrassing Mexican authorities; he was recaptured in January 2016.) The relative calm was shaken, however, with the kidnapping and murder of 43 male student-teachers in the state of Guerrero in September 2014. They were traveling to the city of Iguala to protest a conference hosted by the mayor's wife; the mayor reportedly ordered police to intercept the students and turn them over to a local drug gang to be killed. The mayor and his wife were arrested after fleeing the state, the governor resigned, and dozens of police officers were arrested. Peña Nieto was roundly criticized for a too-tepid reaction, and the crime and alleged cover-up continue to spark large protests.

The trauma of "Los 43" notwithstanding, Mexico has mostly disappeared from the front page and reappeared in the travel section. Tourism has bounced back stronger than ever, with record numbers of visitors, especially to Cancún and the Riviera Maya. Low oil prices and a downward creep of the peso's value have persisted into 2016, leaving Mexico with less buying power than expected, though plans to invest over US$1 billion in tourism infrastructure remain mostly on track. Visitors will notice new roads, bridges, and bus and ferry terminals. A visit to Mexico by Pope Francis in 2016 was widely cheered, especially in the Maya world; the pontiff traveled to Chiapas to reiterate support for the use of indigenous languages, including the many forms of Maya, in performing Catholic Mass.

Government and Economy

GOVERNMENT

Mexico enjoys a constitutional democracy modeled after that of the United States, including a president (who serves one six-year term), a two-house legislature, and a judiciary branch. For 66 years (until the year 2000), Mexico was controlled by one party, the so-called moderate Partido Revolucionario Institucional (PRI). A few cities and states elected candidates from the main opposition parties—the conservative Partido de Acción Nacional (PAN) and leftist Partido de la Revolución Democrática (PRD)—but the presidency and most of the important government positions were passed from one handpicked PRI candidate to the next, amid rampant electoral fraud.

Indeed, fraud and corruption have been ugly mainstays of Mexican government for generations. In the 1988 presidential election, PRI candidate Carlos Salinas Gortari officially garnered 51 percent of the vote, a dubious result judging from polls leading up to the election, and rendered laughable after a mysterious "breakdown" in the election tallying system delayed the results for several days.

Salinas Gortari ended his term under the same heavy clouds of corruption and fraud that ushered him in, accused of having stolen millions of dollars from the federal government during his term. That said, Salinas pushed through changes such as increasing the number of Senate seats and reorganizing the federal electoral commission that helped usher in freer and fairer elections. He also oversaw the adoption of NAFTA in 1993, which has sped up Mexico's manufacturing industry but seriously damaged other sectors, especially small farmers, many of whom are indigenous.

The 1994 presidential election was marred by the assassination in Tijuana of the PRI candidate Luis Donaldo Colosio, the country's first major political assassination since 1928. Colosio's campaign manager, technocrat Ernesto Zedillo, was nominated to fill the candidacy and eventually elected. Zedillo continued with reforms, and in 2000, for the first time in almost seven decades, the opposition candidate officially won. PAN candidate Vicente Fox, a businessman and former Coca-Cola executive from Guanajuato, took the reins, promising continued electoral reforms, a stronger private sector, and closer relations with the United States. He knew U.S. president-elect George W. Bush personally, having worked with him on border issues during Bush's term as governor of Texas. Progress was being made until the terrorist attacks of September 11, 2001, pushed Mexico far down

bird's eye view of Cancún's Zona Hotelera

reduce poverty and strengthen social services. Both men claimed victory after Election Day; when Calderón was declared the winner, López Obrador alleged widespread fraud and called for a total recount. His supporters blocked major thoroughfares throughout the country for weeks. The Mexican Electoral Commission did a selective recount and affirmed a Calderón victory; the official figures set the margin at under 244,000 votes out of 41 million cast, a difference of just 0.5 percent. Calderón's inauguration was further marred by legislators fist-fighting in the chamber and the new president shouting his oath over jeers and general ruckus.

Calderón was confronted with a number of thorny problems upon inauguration, including a protest in Oaxaca that had turned violent, and spiraling corn prices that in turn drove up the cost of tortillas, the most basic of Mexican foods. While addressing those and other issues, he pressed forward with promised law-and-order reforms, raising police officers' wages and dispatching the Mexican military to staunch rampant gang- and drug-related crime in cities like Tijuana and Juárez. The latter sparked an all-out war between cartels, police, and the military.

In 2012, Mexicans elected Enrique Peña Nieto, the PRI candidate, as president. The results may be less a sign that Mexicans have forgiven the PRI its misdeeds of the not-so-distant past, and rather that they're simply exhausted by the violence that's taken place under the PAN (whose candidate finished a distant third). Peña Nieto has quietly shifted the federal government's focus to addressing drug abuse, unemployment, and corruption on a local level, while still pursuing arrests of high-profile cartel leaders. His term runs until 2018.

ECONOMY
Oil

Oil is a leading industry on the Yucatán Peninsula and throughout the Gulf coast, from Campeche to the Texas border. Mexico has long been one of the largest oil producers

on the U.S. administration's priority list. With Mexico serving a term on the U.N. Security Council, Fox came under intense pressure from the United States to support an invasion of Iraq. He ultimately refused—Mexican people were overwhelmingly opposed to the idea—but it cost Fox dearly in his relationship with Bush. The reforms he once seemed so ideally poised to achieve were largely incomplete by the time Fox's term ended.

The presidential elections of 2006 were bitterly contested and created—or exposed—a deep schism in the country. The eventual winner was PAN candidate Felipe Calderón Hinojosa, a former secretary of energy under Fox. His main opponent, Andrés Manuel López Obrador, was a former mayor of Mexico City and member of the left-leaning PRD. Though fraught with accusations and low blows, the campaign also was a classic clash of ideals, with Calderón advocating increased foreign investment and free trade, and López Obrador assailing the neoliberal model and calling for government action to in the Western Hemisphere and the world, and for years it was a net exporter of crude oil and natural gas to the United States and elsewhere. However, declining crude oil production in the Gulf of Mexico, a lack of refining capacity in Mexico, and the rapid expansion of U.S. natural gas production (and high Mexican demand for natural gas) has turned the relationship on its head. Mexico still exports crude oil to the United States, but is one of the main importers of American refined products like gasoline. Mexico also imports natural gas and liquefied natural gas from the United States, spurring plans for cross-border pipelines. Cities in the Yucatán Peninsula have long benefitted from Mexico's strong energy sector, but the effects of the worldwide decline in oil prices, coupled with a shifting relationship with the United States, may change spell changes for the future.

Fishing

Yucatecan fisheries also are abundant along the Gulf coast. At one time fishing was not much more than a family business, but today fleets of large purse seiners with their adjacent processing plants can be seen on the Gulf of Mexico. With the renewed interest in preserving fishing grounds for the future, the industry could continue to thrive for many years.

Tourism

Until the 1970s, Quintana Roo's economy amounted to very little. For a few years the chicle boom brought a flurry of activity up and down the state—it was shipped from the harbor of Isla Cozumel. Native and hardwood trees have always been in demand; coconuts and fishing were the only other natural resources that added to the economy, but neither on a large scale.

With the development of an offshore sandbar—Cancún—into a multimillion-dollar resort town, tourism became the region's number one moneymaker. The development of the Riviera Maya (extending from Cancún to Tulum)—and now, the Costa Maya (south of Sian Ka'an to the border of Belize)—only guaranteed the continued success of the economy. New roads now give access to previously unknown beaches and Maya structures. Extra attention is going to archaeological zones ignored for hundreds of years. All but the smallest have restrooms, ticket offices, and gift shops.

People and Culture

DEMOGRAPHICS

Today, 75-80 percent of the Mexican population is estimated to be mestizo (a combination of the indigenous and Spanish-Caucasian races). Only 10-15 percent are considered to be indigenous peoples. For comparison, as recently as 1870, the indigenous made up more than 50 percent of the population. While there are important native communities throughout Mexico, the majority of the country's indigenous peoples live in the Yucatán Peninsula, Oaxaca, and Chiapas.

RELIGION

The vast majority of Mexicans are Roman Catholic, especially in the generally conservative Yucatán Peninsula. However, a vigorous evangelical movement gains more and more converts every year.

LANGUAGE

The farther away you are from a city in the Yucatán—and Mexico in general—the less Spanish you'll hear and the more dialects of indigenous languages you'll encounter. The government estimates that of the 10 million indigenous people in the country, about 25 percent do not speak Spanish. Of the original

Regional Holidays and Celebrations

- Jan. 1: **New Year's Day**

- Jan. 6: **Día de los Reyes Magos:** Three Kings Day—Christmas gifts exchanged

- Feb. 2: **Virgen de la Candelaria:** Religious candlelight processions light up several towns

- Feb./Mar.: **Carnaval:** Seven-day celebration before Ash Wednesday; celebrated big on Isla Cozumel

- Mar. 21: **Birthday of Benito Juárez:** President of Mexico for five terms; born in 1806

- Mar. 21: **Vernal Equinox in Chichén Itzá:** A phenomenon of light and shadow displays a serpent slithering down the steps of El Castillo

- Apr. 19: **Festival de San Telmo:** Culmination of a two-week festival celebrating the patron saint of fishermen; celebrated on Isla Holbox

- May 1: **Día del Trabajador:** Labor Day

- May 3: **Day of the Holy Cross:** Dance of the Pigs' Head performed in Carrillo Puerto and El Cedral

- May 5: **Cinco de Mayo:** Commemoration of the Mexican army's 1862 defeat of the French at the Battle of Puebla

- Early July: **Founding of Ticul:** Celebrations to commemorate the city's founding by the Spanish in 1549. Festivities include dance and theater performances.

- Sept. 16: **Independence Day:** Celebrated on the night of the 15th

- Sept. 27-Oct. 14: **El Señor de las Ampollas:** Religious celebration in Mérida

- Sept. 29: **Fiesta de San Miguel Arcángel:** Celebration of Isla Cozumel's patron saint

- Oct. 4: **Feast Day of San Francisco de Asisi:** Religious celebrations in Conkal and Telchac Puerto

- Oct. 12: **Día de la Raza:** Indigenous Peoples Day; celebrated instead of Columbus Day

- Oct. 18-28: **El Cristo de Sitilpech:** Religious celebration in Izamal—the peak is on the 25th

- Nov. 1-2: **All Souls' Day and Day of the Dead:** Church ceremonies and graveside celebrations in honor of the deceased

- Nov. 20: **Día de la Revolución:** Celebration of the beginning of the Mexican Revolution in 1910

- Dec. 8: **Feast of the Immaculate Conception:** Religious celebrations in Izamal and Celestún

- Dec. 12: **Virgen de Guadalupe:** Religious celebration in honor of Mexico's patron saint

- Dec. 25: **Christmas:** Celebrated on the night of the 24th

125 native languages, 70 are still spoken, 20 of which are classified as Maya languages, including Tzeltal, Tzotzil, Chol, and Yucatec.

Although education was made compulsory for children in 1917, this law was not enforced in the Yucatán Peninsula until recently. Today, schools throughout the peninsula use Spanish-language books, even though many children do not speak the language. In some of the rural schools, bilingual teachers are recruited to help children make the transition.

ART

Mexico has an incredibly rich colonial and folk-art tradition. While not considered art to the people who make and use it, traditional indigenous clothing is beautiful, and travelers and collectors are increasingly able to buy it in local shops and markets. Prices for these items can be high, for the simple fact that they are handwoven and can literally take months to complete. Valladolid is an especially good place to purchase pottery, carving, and textiles from around the Yucatán and beyond.

HOLIDAYS AND FESTIVALS

Mexicans take celebrations and holidays seriously—of their country, their saints, and their families. You'll be hard-pressed to find a two-week period when something or someone isn't being celebrated. On major holidays—Christmas, New Year's Eve, and Easter—be prepared for crowds at the beaches and ruins. Be sure to book your hotel and buy your airline and bus tickets well in advance; during

Papel Picado

Mexicans are famous for their celebrations—whether it's to honor a patron saint or to celebrate a neighbor's birthday, partying is part of the culture. Typically, fiestas feature live music, lots of food, fireworks, and brightly colored decorations, often including *papel picado* (literally, diced paper).

Papel picado is tissue paper cut or stamped with a design that reflects the occasion in some way: a manger scene at Christmas, church bells for a wedding, skeletons in swooping hats for Day of the Dead. Once cut, row upon row of *papel picado* is strung across city streets, in front of churches, or in people's backyards. It typically stays up until wind or rain leaves just a thin cord and a few bits of torn paper as a reminder of the celebration that was.

holidays, the travel industry is saturated with Mexican travelers.

In addition to officially recognized holidays, villages and cities hold numerous festivals and celebrations: for patron saints, birthdays of officials, a good crop, a birth of a child. You name it, it's probably been celebrated. Festivals typically take place in and around the central plaza of a town with dancing, live music, colorful decorations, and fireworks. Temporary food booths are set up around the plaza and typically sell tamales (both sweet and meat), *buñuelos* (sweet rolls), tacos, *churros* (fried dough dusted with sugar), *carne asada* (barbecued meat), and plenty of regional drinks.

Essentials

Getting There

For centuries, getting to the Yucatán Peninsula required a major sea voyage to one of the few ports on the Gulf of Mexico, only to be followed by harrowing and uncertain land treks limited to mule trains and narrow paths through the tangled jungle. Today, the peninsula is easily accessible. Visitors arrive every day via modern airports, a network of good highways, excellent bus service, or by cruise ship. From just about anywhere in the world, the Yucatán is only hours away.

AIR

The main international airports on the Yucatán Peninsula are in Cancún and Mérida. The **Cancún** airport is by far the busiest, with dozens of daily domestic and international flights. There are smaller airports in **Cozumel, Chetumal, Campeche City,** and **Palenque;** another is reportedly being built in **Tulum,** though it remains far from completion. There also is an airport near **Chichén Itzá,** but currently it only receives chartered flights. In addition, there are small airports in **Mahahual** and **Isla Holbox** for private planes and air taxis.

Most travelers use the Cancún airport—it's well located for those vacationing in the Caribbean as well as for those traveling inland. Fares typically are cheaper to Cancún than to any other airport in the region.

Travelers who are planning to spend their entire time inland often choose to fly to Mérida instead—the city itself is an important destination, and it's close to many of the area's key sights and archaeological ruins.

Similarly, many travelers who only will be visiting Isla Cozumel fly directly there—it's often more expensive than landing in Cancún but avoids the time and hassle of traveling from the mainland to the island (more time to dive and to enjoy the island!).

There also are airports in Chetumal, Campeche City, and Palenque, which are typically used for domestic travel. However, for travelers planning to spend most of their time in the Costa Maya, Campeche, or Chiapas, they may be more convenient.

Departure Tax

There is a departure tax to fly out of any Mexican airport—the cost varies depending on the location (US$48 at the Cancún International Airport, US$14 at the Cozumel International Airport). Most airlines incorporate the tax into their tickets, but it's worth setting aside some cash just in case.

BUS

The Yucatán's main interstate bus hubs are Mérida and Cancún, with service to and from Mexico City, Veracruz, Oaxaca, and other major destinations in the country. There also are buses between Chetumal and cities in Belize and Guatemala. Travel agencies and tour operators in Palenque offer van service to various cities in Guatemala, including Flores, Quetzaltenango, Panajachel, Antigua, and Guatemala City.

CAR

Foreigners driving into Mexico are required to show a valid driver's license, title, registration, and proof of insurance for their vehicle. Mexican authorities do not recognize foreign-issued insurance; Mexican vehicle insurance is available at most border towns 24 hours a day, and several companies also sell policies over the Internet. Do not cross

---

Previous: the main drag in Tulum town; Bike taxis are a common way locals get around town.

Navigating the Cancún Airport

Some travelers find Cancun's airport somewhat daunting to navigate. The key is to not get drawn into any of the many sales pitches you'll encounter. Leaving the plane, simply follow the crowd, queueing first for immigration, then retrieving your luggage, then queueing again for customs, where you're asked to press a button: Green means go, red means stop and have your bags searched. Once through customs, you'll enter a large busy foyer packed with vendor booths, salespeople, and tourist office folks, ranging from peppy to pushy, virtually all of whom you can ignore or politely rebuff. If you're renting a car, look for the booth of the company you've reserved with and let the attendant know you've arrived; he or she will direct you to a shuttle to take you to the rental center. If you need a taxi, look for one of three "Yellow Transfers" booths, the official airport taxi service. To catch a bus, walk out of the terminal—ignoring the hagglers and taxi drivers clustered in front—and look for large ADO buses parked a few steps to your right; you can buy your ticket at the mobile desk set up there. If your resort has arranged transport for you, look for a driver outside the terminal with your name or the name of the resort on a sign. None of the options requires much walking, so you don't really need a porter; if you do use one, a couple dollars per bag is the customary tip.

the border with your car until you have obtained the proper papers.

CRUISE SHIP

Increasing numbers of cruise ships stop along Mexico's Caribbean coast every year, some carrying as many as 5,000 people. Many sail out of Miami and Fort Lauderdale, stopping at Key West before continuing to Punta Venado (Riviera Maya), Isla Cozumel, and Mahahual.

Prices are competitive, and ships vary in services, amenities, activities, and entertainment. Pools, restaurants, nightclubs, and cinemas are commonplace. Fitness centers and shops also make ship life convenient. To hone in on the type of cruise you'd like to go on, research options on the Internet, in the travel section of your local newspaper, and by contacting your travel agent.

If your budget is tight, consider traveling standby. Ships want to sail full and are willing to cut their prices—sometimes up to 50 percent—to do so. Airfare usually is not included. **Note:** Once you're on the standby list, you likely will have no choice of cabin location or size.

NEIGHBORING COUNTRIES

Cancún is an important international hub, not only for tourists from North America and Europe but also for regional flights to Central America and the Caribbean. In southern Quintana Roo, Chetumal is the gateway to Belize, and there's a direct bus to Flores, Guatemala. Most travel to Guatemala, however, is through Chiapas, from the towns of Palenque and San Cristóbal de las Casas. Travel agencies can book tours to Belize and Guatemala, though it's relatively easy to arrange a trip yourself. Most travelers do not need prearranged visas to enter either country, but they may have to pay an entrance fee at the airport or border.

Cancún has long been a major gateway to Cuba, especially for Americans circumventing U.S. travel restrictions to the island. The historic shift in U.S.-Cuba relations announced by President Obama in 2014 makes it significantly easier for Americans to visit Cuba without going through a third country, though Cancún will surely remain a popular and convenient portal.

Getting Around

AIR

Although budget airlines like Interjet are starting to appear on the Mexican airline scene, flying domestically is still relatively expensive, and the Yucatán is no exception. Once you factor in the check-in process, security, and baggage claim, there are very few flights within the region that make sense travel-wise, unless your time is incredibly tight. And if that is the case, you may as well see what you can do by car or bus and start planning a return trip.

BUS

Mexico's bus and public transportation system is one of the best in Latin America, if not the Western Hemisphere. In the Yucatán Peninsula, ADO and its affiliate bus lines practically have a monopoly, but that has not made bus travel any less efficient or less affordable. Dozens of buses cover every major route many times per day, and even smaller towns have frequent and reliable service.

Buses come in three main categories:

First Class: Known as *primera clase* or sometimes *ejecutivo,* first class is the most common and the one travelers use most often. Buses have reclining seats and TVs where movies are played on long trips. First-class buses make some intermediate stops but only in large towns. The main first-class lines in the Yucatán are ADO and OCC (primarily serving Chiapas).

Deluxe Class: Usually called *lujo* (luxury), deluxe class is a step up; they often are slightly faster since they're typically nonstop. The main deluxe line is ADO-GL, which costs 10-25 percent more than regular ADO. ADO-GL buses have nicer seats and better televisions (and even more recent movies!). Sometimes there are even free bottles of water in a cooler at the back. Even nicer are ADO-Platino buses, which often charge twice as much as regular ADO. Platino offers cushy,

extra-wide seats (only three across instead of four), headphones, and sometimes a light meal like a sandwich and soda.

Second Class: *Segunda clase,* or second class, is significantly slower and less comfortable than first class, and they're not all that much cheaper. Whenever possible, pay the dollar or two extra for first class. Second-class buses are handy in that you can flag them down anywhere on the roadside, but that is also precisely the reason they're so slow. In smaller towns, second class may be the only service available, and it's fine for shorter trips. The main second-class lines in the Yucatán are Mayab, Oriente, Noreste, and ATS.

For overnight trips, definitely take first-class or deluxe. Not only will you be much more comfortable, but second-class buses are sometimes targeted by roadside thieves since they drive on secondary roads and stop frequently.

Wherever bus service is thin, you can count on there being frequent *colectivos* or *combis*—vans or minibuses—that cover local routes. They can be flagged down anywhere along the road.

FERRY

Ferries are used to get to and from the region's most visited islands, including Isla Mujeres (reached from Cancún), Isla Cozumel (reached from Playa del Carmen), and Isla Holbox (reached from Chiquilá). Service is safe, reliable, frequent, and affordable.

CAR

As great as Mexico's bus system is, a car is the best way to tour the Yucatán Peninsula. Most of the sights—ruins, deserted beaches, haciendas, caves, cenotes, wildlife—are well outside the region's cities, down long access roads, or on the way from one town to the next. Having a car also saves you the time and effort of walking or the cost of cabbing to

Catch a ferry between Holbox and the mainland.

in cities like Cancún, Cozumel, and Mérida, and they occasionally have good walk-in deals.

- It's best to book on the car rental company's own website rather than a travel website. The prices are virtually the same, and if there are any problems, the rental office can't blame it on the other website.

- Ask your credit card company if your card provides free collision (liability) insurance on rental cars abroad. (Most do.) Unlike ordinary insurance, you'll have to pay any charges upfront and then file for reimbursement once you return. The coverage is usually better, though, with zero deductible and coverage even on dirt roads. Remember you have to actually use the card to pay for the rental in order to get the benefit!

- Car rental agencies make most of their money off the insurance, not the vehicle. That's why they push so hard for you to buy coverage. They'll warn you that with credit card insurance you'll have to pay 100 percent of any damages upfront; this is true, but it will be reimbursed when you file a claim back home. They may require you to authorize a larger "hold" on your card, as much as US$5,000, for potential damages. This is no big deal—it's not an actual charge—but that amount will be unavailable for other purchases. Consider bringing two or more credit cards, especially if your credit limit is low.

- Third-party insurance is required by law, and rental agencies are technically required to provide it. Lately, however, rental agencies say third-party coverage is free for anyone who also purchases collision insurance. But if you decline their collision insurance (because you get it through your credit card), suddenly there's a charge for third-party coverage. Credit cards typically do not offer third-party coverage, so you end up having to pay it. It's less expensive than collision insurance, but still a bummer to pay.

all those "missing links"; it also allows you to enjoy the sights for as much or as little time as you choose.

If you're here for a short time—a week or less—and want to sightsee, definitely get a car for the simple reason that you'll have the option of seeing and doing twice as much. If renting for your entire vacation isn't feasible moneywise, consider getting a car for just a couple days to explore a bit: Chichén Itzá and other nearby archaeological zones, DIY cenotes, the Puuc Route and the Río Bec archaeological zones, and the less-accessible parts of Quintana Roo like the Sian Ka'an Biosphere Reserve and the Costa Maya. You also may want a car for a day in Cozumel to check out the island. Cars aren't necessary to visit Cancún, Isla Mujeres, or Playa del Carmen.

Car Rental

The best rates (and best vehicles) are typically found online with the major international rental chains like Hertz, Thrifty, Budget, and Avis. That said, there are many local agencies

Before driving off, the attendant will review the car for existing damage—definitely accompany him or her on this part and don't be shy about pointing out every nick, scratch, and ding. Other things to confirm before driving off include:

- There is a spare tire (preferably a full-size, not temporary, one) and a working jack and tire iron.
- All doors lock and unlock, including the trunk.
- The headlights, brake lights, and turn signals work.
- All the windows roll up and down properly.
- The proper—and current—car registration is in the car. In some cases, your car rental contract serves as the registration.
- The amount of gas in the tank—you'll have to return it with the same amount.
- There is a 24-hour telephone number for the rental agency in case of an emergency.

Highways and Road Conditions

Driving in the Yucatán isn't as nerve-wracking as you might think. The highways are in excellent condition, and even secondary roads are well maintained. There are a few dirt and sand roads—mostly along the Costa Maya and in the Sian Ka'an Biosphere Reserve, to some of the lesser-visited archaeological sites in Campeche, and in the Lacandón region of Chiapas. If anything, frequent—and sometimes unexpected—*topes* (speed bumps) in small towns are the biggest driving hazard.

The main highways in the region are Highway 307, which runs the length of Mexico's Caribbean coast; Highway 180, the thoroughfare that links Cancún, Mérida, and Campeche City; and Highway 186, which crosses the southern portion of the Yucatán Peninsula and leads travelers to Campeche's Río Bec region and Comalcalco in Tabasco; and Highways 195, 190, and 200, which crisscross the state of Chiapas.

Taxi Scam

Beware of any taxi driver who tries to convince you that the hotel you're going to is closed, roach infested, flooded, burned down, has no running water, was destroyed by a hurricane (add your disaster of choice). As sincere as the driver might seem, he is more often than not retaliating against hotels that refuse to pay a finder's fee. Taxi drivers in Cancún and throughout the Riviera Maya earn significant commissions—as much as US$10 per person *per night*—for bringing guests to certain establishments. Some hotels refuse to pay the fee, and taxi drivers, in turn, try to take their clients to "cooperative" hotels instead. Don't fall for it. You may have to be firm, but insist that your driver take you to the hotel of your choice. Your best option is to call ahead for a room reservation, which also serves to confirm that the hotel actually is open and operational.

In the entire region, there are only two toll roads, both sections of Highway 180: between Mérida and Cancún (a whopping US$32—US$20 from Cancún to Valladolid, US$12 from Pisté to Mérida) and between Campeche City and the town of Champotón (US$4.75). Although far from cheap, they can save a significant amount of time driving, and are safer for driving at night. Secondary roads are free and pass through picturesque countryside and indigenous villages; they are slower and have more obstacles like pedestrians, bicycles, and speed bumps, but can be a rewarding way to go.

Driving Scams

Most travelers have heard horror stories about Mexican police and worry about being taken for all their money or trundled off to jail without reason. While it is true that there is corruption among the police, they don't target tourists; foreigners are, after all, the economic lifeblood of the region—the police don't want to scare them away.

As long as you are a careful and defensive driver, it is very unlikely you'll have

Driving Distances (Kilometers)

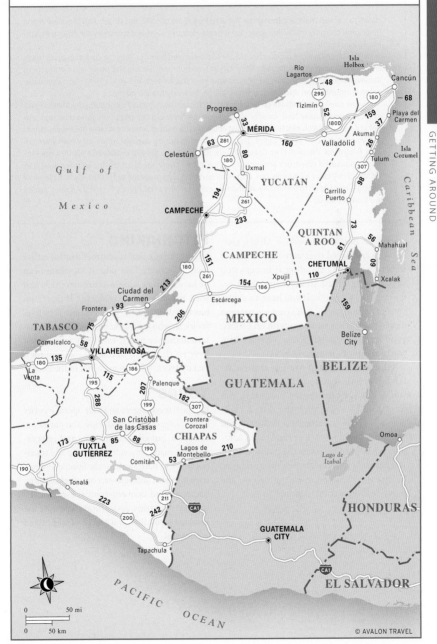

© AVALON TRAVEL

Driving in Mexico

Having a car can make exploring the Yucatán Peninsula quicker and easier, and there are many places you can only reach with your own wheels. Here are some tips to make your driving experience a bit smoother:

Off the highways, the biggest hazard are *topes* (speed bumps). They are common on all roads and highways, save the toll roads. They vary in size, but many are big and burly, and hitting them at even a slow speed can do a number on you, your passengers, and your car. As soon as you see a sign announcing an upcoming town or village, be ready to slow down.

Narrow one-way streets are common in many cities in the Yucatán. Fortunately, the **stop signs** in those areas usually have smaller plaques (beneath the big red one) indicating direction and right of way. A **black rectangle** means you have the right of way, a **red one** means you don't.

If you break down or run out of gas on a main road during daylight hours, stay with your car. **Los Ángeles Verdes** (The Green Angels, toll-free Mex. tel. 078 or 800/903-9200), a government-sponsored tow-truck and repair service, cruise these roads on the lookout for drivers in trouble. They carry a CB radio, gas, and small parts, and are prepared to fix tires. If you have a cell phone—or happen to be near a pay phone—call your car rental agency first; the Ángeles Verdes are a great backup.

any interaction with the police. Most travelers who are pulled over actually have done something wrong—speeding, running a stop sign, turning on red. In those situations, remain calm and polite. If you have an explanation, definitely give it; it is not uncommon to discuss a given situation with an officer. Who knows, you may even convince him you're right—it's happened to us!

Of greater concern are gas station attendants. Full service is the norm here—you pull up, tell the person how much you want, and he or she does the rest. A common scam is for one attendant to distract you with questions about wiper fluid or gas additives while another starts the pump at 50 or 100 pesos. Before you answer any questions, be sure the attendant resets, or "zeroes," the pump before starting to pump.

HITCHHIKING

Hitchhiking is not recommended for either men or women. That said, it sometimes can be hard to know what is a private vehicle and what is a *colectivo* (shared van). If there's no bus terminal nearby, your best bet is to look for locals who are waiting for public transportation and see which vans they take. If you have no choice but to hitch a ride, opt for a pickup truck, where you can sit in the back.

TOURS

Regional travel agents and tour operators offer a vast range of organized trips. You pay extra, of course, but all arrangements and reservations are made for you: from guides and transportation to hotels and meals. Special-interest trips also are common—archaeological tours, hacienda and convent routes, bird-watching and dive trips. Ask around and surf the Internet—you'll find a world of organized adventure.

Visas and Officialdom

PASSPORTS

Gone are the days you could zip down to Mexico with just your driver's license and birth certificate. All nationalities must have a valid passport to enter Mexico by air, land, or sea. (Since January 2007 and March 2010, respectively, U.S. and Canadian citizens are required to have a passport to enter the country.)

VISAS AND TOURIST CARDS

Citizens of most countries, including the United States, Canada, and members of the E.U., do not need to obtain a visa to enter Mexico. All foreigners, however, are issued a white tourist card when they enter, with the number of days that they are permitted to stay in the country written at the bottom, typically 30-60 days. If you plan to stay for more than a month, politely ask the official to give you the amount of time you need; the maximum stay is 180 days.

Hold onto your tourist card! It must be returned to immigration officials when you leave Mexico. If you lose it, you'll be fined and may not be permitted to leave the country (much less the immigration office) until you pay.

To extend your stay up to 180 days, head to the nearest immigration office a week *before* your tourist card expires. Be sure to bring it along with your passport. There, you'll fill out several forms, go to a bank to pay the US$25 processing fee, make photocopies of all the paperwork (including your passport, entry stamp, tourist card, and credit card), and then return to the office to get the extension. For every extra 30 days requested, foreigners must prove that they have US$1,000 available, either in cash or travelers checks, or simply by showing a current credit card. The process can take anywhere from a couple of hours to a week, depending on the office.

CUSTOMS

Plants and fresh foods are not allowed into Mexico, and there are special limits on alcohol, tobacco, and electronic products. Archaeological artifacts, certain antiques, and colonial art cannot be exported from Mexico without special permission.

Above all, do not attempt to bring marijuana or any other narcotic in or out of Mexico. Jail is one place your trusty guidebook won't come in handy.

Returning home, you will be required to declare all items you bought in Mexico. Citizens of the United States are allowed to reenter with US$800 worth of purchases duty-free; the figure for other travelers varies by country.

CONSULATES

The consulates in Cancún and Mérida handle passport issues (replacing a lost one, adding pages, etc.) and can help their citizens if they are in a serious or emergency situation, including hospitalization, assault, arrest, lawsuits, or death. They usually do not help resolve common disputes—with tour operators or hotels, for example.

Foreign consulates and consular agencies in the region include:

AUSTRIA

Cancún: Calle Punta Conoco No. 36, tel. 998/884-1598, konsul_a@yaho.com.mx, 9am-1pm Monday-Friday
Mérida: Av. Colón Norte 501-C, tel. 999/925-6386, bulnesa@prodigy.net.mx, 9:30am-1pm Monday-Friday

BELGIUM

Cancún: Plaza Tropical, Av. Tulum 192, tel. 998/892-2512, www.diplomatie.be, 10am-2pm Monday-Friday

BELIZE

Cancún: Av. Nader 34, tel. 998/887 8415, 9am-5pm Monday-Friday
Chetumal: Av. Genova 369, tel. 983/285-3511, conbelizeqroo@gmail.com, 9am-1pm Monday-Friday
Mérida: Calle 53 btwn Calles 56 and 58, tel. 999/928-6152, consbelice@dutton.com.mx, 9am-1pm Monday-Friday

CANADA

Cancún: Centro Empresarial, Blvd. Kukulcán Km. 12, tel. 998/883-3360, www.canada.org.mx, 9am-1pm Monday-Friday

CUBA

Cancún: Pecari 17, tel. 998/884-3423, www.cubadiplomatica.cu/mexico, 9am-1pm Monday-Friday
Mérida: Calle 1-D btwn Calles 42 and 44, tel. 999/944-4215, www.cubadiplomatica.cu/mexico, 8:30am-1:30pm Monday-Friday

DENMARK

Cancún: Omni Hotel, Blvd. Kukulcán Km. 16.5, tel. 998/881-0600, apresidencia@grupocancun.net, 9am-1pm Monday-Friday

FINLAND

Cancún: Edificio Popolnah, Av. Nader 28, tel. 998/884-1600, notariacancun@prodigy.net.mx, 9am-2pm and 5pm-8pm Monday-Friday

FRANCE

Cancún: Colegio Británico, Calle Pargo 24, tel. 998/883-9816, consulatcancun@aol.com, by appointment only
Mérida: Calle 60 btwn Calles 41 and 43, tel. 999/930-1542, consuladofrancia@sipse.com.mx, 9am-5pm Monday-Friday

GERMANY

Cancún: Calle Punta Conocó 36, tel. 998/884-1598, konsul_d@yahoo.com.mx, 9am-noon Monday-Friday

GUATEMALA

Cancún: Edificio Barcelona, Av. Nader 148, 998/884-8296, 9am-1pm Monday-Friday
Chetumal: Avenida Héroes de Chapultepec 356, tel. 983/832-3045, 9am-1pm Monday-Friday

IRELAND

Cancún: Av. Cobá 15, tel. 555/5520-5803, consul@gruporoyale.com, 9am-1pm Monday-Friday

ITALY

Cancún: Parque Las Palapas, Alcatraces 39, tel. 998/884-1261, conitaca@prodigy.net.mx, 9am-2pm Monday-Friday

NETHERLANDS

Cancún: Pabellón Caribe, Av. Nichupté s/n, tel. 998/884-8672, nlconsulcancun@prodigy.net.mx, 9am-1pm Monday-Friday
Mérida: Calle 64 btwn Calles 47 and 49, tel. 999/924-3122, pixan2003@prodigy.net.mx, 8am-5pm Monday-Friday

NORWAY

Cancún: Calle Venado 30, tel. 998/887-4412, noruega@aviomar.com.mx, 9am-1pm Monday-Friday

SPAIN

Cancún: Blvd. Kukulcán at Calle Cenzontle, tel. 998/848-9918, consules@sercc.com.mx, 10am-1pm Monday-Friday
Mérida: Calle 50 at Calle 33, tel. 999/948-3489, consulado.es.mid@gmail.com, 10am-1pm Monday-Friday

SWEDEN

Cancún: Omni Cancún Hotel & Villas, Blvd. Kukulcán Km. 16.5, tel. 998/881-0600, msalinas@omnicancun.com.mx, tel. 998/881-0600, 9am-6pm Monday-Friday

SWITZERLAND

Cancún: above Rolandi's restaurant, Av. Cobá 12, tel. 998/884-8486, 9am-2pm Monday-Friday

UNITED KINGDOM

Cancún: The Royal Sands Resort & Spa, Blvd. Kukulcán Km. 13.5, tel. 998/881-0100, www.ukinmexico.fco.gov.uk/en, 9am-3pm Monday-Friday

UNITED STATES

Cancún: Torre La Europea, Blvd. Kukulcán Km. 13, tel. 998/883-0272, ConAgencyCancun@state.gov, 8am-1pm Monday-Friday, appointment required for some services

Mérida: Calle 60 No. 338-K btwn Calles 29 and 31, tel. 999/942-5700, http://merida.usconsulate.gov, 7:30am-4:30pm Monday-Friday, appointment required for some services

Playa del Carmen: La Palapa, Calle 1 btwn Avs. 15 and 20, tel. 984/873-0303, ConAgencyCancun@state.gov, 9am-1pm Monday-Friday

UNDERAGE TRAVELERS

In the United States, anyone under 18 traveling internationally without *both* parents or legal guardians must present a signed, notarized letter from the parent(s) or guardian(s) granting the minor permission to leave the country. This requirement is aimed at preventing international abductions, but it causes frequent and major disruptions for vacationers.

Food and Accommodations

FOOD

Considered among the most distinct cuisines of the country, Yucatecan food reflects the influences of its Maya, European, and Caribbean heritage. Some of the most popular menu items include:

Cochinita Pibil: pork marinated in achiote, orange juice, and other spices then wrapped in banana leaves and baked.

Dzoto-bichay: tamales made of *chaya* (a spinach-like leafy vegetable) and eggs, smothered in tomato sauce.

Empanizado: breaded and fried pork or chicken slices—often served with salad, rice, and beans.

Panucho: small thick tortillas stuffed with refried beans and covered with shredded turkey, pickled onion, and avocado.

Papadzules: hard-boiled eggs chopped and rolled into a corn tortilla, smothered in a creamy pumpkin-seed sauce.

Poc-Chuc: slices of pork marinated in orange juice and coated with a tangy sauce.

Salbute: small handmade tortillas topped with shredded turkey, pickled onion, and slices of avocado.

Sopa de Lima: turkey stock soup with shredded turkey, fried tortilla strips, and *lima* juice.

ACCOMMODATIONS

Lodging in the Yucatán Peninsula truly runs the gamut: campgrounds, hostels, small hotels, bed-and-breakfasts, boutique hotels, large modern hotels, and all-inclusive resorts. There are a handful of fishing lodges in places like Sian Ka'an Biosphere Reserve, and a number of large ex-haciendas that have been converted into deluxe hotels, primarily in Yucatán and Campeche states.

Taxes on your hotel bill, referred to generally as I.V.A. (value-added tax; pronounced EE-va in Spanish), are usually 12 percent but can be as high as 17-22 percent. Be sure to ask if the rate you're quoted includes taxes (*¿Incluye impuestos?*); in many cases, especially at smaller hotels, the taxes are applied only if you pay by credit card.

You may be required to make a deposit in order to reserve a room, especially in popular areas during high season. However, in Mexico credit cards cannot be charged without a physical signature, so they aren't much help as a deposit. Many hotels utilize PayPal or a similar service; those that do not will give you the name of their bank and account number, and you must stop by a branch and make the deposit with the teller. Be sure to get a receipt, and notify the hotel after making the deposit.

Cancellation policies tend to be rather unforgiving, especially during high season; you may be required to give a month or more advance notice to receive even a partial refund. Trip insurance is a good idea if your plans are less than concrete.

Conduct and Customs

CLOTHING

Perhaps the single most-abused social custom in Mexico is the use of shorts. Mexicans rarely wear them outside the home or off the beach, while many foreign travelers seem to have packed nothing but shorts. There is a bit more flexibility in beach areas, but it's worth getting in the habit of wearing long pants or skirts whenever going to dinner, attending performances, and especially when entering churches and government offices, where shorts and tank tops are considered inappropriate (and, in some cases, disrespectful).

Topless and nude sunbathing are not customary on Mexican beaches, and are rarely practiced in Cancún and other areas frequented by Americans and Canadians. However, on beaches popular with Europeans, especially Playa del Carmen and Tulum, it is more commonplace. Wherever you are, take a look around to help decide whether baring some or all is appropriate.

PHOTOGRAPHING LOCALS

No one enjoys having a stranger take his or her picture for no good reason, and Mexicans—indigenous or otherwise—are no different. The best policy is simply not to take these photographs unless you've first asked the person's permission and he or she has agreed. **Tip:** If the potential subject of your photo is a vendor, buy something and *then* ask if you can take a photo—you're more likely to get a positive response.

GREETINGS

Even a small amount of Spanish can go a long way in showing respect and consideration for people you encounter. Make a point of learning basic greetings like *buenos días* (good morning) and *buenas tardes* (good afternoon) and using them in passing, or as preface to a conversation; it is considered somewhat impolite to launch into a discussion without greeting the other person first.

Travel Tips

WHAT TO PACK

Essentials for the Yucatán include sunscreen, sunglasses, and a billed hat. If you wear contacts or glasses, bring a replacement set. A good pair of shoes—or at least Teva-style sandals—are vital for exploring Maya ruins safely, and insect repellent definitely can come in handy. If you lose or forget something, Cancún, Cozumel, Playa del Carmen, Tulum, Chetumal, Mérida, and Campeche all have huge supermarkets, including Walmart.

ACCESS FOR TRAVELERS WITH DISABILITIES

Mexico has made many improvements for the blind and people in wheelchairs—many large stores and tourist centers have ramps or elevators. A growing number of hotels also have rooms designed for guests with disabilities, and museums occasionally create exhibits with, for example, replicas of Maya artifacts or folk art that visually impaired travelers can hold and touch. (None were currently on display at the time of research, however.) That said, Mexico is still a hard place to navigate if you have a disability. Smaller towns are the most problematic, as their sidewalks can be narrow, and even some main streets are not paved. Definitely ask for help—for what Mexico lacks in infrastructure, its people often make up for in graciousness.

TRAVELING WITH CHILDREN

The Yucatán Peninsula is a great place to take kids, whether youngsters or teenagers. The variety of activities and relative ease of transportation help keep everyone happy and engaged. Cancún and the Riviera Maya are especially family friendly, with several different ecoparks and water parks, miles of beaches, and (if all else fails) plenty of malls with movie theaters, arcades, bowling, mini-golf, aquariums, and more. Perhaps best of all, Mexico is a country where family is paramount, so kids—even fussy ones—are welcome just about everywhere.

WOMEN TRAVELING ALONE

Solo women should expect a certain amount of unwanted attention, mostly in the form of whistles and catcalls. It typically happens as they walk down the street and sometimes comes from the most unlikely sources—we saw a man dressed as a clown turn mid-balloon animal to whistle at a woman walking by. Two or more women walking together attract much less unwanted attention, and a woman and man walking together will get none at all (at least of this sort—street vendors are a different story). While annoying and often unnerving, this sort of attention is almost always completely benign, and ignoring it is definitely the best response. Making eye contact or snapping a smart retort only will inspire more attention. Occasionally men will hustle alongside a woman and try to strike up a conversation—if you don't want to engage, a brief *no, gracias* should make that clear. To minimize unwanted attention, avoid revealing clothing, such as tight jeans, low-cut shirts, or bikini tops, as street wear. Carrying a notebook—or creating the appearance of working—also helps.

SENIOR TRAVELERS

Seniors should feel very welcome and safe visiting the Yucatán. Mexico is a country that affords great respect to *personas de la tercera edad* (literally, "people of the third age"), and especially in the tradition-minded Yucatán Peninsula. But as anywhere, older travelers should take certain precautions. The Yucatán, particularly Mérida and inland areas, is known to be extremely hot and humid, especially May-July. Seniors should take extra care to stay cool and hydrated. Exploring the Maya ruins also can be hot, not to mention exhausting. Bring water and snacks, especially to smaller sites where they may not be commonly sold. Travelers with balance or mobility concerns should think twice about climbing any of the pyramids or other structures. They can be deceptively treacherous, with steps that are steep, uneven, and slick.

Cancún, Playa del Carmen, and Mérida have state-of-the-art hospitals, staffed by skilled doctors, nurses, and technicians, many of whom speak English. Most prescription medications are available in Mexico, often at discount prices. However, pharmacists are woefully under-trained, and you should always double-check the active ingredients and dosage of any pills you buy here.

GAY AND LESBIAN TRAVELERS

While openly gay women are still rare in Mexico, gay men are increasingly visible in large cities and certain tourist areas. Mérida has a fairly large gay community, of which a number of expat hotel and guesthouse owners are a prominent part. Cancún and Playa del Carmen also both have a visible gay presence and a number of gay-friendly venues. Nevertheless, many locals—even in large cities—are not accustomed to open displays of homosexuality and may react openly and negatively. Many hotel attendants also simply don't understand that two travel companions of the same gender may prefer one bed—in some cases they will outright refuse to grant the request. Some couples find it easier to book a room with two queen-size beds and just sleep in one.

TRAVELING WITH IMPORTANT DOCUMENTS

Scan and/or make copies of your passport, tourist card, and airline tickets. Whether you're traveling solo or with others, leave a copy with someone you trust at home. Store another copy online (i.e., your email account or on the cloud), and if you have a travel companion, give a copy to him or her. Be sure to carry a *copy* of your passport and tourist card in your purse or wallet and leave the originals in the hotel safe or locked in your bag; they're a lot more likely to be lost or stolen on the street than taken by hotel staff. When you move from place to place, carry your passport and important documents in a travel pouch, always under your clothing. Write down your credit card and ATM numbers and the 24-hour service numbers and keep those in a safe place.

Health and Safety

SUNBURN

Common sense is the most important factor in avoiding sunburn. Use waterproof and sweatproof sunscreen with a high SPF. Reapply regularly—even the most heavy-duty waterproof sunscreen washes off faster than it claims to on the bottle (or gets rubbed off when you use your towel to dry off). Be extra careful to protect parts of your body that aren't normally exposed to the sun—a good way to cover every inch is to apply sunscreen *before* you get dressed—and give your skin a break from direct sun every few hours. Remember that redness from a sunburn takes several hours to appear—that is, you can be sunburned long before you *look* sunburned.

If you get sunburned, treat it like any other burn by running cool water over it for as long and as often as you can. Do not expose your skin to more sun. Re-burning the skin can result in painful blisters that can easily become infected. There are a number of products designed to relieve sunburns, most with aloe extracts. Finally, be sure to drink plenty of water to keep your skin hydrated.

HEAT EXHAUSTION AND HEAT STROKE

The symptoms of heat exhaustion are cool moist skin, profuse sweating, headache, fatigue, and drowsiness. It is associated with dehydration and commonly happens during or after a strenuous day in the sun, such as while visiting ruins. You should get out of the sun, remove any tight or restrictive clothing, and sip a sports drink such as Gatorade. Cool compresses and raising your feet and legs helps too.

Heat exhaustion is not the same as heat stroke, which is distinguished by a high body temperature, a rapid pulse, and sometimes delirium or even unconsciousness. It is an extremely serious, potentially fatal condition, and victims should be taken to the hospital immediately. In the meantime, wrap the victim in wet sheets, massage the arms and legs to increase circulation, and do not administer large amounts of liquids. Never give liquids if the victim is unconscious.

DIARRHEA

Diarrhea is not an illness in itself, but your body's attempt to get rid of something bad in a hurry; that something can be any one of a number of strains of bacteria, parasites, or amoebae that are often passed from contaminated water. No fun, it is usually accompanied by cramping, dehydration, fever, and of course, frequent trips to the bathroom.

If you get diarrhea, it should pass in a day or two. Anti-diarrheals such as Lomotil and Imodium A-D will plug you up but don't cure you—use them only if you can't be near a bathroom. The malaise you feel from diarrhea typically is from dehydration, not the actual infection, so be sure to drink plenty of fluids—a sports drink such as Gatorade is best. If it's especially bad, ask at your hotel for the nearest *laboratorio* (laboratory or clinic), where a stool sample can be analyzed for around US$5 and tell you if you have a

parasitic infection or a virus. If it's a common infection, the lab technician will tell you what medicine to take. Be aware that medicines for stomach infection are seriously potent, killing not only the bad stuff but the good stuff as well; they'll cure you but leave you vulnerable to another infection. Avoid alcohol and spicy foods for several days afterward.

A few tips for avoiding diarrhea include:

- Only drink bottled water. Avoid using tap water even for brushing your teeth.

- Avoid raw fruits or vegetables that you haven't disinfected and cut yourself. Lettuce is particularly dangerous since water is easily trapped in the leaves. Also, as tasty as they look, avoid the bags of sliced fruit sold from street carts.

- Order your meat dishes well done, even if it's an upscale restaurant. If you've been to a market, you'll see that meat is handled very differently here.

INSECTS

Insects are not of particular concern in the Yucatán, certainly not as they are in other parts of the tropics. Mosquitoes are common, but are not known to carry malaria. Dengue fever, also transmitted by mosquitoes, is present but still rare. The Zika virus is a concern, of course: As of early 2016, Mexico had a few dozen confirmed cases, the majority in Chiapas. The numbers are expected to grow, but the Yucatán has the benefit of robust anti-mosquito measures already in place, thanks to dengue and chikungunya outbreaks in years past. Just as those diseases have been fairly well-contained, regional health and tourism officials believe Zika will not pose a major threat to locals or visitors. Needless to say, be sure to review the latest information before traveling, and take sensible precautions, like wearing repellent and long pants and sleeves.

Finally, some remote beaches, like Isla Holbox and the Costa Maya, may have sand flies or horseflies, but they have been all but eliminated in the more touristed areas. Certain destinations are more likely to be buggy, like forested archaeological zones and coastal bird-watching areas, and travelers should bring and use insect repellent there, if only for extra comfort.

CRIME

The Yucatán Peninsula is generally quite safe, and few travelers report problems with crime of any kind. Cancún is the one area where particular care should be taken, however. You may find illicit drugs relatively easy to obtain, but bear in mind that drug crimes are prosecuted vigorously in Mexico (especially ones involving foreigners), and your country's embassy can do very little to help. Sexual assault and rape have been reported by women at nightclubs, sometimes after having been slipped a "date rape" drug. While the clubs are raucous and sexually charged by definition, women should be especially alert to the people around them and wary of accepting drinks from strangers. In all areas, common-sense precautions are always recommended, such as taking a taxi at night instead of walking (especially if you've been drinking) and avoiding flashing your money and valuables, or leaving them unattended on the beach or elsewhere. Utilize the safety deposit box in your hotel room, if one is available; if you rent a car, get one with a trunk so your bags will not be visible through the window.

Information and Services

MONEY
Currency and Exchange Rates

Mexico's official currency is the peso, divided into 100 centavos. It is typically designated with the symbol $, but you may also see MN$ (*moneda nacional,* or national currency). We've listed virtually all prices in their U.S. dollar equivalent, but occasionally use M$ to indicate the price is in Mexican pesos.

U.S. dollars and E.U. euros are accepted in a few highly touristed locations like the Zona Hotelera in Cancún and the shopping districts of Cozumel and Playa del Carmen. However, you'll want and need pesos everywhere else, as most shopkeepers appreciate visitors paying in the local currency. **Note:** Foreign bills only are accepted because coins can't be changed to pesos.

At the time of research, US$1 was equal to M$16, slightly less for Canadian dollars, and M$18 for euros.

ATMs

Almost every town in the Yucatán Peninsula has an ATM, and they are without question the easiest, fastest, and best way to manage your money. Be aware that you may be charged a transaction fee by the ATM (US$2-3 typically) as well as your home bank (as much as US$10). It's worth asking your bank if it partners with a Mexican bank, and whether transaction fees are lower if you use that bank's cash machines. Also, be sure to use ATMS that are affiliated with a recognizable bank in order to avoid exorbitant service charges.

Travelers Checks

With the spread of ATMs, travelers checks have stopped being convenient for most travel, especially in a country as developed as Mexico. If you do bring them, you will have to exchange them at a bank or a *casa de cambio* (exchange booth).

Credit Cards

Visa and MasterCard are accepted at all large hotels and many medium and small ones, upscale restaurants, main bus terminals, travel agencies, and many shops throughout Mexico. American Express is accepted much less frequently. Some merchants tack on a 3-10 percent surcharge for any credit card purchase—ask before you pay.

Cash

It's a good idea to bring a small amount of U.S. cash, on the off chance that your ATM or credit cards suddenly stop working; a US$200 reserve should be more than enough. Stow it away with your other important documents, to be used only if necessary.

Tax

A 12 percent value-added tax (*IVA* in Spanish) applies to hotel rates, restaurant and bar tabs, and gift purchases. When checking in or making reservations at a hotel, ask if tax has already been added. In some cases, the tax is 17 percent.

Bargaining

Bargaining is common and expected in street and artisans' markets, but try not to be too aggressive. Some tourists derive immense and almost irrational pride from haggling over every last cent, and then turn around and spend several times that amount on beer or snacks. The fact is, most bargaining comes down to the difference of a few dollars or even less, and earning those extra dollars is a much bigger deal for most artisans than spending them is to most tourists.

Tipping

While tipping is always a choice, it is a key supplement to many workers' paychecks. In fact, for some—like baggers at the grocery store—the tip is the *only* pay they receive. And while dollars and euros are appreciated, pesos are preferred. **Note:** Foreign coins can't be changed to pesos, so are useless to workers. Average gratuities in the region include:

- Archaeological zone guides: 10-15 percent if you're satisfied with the service; for informal guides (typically boys who show you around the site), US$2-3 is customary.

- Gas station attendants: around US$0.50 if your windshield has been cleaned, tires have been filled, or the oil and water have been checked; no tip is expected for simply pumping gas.

- Grocery store baggers: US$0.25-0.50.

- Housekeepers: US$1.50-2 per day; either left daily or as a lump sum at the end of your stay.

- Porters: about US$1-2 per bag.

- Taxi drivers: Tipping is not customary.

- Tour guides: 10-15 percent; don't forget the driver—US$1-2 is typical.

- Waiters: 10-15 percent; make sure the gratuity is not already included in the bill.

COMMUNICATIONS AND MEDIA
Postal Service

Mailing letters and postcards from Mexico is neither cheap nor necessarily reliable. Delivery times vary greatly, and letters get "lost" somewhat more than postcards. Letters (under 20 grams) and postcards cost US$1 to the United States and Canada, US$1.20 to Europe and South America, and US$1.35 to the rest of the world. Visit the Correos de México website (www.correosde-mexico.com.mx) for pricing on larger packages and other services.

Telephone

Ladatel—Mexico's national phone company—maintains good public phones all over the peninsula and country. Plastic phone cards with little chips in them are sold at most mini-marts and supermarkets in 30-, 50-, 100-, and 200-peso denominations. Ask for a *tarjeta* Ladatel—they are the size and stiffness of a credit card, as opposed to the thin cards used for cell phones. Insert the card into any public pay phone, and the amount on the card will be displayed on the screen. Rates and dialing instructions (in Spanish and English) are inside the phone cabin. At the time of research, rates were roughly US$0.10 per minute for local calls, US$0.40 per minute for national calls, and US$0.50 per minute for calls to the United States and Canada.

A number of Internet cafés offer inexpensive **Web-based phone service**, especially in the larger cities where broadband

Useful Telephone Numbers

TRAVELER ASSISTANCE

- Emergencies: 060 or 066
- Ángeles Verdes (Green Angels): 078 or 800/903-9200
- Directory Assistance: 044

LONG-DISTANCE DIRECT DIALING

- Domestic long-distance: 01 + area code + number
- International long-distance (United States only): 001 + area code + number
- International long-distance (rest of the world): 00 + country code + area code + number

LONG-DISTANCE COLLECT CALLS

- Domestic long-distance operator: 02
- International long-distance operator (English-speaking): 09

connections are fastest. Rates tend to be significantly lower than those of Ladatel, and you don't have to worry about your card running out.

Beware of phones offering "free" collect or credit card calls; far from being free, their rates are outrageous.

If you've got an unlocked GSM cell phone, you can purchase a local SIM card for around US$15, including US$5 credit, for use during your trip. Calls are expensive, but text messaging is relatively cheap, including to the United States; having two local phones/chips can be especially useful for couples or families traveling together.

Internet Access

Internet cafés can be found in virtually every town in the region. Most charge around US$1 per hour, though prices can be much higher in malls and heavily touristed areas. Most places also will burn digital photos onto a CD or DVD—they typically sell blank discs, but travelers should bring their own USB cable.

Wireless Internet is also becoming popular at all levels of hotels; if you need to stay connected while you're on the road, and you're

willing to travel with a laptop or tablet, it's easy—and free—to access the Internet.

Newspapers

The most popular daily newspapers in the Yucatán Peninsula are *Novedades Quintana Roo* (www.sipse.com/novedades/), *¡Por Esto!* (www.poresto.net), *El Diario de Yucatán* (www.yucatan.com.mx), *Tribuna de Campeche* (www.tribunacampeche.com), *Novedades Campeche* (www.novedadesdecampeche.com.mx), and *El Sur de Campeche* (www.elsur.mx). The main national newspapers are also readily available, including *Reforma (www.reforma.com), La Prensa* (www.la-prensa.com.mx), and *La Jornada* (www.jornada.unam.mx). For news in English, you'll find *USA Today* (www.usatoday.com) and *Miami Herald Cancún Edition* in Cancún and occasionally in Playa del Carmen, Isla Cozumel, and Mérida.

Radio and Television

Most large hotels and a number of midsize and small ones have cable or satellite TV, which usually includes CNN (though sometimes in Spanish only), MTV, and other U.S.

Cell Phone Calls

MEXICAN LANDLINE TO MEXICAN CELL PHONE:

- Within the same area code: 044 + 3-digit area code + 7-digit phone number
- Different area code: 045 + 3-digit area code + 7-digit phone number

MEXICAN CELL PHONE TO MEXICAN CELL PHONE:

- Within the same area code: 7-digit number only
- Different area code: 3-digit area code + 7-digit number

INTERNATIONAL LANDLINE/ CELL PHONE TO MEXICAN CELL PHONE:

- From U.S. or Canada: 011 + 52 + 1 + 3-digit area code + 7-digit number
- From other countries: international access code + 52 + 1 + 3-digit area code + 7-digit number

channels. AM and FM radio options are surprisingly bland—you're more likely to find a good *rock en español* station in California than you are in the Yucatán.

MAPS AND TOURIST INFORMATION

Maps

A husband-and-wife team creates **MapChick maps** (www.cancunmap.com), outstanding and exhaustively detailed maps of Cancún, Playa del Carmen, the Riviera Maya, Isla Cozumel, Isla Mujeres, and inland archaeological zones. They're as much guidebooks as maps, with virtually every building and business identified, many with short personal reviews, plus useful information like taxi rates, driving distances, ferry schedules, and more. Maps cost around US$15 and often come with a couple of smaller secondary maps; they're sold on the MapChick website as well as at www.amazon.com.

Dante (Calle 61 near Calle 62, tel. 999/928-2611, 8am-10:30pm daily) produces reasonably reliable maps of the entire Yucatán Peninsula; it also operates a chain of excellent bookstores in Mérida and at various archaeological sites.

Most local tourist offices distribute maps to tourists free of charge, though quality varies considerably. Car rental agencies often have maps, and many hotels create maps for their guests of nearby restaurants and sights.

Tourist Offices

Most cities in the region have a tourist information office or kiosk. Some are staffed with friendly and knowledgeable people and have a good sense of what tourists are looking for. At others, you'll seriously wonder how the people there were hired. It is certainly worth stopping in if you have a question—you may well get it answered, but don't be surprised if you don't.

Photography and Video

Digital cameras are as ubiquitous in Mexico as they are everywhere else, but memory sticks and other paraphernalia can be prohibitively expensive; bring a spare chip in case your primary one gets lost or damaged. If your chip's capacity is relatively small and you're not bringing your laptop along, pack a couple of blank DVDs and a USB cable to download and burn photos, which you can do at most Internet cafés.

Video is another great way to capture the color and movement of the region. Be aware that all archaeological sites charge an additional US$3.50 to bring in a video camera; tripods often are prohibited.

WEIGHTS AND MEASURES
Measurements

Mexico uses the metric system, so distances are in kilometers, weights are in kilograms, gasoline is sold by the liter, and temperatures are given in Celsius.

Time Zone

The entire Yucatán Peninsula and Chiapas used to be part of the Central Standard time zone (along with Mexico City and much of central Mexico), with a region-wide shift in fall and spring for daylight savings. However, in 2015, the state of Quintana Roo (which includes Cancún, Playa del Carmen, Cozumel, Tulum, and the Costa Maya) joined the Eastern Standard Zone from October to April only. Put another way, while the rest of the Yucatán and Central Time Zone "fall back" in October, Quintana Roo now stays on daylight saving time, making it one hour ahead of its neighbors (and thus the same as the Eastern Time Zone). In April, Central Time Zone "catches up," and the entire region is on the same hour again. The change is meant to give the Riviera Maya a longer-feeling day during the winter months and make travel from the U.S. East Coast easier. It's sure to make travel to and from the Yucatecan interior a bit more confusing, however; be sure to double-check your flight and bus times to avoid missed connections.

Electricity

Mexico uses the 60-cycle, 110-volt AC current common in the United States. Bring a surge protector if you plan to plug in a laptop.

Resources

Spanish Glossary

SPANISH GLOSSARY

The form of Spanish spoken in the Yucatán Peninsula is quite clear and understandable, and far less clipped or colloquial than in other countries. That's good news for anyone new to the language, and hoping to use their trip to learn more.

abarrotería: small grocery store
alcalde: mayor or municipal judge
alfarería: pottery
alfarero, alfarera: potter
amigo, amiga: friend
andador: walkway or strolling path
antojitos: Mexican snacks, such as huaraches, flautas, and quesadillas
artesanías: handicrafts, as distinguished from *artesano, artesana,* the person who makes handicrafts
audiencia: one of the royal executive-judicial panels sent to rule areas of Latin America during the 16th century
ayuntamiento: either the town council or the building where it meets
bienes raíces: literally "good roots," but popularly, real estate
boleto: ticket, boarding pass
bucear, buzo: to scuba dive, scuba diver
caballero: gentleman
cabecera: head town of a municipal district, or headquarters in general
cabrón: a bastard; sometimes used affectionately
cacique: chief or boss
calesa: early 1800s-style horse-drawn carriage; also called *calandria*

camionera central: central bus station; alternatively, *terminal camionera*
campesino: country person; farm worker
canasta: basket
cárcel: jail
casa de huéspedes: guesthouse, often operated in a family home
caudillo: dictator or political chief
charro, charra: cowboy, cowgirl
churrigueresque: Spanish baroque architectural style incorporated into many Mexican colonial churches, named after José Churriguera (1665-1725)
cofradía: Catholic fraternal service association, either male or female, mainly in charge of financing and organizing religious festivals
colectivo: a shared public taxi or minibus that picks up and drops off passengers along a designated route; alternatively, *combi*
colegio: preparatory school
colonia: city neighborhood or subdivision; similar to *fraccionamiento* or *barrio*
combi: a shared public minibus; alternatively, *colectivo*
comedor: small restaurant
correo: post office
criollo: person of all-Spanish descent born in the New World
cuadra: city block
Cuaresma: Lent
cuota: literally "toll," commonly refers to a toll highway
curandero, curandera: indigenous medicine man or woman
dama: lady
Domingo de Ramos: Palm Sunday

Don, Doña: title of respect, generally used for an older man or woman

ejido: a constitutional, government-sponsored form of community, with shared land ownership and cooperative decision-making

encomienda: colonial award of tribute from a designated indigenous district

farmacia: pharmacy or drugstore

finca: farm

fraccionamiento: city sector or subdivision; similar to *colonia* or *barrio*

gasolinera: gasoline station

gringo: term referring to North American Caucasians, sometimes derogatorily, sometimes not

grito: impassioned cry; *El Grito* commonly refers to Mexican Independence Day celebrations, from Hidalgo's *Grito de Dolores*

hacienda: large landed estate; also the government treasury

impuestos, I.V.A. (pronounced EE-va): taxes, value-added tax

indígena: indigenous person; commonly, but incorrectly, an indian (*indio*)

jardín: garden or small park

jejenes: "no-see-um" biting gnats

judiciales: the federal or state police, best known to motorists for their highway checkpoint inspections; alternatively, *federales*

lancha: small motorboat; alternatively, *panga*

larga distancia: long-distance telephone service, or the *caseta* (booth) where it's provided

licenciado: academic degree (abbr. Lic.) approximately equivalent to a bachelor's degree

lonchería: small lunch counter, usually serving juices, sandwiches, and *antojitos* (Mexican snacks)

machismo; macho: exaggerated sense of maleness; person who holds such a sense of himself

mescal: alcoholic beverage distilled from the fermented hearts of maguey (century plant)

mestizo: person of mixed European/indigenous descent

milpa: native farm plot, usually of corn, squash, and/or beans

mordida: slang for bribe; literally, "little bite"

palapa: thatched-roof structure, often open air

panga: small motorboat; alternatively, *lancha*

parque central: town plaza or central square; alternatively, *zócalo*

PEMEX: government gasoline station, acronym for "Petróleos Mexicanos," Mexico's national oil corporation

peninsulares: the Spanish-born ruling colonial elite

petate: a mat, traditionally woven of palm leaf

plan: political manifesto, usually by a leader or group consolidating or seeking power

plaza: shopping mall

policía: municipal police, alternatively *preventativa*

Porfiriato: the 34-year (1876-1910) ruling period of president-dictator Porfirio Díaz

pozole: popular stew of hominy in broth, usually topped by shredded pork, cabbage, and diced onion

presidencia municipal: the headquarters, like a U.S. city or county hall, of a Mexican *municipio*, a county-like local governmental unit

propina: tip, as at a restaurant or hotel; alternatively, *servicio*

pueblo: town or people

puta: whore

quinta: a villa or country house

retorno: highway turnaround

Semana Santa: literally Holy Week, the week before Easter, a popular travel period for Mexicans

temporada: season, as in *temporada alta/baja* (high/low season)

tenate: soft, pliable basket, without handle, woven of palm leaf

terminal camionera: central bus station; alternatively, *camionera central*

vecinidad: neighborhood, alternatively *barrio*

zócalo: town plaza or central square; alternatively, *parque central*

Abbreviations

Av.: *avenida* (avenue)

Blvd.: *bulevar* (boulevard)

Calz.: *calzada* (thoroughfare, main road)

Carr.: *carretera* (highway)

Col.: *colonia* (subdivision)

Nte.: *norte* (north)

Yucatec Maya Glossary

The Maya language family includes 30 distinct languages, together spoken by nearly six million people in Mexico, Guatemala, and Belize. Yucatec Maya is spoken by around 800,000 people, and is the most commonly spoken Maya language in the Yucatán Peninsula (and second overall, after K'iche in Guatemala). Most ancient glyphs were written in early forms of Yucatec Maya or another Maya language, Ch'ol.

MAYA GODS AND CEREMONIES

Acanum: protective deity of hunters

Ahau Can: serpent lord and highest priest

Ahau Chamehes: deity of medicine

Ah Cantzicnal: aquatic deity

Ah Chuy Kak: god of violent death and sacrifice

Ahcit Dzalmalcum: protective god of fishermen

Ah Cup Cacap: god of the underworld who denies air

Ah Itzám: the water witch

Ah kines: priests that consult the oracles and preside over ceremonies and sacrifices

Ahpua: god of fishing

Ah Puch: god of death

Ak'Al: sacred marsh where water abounds

Bacaboob: supporters of the sky and guardians of the cardinal points, who form a single god, Ah Cantzicnal Becabs

Bolontiku: the nine lords of the night

Chaac: god of rain and agriculture

Chac Bolay Can: butcher serpent living in the underworld

Chaces: priests' assistants in agricultural and other ceremonies

Cihuateteo: women who become goddesses through death in childbirth

Cit Chac Coh: god of war

Hetzmek: ceremony when the child is first carried astride the hip

Hobnil Bacab: bee god, protector of beekeepers

Holcanes: warriors charged with obtaining slaves for sacrifice

Hunab Ku: giver of life, builder of the universe, and father of Itzámna

Ik: god of the wind

Itzámna: lord of the skies, creator of the beginning, god of time

Ixchel: goddess of birth, fertility, and medicine; credited with inventing spinning

Ixtab: goddess of the cord and of suicide by hanging

Kinich: face of the sun

Kukulcán: quetzal-serpent, plumed serpent

Metnal: the underworld, place of the dead

Nacom: warrior chief

Noh Ek: Venus

Pakat: god of violent death

Zec: spirit lords of beehives

FOOD AND DRINK

alche: inebriating drink, sweetened with honey and used for ceremonies and offerings

ic: chili

itz: sweet potato

kabaxbuul: heaviest meal of the day, eaten at dusk and containing cooked black beans

kah: pinole flour

kayem: ground maize

macal: a root

muxubbak: tamale

on: avocado

op: plum

p'ac: tomatoes

put: papaya

tzamna: black bean

uah: tortillas

za: maize drink

ANIMALS

acehpek: dog used for deer hunting
ah maax cal: prattling monkey
ah maycuy: chestnut deer
ah sac dziu: white thrush
ah xixteel ul: rugged land conch
bil: hairless dog reared for food
cutz: wild turkey
cutzha: duck
hoh: crow
icim: owl
jaleb: hairless dog
keh: deer
kitam: wild boar
muan: evil bird related to death
que: parrot
thul: rabbit
tzo: domestic turkey
utiu: coyote

MUSIC AND FESTIVALS

ah paxboob: musicians
bexelac: turtle shell used as percussion instrument
chohom: dance performed in ceremonies related to fishing
chul: flute
hom: trumpet
kayab: percussion instrument fashioned from turtle shell
Oc na: festival where old idols of a temple are broken and replaced with new ones
okot uil: dance performed during the Pocan ceremony
Pacum chac: festival in honor of the war gods
tunkul: drum
zacatan: drum made from a hollowed tree trunk; one opening is covered with hide

ELEMENTS OF TIME

baktun: 144,000-day Maya calendar
chumuc akab: midnight
chumuc kin: midday
emelkin: sunset
haab: solar calendar of 360 days plus five extra days of misfortune, which complete the final month
kaz akab: dusk

kin: the sun, the day, the unity of time
potakab: time before dawn
yalhalcab: dawn

NUMBERS

hun: one
ca: two
ox: three
can: four
ho: five
uac: six
uuc: seven
uacax: eight
bolon: nine
iahun: ten
buluc: eleven
iahca: twelve
oxlahum: thirteen
canlahum: fourteen
holahun: fifteen
uaclahun: sixteen
uuclahun: seventeen
uacaclahun: eighteen
bolontahun: nineteen
hunkal: twenty

PLANTS AND TREES

ha: cacao seed
kan ak: plant that produces a yellow dye
ki: sisal
kiixpaxhkum: chayote
kikche: tree trunk that is used to make canoes
kuche: red cedar tree
k'uxub: annatto tree
piim: fiber of the cotton tree
taman: cotton plant
tauch: black zapote tree
tazon te: moss

MISCELLANEOUS WORDS

ah kay kin bak: meat-seller
chaltun: water cistern
cha te: black vegetable dye
chi te: eugenia, plant for dyeing
ch'oh: indigo
ek: dye
hadzab: wooden swords

halach uinic: leader
mayacimil: smallpox epidemic
palapa: traditional Maya structure constructed without nails or tools
pic: underskirt
ploms: rich people

suyen: square blanket
xanab: sandals
xicul: sleeveless jacket decorated with feathers
xul: stake with a pointed, fire-hardened tip
yuntun: slings

Spanish Phrasebook

Whether you speak a little or a lot, using your Spanish will surely make your vacation a lot more fun. You'll soon see that Mexicans truly appreciate your efforts and your willingness to speak their language.

Spanish commonly uses 30 letters—the familiar English 26, plus four straightforward additions: ch, ll, ñ, and rr.

PRONUNCIATION

Once you learn them, Spanish pronunciation rules—in contrast to English and other languages—generally don't change. Spanish vowels generally sound softer than in English.

Vowels

a like ah, as in "hah": *agua* AH-gooah (water), *pan* PAHN (bread), and *casa* CAH-sah (house)

e like eh, as in "hem": *mesa* MEH-sah (table), *tela* TEH-lah (cloth), and *de* DEH (of, from)

i like ee, as in "need": *diez* dee-EHZ (ten), *comida* ko-MEE-dah (meal), and *fin* FEEN (end)

o like oh, as in "go": *peso* PEH-soh (weight), *ocho* OH-choh (eight), and *poco* POH-koh (a bit)

u like oo, as in "cool": *uno* OO-noh (one), *cuarto* KOOAHR-toh (room), and *usted* oos-TEHD (you); when it follows a "q" the **u** is silent: *quiero* ki-EH-ro (I want); when it follows an "h" or has an umlaut, it's pronounced like "w": *huevo* WEH-vo (egg)

Consonants

b, d, f, k, l, m, n, p, q, s, t, v, w, x, y, z, and

ch pronounced almost as in English; **h** is silent

c like k, as in "keep": *cuarto* KOOAR-toh (room), *Tepic* tay-PEEK (capital of Nayarit state); when it precedes "e" or "i," pronounce **c** like s, as in "sit": *cerveza* sehr-VEH-sah (beer), *encima* ehn-SEE-mah (atop)

g like g, as in "gift" when it precedes "a," "o," "u," or a consonant: *gato* GAH-toh (cat), *hago* AH-goh (I do, make); otherwise, pronounce **g** like h, as in "hat": *giro* HEE-roh (money order), *gente* HEN-tay (people)

j like h, as in "has": *Jueves* HOOEH-vehs (Thursday), *mejor* meh-HOR (better)

ll like y, as in "yes": *toalla* toh-AH-yah (towel), *ellos* EH-yohs (they, them)

ñ like ny, as in "canyon": *año* AH-nyo (year), *señor* SEH-nyor (mister, sir)

r is lightly trilled: *pero* PEH-roh (but), *tres* TREHS (three), *cuatro* KOOAH-troh (four)

rr like a Spanish r, but with much more emphasis and trill: *burro* (donkey), *carretera* (highway), *ferrocarril* (railroad)

Note: The single exception to the above is the pronunciation of **y** when it's being used as the Spanish word for "and," as in *Eva y Leo.* In such case, pronounce it like the English ee, as in "keep": Eva "ee" Leo (Eva and Leo).

Accent

The rule for accent, the relative stress given to syllables within a given word, is straightforward. If a word ends in a vowel, an "n," or an "s," accent the next-to-last syllable; if not, accent the last syllable.

Pronounce *gracias* GRAH-seeahs (thank you), *orden* OHR-dehn (order), and *carretera* kah-reh-TEH-rah (highway) with the stress on the next-to-last syllable.

Otherwise, accent the last syllable: *venir* vay-NEER (to come), *ferrocarril* feh-roh-cah-REEL (railroad), and *edad* eh-DAHD (age).

Exceptions to the accent rule are always marked with an accent sign: (á, é, í, ó, or ú), such as *teléfono* teh-LEH-foh-noh (telephone), *jabón* hah-BON (soap), and *rápido* RAH-pee-doh (rapid).

BASIC AND COURTEOUS EXPRESSIONS

Most Spanish-speakers consider formalities important. Whenever approaching anyone, try to say the appropriate salutation—good morning, good evening, etc. Standing alone, the greeting *hola* (hello) can sound brusque.

Hello. *Hola.*
Good morning. *Buenos días.*
Good afternoon. *Buenas tardes.*
Good evening. *Buenas noches.*
How are you? *¿Cómo está Usted?*
Very well, thank you. *Muy bien, gracias.*
Okay; good. *Bien.*
Not okay; bad. *No muy bien; mal.*
So-so. *Más o menos.*
And you? *¿Y usted?*
Thank you. *Gracias.*
Thank you very much. *Muchas gracias.*
You're very kind. *Muy amable.*
You're welcome. *De nada.*
Good-bye. *Adios.*
See you later. *Hasta luego.*
please *por favor*
yes *sí*
no *no*
I don't know. *No sé.*
Just a moment, please. *Un momento, por favor.*
Excuse me, please (when you're trying to get attention). *Disculpe* or *Con permiso.*
Excuse me (when you've made a mistake). *Lo siento.*
Pleased to meet you. *Mucho gusto.*

Do you speak English? *¿Habla Usted inglés?*
Is English spoken here? *¿Se habla inglés?*
I don't speak Spanish well. *No hablo bien el español.*
I don't understand. *No entiendo.*
How do you say . . . in Spanish? *¿Cómo se dice . . . en español?*
What is your name? *¿Cómo se llama Usted?*
My name is . . . *Me llamo . . .*
Would you like . . . *¿Quisiera Usted . . .*
Let's go to . . . *Vamos a . . .*

TERMS OF ADDRESS

When in doubt, use the formal *Usted* (you) as a form of address.

I *yo*
you (formal) *Usted*
you (familiar) *tu*
he/him *él*
she/her *ella*
we/us *nosotros*
you (plural) *ustedes*
they/them *ellos* (all males or mixed gender); *ellas* (all females)
mister, sir *señor*
missus, ma'am *señora*
miss, young lady *señorita*
wife *esposa*
husband *esposo*
friend *amigo* (male); *amiga* (female)
boyfriend; girlfriend *novio; novia*
son; daughter *hijo; hija*
brother; sister *hermano; hermana*
father; mother *padre; madre*
grandfather; grandmother *abuelo; abuela*

TRANSPORTATION

Where is . . . ? *¿Dónde está . . . ?*
How far is it to . . . ? *¿A cuánto está . . . ?*
from . . . to . . . *de . . . a . . .*
How many blocks? *¿Cuántas cuadras?*
Where (Which) is the way to . . . ? *¿Dónde está el camino a . . . ?*
the bus station *la terminal de autobuses*

the bus stop *la parada de autobuses*
Where is this bus going? *¿Adónde va este autobús?*
the taxi stand *la parada de taxis*
the train station *la estación de ferrocarril*
the boat *el barco* or *la lancha*
the airport *el aeropuerto*
I'd like a ticket to . . . *Quisiera un boleto a . . .*
first (second) class *primera (segunda) clase*
round-trip *ida y vuelta*
reservation *reservación*
baggage *equipaje*
Stop here, please. *Pare aquí, por favor.*
the entrance *la entrada*
the exit *la salida*
the ticket office *la taquilla*
(very) near; far *(muy) cerca; lejos*
to; toward *a*
by; through *por*
from *de*
the right *la derecha*
the left *la izquierda*
straight ahead *derecho; directo*
in front *en frente*
beside *al lado*
behind *atrás*
the corner *la esquina*
the stoplight *el semáforo*
a turn *una vuelta*
here *aquí*
somewhere around here *por aquí*
right there *allí*
somewhere around there *por allá*
street; boulevard *calle; bulevar*
highway *carretera*
bridge *puente*
toll *cuota*
address *dirección*
north; south *norte; sur*
east; west *oriente (este); poniente (oeste)*

ACCOMMODATIONS

hotel *hotel*
Is there a room? *¿Hay cuarto?*
May I (may we) see it? *¿Podría (podríamos) verlo?*
What is the rate? *¿Cuál es la tarifa?*

Is that your best rate? *¿Es su mejor precio?*
Is there something cheaper? *¿Hay algo más económico?*
a single room *un cuarto sencillo*
a double room *un cuarto doble*
double bed *cama matrimonial*
twin bed *cama individual*
with private bath *con baño privado*
hot water *agua caliente*
shower *ducha; regadera*
towels *toallas*
soap *jabón*
toilet paper *papel higiénico*
blanket *cobija*
sheets *sábanas*
air-conditioned *aire acondicionado*
fan *abanico; ventilador*
key *llave*
manager *gerente*

FOOD

I'm hungry. *Tengo hambre.*
I'm thirsty. *Tengo sed.*
menu *carta; menú*
order *orden*
glass *vaso*
fork *tenedor*
knife *cuchillo*
spoon *cuchara*
napkin *servilleta*
soft drink *refresco*
coffee *café*
tea *té*
drinking water *agua pura; agua potable*
carbonated water *agua mineral*
bottled uncarbonated water *agua sin gas*
beer *cerveza*
wine *vino*
milk *leche*
juice *jugo*
cream *crema*
sugar *azúcar*
cheese *queso*
snack *antojito; botana*
breakfast *desayuno*
lunch *almuerzo* or *comida*
daily lunch special *comida corrida*

dinner *cena*
the check *la cuenta*
eggs *huevos*
bread *pan*
salad *ensalada*
fruit *fruta*
mango *mango*
watermelon *sandía*
papaya *papaya*
banana *plátano*
apple *manzana*
orange *naranja*
lime *limón*
fish *pescado*
shellfish *mariscos*
shrimp *camarones*
meat (without) *(sin) carne*
chicken *pollo*
pork *puerco*
beef; steak *res; bistec*
bacon; ham *tocino; jamón*
fried *frito*
roasted *asado*
barbecue; barbecued *barbacoa; al carbón*
food to go *comida para llevar; para llevar*
delivery service *servicio a domicilio*

SHOPPING

money *dinero*
money-exchange bureau *casa de cambio*
I would like to exchange travelers
  checks. *Quisiera cambiar cheques de
  viajero.*
What is the exchange rate? *¿Cuál es el
  tipo de cambio?*
How much is the commission? *¿Cuánto
  cuesta la comisión?*
Do you accept credit cards? *¿Aceptan
  tarjetas de crédito?*
money order *giro*
How much does it cost? *¿Cuánto cuesta?*
What is your final price? *¿Cuál es su
  último precio?*
expensive *caro*
cheap *barato; económico*
more *más*
less *menos*
a little *un poco*

too much *demasiado*

HEALTH

Help me please. *Ayúdeme por favor.*
I am ill. *Estoy enfermo.*
Call a doctor. *Llame un doctor.*
Take me to... *Lléveme a...*
hospital *hospital; clinica medica*
drugstore *farmacia*
pain *dolor*
fever *fiebre*
headache *dolor de cabeza*
stomachache *dolor de estómago*
burn *quemadura*
cramp *calambre*
nausea *náusea*
vomiting *vomitar*
medicine *medicina*
antibiotic *antibiótico*
pill; tablet *pastilla*
aspirin *aspirina*
ointment; cream *pomada; crema*
bandage *venda*
cotton *algodón*
sanitary napkins *Kotex*
birth control pills *pastillas anticonceptivas*
contraceptive foam *espuma
  anticonceptiva*
condoms *preservativos; condones*
contact lenses *pupilentes*
glasses *lentes*
dental floss *hilo dental*
dentist *dentista*
toothbrush *cepillo de dientes*
toothpaste *pasta de dientes*
toothache *dolor de dientes*
delivery service *servicio a domicilio*

POST OFFICE AND COMMUNICATIONS

long-distance telephone *teléfono de
  larga distancia*
I would like to call... *Quisiera llamar a...*
collect *por cobrar*
person to person *persona a persona*
credit card *tarjeta de crédito*
post office *correo*
letter *carta*

stamp *estampilla, timbre*
postcard *tarjeta*
air mail *correo aereo*
registered *registrado*
money order *giro*
package; box *paquete; caja*
string; tape *cuerda; cinta*
Internet *internet*
Internet café *ciber café; ciber*
website *página web*
Web search *búsqueda*
link *enlace*
email *correo electrónico*
Skype *Skype*
Facebook *face*

AT THE BORDER

border *frontera*
customs *aduana*
immigration *migración*
tourist card *tarjeta de turista*
inspection *inspección; revisión*
passport *pasaporte*
profession *profesión*
marital status *estado civil*
single *soltero*
married; divorced *casado; divorciado*
widowed *viudado* (male); *viudada*
  (female)
insurance *seguro*
title *título*
driver's license *licencia de manejar*

AT THE GAS STATION

gas station *gasolinera*
gasoline *gasolina*
unleaded *sin plomo*
Fill it up, please. *Lleno, por favor.*
tire *llanta*
tire repair shop *vulcanizadora*
air *aire*
water *agua*
oil; oil change *aceite; cambio de aceite*
grease *grasa*
My ... doesn't work. *Mi ... no sirve.*
battery *batería*
radiator *radiador*
alternator *alternador*

generator *generador*
tow truck *grúa*
repair shop *taller mecánico*
tune-up *afinación*
auto parts store *refaccionería*

VERBS

In Spanish, verbs employ mostly predictable forms and come in three classes, which end in *ar, er,* and *ir.* Note that the first-person (*yo*) verb form is often irregular.

to buy *comprar*
I buy, you (he, she, it) buys *compro, compra*
we buy, you (they) buy *compramos, compran*

to eat *comer*
I eat, you (he, she, it) eats *como, come*
we eat, you (they) eat *comemos, comen*

to climb *subir*
I climb, you (he, she, it) climbs *subo, sube*
we climb, you (they) climb *subimos, suben*

Here are more (with irregularities indicated):

to do or make *hacer* (regular except for *hago,* I do or make)
to go *ir* (very irregular: *voy, va, vamos, van*)
to go (walk) *andar*
to love *amar*
to work *trabajar*
to want *desear, querer*
to need *necesitar*
to read *leer*
to write *escribir*
to repair *reparar*
to stop *parar*
to get off (the bus) *bajar*
to arrive *llegar*
to stay (remain) *quedar*
to stay (lodge) *hospedar*
to leave *salir* (regular except for *salgo,* I leave)

to look at *mirar*
to look for *buscar*
to give *dar* (regular except for *doy*, I give)
to carry *llevar*
to have *tener* (irregular but important:
  tengo, tiene, tenemos, tienen)
to come *venir* (similarly irregular: *vengo,
  viene, venimos, vienen*)

Spanish has two forms of "to be":

to be *estar* (regular except for *estoy*, I am)
to be *ser* (very irregular: *soy, es, somos,
  son*)

Use *estar* when speaking of location or a temporary state of being: "I am at home." *"Estoy en casa."* "I'm sick." *"Estoy enfermo."* Use *ser* for a permanent state of being: "I am a doctor." *"Soy doctora."*

NUMBERS
zero *cero*
one *uno*
two *dos*
three *tres*
four *cuatro*
five *cinco*
six *seis*
seven *siete*
eight *ocho*
nine *nueve*
10 *diez*
11 *once*
12 *doce*
13 *trece*
14 *catorce*
15 *quince*
16 *dieciseis*
17 *diecisiete*
18 *dieciocho*
19 *diecinueve*
20 *veinte*
21 *veintiuno*
30 *treinta*
40 *cuarenta*
50 *cincuenta*
60 *sesenta*

70 *setenta*
80 *ochenta*
90 *noventa*
100 *cien*
101 *cientiuno*
200 *doscientos*
500 *quinientos*
1,000 *mil*
10,000 *diez mil*
100,000 *cien mil*
1,000,000 *millón*
one half *medio*
one third *un tercio*
one fourth *un cuarto*

TIME
What time is it? *¿Qué hora es?*
It's one o'clock. *Es la una.*
It's three in the afternoon. *Son las tres
  de la tarde.*
It's 4am. *Son las cuatro de la mañana.*
six-thirty *seis y media*
a quarter till eleven *un cuarto para las
  once*
a quarter past five *las cinco y cuarto*
an hour *una hora*

DAYS AND MONTHS
Monday *lunes*
Tuesday *martes*
Wednesday *miércoles*
Thursday *jueves*
Friday *viernes*
Saturday *sábado*
Sunday *domingo*
today *hoy*
tomorrow *mañana*
yesterday *ayer*
January *enero*
February *febrero*
March *marzo*
April *abril*
May *mayo*
June *junio*
July *julio*
August *agosto*
September *septiembre*
October *octubre*

November *noviembre*	**after** *después*
December *diciembre*	**before** *antes*
a week *una semana*	
a month *un mes*	

Suggested Reading

The following titles provide insight into the Yucatán Peninsula and the Maya people. A few of these books are more easily obtained in Mexico, but all of them will cost less in the United States. Most are nonfiction, though several are fiction and great to throw into your carry-on for a good read on the plane, or for when you're in a Yucatecan mood. Happy reading!

Beletsky, Les. *Travellers' Wildlife Guides: Southern Mexico.* Northampton, MA: Interlink Books, 2006. A perfect companion guide if you plan on bird-watching, diving/snorkeling, hiking, or canoeing your way through your vacation. Excellent illustrations.

Coe, Andrew. *Archaeological Mexico: A Guide to Ancient Cities and Sacred Sites.* Emeryville, CA: Avalon Travel Publishing, 2001.

Coe, Michael D. *Breaking the Maya Code.* New York: Thames and Hudson, 2012. A fascinating account of how epigraphers, linguists, and archaeologists succeeded in deciphering Maya hieroglyphics.

Coe, Michael D. *The Maya.* New York: Thames and Hudson, 2011. A well-illustrated, easy-to-read volume on the Maya people.

Cortés, Hernán. *Five Letters.* New York: Gordon Press, 1991. Cortés's letters to the king of Spain, telling of his accomplishments and justifying his actions in the New World.

Davies, Nigel. *The Ancient Kingdoms of Mexico.* New York: Penguin Books, 1991. An excellent study of the preconquest of the indigenous peoples of Mexico.

De Landa, Bishop Diego. *Yucatán Before and After the Conquest.* New York: Dover Publications, 2012. This book, translated by William Gates from the original 1566 volume, has served as the basis for much of the research that has taken place since.

Díaz del Castillo, Bernal. *The Conquest of New Spain.* New York: Penguin Books, 1963. History straight from the adventurer's reminiscences, translated by J. M. Cohen.

Fehrenbach, T. R. *Fire and Blood: A History of Mexico.* New York: Collier Books, 1995. Over 3,000 years of Mexican history, related in a way that will keep you reading.

Ferguson, William M. *Maya Ruins of Mexico in Color.* Norman, OK: University of Oklahoma Press, 1985. Good reading before you go, but too bulky to carry along. Oversized with excellent drawings and illustrations of the archaeological structures of the Maya.

Franz, Carl, and Lorena Havens. *The People's Guide to Mexico.* Berkeley, CA: Avalon Travel, 2012. A humorous guide filled with witty anecdotes and helpful general information for visitors to Mexico. Don't expect any specific city information, just nuts-and-bolts hints for traveling south of the border.

Greene, Graham. *The Power and the Glory.* New York: Penguin Books, 2003. A novel that takes place in the 1920s about a priest and the antichurch movement that gripped Mexico.

Heffern, Richard. *Secrets of the Mind-Altering Plants of Mexico*. New York: Pyramid Books, 1974. A fascinating study of many substances, from ancient ritual hallucinogens to today's medicines that are found in Mexico.

Maya: Divine Kings of the Rain Forest. Cologne: Könemann, 2006. A beautifully compiled book of essays, photographs, and sketches relating to the Maya, past and present. Too heavy to take on the road but an excellent read.

McNay Brumfield, James. *A Tourist in the Yucatán*. Watsonville, CA: Tres Picos Press, 2004. A decent thriller that takes place in the Yucatán Peninsula; good for the beach or a long bus ride.

Meyer, Michael, and William Sherman. *The Course of Mexican History*. New York: Oxford University Press, 2013. A concise one-volume history of Mexico.

Nelson, Ralph. *Popul Vuh: The Great Mythological Book of the Ancient Maya*. Boston: Houghton Mifflin, 1974. An easy-to-read translation of myths handed down orally by the Quiche Maya, family to family, until written down after the Spanish conquest.

Perry, Richard, and Rosalind Perry. *Maya Missions: Exploring Colonial Yucatán*. Santa Barbara, CA: Espadaña Press, 2002. Detailed and informative guide, including excellent hand-drawn illustrations, about numerous colonial missions and structures in the Yucatán Peninsula.

Sodi, Demetrio M. (in collaboration with Adela Fernández). *The Mayas*. Mexico City: Panama Editorial S.A., 1987. This small book presents a fictionalized account of life among the Maya before the conquest. Easy reading for anyone who enjoys fantasizing about what life *might* have been like before recorded history in the Yucatán.

Stephens, John L. *Incidents of Travel in Central America, Chiapas, and Yucatán*. 2 vols. New York: Cosimo Classics, 2008. Good companions to refer to when traveling in the area. Stephens and illustrator Frederick Catherwood rediscovered many of the Maya ruins on their treks that took place in the mid-1800s. Easy reading.

Thompson, J. Eric. *Maya Archaeologist*. Norman, OK: University of Oklahoma Press, 1974. Thompson, a noted Maya scholar, traveled and worked at many of the Maya ruins in the 1930s.

Thompson, J. Eric. *The Rise and Fall of the Maya Civilization*. Norman, OK: University of Oklahoma Press, 1973. One man's story of the Maya. Excellent reading.

Webster, David. *The Fall of the Ancient Maya*. New York: Thames and Hudson, 2002. A careful and thorough examination of the possible causes of one of archaeology's great unsolved mysteries—the collapse of the Classic Maya in the 8th century.

Werner, David. *Where There Is No Doctor*. Palo Alto, CA: The Hesperian Foundation, 1992. This is an invaluable medical aid to anyone traveling not only to isolated parts of Mexico but to any place in the world where there's not a doctor (or the Internet).

Wolf, Eric. *Sons of the Shaking Earth*. Chicago: University of Chicago Press, 1962. An anthropological study of the indigenous and mestizo people of Mexico and Guatemala.

Wright, Ronald. *Time Among the Maya*. New York: Grove Press, 2000. A narrative that takes the reader through the Maya country of today, with historical comments that help put the puzzle together.

Internet Resources

www.almalibrebooks.com
Bookstore website that's packed with information about Puerto Morelos; also has listings for short- and long-term rentals.

www.bacalarmosaico.com
Laguna Bacalar's online resource for tourists and locals—a mishmash of information, in a good way.

www.backyardnature.net/yucatan
Notes and observations by an experienced naturalist about the major plants and animal species in the northern Yucatán Peninsula.

www.campeche.gob.mx
Official website of Campeche state, including information for tourists.

www.cancunmap.com
An excellent source of detailed maps of the Riviera Maya and some inland archaeological zones.

www.cancuntips.com.mx
The online version of Cancún's main tourist magazine, with tons of listings, travel tips, and tourist resources.

www.colonial-mexico.com
Photos and text on colonial Mexico by Richard and Rosalind Perry, authors of the *Maya Missions* handbook.

www.cozumelinsider.com
Good website covering Cozumel, including current tourist information and issues important to locals.

www.cozumelmycozumel.com
Website offering a host of information to travelers and people considering a move to Isla Cozumel, moderated by longtime expats.

www.cozumeltoday.com
Website with articles geared toward travelers; affiliated with *Cozumel Today* magazine.

www.cruiseportinsider.com
A good source of information for travelers arriving to the region via cruise ship, including maps and shore excursion descriptions.

www.holboxisland.com
Website focused on Isla Holbox, with information on charter air tours and a handful of other tours and sights.

www.intheroo.com
Searchable listings of all kinds (housing, wedding planners, legal services, etc.) for all major Riviera Maya cities, plus maps, articles, and user forums.

www.islamujeres.gob.mx
Official website of the island of Isla Mujeres, including information for tourists.

www.islamujeres.info
Excellent resource for the goings-on about Isla Mujeres, including activities, ferry schedules, and even a message board with participation by longtime expats.

www.isla-mujeres.net
Informative and easy-to-use website covering Isla Mujeres, with lodging, restaurants, activities, maps, FAQs, coupons, island history, even a Spanish primer.

www.locogringo.com
Website with extensive business listings for the Riviera Maya.

www.mapapocketcancun.com
Online resource for Cancun's restaurants, including menus, reviews, and discount coupons.

www.mesoweb.com

Website relating to Mesoamerican cultures, including detailed reports and photos of past and current archaeological digs.

www.mostlymaya.com

Eclectic but informative website on various Maya topics; especially useful for info on Maya languages.

www.playa.info

Established website with lots of travel planning information to Playa and the Riviera Maya. It also has a popular forum for asking questions and sharing tips.

www.puertoaventuras.com

Good website with updated information about Puerto Aventuras.

www.qroo.gob.mx

Official website of Quintana Roo state, including information for tourists.

www.sac-be.com

Buggy online version of an English-language Riviera Maya newspaper, with longish articles and reviews of a wide smattering of area destinations, excursions, and restaurants.

www.thisiscozumel.com

Excellent website for Cozumel, including up-to-date tourist information.

www.todotulum.com

Great resource for Tulum—everything from nightlife to real estate.

www.travelyucatan.com

Detailed information and practical advice about traveling to and around the Yucatán Peninsula.

www.turismochiapas.gob.mx

Official tourism website for the state of Chiapas, with detailed information about sights, cities, and events.

www.visitcalakmul.com

Information about visiting the Calakmul ruins and surrounding areas; includes listings of guides, hotels and restaurants, bus schedules, and more.

www.visitmahahual.com

Website with information on activities, hotels, and restaurants in Mahahual.

www.yucatan.gob.mx

Official website of Yucatán state, including information for tourists.

www.yucatanliving.com

Award-winning website about living in Mérida and Yucatán state, with helpful travel info like up-to-date event listings.

www.yucatantoday.com

Website of the monthly tourist magazine of the same name. Based in Mérida but contains coverage of all of Yucatán state.

Index

XYZ

List of Maps

Photo Credits

Title page photo: © Liza Prado
page 4 © Liza Prado; page 5 © Liza Prado; page 6 (top left) © Liza Prado, (top right) © Liza Prado, (bottom) © Liza Prado; page 7 (top) © Liza Prado, (bottom left) © Liza Prado, (bottom right) © Liza Prado; page 8 © H.W. Prado; page 9 (top) © Liza Prado, (bottom left) © Liza Prado, (bottom right) © Liza Prado; page 12 © H.W. Prado; page 14 (top left) © H.W. Prado, (top right) © Liza Prado; page 16 © Liza Prado; page 18 © Liza Prado; page 19 © Liza Prado; page 21 © Liza Prado; page 23 © Liza Prado; page 25 (top) © Liza Prado, (bottom) © Liza Prado; page 27 © Liza Prado; page 33 © Gary Chandler; page 36 © Gary Chandler; page 37 © Gary Chandler; page 41 © Liza Prado; page 42 © Liza Prado; page 44 © Gary Chandler; page 50 © Liza Prado; page 54 © H.W. Prado; page 56 © Liza Prado; page 67 © Liza Prado; page 68 © Liza Prado; page 70 © Liza Prado; page 72 © Liza Prado; page 74 © Liza Prado; page 82 © Liza Prado; page 84 © Liza Prado; page 86 © Liza Prado; page 91 © Liza Prado; page 93 © Liza Prado; page 95 (top) © Gary Chandler, (bottom) © Liza Prado; page 97 © Liza Prado; page 101 © Liza Prado; page 107 © H.W. Prado; page 111 © Liza Prado; page 112 © Liza Prado; page 116 © Liza Prado; page 119 © Liza Prado; page 120 © Liza Prado; page 122 © Liza Prado; page 126 © Liza Prado; page 128 © Gary Chandler; page 132 © Liza Prado; page 137 © Gary Chandler; page 139 (top) © H.W. Prado, (bottom) © Liza Prado; page 141 © Gary Chandler; page 145 © Liza Prado; page 146 © H.W. Prado; page 149 © Liza Prado; page 155 © Liza Prado; page 159 © H.W. Prado; page 161 © H.W. Prado; page 164 © Liza Prado; page 167 © Liza Prado; page 176 © Liza Prado; page 178 © Liza Prado; page 183 © H.W. Prado; page 190 © Gary Chandler; page 192 © Liza Prado; page 194 (top) © Liza Prado, (bottom) © Liza Prado; page 195 © Gary Chandler; page 200 © Liza Prado; page 204 © Liza Prado; page 205 © Liza Prado; page 207 © H.W. Prado; page 209 © Liza Prado; page 216 © Liza Prado; page 224 © Liza Prado; page 226 © Liza Prado; page 228 © Liza Prado; page 231 © Liza Prado; page 234 © Liza Prado; page 241 © Liza Prado; page 242 © Liza Prado; page 247 © Liza Prado; page 249 © Liza Prado; page 251 © Liza Prado; page 254 © Liza Prado; page 257 © Liza Prado; page 264 © Liza Prado; page 267 (top) © Liza Prado, (bottom) © Liza Prado; page 269 © Liza Prado; page 273 © Liza Prado; page 277 © Liza Prado; page 280 © Liza Prado; page 281 © Liza Prado; page 283 © Liza Prado; page 287 © Liza Prado; page 298 © Liza Prado; page 299 © Liza Prado; page 300 © Liza Prado; page 301 © Liza Prado; page 303 © Liza Prado; page 304 © Liza Prado; page 305 (top) © Liza Prado, (bottom) © Liza Prado; page 307 © Liza Prado; page 312 © Liza Prado; page 313 © Liza Prado; page 321 © Liza Prado; page 325 © Liza Prado; page 330 © Liza Prado; page 341 © Liza Prado; page 345 © Liza Prado; page 346 © Liza Prado; page 349 © Liza Prado; page 355 © Liza Prado; page 356 © Liza Prado; page 357 © Liza Prado; page 358 © Liza Prado; page 365 © Liza Prado; page 367 © Liza Prado; page 376 © Liza Prado; page 377 © Liza Prado; page 381 © Liza Prado; page 388 © Liza Prado; page 389 © Liza Prado; page 395 © Liza Prado; page 400 © Liza Prado; page 403 © Liza Prado; page 406 © Liza Prado; page 407 © Liza Prado; page 410 © Liza Prado; page 412 © Liza Prado; page 416 © Liza Prado; page 419 © Liza Prado; page 423 © Liza Prado; page 425 © Liza Prado; page 431 (top) © Liza Prado, (bottom) © Liza Prado; page 433 © Liza Prado; page 437 © Liza Prado; page 441 © Liza Prado; page 444 © Liza Prado; page 447 © Liza Prado; page 452 © Gary Chandler; page 453 © Gary Chandler; page 457 © Gary Chandler; page 461 © Liza Prado; page 462 © Liza Prado; page 463 © Liza Prado; page 467 © Liza Prado; page 470 © Liza Prado; page 471 (top) © Liza Prado, (bottom) © Liza Prado; page 473 © Liza Prado; page 475 © Liza Prado; page 479 © Liza Prado; page 480 © Liza Prado; page 482 © Liza Prado; page 483 © Liza Prado; page 484 © Liza Prado; page 491 © Liza Prado; page 495 (top) © Liza Prado, (bottom) © Liza Prado; page 499 © Liza Prado

Also Available

SAN MIGUEL DE ALLENDE

Including Guanajuato & Querétaro

JULIE DOHERTY MEADE

CANCÚN & COZUMEL

Including Playa del Carmen, Tulum & the Riviera Maya

GARY CHANDLER & LIZA PRADO

OAXACA

JUSTIN HENDERSON

PUERTO VALLARTA

Including Sayulita & the Riviera Nayarit

JUSTIN HENDERSON

MAP SYMBOLS

≡≡≡	Expressway	○	City/Town	✈	Airport	⚬	Golf Course
▬▬	Primary Road	◉	State Capital	✈	Airfield	P	Parking Area
▭▭	Secondary Road	⊛	National Capital	▲	Mountain	⛢	Archaeological Site
▢▢	Unpaved Road	★	Point of Interest	✦	Unique Natural Feature	♦	Church
▬▬	Feature Trail	•	Accommodation			⛽	Gas Station
------	Other Trail	▼	Restaurant/Bar	⟆	Waterfall		
··········	Ferry	■	Other Location	▲	Park	⬭	Glacier
▬▬	Pedestrian Walkway			⊓	Trailhead	▦	Mangrove
▭▭▭	Stairs	Λ	Campground	⛷	Skiing Area	⟿	Reef
						▦	Swamp

CONVERSION TABLES

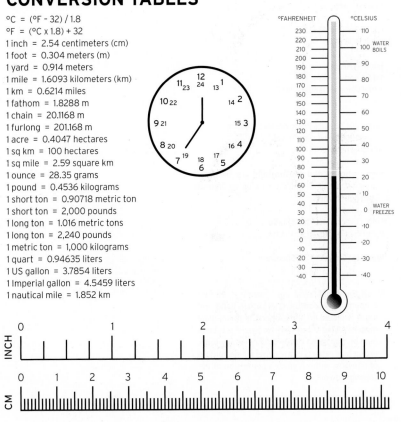

°C = (°F - 32) / 1.8
°F = (°C x 1.8) + 32
1 inch = 2.54 centimeters (cm)
1 foot = 0.304 meters (m)
1 yard = 0.914 meters
1 mile = 1.6093 kilometers (km)
1 km = 0.6214 miles
1 fathom = 1.8288 m
1 chain = 20.1168 m
1 furlong = 201.168 m
1 acre = 0.4047 hectares
1 sq km = 100 hectares
1 sq mile = 2.59 square km
1 ounce = 28.35 grams
1 pound = 0.4536 kilograms
1 short ton = 0.90718 metric ton
1 short ton = 2,000 pounds
1 long ton = 1.016 metric tons
1 long ton = 2,240 pounds
1 metric ton = 1,000 kilograms
1 quart = 0.94635 liters
1 US gallon = 3.7854 liters
1 Imperial gallon = 4.5459 liters
1 nautical mile = 1.852 km

MOON YUCATÁN PENINSULA

Avalon Travel
An imprint of Perseus Books
A Hachette Book Group company
1700 Fourth Street
Berkeley, CA 94710, USA
www.moon.com

Editor: Kimberly Ehart
Series Manager: Kathryn Ettinger
Copy Editor: Ann Seifert
Graphics and Production Coordinator:
   Sarah Wildfang
Cover Design: Faceout Studios, Charles Brock
Interior Design: Domini Dragoone
Moon Logo: Tim McGrath
Map Editor: Kat Bennett
Cartographers: Kat Bennett, Austin Ehrhardt
Proofreader: Alissa Cyphers
Indexer: Greg Jewett

ISBN-13: 978-1-63121-410-3
ISSN: 1098-6707

Printing History
1st Edition — 1986
12th Edition — January 2017
5 4 3 2 1

All recommendations, including those for sights,
   activities, hotels, restaurants, and shops, are
   based on each author's individual judgment. We
   do not accept payment for inclusion in our travel
   guides, and our authors don't accept free goods or
   services in exchange for positive coverage.

Although every effort was made to ensure that the
   information was correct at the time of going to
   press, the author and publisher do not assume
   and hereby disclaim any liability to any party for
   any loss or damage caused by errors, omissions,
   or any potential travel disruption due to labor
   or financial difficulty, whether such errors or
   omissions result from negligence, accident, or
   any other cause.